HIGHER
GCSE MATHEMATICS
FOR OCR

Howard Baxter, Michael Handbury,
John Jeskins, Jean Matthews,
Mark Patmore

Hodder Murray
www.hoddereducation.co.uk

Series Editor
Brian Seager

The Publishers would like to thank the following for permission to reproduce copyright material:
Acknowledgements p.372 Kidshealth.org/The Nemours Foundation
Every effort has been made to trace all copyright holders, but if any have been inadvertently overlooked the Publishers will be pleased to make the necessary arrangements at the first opportunity.

Although every effort has been made to ensure that website addresses are correct at time of going to press, Hodder Murray cannot be held responsible for the content of any website mentioned in this book. It is sometimes possible to find a relocated web page by typing in the address of the home page for a website in the URL window of your browser.

Orders: please contact Bookpoint Ltd, 130 Milton Park, Abingdon, Oxon OX14 4SB. Telephone: (44) 01235 827720. Fax: (44) 01235 400454. Lines are open 9 a.m. to 5 p.m., Monday to Saturday, with a 24-hour message-answering service. Visit our website at www.hoddereducation.co.uk.

© Howard Baxter, Michael Handbury, John Jeskins, Jean Matthews, Mark Patmore, Brian Seager, Eddie Wilde 2006
First published in 2006 by
Hodder Murray, an imprint of Hodder Education,
a member of the Hodder Headline Group
338 Euston Road
London NW1 3BH

Impression number   10 9 8 7 6 5 4 3 2 1
Year   2011 2010 2009 2008 2007 2006

All rights reserved. Apart from any use permitted under UK copyright law, no part of this publication may be reproduced or transmitted in any form or by any means, electronic or mechanical, including photocopying and recording, or held within any information storage and retrieval system, without permission in writing from the publisher or under licence from the Copyright Licensing Agency Limited. Further details of such licences (for reprographic reproduction) may be obtained from the Copyright Licensing Agency Limited, 90 Tottenham Court Road, London W1T 4LP.

Cover photo © Charles D. Winters/Science Photo Library
Illustrations © Barking Dog Art
Typeset in 10/12pt Times Ten by Tech-Set Ltd, Gateshead, Tyne and Wear
Printed in Italy

A catalogue record for this title is available from the British Library

ISBN-10: 0340 889535
ISBN-13: 978 0340 889 534

CONTENTS

Introduction		**vi**
1	**Integers, powers and roots**	**1**
	Prime numbers and factors	1
	Writing a number as a product of its prime factors	2
	Highest common factors and lowest common multiples	4
	Multiplying and dividing by negative numbers	7
	Powers and roots	11
	Reciprocals	15
2	**Algebraic manipulation 1**	**19**
	Expanding brackets	19
	Combining terms	21
	Factorising	24
	Expanding pairs of brackets	25
	Index notation	28
3	**Properties of shapes**	**31**
	The area of a triangle	31
	The area of a parallelogram	34
	Angles made with parallel lines	37
	The angles in a triangle	40
	The angles in a quadrilateral	42
	Special quadrilaterals	44
	The angles in a polygon	46
4	**Fractions, decimals and percentages**	**53**
	Comparing fractions	53
	Adding and subtracting fractions and mixed numbers	54
	Multiplying and dividing fractions and mixed numbers	59
	Fractions on your calculator	64
	Changing fractions to decimals	67
	Mental arithmetic with decimals	69
	Multiplying and dividing decimals	70
	Percentage increase and decrease	74
5	**Statistical diagrams**	**79**
	Frequency diagrams	79
	Frequency polygons	83
	Stem-and-leaf diagrams	84
	Scatter diagrams	87
6	**Areas, volumes and 2-D representation**	**93**
	Circles	93
	Area of complex shapes	97
	Volume of complex shapes	99
	Volume of a prism	101
	Volume of a cylinder	103
	Surface area of a cylinder	104
	Plans and elevations	107
7	**Equations and inequalities 1**	**114**
	Solving equations	114
	Solving equations with brackets	115
	Equations with x on both sides	116
	Fractions in equations	118
	Inequalities	119
8	**Ratio and proportion**	**122**
	What is a ratio?	122
	Writing a ratio in the form $1:n$	125
	Using ratios	126
	Dividing a quantity in a given ratio	130
	Best value	132
9	**Statistical calculations**	**136**
	The mean from a frequency table	136
	Grouped data	143
	Continuous data	148
10	**Pythagoras**	**155**
	Pythagoras' theorem	155
	Using Pythagoras' theorem	157
	Pythagorean triples	160
	Midpoints	161
	Three-dimensional (3-D) coordinates	163
11	**Mental methods**	**169**
	Mental strategies	169
	Rounding to 1 significant figure	172
	Rounding to a given number of significant figures	174
	Using π without a calculator	176
	Deriving unknown facts from those you know	178
12	**Formulae 1**	**181**
	Using formulae	181
	Rearranging formulae	184
	Solving equations by trial and improvement	187
13	**Transformations**	**191**
	Reflections	191
	Rotations	194
	Translations	200
	Enlargements	204

14	**Probability 1**	**211**
	Probability of an outcome not happening	211
	Probability involving a given number of different outcomes	212
	Expected frequency	215
	Relative frequency	216
15	**Graphs 1**	**221**
	Drawing straight-line graphs	221
	Harder straight-line graphs	223
	Distance–time graphs	225
	Interpreting graphs	226
	Quadratic graphs	231
16	**Measures**	**242**
	Converting between measures	242
	Accuracy in measurement	244
	Working to a sensible degree of accuracy	246
	Compound measures	247
17	**Planning and collecting**	**251**
	Statistical questions	251
18	**Sequences**	**257**
	Using rules to find terms of sequences	257
	Finding the nth term of a linear sequence	260
19	**Constructions and loci**	**267**
	Constructions	267
	Intersecting loci	275
20	**Solving problems**	**279**
	Order of operations	279
	Estimating and checking	281
	Compound measures	285
	Time	286
	Solving problems	287
21	**Graphs 2**	**293**
	Finding the gradient of a straight-line graph	293
	Finding the equation of a straight-line graph	296
	Solving simultaneous equations graphically	298
	Solving simultaneous equations algebraically	300
	Solving harder simultaneous equations algebraically	302
22	**Further percentages**	**306**
	Repeated percentage change	306
	Repeated fractional change	307
	Reverse percentage and fraction problems	310
23	**Sampling**	**316**
	Sampling	316
	Bias	322
24	**Trigonometry 1**	**325**
	The distance between two points	325
	Labelling sides	327
	Using the ratios 1	330
	Using the ratios 2	333
	Using the ratios 3	335
25	**Representing and interpreting data**	**343**
	Cumulative frequency diagrams	343
	Histograms	354
	Time series	361
	Interpreting other graphs and diagrams	365
26	**Indices and standard form**	**373**
	Raising a power to another power	373
	Other powers	373
	Using a calculator	377
	Using the rules of indices with numbers and letters	380
	Standard form	381
	Calculating with numbers in standard form	383
27	**Similarity and enlargement**	**388**
	Similarity of triangles and other plane shapes	388
	Enlargement	392
	The area and volume of similar figures	395
28	**Algebraic manipulation 2**	**400**
	Simplifying algebraic fractions	400
	Factorising quadratic expressions	402
	Difference of two squares	403
	Simplifying algebraic fractions involving indices	405
	Factorising quadratic expressions where the coefficient of $x^2 \neq 1$	407
	Simplifying fractions involving quadratic expressions	408
29	**Using a calculator**	**412**
	The efficient use of a calculator	412
	Exponential growth and decay	415
	Bounds of measurements	418
	Further calculations involving bounds of measurements	419
30	**Equations and inequalities 2**	**423**
	Equations	423
	Inequalities	429
	Solving inequalities with two unknowns	431

31	**Three-dimensional geometry**	**435**
	Finding lengths and angles in three dimensions	435
	The angle between a line and a plane	439
32	**Formulae 2**	**444**
	Formulae where the new subject occurs more than once	444
	Formulae where the new subject is raised to a power	446
33	**Proportion and variation**	**449**
	Direct proportion	449
	Inverse proportion	452
	Finding formulae	454
	Other types of proportion	456
34	**Linear equations**	**463**
	Finding the equation of a straight line in the form $y = mx + c$	463
	Exploring gradients	467
35	**Congruence and proof**	**474**
	Angle properties of triangles	474
36	**Quadratic equations**	**482**
	Solving quadratic equations	482
	Solving quadratic equations by factorising	484
	Equations that need rearranging first	486
	Completing the square	488
	Solving quadratic equations by completing the square	491
	Solving quadratic equations by using the formula	493
37	**Simultaneous equations**	**498**
	Solving simultaneous equations using the method of elimination	498
	Solving simultaneous equations by substitution	502
38	**Decimals and surds**	**508**
	Terminating and recurring decimals	508
	Surds	512
39	**Graphs 3**	**518**
	Velocity–time graphs	518
	Solving simultaneous equations graphically	521
	Using graphs to solve quadratic equations	522
	Drawing and recognising other curves	524
40	**Trigonometry 2**	**531**
	The area of a triangle	531
	The sine rule	534
	The cosine rule	538
	Graphs of trigonometrical functions	543
	Other trigonometrical functions	546
41	**Functions**	**554**
	Function notation	554
	Translations	557
	One-way stretches	562
42	**Length, area and volume**	**569**
	Dimension analysis	569
	Arcs and sectors	571
	Pyramids, cones and spheres	574
	Compound shapes and problems	577
43	**Probability 2**	**583**
	The addition rule for mutually exclusive events	583
	The multiplication rule for independent events	585
	Probability tree diagrams	588
	Dependent events	592
44	**Vectors**	**597**
	The definition of a vector	597
	Multiplying a vector by a scalar	598
	Addition and subtraction of vectors	602
45	**Algebraic fractions**	**611**
	Adding and subtracting algebraic fractions	611
	Adding and subtracting more complex algebraic fractions	613
	Solving equations involving algebraic fractions	615
46	**Circle theorems**	**619**
	The perpendicular from the centre to a chord bisects the chord	619
	The angle subtended by an arc at the centre of a circle is twice the angle that it subtends at any point on the circumference	620
	The angle subtended at the circumference in a semicircle is a right angle	621
	Angles in the same segment of a circle are equal	622
	The opposite angles of a cyclic quadrilateral add up to 180°	623
	The two tangents to a circle from an external point are equal in length	626
	The angle between a tangent and a chord is equal to the angle subtended by the chord in the alternate segment	628

INTRODUCTION

About this book

This book covers the complete specification for the Higher Tier of GCSE Mathematics. It has been written especially for students following OCR's 2006 Linear Specification A.

- Each chapter is presented in a way which will help you to understand the mathematics, with straightforward explanations and worked examples covering every type of problem.
- At the start of each chapter are two lists, one of what you should already know before you begin and the other of the topics you will be learning about in that chapter.
- There are 'Check ups' to check understanding of work already covered.
- 'Discoveries' encourage you to find out something for yourself, either from an external source such as the internet, or through a guided activity.
- 'Challenges' are rather more searching and are designed to make you think mathematically.
- There are plenty of exercises to work through to practise your skills.
- Some questions are designed to be done without a calculator so that you can practise for the non-calculator paper.
- Look out for the 'Tips' – these give advice on how to improve examination performance, direct from the experienced examiners who have written this book.
- At the end of each chapter there is a short summary of what you have learned.
- Finally, there is a 'Mixed exercise' to help you revise all the topics covered in that chapter.

Other components in the series

- A Homework Book
  This contains parallel exercises to those in this book to give you more practice. Included with the Homework Book is a Personal Tutor CD-ROM. This will help you if you have to miss a lesson or if you need a reminder of something taught in class.
- An Assessment Pack
  This teaching resource contains revision exercises and practice papers that your teacher can photocopy and give to the class to help you prepare for the examination. Some of the questions in the examination will offer you little help to get started. These are called 'unstructured' or 'multi-step' questions. Instead of the question having several parts, each of which helps you to answer the next, you have to work out the necessary steps to find the answer. There will be examples of this kind of question in the Assessment Pack.
  Also in the Assessment Pack is information about coursework and how to tackle it.
- An Interactive Investigations CD-ROM
  This teaching resource contains whole-class presentations and individual activities that your teacher can use in your lessons.
  It helps you understand how you can best use ICT to do your homework and coursework tasks.

Top ten tips

Here are some general tips from the examiners who wrote this book to help you to do well in your tests and examinations.

Practise
1. **taking time** to work through each question carefully.
2. answering questions **without** a calculator.
3. wering questions which require **explanations**.
4. answering **unstructured** questions.
5. **accurate** drawing and construction.
6. answering questions which **need a calculator**, trying to use it efficiently.
7. **checking answers**, especially for reasonable size and degree of accuracy.
8. making your work **concise** and well laid out.
9. checking that you have **answered the question**.
10. **rounding** numbers, but only at the appropriate stage.

 Introduction

1 → INTEGERS, POWERS AND ROOTS

> **THIS CHAPTER IS ABOUT**
> - Prime numbers and factors
> - Writing a number as a product of its prime factors
> - Highest common factors and lowest common multiples
> - Multiplying and dividing by negative numbers
> - Powers, roots and reciprocals

> **YOU SHOULD ALREADY KNOW**
> - How to add and subtract, multiply and divide integers
> - How to use index notation for squares, cubes and powers of ten
> - The meaning of the words *factor, multiple, square, cube, square root*

Prime numbers and factors

You already know that a **factor** of a number is any number that divides exactly into that number. This includes 1 and the number itself.

> **Check up 1.1**
>
> The factors of 2 are 1 and 2.
> The factors of 22 are 1, 2, 11 and 22.
>
> Write down all the factors of these numbers.
> (a) 14   (b) 16   (c) 40

> **Discovery 1.1**
>
> (a) Write down all the factors of the other numbers from 1 to 20.
>
> (b) Write down all the numbers under 20 that have two, and only two, different factors.

The numbers you found in part **(b)** of Discovery 1.1 are called **prime numbers**. Notice that 1 is not a prime number as it only has one factor.

> **TIP** It is useful to learn the prime numbers up to 50.

Prime numbers and factors   1

Check up 1.2

Find all the prime numbers up to 50.
If you have time, go further.

Writing a number as a product of its prime factors

When you multiply two or more numbers together the result is a **product**.

When you write a number as a product of its prime factors you work out which prime numbers are multiplied together to give the number.

The number 6 written as a product of its prime factors is 2×3.

It is easy to write down the prime factors of 6 because it is a small number. To write a larger number as a product of its prime factors, use this method.

- Try dividing the number by 2.
- If it divides by 2 exactly, try dividing by 2 again.
- Continue dividing by 2 until your answer will not divide by 2.
- Next try dividing by 3.
- Continue dividing by 3 until your answer will not divide by 3.
- Then try dividing by 5.
- Continue dividing by 5 until your answer will not divide by 5.
- Continue to work systematically through the prime numbers.
- Stop when your answer is 1.

EXAMPLE 1.1

(a) Write 12 as a product of its prime factors.
(b) Write 126 as a product of its prime factors.

Solution

(a) $2\overline{)12}$
$2\overline{)6}$
$3\overline{)3}$
1

$12 = 2 \times 2 \times 3$

You already know that you can write 2×2 as 2^2.

So you can write $2 \times 2 \times 3$ in a shorter way as $2^2 \times 3$.

(b) $\quad\begin{array}{r|r}2&126\\\hline3&63\\\hline3&21\\\hline7&7\\\hline&1\end{array}$

$126 = 2 \times 3 \times 3 \times 7 = 2 \times 3^2 \times 7$

Remember 3^2 means 3 squared and this is the special name for 3 to the power 2.

The power, 2 in this case, is called the **index**.

> **TIP:** Check your answer by multiplying the prime factors together. Your answer should be the original number.

EXERCISE 1.1

Write each of these numbers as a product of its prime factors.

| **1** 6 | **2** 10 | **3** 15 | **4** 21 | **5** 32 |
| **6** 36 | **7** 140 | **8** 250 | **9** 315 | **10** 420 |

Challenge 1.1

The factors of 24 are 1, 2, 3, 4, 6, 8, 12, 24.

This is eight different factors. You can write this as F(24) = 8.

24 written as a product of its prime factors is $2 \times 2 \times 2 \times 3 = 2^3 \times 3^1$.

(You do not usually include the index if it is 1 but you need it for this activity.)

Now add 1 to each of the indices: $(3 + 1) = 4$ and $(1 + 1) = 2$.
Then multiply these numbers: $4 \times 2 = 8$.

Your answer is the same as F(24), the number of factors of 24.

Here is another example.

The factors of 8 are 1, 2, 4, 8.

This is four different factors so F(8) = 4.

8 written as a product of its prime factors is 2^3.

There is just one power this time.

Add 1 to the index: $(3 + 1) = 4$.

continues ...

Writing a number as a product of its prime factors

> **Challenge 1.1 continued**
>
> This is the same as F(8), the number of factors of 8.
> (a) Try this for 40.
> (b) Investigate if there is a similar connection between the number of factors and powers of the prime factors for some other numbers.

Highest common factors and lowest common multiples

The **highest common factor (HCF)** of a set of numbers is the largest number that will divide exactly into each of the numbers.

The largest number that will divide into both 8 and 12 is 4.
So 4 is the highest common factor of 8 and 12.

You can find the highest common factor of 8 and 12 without using any special methods. You list, perhaps mentally, the factors of 8 and 12 and compare the lists to find the largest number that appears in both lists.

When you can give the answer without using any special methods it is called finding **by inspection**.

> **Check up 1.3**
>
> Find, by inspection, the highest common factor (HCF) of these pairs of numbers.
> (a) 12 and 18   (b) 27 and 36   (c) 48 and 80

TIP: The HCF is never bigger than the smaller of the numbers.

You probably found parts **(a)** and **(b)** of Check up 1.3 fairly easy but part **(c)** more difficult.

This is the method to use when it is not easy to find the highest common factor by inspection.

- Write each number as a product of its prime factors.
- Choose the common factors.
- Multiply them together.

This method is shown in the next example.

4   1 Integers, powers and roots

EXAMPLE 1.2

Find the highest common factor of these pairs of numbers.
(a) 28 and 72   (b) 96 and 180

Solution

(a) Write each number as the product of its prime factors.

$28 = ②×②×7 \quad\quad = 2^2 × 7$
$72 = ②×②×2×3×3 \quad = 2^3 × 3^2$

The common factors are 2 and 2.
The highest common factor is $2 × 2 = 2^2 = 4$.

(b) Write each number as the product of its prime factors.

$96 = ②×②×2×2×2×③ \quad = 2^5 × 3$
$180 = ②×②×③×3×5 \quad = 2^2 × 3^2 × 5$

The common factors are 2, 2 and 3.
The highest common factor is $2 × 2 × 3 = 2^2 × 3 = 12$.

The **lowest common multiple (LCM)** of a set of numbers is the smallest number into which all the members of the set will divide.

The smallest number into which both 8 and 12 will divide is 24.

So 24 is the lowest common multiple of 8 and 12.

As for the highest common factor, you can find the lowest common multiple of small numbers by inspection. One way is to list the multiples of each of the numbers and compare the lists to find the smallest number that appears in both lists.

Check up 1.4

Find, by inspection, the lowest common multiple (LCM) of these pairs of numbers.

(a) 3 and 5   (b) 12 and 16   (c) 48 and 80

TIP

The LCM is never smaller than the larger of the numbers.

You probably found parts **(a)** and **(b)** of Check up 1.4 fairly easy but part **(c)** more difficult.

This is the method to use when it is not easy to find the lowest common multiple by inspection.

- Write each number as a product of its prime factors.
- Choose the highest power of each of the factors that occur in either of the lists.
- Multiply the numbers you choose together.

This method is shown in the next example.

EXAMPLE 1.3

Find the lowest common multiple of these pairs of numbers.
(a) 28 and 42
(b) 96 and 180

Solution

(a) Write each number as the product of its prime factors.

$28 = 2 \times 2 \times 7 = 2^2 \times 7$
$42 = 2 \times 3 \times 7$

The highest power of 2 is 2^2.
The highest power of 3 is $3^1 = 3$.
The highest power of 7 is $7^1 = 7$.

The lowest common multiple is $2^2 \times 3 \times 7 = 84$.

Notice that a number can be written as that number to the power 1. For example 3 was written as 3^1. A number to the power 1 is equal to the number. $3^1 = 3$.

(b) Write each number as the product of its prime factors.

$96 = 2 \times 2 \times 2 \times 2 \times 2 \times 3 = 2^5 \times 3$
$180 = 2 \times 2 \times 3 \times 3 \times 5 = 2^2 \times 3^2 \times 5$

The highest power of 2 is 2^5.
The highest power of 3 is 3^2.
The highest power of 5 is $5^1 = 5$.

The lowest common multiple is $2^5 \times 3^2 \times 5 = 1440$.

Summary

- To find the highest common factor (HCF), use the prime numbers that appear in *both* lists and use the *lower* power for each prime.
- To find the lowest common multiple (LCM), use all the prime numbers that appear in the lists and use the *higher* power of each prime.

TIP

Check your answers.

Does the HCF divide into both numbers?

Do both numbers divide into the LCM?

1 Integers, powers and roots

EXERCISE 1.2

For each of these pairs of numbers
- write the numbers as products of their prime factors.
- state the highest common factor.
- state the lowest common multiple.

| **1** 4 and 6 | **2** 12 and 16 | **3** 10 and 15 | **4** 32 and 40 | **5** 35 and 45 |
| **6** 27 and 63 | **7** 20 and 50 | **8** 48 and 84 | **9** 50 and 64 | **10** 42 and 49 |

Challenge 1.2

The students in Year 11 at a school are to be split into groups of equal size. Two possible sizes for the groups are 16 and 22.

What is the smallest number of students that there can be in Year 11?

Multiplying and dividing by negative numbers

Discovery 1.2

(a) Work out this sequence of calculations.

$5 \times 5 = 25$
$5 \times 4 = 20$
$5 \times 3 =$
$5 \times 2 =$
$5 \times 1 =$
$5 \times 0 =$

What is the pattern in the answers?
Use the pattern to continue the sequence.

$5 \times -1 =$
$5 \times -2 =$
$5 \times -3 =$
$5 \times -4 =$

(b) Work out this sequence of calculations.

$5 \times 4 =$
$4 \times 4 =$
$3 \times 4 =$
$2 \times 4 =$
$1 \times 4 =$
$0 \times 4 =$

Spot the pattern and continue the sequence.

You should have found in Discovery 1.2 that a positive number multiplied by a negative number gives a negative answer.

Discovery 1.3

Work out this sequence of calculations.

$-3 \times 5 =$
$-3 \times 4 =$
$-3 \times 3 =$
$-3 \times 2 =$
$-3 \times 1 =$
$-3 \times 0 =$

What is the pattern in the answers?
Use the pattern to continue the sequence.

$-3 \times -1 =$
$-3 \times -2 =$
$-3 \times -3 =$
$-3 \times -4 =$
$-3 \times -5 =$

Your answers to Discoveries 1.2 and 1.3 suggest these rules.

$$+ \times - = -$$
and
$$- \times + = -$$

$$+ \times + = +$$
and
$$- \times - = +$$

EXAMPLE 1.4

Work out these.
(a) 6×-4
(b) -7×-3
(c) -5×8

Solution

(a) $+ \times - = -$
$6 \times 4 = 24$
So $6 \times -4 = -24$

(b) $- \times - = +$
$7 \times 3 = 21$
So $-7 \times -3 = +21 = 21$

(c) $- \times + = -$
$5 \times 8 = 40$
So $-5 \times 8 = -40$

1 Integers, powers and roots

Discovery 1.4

$4 \times 3 = 12$ From this calculation you can say that $12 \div 4 = 3$ and $12 \div 3 = 4$.

$10 \times 6 = 60$ From this calculation you can say that $60 \div 6 = 10$ and $60 \div 10 = 6$.

In Example 1.4 you saw that $6 \times -4 = -24$.

In the same way as for the calculations above you can write down these two division sums.

$$-24 \div 6 = -4 \quad \text{and} \quad -24 \div -4 = 6$$

(a) Work out 2×-9.
Then write two division sums in the same way as above.

(b) Work out -7×-4.
Then write two division sums in the same way as above.

Your answers to Discovery 1.4 suggest these rules.

$$+ \div - = -$$
$$\text{and}$$
$$- \div + = -$$

$$+ \div + = +$$
$$\text{and}$$
$$- \div - = +$$

You now have a complete set of rules for multiplying and dividing positive and negative numbers.

$$+ \times - = -$$
$$+ \div - = -$$
$$- \times + = -$$
$$- \div + = -$$

$$+ \times + = +$$
$$+ \div + = +$$
$$- \times - = +$$
$$- \div - = +$$

Here is another way of thinking of these rules.

Signs different: answer negative   Signs the same: answer positive

EXAMPLE 1.5

Work out these.
(a) 5×-3 **(b)** -2×-3 **(c)** $-10 \div 2$ **(d)** $-15 \div -3$

Solution

First work out the signs. Then work out the numbers.

(a) -15 $(+ \times - = -)$ **(b)** $+6 = 6$ $(- \times - = +)$
(c) -5 $(- \div + = -)$ **(d)** $+5 = 5$ $(- \div - = +)$

Multiplying and dividing by negative numbers

You can extend the rules to calculations with more than two numbers.

If there is an even number of negative signs the answer is positive.
If there is an odd number of negative signs the answer is negative.

EXAMPLE 1.6

Work out $-2 \times 6 \div -4$.

Solution

You can work this out by taking each part of the calculation in turn.

$-2 \times 6 = -12 \quad (- \times + = -)$
$-12 \div -4 = 3 \quad (- \div - = +)$

Or you can count the number of negative signs and then work out the numbers.

There are two negative signs so the answer is positive.

$-2 \times 6 \div -4 = 3$

EXERCISE 1.3

Work out these.

1. 4×3
2. -5×4
3. -6×-5
4. -9×6
5. 4×-7
6. -2×8
7. -3×-6
8. $24 \div -6$
9. $-25 \div -5$
10. $-32 \div 4$
11. $18 \div 6$
12. $-14 \div -7$
13. $-45 \div 5$
14. $49 \div -7$
15. $36 \div -9$
16. $6 \times 10 \div -5$
17. $-84 \div -12 \times -3$
18. $4 \times 9 \div -6$
19. $-3 \times -6 \div -2$
20. $-6 \times 2 \times -5 \div -3$

Challenge 1.3

Find the value of each of these expressions when $x = -3$, $y = 4$ and $z = -1$.

(a) $5xy$ (b) $x^2 + 2x$ (c) $2y^2 - 2yz$ (d) $3xz - 2xy + 3yz$ (e) $4xyz$

Powers and roots

The **square** of a number is the number multiplied by itself.
For example 2 squared is written 2^2 and equals $2 \times 2 = 4$.
The **cube** of a number is the number $\times$ number $\times$ number.
For example 2 cubed is written 2^3 and equals $2 \times 2 \times 2 = 8$.
It is useful to know the squares of the numbers 1 to 15 and the cubes of the numbers 1 to 5 and of 10.

Check up 1.5

(a) What are the squares of the numbers 1 to 15?

(b) What are the cubes of the numbers 1 to 5 and of 10?

The squares of integers are called **square numbers**.

The cubes of integers are called **cube numbers**.

Because $4^2 = 4 \times 4 = 16$, the **square root** of 16 is 4.
This is written as $\sqrt{16} = 4$.

But $(-4)^2 = -4 \times -4 = 16$.
So the square root of 16 is also -4.

This is often written as $\sqrt{16} = \pm 4$.
Similarly $\sqrt{81} = \pm 9$ and so on.

In many practical problems where the answer is a square root, the negative answer has no meaning and should be left out.

Because $5^3 = 5 \times 5 \times 5 = 125$, the **cube root** of 125 is 5.
This is written as $\sqrt[3]{125} = 5$.
It can only be positive.

$(-5)^3 = -5 \times -5 \times -5 = -125$.
So $\sqrt[3]{-125} = -5$.

Finding the square root is the reverse operation to squaring. Finding the cube root is the reverse operation to cubing. So you can find the square roots and cube roots of the squares and cubes you know.

Make sure you also know how to use your calculator to work out square roots and cube roots.

> **TIP** A common error is to think $1^2 = 2$ rather than 1.

EXAMPLE 1.7

(a) Find the square root of 57. Give your answer to 2 decimal places.
(b) Find the cube root of 86. Give your answer to 2 decimal places.

Solution

(a) $\sqrt{57} = \pm 7.55$ You press $\sqrt{}$ 5 7 on your calculator.

(b) $\sqrt[3]{86} = 4.41$ You press $\sqrt[3]{}$ 8 6 on your calculator.

EXERCISE 1.4

Do not use your calculator for questions **1** and **2**.

1 Write down the value of each of these.
 (a) 7^2 (b) 11^2 (c) $\sqrt{36}$ (d) $\sqrt{144}$
 (e) 2^3 (f) 10^3 (g) $\sqrt[3]{64}$ (h) $\sqrt[3]{1}$

2 A square has an area of 36 cm². What is the length of one side?

You may use your calculator for questions **3** to **7**.

3 Find the square of each of these numbers.
 (a) 25   (b) 40   (c) 35   (d) 32   (e) 1.2

4 Find the cube of each of these numbers.
 (a) 12   (b) 2.5   (c) 6.1   (d) 30   (e) 5.4

5 Find the square root of each of these numbers.
 Where necessary, give your answer correct to 2 decimal places.
 (a) 400   (b) 575   (c) 1284   (d) 3684   (e) 15 376

12 1 Integers, powers and roots

6 Find the cube root of each of these numbers.
Where necessary, give your answer correct to 2 decimal places.
  (a) 512 (b) 676 (c) 8000 (d) 9463 (e) 10 000

7 Find two numbers less than 200 which are both a square number and a cube number.

Challenge 1.4

(a) A cube has edges of length 14 cm.
What is its volume?

(b) A square has an area of 29 cm².
What is the length of each side? Give your answer correct to 2 decimal places.

(c) The volume of a cube is 96 cm³.
What is the area of one face of the cube? Give your answer correct to 2 decimal places.

Discovery 1.5

$2^2 \times 2^5 = (2 \times 2) \times (2 \times 2 \times 2 \times 2 \times 2) = (2 \times 2 \times 2 \times 2 \times 2 \times 2 \times 2) = 2^7$

$3^5 \div 3^2 = (3 \times 3 \times 3 \times 3 \times 3) \div (3 \times 3) = (3 \times 3 \times 3) = 3^3$

Copy and complete the following.

(a) $5^2 \times 5^3 = (5 \times 5) \times (\ldots\ldots\ldots\ldots) = (\ldots\ldots\ldots\ldots) = \ldots\ldots\ldots\ldots$

(b) $2^4 \times 2^2 =$ (c) $6^5 \times 6^3 =$ (d) $5^5 \div 5^3 =$ (e) $3^6 \div 3^3 =$ (f) $7^5 \div 7^2 =$

What do you notice?

Your answers to Discovery 1.5 were examples of these two rules.

$$n^a \times n^b = n^{a+b} \quad \text{and} \quad n^a \div n^b = n^{a-b}$$

You have already met a number with an index of 1 in Example 1.3.
A number to the power 1 equals the number itself.

$n^1 = n$ For example: $3^1 = 3$.

Any number with an index 0 is 1.

$n^0 = 1$ For example: $3^0 = 1$.

TIP To confirm this, put $a = b$ in $n^a \div n^b = n^{a-b}$.
$n^a \div n^a = 1$ and $n^{a-a} = n^0$.

Powers and roots

EXAMPLE 1.8

Write each of these as a single power of 3.

(a) $3^4 \times 3^2$ (b) $3^7 \div 3^2$ (c) $\dfrac{3^5 \times 3}{3^6}$

Solution

(a) When you multiply powers you add the indices.
$3^4 \times 3^2 = 3^{4+2} = 3^6$

(b) When you divide powers you subtract the indices.
$3^7 \div 3^2 = 3^{7-2} = 3^5$

(c) You can also combine operations.
$\dfrac{3^5 \times 3}{3^6} = 3^{5+1-6} = 3^0$

TIP: $3^0 = 1$ but you have been asked to write your answer as a power of 3 so you leave your answer as 3^0.

If you are asked to simplify the expression, you write $3^0 = 1$.

EXERCISE 1.5

1. Write these in simpler form using indices.
   (a) $3 \times 3 \times 3 \times 3 \times 3$
   (b) $7 \times 7 \times 7$
   (c) $3 \times 3 \times 3 \times 3 \times 5 \times 5$
   Hint: Write the 3s separately from the 5s.

2. Work out these, giving your answers in index form.
   (a) $5^2 \times 5^3$ (b) $10^5 \times 10^2$ (c) 8×8^3
   (d) $3^6 \times 3^4$ (e) $2^5 \times 2$

3. Work out these, giving your answers in index form.
   (a) $5^4 \div 5^2$ (b) $10^5 \div 10^2$ (c) $8^6 \div 8^3$
   (d) $3^6 \div 3^4$ (e) $2^3 \div 2^3$

4. Work out these, giving your answers in index form.
   (a) $5^4 \times 5^2 \div 5^2$ (b) $10^7 \times 10^6 \div 10^2$ (c) $8^4 \times 8 \div 8^3$ (d) $3^5 \times 3^3 \div 3^4$

5. Work out these, giving your answers in index form.
   (a) $\dfrac{2^6 \times 2^3}{2^4}$ (b) $\dfrac{3^6}{3^2 \times 3^2}$ (c) $\dfrac{5^3 \times 5^4}{5 \times 5^2}$ (d) $\dfrac{7^4 \times 7^4}{7^2 \times 7^3}$

Reciprocals

The **reciprocal** of a number is $\dfrac{1}{\text{the number}}$.

For example, the reciprocal of 2 is $\tfrac{1}{2}$.

The reciprocal of n is $\dfrac{1}{n}$.

The reciprocal of $\dfrac{1}{n}$ is n.

The reciprocal of $\dfrac{a}{b}$ is $\dfrac{b}{a}$.

0 does not have a reciprocal.

To find the reciprocal of a number without a calculator you divide 1 by the number. To find the reciprocal of a number with a calculator you use the $\boxed{x^{-1}}$ button.

EXAMPLE 1.9

Without using a calculator, find the reciprocal of each of these.
(a) 5 (b) $\tfrac{5}{8}$ (c) $1\tfrac{1}{8}$

Solution

(a) To find the reciprocal of a number, divide 1 by the number.
The reciprocal of 5 is $\tfrac{1}{5}$ or 0.2.

(b) The reciprocal of $\tfrac{5}{8}$ is $\tfrac{8}{5} = 1\tfrac{3}{5}$.
Note: You should always convert improper fractions to mixed numbers unless you are told not to.

(c) First convert $1\tfrac{1}{8}$ to an improper fraction: $\quad 1\tfrac{1}{8} = \tfrac{9}{8}$
The reciprocal of $\tfrac{9}{8} = \tfrac{8}{9}$.

EXAMPLE 1.10

Use your calculator to find the reciprocal of 1.25.
Give your answer as a decimal.

Solution

This is the sequence of keys to press.

$\boxed{1}\ \boxed{.}\ \boxed{2}\ \boxed{5}\ \boxed{x^{-1}}\ \boxed{=}$

The display should read 0.8.

Check up 1.6

Write down the reciprocal of each of these numbers.

(a) 2   (b) 5   (c) 10   (d) $\frac{3}{5}$

Discovery 1.6

(a) Multiply each of the numbers in Check up 1.6 by its reciprocal. What do you notice about your answers?

(b) Now try these products on your calculator.
  (i) 55×2 (press =) $\times \frac{1}{2}$ (press =)
  (ii) 15×4 (press =) $\times \frac{1}{4}$ (press =)
  (iii) 8×10 (press =) $\times 0.1$ (press =)
  What do you notice about your answers?

(c) Try some more calculations and explain what is happening.

Challenge 1.5

An **inverse operation** takes you back to the previous number.

Multiplying by a number and multiplying by its reciprocal are inverse operations.

Write down as many operations and their inverse operations as you can.

1 Integers, powers and roots

EXERCISE 1.6

Do not use your calculator for questions **1** to **3**.

1 Write down the reciprocal of each of these numbers.
   (a) 3   (b) 6   (c) 49   (d) 100   (e) 640

2 Write down the numbers of which these are the reciprocals.
   (a) $\frac{1}{16}$ (b) $\frac{1}{9}$ (c) $\frac{1}{52}$ (d) $\frac{1}{67}$ (e) $\frac{1}{1000}$

3 Find the reciprocal of each of these numbers.
   Give your answers as fractions or mixed numbers.
   (a) $\frac{4}{5}$ (b) $\frac{3}{8}$ (c) $1\frac{3}{5}$ (d) $3\frac{1}{3}$ (e) $\frac{2}{25}$

You may use your calculator for question **4**.

4 Find the reciprocal of each of these numbers.
   Give your answers as decimals.
   (a) 2.5   (b) 0.5   (c) 125   (d) 0.16   (e) 3.2

WHAT YOU HAVE LEARNED

- **A prime number has two factors only, 1 and itself**
- **How to write a number as the product of its prime factors**
- **The highest common factor (HCF) of a set of numbers is the largest number that will divide exactly into each of the numbers**
- **How to find the highest common factor of a pair of numbers using prime factors**
- **The lowest common multiple (LCM) of a set of numbers is the smallest number into which all the members of the set will divide**
- **How to find the lowest common multiple using prime factors**
- **That, when multiplying or dividing positive and negative numbers,**
  $+ \times + = +$ $- \times - = +$ $+ \times - = -$ $- \times + = -$
  $+ \div + = +$ $- \div - = +$ $+ \div - = -$ $- \div + = -$
- $5^3 = 5 \times 5 \times 5 = 125$, **so the cube root of 125 is 5**
- **That, when multiplying and dividing powers,**
  $n^a \times n^b = n^{a+b}$ **and** $n^a \div n^b = n^{a-b}$
- **The reciprocal of a number is 1 divided by the number: the reciprocal of n is $\frac{1}{n}$**
- **The reciprocal of $\frac{a}{b}$ is $\frac{b}{a}$**
- **0 does not have a reciprocal**

Reciprocals

MIXED EXERCISE 1

1. Write each of these numbers as a product of its prime factors.
   (a) 75
   (b) 140
   (c) 420

2. For each of these pairs of numbers
   • write the numbers as products of their prime factors.
   • state the highest common factor.
   • state the lowest common multiple.
   (a) 24 and 60
   (b) 100 and 150
   (c) 81 and 135

Do not use your calculator for questions **3** to **6**.

3. Work out these.
   (a) 4×-3
   (b) -2×8
   (c) $-48 \div -6$
   (d) $2 \times -6 \div -4$

4. Write down the square and the cube of each of these numbers.
   (a) 4
   (b) 6
   (c) 10

5. Write down the square root of each of these numbers.
   (a) 64
   (b) 196

6. Write down the cube root of each of these numbers.
   (a) 125
   (b) 27

You may use your calculator for questions **7** and **8**.

7. Find the square and the cube of each of these numbers.
   (a) 4.6
   (b) 21
   (c) 2.9

8. Find the square root and the cube root of each of these numbers. Give your answers correct to 2 decimal places.
   (a) 89
   (b) 124
   (c) 986

9. Work out these, giving your answers in index form.
   (a) $5^5 \times 5^2$
   (b) $10^5 \div 10^2$
   (c) $8^4 \times 8^3 \div 8^5$
   (d) $\dfrac{2^4 \times 2^4}{2^2}$
   (e) $\dfrac{3^9}{3^4 \times 3^2}$

10. Find the reciprocal of each of these numbers.
    (a) 5
    (b) 8
    (c) $\frac{1}{8}$
    (d) 0.1
    (e) 1.6

1 Integers, powers and roots

2 ALGEBRAIC MANIPULATION 1

THIS CHAPTER IS ABOUT
- Expanding brackets in algebra
- Factorising expressions
- Index notation in algebra

YOU SHOULD ALREADY KNOW
- Letters can be used to stand for numbers

Expanding brackets

Joe has a job making cheese sandwiches.
He uses two slices of bread and one slice of cheese for each sandwich.
He wants to know how much it will cost to make 25 sandwiches.

Joe uses 50 slices of bread and 25 slices of cheese to make 25 sandwiches.

You could use letters to represent the cost of the sandwich ingredients.
Let b represent the cost of each slice of bread in pence.
Let c represent the cost of each slice of cheese in pence.

You could then write one sandwich costs $2b + c$.

(You write $1c$ as just c.)

25 sandwiches cost 25 times this amount. You could write $25(2b + c)$.

$2b$ and c are called **terms**. $25(2b + c)$ is called an **expression**.

To work out the cost of 25 sandwiches you could write

$25(2b + c) = 50b + 25c$.

This is is called **expanding the brackets**. You multiply *each* term inside the brackets by the number outside the brackets.

EXAMPLE 2.1

Work out these.
(a) $10(2b + c)$
(b) $35(2b + c)$
(c) $16(2b + c)$
(d) $63(2b + c)$

Solution

(a) $10(2b + c) = 10 \times 2b + 10 \times c$
$= 20b + 10c$

(b) $35(2b + c) = 35 \times 2b + 35 \times c$
$= 70b + 35c$

(c) $16(2b + c) = 16 \times 2b + 16 \times c$
$= 32b + 16c$

(d) $63(2b + c) = 63 \times 2b + 63 \times c$
$= 126b + 63c$

You expand brackets with other letters or other signs, with numbers or with more terms in the same way.

EXAMPLE 2.2

Expand these.
(a) $12(2b + 7g)$
(b) $6(3m - 4n)$
(c) $8(2x - 5)$
(d) $3(4p + 2v - c)$

Solution

(a) $12(2b + 7g) = 12 \times 2b + 12 \times 7g$
$= 24b + 84g$

(b) $6(3m - 4n) = 6 \times 3m - 6 \times 4n$
$= 18m - 24n$

(c) $8(2x - 5) = 8 \times 2x - 8 \times 5$
$= 16x - 40$

(d) $3(4p + 2v - c) = 3 \times 4p + 3 \times 2v - 3 \times c$
$= 12p + 6v - 3c$

EXERCISE 2.1

Expand these.

1 10(2a + 3b)
2 3(2c + 7d)
3 5(3e − 8f)
4 7(4g − 3h)
5 5(2u + 3v)
6 6(5w + 3x)
7 7(3y + z)
8 8(2v + 5)
9 6(2 + 7w)
10 4(3 − 8a)
11 2(4g − 3)
12 5(7 − 4b)
13 2(3i + 4j − 5k)
14 4(5m − 3n + 2p)
15 6(2r − 3s − 4t)

Challenge 2.1

The diagram shows a rectangular room with a square rug at one end.

Write an expression for
(a) the length of the uncovered section of the room.
(b) the area of the uncovered section of the room.

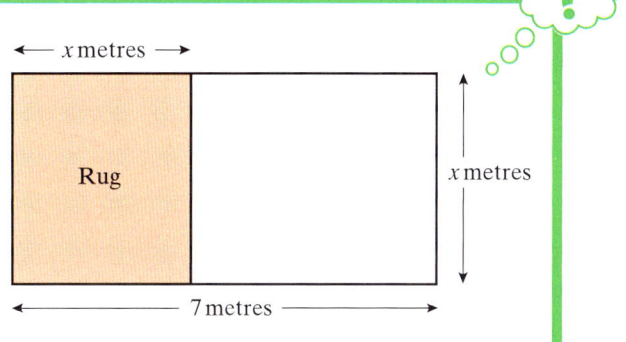

Combining terms

Terms with the same letter are called **like terms**. Like terms can be added.

One weekend Joe works on both Saturday and Sunday.
On Saturday he makes 75 cheese sandwiches and on Sunday he makes 45 cheese sandwiches

You can calculate the total cost of the bread and the cost of the cheese he uses as follows.

Write expressions for the two days and expand the brackets.

$75(2b + c) + 45(2b + c) = 150b + 75c + 90b + 45c$

Simplify the expression by collecting like terms.

$150b + 75c + 90b + 45c = 150b + 90b + 75c + 45c$
$= 240b + 120c$

EXAMPLE 2.3

Expand the brackets and simplify these.
(a) $10(2b + c) + 5(2b + c)$ **(b)** $35(b + c) + 16(2b + c)$
(c) $16(2b + c) + 63(b + 2c)$ **(d)** $30(b + 2c) + 18(b + c)$

Solution

(a) $10(2b + c) + 5(2b + c) = 20b + 10c + 10b + 5c$
$= 20b + 10b + 10c + 5c$
$= 30b + 15c$

(b) $35(b + c) + 16(2b + c) = 35b + 35c + 32b + 16c$
$= 35b + 32b + 35c + 16c$
$= 67b + 51c$

(c) $16(2b + c) + 63(b + 2c) = 32b + 16c + 63b + 126c$
$= 32b + 63b + 16c + 126c$
$= 95b + 142c$

(d) $30(b + 2c) + 18(b + c) = 30b + 60c + 18b + 18c$
$= 30b + 18b + 60c + 18c$
$= 48b + 78c$

You expand and simplify brackets with other letters or other signs or with numbers in the same way. You have to take particular care when there are minus signs in the expression.

EXAMPLE 2.4

Expand the brackets and simplify these.
(a) $2(3c + 4d) + 5(3c + 2d)$
(b) $5(4e + f) - 3(2e - 4f)$
(c) $5(4g + 3) - 2(3g + 4)$

Solution

(a) Multiply all terms in the first bracket by the number in front of that bracket.

Multiply all the terms in the second bracket by the number in front of that bracket.

Then collect like terms together.

$2(3c + 4d) + 5(3c + 2d) = 6c + 8d + 15c + 10d$
$= 6c + 15c + 8d + 10d$
$= 21c + 18d$

(b) Take care with the signs.
Think of the second part of the expression, $-3(2e - 4f)$, as $+(-3) \times (2e + (-4f))$.
You need to multiply both the terms in the second bracket by -3.
You learned the rules for calculating with negative numbers in Chapter 1.

$$\begin{aligned}5(4e + f) - 3(2e - 4f) &= 5(4e + f) + (-3) \times (2e + (-4f)) \\ &= 5 \times 4e + 5 \times f + (-3) \times 2e + (-3) \times (-4f) \\ &= 20e + 5f + (-6e) + (+12f) \\ &= 20e + (-6e) + 5f + 12f \\ &= 20e - 6e + 5f + 12f \\ &= 14e + 17f\end{aligned}$$

(c) Again you need to take need to care with the signs.
Think of the second part of the expression, $-2(3g + 4)$, as $+(-2) \times (3g + 4)$.
You need to multiply both the terms in the second bracket by -2.

$$\begin{aligned}5(4g + 3) - 2(3g + 4) &= 5(4g + 3) + (-2) \times (3g + 4) \\ &= 20g + 15 + (-2) \times 3g + (-2) \times 4 \\ &= 20g + 15 + (-6g) + (-8) \\ &= 20g + (-6g) + 15 + (-8) \\ &= 20g - 6g + 15 - 8 \\ &= 14g + 7\end{aligned}$$

EXERCISE 2.2

Expand the brackets and simplify these.

1   **(a)** $8(2a + 3) + 2(2a + 7)$ **(b)** $5(3b + 7) + 6(2b + 3)$
    (c) $2(3 + 8c) + 3(2 + 7c)$ **(d)** $6(2 + 3a) + 4(5 + a)$

2   **(a)** $5(2s + 3t) + 4(2s + 7t)$ **(b)** $2(2v + 7w) + 5(2v + 7w)$
    (c) $7(3x + 8y) + 3(2x + 7y)$ **(d)** $3(2v + 5w) + 4(8v + 3w)$

3   **(a)** $4(3x + 5) + 3(3x - 4)$ **(b)** $2(4y + 5) + 3(2y - 3)$
    (c) $5(2 + 7z) + 4(3 - 8z)$ **(d)** $3(2 + 5x) + 5(6 - x)$

4   **(a)** $3(2n + 7p) + 2(5n - 6p)$ **(b)** $5(3q + 8r) + 3(2q - 9r)$
    (c) $7(2d + 3e) + 3(3d - 5e)$ **(d)** $4(2f + 7g) + 3(2f - 9g)$
    (e) $3(3h - 8j) - 5(2h - 7j)$ **(f)** $6(2k - 3m) - 3(2k - 7m)$

Factorising

You learned in Chapter 1 that the highest common factor of a set of numbers is the largest number that will divide into all of the numbers in the set.

Remember that in algebra you use letters to stand for numbers. For example, $2x = 2 \times x$ and $3x = 3 \times x$.
You do not know what x is but you do know that $2x$ and $3x$ both divide by x. So x is the highest common factor of $2x$ and $3x$.

When you have unlike terms, for example $2x$ and $4y$, you must assume that x and y do not have any common factors. However, you can look for common factors in the numbers. The highest common factor of 2 and 4 is 2 so the highest common factor of $2x$ and $4y$ is 2.

Factorising is the reverse of expanding brackets. You divide each of the terms in the bracket by the highest common factor and write this common factor outside the bracket.

EXAMPLE 2.5

Factorise these.
(a) $(12x + 16)$ (b) $(x - x^2)$ (c) $(8x^2 - 12x)$

Solution

(a) $(12x + 16)$ The common factor of $12x$ and 16 is 4.
   $4(\quad)$ You write this factor outside the bracket.
   You then divide each term inside the original bracket by the common factor, 4.
   $12x \div 4 = 3x$ and $16 \div 4 = 4$.
   $4(3x + 4)$ You write the new terms inside the bracket.
   $(12x + 16) = 4(3x + 4)$

> **TIP** Check that your answer is correct by expanding it.
> $4(3x + 4) = 4 \times 3x + 4 \times 4 = 12x + 16$

(b) $(x - x^2)$ The common factor of x and x^2 is x.
   (Remember that x^2 is $x \times x$.)
   $x(\quad)$ You write this factor outside the bracket.
   You then divide each term inside the original bracket by the common factor, x.
   $x \div x = 1$ and $x^2 \div x = x$
   $(x - x^2) = x(1 - x)$

24 2 Algebraic manipulation 1

(c) $(8x^2 - 12x)$ Think about the numbers and the letters separately and then combine them. The common factor of 8 and 12 is 4 and the common factor of x^2 and x is x. Therefore, the common factor of $8x^2$ and $12x$ is $4 \times x = 4x$.

$4x(\quad)$ You write this factor outside the bracket.
You then divide each term inside the original bracket by the common factor, $4x$.
$8x^2 \div 4x = 2x$ and $12x \div 4x = 3$
$(8x^2 - 12x) = 4x(2x - 3)$

EXERCISE 2.3

Factorise these.

1 (a) $(10x + 15)$ (b) $(2x + 6)$ (c) $(8x - 12)$ (d) $(4x - 20)$

2 (a) $(14 + 7x)$ (b) $(8 + 12x)$ (c) $(15 - 10x)$ (d) $(9 - 12x)$

3 (a) $(3x^2 + 5x)$ (b) $(5x^2 + 20x)$ (c) $(12x^2 - 8x)$ (d) $(6x^2 - 8x)$

Expanding pairs of brackets

Earlier in this chapter you learned how to expand brackets of the type $25(2b + c)$. In that case you were multiplying a bracket by a single term. A term can be a number or a letter or a combination of the two, such as $3x$.

You can also expand pairs of brackets. In this case you are multiplying a bracket by another bracket. You must multiply each term inside the second bracket by each term inside the first bracket. The examples which follow show two methods for doing this.

EXAMPLE 2.6

Expand these.
(a) $(a + 2)(a + 5)$
(b) $(b + 4)(2b + 7)$
(c) $(2m + 5)(3m - 4)$

Solution

(a) Method 1
Use a grid to multiply each of the terms in the second bracket by each of the terms in the first.

×	a	+2
a	a^2	+2a
+5	+5a	+10

$= a^2 + 2a + 5a + 10$ Collect like terms together: $2a + 5a = 7a$.
$= a^2 + 7a + 10$

Method 2
Use the word FOIL to make sure you multiply each term in the second bracket by each term in the first.
F: first × first
O: outer × outer
I: inner × inner
L: last × last
If you draw arrows to show the multiplications, you can think of a smiley face.

$(a + 2)(a + 5)$

$= a \times a + a \times 5 + 2 \times a + 2 \times 5$
$= a^2 + 5a + 2a + 10$
$= a^2 + 7a + 10$

(b) Method 1

×	b	+4
2b	$2b^2$	+8b
+7	+7b	+28

$= 2b^2 + 8b + 7b + 28$
$= 2b^2 + 15b + 28$

Method 2

$(b + 4)(2b + 7)$

$= b \times 2b + b \times 7 + 4 \times 2b + 4 \times 7$
$= 2b^2 + 7b + 8b + 28$
$= 2b^2 + 15b + 28$

(c) Method 1

×	2m	+5
3m	$6m^2$	+15m
−4	−8m	−20

$= 6m^2 + 15m - 8m - 20$
$= 6m^2 + 7m - 20$

Method 2

$(2m + 5)(3m - 4)$

$= 2m \times 3m + 2m \times -4 + 5 \times 3m + 5 \times -4$
$= 6m^2 - 8m + 15m - 20$
$= 6m^2 + 7m - 20$

TIP Choose the method you prefer and stick to it.

EXERCISE 2.4

Expand the brackets and simplify these. Use the method you prefer.

1. (a) $(a + 3)(a + 7)$ (b) $(b + 7)(b + 4)$ (c) $(3 + c)(2 + c)$
2. (a) $(3d + 5)(3d - 4)$ (b) $(4e + 5)(2e - 3)$ (c) $(2 + 7f)(3 - 8f)$
3. (a) $(2g - 3)(2g - 7)$ (b) $(2h - 7)(2h - 7)$ (c) $(3j - 8)(2j - 7)$
4. (a) $(2k + 7)(5k - 6)$ (b) $(3 + 8m)(2 - 9m)$ (c) $(2 + 3n)(3 - 5n)$
5. (a) $(2 + 7p)(2 - 9p)$ (b) $(3r - 8)(2r - 7)$ (c) $(2s - 3)(2s - 7)$

Challenge 2.2

What pairs of brackets have been expanded to give each of these expressions?
(a) $m^2 + 3m + 2$ (b) $x^2 - 5x + 6$ (c) $2y^2 + 3y - 2$

Challenge 2.3

The diagram shows a rectangular garden with a shed in one corner.

(a) Write an expression for
  (i) the length of the garden.
  (ii) the width of the garden.

(b) Write an expression for the area of the garden.
Simplify the expression.

Challenge 2.4

The diagram shows a rectangular picture hanging on a rectangular wall in a gallery.

The picture is placed so that it is 1 metre from the top of the wall and 1 metre from the bottom of the wall.

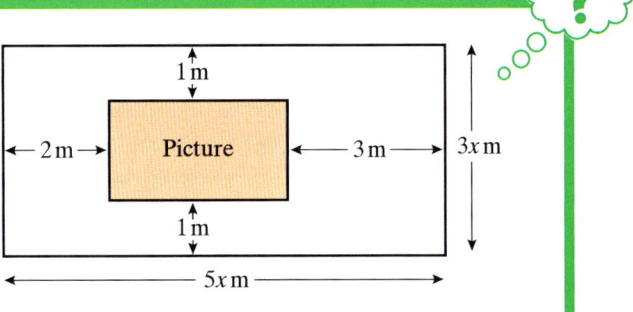

continues …

Expanding pairs of brackets

Challenge 2.4 continued

The picture is also 2 metres from the left-hand end of the wall and 3 metres from the right-hand end of the wall.

(a) Write an expression for
  (i) the length of the picture.
  (ii) the width of the picture.

(b) Write an expression for the area of the wall occupied by the picture. Simplify the expression.

Index notation

In Chapter 1 you learned that you can write 2 to the power 4 as 2^4 and that the power, 4 in this case, is called the index. You can say that 2^4 is written in **index notation**.

You can use index notation in algebra too. You have already met x^2. This means x squared or x to the power 2.

y^5 is another example of an expression written using index notation. It means y to the power 5 or $y \times y \times y \times y \times y$. The index is 5.

EXAMPLE 2.7

Write these using index notation.
(a) $5 \times 5 \times 5 \times 5 \times 5 \times 5$
(b) $x \times x \times x \times x \times x \times x \times x$
(c) $p \times p \times p \times p \times r \times r \times r$
(d) $3w \times 4w \times 5w$

Solution

(a) $5 \times 5 \times 5 \times 5 \times 5 \times 5 = 5$ to the power $6 = 5^6$

(b) $x \times x \times x \times x \times x \times x \times x = x$ to the power $7 = x^7$

(c) $p \times p \times p \times p \times r \times r \times r = p^4 \times r^3 - p^4 r^3$

(d) $3w$, $4w$ and $5w$ are like terms so you multiply the numbers together first, then the letters.
$3w \times 4w \times 5w = (3 \times 4 \times 5) \times (w \times w \times w) = 60 \times w^3 = 60w^3$

EXERCISE 2.5

Simplify each of the following, writing your answer using index notation.

1. (a) $3 \times 3 \times 3 \times 3$ (b) $7 \times 7 \times 7$ (c) $10 \times 10 \times 10 \times 10 \times 10$

2. (a) $x \times x \times x \times x \times x$ (b) $y \times y \times y \times y$ (c) $z \times z \times z \times z \times z \times z$

3. (a) $m \times m \times n \times n \times n \times n$
   (b) $f \times f \times f \times f \times g \times g \times g \times g \times g$
   (c) $p \times p \times p \times r \times r \times r \times r$

4. (a) $2k \times 4k \times 7k$ (b) $3y \times 5y \times 8y$ (c) $4d \times 2d \times d$

Challenge 2.5

Simplify each of the following, writing your answer using index notation.

(a) $m^2 \times m^4$ (b) $x^3 \times 5x^6$ (c) $5y^4 \times 3y^3$ (d) $2b^3 \times 3b^2 \times 4b$

WHAT YOU HAVE LEARNED

- When you expand brackets such as $25(2b + c)$ you multiply each of the terms inside the bracket by the number (or term) outside the bracket
- When you expand brackets such as $(a + 2)(a + 5)$ you multiply each of the terms in the second bracket by each of the terms in the first bracket
- One way to expand brackets is to use a grid. Another way is to use the word FOIL to make sure you perform all the multiplications
- Factorising expressions is the reverse of expanding brackets
- To factorise an expression you take the common factors outside the bracket
- How to use index notation in algebra

Index notation

MIXED EXERCISE 2

1 Expand these.
(a) $8(3a + 2b)$
(b) $5(4a + 3b)$
(c) $12(3a - 5b)$
(d) $9(a - 2b)$
(e) $3(4x + 5y)$
(f) $6(3x - 2y)$
(g) $4(5x - 3y)$
(h) $2(4x + y)$
(i) $5(3f - 4g)$
(j) $3(2j + 5k)$
(k) $7(r + 2s)$
(l) $4(3v - w)$

2 Expand the brackets and simplify these.
(a) $2(3x + 4) + 3(2x + 1)$
(b) $4(2x + 3) + 3(4x + 5)$
(c) $2(2x + 3) + 3(x + 2)$
(d) $5(2y + 3) + 2(3y - 5)$
(e) $3(3y + 5) + 2(3y - 4)$
(f) $3(5y + 2) + 2(3y - 1)$
(g) $3(2a + 4) - 3(a + 2)$
(h) $2(6m + 2) - 3(2m + 1)$
(i) $6(3p + 4) - 3(4p + 2)$
(j) $4(5t + 3) - 3(2t - 4)$
(k) $2(4j + 8) - 3(3j - 5)$
(l) $6(2w + 5) - 4(3w - 4)$

3 Factorise these.
(a) $(4x + 8)$
(b) $(6x + 12)$
(c) $(9x - 6)$
(d) $(12x - 18)$
(e) $(6 - 10x)$
(f) $(10 - 15x)$
(g) $(24 + 8x)$
(h) $(16x + 12)$
(i) $(6x + 8)$
(j) $(32x - 12)$
(k) $(20 - 16x)$
(l) $(15 + 20x)$
(m) $(2x - x^2)$
(n) $(3y - 7y^2)$
(o) $(5z^2 + 2z)$

4 Expand the brackets and simplify these.
(a) $(a + 5)(a + 4)$
(b) $(a + 2)(a + 3)$
(c) $(3 + a)(4 + a)$
(d) $(x - 1)(x + 8)$
(e) $(x + 9)(x - 5)$
(f) $(x - 2)(x - 1)$
(g) $(3x + 4)(x + 9)$
(h) $(y - 3)(2y + 7)$
(i) $(2 - 3p)(7 - 2p)$
(j) $(2p + 4)(3p - 2)$
(k) $(t - 5)(4t - 3)$
(l) $(2a - 3)(3a + 5)$

5 Simplify each of the following, writing your answer using index notation.
(a) $4 \times 4 \times 4 \times 4 \times 4 \times 4$
(b) $5 \times 5 \times 5 \times 5$
(c) $2 \times 2 \times 2 \times 2 \times 2$
(d) $a \times a \times a \times a \times a \times a \times a$
(e) $j \times j \times j$
(f) $t \times t \times t \times t \times t \times t$
(g) $v \times v \times v \times w \times w \times w$
(h) $d \times d \times d \times e \times e \times e \times e \times e \times e$
(i) $x \times x \times x \times y \times y \times y \times y \times y$
(j) $5p \times 4p \times 3p$

3 → PROPERTIES OF SHAPES

THIS CHAPTER IS ABOUT

- Finding the area of a triangle and parallelogram
- The angle properties associated with parallel lines
- The angle sum of a triangle, of a quadrilateral and of any polygon
- Exterior angles of triangles and of other polygons
- The properties of special quadrilaterals

YOU SHOULD ALREADY KNOW

- The common metric units for length and area
- How to find the area of a rectangle
- Angles on a straight line add up to 180°
- Angles around a point add up to 360°
- When two straight lines cross, the vertically opposite angles are equal
- The meaning of the word *parallel*
- That a quadrilateral has four sides
- Some properties of special quadrilaterals

The area of a triangle

You already know that

Area of a rectangle = Length × Width

or

Area of a rectangle = $l \times w$.

Look at this diagram.

Area of rectangle ABCD = $l \times w$

You can see that

Area of triangle ABC = $\frac{1}{2} \times$ area of ABCD
$= \frac{1}{2} \times l \times w$.

Now look at a different triangle.
From the diagram you can see that

Area of triangle ABC = $\frac{1}{2}$ area of BEAF + $\frac{1}{2}$ area of FADC
$= \frac{1}{2}$ area of BEDC
$= \frac{1}{2} \times l \times w$.

The area of a triangle   31

This shows that the area of any triangle can be found using the formula

> Area of a triangle = $\frac{1}{2}$ × base × height
> or
> $A = \frac{1}{2} \times b \times h$.

Note that the height of a triangle, h, is measured at right angles to the base. It is the **perpendicular height** or **altitude** of the triangle.

TIP You can use any of the sides as the base provided that you use the perpendicular height that goes with it.

EXAMPLE 3.1

Find the area of this triangle.

Solution

Use the formula.
$A = \frac{1}{2} \times b \times h$
$= \frac{1}{2} \times 10 \times 6$
$= 30 \text{ cm}^2$

TIP Do not forget the units, but notice how you only need to put the units in the answer. Remember that the two measurements used must have the same units.

3 Properties of shapes

EXERCISE 3.1

Find the area of each of these triangles.

1 8 cm base, 4 cm height

2 base 10 cm, height 10 cm

3 base 20 m, height 16 m

4 base 10 mm, height 15 mm

5 base 8 cm, height 16 cm

6 base 7 cm, height 5 cm

7 base 11 cm, height 10 cm

8 base 24 cm, height 12 cm

9 sides 15 m, 20 m, 25 m with height 12 m

10 base 15 m (with sides 17 m, 17 m), height 16 m

Challenge 3.1

The vertices of a triangle are at (2, 2), (7, 2) and (4, 6).

Draw the triangle on squared paper and calculate its area.

Challenge 3.2

A triangle has an area of 12 cm². Its base is 4 cm long.

Work out the perpendicular height of this triangle.

Challenge 3.3

In triangle ABC, AB = 6 cm, BC = 8 cm and AC = 10 cm. Angle ABC = 90°.

(a) Find the area of triangle ABC.

H is the point on AC such that angle BHC = 90°.

(b) Find BH.

The area of a parallelogram

There are two ways to find the area of a parallelogram.

It can be cut and rearranged to form a rectangle. So,

$A = b \times h$.

Or it can be split into two congruent triangles along a diagonal.
(Remember that congruent means exactly the same size.)

The area of each triangle is $A = \frac{1}{2} \times b \times h$, so the total area of the parallelogram is

$A = 2 \times \frac{1}{2} \times b \times h$
$= b \times h$.

Note that the height of the parallelogram is the *perpendicular* height, just as in the formula for the area of a triangle.

> Area of a parallelogram = $b \times h$
>
> or
>
> $A = b \times h$

34 3 Properties of shapes

EXAMPLE 3.2

Find the area of this parallelogram.

Solution

Use the formula. Make sure you choose the correct measurement for the height.

$A = b \times h$
$= 6 \times 4$
$= 24 \, cm^2$

EXERCISE 3.2

Find the area of each of these parallelograms.

1. 4 cm, 6 cm
2. 8 cm, 9 cm
3. 10 m, 6.4 m
4. 5 cm, 7 cm, 6 cm
5. 5 cm, 4 cm, 3.5 cm
6. 7.5 cm, 4 cm
7. 7 cm, 6 cm
8. 12 m, 15 m, 12 m
9. 8.4 cm, 5 cm, 6 cm
10. 8 cm, 6 cm, 2 cm, 10 cm

The area of a parallelogram 35

Challenge 3.4

Use appropriate measurements to find the area of each of these parallelograms.

(a)

(b)

Challenge 3.5

Find the lengths x and y.

(a) Area = 36 cm², 9 cm, x

(b) 5 cm, Area = $37\frac{1}{2}$ cm², y

Challenge 3.6

OABC is a parallelogram with vertices at O(0, 0), A(4, 2), B(6, 0) and C(2, −2).

(a) Draw the parallelogram OABC on squared paper.
(b) Work out the area of OABC.

3 Properties of shapes

Angles made with parallel lines

Discovery 3.1

This is a map of part of New York.

(a) Find Broadway and W 32nd Street on the map.
Find some more angles equal to the angle between Broadway and W 32nd Street.

Two angles that add up to 180° are called **supplementary** angles.

(b) Find an angle that is supplementary to the angle between Broadway and W 32nd Street.

(c) Explain you results.

In Discovery 3.1 you should have found three sorts of angles made with parallel lines.

Corresponding angles

The diagrams show equal angles made by a line cutting across a pair of parallel lines. These equal angles are called **corresponding** angles. Corresponding angles occur in an F-shape.

Angles made with parallel lines 37

Alternate angles

These diagrams also show equal angles made by a line cutting across a pair of parallel lines. These equal angles are called **alternate** angles. Alternate angles occur in a Z-shape.

Allied angles

You can see that the two angles marked in these diagrams are not equal. Instead, they are supplementary. (Remember that supplementary angles add up to 180°.) These angles are called **allied** angles or **co-interior** angles and occur in a C-shape.

> **TIP**
> Questions about finding the size of angles often ask you to give reasons for your answers. This means that you must say why, for example, angles are equal. Stating that the angles are alternate angles or corresponding angles would be possible reasons. This is shown in the next example.

EXAMPLE 3.3

Work out the size of the lettered angles. Give a reason for each answer.

Solution

$a = 70°$ Corresponding angles
$b = 45°$ Alternate angles
$c = 65°$ Angles on a straight line add up to 180°
           or Allied angles add up to 180°
           or Angles in a triangle add up to 180°

3 Properties of shapes

EXERCISE 3.3

Find the size of the lettered angles. Give a reason for each answer.

1. 74°, a

2. 115°, b

3. 125°, c

4. 65°, d, e

5. 110°, f, g

6. i, j, h, 125°

7. 65°, l, n, m, k

8. 101°, o, q, p

9. t, s, 68°, r, 83°

10. u, v, w, 45°, 67°

Angles made with parallel lines

Challenge 3.7

One of the angles in a parallelogram is 125°.

(a) Make a sketch of the parallelogram and mark this angle.

(b) Calculate the other three angles and mark them on your diagram. Give a reason for each of your answers.

Challenge 3.8

Make a list of capital letters which contain parallel lines.

Mark pairs of equal angles on each sketch.

Give a reason for each of the pairs of angles.

Challenge 3.9

ABCD is a parallelogram.

Show that triangles ABD and CDB contain the same angles.

Give a reason for each step of your work.

Challenge 3.10

Draw a circle using compasses.
Draw a quadrilateral with its vertices on the edge of the circle. Measure the opposite angles of the quadrilateral and add each pair together.

What did you get for your two answers?

Try this again with a different sized circle and a different shaped quadrilateral.

Check your answers with your classmates. Did they get the same?

The angles in a triangle

You already know that the angles in a triangle add up to 180°. You can use the properties of angles associated with parallel lines to prove this fact.

Proof 3.1

You draw a line parallel to the base of a triangle.

$x + a + y = 180°$ Angles on a straight line add up to 180°
$b = x$ Alternate angles
$c = y$ Alternate angles

So

$b + a + c = 180°$ Since $b = x$ and $c = y$

This proves that the three angles in any triangle add up to 180°.

The angles inside a triangle (or any polygon) are called **interior** angles. If you extend a side of the triangle, there is an angle between the extended side and the next side. This angle is called an **exterior** angle.

The exterior angle of a triangle is equal to the sum of the opposite, interior angles.

Here is a proof of this fact.

Proof 3.2

One side is extended, as shown in the diagram.

$x + c = 180°$ Angles on a straight line add up to 180°
$a + b + c = 180°$ Angles in a triangle add up to 180°

So $x = a + b$

     Since $x = 180° - c$ and $a + b = 180° - c$

This proves that the exterior angle of a triangle is equal to the sum of the opposite, interior angles.

The angles in a triangle

Challenge 3.11

There is another way to prove that the exterior angle of a triangle is equal to the sum of the opposite, interior angles. It uses angle facts associated with parallel lines.

Complete a proof for this diagram. Remember to give a reason for each step.

You can use the angle facts associated with triangles to work out missing angles. This is shown in the next example.

EXAMPLE 3.4

Work out the size of the lettered angles. Give a reason for each answer.

Solution

$d = 180° − (51° + 90°)$ Angles in a triangle add up to 180°

$d = 39°$

$e = 51° + 90°$ Exterior angle of a triangle equals the sum

$e = 141°$ of the opposite interior angles

The angles in a quadrilateral

A quadrilateral is a four-sided shape.

> The angles in a quadrilateral add up to 360°.

You can divide a quadrilateral into two triangles. You can then use the fact that angles in a triangle add up to 180° to prove this fact.

Proof 3.3

A quadrilateral is divided into two triangles, as shown in the diagram.

$a + b + c = 180°$ Angles in a triangle add up to 180°
$p + q + r = 180°$ Angles in a triangle add up to 180°
$a + b + c + p + q + r = 360°$, so

the interior angles of a quadrilateral add up to 360°.

You can use this fact to work out missing angles in quadrilaterals.

EXAMPLE 3.5

Work out the size of angle x.
Give a reason for your answer.

Solution

$x = 360° - (126° + 90° + 74°)$ Angles in a quadrilateral add up to 360°
$x = 70°$

EXERCISE 3.4

Find the size of the lettered angles. Give a reason for each answer.

1. (triangle with angles 85°, 60°, a)
2. (triangle with angles b, 116°, 23°)
3. (triangle with angles 90°, 47°, c)
4. (triangle with angles d, 110°, d)

The angles in a quadrilateral   43

5 — triangle with angles e, e, e and tick marks on all sides

6 — triangle with angles 65°, 120°, f

7 — 51°, right angle, h, g

8 — quadrilateral with 45°, 60°, 140°, i

9 — 67°, 110°, k, j, 60°

10 — quadrilateral with 72°, m, 80°, l, 104°

Special quadrilaterals

You already know about the special quadrilaterals: square, rectangle, parallelogram, rhombus, kite, arrowhead and trapezium. There is also a special type of trapezium called an isosceles trapezium.

Square

Rectangle

Parallelogram

Rhombus

Kite

Arrowhead

Trapezium

Isosceles trapezium

Challenge 3.12

Copy this decision tree.

Take each of the eight special quadrilaterals in turn.

Work through the decision tree with each shape and fill in the boxes at the bottom.

```
                          Quadrilateral
                                │
                                ▼
                        ┌───────────────┐
                        │ Both pairs of │  No    ┌───────────────┐  No
                        │ sides         │──────▶ │ One pair of   │──────▶
                        │ parallel?     │        │ sides         │
                        └───────┬───────┘        │ parallel?     │
                                │ Yes            └───────┬───────┘
                                ▼                        │ Yes
                        ┌───────────────┐
                  No    │ All sides     │
              ◀─────────│ equal?        │
                        └───────┬───────┘
                                │ Yes
                                ▼
   ┌──────────┐          ┌──────────┐       ┌───────────────┐   No     ┌──────────┐   No
   │ All      │   No     │ All      │       │ Two pairs of  │──────▶   │ Is one   │──────▶
No │ angles   │◀──       │ angles   │       │ angles equal? │          │ angle    │
◀──│ equal?   │          │ equal?   │       └───────┬───────┘          │ reflex?  │
   └────┬─────┘          └────┬─────┘               │ Yes              └────┬─────┘
        │ Yes                 │ Yes                 │                       │ Yes
        ▼                     ▼                     ▼                       ▼
     ┌────┐  ┌────┐    ┌────┐  ┌────┐        ┌────┐  ┌────┐           ┌────┐  ┌────┐
     │    │  │    │    │    │  │    │        │    │  │    │           │    │  │    │
     └────┘  └────┘    └────┘  └────┘        └────┘  └────┘           └────┘  └────┘
```

Check up 3.1

Look again at the diagram of the kite. It has one pair of opposite angles equal. Sides next to each other are called **adjacent** sides. A kite has two pairs of adjacent sides equal. Look at the diagonals. They cross at right angles and one of the diagonals is cut into two equal parts, or **bisected**, by the other.

Copy and complete this table for each of the special quadrilaterals.

Name	Diagram	Angles	Length of sides	Parallel sides	Diagonals

Special quadrilaterals

EXERCISE 3.5

1 Name each of these quadrilaterals.

2 Name the quadrilateral or quadrilaterals which have the following properties.
   (a) All sides the same length
   (b) Two pairs of sides equal in length
   (c) Opposite sides the same length but not all four sides the same length
   (d) Just two sides parallel
   (e) Diagonals that cross at 90°

3 Plot each set of points on squared paper and join them in order to make a quadrilateral. Use a different grid for each part.
Write down the special name of each quadrilateral.
   (a) (3, 0), (5, 4), (3, 8), (1, 4)   **(b)** (8, 1), (6, 3), (2, 3), (1, 1)
   (c) (1, 2), (3, 1), (7, 2), (5, 3)   **(d)** (6, 2), (2, 3), (1, 2), (2, 1)

4 A rectangle is a special type of parallelogram.
What extra properties does a rectangle have?

5 A quadrilateral has angles of 70°, 70°, 110° and 110°.
Which special quadrilaterals could have these as their angles?
Draw each of these quadrilaterals and mark on the angles.

The angles in a polygon

A polygon is a closed shape made with straight sides.

Earlier in this chapter you saw how, by dividing a quadrilateral into two triangles, you could see that the interior angles of a quadrilateral add up to 360°.

In the same way you can divide a polygon into triangles to find the sum of the interior angles of any polygon.

Discovery 3.2

Copy and complete this table.

Number of sides	Diagram	Name	Sum of interior angles
3		Triangle	$1 \times 180° = 180°$
4		Quadrilateral	$2 \times 180° = 360°$
5			$3 \times 180° =$
6			
7			
8			
9			
10			
n			

The angles in a polygon 47

At each **vertex**, or corner, of a polygon there is an interior angle and an exterior angle.

Since these form a straight line you know the sum of the angles.

Interior angle + Exterior angle = 180°

Discovery 3.3

Here is a pentagon showing all its exterior angles.

(a) Measure each of the exterior angles and find the total.
Check with your neighbour. Do you both have the same total?

(b) Draw another polygon.
Extend its sides and measure each of the exterior angles.
Is the total of these angles the same as for the pentagon?

You may have noticed that the five exterior angles of the pentagon go round in a full circle. This gives you another fact about the angles of a polygon.

The sum of the exterior angles of a polygon is 360°.

EXAMPLE 3.6

Two of the exterior angles of this pentagon are equal. Find their size.

Solution

$$x + x + 72° + 80° + 86° = 360°$$
$$2x = 360° - 238°$$
$$2x = 122°$$
$$x = 61°$$

Exterior angles of a polygon add up to 360°

Regular polygons

You already know that, for a regular polygon, the sides are all the same length and the interior angles are all the same size. You can see now that the exterior angles are also all the same size.

EXAMPLE 3.7

Find the size of the exterior and interior angles of a regular octagon.

Solution

An octagon has eight sides.

Exterior angle $= \dfrac{360°}{8}$ Since the sum of the exterior angles of any polygon is 360°

Exterior angle $= 45°$

Interior angle $= 180° - 45°$ Since the interior angle and the exterior angle add up to 180°

Interior angle $= 135°$

Check up 3.2

Calculate the exterior and interior angles of each of these regular polygons: triangle (equilateral triangle), quadrilateral (square), pentagon, hexagon, heptagon, nonagon (nine sides) and decagon.

Remember that, for any regular polygon,

$$\text{The angle at the centre} = \frac{360°}{\text{Number of sides}}.$$

Note that the size of the angle at the centre of a polygon is the same as the exterior angle of the polygon. Can you see why?

Check up 3.3

Lines are drawn from the centre of a regular pentagon to each of its vertices.

(a) What can you say about the triangles formed?
(b) What sort of triangles are they?
(c) Calculate the size of the lettered angles. Give a reason for each of your answers.

EXERCISE 3.6

1 A polygon has 15 sides.
   Work out the sum of the interior angles of this polygon.

2 A polygon has 20 sides.
   Work out the sum of the interior angles of this polygon.

3 Three of the exterior angles of a quadrilateral are 94°, 50° and 85°.
   (a) Work out the size of the fourth exterior angle.
   (b) Work out the size of the interior angles of the quadrilateral.

4 Four of the exterior angles of a pentagon are 90°, 80°, 57° and 75°.
   (a) Work out the size of the other exterior angle.
   (b) Work out the size of the interior angles of the pentagon.

5 A regular polygon has 12 sides.
   Find the size of the exterior and interior angles of this polygon.

6 A regular polygon has 100 sides.
   Find the size of the exterior and interior angles of this polygon.

7 A regular polygon has an exterior angle of 24°.
   Work out the number of sides that the polygon has.

8 A regular polygon has an interior angle of 162°.
   Work out the number of sides that the polygon has.

3 Properties of shapes

WHAT YOU HAVE LEARNED

- The area of a triangle = $\frac{1}{2}$ × base × perpendicular height or $A = \frac{1}{2} \times b \times h$
- The area of a parallelogram = base × perpendicular height or $A = b \times h$
- When a line crosses a pair of parallel lines, corresponding angles are equal
- When a line crosses a pair of parallel lines, alternate angles are equal
- When a line crosses a pair of parallel lines, allied angles add up to 180°
- The interior angles of a triangle add up to 180°
- The exterior angle of a triangle is equal to the sum of the opposite, interior angles
- The interior angles of a quadrilateral add up to 360°
- The properties of special quadrilaterals
- The sum of the interior angles of a polygon with n sides = 180° × (n − 2)
- The interior angle and the exterior angle of a polygon add up to 180°
- The sum of the exterior angles of a polygon is 360°
- The angle at the centre of a regular polygon with n sides is $\dfrac{360°}{n}$

MIXED EXERCISE 3

1 Find the area of each of these triangles.

(a) 3 cm, 6 cm

(b) 8 cm, 2 cm

(c) 5 cm, 13 cm, 12 cm

2 Find the area of each of these parallelograms.

(a) 4 cm, 7 cm

(b) 12 cm, 25 cm

(c) 5 cm, 6 cm, 4.5 cm

3 Find the size of the lettered angles. Give a reason for each answer.
   (a) (b) (c)

4 Find the size of the lettered angles. Give a reason for each answer.
   (a) (b) (c)

5 Find the size of the lettered angles. Give a reason for each answer.
   (a) (b)

6 Write down the name of the quadrilateral or quadrilaterals which
   (a) can be made using lengths of 10 cm, 10 cm, 5 cm and 5 cm.
   (b) can be made using angles of 110°, 110°, 70° and 70°.
   (c) has both diagonals equal in length.

7 (a) A polygon has seven sides.
       Work out the sum of the interior angles of this polygon.
   (b) A regular polygon has 15 sides.
       Find the size of the exterior and interior angles of this polygon.
   (c) A regular polygon has an exterior angle of 10°.
       Work out the number of sides that the polygon has.

3 Properties of shapes

4 → FRACTIONS, DECIMALS AND PERCENTAGES

THIS CHAPTER IS ABOUT

- Comparing fractions
- Adding, subtracting, multiplying and dividing fractions and mixed numbers
- The meaning and use of *reciprocals*
- Changing fractions to decimals
- Recurring decimals
- Adding and subtracting decimals
- Multiplying and dividing decimals
- Percentage increase and decrease

YOU SHOULD ALREADY KNOW

- How to find equivalent fractions
- How to find fractions of a given quantity
- How to change improper ('top-heavy') fractions into mixed numbers
- How to multiply simple decimals
- How to calculate percentage increase and decrease

Comparing fractions

Sometimes it is obvious which of two fractions is the bigger. If not, the best way is to use equivalent fractions.

To find suitable equivalent fractions, you first need to look for a number that the two denominators (bottom numbers) will divide into exactly.

For example, if you want to compare $\frac{1}{2}$ and $\frac{1}{3}$ you need to find a number that 2 and 3 divide into exactly. Because 2 and 3 are both factors of 6, you can convert both fractions into sixths.

To convert $\frac{1}{2}$ into sixths you need to multiply both the denominator and the numerator by $6 \div 2 = 3$.

To convert $\frac{1}{3}$ into sixths you need to multiply both the denominator and the numerator by $6 \div 3 = 2$.

$$\frac{1 \times 3}{2 \times 3} = \frac{3}{6} \text{ and } \frac{1 \times 2}{3 \times 2} = \frac{2}{6}$$

Now that both fractions are expressed as sixths, you can easily tell which is the bigger by looking at the numerators.

Fractions with the same denominator are said to have a **common denominator**.

EXAMPLE 4.1

Which is the bigger, $\frac{3}{4}$ or $\frac{5}{6}$?

Solution

First find a common denominator. 24 is an obvious one, as $4 \times 6 = 24$, but a smaller one is 12.
12 is the lowest common multiple (LCM) of 4 and 6. You learned how to find LCMs in Chapter 1.

Then convert both fractions into twelfths.

$$\frac{3 \times 3}{4 \times 3} = \frac{9}{12}, \qquad \frac{5 \times 2}{6 \times 2} = \frac{10}{12}$$

$\frac{10}{12}$ is bigger than $\frac{9}{12}$, so $\frac{5}{6}$ is bigger than $\frac{3}{4}$.

> **TIP** Multiplying the two denominators together will always work to find a common denominator but the LCM is sometimes smaller.

Check up 4.1

Which of these fractions is the bigger?

(a) $\frac{3}{4}$ or $\frac{5}{8}$ (b) $\frac{7}{9}$ or $\frac{5}{6}$ (c) $\frac{3}{10}$ or $\frac{4}{15}$

> **TIP** In each case the LCM is smaller than the number you get by simply multiplying the two denominators together.

Check up 4.2

Put these fractions in order, smallest first.

$\frac{2}{5}, \quad \frac{1}{2}, \quad \frac{9}{20}, \quad \frac{17}{40}, \quad \frac{3}{8}$

Adding and subtracting fractions and mixed numbers

You can only add and subtract fractions if they have a common denominator. Sometimes this means you have to find the common denominator first.

Adding and subtracting fractions with a common denominator

This rectangle is divided into twelfths.

$\frac{4}{12}$ of the rectangle is shaded blue and $\frac{3}{12}$ is shaded red. The total fraction shaded is $\frac{7}{12}$.

This shows that $\frac{4}{12} + \frac{3}{12} = \frac{7}{12}$.

To add fractions with a common denominator, simply add the numerators.

Do *not* add the denominators.

You subtract fractions in a similar way.

You may need to cancel the answer, to give the fraction in its lowest terms.

For example, $\frac{7}{12} - \frac{5}{12} = \frac{2}{12} = \frac{1}{6}$.

> **TIP** Unless you are told not to, always cancel your answer.

Adding and subtracting fractions with different denominators

To add and subtract fractions with different denominators, you use the same method as when comparing fractions.

EXAMPLE 4.2

Work out $\frac{3}{8} + \frac{1}{4}$.

Solution

First find the common denominator. The LCM of 4 and 8 is 8.

$\frac{3}{8}$ already has a denominator of 8.

$\frac{1}{4} = \frac{2}{8}$ Multiply the numerator and the denominator by 2.

$\frac{3}{8} + \frac{1}{4} = \frac{3}{8} + \frac{2}{8} = \frac{5}{8}$ Add the numerators only.

> **TIP** Remember that you add the numerators but not the denominators.

Adding and subtracting fractions and mixed numbers

EXAMPLE 4.3

Work out $\frac{2}{3} - \frac{3}{5}$.

Solution

First find the common denominator. The LCM of 3 and 5 is 15.

$\frac{2}{3} = \frac{10}{15}$ Multiply the numerator and the denominator by 5.

$\frac{3}{5} = \frac{9}{15}$ Multiply the numerator and the denominator by 3.

$\frac{10}{15} - \frac{9}{15} = \frac{1}{15}$ Subtract the numerators only.

EXAMPLE 4.4

Work out $\frac{3}{4} + \frac{2}{5}$.

Solution

The common denominator is 20.

$\frac{3}{4} + \frac{2}{5} = \frac{15}{20} + \frac{8}{20}$

$\phantom{\frac{3}{4} + \frac{2}{5}} = \frac{23}{20}$ $\frac{23}{20}$ is an improper ('top-heavy') fraction.

$\phantom{\frac{3}{4} + \frac{2}{5}} = 1\frac{3}{20}$ You need to change it to a mixed number.

Adding and subtracting mixed numbers

To add mixed numbers you add the whole number parts and then add the fraction parts.

EXAMPLE 4.5

Work out $1\frac{1}{4} + 2\frac{1}{2}$.

Solution

$1\frac{1}{4} + 2\frac{1}{2} = 1 + 2 + \frac{1}{4} + \frac{1}{2}$

$\phantom{1\frac{1}{4} + 2\frac{1}{2}} = 3 + \frac{1}{4} + \frac{1}{2}$ Add the whole numbers first.

$\phantom{1\frac{1}{4} + 2\frac{1}{2}} = 3 + \frac{1}{4} + \frac{2}{4}$ Change the fractions into equivalent fractions with a common denominator.

$\phantom{1\frac{1}{4} + 2\frac{1}{2}} = 3\frac{3}{4}$ Add the fractions.

EXAMPLE 4.6

Work out $2\frac{3}{5} + 4\frac{2}{3}$.

Solution

$2\frac{3}{5} + 4\frac{2}{3} = 6 + \frac{3}{5} + \frac{2}{3}$ Add the whole numbers first.

$\phantom{2\frac{3}{5} + 4\frac{2}{3}} = 6 + \frac{9}{15} + \frac{10}{15}$ Change the fractions into equivalent fractions with a common denominator.

$\phantom{2\frac{3}{5} + 4\frac{2}{3}} = 6 + \frac{19}{15}$ Add the fractions. $\frac{19}{15}$ is an improper fraction. You need to change it into a mixed number and add the whole number to the 6 you already have.

$\phantom{2\frac{3}{5} + 4\frac{2}{3}} = 7\frac{4}{15}$ $\frac{19}{15} = 1\frac{4}{15}$ and $6 + 1 = 7$.

You subtract mixed numbers in a similar way.

EXAMPLE 4.7

Work out $3\frac{3}{4} - 1\frac{1}{3}$.

Solution

$3\frac{3}{4} - 1\frac{1}{3} = 3 - 1 + \frac{3}{4} - \frac{1}{3}$ Split the calculation into two parts.

$\phantom{3\frac{3}{4} - 1\frac{1}{3}} = 2 + \frac{3}{4} - \frac{1}{3}$ Subtract the whole numbers first.

$\phantom{3\frac{3}{4} - 1\frac{1}{3}} = 2 + \frac{9}{12} - \frac{4}{12}$ Change the fractions into equivalent fractions with a common denominator.

$\phantom{3\frac{3}{4} - 1\frac{1}{3}} = 2\frac{5}{12}$ Subtract the fractions.

EXAMPLE 4.8

Work out $5\frac{3}{10} - 2\frac{3}{4}$.

Solution

$5\frac{3}{10} - 2\frac{3}{4} = 5 - 2 + \frac{3}{10} - \frac{3}{4}$ Split the calculation into two parts.

$\phantom{5\frac{3}{10} - 2\frac{3}{4}} = 3 + \frac{3}{10} - \frac{3}{4}$ Subtract the whole numbers first.

$\phantom{5\frac{3}{10} - 2\frac{3}{4}} = 3 + \frac{6}{20} - \frac{15}{20}$ Change the fractions into equivalent fractions with a common denominator.

$\phantom{5\frac{3}{10} - 2\frac{3}{4}} = 2 + \frac{20}{20} + \frac{6}{20} - \frac{15}{20}$ $\frac{6}{20}$ is smaller than $\frac{15}{20}$ and would give a negative answer. Take 1 of the whole units and change it to $\frac{20}{20}$.

$\phantom{5\frac{3}{10} - 2\frac{3}{4}} = 2 + \frac{26}{20} - \frac{15}{20}$ Add it to $\frac{6}{20}$.

$\phantom{5\frac{3}{10} - 2\frac{3}{4}} = 2\frac{11}{20}$ Subtract the fractions.

EXERCISE 4.1

1 For each pair of fractions
- find the common denominator.
- state which is the bigger fraction.

(a) $\frac{2}{3}$ or $\frac{7}{9}$ (b) $\frac{5}{6}$ or $\frac{7}{8}$ (c) $\frac{3}{8}$ or $\frac{7}{20}$

2 Work out these.

(a) $\frac{2}{9} + \frac{5}{9}$ (b) $\frac{4}{11} + \frac{3}{11}$ (c) $\frac{5}{12} - \frac{1}{12}$ (d) $\frac{7}{13} - \frac{2}{13}$

(e) $\frac{7}{12} + \frac{3}{12}$ (f) $\frac{5}{8} + \frac{4}{8}$ (g) $\frac{8}{9} - \frac{5}{9}$ (h) $\frac{7}{10} + \frac{9}{10}$

(i) $1\frac{5}{12} + 2\frac{1}{12}$ (j) $3\frac{5}{8} - 1\frac{3}{8}$ (k) $4\frac{5}{9} - \frac{4}{9}$ (l) $5\frac{4}{7} - 2\frac{5}{7}$

3 Work out these.

(a) $\frac{1}{2} + \frac{3}{8}$ (b) $\frac{4}{9} + \frac{1}{3}$ (c) $\frac{5}{6} - \frac{1}{4}$ (d) $\frac{11}{12} - \frac{2}{3}$

(e) $\frac{4}{5} + \frac{1}{2}$ (f) $\frac{5}{7} + \frac{3}{4}$ (g) $\frac{8}{9} - \frac{1}{6}$ (h) $\frac{7}{10} + \frac{4}{5}$

(i) $\frac{8}{9} + \frac{5}{6}$ (j) $\frac{7}{15} + \frac{3}{10}$ (k) $\frac{4}{9} - \frac{1}{12}$ (l) $\frac{7}{20} + \frac{5}{8}$

4 Work out these.

(a) $3\frac{1}{2} + 2\frac{1}{5}$ (b) $4\frac{7}{8} - 1\frac{3}{4}$ (c) $4\frac{2}{7} + \frac{1}{2}$ (d) $6\frac{5}{12} - 3\frac{1}{3}$

(e) $4\frac{3}{4} + 2\frac{5}{8}$ (f) $5\frac{5}{6} - 1\frac{1}{4}$ (g) $4\frac{7}{9} + 2\frac{5}{6}$ (h) $4\frac{7}{13} - 4\frac{1}{2}$

(i) $3\frac{5}{7} + 2\frac{1}{3}$ (j) $7\frac{2}{5} - 1\frac{3}{4}$ (k) $5\frac{2}{7} - 3\frac{1}{2}$ (l) $4\frac{1}{12} - 3\frac{1}{4}$

Challenge 4.1

Brittany has some sweets.

$\frac{1}{4}$ of her sweets are red, $\frac{2}{5}$ are yellow and the rest are orange.

What fraction are orange?

Challenge 4.2

Simon says that $\frac{1}{3}$ of his class come to school by car, $\frac{1}{6}$ walk and $\frac{5}{8}$ come on the bus.

Show how you know that he must be wrong.

4 Fractions, decimals and percentages

Challenge 4.3

Find a formula to add these fractions.

$$\frac{a}{b} + \frac{c}{d}$$

Multiplying and dividing fractions and mixed numbers

You already know how to multiply a fraction by a whole number. You can also multiply two fractions together.

Multiplying proper fractions

You know that $\frac{1}{3}$ is the same as $1 \div 3$.

To multiply another fraction, for example $\frac{2}{5}$ by $\frac{1}{3}$, you divide $\frac{2}{5}$ by 3.

The diagram shows $\frac{2}{5}$ divided by 3, which is the same as $\frac{1}{3}$ of $\frac{2}{5}$.
$\frac{1}{3}$ of $\frac{2}{5}$ is $\frac{2}{15}$.

Notice that $1 \times 2 = 2$ (the numerators) and $3 \times 5 = 15$ (the denominators).

So $\dfrac{1}{3} \times \dfrac{2}{5} = \dfrac{1 \times 2}{3 \times 5} = \dfrac{2}{15}$.

To multiply fractions you

> multiply the numerators and multiply the denominators.

EXAMPLE 4.9

Work out $\frac{2}{3} \times \frac{5}{7}$.

Solution

$$\frac{2}{3} \times \frac{5}{7} = \frac{2 \times 5}{3 \times 7} = \frac{10}{21}$$

EXAMPLE 4.10

Find $\frac{3}{4}$ of $\frac{6}{7}$.

Solution

$\frac{3}{4} \times \frac{6}{7} = \frac{18}{28}$ 'of' means the same as '×'.

$\frac{18}{28} = \frac{9}{14}$ Cancel by dividing the numerator and the denominator by 2.

Look again at Example 4.10. $\frac{3}{4} \times \frac{6}{7}$

The numbers 4 and 6 are both multiples of 2.

This means that you can cancel before you multiply the fractions. This makes the arithmetic easier.

$\frac{3}{\cancel{4}_2} \times \frac{\cancel{6}^3}{7} = \frac{9}{14}$ Divide both 4 and 6 by 2, then multiply the numerators and denominators.

EXAMPLE 4.11

Work out $4 \times \frac{3}{10}$.

Solution

$4 \times \frac{3}{10} = \frac{4}{1} \times \frac{3}{10}$ First write 4 as $\frac{4}{1}$.

$= \frac{\cancel{4}^2}{1} \times \frac{3}{\cancel{10}_5}$ Cancel by dividing the 4 and the 10 by 2.

$= \frac{6}{5} = 1\frac{1}{5}$

Dividing proper fractions

When you work out $6 \div 3$, you are finding how many 3s there are in 6.

Finding $6 \div \frac{1}{3}$ is the same as finding how many $\frac{1}{3}$s there are in 6, which is $6 \times 3 = 18$.

So dividing by $\frac{1}{3}$ is the same as multiplying by 3.

Notice that $\frac{1}{3}$ is the reciprocal of 3.

To find $6 \div \frac{2}{3}$, you need to multiply by 3 and also divide by 2, because there will be half as many $\frac{2}{3}$s as there are $\frac{1}{3}$s. That means multiply by $\frac{3}{2}$, the reciprocal of $\frac{2}{3}$.

$6 \div \frac{2}{3} = \frac{6}{1} \times \frac{3}{2} = \frac{18}{2} = 9$

Dividing by a fraction is the same as multiplying by the reciprocal of the fraction.

> **TIP** The reciprocal of a fraction is a fraction with the numerator and denominator swapped round. You can think of this as 'turning the fraction upside down'.

EXAMPLE 4.12

Work out $\frac{3}{4} \div \frac{2}{7}$.

Solution

$\frac{3}{4} \div \frac{2}{7} = \frac{3}{4} \times \frac{7}{2}$ The reciprocal of $\frac{2}{7}$ is $\frac{7}{2}$.

$= \frac{21}{8}$ Multiply the numerators and denominators.

$= 2\frac{5}{8}$ Change the improper fraction into a mixed number.

EXAMPLE 4.13

Work out $\frac{5}{8} \div \frac{3}{4}$.

Solution

$\frac{5}{8} \div \frac{3}{4} = \frac{5}{8} \times \frac{4}{3}$ The reciprocal of $\frac{3}{4}$ is $\frac{4}{3}$.

$= \frac{5}{\cancel{8}_2} \times \frac{\cancel{4}^1}{3}$ Cancel by dividing the 4 and the 8 by 4.

$= \frac{5}{6}$

TIP Never cancel fractions at the divide stage. Wait until it has changed to a multiplication.

Challenge 4.4

(a) Calculate the area of this rectangle.
(b) Find the perimeter of this rectangle.

Give your answers in their lowest terms.

$5\frac{1}{4}$ cm

$3\frac{2}{3}$ cm

Reciprocals

Discovery 4.1

Work out these.

(a) $1 \div \frac{3}{4}$ (b) $1 \div \frac{5}{6}$ (c) $1 \div \frac{5}{3}$

What do you notice?

In Chapter 1 you learned that the reciprocal of a number is 1 ÷ the number. You can see now that this definition also applies to fractions.

Your calculator has a reciprocal button. It may be labelled $\boxed{x^{-1}}$.

Use your calculator to try to work out the reciprocal of 0 (zero).

You should get 'error'. This is because you cannot divide by zero. Zero has no reciprocal.

Multiplying and dividing mixed numbers

When multiplying and dividing mixed numbers, you first have to change the mixed numbers into improper fractions.

Discovery 4.2

(a) (i) How many halves are there in two whole units?
(ii) How many halves are there in $2\frac{1}{2}$?

(b) (i) How many quarters are there in three whole units?
(ii) How many quarters are there in $3\frac{3}{4}$?

(c) (i) How many fifths are there in two whole units?
(ii) How many fifths are there in $2\frac{4}{5}$?

What do you notice about your answers to part (ii) of these questions?

To change a mixed number into an improper fraction, you multiply the whole number by the denominator and add it to the numerator.

EXAMPLE 4.14

Change $3\frac{2}{3}$ into an improper fraction.

Solution

$3\frac{2}{3} = \dfrac{3 \times 3 + 2}{3}$ Multiply the whole number (3) by the denominator (3) and add it to the numerator (2).
$= \dfrac{11}{3}$ This gives you the numerator of the improper fraction. The denominator stays the same.

EXAMPLE 4.15

Change $4\frac{3}{5}$ to an improper fraction.

Solution

$4\frac{3}{5} = \dfrac{4 \times 5 + 3}{5}$
$= \dfrac{23}{5}$

Multiplying and dividing mixed numbers is the same as multiplying and dividing fractions, after you have changed the mixed numbers to improper fractions.

EXAMPLE 4.16

Work out $2\frac{1}{2} \times 4\frac{3}{5}$.

Solution

$2\frac{1}{2} \times 4\frac{3}{5} = \frac{5}{2} \times \frac{23}{5}$ First change the mixed numbers into improper fractions.

$= \frac{\cancel{5}^1}{2} \times \frac{23}{\cancel{5}_1}$ Cancel out the two 5s. This makes the arithmetic much easier.

$= \frac{23}{2}$ Multiply the numerator and the denominator.

$= 11\frac{1}{2}$ Give your answer as a mixed number.

EXAMPLE 4.17

Work out $2\frac{3}{4} \div 1\frac{5}{8}$.

Solution

$2\frac{3}{4} \div 1\frac{5}{8} = \frac{11}{4} \div \frac{13}{8}$ Change the mixed numbers into improper fractions. You must do this before turning the calculation into a multiplication.

$= \frac{11}{\cancel{4}_1} \times \frac{\cancel{8}^2}{13}$ The reciprocal of $\frac{13}{8}$ is $\frac{8}{13}$. The numbers 4 and 8 are both multiples of 4.

$= \frac{22}{13}$

$= 1\frac{9}{13}$ Give your answer as a mixed number.

TIP: If you are multiplying or dividing by a whole number, for example 6, you can write it as $\frac{6}{1}$.

EXERCISE 4.2

1 Change these mixed numbers to improper fractions.
  (a) $4\frac{3}{4}$
  (b) $5\frac{2}{3}$
  (c) $6\frac{1}{2}$
  (d) $2\frac{5}{8}$
  (e) $3\frac{2}{7}$
  (f) $1\frac{5}{12}$
  (g) $2\frac{5}{6}$
  (h) $5\frac{7}{11}$

2 Work out these.
Write your answers as proper fractions or mixed numbers in their lowest terms.
(a) $\frac{3}{5} \times 4$ (b) $\frac{3}{4} \times 6$ (c) $\frac{2}{3} \div 5$
(d) $7 \times \frac{5}{8}$ (e) $\frac{5}{7} \div 3$ (f) $6 \div \frac{2}{3}$

3 Work out these.
Write your answers as proper fractions or mixed numbers in their lowest terms.
(a) $\frac{1}{2} \times \frac{3}{8}$ (b) $\frac{4}{9} \times \frac{1}{3}$ (c) $\frac{5}{6} \times \frac{1}{4}$ (d) $\frac{11}{12} \div \frac{2}{3}$
(e) $\frac{4}{5} \div \frac{1}{2}$ (f) $\frac{5}{7} \times \frac{3}{4}$ (g) $\frac{8}{9} \times \frac{1}{6}$ (h) $\frac{7}{10} \div \frac{4}{5}$
(i) $\frac{8}{9} \times \frac{5}{6}$ (j) $\frac{7}{15} \div \frac{3}{10}$ (k) $\frac{4}{9} \div \frac{1}{12}$ (l) $\frac{7}{20} \times \frac{5}{8}$

4 Work out these.
Write your answers as proper fractions or mixed numbers in their lowest terms.
(a) $3\frac{1}{2} \times 2\frac{1}{5}$ (b) $4\frac{2}{7} \times \frac{1}{2}$ (c) $2\frac{3}{4} \div 1\frac{3}{4}$ (d) $1\frac{5}{12} \div 3\frac{1}{3}$
(e) $3\frac{1}{5} \times 2\frac{5}{8}$ (f) $2\frac{7}{8} \div 1\frac{3}{5}$ (g) $2\frac{7}{9} \times 3\frac{3}{5}$ (h) $5\frac{5}{6} \div 1\frac{3}{4}$
(i) $3\frac{5}{7} \times 2\frac{1}{13}$ (j) $5\frac{2}{5} \div 2\frac{1}{4}$ (k) $5\frac{2}{7} \times 3\frac{1}{2}$ (l) $4\frac{1}{12} \div 3\frac{1}{4}$

Challenge 4.5

Work out these.
(a) $\left(3\frac{1}{2} + 2\frac{4}{5}\right) \times 2\frac{1}{12}$ (b) $5\frac{1}{3} \div 3\frac{3}{5} + 2\frac{1}{3}$
(c) $4\frac{2}{3} \times 2\frac{2}{7} - 4\frac{7}{8}$ (d) $\left(2\frac{4}{5} + 3\frac{1}{4}\right) \div \left(3\frac{1}{3} - 2\frac{3}{4}\right)$

Fractions on your calculator

You need to be able to calculate with fractions without a calculator.
However, when a calculator is allowed you can use the fraction button.

The fraction button looks like this $\boxed{a^{b/c}}$.

To enter a fraction such as $\frac{2}{5}$ into your calculator you press $\boxed{2}$ $\boxed{a^{b/c}}$ $\boxed{5}$ $\boxed{=}$.

Your display will look like this. $\boxed{2 \lrcorner 5}$

This is the calculator's way of showing the fraction $\frac{2}{5}$.

Discovery 4.3

Some calculators may have the $\lrcorner$ symbol a different way round.
Check now what you see when you press $\boxed{2}$ $\boxed{a^{b/c}}$ $\boxed{5}$ $\boxed{=}$.

To do a calculation like $\frac{2}{5} + \frac{1}{2}$, the sequence of buttons is

[2] [ab/c] [5] [+] [1] [ab/c] [2] [=].

This is what you should see on your display. [9 ⌐ 10]

You must, of course, write this down as $\frac{9}{10}$ for your answer.

EXAMPLE 4.18

Use your calculator to work out $\frac{3}{4} + \frac{5}{6}$.

Solution

This is the sequence of buttons to press.

[3] [ab/c] [4] [+] [5] [ab/c] [6] [=]

The display on your calculator should look like this. [1 ⌐ 7 ⌐ 12]

This is the calculator's way of showing the mixed number $1\frac{7}{12}$.

So the answer is $1\frac{7}{12}$.

To enter a mixed number such as $2\frac{3}{5}$ into your calculator you press

[2] [ab/c] [3] [ab/c] [5] [=].

Your display will look like this. [2 ⌐ 3 ⌐ 5]

EXAMPLE 4.19

Use your calculator to work out these.
(a) $2\frac{3}{5} - 1\frac{1}{4}$ (b) $2\frac{2}{3} \times 3\frac{3}{4}$

Solution

(a) This is the sequence of buttons to press.

[2] [ab/c] [3] [ab/c] [5] [−] [1] [ab/c] [1] [ab/c] [4] [=]

The display on your calculator should look like this. [1 ⌐ 7 ⌐ 20]

So the answer is $1\frac{7}{20}$.

(b) This is the sequence of buttons to press.

[2] [ab/c] [2] [ab/c] [3] [×] [3] [ab/c] [3] [ab/c] [4] [=]

The answer is 10.

Fractions on your calculator

Cancelling fractions

To **cancel** fractions to their **lowest terms** you divide the numerator and the denominator by the same number.

For example $\frac{8}{12} = \frac{2}{3}$ (by dividing both the numerator and the denominator by 4).

You can also do this on a calculator.

When you press $\boxed{8}$ $\boxed{a^{b}/_{c}}$ $\boxed{1}$ $\boxed{2}$, you should see $\boxed{8 \lrcorner 12}$.

When you press $\boxed{=}$, the display changes to $\boxed{2 \lrcorner 3}$, meaning $\frac{2}{3}$.

When you do calculations with fractions on your calculator, it will automatically give the answer as a fraction in its lowest terms.

If you do a calculation which is a mixture of fractions and decimals, your calculator will give the answer as a decimal.

EXAMPLE 4.20

Use your calculator to work out $2\frac{3}{4} \times 1.5$.

Solution

This is the sequence of buttons to press.

$\boxed{2}$ $\boxed{a^{b}/_{c}}$ $\boxed{3}$ $\boxed{a^{b}/_{c}}$ $\boxed{4}$ $\boxed{\times}$ $\boxed{1}$ $\boxed{.}$ $\boxed{5}$ $\boxed{=}$

The answer is 4.125.

Improper fractions

If you enter an improper fraction into your calculator and press the $\boxed{=}$ button, the calculator will automatically change it to a mixed number.

EXAMPLE 4.21

Use your calculator to change $\frac{187}{25}$ to a mixed number.

Solution

This is the sequence of buttons to press.

$\boxed{1}$ $\boxed{8}$ $\boxed{7}$ $\boxed{a^{b}/_{c}}$ $\boxed{2}$ $\boxed{5}$ $\boxed{=}$

The display on your calculator should look like this. $\boxed{7 \lrcorner 12 \lrcorner 25}$

So the answer is $7\frac{12}{25}$.

EXERCISE 4.3

1 Work out these.
(a) $\frac{2}{7} + \frac{1}{3}$
(b) $\frac{3}{4} - \frac{2}{5}$
(c) $\frac{5}{8} \times \frac{4}{11}$
(d) $\frac{11}{12} \div \frac{5}{8}$
(e) $2\frac{3}{7} + 3\frac{1}{2}$
(f) $5\frac{2}{3} - 3\frac{3}{4}$
(g) $4\frac{2}{7} \times 3$
(h) $5\frac{7}{8} \div 1\frac{5}{6}$

2 Write these fractions in their lowest terms.
(a) $\frac{24}{60}$
(b) $\frac{35}{56}$
(c) $\frac{84}{180}$
(d) $\frac{175}{400}$
(e) $\frac{18}{162}$

3 Write these improper fractions as mixed numbers.
(a) $\frac{124}{60}$
(b) $\frac{130}{17}$
(c) $\frac{73}{15}$
(d) $\frac{168}{35}$
(e) $\frac{107}{13}$

4 Calculate
(a) the perimeter of this rectangle.
(b) the area of this rectangle.

$6\frac{3}{4}$ cm

$3\frac{2}{3}$ cm

Changing fractions to decimals

Since a fraction like $\frac{5}{8}$ means the same as $5 \div 8$, you can use division to change a fraction into a decimal.

EXAMPLE 4.22

Convert $\frac{5}{8}$ to a decimal.

Solution

First write 5 as 5.000.

You may need more or fewer zeros depending on the fraction.

Now work out $5.000 \div 8$.

$0.6\,2\,5$
$8)\overline{5.0^20^40}$

If the division is not exact, you may need to round your answer to a given number of decimal places.

Challenge 4.6

Are these numbers equal?

$\frac{1}{3}$,   0.3,   0.33,   0.333 33

Which is exact?

Changing fractions to decimals   67

Some fractions, such as $\frac{5}{8}$, convert to decimals which stop. These are **terminating decimals**. Others, such as $\frac{1}{3}$, just keep going. These are called **recurring decimals**.

> **TIP** There is always a pattern in recurring decimals.

Discovery 4.4

Convert the following fractions into decimals.
- (a) $\frac{1}{2}$
- (b) $\frac{1}{3}$
- (c) $\frac{3}{4}$
- (d) $\frac{2}{5}$
- (e) $\frac{5}{6}$
- (f) $\frac{2}{7}$
- (g) $\frac{7}{8}$
- (h) $\frac{8}{9}$

Try some more conversions of your own.

What can you say about the numbers in the denominators of the fractions giving terminating decimals?

EXAMPLE 4.23

State whether each of these fractions gives a terminating or a recurring decimal.
- (a) $\frac{1}{6}$
- (b) $\frac{1}{5}$
- (c) $\frac{1}{7}$
- (d) $\frac{1}{11}$

Solution

(a) $\frac{1}{6}$ is a recurring decimal $1 \div 6 = 0.166\,666\ldots$

(b) $\frac{1}{5}$ is a terminating decimal $1 \div 5 = 0.2$

(c) $\frac{1}{7}$ is a recurring decimal $1 \div 7 = 0.142\,857\,142\ldots$

(d) $\frac{1}{11}$ is a recurring decimal $1 \div 11 = 0.090\,909\ldots$

> **TIP** If the denominator of a fraction has only factors which are factors of 10, it will give a terminating decimal.
>
> If the denominator of a fraction has factors which are not factors of 10, it will give a recurring decimal.

EXERCISE 4.4

1 Change each of these fractions to a decimal. If necessary, give your answer to 3 decimal places.
- (a) $\frac{4}{5}$
- (b) $\frac{3}{8}$
- (c) $\frac{2}{11}$
- (d) $\frac{1}{9}$
- (e) $\frac{9}{20}$

2 State whether each of these fractions gives a recurring or a terminating decimal. Give your reasons.
- (a) $\frac{3}{5}$
- (b) $\frac{2}{3}$
- (c) $\frac{4}{9}$
- (d) $\frac{1}{16}$
- (e) $\frac{3}{7}$

3 (a) Find the recurring decimal equivalent to $\frac{5}{7}$.
   (b) How many digits are there in the repeating pattern?

Challenge 4.7

(a) In Exercise 4.4 question **1**, you found these.

$\frac{1}{9} = 0.111\,111\,111\ldots$ $\qquad$ $\frac{4}{9} = 0.444\,444\,444\ldots$

Write down the decimal equivalent of these without using your calculator.

$\frac{2}{9}, \frac{3}{9}, \frac{5}{9}, \frac{6}{9}, \frac{7}{9}, \frac{8}{9}$

(b) In Example 4.23 you found that $\frac{1}{11} = 0.090\,909\,090\ldots$.

In addition, $\frac{2}{11} = 0.181\,818\,181\ldots$ and $\frac{5}{11} = 0.454\,545\,454\ldots$.

Write down the decimal equivalent of these without using your calculator.

$\frac{3}{11}, \frac{4}{11}, \frac{6}{11}, \frac{7}{11}, \frac{8}{11}, \frac{9}{11}, \frac{10}{11}$

Mental arithmetic with decimals

You should be able to add and subtract simple decimals in your head. It is similar to adding and subtracting whole numbers.

For example, you can do 63 + 24 by adding 20 to get 83 and then adding 4 to get 87.

In the same way, you can do 6.3 + 2.4 by adding 2 to get 8.3 and then adding 0.4 to get 8.7.

Subtraction can also be done in stages.

EXAMPLE 4.24

Work out these.

(a) 5.8 + 7.3 $\qquad$ **(b)** 8.5 − 3.7

Solution

(a) 5.8 + 7 = 12.8 $\qquad$ Add the units first.
12.8 + 0.3 = 13.1 $\qquad$ Then add the tenths.

(b) 8.5 − 3 = 5.5 $\qquad$ Subtract the units first.
5.5 − 0.5 = 5 $\qquad$ You need to subtract 7 tenths. Subtract 5 tenths first.
5 − 0.2 = 4.8 $\qquad$ Then subtract the remaining 2 tenths.

Check up 4.3

Work in pairs. Take it in turns to work out a decimal addition on a calculator. Make sure that each number has only one decimal place. Ask your partner to do the calculation in their head. Check your answers using the calculator.

Now try some decimal subtraction.

EXERCISE 4.5

Work out these. As far as possible, write down only your final answer.

1 $4.2 + 3.5$
2 $5.1 + 2.8$
3 $7.8 - 4.2$
4 $5.6 - 3.4$
5 $5.8 + 1.3$
6 $4.6 + 3.5$
7 $6.5 - 0.8$
8 $6.4 - 2.6$
9 $7.9 + 4.3$
10 $7.8 + 8.7$
11 $7.8 - 6.9$
12 $7.6 - 1.8$

Multiplying and dividing decimals

Check up 4.4

Work out these.

(a) (i) 5×3 (ii) 5×0.3 (iii) 0.5×3 (iv) 0.5×0.3
(b) (i) 4×2 (ii) 4×0.2 (iii) 0.4×2 (iv) 0.4×0.2

This section shows you how to extend the techniques you used for multiplying simple decimals to multiplying any decimals.

Discovery 4.5

(a) $39 \times 8 = 312$.
   Without using your calculator, write down the answers to these.
   (i) 3.9×8 (ii) 39×0.8 (iii) 0.39×8 (iv) 0.39×0.8

(b) $37 \times 56 = 2072$.
   Without using your calculator, write down the answers to these.
   (i) 3.7×56 (ii) 37×5.6 (iii) 3.7×5.6
   (iv) 0.37×56 (v) 0.37×5.6 (vi) 0.37×0.56

Now check your answers with your calculator.

Look again at your answers to Discovery 4.5. These are the steps you take to multiply decimals.

1. Carry out the multiplication ignoring the decimal points. The digits in the answer will be the same as the digits in the final answer.
2. Count the total number of decimal places in the two numbers to be multiplied.
3. Put the decimal point in the answer you got in step 1 so that the final answer has the same number of decimal places as you found in step 2.

EXAMPLE 4.25

Work out 8×0.7.

Solution

1. First do $8 \times 7 = 56$.
2. The total number of decimal places in 8 and $0.7 = 0 + 1 = 1$.
3. The answer is 5.6.

> **TIP**: Notice that when you multiply by a number between 0 and 1, such as 0.7, you decrease the original number (8 to 5.6).

EXAMPLE 4.26

Work out 8.3×3.4.

Solution

1. First do 83×34.

$$\begin{array}{r} 8\,3 \\ \times\ \ 3\,4 \\ \hline 2\,4\,9\,0 \\ 3\,3\,2 \\ \hline 2\,8\,2\,2 \end{array}$$

The method used here is the traditional long multiplication. You may have learnt another method.

2. The total number of decimal places in 8.3 and $3.4 = 1 + 1 = 2$.
3. The answer is 28.22.

EXAMPLE 4.27

Work out 8.32×2.6.

Solution

1. First do 832×26.

$$\begin{array}{r} 8\,3\,2 \\ \times\ \ \ 2\,6 \\ \hline 1\,6\,6\,4\,0 \\ 4\,9\,9\,2 \\ \hline 2\,1\,6\,3\,2 \end{array}$$

2. The total number of decimal places in 8.32 and $2.6 = 2 + 1 = 3$.
3. The answer is 21.632.

Multiplying and dividing decimals

Discovery 4.6

(a) Do these calculations on your calculator.
   (i) $26 \div 1.3$
   (ii) $260 \div 13$
(b) What do you notice?
(c) Now do these calculations on your calculator.
   (i) $5.92 \div 3.7$
   (ii) $59.2 \div 37$
   (iii) $3.995 \div 2.35$
   (iv) $399.5 \div 235$
(d) Can you explain your results?

The result of a division sum is unchanged when you multiply both numbers by 10 (i.e. move the decimal point one place in both numbers).

The result is also unchanged when you multiply both numbers by 100 (i.e. move the decimal point two places in both numbers).

This rule is exactly the same as when you are writing equivalent fractions.

For example, $\frac{3}{5} = \frac{30}{50} = \frac{300}{500}$.

You use this rule when you are dividing decimals.

EXAMPLE 4.28

Work out $6 \div 0.3$.

Solution

First multiply both numbers by 10, so that the number you are dividing by is a whole number.

The calculation becomes $60 \div 3$.

$60 \div 3 = 20$

so $6 \div 0.3$ is also 20.

TIP: Notice that when you divide by a number between 0 and 1, such as 0.3, you increase the original number (6 to 20).

EXAMPLE 4.29

Work out $4.68 \div 0.4$.

Solution

First multiply both numbers by 10 (move the decimal point one place).

The calculation becomes $46.8 \div 4$.

$$\begin{array}{r} 11.7 \\ 4\overline{)46.^28} \end{array}$$

The decimal point in the answer goes above the decimal point in 46.8.

$4.68 \div 0.4$ is also 11.7.

EXAMPLE 4.30

Work out $3.64 \div 1.3$.

Solution

First multiply both numbers by 10 (move the decimal point one place).

The calculation becomes $36.4 \div 13$.

$$13 \overline{)36.^{10}4}^{\ 2.8}$$

You may have been taught to do this by long division rather than by short division.

$3.64 \div 1.3$ is also 2.8.

EXERCISE 4.6

1 Work out these.
- (a) 4×0.3
- (b) 0.5×7
- (c) 3×0.6
- (d) 0.8×9
- (e) 0.6×0.4
- (f) 0.8×0.6
- (g) 40×0.3
- (h) 0.5×70
- (i) 0.3×0.2
- (j) 0.8×0.1
- (k) $(0.7)^2$
- (l) $(0.3)^2$

2 Work out these.
- (a) $8 \div 0.2$
- (b) $1.2 \div 0.3$
- (c) $2.8 \div 0.7$
- (d) $3.6 \div 0.4$
- (e) $24 \div 1.2$
- (f) $50 \div 2.5$
- (g) $9 \div 0.3$
- (h) $15 \div 0.3$
- (i) $16 \div 0.2$
- (j) $24 \div 0.8$
- (k) $1.55 \div 0.5$
- (l) $48.8 \div 0.4$

3 Work out these.
- (a) 4.2×1.5
- (b) 6.2×2.3
- (c) 5.9×6.1
- (d) 7.2×2.7
- (e) 63×1.8
- (f) 72×5.4
- (g) 5.6×8.9
- (h) 10.9×2.4
- (i) 12.7×0.4
- (j) 2.34×0.8
- (k) 5.46×0.7
- (l) 6.23×1.6

4 Work out these.
- (a) $14.7 \div 0.3$
- (b) $13.6 \div 0.8$
- (c) $14.4 \div 0.6$
- (d) $22.4 \div 0.7$
- (e) $47.7 \div 0.9$
- (f) $85.8 \div 1.1$
- (g) $3.42 \div 0.6$
- (h) $1.96 \div 0.4$
- (i) $1.45 \div 0.5$
- (j) $3.51 \div 1.3$
- (k) $5.55 \div 1.5$
- (l) $6.3 \div 1.4$

Multiplying and dividing decimals

Challenge 4.8

In a 4 by 400-metres relay race, the four members of a team run the following times.

44.5 seconds, 45.6 seconds, 45.8 seconds and 43.9 seconds

What was their average time?

Challenge 4.9

(a) Calculate the area of this rectangle.

6.3 cm

2.6 cm

(b) This rectangle has the same area as the one in part (a).
Calculate the length of this rectangle.

3.9 cm

Percentage increase and decrease

You already know how to find a percentage of a quantity.

Percentage increase

To increase £240 by 23% you first work out 23% of £240. $240 \times 0.23 = £55.20$
Then you add £55.20 to £240. $240 + 55.20 = £295.20$

There is a quicker way to do the same calculation.

To increase a quantity by 23% you need to find the original quantity plus 23%.

This means that to increase £240 by 23% you need to find 100% of £240 + 23% of £240 = 123% of £240.

The decimal equivalent of 123% is 1.23.

The calculation can therefore be done in one stage: $240 \times 1.23 = £295.20$

The number that you multiply the original quantity by (here 1.23) is called the **multiplier**.

74   4 Fractions, decimals and percentages

EXAMPLE 4.31

Amir's salary is £17 000 per year. He receives a 3% increase.
Find his new salary.

Solution

Amir's new salary is 103% of his original salary. So the multiplier is 1.03.

£17 000 × 1.03 = £17 510

This method is much quicker when repeated calculations are needed.

EXAMPLE 4.32

Invest now and receive a guaranteed 6% compound interest over 5 years.

Compound interest means that interest is paid on the total amount in the account. It is different from simple interest, when interest is paid only on the original amount invested.

Jane invests £1500 for the full 5 years.
What will her investment be worth at the end of the 5 years?

Solution

At the end of year 1 the investment will be worth	£1500 × 1.06 = £1590.00
At the end of year 2 the investment will be worth	£1590 × 1.06 = £1685.40
This is the same as	£1500 × 1.06 × 1.06 = £1685.40
	or £1500 × 1.06^2 = £1685.40
At the end of year 3 the investment will be worth	£1685.40 × 1.06 = £1786.524
This is the same as	£1500 × 1.06 × 1.06 × 1.06 = £1786.524
	or £1500 × 1.06^3 = £1786.524
At the end of year 4 the investment will be worth	£1786.524 × 1.06 = £1893.7154
This is the same as	£1500 × 1.06 × 1.06 × 1.06 × 1.06 = £1893.7154
	or £1500 × 1.06^4 = £1893.7154
At the end of year 5 the investment will be worth	£1893.7154 × 1.06 = £2007.34
This is the same as	£1500 × 1.06 × 1.06 × 1.06 × 1.06 × 1.06 = £2007.34
	or £1500 × 1.06^5 = £2007.34
	(to the nearest penny)

Notice that at the end of year n you multiply £1500 by 1.06^n.

> **TIP** Use the power button (^ or x^y or y^x) on your calculator.

Percentage increase and decrease

Percentage decrease

Percentage decrease can be done in a similar way.

EXAMPLE 4.33

In a sale there is 15% off everything.

Kieran buys a DVD recorder in the sale. The original price was £225. Calculate the sale price.

Solution

£225 × 0.85 = £191.25   A percentage decrease of 15% is the same as 100% − 15% = 85%. So the multiplier is 0.85.

Again, this method is very useful for repeated calculations.

EXAMPLE 4.34

The value of a car decreases by 12% every year.
Zara's car cost £9000 when new.
Calculate its value 4 years later. Give your answer to the nearest pound.

Solution

100% − 12% = 88%

Value after 4 years = £9000 × 0.88^4 At the end of year 4 you multiply £9000 by 0.88^4.
 = £5397.26
 = £5397 to the nearest pound

EXERCISE 4.7

1. Write down the multiplier that will increase an amount by
   (a) 13%. (b) 20%. (c) 68%. (d) 8%.
   (e) 2%.   (f) 17.5%. (g) 100%. (h) 150%.

2. Write down the multiplier that will decrease an amount by
   (a) 14%. (b) 20%. (c) 45%. (d) 7%.
   (e) 3%.   (f) 23%. (g) 86%. (h) 16.5%.

3. Sanjay earns £4.60 per hour from his Saturday job.
   If he receives a 4% increase, how much will he earn?
   Give your answer to the nearest penny.

4. In a sale all items were reduced by 30%. Abi bought a pair of shoes.
   The original price was £42. What was the sale price?

5 Mark invested £2400 at 5% compound interest.
What was the investment worth at the end of 4 years?
Give your answer to the nearest pound.

6 This painting was worth £15 000 in 1998.
The painting increased in value by 15% every year for 6 years.
How much was it worth at the end of the 6 years?
Give your answer to the nearest pound.

7 The value of a car decreased by 9% per year.
When it was new it was worth £14 000.
What was its value after 5 years?
Give your answer to the nearest pound.

8 House prices rose by 12% in 2003, 11% in 2004 and 7% in 2005.
At the start of 2003 the price of a house was £120 000.
What was the price at the end of 2005?
Give your answer to the nearest pound.

9 The value of an investment rose by 8% in 2004 and fell by 8% in 2005. If the value of the investment was £3000 at the start of 2004, what was the value at the end of 2005?

WHAT YOU HAVE LEARNED

- To add and subtract fractions you use a common denominator
- To add or subtract mixed numbers you deal with the whole numbers first and then the fraction parts
- To multiply fractions you multiply the numerators and multiply the denominators
- Sometimes you can cancel before doing the multiplication
- To divide fractions you find the reciprocal of the second fraction (turn it upside down) and then multiply
- To multiply and divide mixed numbers, you must change the mixed numbers to improper fractions first
- How to work with fractions and mixed numbers on your calculator using the $a^{b/c}$ button
- To change a fraction to a decimal you divide the numerator by the denominator
- To multiply decimals, multiply the numbers without the decimal point and then count the total number of decimal places in the two numbers
- To divide by a decimal with one decimal place, multiply both numbers by 10 (move the decimal point to the right one place) and then do the division
- A quick way of increasing by e.g. 12% or 7% is to multiply by 1.12 or 1.07
- A quick way of decreasing by e.g. 15% or 8% is to multiply by 0.85 or 0.92

MIXED EXERCISE 4

Do not use your calculator for questions **1** to **6**.

1 For each pair of fractions
- find the common denominator.
- state which is the bigger fraction.

(a) $\frac{4}{5}$ or $\frac{5}{6}$ (b) $\frac{1}{3}$ or $\frac{2}{7}$ (c) $\frac{13}{20}$ or $\frac{5}{8}$

2 Work out these.

(a) $\frac{3}{5} + \frac{4}{5}$ (b) $\frac{3}{7} + \frac{2}{3}$ (c) $\frac{5}{8} - \frac{1}{6}$ (d) $\frac{7}{10} + \frac{2}{15}$ (e) $\frac{11}{12} - \frac{3}{8}$

(f) $3\frac{1}{4} + 2\frac{1}{6}$ (g) $4\frac{3}{4} - 1\frac{2}{5}$ (h) $5\frac{1}{2} + 2\frac{7}{8}$ (i) $3\frac{5}{6} + 2\frac{2}{9}$ (j) $4\frac{1}{4} - 2\frac{3}{5}$

(k) $\frac{3}{5} \times \frac{2}{3}$ (l) $\frac{4}{7} \times \frac{5}{6}$ (m) $\frac{5}{8} \div \frac{2}{3}$ (n) $\frac{9}{10} \div \frac{3}{7}$ (o) $\frac{15}{16} \times \frac{12}{25}$

(p) $1\frac{2}{3} \times 2\frac{1}{5}$ (q) $2\frac{5}{6} \div 1\frac{3}{4}$ (r) $2\frac{5}{8} \times 1\frac{3}{7}$ (s) $1\frac{7}{10} \div 4\frac{2}{5}$ (t) $2\frac{3}{4} \times 3\frac{3}{7}$

3 Change each of these fractions to a decimal.
Where necessary, give your answer correct to 3 decimal places.

(a) $\frac{1}{8}$ (b) $\frac{2}{9}$ (c) $\frac{5}{7}$ (d) $\frac{3}{11}$

4 Work out these.

(a) $4.3 + 5.4$ (b) $9.6 - 4.3$ (c) $5.8 + 2.9$ (d) $6.4 - 1.8$

5 Work out these.

(a) 5×0.4 (b) 0.7×0.1 (c) 0.9×0.8

(d) 1.8×6 (e) 2.7×3.4 (f) 5.2×3.6

6 Work out these.

(a) $9 \div 0.3$ (b) $3.2 \div 0.4$ (c) $6.9 \div 2.3$

(d) $56 \div 0.7$ (e) $86.9 \div 1.1$ (f) $5.22 \div 0.6$

You may use your calculator for questions **7** to **9**.

7 Use your calculator to work out these.

(a) $\frac{2}{11} + \frac{5}{6}$ (b) $\frac{7}{8} - \frac{3}{5}$ (c) $2\frac{2}{7} \times 1\frac{3}{8}$ (d) $8\frac{2}{5} \div 2\frac{7}{10}$

8 Sam invested £3500 at 6% compound interest.
What was the investment worth at the end of 7 years?
Give your answer to the nearest pound.

9 In a sale, prices were reduced by 10% every day.
A pair of jeans originally cost £45.
Nicola bought a pair of jeans on the fourth day of the sale.
How much did she pay for them? Give your answer to the nearest penny.

4 Fractions, decimals and percentages

5 STATISTICAL DIAGRAMS

THIS CHAPTER IS ABOUT
- Drawing and interpreting a variety of statistical diagrams and tables

YOU SHOULD ALREADY KNOW
- That a large amount of data can be displayed in a diagram, such as a bar graph
- The difference between discrete and continuous data
- The meaning of *mode* and *median*
- How to plot points on a coordinate grid

Frequency diagrams

When you have a lot of data it is often more convenient to group the data into bands or intervals. You have already drawn bar charts to display grouped discrete data.

To display **grouped continuous data**, you can use a **frequency diagram**. This is very like a bar chart: the main difference is that there are no gaps between the bars.

> **TIP:** Remember that the intervals should usually be of equal size.

EXAMPLE 5.1

Saul measured the heights of 34 students.
He grouped the data into intervals of 5 cm.
Here is his table of values.

Height (h cm)	$140 < h \leq 145$	$145 < h \leq 150$	$150 < h \leq 155$	$155 < h \leq 160$	$160 < h \leq 165$	$165 < h \leq 170$
Frequency	3	8	8	9	2	4

(a) Draw a grouped frequency diagram to show these data.
(b) Which of the intervals is the modal class?
(c) Which of the intervals contains the median value?

> **TIP:** $145 < h \leq 150$ means all heights, h, which are bigger than 145 cm (but not equal to 145 cm) and up to and including 150 cm.

Frequency diagrams 79

Solution

(a)

[Frequency diagram showing heights: 140-145: 3, 145-150: 8, 150-155: 8, 155-160: 9, 160-165: 2, 165-170: 4. Vertical axis: Frequency. Horizontal axis: Height (cm).]

Don't forget to label the axes.

The horizontal axis shows the type of data being collected.

The vertical axis shows the **frequency**, or how many data items there are in each of the intervals.

(b) $155 < h \leq 160$ The modal class is the one with the highest frequency. It has the highest number in the 'frequency' row of the table, and the highest bar in the frequency diagram.

(c) The median value is the value halfway along the ordered list.
As there are 34 values, the median will lie between the 17th and 18th values.
Add on the frequency for each interval until you find the interval containing the 17th and 18th values:

                            3 is smaller than 17. The 17th and 18th values do not lie in interval $140 < h \leq 145$.

$3 + 8 = 11$ 11 is smaller than 17. The 17th and 18th values do not lie in interval $145 < h \leq 150$.

$11 + 8 = 19$ 19 is larger than 18. The 17th and 18th values must lie in interval $150 < h \leq 155$.

Interval $150 < h \leq 155$ contains the median value.

EXERCISE 5.1

1 The manager of a leisure centre recorded the ages of the women who used the swimming pool one morning. Here are his results.

Age (a years)	$15 \leq a < 20$	$20 \leq a < 25$	$25 \leq a < 30$	$30 \leq a < 35$	$35 \leq a < 40$	$40 \leq a < 45$	$45 \leq a < 50$
Frequency	4	12	17	6	8	3	12

Draw a frequency diagram to show these data.

5 Statistical diagrams

2 In a survey, the annual rainfall was measured at 100 different towns.
Here are the results of the survey.

Rainfall (r cm)	$50 \leq r < 70$	$70 \leq r < 90$	$90 \leq r < 110$	$110 \leq r < 130$	$130 \leq r < 150$	$150 \leq r < 170$
Frequency	14	33	27	8	16	2

(a) Draw a frequency diagram to show these data.
(b) Which of the intervals is the modal class?
(c) Which of the intervals contains the median value?

3 As part of a fitness campaign, a business measured the weight of all of its workers.
Here are the results.

Weight (w kg)	$60 \leq w < 70$	$70 \leq w < 80$	$80 \leq w < 90$	$90 \leq w < 100$	$100 \leq w < 110$
Frequency	3	18	23	7	2

(a) Draw a frequency diagram to show these data.
(b) Which of the intervals is the modal class?
(c) Which of the intervals contains the median value?

4 Here is a frequency diagram.

Use the frequency diagram to make a grouped frequency table like those in questions **1** to **3**.

Frequency diagrams

> **TIP**
> When you choose the size of the interval, make sure you don't end up with too many, or too few, groups. Between five and ten intervals is usually about right. Remember that the intervals should be equal.

Discovery 5.1

(a) Measure the height of everyone in your class and record the data in two lists, one for boys and one for girls.
(b) Choose suitable intervals for the data and organise the data in a two-way table.
(c) Draw two frequency diagrams, one for the boys' data and one for the girls'. Use the same scales for both diagrams so that they can be compared easily.
(d) Compare the two diagrams.
What do the shapes of the graphs tell you, in general, about the heights of the boys and girls in your class?
(e) Compare your frequency diagrams with others in your class.
Have they used the same intervals for the data as you?
If they haven't, has this made a difference to their answers to part (d)?
Which of the diagrams looks the best? Why?

Challenge 5.1

Lisa checked the price of kettles on the internet.
Here are the prices of the first 30 she saw.

£9.60	£6.54	£8.90	£12.95	£13.90	£13.95
£14.25	£16.75	£16.90	£17.75	£17.90	£19.50
£19.50	£21.75	£22.40	£23.25	£24.50	£24.95
£26.00	£26.75	£27.00	£27.50	£29.50	£29.50
£29.50	£29.50	£32.25	£34.50	£35.45	£36.95

Complete a tally chart and draw a frequency diagram to show these data.
Use appropriate intervals for your groups.

Frequency polygons

A **frequency polygon** is another way of representing grouped continuous data.

A frequency polygon is formed by joining, with straight lines, the midpoints of the tops of the bars in a frequency diagram. The bars are not drawn. This means that several frequency polygons can be drawn on one grid, which makes them easier to compare.

To find the midpoint of each interval, add the bounds of each interval and divide the sum by 2.

EXAMPLE 5.2

The grouped frequency table shows the number of days that students in a tutor group were absent one term.

Days absent (d)	$0 \leqslant d < 5$	$5 \leqslant d < 10$	$10 \leqslant d < 15$	$15 \leqslant d < 20$	$20 \leqslant d < 25$
Frequency	11	8	6	0	5

Draw a frequency polygon to show these data.

Solution

First find the midpoint of each class.

$$\frac{0+5}{2} = 2.5 \quad \frac{5+10}{2} = 7.5 \quad \frac{10+15}{2} = 12.5 \quad \frac{15+20}{2} = 17.5 \quad \frac{20+25}{2} = 22.5$$

> **TIP** Notice that the midpoints go up in fives: this is because the interval size is five.

Now you can draw your frequency polygon.

Frequency polygons   83

EXERCISE 5.2

1. The table shows the weight loss of people in a slimming club over 6 months.

Weight (w kg)	$0 \leqslant w < 6$	$6 \leqslant w < 12$	$12 \leqslant w < 18$	$18 \leqslant w < 24$	$24 \leqslant w < 30$
Frequency	8	14	19	15	10

   Draw a frequency polygon to show these data.

2. The table shows the length of time that cars stayed in a car park one day.

Time (t mins)	$15 \leqslant t < 30$	$30 \leqslant t < 45$	$45 \leqslant t < 60$	$60 \leqslant t < 75$	$75 \leqslant t < 90$	$90 \leqslant t < 105$
Frequency	56	63	87	123	67	22

   Draw a frequency polygon to show these data.

3. The table shows the heights of 60 students.

Height (h cm)	$168 \leqslant h < 172$	$172 \leqslant h < 176$	$176 \leqslant h < 180$	$180 \leqslant h < 184$	$184 \leqslant h < 188$	$188 \leqslant h < 192$
Frequency	2	6	17	22	10	3

   Draw a frequency polygon to show these data.

4. The table shows the number of words per sentence in the first 50 sentences of two books.

No. of words (w)	$0 < w \leqslant 10$	$10 < w \leqslant 20$	$20 < w \leqslant 30$	$30 < w \leqslant 40$	$40 < w \leqslant 50$	$50 < w \leqslant 60$	$60 < w \leqslant 70$
Frequency Book 1	2	9	14	7	4	8	6
Frequency Book 2	27	11	9	0	3	0	0

   (a) On the same grid, draw a frequency polygon for each book.
   (b) Use the frequency polygons to compare the number of words per sentence in each book.

Stem-and-leaf diagrams

Another way of presenting data is to show them in a **stem-and-leaf diagram**.

Stem-and-leaf diagrams are useful because the data is grouped but the individual values are not lost.

Often the stem shows the tens digit of each value and the leaves show the units digits. If you put them together you get the original value. For example, 3|1 represents 31.

Or the stem might show the units digit of each value and the leaves might show the tenths digits. For example, 1|7 represents 1.7.

A stem-and-leaf diagram should have a key. The key tells you how to read the numbers.

EXAMPLE 5.3

Here are the marks gained by a group of students in a maths test.

63	58	63	52	59	65	69	75	70	54
57	63	76	81	63	68	59	40	65	74
80	44	47	53	70	81	68	49	57	61

(a) Construct a stem-and-leaf diagram to represent these data.
(b) What is the mode of these data?
(c) What is the modal class?
(d) What is the median?

Solution

(a) First draw the stem of the diagram.

```
4|
5|
6|
7|
8|
```

The smallest value in the list is 40 and the largest is 81.
The stem of the diagram will be the tens digits from 4 to 8.

Now work through the data values and put the second digit on the appropriate row.

```
4| 0 4 7 9
5| 8 2 9 4 7 9 3 7
6| 3 3 5 9 3 3 8 5 8 1
7| 5 0 6 4 0
8| 1 0 1
```

For the first value, 63, the 3 will go on the 6 row.

The numbers on the right of the diagram are the leaves.

Finally rewrite the diagram with all the leaves in order, with the smallest nearest to the stem. Remember to include a key.

```
4| 0 4 7 9
5| 2 3 4 7 7 8 9 9
6| 1 3 3 3 3 5 5 8 8 9
7| 0 0 4 5 6
8| 0 1 1
```

Key: 8|0 represents a mark of 80

(b) The mode is 63.   It is easy to see from the stem-and-leaf diagram that this is the value that occurs most often.

(c) The modal class is the 60 to 69 class.   Even though there is no value 60, the 6 row of the table covers all values from 60 to 69.

(d) As there are 30 values, the median will lie between the 15th and 16th values.
Count the values in the stem-and-leaf diagram to find the 15th and 16th values.
Since these are both 63, the median is 63.

EXERCISE 5.3

1 The data shows the weights, in kilograms, of 30 children.

```
41  30  40  30  34  37  55  27  45  39
65  47  36  44  32  31  58  41  41  28
49  53  49  37  33  30  34  59  34  68
```

Construct a stem-and-leaf diagram to show these weights.

2 The data shows the ages of 25 employees in a business.

```
19  17  26  33  31  41  41  27  25  28  24  28  32
40  31  29  29  39  26  36  26  35  38  42  38
```

(a) Construct a stem-and-leaf diagram to show these ages.
(b) What is the modal age?
(c) What is the median age?

3 The data shows the times, in seconds, 45 students took to swim one length of a swimming pool.

```
14.6  15.2  15.7  19.4  18.5  14.7  16.1  18.5  15.9  19.5  16.2  15.6
21.7  20.0  18.4  17.1  17.8  16.2  17.7  15.1  17.0  15.8  16.1
18.1  16.2  14.9  15.5  18.6  17.4  18.3  16.3  19.2  16.4  15.5
18.7  14.9  18.3  14.1  17.4  19.8  16.4  16.3  21.2  15.8  16.8
```

(a) Construct a stem-and-leaf diagram to show these times.
Use the key: 14|6 represents 14.6 seconds.
(b) Students who swam the length in less than 15 seconds qualified for the school team.
How many students qualified?
(c) What was the median time?

4 For their mock examinations, a group of 41 students take two maths papers.
Here are their results.

Paper 1
```
25  46  33  76  55  40  86  83  83  92  36
38  69  45  87  65  53  52  95  94  80
49  78  57  31  74  65  63  61  70  92
24  23  66  42  86  74  73  71  82  91
```

Paper 2

38	26	34	32	20	69	64	75	61	87	48
49	35	46	45	32	31	52	50	72	83	
26	48	58	57	45	42	52	63	89	95	
37	22	21	69	56	52	64	73	70	91	

(a) Construct a stem-and-leaf diagram for each set of scores.
(b) Which paper do you think was the harder? Give a reason for your answer.
(c) Find the median mark for each paper.
(d) The pass mark was 40 on each paper. How many students passed each paper?

Challenge 5.2

A 'stretched' stem-and-leaf diagram is one where the leaves are split into two parts. Each stem appears in the diagram twice.

1 | leaves 0 to 4
1 | leaves 5 to 9
2 | leaves 0 to 4
2 | leaves 5 to 9

(a) Look back at the solution to Example 5.3.
Draw a stretched stem-and-leaf diagram for this data.
(b) When do you think that it is necessary to use this technique?
(c) Draw stretched stem-and-leaf diagrams for questions **1** and **2** of Exercise 5.3.

Scatter diagrams

A scatter diagram is used to find out whether there is a **correlation**, or relationship, between two sets of data.

Data are presented as pairs of values each of which is plotted as a coordinate point on a graph.

Here are some examples of what a scatter diagram could look like and how we might interpret them.

Strong positive correlation

Here, one quantity increases as the other increases.
This is called **positive correlation**.

The trend is bottom left to top right.

When the points are closely in line, we say that the correlation is **strong**.

Weak positive correlation

Here the points again display positive correlation.
The points are more scattered so we say that the correlation is **weak**.

Strong negative correlation

Here, one quantity decreases as the other increases.
This is called **negative correlation**.

The trend is from top left to bottom right.

Again, the points are closely in line, so we say that the correlation is **strong**.

Weak negative correlation

Here the points again display negative correlation.
The points are more scattered so the correlation is **weak**.

No correlation

When the points are totally scattered and there is no clear pattern we say that there is **no correlation** between the two quantities.

If a scatter diagram shows correlation, you can draw a **line of best fit** on it. Try putting your ruler in various positions on the scatter diagram until you have a slope which matches the general slope of the points. There should be roughly the same number of points on each side of the line.

You cannot draw a line of best fit on a scatter diagram with no correlation.

88   5 Statistical diagrams

You can use the line of best fit to predict a value when only one of the pair of quantities is known.

EXAMPLE 5.4

The table shows the weights and heights of 12 people.

Height (cm)	150	152	155	158	158	160	163	165	170	175	178	180
Weight (kg)	56	62	63	64	57	62	65	66	65	70	66	67

(a) Draw a scatter diagram to show these data.
(b) Comment on the strength and type of correlation between these heights and weights.
(c) Draw a line of best fit on your scatter diagram.
(d) Tom is 162 cm tall. Use your line of best fit to estimate his weight.

Solution

(a), (c)

(b) Weak positive correlation.

(d) Draw a line from 162 cm on the Height axis, to meet your line of best fit. Now draw a horizontal line and read off the value where it meets the Weight axis.
Tom's probable weight is about 63 kg.

EXERCISE 5.4

1 The table shows the number of bad peaches per box after different delivery times.

Delivery time (hours)	10	4	14	18	6
Number of bad peaches	2	0	4	5	6

(a) Draw a scatter diagram to show this information.
(b) Describe the correlation shown in the scatter diagram.
(c) Draw a line of best fit on your scatter diagram.
(d) Use your line of best fit to estimate the number of bad peaches expected after a 12 hour delivery time.

2 The table shows the marks of 15 students taking Paper 1 and Paper 2 of a maths exam. Both papers were marked out of 40.

Paper 1	36	34	23	24	30	40	25	35	20	15	35	34	23	35	27
Paper 2	39	36	27	20	33	35	27	32	28	20	37	35	25	33	30

(a) Draw a scatter diagram to show this information.
(b) Describe the correlation shown in the scatter diagram.
(c) Draw a line of best fit on your scatter diagram.
(d) Joe scored 32 on Paper 1 but was absent for Paper 2.
Use your line of best fit to estimate his score on Paper 2.

3 The table shows the engine size and petrol consumption of nine cars.

Engine size (litres)	1.9	1.1	4.0	3.2	5.0	1.4	3.9	1.1	2.4
Petrol consumption (mpg)	34	42	23	28	18	42	27	48	34

(a) Draw a scatter diagram to show this information.
(b) Describe the correlation shown in the scatter diagram.
(c) Draw a line of best fit on your scatter diagram.
(d) Another car has an engine size of 2.8 litres.
Use your line of best fit to estimate the petrol consumption of this car.

4 Tracy thinks that the larger your head, the cleverer you are.
The table shows the number of marks scored in a test by ten students, and the circumference of their heads.

Circumference of head (cm)	600	500	480	570	450	550	600	460	540	430
Mark	43	33	45	31	25	42	23	36	24	39

5 Statistical diagrams

(a) Draw a scatter diagram to show this information.
(b) Describe the correlation shown in the scatter diagram.
(c) Is Tracy correct?
(d) Can you think of any reasons why the comparison may not be valid?

Challenge 5.3

(a) What type of correlation, if any, would you expect to find if you drew a scatter diagram for each of the following data?
   (i)   Sales of CDs and amount spent on advertising
   (ii) Number of accidents and number of speed cameras
   (iii) Height of adults and age of adults

(b) Write down your own examples of data which would show
   (i)   positive correlation.
   (ii) negative correlation.
   (iii) no correlation.

WHAT YOU HAVE LEARNED

- How to construct and interpret frequency diagrams, two-way tables, frequency polygons, stem-and-leaf diagrams and scatter diagrams
- About the different types of correlation
- How to draw and use lines of best fit

MIXED EXERCISE 5

1 Emma kept a record of the time, in minutes, that she had to wait for the school bus each morning for 4 weeks.

11 5 7 4 2 18 3 10 8 1
13 4 9 10 14 4 5 17 6 7

(a) Make a frequency table for these values using the groups
$0 \leqslant t < 5$, $5 \leqslant t < 10$, $10 \leqslant t < 15$ and $15 \leqslant t < 20$.
(b) Draw a frequency diagram for these data.
(c) Which of the intervals is the modal class?
(d) Which of the intervals contains the median value?

2 The table shows the marks gained by students in an examination.

Mark	$30 \leq m < 40$	$40 \leq m < 50$	$50 \leq m < 60$	$60 \leq m < 70$	$70 \leq m < 80$	$80 \leq m < 90$
Frequency	8	11	18	13	8	12

  (a) Draw a frequency polygon to show these data.
  (b) Describe the distribution of the marks.
  (c) Which is the modal class?
  (d) How many students took the examination?
  (e) What fraction of students scored 70 or more in the examination?
      Give your answer in its simplest form.

3 The data show the number of seats empty at a local theatre during each performance over the pantomime season.

```
19   1   8  11  15  19  21  43  17   1  23  19  11
12  15  40  21  11   8   4  27  21  20  14  18   7
11  23  31  16   8   2   8   6  10  11  15   9   8
 6   2   3   8  21  41  27  32  37   4
```

  (a) Construct a stem-and-leaf diagram to show these data.
  (b) There is one performance each day.
      For how many weeks did the pantomime season run?
  (c) What was the median number of empty seats?
  (d) The theatre makes a loss if the number of empty seats is over 40.
      For how many performances does the theatre make a loss?

4 A pet shop owner carried out a survey to investigate the average weight of a breed of rabbit at various ages. The table shows his results.

Age of rabbit (months)	1	2	3	4	5	6	7	8
Average weight (g)	90	230	490	610	1050	1090	1280	1560

  (a) Draw a scatter diagram to show this information.
  (b) Describe the correlation shown in the scatter diagram.
  (c) Draw a line of best fit on your scatter diagram.
  (d) Use your line of best fit to estimate
      (i) the weight of a rabbit of this breed which is $4\frac{1}{2}$ months old.
      (ii) the weight of a rabbit of this breed which is 9 months old.
  (e) If the line of best fit was extended you could estimate the weight of a rabbit of this breed which is 20 months old.
      Would this be sensible? Give a reason for your answer.

6 AREAS, VOLUMES AND 2-D REPRESENTATION

THIS CHAPTER IS ABOUT

- The meaning of terms related to circles
- Circumference and area of a circle
- Area and volume of complex shapes
- Volume of prisms
- Volume and surface area of a cylinder
- Plans and elevations

YOU SHOULD ALREADY KNOW

- The meaning of *circumference*, *diameter* and *radius*
- The meaning of *area* and *volume*
- How to find the area of rectangles and triangles
- How to find the volume of cuboids

Circles

The distance all the way round a circle is its **circumference**.

A **diameter** is a line all the way across a circle and passing through its centre.

A line from the centre of a circle to the circumference is called a **radius**.
For any circle, the radius is always the same, that is, it is constant.

TIP *Radius* is a Latin word. The plural is **radii**.

Here are some other terms relating to circles.

A **tangent** 'touches' a circle and is at right angles to the radius.
An **arc** is part of the circumference.
A **sector** is part of a circle between two radii, like a slice of cake.
A **chord** is a straight line dividing the circle in two parts.
A **segment** is the part cut off by a chord. The one shown is the **minor segment**. On the other side of the chord is the **major segment**.

You should use these mathematical terms when talking about parts of a circle.

Circumference of a circle

Discovery 6.1

Find a number of circular or cylindrical items.
Measure the circumference and diameter of each item and complete a table like this.

Item name	Circumference	Diameter	Circumference ÷ Diameter

What do you notice?

For any circle, $\dfrac{\text{circumference}}{\text{diameter}} \approx 3$.

If it were possible to take very accurate measurements, you would find that $\dfrac{\text{circumference}}{\text{diameter}} = 3.141\,592\,...$

This number is called **pi** and is represented by the symbol π.

This means that you can write a formula for the circumference of any circle.

> Circumference = $\pi \times$ diameter   or $C = \pi d$.

π is a decimal number which does not terminate and does not recur: it goes on for ever. In calculations, you can either use the $\boxed{\pi}$ button on your calculator or use an approximation: 3.142 is suitable.

EXAMPLE 6.1

Find the circumference of a circle with a diameter of 45 cm.

Solution

Circumference = $\pi \times$ diameter
            = 3.142 × 45
            = 141.39
            = 141.4 cm

3.142 is an approximation for π so your answer is not exact and should be rounded. You will often be told to what accuracy to give your answer. Here the answer is given correct to 1 decimal place.

> **TIP**
> You could do this calculation on your calculator, using the π button.
> Input π × 4 5 = . The answer on your display will be 141.371 67.

EXERCISE 6.1

Use the formula to find the circumferences of circles with these diameters.

1 12 cm   **2** 25 cm   **3** 90 cm   **4** 37 mm   **5** 66 mm   **6** 27 cm
7 52 cm   **8** 4.7 cm   **9** 9.2 cm   **10** 7.3 m   **11** 2.9 m   **12** 1.23 m

Challenge 6.1

Find the circumferences of circles with these radii.
(a) 8 cm   (b) 30 cm   (c) 65 cm   (d) 59 mm   (e) 0.7 m   (f) 1.35 m

Challenge 6.2

The wheel of a bicycle has a diameter of 66 cm.

How many complete revolutions will the wheel complete in a journey of 1 kilometre?

Area of a circle

The area of a circle is the space it covers.

Discovery 6.2

Take a disc of paper and cut it into 12 narrow sectors, all the same size.

Arrange them, reversing every other piece, like this.

This is nearly a rectangle. If you had cut the disc into 100 sectors it would be more accurate.

(a) What are the dimensions of the rectangle?
(b) What is its area?

Circles

The height of the rectangle in Discovery 6.2 is the radius of the circle, r.

The width is half the circumference of the circle, $\frac{1}{2}\pi d$ or πr.

This gives a formula to calculate the area of a circle.

> Area = πr^2 where r is the radius of the circle.

TIP
The formula is Area = πr^2. This means $\pi \times r^2$: that is, square r first then multiply by π. Do not work out $(\pi r)^2$.

EXAMPLE 6.2

Find the area of a circle with a radius of 23 cm.

Solution

Area = πr^2
= 3.142 × 23²
= 1662.118
= 1662 cm² (to the nearest whole number)

TIP
You could do this calculation on your calculator, using the π button.

Input π × 2 3 x^2 =. The answer on your display will be 1661.9025.

EXERCISE 6.2

1 Use the formula to find the areas of circles with the following radii.
(a) 14 cm
(b) 28 cm
(c) 80 cm
(d) 35 mm
(e) 62 mm
(f) 43 cm
(g) 55 cm
(h) 4.9 cm
(i) 9.7 cm
(j) 3.4 m
(k) 2.6 m
(l) 1.25 m

2 Use the formula to find the areas of circles with the following diameters.
(a) 16 cm
(b) 24 cm
(c) 70 cm
(d) 36 mm
(e) 82 mm
(f) 48 cm
(g) 54 cm
(h) 4.4 cm
(i) 9.8 cm
(j) 3.8 m
(k) 2.8 m
(l) 2.34 m

Challenge 6.3

A metal washer has the dimensions shown in the diagram.
Calculate the area of the washer.

14 mm

10 mm

Area of complex shapes

The formula for the area of a rectangle is

$$\text{Area} = \text{length} \times \text{width} \quad \text{or} \quad A = l \times w.$$

The formula for the area of a triangle is

$$\text{Area} = \tfrac{1}{2} \times \text{base} \times \text{height} \quad \text{or} \quad A = \tfrac{1}{2} \times b \times h.$$

You can use these formulae to find the area of more complex shapes, which can be broken down into rectangles and right-angled triangles.

EXAMPLE 6.3

Find the area of this shape.

5 cm
7 cm
A   B   C
3 cm   4 cm

Solution

Work out the area of the rectangle and each of the triangles separately and then add them together to find the area of the whole shape.

Area of shape = area of triangle **A** + area of rectangle **B** + area of triangle **C**

$$= \frac{3 \times 7}{2} \quad + \quad 5 \times 7 \quad + \quad \frac{4 \times 7}{2}$$

$$= \quad 10.5 \quad + \quad 35 \quad + \quad 14$$

$$= 59.5 \text{ cm}^2$$

EXERCISE 6.3

Find the area of each of these shapes.
Break them down into rectangles and right-angled triangles first.

1 13 cm, 4 cm, 7 cm, 18 cm

2 12 cm, 3 cm, 6 cm, 13 cm, 12 cm

3 19 cm, 7 cm, 25 cm, 12 cm, 10 cm

4 15 cm, 5 cm, 7 cm, 7 cm, 5 cm

5 8 cm, 6 cm, 6 cm, 10 cm, 6 cm, 6 cm, 8 cm

6 15 cm, 6 cm, 18 cm, 8 cm, 8 cm

Challenge 6.4

A kite has the dimensions shown in the diagram.
Calculate the area of the kite.

0.5 m, 0.7 m, 1.2 m

98   6 Areas, volumes and 2-D representation

Challenge 6.5

A blade for a lawnmower has the dimensions shown in the diagram.

Calculate the area of the blade.

Volume of complex shapes

The formula for the volume of a cuboid is

Volume = length × width × height   or $V = l \times w \times h$.

It is possible to find the volume of shapes made from cuboids by breaking them down into smaller parts.

EXAMPLE 6.4

Find the volume of this shape.

Solution

This shape can be broken down into two cuboids, **A** and **B**.
Work out the volumes of these two cuboids and add them together to find the volume of the whole shape.

Volume of shape = volume of cuboid **A** + volume of cuboid **B**
$$= 8 \times 11 \times 10 + 13 \times 11 \times 5$$
$$= 880 + 715$$
$$= 1595 \text{ cm}^3$$

The width of cuboid **B** is the same as the width of cuboid **A**.

EXERCISE 6.4

1 Find the volume of each of these shapes.

(a) 6 cm, 5 cm, 8 cm, 5 cm, 13 cm, 5 cm, 11 cm

(b) 8 cm, 14 cm, 8 cm, 15 cm, 18 cm

(c) 2 cm, 2 cm, 4 cm, 7.5 cm, 4.8 cm, 8.5 cm

(d) 6 cm, 11.5 cm, 8.5 cm, 3 cm, 15 cm

(e) 3 cm, 3 cm, 3 cm, 5 cm, 7 cm, 4 cm, 15 cm

(f) 4 cm, 3 cm, 14 cm, 4 cm, 5 cm, 7 cm, 12 cm

2 The diagram shows a concrete lintel used by builders. Calculate the volume of concrete needed to make the lintel.

(Note: The diagram is *not* drawn to scale.)

15 cm, 90 cm, 8 cm, 10 cm, 20 cm, 8 cm, 4 cm, 10 cm

100 6 Areas, volumes and 2-D representation

Volume of a prism

A **prism** is a three-dimensional object that is the same 'shape' throughout. The correct definition is that the object has a **uniform cross-section**.

In this diagram the shaded area is the cross-section.

Looking at the shape from point F you see the cross-section as an L-shape. If you were to cut through the shape along the dotted line you would still see the same cross-section.

You could cut the shape into slices, each 1 cm thick. The volume of each slice, in centimetres cubed, would be the area of the cross-section × 1.
As the shape is 11 cm thick, you would have 11 identical slices. So the volume of the whole shape would be the area of the cross-section × 11.

This tells you that the formula for the volume of a prism is

$$\text{Volume} = \text{area of cross-section} \times \text{length}.$$

The area of the cross-section (shaded) = (10 × 8) + (13 × 5)
$= 80 + 65$
$= 145 \text{ cm}^2$

Volume = 145 × 11
$= 1595 \text{ cm}^3$

This is the same answer as in Example 6.4, when the volume of this shape was found by breaking it down into cuboids.

The formula works for any prism.

EXAMPLE 6.5

This prism has a cross-section of area 374 cm², and is 26 cm long.
Find its volume.

Solution

Volume = area of cross-section × length
$= 374 \times 26$
$= 9724 \text{ cm}^3$

Volume of a prism 101

EXERCISE 6.5

1 Find the volume of each of these prisms.

(a) 9 cm, 137 cm²

(b) 321 cm², 54 cm

(c) 65.4 cm², 32 cm

(d) 24.8 cm², 16 cm

(e) 96.3 cm², 23.4 cm

(f) 27.4 cm², 19.3 cm

2 The diagram shows a clay plant pot support with a uniform cross-section.

The area of the cross-section is 3400 mm² and the length of the support is 35 mm.
What is the volume of the clay in the support?

35 mm

102 6 Areas, volumes and 2-D representation

Volume of a cylinder

A **cylinder** is a special kind of prism: the cross-section is always a circle.

Cylinder **A** and cylinder **B** are identical prisms.

You can find the volume of both cylinders using the formula for the volume of a prism.

Volume of cylinder **A** = area of cross-section × length
= 77 × 18
= 1386 cm³

Volume of cylinder **B** = area of cross-section (area of circle)
× length (height)
= $\pi r^2 \times h$ cm³

This gives you the formula for the volume of any cylinder:

> Volume = $\pi r^2 h$ where r is the radius of the circle and h is the height of the cylinder.

EXAMPLE 6.6

Find the volume of a cylinder with radius 13 cm and height 50 cm.

Solution

Volume = $\pi r^2 h$
= 3.142 × 13² × 50
= 26 549.9
= 26 550 cm³ (to the nearest whole number)

TIP

You could do this calculation on your calculator, using the $\boxed{\pi}$ button.

Input $\boxed{\pi}$ $\boxed{\times}$ $\boxed{1}$ $\boxed{3}$ $\boxed{x^2}$ $\boxed{\times}$ $\boxed{5}$ $\boxed{0}$ $\boxed{=}$. The answer on your display will be 26 546.458.

Rounded to the nearest whole number, this is 26 546 cm³. This is different from the answer you get using 3.142 as an approximation for π because your calculator uses a more accurate value for π.

EXERCISE 6.6

1 Use the formula to find the volumes of cylinders with these dimensions.
   (a) Radius 8 cm and height 35 cm
   (b) Radius 14 cm and height 42 cm
   (c) Radius 20 cm and height 90 cm
   (d) Radius 12 mm and height 55 mm
   (e) Radius 25 mm and height 6 mm
   (f) Radius 0.7 mm and height 75 mm
   (g) Radius 3 m and height 25 m
   (h) Radius 5.8 m and height 3.5 m

2 A capping stone for the top of a wall is in the shape of a half cylinder as shown in the diagram.

Calculate the volume of the capping stone.

45 cm
25 cm

Challenge 6.6

A water tank in a factory is a cylinder, as shown in the diagram.

The tank is full and the water is pumped out at a rate of 600 litres per minute.

How long does it take to empty the tank?

3.2 m
4.5 m²

Surface area of a cylinder

You can probably think of lots of examples of cylinders. Some of them, like the inner tube of a roll of kitchen paper, have no ends: these are called **open cylinders**. Others, like a can of beans, do have ends: these are called **closed cylinders**.

Curved surface area

If you took an open cylinder, cut straight down its length and opened it out, you would get a rectangle. The **curved surface area** of the cylinder has become a flat shape.

104 6 Areas, volumes and 2-D representation

The area of the rectangle is circumference × height.

You know that the formula for the circumference of a circle is

$$\text{Circumference} = \pi \times \text{diameter} \quad \text{or} \quad C = \pi d.$$

So the formula for the area of the curved surface of any cylinder is:

$$\text{Curved surface area} = \pi \times \text{diameter} \times \text{height} \quad \text{or} \quad \pi d h.$$

This formula is usually written in terms of the radius. You know that the radius is half the length of the diameter, or $d = 2r$.

So you can also write the formula for the area of the curved surface area of any cylinder as

$$\text{Curved surface area} = 2 \times \pi \times \text{radius} \times \text{height} \quad \text{or} \quad 2\pi r h.$$

EXAMPLE 6.7

Find the curved surface area of a cylinder with radius 4 cm and height 0.7 cm.

Solution

Curved surface area $= 2\pi rh$
$= 2 \times 3.142 \times 4 \times 0.7$
$= 17.5952$
$= 17.6 \text{ cm}^2$ (correct to 1 decimal place)

TIP

You could do this calculation on your calculator, using the π button.

Input $2 \times \pi \times 4 \times 0 . 7 =$. The answer on your display will be 17.592 919.

Total surface area

The total surface area of a closed cylinder is made up of the curved surface area and the area of the two circular ends.

So the formula for the total surface area of a (closed) cylinder is

$$\text{Total surface area} = 2\pi rh + 2\pi r^2.$$

EXAMPLE 6.8

Find the total surface area of a cylinder with radius 13 cm and height 1.5 cm.

Solution

Total surface area = $2\pi rh + 2\pi r^2$
= $(2 \times 3.142 \times 13 \times 1.5) + (2 \times 3.142 \times 13^2)$
= $122.538 + 1061.996 = 1184.534$
= 1185 cm^2 (to the nearest whole number)

TIP

You could do this calculation on your calculator, using the π button.

Input $(2 \times \pi \times 1 3 \times 1 . 5) + (2 \times \pi \times 1 3 \; x^2) =$.

The answer on your display will be 1184.3804.

Rounded to the nearest whole number, this is 1184 cm². This is different from the answer you get using 3.142 as an approximation for π because your calculator uses a more accurate value for π.

EXERCISE 6.7

1 Find the curved surface areas of cylinders with these dimensions.
   (a) Radius 12 cm and height 24 cm
   (b) Radius 11 cm and height 33 cm
   (c) Radius 30 cm and height 15 cm
   (d) Radius 18 mm and height 35 mm
   (e) Radius 15 mm and height 4 mm
   (f) Radius 1.3 mm and height 57 mm
   (g) Radius 2.1 m and height 10 m
   (h) Radius 3.5 m and height 3.5 m

2 The cardboard tube in a toilet roll is in the shape of a cylinder.
The diameter of the tube is 4.4 cm and the tube is 11 cm long.
Find the area of card used to make the tube.

3 Find the total surface areas of cylinders with these dimensions.
   (a) Radius 14 cm and height 10 cm
   (b) Radius 21 cm and height 32 cm
   (c) Radius 35 cm and height 12 cm
   (d) Radius 18 mm and height 9 mm
   (e) Radius 25 mm and height 6 mm
   (f) Radius 3.5 mm and height 50 mm
   (g) Radius 1.8 m and height 15 m
   (h) Radius 2.5 m and height 1.3 m

Challenge 6.7

The curved surface area of an open cylinder is 550 cm², to the nearest whole number.

The height of the cylinder is 19.5 cm.

Find the diameter of the cylinder.

Challenge 6.8

The total surface area of a closed cylinder is 2163 cm², to the nearest whole number.

The radius of the cylinder is 8.5 cm.

Find the height of the cylinder.

Plans and elevations

This diagram is part of a builder's plan for a housing estate.

It shows the shapes of the houses as seen from above. You may have heard the term 'bird's eye view' for this sort of picture. The mathematical term is **plan view**.

From the plan you can tell only what shape the buildings are from above. You cannot tell whether they are bungalows, two-storey houses or even blocks of flats.

The view of the front of an object is called a **front elevation**, the view from the side is called a **side elevation** and the view from the back is called a **back elevation**. An elevation shows you the height of an object.

EXAMPLE 6.9

For house A, sketch

(a) a possible view from F.   **(b)** a possible view from S.

Solution

(a) View from F   **(b) View from S**

Roof

Wall

The dotted lines show hidden detail.

Plans and elevations 107

EXAMPLE 6.10

For this shape, draw
(a) the plan.
(b) the front elevation (view from F).
(c) the side elevation from S.

Solution

(a) **Plan**

The cross shows the edges of the pyramid on top of the tower. The rectangle on the right is the flat top of the lower part of the shape.

(b) **Front elevation**

(c) **Side elevation**

EXAMPLE 6.11

Draw the plan view, front elevation and side elevation of this child's building block.

Solution

Plan

You can use dotted lines to show hidden detail.

In the plan, the dotted lines show the sides of the tunnel at floor level.

In the side elevation, the dotted line shows the top of the tunnel.

Front elevation

Side elevation

EXERCISE 6.8

Draw the plan view, front elevation and side elevation of each of these objects.

1.
2.
3.
4.
5.
6.

WHAT YOU HAVE LEARNED

- The names of parts of a circle
- The formula for the circumference of a circle is Circumference = πd or $2\pi r$
- The formula for the area of a circle is Area = πr^2
- The area of a complex shape can be found by breaking the shape down into rectangles and right-angled triangles
- The volume of a complex shape can be found by breaking the shape down into cuboids
- A prism is a three-dimensional object that has a uniform cross-section
- The formula for the volume of a prism is Volume = area of cross-section × length
- A cylinder is a special kind of prism whose cross-section is always a circle
- The formula for the volume of a cylinder is Volume = $\pi r^2 h$
- The formula for the curved surface area of a cylinder is
  Curved surface area = $2\pi rh$ or πdh

- The formula for the total surface area of a (closed) cylinder is
  Total surface area = $2\pi rh + 2\pi r^2$
- A plan view of an object is the shape of the object viewed from above
- An elevation of an object is the shape of the object viewed from the front, back or side

MIXED EXERCISE 6

1 Find the circumferences of circles with these diameters.
   (a) 14.2 cm   (b) 29.7 cm
   (c) 65 cm   (d) 32.1 mm

2 Find the areas of circles with these dimensions.
   (a) Radius 6.36 cm   (b) Radius 2.79 m
   (c) Radius 8.7 mm   (d) Diameter 9.4 mm
   (e) Diameter 12.6 cm   (f) Diameter 9.58 m

3 Draw a circle with radius 4 cm. On it draw and label
   (a) a chord.
   (b) a sector.
   (c) a tangent.

4 Work out the area of each of these shapes.

(a) 8.3 cm, 8.7 cm, 3.9 cm, 15.4 cm

(b) 3.5 cm, 2.5 cm, 4 cm, 8 cm, 10.5 cm

(c) 6 cm, 15 cm, 9 cm, 7 cm, 11 cm

(d) 17.9 cm, 6 cm, 11.7 cm, 6 cm, 6.5 cm, 12.7 cm

Mixed exercise 6

5   Find the volume of each of these shapes.

(a) 2 cm, 7 cm, 12 cm, 4 cm, 6 cm

(b) 3 cm, 3 cm, 6 cm, 4 cm, 10 cm

(c) 4 cm, 4.7 cm, 7.2 cm, 5.7 cm, 9.6 cm

(d) 3 cm, 4 cm, 4 cm, 5 cm, 2 cm, 8 cm, 10 cm

(e) 3.4 cm, 4.2 cm, 1.8 cm, 7.2 cm, 8 cm, 10.6 cm, 8.4 cm

(f) 8.4 cm, 6.6 cm, 6.6 cm, 2 cm, 4 cm, 2 cm, 6.6 cm, 4 cm, 7 cm, 6.6 cm, 2 cm, 2 cm, 8.4 cm

6   Find the volume of each of these prisms.

(a) 543 cm², 37.4 cm

(b) 93.4 mm², 16.9 mm

112   6 Areas, volumes and 2-D representation

(c) 74.9 cm² 75 cm

(d) 0.58 m² 1.53 m

7 Find the volumes of cylinders with these dimensions.
 (a) Radius 6 mm and height 23 mm
 (b) Radius 17 mm and height 3.6 mm
 (c) Radius 22 cm and height 70 cm
 (d) Radius 12 cm and height 0.4 cm
 (e) Radius 35 m and height 6 m
 (f) Radius 1.8 m and height 2.7 m

8 Find the curved surface areas of cylinders with these dimensions.
 (a) Radius 9.6 m and height 27.5 m
 (b) Radius 23.6 cm and height 16.4 cm
 (c) Radius 1.7 cm and height 1.5 cm
 (d) Radius 16.7 mm and height 6.4 mm

9 Find the total surface areas of cylinders with these dimensions.
 (a) Radius 23 mm and height 13 mm
 (b) Radius 3.6 m and height 1.4 m
 (c) Radius 2.65 cm and height 7.8 cm
 (d) Radius 4.7 cm and height 13.8 cm

10 Draw the plan view, front elevation and side elevation of these objects.

(a)

(b)

(c)

(d)

Mixed exercise 6

7 → EQUATIONS AND INEQUALITIES 1

THIS CHAPTER IS ABOUT
- Solving simple equations
- Solving simple inequalities

YOU SHOULD ALREADY KNOW
- How to collect like terms
- How to add, subtract, multiply and divide with negative numbers
- The squares of whole numbers up to 10

Solving equations

Sometimes the x term in the equation is squared (x^2). If there is an x squared term and no other x term in the equation, you can solve it as you would normally. However, you must remember that if you square a negative number, the result is positive. For example, $(-6)^2 = 36$.

When you solve an equation involving x^2, there will usually be two values that satisfy the equation.

EXAMPLE 7.1

Solve these equations.
(a) $5x + 1 = 16$
(b) $x^2 + 3 = 39$

TIP: Remember that you must always do each operation to the whole of both sides of the equation.

Solution

(a) $\quad 5x + 1 = 16$
$\quad 5x + 1 - 1 = 16 - 1$ First subtract 1 from each side.
$\quad\quad\quad\quad 5x = 15$
$\quad 5x \div 5 = 15 \div 5$ Now divide each side by 5.
$\quad\quad\quad\quad x = 3$

(b) $\quad x^2 + 3 = 39$
$\quad\quad\quad x^2 = 36$ First subtract 3 from each side.
$\quad\quad\quad x = 6$ Now find the square root of each side.
$\quad$ or $\quad x = -6$

EXERCISE 7.1

Solve these equations.

1. $2x - 1 = 13$
2. $2x - 1 = 0$
3. $2x - 13 = 1$
4. $3x - 2 = 19$
5. $6x + 12 = 18$
6. $3x - 7 = 14$
7. $4x - 8 = 12$
8. $4x + 12 = 28$
9. $3x - 6 = 24$
10. $5x - 10 = 20$
11. $x^2 + 3 = 28$
12. $x^2 - 4 = 45$
13. $y^2 - 2 = 62$
14. $m^2 + 3 = 84$
15. $m^2 - 5 = 20$
16. $x^2 + 10 = 110$
17. $x^2 - 4 = 60$
18. $20 + x^2 = 36$
19. $16 - x^2 = 12$
20. $200 - x^2 = 100$

Solving equations with brackets

You learned how to **expand brackets** in Chapter 2.

If you are solving an equation with brackets in it, expand the brackets first.

> **TIP**
> Remember to multiply *each* term inside the brackets by the number outside the brackets.

EXAMPLE 7.2

Solve these equations.
(a) $3(x + 4) = 24$
(b) $4(p - 3) = 20$

Solution

(a) $3(x + 4) = 24$
$3x + 12 = 24$ Multiply each term inside the brackets by 3.
$3x = 12$ Subtract 12 from each side.
$x = 4$ Divide each side of the equation by 3.

(b) $4(p - 3) = 20$
$4p - 12 = 20$ Multiply each term inside the brackets by 4.
$4p = 32$ Add 12 to each side.
$p = 8$ Divide each side by 4.

EXERCISE 7.2

Solve these equations.

1 $3(p - 4) = 36$
2 $3(4 + x) = 21$
3 $6(x - 6) = 6$
4 $4(x + 3) = 16$
5 $2(x - 8) = 14$
6 $2(x + 4) = 10$
7 $2(x - 4) = 20$
8 $5(x + 1) = 30$
9 $3(x + 7) = 9$
10 $2(x - 7) = 6$
11 $5(x - 6) = 20$
12 $7(a + 3) = 28$
13 $3(2x + 3) = 40$
14 $5(3x - 1) = 40$
15 $2(5x - 3) = 14$
16 $4(3x - 2) = 28$
17 $7(x - 4) = 28$
18 $3(5x - 12) = 24$
19 $2(4x + 2) = 20$
20 $2(2x - 5) = 12$

Equations with x on both sides

Some equations, such as $2x + 5 = 4 + 3x$, have x on both sides.

You could start to solve the equation in two different ways.

Subtract $3x$ from both sides
$2x + 5 - 3x = 4 + 3x - 3x$
$-x + 5 = 4$

or Subtract $2x$ from both sides
$2x + 5 - 2x = 4 + 3x - 2x$
$5 = 4 + x$

Subtracting $3x$ gives a negative x term. It is much easier to work with a positive x term, so for this equation it is better to start by subtracting $2x$.

EXAMPLE 7.3

Solve these equations.
(a) $8x - 3 = 3x + 7$
(b) $18 - 6x = 3x + 9$

Solution

(a) $8x - 3 = 3x + 7$
$8x - 3 - 3x = 3x + 7 - 3x$
$5x - 3 = 7$
$5x = 10$
$x = 2$

You could start by subtracting $8x$ from each side, but this would give a negative x term. So subtract $3x$ from each side.
Add 3 to each side.
Divide each side by 5.

(b) $18 - 6x = 3x + 9$
$18 - 6x + 6x = 3x + 9 + 6x$
$18 = 9x + 9$
$9 = 9x$
$1 = x$ or $x = 1$

You could start by subtracting $3x$ from each side, but this would give a negative x term. So add $6x$ to each side.
Subtract 9 from each side.
Divide each side by 9.

EXERCISE 7.3

Solve these equations.

1. $7x - 4 = 3x + 8$
2. $5x + 4 = 2x + 13$
3. $6x - 2 = x + 8$
4. $5x + 1 = 3x + 21$
5. $9x - 10 = 3x + 8$
6. $5x - 12 = 2x - 6$
7. $4x - 23 = x + 7$
8. $8x + 8 = 3x - 2$
9. $11x - 7 = 6x + 8$
10. $5 + 3x = x + 9$
11. $2x - 3 = 7 - 3x$
12. $4x - 1 = 2 + x$
13. $2x - 7 = x - 4$
14. $3x - 2 = x + 7$
15. $x - 5 = 2x - 9$
16. $x + 9 = 3x - 3$
17. $3x - 4 = 2 - 3x$
18. $5x - 6 = 16 - 6x$
19. $3(x + 1) = 2x$
20. $49 - 3x = x + 21$

Challenge 7.1

The length of a rectangular field is 10 metres more than its width.

The perimeter of the field is 220 metres.

What are the width and length of the field?

Hint: let x represent the width and draw a sketch of the rectangle.

Challenge 7.2

A rectangle measures $(2x + 1)$ cm by $(x + 9)$ cm.

Find the value of x for which the rectangle is a square.

Challenge 7.3

Here is an equation with boxes instead of numbers.

$\square x + \square = \square x + \square$

Jake found four numbers to put in the boxes by rolling a dice four times. He then tried to solve the equation he had made.

(a) What is the largest possible solution?
(b) What is the smallest possible solution?
(c) Find an equation he cannot solve.

Fractions in equations

You know that $k \div 6$ can be written as $\dfrac{k}{6}$.

You solve an equation like $\dfrac{k}{6} = 2$ by multiplying both sides of the equation by the denominator of the fraction.

Check up 7.1

Solve these equations.

(a) $\dfrac{x}{3} = 10$ (b) $\dfrac{m}{4} = 2$ (c) $\dfrac{m}{2} = 6$ (d) $\dfrac{p}{3} = 9$ (e) $\dfrac{y}{7} = 4$

Some equations involving fractions take more than one step to solve. These are solved using the same method as equations without fractions. You can get rid of the fraction, by multiplying both sides of the equation by the denominator of the fraction, at the end.

EXAMPLE 7.4

Solve the equation $\dfrac{x}{8} + 3 = 5$.

Solution

$\dfrac{x}{8} + 3 = 5$

$\dfrac{x}{8} = 2$ Subtract 3 from each side.

$x = 16$ Multiply each side by 8.

EXERCISE 7.4

Solve these equations.

1 $\dfrac{x}{4} + 3 = 7$ 2 $\dfrac{a}{5} - 2 = 6$ 3 $\dfrac{x}{4} - 2 = 3$ 4 $\dfrac{y}{5} - 5 = 5$

5 $\dfrac{y}{6} + 3 = 8$ 6 $\dfrac{p}{7} - 4 = 1$ 7 $\dfrac{m}{3} + 4 = 12$ 8 $\dfrac{x}{8} + 8 = 16$

9 $\dfrac{x}{9} + 7 = 10$ 10 $\dfrac{y}{3} - 9 = 2$

Challenge 7.4

Try to solve this ancient puzzle.

A number plus its three-quarters, plus its half, plus its fifth makes 49. What is the number?

Challenge 7.5

I think of a number. I square it and add 1. The answer divided by 10 gives 17. What is the number?

Inequalities

If you want to buy a packet of sweets costing 79p, you need at least 79p.

You may have more than that in your pocket. The amount in your pocket must be greater than or equal to 79p.

If the amount in your pocket is x, then this can be written as $x \geq 79$. This is an inequality.

The symbol $\geq$ means 'greater than or equal to'.
The symbol $>$ means 'greater than'.
The symbol $\leq$ means 'less than or equal to'.
The symbol $<$ means 'less than'.

On a number line you use an open circle to represent $>$ and $<$ and a solid circle to represent $\geq$ and $\leq$.

Inequalities are solved in a similar way to equations.

EXAMPLE 7.5

Solve the inequality $2x - 1 > 8$.

Show the solution on a number line.

Solution

$2x - 1 > 8$
$\quad 2x > 9$ Add 1 to each side.
$\quad\;\; x > 4.5$ Divide each side by 2.

Negative inequalities work a bit differently. It is best to make sure that you do not end up with a negative x term.

EXAMPLE 7.6

Solve the inequality $7 - 3x \leq 1$.

Show the solution on a number line.

Solution

$7 - 3x \leq 1$	You could start by subtracting 7 from each side, but
$7 \leq 1 + 3x$	this would give a negative x term. So add $3x$ to each side.
$6 \leq 3x$	Subtract 1 from each side.
$2 \leq x$	Divide each side by 3.
$x \geq 2$	Rewrite the inequality so that x is on the left. Remember to turn the inequality sign round as well.

EXERCISE 7.5

For each of questions **1** to **6**, solve the inequality and show the solution on a number line.

1 $x - 3 > 10$ **2** $x + 1 < 5$ **3** $5 > x - 8$

4 $2x + 1 \leq 9$ **5** $3x - 4 \geq 5$ **6** $10 \leq 2x - 6$

For each of questions **7** to **20**, solve the inequality.

7 $5x < x + 8$ **8** $2x \geq x - 5$ **9** $4 + x < -5$

10 $2(x + 1) > x + 3$ **11** $6x > 2x + 20$ **12** $3x + 5 \leq 2x + 14$

13 $5x + 3 \leq 2x + 9$ **14** $8x + 3 > 21 + 5x$ **15** $5x - 3 > 7 + 3x$

16 $6x - 1 < 2x$ **17** $5x < 7x - 4$ **18** $9x + 2 \geq 3x + 20$

19 $5x - 4 \leq 2x + 8$ **20** $5x < 2x + 12$

> **WHAT YOU HAVE LEARNED**
>
> - To solve equations involving brackets, expand the brackets first
> - To solve equations with x on both sides, avoid ending up with a negative x term
> - Solve equations involving fractions in the same way as equations without fractions, and deal with the fraction at the end
> - The symbol $\geq$ means 'greater than or equal to', $>$ means 'greater than', $\leq$ means 'less than or equal to' and $<$ means 'less than'
> - $x \geq 4$, $x > 3$, $y \leq 6$ and $y < 7$ are inequalities
> - Inequalities can be solved in a similar way to equations

MIXED EXERCISE 7

Solve these equations.

1. $2(m - 4) = 10$
2. $5(p + 6) = 40$
3. $7(x - 2) = 42$
4. $3(4 + x) = 21$
5. $4(p - 3) = 20$
6. $3x^2 = 48$
7. $2x^2 = 72$
8. $5p^2 + 1 = 81$
9. $4x^2 - 3 = 61$
10. $2a^2 - 3 = 47$
11. $\dfrac{x}{5} - 1 = 4$
12. $\dfrac{x}{6} + 5 = 10$
13. $\dfrac{y}{3} + 7 = 13$
14. $\dfrac{y}{7} - 6 = 1$
15. $\dfrac{a}{4} - 8 = 1$

Solve each of these inequalities and show the solution on a number line.

16. $5x + 1 \leq 11$
17. $10 + 3x \leq 5x + 4$
18. $7x + 3 < 5x + 9$
19. $6x - 8 > 4 + 3x$
20. $5x - 7 > 7 - 2x$

8 → RATIO AND PROPORTION

> **THIS CHAPTER IS ABOUT**
> - Understanding ratio and its notation
> - Writing a ratio in its lowest terms
> - Writing a ratio in the form $1:n$
> - Using ratios in proportion calculations
> - Dividing a quantity in a given ratio
> - Comparing proportions

> **YOU SHOULD ALREADY KNOW**
> - How to multiply and divide without a calculator
> - How to find common factors
> - How to simplify fractions
> - What is meant by an enlargement
> - How to change between metric units

What is a ratio?

A ratio is used to compare two or more quantities.

If you have three sweets and decide to keep one and give two to your best friend, you and your friend have sweets in the ratio $1:2$. You say this as '1 to 2'.

Larger numbers can also be compared in a ratio.

If you have six sweets and decide to keep two and give four to your best friend, you and your friend have sweets in the ratio $2:4$.

You already know how to give a fraction in its **lowest terms**, by **cancelling**. You can do the same with ratios.

$2:4 = 1:2$ 2 and 4 are both multiples of 2. So you can divide each part of the ratio by 2.

EXAMPLE 8.1

The salaries of three people are £16 000, £20 000 and £32 000.
Write this as a ratio in its lowest terms.

Solution

 16 000 : 20 000 : 32 000   First write the salaries as a ratio.
$=$ 16 : 20 : 32   Divide each part of the ratio by 1000.
$=$ 8 : 10 : 16   Divide each part by 2.
$=$ 4 : 5 : 8   Divide each part by 2.

Notice that your answer should not include units. £4 : £5 : £8 would be wrong.

TIP
To write a ratio in its lowest terms in one step, find the highest common factor (HCF) of the numbers in the ratio.

Then divide each part of the ratio by the HCF.

EXAMPLE 8.2

Write these ratios in their lowest terms.
(a) $20:50$ (b) $16:24$ (c) $9:27:54$

Solution

(a) $20:50 = 2:5$ Divide each part by 10.
(b) $16:24 = 2:3$ Divide each part by 8.
(c) $9:27:54 = 1:3:6$ Divide each part by 9.

Check up 8.1

(a) Jane is 4 years old and Petra is 8 years old.
Write the ratio of their ages in its lowest terms.

(b) A recipe uses 500 g of flour, 300 g of sugar and 400 g of raisins.
Write the ratio of these amounts in its lowest terms.

Sometimes you have to change the units of one part of the ratio first.

EXAMPLE 8.3

Write each of these ratios in its lowest terms.
(a) 1 millilitre : 1 litre   (b) 1 kilogram : 200 grams

Solution

(a) 1 millilitre : 1 litre = 1 millilitre : 1000 millilitres   Write each part in the same units.
             $= 1:1000$ When the units are the same, you do not include them in the ratio.

(b) 1 kilogram : 200 grams = 1000 grams : 200 grams   Write each part in the same units.
             $= 5:1$ Divide each part by 200.

What is a ratio? 123

EXAMPLE 8.4

Write each of these ratios in its lowest terms.
(a) 50p : £2
(b) 2 cm : 6 mm
(c) 600 g : 2 kg : 750 g

Solution

(a) 50p : £2 = 50p : 200p   Write each part in the same units.
           = 1 : 4   Divide each part by 50.

(b) 2 cm : 6 mm = 20 mm : 6 mm   Write each part in the same units.
                = 10 : 3   Divide each part by 2.

(c) 600 g : 2 kg : 750 g = 600 g : 2000 g : 750 g   Write each part in the same units.
                        = 12 : 40 : 15   Divide each part by 50.

EXERCISE 8.1

1 Write each of these ratios in its lowest terms.
   (a) 6 : 3
   (b) 25 : 75
   (c) 30 : 6
   (d) 5 : 15 : 25
   (e) 6 : 12 : 8

2 Write each of these ratios in its lowest terms.
   (a) 50 g : 1000 g
   (b) 30p : £2
   (c) 2 minutes : 30 seconds
   (d) 4 m : 75 cm
   (e) 300 ml : 2 litres

3 At a concert there are 350 men and 420 women.
   Write the ratio of men to women in its lowest terms.

4 Al, Peta and Dave invest £500, £800 and £1000 respectively in a business.
   Write the ratio of their investments in its lowest terms.

5 A recipe for vegetable soup uses 1 kg of potatoes, 500 g of leeks and 750 g of celery.
   Write the ratio of the ingredients in its lowest terms.

Challenge 8.1

(a) Explain why the ratio 20 minutes : 1 hour is not 20 : 1.

(b) What should it be?

Writing a ratio in the form $1:n$

It is sometimes useful to have a ratio with 1 on the left.
A common scale for a scale model is $1:24$.
The scale of a map or enlargement is often given as $1:n$.

To change a ratio to this form, divide both numbers by the one on the left. This can be written in a general form as $1:n$.

EXAMPLE 8.5

Write these ratios in the form $1:n$.
(a) $2:5$
(b) $8\,mm:3\,cm$
(c) $25\,mm:1.25\,km$

Solution

(a) $2:5 = 1:2.5$ Divide each side by 2.

(b) $8\,mm:3\,cm = 8\,mm:30\,mm$ Write each side in the same units.
$\qquad\qquad\quad = 1:3.75$ Divide each side by 8.

(c) $25\,mm:1.25\,km = 25:1\,250\,000$ Write each side in the same units.
$\qquad\qquad\qquad\quad = 1:50\,000$ Divide each side by 25.

$1:50\,000$ is a common map scale. It means that 1 cm on the map represents 50 000 cm, or 500 m, on the ground.

> **TIP**
> Use a calculator if necessary to convert the ratio to the form $1:n$.

EXERCISE 8.2

1 Write each of these ratios in the form $1:n$.
(a) $2:6$
(b) $3:15$
(c) $6:15$
(d) $4:7$
(e) $20p:£1.50$
(f) $4\,cm:5\,m$
(g) $10:2$
(h) $2\,mm:1\,km$

2 On a map a distance of 8 mm represents a distance of 2 km.
What is the scale of the map in the form $1:n$?

3 A negative for a photograph is 35 mm long. An enlargement is 21 cm long.
What is the ratio of the negative to the enlargement in the form $1:n$?

Using ratios

Sometimes you know one of the quantities in the ratio, but not the other.

If the ratio is in the form $1:n$, you can work out the second quantity by multiplying the first by n.

You can work out the first quantity by dividing the second quantity by n.

EXAMPLE 8.6

(a) A negative is enlarged in the ratio $1:20$ to make a picture.
The negative measures 36 mm by 24 mm.
What size is the enlargement?

(b) Another $1:20$ enlargement measures 1000 mm × 1000 mm.
What size is the negative?

Solution

(a) $36 \times 20 = 720$ The enlargement will be 20 times bigger than
$24 \times 20 = 480$ the negative, so multiply both dimensions by 20.

The enlargement measures 720 mm by 480 mm.

(b) $1000 \div 20 = 50$ The negative will be 20 times smaller than the negative, so divide the dimensions by 20.

The negative measures 50 mm × 50 mm.

EXAMPLE 8.7

A map is drawn to a scale of $1 \text{ cm} : 2 \text{ km}$.

(a) On the map, the distance between Amhope and Didburn is 5.4 cm.
What is the actual distance in kilometres?

(b) The length of a straight railway track between two stations is 7.8 km.
How long is this track on the map in centimetres?

Solution

(a) $2 \times 5.4 = 10.8$ The actual distance, in kilometres, is
Real distance = 10.8 km twice as large as the map distance, in centimetres. So multiply by 2.

(b) $7.8 \div 2 = 3.9$ The map distance, in centimetres, is
Map distance = 3.9 cm half as large as the actual distance, in kilometres. So divide by 2.

Challenge 8.2

What would the answer to part **(a)** of Example 8.7 be in centimetres?

What ratio could you use to work this out?

Sometimes you have to work out quantities using a ratio that is not in the form $1:n$.

To work out an unknown quantity, you multiply each part of the ratio by the same number to get an equivalent ratio which contains the quantity you know. This number is called the **multiplier**.

EXAMPLE 8.8

To make jam, fruit and sugar are mixed in the ratio $2:3$.
This means that if you have 2 kg of fruit, you need 3 kg of sugar; if you have 4 kg of fruit, you need 6 kg of sugar.
How much sugar do you need if your fruit weighs

(a) 6 kg? (b) 10 kg? (c) 500 g?

Solution

(a) $6 \div 2 = 3$ Divide the quantity of fruit by the fruit part of the ratio to find the multiplier.
   $2:3 = 6:9$ Multiply each part of the ratio by the multiplier, 3.
   9 kg of sugar

(b) $10 \div 2 = 5$ Divide the quantity of fruit by the fruit part of the ratio to find the multiplier.
   $2:3 = 10:15$ Multiply each part of the ratio by the multiplier, 5.
   15 kg of sugar

(c) $500 \div 2 = 250$ Divide the quantity of fruit by the fruit part of the ratio to find the multiplier.
   $2:3 = 500:750$ Multiply each part of the ratio by the multiplier, 250.
   750 g of sugar

EXAMPLE 8.9

Two photos are in the ratio $2:5$.
(a) What is the height of the larger photo?
(b) What is the width of the smaller photo?

5 cm

9 cm

Using ratios 127

Solution

(a) $5 \div 2 = 2.5$ Divide the height of the smaller photo by the smaller part of the ratio to find the multiplier.
$2:5 = 5:12.5$ Multiply each part of the ratio by the multiplier, 2.5.
Height of the larger photo = 12.5 cm

(b) $9 \div 5 = 1.8$ Divide the width of the larger photo by the larger part of the ratio to find the multiplier.
$2:5 = 3.6:9$ Multiply each part of the ratio by the multiplier, 1.8.
Width of the smaller photo = 3.6 cm

EXAMPLE 8.10

To make grey paint, white paint and black paint are mixed in the ratio $5:2$.
(a) How much black paint is mixed with 800 ml of white paint?
(b) How much white paint is mixed with 300 ml of black paint?

Solution

A table is often useful for this sort of question.

	Paint	White	Black
	Ratio	5	2
(a)	Amount	800 ml	$2 \times 160 = 320$ ml
	Multiplier	$800 \div 5 = 160$	
(b)	Amount	$5 \times 150 = 750$ ml	300 ml
	Multiplier		$300 \div 2 = 150$

TIP Make sure you haven't made a silly mistake by checking that the bigger side of the ratio has the bigger quantity.

(a) Black paint = 320 ml   (b) White paint = 750 ml

EXAMPLE 8.11

To make stew for four people, a recipe uses 1.6 kg of beef.
How much beef is needed using the recipe for six people?

Solution

The ratio of people is $4:6$.

$4:6 = 2:3$ Write the ratio in its lowest terms.
$1.6 \div 2 = 0.8$ Divide the quantity of beef needed for four people by the first part of the ratio to find the multiplier.
$0.8 \times 3 = 2.4$ Multiply the second part of the ratio by the multiplier, 0.8.
Beef needed for six people = 2.4 kg

EXERCISE 8.3

1. The ratio of the lengths of two squares is 1 : 6.
   (a) The length of the side of the small square is 2 cm.
       What is the length of the side of the large square?
   (b) The length of the side of the large square is 21 cm.
       What is the length of the side of the small square?

2. The ratio of helpers to babies in a crèche must be 1 : 4.
   (a) There are six helpers on a Tuesday.
       How many babies can there be?
   (b) There are 36 babies on a Thursday.
       How many helpers must there be?

3. Sanjay is mixing pink paint.
   To get the shade he wants, he mixes red and white paint in the ratio 1 : 3.
   (a) How much white paint should he mix with 2 litres of red paint?
   (b) How much red paint should he mix with 12 litres of white paint?

4. The negative of a photo is 35 mm long. An enlargement of 1 : 4 is made.
   What is the length of the enlargement?

5. A road atlas of Great Britain is to a scale of 1 inch to 4 miles.
   (a) On the map the distance between Forfar and Montrose is 7 inches.
       What is the actual distance between the two towns in miles?
   (b) It is 40 miles from Newcastle to Middlesbrough. How far is this on the map?

6. For a recipe, Chelsy mixes water and lemon curd in the ratio 2 : 3.
   (a) How much lemon curd should she mix with 20 ml of water?
   (b) How much water should she mix with 15 teaspoons of lemon curd?

7. To make a solution of a chemical a scientist mixes 3 parts chemical with 20 parts water.
   (a) How much water should he mix with 15 ml of chemical?
   (b) How much chemical should he mix with 240 ml of water?

8. An alloy is made by mixing 2 parts silver with 5 parts nickel.
   (a) How much nickel must be mixed with 60 g of silver?
   (b) How much silver must be mixed with 120 g of nickel?

9. Sachin and Rehan share a flat. They agree to share the rent in the same ratio as their wages.
   Sachin earns £600 a month and Rehan earns £800 a month.
   If Sachin pays £90, how much does Rehan pay?

10. A recipe for hotpot uses onions, carrots and stewing steak in the ratio, by mass, of 1 : 2 : 5.
    (a) What quantity of steak is needed if 100 g of onion is used?
    (b) What quantity of carrots is needed if 450 g of steak is used?

Dividing a quantity in a given ratio

Discovery 8.1

Maya has an evening job making up party bags for a children's party organiser. She shares out lemon sweets and raspberry sweets in the ratio 2 : 3. Each bag contains 5 sweets.

(a) On Monday Maya makes up 10 party bags.
  (i) How many sweets does she use in total?
  (ii) How many lemon sweets does she use?
  (iii) How many raspberry sweets does she use?

(b) On Tuesday Maya makes up 15 party bags.
  (i) How many sweets does she use in total?
  (ii) How many lemon sweets does she use?
  (iii) How many raspberry sweets does she use?

What do you notice?

A ratio represents the number of shares in which a quantity is divided. The total quantity divided in a ratio is found by adding the parts of the ratio together.

To find the quantities shared in a ratio:
- Find the total number of shares.
- Divide the total quantity by the total number of shares to find the multiplier.
- Multiply each part of the ratio by the multiplier.

TIP: The multiplier may not be a whole number. Work with the decimal or fraction and round the final answer if necessary.

EXAMPLE 8.12

To make fruit punch, orange juice and grapefruit juice are mixed in the ratio 5 : 3.
Jo wants to make 1 litre of punch.
(a) How much orange juice does she need in millilitres?
(b) How much grapefruit juice does she need in millilitres?

8 Ratio and proportion

Solution

5 + 3 = 8   First work out the total number of shares.
1000 ÷ 8 = 125   Convert 1 litre to millilitres and divide by 8 to find the multiplier.

A table is often helpful for this sort of question.

Punch	Orange	Grapefruit
Ratio	5	3
Amount	5 × 125 = 625 ml	3 × 125 = 375 ml

(a) Orange juice = 625 ml   **(b)** Grapefruit juice = 375 ml

> **TIP** To check your answers, add the parts together: they should equal the total quantity. For example, 625 ml + 375 ml = 1000 ml ✓

EXERCISE 8.4

Do not use your calculator for questions **1** to **5**.

1 Share £20 between Dave and Sam in the ratio 2 : 3.

2 Paint is mixed in the ratio 3 parts red to 5 parts white to make 40 litres of pink paint.
   (a) How much red paint is used?   **(b)** How much white paint is used?

3 Asif is making mortar by mixing sand and cement in the ratio 5 : 1.
   How much sand is needed to make 36 kg of mortar?

4 To make a solution of a chemical a scientist mixes 1 part chemical with 5 parts water.
   She makes 300 ml of the solution.
   (a) How much chemical does she use?   **(b)** How much water does she use?

5 Amit, Bree and Chris share £1600 between them in the ratio 2 : 5 : 3.
   How much does each receive?

You may use your calculator for questions **6** to **8**.

6 In a local election, 5720 people vote.
   They vote for Labour, Conservative and other parties in the ratio 6 : 3 : 2.
   How many people vote Conservative?

Dividing a quantity in a given ratio

7 St Anthony's College Summer Fayre raised £1750. The governors decided to share the money between the college and a local charity in the ratio 5 to 1.
   How much did the local charity receive? Give your answer correct to the nearest pound.

8 Sally makes breakfast cereal by mixing bran, currants and wheatgerm in the ratio 8 : 3 : 1 by mass.
   (a) How much bran does she use to make 600 g of the cereal?
   (b) One day, she only has 20 g of currants.
       How much cereal can she make? She has plenty of bran and wheatgerm.

Challenge 8.3

Okera has a photo measuring 13 cm by 17 cm. He wants to have it enlarged.
Supa Print offer two sizes: 24 inches by 32 inches and 20 inches by 26.5 inches.
He wants to keep the same proportions, or as near as possible.

(a) Which of the two enlargements should he choose? Show how you make your decision.

(b) Why might he choose the other one?

Best value

Discovery 8.2

Two packets of cornflakes are available at a supermarket.

Which is the better value for money?

CORN FLAKES 1.5 kg £4.99

CORN FLAKES 500g £1.70

To compare value, you need to compare either
- how much you get for a certain amount of money or
- how much a certain quantity (for example, volume or mass) costs.

In each case you are comparing **proportions**, either of size or of cost.

The better value item is the one with the **lower unit cost** or the **greater number of units per penny** (or pound).

EXAMPLE 8.13

Sunflower oil is sold in 700 ml bottles for 95p and in 2 litre bottles for £2.45.
Show which bottle is the better value.

Solution

Method 1

Work out the price per millilitre for each bottle.

Size	Small	Large
Capacity	700 ml	2 litre = 2000 ml
Price	95p	£2.45 = 245p
Price per ml	95 ÷ 700 = 0.14p	245 ÷ 2000 = 0.1225p

Use the same units for each bottle.

Round your answers to 2 decimal places if necessary.

The price per ml of the 2 litre bottle is lower. It has the lower unit cost. In this case the unit is a millilitre.

The 2 litre bottle is the better value.

Method 2

Work out the amount per penny for each bottle.

Size	Small	Large
Capacity	700 ml	2 litre = 2000 ml
Price	95p	£2.45 = 245p
Amount per penny	700 ÷ 95 = 7.37 ml	2000 ÷ 245 = 8.16 ml

Again, use the same units for each bottle.

Round your answers to 2 decimal places if necessary.

The amount per pence is greater for the 2 litre bottle. It has the greater number of units per penny.

The 2 litre bottle is the better value.

> **TIP**: Make it clear whether you are working out the cost per unit or the amount per penny, and include the units in your answers. Always show your working.

EXERCISE 8.5

1. A 420 g bag of Choco bars costs £1.59 and a 325 g bag of Choco bars costs £1.09. Which is the better value for money?

2. Spa water is sold in 2 litre bottles for 85p and in 5 litre bottles for £1.79. Show which is the better value.

3. Wallace bought two packs of cheese, a 680 g pack for £3.20 and a 1.4 kg pack for £5.40. Which was the better value?

4. One-inch nails are sold in packets of 50 for £1.25 and in packets of 144 for £3.80. Which packet is the better value?

5. Toilet rolls are sold in packs of 12 for £1.79 and in packs of 50 for £7.20. Show which is the better value.

6. Brillo white toothpaste is sold in 80 ml tubes for £2.79 and in 150 ml tubes for £5.00. Which tube is the better value?

7. A supermarket sells cola in three different sized bottles: a 3 litre bottle costs £1.99, a 2 litre bottle costs £1.35 and a 1 litre bottle costs 57p. Which bottle gives the best value?

8. Crispy cornflakes are sold in three sizes: 750 g for £1.79, 1.4 kg for £3.20 and 2 kg for £4.89. Which packet gives the best value?

WHAT YOU HAVE LEARNED

- To write a ratio in its lowest terms, divide all parts of the ratio by their highest common factor (HCF)
- To write a ratio in the form $1:n$, divide both numbers by the one on the left
- If the ratio is in the form $1:n$, you can work out the second quantity by multiplying the first by n, and you can work out the first quantity by dividing the second quantity by n
- To find an unknown quantity, each part of the ratio must be multiplied by the same number, called the multiplier
- To find the quantities shared in a given ratio, first find the total number of shares, then divide the total quantity by the total number of shares to find the multiplier, then multiply each part of the ratio by the multiplier
- To compare value, work out the cost per unit or the number of units per penny (or pound). The better value item is the one with the lower cost per unit or the greater number of units per penny (or pound)

MIXED EXERCISE 8

1 Write each ratio in its simplest form.
   (a) 50 : 35
   (b) 30 : 72
   (c) 1 minute : 20 seconds
   (d) 45 cm : 1 m
   (e) 600 ml : 1 litre

2 Write these ratios in the form $1 : n$.
   (a) 2 : 8
   (b) 5 : 12
   (c) 2 mm : 10 cm
   (d) 2 cm : 5 km
   (e) 100 : 40

3 A notice is enlarged in the ratio 1 : 20.
   (a) The original is 3 cm wide.
       How wide is the enlargement?
   (b) The enlargement is 100 cm long.
       How long is the original?

4 To make 12 scones Maureen uses 150 g of flour.
   How much flour does she use to make 20 scones?

5 To make a fruit and nut mixture, raisins and nuts are mixed in the ratio 5 : 3, by mass.
   (a) What mass of nuts is mixed with 100 g of raisins?
   (b) What mass of raisins is mixed with 150 g of nuts?

6 Panache made a fruit punch by mixing orange, lemon and grapefruit juice in the ratio 5 : 1 : 2.
   (a) He made a 2 litre bowl of fruit punch.
       How many millilitres of grapefruit juice did he use?
   (b) How much fruit punch could he make with 150 ml of orange juice?

7 Show which is the better buy: 5 litres of oil for £18.50 or 2 litres of oil for £7.00.

8 Supershop sells milk in pints at 43p and in litres at 75p.
   A pint is equal to 568 ml.
   Which is the better buy?

9 STATISTICAL CALCULATIONS

THIS CHAPTER IS ABOUT
- Calculating the mean and range for grouped data
- Calculating the mean, range and median for continuous data
- Using statistical functions on a calculator or computer

YOU SHOULD ALREADY KNOW
- How to calculate the mean, mode, median and range for discrete data

The mean from a frequency table

The **mean** of a set of data is found by adding the values together and dividing the total by the number of values used.

For example, the following data shows the number of pets owned by nine Year 10 students.

| 8 | 4 | 4 | 6 | 3 | 7 | 3 | 2 | 8 |

The mean is $45 \div 9 = 5$.

What you are working out is (the total number of pets) ÷ (the total number of students surveyed).

If you surveyed 150 people you would have a list of 150 numbers. You could find the mean by adding them all up and dividing by 150, but this would take a long time.

Instead, you can put the data in a frequency table and work out the mean using a different method.

EXAMPLE 9.1

Skye asked all the students in Year 10 at her local girls' school how many brothers they had. The table shows her results.

Work out the mean number of brothers for these students.

Number of brothers	Frequency (number of girls)
0	24
1	60
2	47
3	11
4	5
5	2
6	0
7	0
8	1
Total	150

Solution

The mean of this data is (the total number of brothers) ÷ (the total number of girls surveyed).

First you need to work out the total number of brothers.

You can see from the table that
- 24 girls do not have any brothers. They have 24 × 0 = 0 brothers between them.
- 60 girls have one brother each. They have 60 × 1 = 60 brothers between them.
- 47 girls have two brothers each. They have 47 × 2 = 94 brothers between them.

and so on.

If you add the results for each row of the table together, you will get the total number of brothers.

You can add some more columns to the table to show this.

Number of brothers (x)	Number of girls (f)	Number of brothers × frequency	Total number of brothers (fx)
0	24	0 × 24	0
1	60	1 × 60	60
2	47	2 × 47	94
3	11	3 × 11	33
4	5	4 × 5	20
5	2	5 × 2	10
6	0	6 × 0	0
7	0	7 × 0	0
8	1	8 × 1	8
Total	150		225

> **TIP**
> The 'Number of brothers' column is the variable and is usually labelled x.
> The 'Number of girls' column is the frequency and is usually labelled f.
> The 'Total number of brothers' column is usually labelled fx because it represents (Number of brothers) × (Number or girls) = $x \times f$.

The total number of brothers = 225
The total number of girls surveyed = 150
So the mean = 225 ÷ 150 = 1.5 brothers.

> **TIP**
> You can enter the calculations into your calculator as a chain of numbers and then press the $=$ key to find the total before dividing by 150.
>
> Input [0][×][2][4][+][1][×][6][0][+][2][×][4][7][+][3][×][1][1][+][4][×][5]
> [+][5][×][2][+][6][×][0][+][7][×][0][+][8][×][1][=][÷][1][5][0][=]

You can also work out the **mode**, **median** and **range** from the table.

The mode of the number of brothers is 1.
This is the number of brothers with the highest frequency (60).

The median number of brothers is 1.
As there are 150 values, the median will lie between the 75th and 76th values.
Add on the frequency for each number of brothers (row) until you find the interval containing the 75th and 76th values:

24 is smaller than 75. The 75th and 76th values do not lie in row 0.
24 + 60 = 84   84 is larger than 76. The 75th and 76th values must lie in row 1.

The range of the number of brothers is 8.
This is (the largest number of brothers) − (the smallest number of brothers) = 8 − 0 = 8.

Using a spreadsheet to find the mean

You can also calculate the mean using a computer spreadsheet. Follow these steps to work out the mean for the data in Example 9.1.

> **TIP**
> Type the bold text carefully: do not put in any spaces.

1 Open a new spreadsheet.

2 In cell A1 type the title 'Number of brothers (x)'.
   In cell B1 type the title 'Number of girls (f)'.
   In cell C1 type the title 'Total number of brothers (fx)'.

3 In cell A2 type the number 0. Then type the numbers 1 to 8 in cells A3 to A10.

4 In cell B2 type the number 24. Then type the other frequencies in cells B3 to B10.

5 In cell C2 type **=A2*B2** and press the enter key.
Click on cell C2, click on Edit in the toolbar and select Copy.
Click on cell C3, and hold down the mouse key and drag down to cell C10. Then click on Edit in the toolbar and select Paste.

6 In cell A11 type the word 'Total'.

7 In cell B11 type **=SUM(B2:B10)** and press the enter key.
In cell C11 type **=SUM(C2:C10)** and press the enter key.

8 In cell A12 type the word 'Mean'.

9 In cell B12 type **=C11/B11** and press the enter key.

Your spreadsheet should look like this.

	A	B	C
1	Number of brothers (x)	Number of girls (f)	Total number of brothers (fx)
2	0	24	0
3	1	60	60
4	2	47	94
5	3	11	33
6	4	5	20
7	5	2	10
8	6	0	0
9	7	0	0
10	8	1	8
11	Total	150	225
12	Mean	1.5	

Answer one of the questions in the next exercise using a computer spreadsheet.

EXERCISE 9.1

1 For each of these sets of data
  (i) find the mode.
  (ii) find the median.
  (iii) find the range.
  (iv) calculate the mean.

(a)

Score on dice	Number of times thrown
1	89
2	77
3	91
4	85
5	76
6	82
Total	500

(b)

Number of matches	Number of boxes
47	78
48	82
49	62
50	97
51	86
52	95
Total	500

(c)

Number of accidents	Number of drivers
0	65
1	103
2	86
3	29
4	14
5	3
Total	300

(d)

Number of cars per house	Number of students
0	15
1	87
2	105
3	37
4	6
Total	250

2 Calculate the mean for each of these sets of data.

(a)

Number of passengers in taxi	Frequency
1	84
2	63
3	34
4	15
5	4
Total	200

(b)

Number of pets owned	Frequency
0	53
1	83
2	23
3	11
4	5
Total	175

(c)

Number of books read in a month	Frequency
0	4
1	19
2	33
3	42
4	29
5	17
6	6
Total	150

(d)

Number of drinks in a day	Frequency
3	81
4	66
5	47
6	29
7	18
8	9
Total	250

3 Calculate the mean for each of these sets of data.

(a)

x	Frequency
1	47
2	36
3	28
4	57
5	64
6	37
7	43
8	38

(b)

x	Frequency
23	5
24	9
25	12
26	15
27	13
28	17
29	14
30	15

(c)

x	Frequency
10	5
11	8
12	6
13	7
14	3
15	9
16	2

(d)

x	Frequency
0	12
1	59
2	93
3	81
4	43
5	67
6	45

The mean from a frequency table

4 In Barnsfield, bus tickets cost 50p, £1.00, £1.50 or £2.00 depending on the length of the journey. The frequency table shows the numbers of tickets sold on one Friday. Calculate the mean fare paid on that Friday.

Price of ticket (£)	0.50	1.00	1.50	2.00
Number of tickets	140	207	96	57

5 800 people were asked how many newspapers they had bought one week. The table shows the data.
Calculate the mean number of newspapers bought.

Number of newspapers	Frequency
0	20
1	24
2	35
3	26
4	28
5	49
6	97
7	126
8	106
9	54
10	83
11	38
12	67
13	21
14	26

Challenge 9.1

(a) Design a data collection sheet for the number of pairs of trainers owned by each of the students in your class.

(b) Collect the data for your class.

(c) (i) Find the mode of your data.
  (ii) Find the range of your data.
  (iii) Calculate the mean number of pairs of trainers owned by the students in your class.

Grouped data

The table shows the number of CDs bought in January by a group of 75 people.

Number of CDs purchased	Number of people
0–4	35
5–9	21
10–14	12
15–19	5
20–24	2

Grouping data makes it easier to work with, but it also causes some problems when calculating the mode, median, mean or range.

For example, the modal class of these data is 0–4, because that is the class with the highest frequency.

However, it is impossible to say which number of CDs was the mode because we do not know exactly how many people in this class bought what number of CDs.

It is possible (though not very likely) that seven people bought no CDs, seven people bought one CD, seven people bought two CDs, seven people bought three CDs and seven people bought four CDs. If eight or more people bought nine CDs, then the mode would actually be 9, even though the modal class is 0–4!

The median presents a similar problem: you can see which class contains the median value, but you cannot work out what the median value actually is.

It is also impossible to work out the exact mean from a grouped frequency table. You can, however, calculate an estimate using a single value to represent each class: it is usual to use the middle value.

These middle values can also be used to calculate an estimate for the range. You cannot find the exact range because it is impossible to say for certain what the highest and lowest numbers of CDs purchased are. The maximum possible purchase is 24 but you cannot tell whether anyone did actually buy 24. The minimum possible purchase is 0 but, again, you cannot tell whether anyone did actually buy no CDs.

EXAMPLE 9.2

Use the data in the table above to calculate
(a) an estimate of the mean number of CDs purchased.
(b) an estimate of the range of the number of CDs purchased.
(c) which of the classes contains the median value.

Solution

(a)

Number of CDs purchased (x)	Number of people (f)	Middle (x) value	f × middle x	fx
0–4	35	2	35 × 2	70
5–9	21	7	21 × 7	147
10–14	12	12	12 × 12	144
15–19	5	17	5 × 17	85
20–24	2	22	2 × 22	44
Total	75			490

The estimate of the mean number of CDs purchased is
490 ÷ 75 = 6.5 (to 1 d.p.).

> **TIP**
> There are five groups in the table but the total number of people is 75.
>
> Do not be tempted to divide by 5!

(b) The estimate of the range of the number of CDs purchased is
22 − 2 = 20 but it could be as high as 24 or as low as 16.

(c) As there are 75 values, the median will be the 38th value.
Add on the frequency for each class until you find the class containing the 38th value.

                35 is smaller than 38. The 38th value does not lie in class 0–4.
35 + 21 = 56   56 is larger than 38. The 38th value must lie in class 5–9.
So the 5–9 class contains the median value.

Using a spreadsheet to find the mean of grouped data

An estimate of the mean of grouped data can also be calculated using a computer spreadsheet. The method is the same as before, except for the addition of a 'Middle (x) value' column. This column can then also be used to calculate an estimate of the range.

Follow these steps to calculate estimates of the mean and range of the data in Example 9.2.

> **TIP**
> Type the bold text carefully: do not put in any spaces.

1 Open a new spreadsheet.

2 In cell A1 type the title 'Number of CDs purchased (x)'.
In cell B1 type the title 'Number of people (f)'.
In cell C1 type the title 'Middle (x) value'.
In cell D1 type the title 'Total number of CDs purchased (fx)'.

3 In cell A2 type 0–4. Then type the other classes in cells A3 to A6.

4 In cell B2 type the number 35. Then type the other frequencies in cells B3 to B6.

5 In cell C2 type **=(0+4)/2** and press the enter key.
In cell C3 type **=(5+9)/2** and press the enter key.
In cell C4 type **=(10+14)/2** and press the enter key.
In cell C5 type **=(15+19)/2** and press the enter key.
In cell C6 type **=(20+24)/2** and press the enter key.

6 In cell D2 type **=B2*C2** then press the enter key.
Click on cell D2, click on Edit in the toolbar and select Copy.
Click on cell D3, and hold down the mouse key and drag down to cell D6. Then click on Edit in the toolbar and select Paste.

7 In cell A7 type the word 'Total'.

8 In cell B7 type **=SUM(B2:B6)** and press the enter key.
In cell D7 type **=SUM(D2:D6)** and press the enter key.

9 In cell A8 type the word 'Mean'.

10 In cell B8 type **=D7/B7** and press the enter key.

11 In cell A9 type the word 'Range'.

12 In cell B9 type **=C6−C2** and press the enter key.

Your spreadsheet should look like this.

	A	B	C	D
1	Number of CDs purchased (x)	Number of people (f)	Middle (x) value	Total number of CDs purchased (fx)
2	0-4	35	2	70
3	5-9	21	7	147
4	10-14	12	12	144
5	15-19	5	17	85
6	20-24	2	22	44
7	Total		75		490
8	Mean	6.533333333		
9	Range	20		

Answer one of the questions in the next exercise using a computer spreadsheet.

EXERCISE 9.2

1 For each of these sets of data calculate an estimate of
  (i) the range. **(ii)** the mean.

(a)
Number of texts received in a day	Number of people	Middle value
0–9	99	4.5
10–19	51	14.5
20–29	28	24.5
30–39	14	34.5
40–49	7	44.5
50–59	1	54.5
Total	200	

(b)
Number of telephone calls made in a day	Number of people	Middle value
0–4	118	2
5–9	54	7
10–14	39	12
15–19	27	17
20–24	12	22
Total	250	

(c)
Number of texts sent	Number of people	Middle value
0–9	79	4.5
10–19	52	14.5
20–29	31	24.5
30–39	13	34.5
40–49	5	44.5
Total	180	

(d)
Number of calls received	Frequency	Middle value
0–4	45	2
5–9	29	7
10–14	17	12
15–19	8	17
20–24	1	22
Total	100	

2 For each of these sets of data
  (i) find the modal class.
  (ii) calculate an estimate of the range.
  (iii) calculate an estimate of the mean.

(a)
Number of DVDs owned	Number of people
0–4	143
5–9	95
10–14	54
15–19	26
20–24	12
Total	330

(b)
Number of books owned	Number of people
0–9	54
10–19	27
20–29	19
30–39	13
40–49	7
Total	120

(c)

Number of train journeys in a year	Number of people
0–49	118
50–99	27
100–149	53
150–199	75
200–249	91
250–299	136

(d)

Number of flowers on a plant	Frequency
0–14	25
15–29	52
30–44	67
45–59	36

3 For each of these sets of data
  (i) find the modal class.
  (ii) calculate an estimate of the mean.

(a)

Number of eggs in a nest	Frequency
0–2	97
3–5	121
6–8	43
9–11	7
12–14	2

(b)

Number of peas in a pod	Frequency
0–3	15
4–7	71
8–11	63
12–15	9
16–19	2

(c)

Number of leaves on a branch	Frequency
0–9	6
10–19	17
20–29	27
30–39	34
40–49	23
50–59	10
60–69	3

(d)

Number of bananas in a bunch	Frequency
0–24	1
25–49	29
50–74	41
75–99	52
100–124	24
125–149	3

4 A company record the number of complaints they receive each week about their products.
The table shows the data for one year.

Calculate an estimate of the mean number of complaints each week.

Number of complaints	Frequency
1–10	12
11–20	5
21–30	10
31–40	8
41–50	9
51–60	5
61–70	2
71–80	1

5 An office manager records the number of photocopies made by his staff each day in September.
The data is shown in the table.

Calculate an estimate of the mean number of copies each day.

Number of photocopies	Frequency
0–99	13
100–199	8
200–299	3
300–399	0
400–499	5
500–599	1

Challenge 9.2

(a) Design a data collection sheet, using appropriate groupings, for the number of CDs owned by the students in your class.

(b) Collect the data for your class.

(c) (i) Estimate the range of your data.
   (ii) Calculate an estimate of the mean number of CDs owned by the students in your class.

Continuous data

So far all the data in this chapter has been **discrete data** (the result of objects beings counted).

When dealing with **continuous data** (the result of measurement) you estimate the mean in the same way as for grouped discrete data.

EXAMPLE 9.3

A manager records the lengths of telephone calls made by her employees. The table shows the results for one week.

Duration of telephone call in minutes (x)	Frequency (f)
$0 \leq x < 5$	86
$5 \leq x < 10$	109
$10 \leq x < 15$	54
$15 \leq x < 20$	27
$20 \leq x < 25$	16
$25 \leq x < 30$	8
Total	300

TIP: Remember that $15 \leq x < 20$ means all times, x, which are greater than or equal to 15 minutes but less than 20 minutes.

Solution

Duration of telephone call in minutes (x)	Frequency (f)	Middle (x) value	$f \times$ middle x
$0 \leq x < 5$	86	2.5	215
$5 \leq x < 10$	109	7.5	817.5
$10 \leq x < 15$	54	12.5	675
$15 \leq x < 20$	27	17.5	472.5
$20 \leq x < 25$	16	22.5	360
$25 \leq x < 30$	8	27.5	220
Total	300		2760

The estimate of the mean is $2760 \div 300 = 9.2$ minutes or 9 minutes and 12 seconds.

TIP: Remember that there are 60 seconds in 1 minute. $60 \times 0.2 = 12$ seconds.

Continuous data

EXERCISE 9.3

Use a spreadsheet to answer one of the questions in this exercise.

1. For each of these sets of data, calculate an estimate of
   (i) the range.
   (ii) the mean.

(a)

Height of plant in centimetres (x)	Number of plants (f)
$0 \leq x < 10$	5
$10 \leq x < 20$	11
$20 \leq x < 30$	29
$30 \leq x < 40$	26
$40 \leq x < 50$	18
$50 \leq x < 60$	7
Total	96

(b)

Weight of egg in grams (x)	Number of eggs (f)
$0 \leq x < 8$	3
$8 \leq x < 16$	18
$16 \leq x < 24$	43
$24 \leq x < 32$	49
$32 \leq x < 40$	26
$40 \leq x < 48$	5
Total	144

(c)

Length of string in centimetres (x)	Frequency (f)
$60 \leq x < 64$	16
$64 \leq x < 68$	28
$68 \leq x < 72$	37
$72 \leq x < 76$	14
$76 \leq x < 80$	5
Total	100

(d)

Rainfall per day in millimetres (x)	Frequency (f)
$0 \leq x < 10$	151
$10 \leq x < 20$	114
$20 \leq x < 30$	46
$30 \leq x < 40$	28
$40 \leq x < 50$	17
$50 \leq x < 60$	9
Total	365

2. For each of these sets of data
   (i) write down the modal class.
   (ii) calculate an estimate of the mean.

(a)

Age of chick in days (x)	Number of chicks (f)
$0 \leq x < 3$	61
$3 \leq x < 6$	57
$6 \leq x < 9$	51
$9 \leq x < 12$	46
$12 \leq x < 15$	44
$15 \leq x < 18$	45
$18 \leq x < 21$	46

(b)

Weight of apple in grams (x)	Number of apples (f)
$90 \leq x < 100$	5
$100 \leq x < 110$	24
$110 \leq x < 120$	72
$120 \leq x < 130$	81
$130 \leq x < 140$	33
$140 \leq x < 150$	10

9 Statistical calculations

(c)

Length of runner bean in centimetres (x)	Frequency (f)
$10 \leq x < 14$	16
$14 \leq x < 18$	24
$18 \leq x < 22$	25
$22 \leq x < 26$	28
$26 \leq x < 30$	17
$30 \leq x < 34$	10

(d)

Time to complete race in minutes (x)	Frequency (f)
$40 \leq x < 45$	1
$45 \leq x < 50$	8
$50 \leq x < 55$	32
$55 \leq x < 60$	26
$60 \leq x < 65$	5
$65 \leq x < 70$	3

3 The table shows the weekly wages of the manual workers in a factory.

Wage in £ (x)	$150 \leq x < 200$	$200 \leq x < 250$	$250 \leq x < 300$	$300 \leq x < 350$
Frequency (f)	4	14	37	15

(a) What is the modal class?   **(b)** In which class is the median wage?
(c) Calculate an estimate of the mean wage.

4 The table shows the masses, in grams, of the first 100 letters posted one day.

Mass in grams (x)	$0 \leq x < 15$	$15 \leq x < 30$	$30 \leq x < 45$	$45 \leq x < 60$
Frequency (f)	48	36	12	4

Calculate an estimate of the mean mass of a letter.

5 The table shows the prices paid for birthday cards sold in one day by a greetings card shop.

Calculate an estimate of the mean price paid for a birthday card that day.

Price of birthday card in pence (x)	Frequency (f)
$100 \leq x < 125$	18
$125 \leq x < 150$	36
$150 \leq x < 175$	45
$175 \leq x < 200$	31
$200 \leq x < 225$	17
$225 \leq x < 250$	9

Challenge 9.3

(a) Design a data collection sheet, using appropriate groupings, and carry out one of the following tasks. Use the students in your class as the source of your data.
- Ask each person the amount of money they spent on lunch on a particular day.
- Obtain a piece of string, arrange it in a non-straight line and ask each person to estimate its length.

(b) (i) Estimate the range of your data.   **(ii)** Calculate an estimate of the mean of your data.

> **WHAT YOU HAVE LEARNED**
>
> - How to find the mean from a frequency table
> - How to estimate the mean for grouped data
> - How to estimate the range for grouped data
> - How to find the class in which the median value lies in large data sets
> - How to use a spreadsheet to calculate the mean and range of grouped data

MIXED EXERCISE 9

1 For each of these sets of data
   (i) find the mode.   **(ii)** find the range.   **(iii)** calculate the mean.

(a)

Score on octagonal dice	Number of times thrown
1	120
2	119
3	132
4	126
5	129
6	142
7	123
8	109
Total	1000

(b)

Number of marbles in a bag	Number of bags
47	11
48	25
49	47
50	63
51	54
52	38
53	17
54	5
Total	260

(c)

Number of pets per house	Frequency
0	64
1	87
2	41
3	26
4	17
5	4
6	1

(d)

Number of broad beans in a pod	Frequency
4	17
5	36
6	58
7	49
8	27
9	13

9 Statistical calculations

(e)

x	f
1	242
2	266
3	251
4	252
5	259
6	230

(f)

x	f
15	9
16	13
17	18
18	27
19	16
20	7

2 Crazyphone top-ups cost £5, £10, £20 or £50 depending upon the amount of credit bought. The frequency table shows the numbers of each value of top-up sold in one shop on a Saturday.

Price of top-up (£)	5	10	20	50
Number of top-ups	34	63	26	2

Calculate the mean value of top-up bought in the shop that Saturday.

3 A sample of 350 people were asked how many magazines they had bought in September. The table below shows the data.

Number of magazines	0	1	2	3	4	5	6	7	8	9	10
Frequency	16	68	94	77	49	27	11	5	1	0	2

Calculate the mean number of magazines bought in September.

4 For each of these sets of data, calculate an estimate of
  (i) the range.
  (ii) the mean.

(a)

Height of cactus in centimetres (x)	Number of plants (f)
$10 \leqslant x < 15$	17
$15 \leqslant x < 20$	49
$20 \leqslant x < 25$	66
$25 \leqslant x < 30$	38
$30 \leqslant x < 35$	15
Total	185

(b)

Wind speed at noon in km/h (x)	Number of days (f)
$0 \leqslant x < 20$	164
$20 \leqslant x < 40$	98
$40 \leqslant x < 60$	57
$60 \leqslant x < 80$	32
$80 \leqslant x < 100$	11
$100 \leqslant x < 120$	3
Total	365

Mixed exercise 9

(c)

Time holding breath in seconds (x)	Frequency (f)
$30 \leq x < 40$	6
$40 \leq x < 50$	29
$50 \leq x < 60$	48
$60 \leq x < 70$	36
$70 \leq x < 80$	23
$80 \leq x < 90$	8

(d)

Mass of student in kilograms (x)	Frequency (f)
$40 \leq x < 45$	5
$45 \leq x < 50$	13
$50 \leq x < 55$	26
$55 \leq x < 60$	31
$60 \leq x < 65$	17
$65 \leq x < 70$	8

5 The table below shows the lengths, to the nearest minute, of 304 telephone calls.

Length in minutes (x)	$0 \leq x < 10$	$10 \leq x < 20$	$20 \leq x < 30$	$30 \leq x < 40$	$40 \leq x < 50$
Frequency (f)	53	124	81	35	11

(a) What is the modal class?
(b) In which class is the median length of call?
(c) Calculate an estimate of the mean length of call.

6 The table shows the annual wages of the workers in a company.

Annual wage in thousands of £ (x)	Frequency (f)
$10 \leq x < 15$	7
$15 \leq x < 20$	18
$20 \leq x < 25$	34
$25 \leq x < 30$	12
$30 \leq x < 35$	9
$35 \leq x < 40$	4
$40 \leq x < 45$	2
$45 \leq x < 50$	1
$50 \leq x < 55$	2
$55 \leq x < 60$	0
$60 \leq x < 65$	1

Calculate an estimate of the mean annual wage of these workers.

10 → PYTHAGORAS

THIS CHAPTER IS ABOUT

- Calculating the length of a side of a right-angled triangle when you know the other two
- Deciding whether or not a triangle is right-angled
- Finding the coordinates of the midpoint of a line segment
- Using coordinates in three dimensions (3-D)

YOU SHOULD ALREADY KNOW

- How to find squares and square roots on your calculator
- The formula for the area of a triangle
- How to use coordinates in two dimensions

Pythagoras' theorem

Discovery 10.1

Measure all three sides of the right-angled triangle in the diagram.

Use the lengths to work out the area of each of the three coloured squares.

What do you notice?

The area of the yellow square added to the area of the blue square is equal to the area of the red square.

The longest side of a right-angled triangle is called the **hypotenuse**.

What you discovered in Discovery 10.1 is true for all right-angled triangles. It was first 'discovered' by Pythagoras, a Greek mathematician, who lived around 500 BC.

Pythagoras' theorem states that:

> The area of the square on the hypotenuse of a right-angled triangle is equal to the sum of the areas of the squares on the other two sides.

That is:

$$P + Q = R$$

EXERCISE 10.1

For each of these diagrams, find the area of the third square.

1 4 cm², 8 cm², ?

2 15 cm², 70 cm², ?

156 10 Pythagoras

3

60 cm²

10 cm²

?

4

?

22 cm²

50 cm²

Using Pythagoras' theorem

Although the theorem is based on area it is usually used to find the length of a side.

If you drew squares on the three sides of this triangle their areas would be a^2, b^2 and c^2.

So Pythagoras' theorem can also be written as

$$a^2 + b^2 = c^2.$$

EXAMPLE 10.1

For each of these triangles, find the length marked x.

(a)

5 cm
x
8 cm

(b)

x
8.7 cm
6.9 cm

Solution

(a) $c^2 = a^2 + b^2$ The length marked x is the hypotenuse, or c.
$x^2 = 8^2 + 5^2$ Substitute the numbers into the formula.
$x^2 = 64 + 25$
$x^2 = 89$
$x = \sqrt{89}$ Take the square root of both sides.
$x = 9.43$ cm (to 2 d.p.)

(b) $a^2 + b^2 = c^2$ This time the length marked x is the shortest side, or a.
$x^2 + 6.9^2 = 8.7^2$
$\quad x^2 = 8.7^2 - 6.9^2$ Subtract 6.9^2 from each side.
$\quad x^2 = 75.69 - 47.61$
$\quad x^2 = 28.08$
$\quad x = \sqrt{28.08}$ Take the square root of both sides.
$\quad x = 5.30$ (to 2 d.p.)

> **TIP**
>
> Always check whether you are finding the longest side (the hypotenuse) or one of the shorter sides.
>
> If you are finding the longest side: add the squares.
>
> If you are finding a shorter side: subtract the squares.

EXERCISE 10.2

1 For each of these triangles, find the length marked x.
Where the answer is not exact, give your answer correct to 2 decimal places.

(a) 5 cm, 12 cm, x

(b) 5 m, 3 m, x

(c) 5 cm, 8 cm, x

(d) 25 cm, 7 cm, x

(e) 6.1 cm, 4.6 cm, x

(f) 9.3 cm, 6.8 cm, x

(g) 24.7 m, 17.9 m, x

(h) 7.2 m, 11.8 m, x

(i) 4.2 cm, 7.8 cm, x

2 The diagram shows a ladder standing on horizontal ground and leaning against a vertical wall.

The ladder is 4.8 m long and the foot of the ladder is 1.6 m away from the wall.

How far up the wall does the ladder reach?
Give your answer correct to 2 decimal places.

3 The size of a television screen is the length of the diagonal.

The screen size of this television is 27 inches.

If the height of the screen is 13 inches, what is the width?
Give your answer correct to 2 decimal places.

Challenge 10.1

(a) Calculate the area of the isosceles triangle ABC.

Hint: Draw the height AD of the triangle.
Calculate the length of AD.

(b) Calculate the area of each of these isosceles triangles.
Give your answers correct to 1 decimal place.

(i)

(ii)

Using Pythagoras' theorem   159

Pythagorean triples

Look again at the answers to question **1** parts **(a)** and **(d)** in Exercise 10.2.

The answers were exact.

In part **(a)** $5^2 + 12^2 = 13^2$
In part **(d)** $7^2 + 24^2 = 25^2$

These are examples of **Pythagorean triples**, or three numbers that exactly fit the Pythagoras relationship.

Another Pythagorean triple is 3, 4, 5.
You saw this in the diagram at the start of the chapter.

3, 4, 5   5, 12, 13   and   7, 24, 25   are the most well-known Pythagorean triples.

You can also use Pythagoras' theorem in reverse.

If the lengths of the three sides of a triangle form a Pythagorean triple then the triangle is right-angled.

EXERCISE 10.3

Work out whether or not each of these triangles is right-angled.

Show your working.

1 6 cm, 8 cm, 10 cm

2 4 cm, 7 cm, 8 cm

3 8 cm, 8 cm, 11 cm

4 7.5 cm, 18 cm, 19.5 cm

5 12.5 cm, 12 cm, 3.5 cm

6 5 cm, 10 cm, 11 cm

7 4.5 cm, 10 cm, 9 cm

8 28.8 cm, 12 cm, 31.2 cm

Midpoints

Discovery 10.2

For each of these pairs of points:
- Draw a diagram on squared paper. The first one is done for you.
- Find the middle point of the line joining the two points and label it M.
- Write down the coordinates of M.

(a) A(1, 3) and B(5, 7)
(b) C(1, 5) and D(7, 1)
(c) E(2, 5) and F(6, 6)
(d) G(3, 7) and H(6, 0)

What do you notice?

TIP: 'Middle point' is often shortened to **midpoint**.

The coordinates of the midpoint of a line are the means of the coordinates of the two endpoints.

$$\text{Midpoint of line with coordinates } (a, b), (c, d) = \left(\frac{a+c}{2}, \frac{b+d}{2}\right).$$

EXAMPLE 10.2

Find the coordinates of the midpoints of these pairs of points without drawing the graph.
(a) A(2, 1) and B(6, 7)
(b) C(−2, 1) and D(2, 5)

Solution

(a) A(2, 1) and B(6, 7)
$a = 2, b = 1, c = 6, d = 7$
$$\text{Midpoint} = \left(\frac{a+c}{2}, \frac{b+d}{2}\right)$$
$$= \left(\frac{2+6}{2}, \frac{1+7}{2}\right)$$
$$= (4, 4)$$

(b) C(−2, 1) and D(2, 5)
$a = -2, b = 1, c = 2, d = 5$
$$\text{Midpoint} = \left(\frac{a+c}{2}, \frac{b+d}{2}\right)$$
$$\text{Midpoint} = \left(\frac{-2+2}{2}, \frac{1+5}{2}\right)$$
$$= (0, 3)$$

You can check your answers by drawing the graph of the line.

EXERCISE 10.4

1 Find the coordinates of the midpoint of each of the lines in the diagram.

2 Find the coordinates of the midpoint of the line joining each of these pairs of points. Try to do them without plotting the points.

(a) A(1, 4) and B(1, 8)
(b) C(1, 5) and D(7, 3)
(c) E(2, 3) and F(8, 6)
(d) G(3, 7) and H(8, 2)
(e) I(−2, 3) and J(4, 1)
(f) K(−4, −3) and L(−6, −11)

Challenge 10.2

(a) The midpoint of AB is (5, 3).
A is the point (2, 1).
What are the coordinates of B?

(b) The midpoint of CD is (−1, 2).
C is the point (3, 6).
What are the coordinates of D?

Three-dimensional (3-D) coordinates

You already know how to describe a point using coordinates in two dimensions.
You use *x*- and *y*-coordinates.

If you are working in three dimensions you need a third coordinate. This is known as the *z*-coordinate.

> **TIP** Notice that the *x*- and *y*-axes lie flat with the *z*-axis vertical.

The coordinates of point P are (4, 5, 3).
That is, 4 in the *x* direction, 5 in the *y* direction and 3 in the *z* direction.

> **TIP** As with 2-D coordinates, 3-D coordinates are written in alphabetical order: *x* then *y* then *z*.

Check up 10.1

What are the coordinates of the points Q, R, S and T in the diagram above?

EXAMPLE 10.3

A is the point (4, 2, 3) and B is the point (2, 6, 9).
What are the coordinates of the midpoint of AB?

Solution

The coordinates of the midpoint of a line are the means of the coordinates of the two endpoints.

In three dimensions:

Midpoint of line with coordinates (a, b, c) and $(d, e, f) = \left(\dfrac{a+d}{2}, \dfrac{b+e}{2}, \dfrac{c+f}{2}\right)$.

For A(4, 2, 3) and B(2, 6, 9) the coordinates of the midpoint of the line AB are $\left(\dfrac{4+2}{2}, \dfrac{2+6}{2}, \dfrac{3+9}{2}\right) = (3, 4, 6)$.

EXERCISE 10.5

1 The diagram shows the outline of a cuboid.
The coordinates of point A are (5, 0, 0).
The coordinates of point B are (0, 3, 0).
The coordinates of point C are (0, 0, 2).
Write down the coordinates of
(a) point D.
(b) point E.
(c) point F.
(d) point G.

2 VOABC is a square-based pyramid.
A is the point (6, 0, 0).
N is the centre of the base.
The perpendicular height VN of the pyramid is 5 units.
Write down the coordinates of
(a) point C.
(b) point B.
(c) point N.
(d) point V.

3 The diagram shows the outline of a cuboid.
The coordinates of point A are (8, 0, 0).
The coordinates of point B are (0, 6, 0).
The coordinates of point C are (0, 0, 4).
L is the midpoint of AD.
M is the midpoint of EG.
N is the midpoint of FG.
Write down the coordinates of
(a) point D.   (b) point L.
(c) point M.   (d) point N.

Challenge 10.3

(a) For the pyramid in Exercise 10.5, question **2**, calculate these lengths.
   (i) OB   (ii) VB

(b) For the cuboid in Exercise 10.5, question **1**, calculate the length of OG.

Challenge 10.4

The diagram shows a mast supported by three wires.

The mast is vertical and standing on flat horizontal ground.

The mast is 48 metres tall.
Each wire is attached to a point on the ground 17 metres from the foot of the mast.

Find the total length of the three wires.
Give your answer correct to the nearest metre.

WHAT YOU HAVE LEARNED

- The longest side of a right-angled triangle is called the hypotenuse
- Pythagoras' theorem states that the area of the square on the hypotenuse of a right-angled triangle is equal to the sum of the areas of the squares on the other two sides, that is, if the hypotenuse of a right-angled triangle is c and the other sides are a and b, $a^2 + b^2 = c^2$
- To find the length of the longest side using Pythagoras' theorem, add the squares
- To find the length of one of the shorter sides using Pythagoras' theorem, subtract the squares
- If the lengths of the sides are a Pythagorean triple, the triangle is right-angled
- The three most well-known Pythagorean triples are 3, 4, 5; 5, 12, 13 and 7, 24, 25
- The coordinates of the midpoint of the line joining (a, b) to (c, d) are $\left(\dfrac{a+c}{2}, \dfrac{b+d}{2}\right)$
- In three dimensions a point has three coordinates, the third being the z-coordinate

MIXED EXERCISE 10

1 For each of these diagrams, find the area of the third square.

(a)

(b)

2 For each of these triangles, find the length marked x.
Give your answers correct to 2 decimal places.

(a) 7 cm, 9 cm, x

(b) 11 cm, 8 cm, x

(c) 4.3 cm, 7.6 cm, x

(d) 4.2 cm, 2.7 cm, x

3 Work out whether or not each of these triangles is right-angled.
Show your working.

(a) 8 cm, 5 cm, 9 cm

(b) 12 m, 9 m, 15 m

(c) 17.5 cm, 60 cm, 62.5 cm

(d) 5.2 cm, 8.3 cm, 9.7 cm

4 Find the coordinates of the midpoint of the line joining each of these pairs of points.
Try to do them without plotting the points.
  (a) A(2, 1) and B(4, 7)
  (b) C(2, 3) and D(6, 8)
  (c) E(2, 0) and F(7, 9)

5 The diagram shows the end of a shed.
The vertical sides are of height 2.8 m and 2.1 m.
The width of the shed is 1.8 m.
Calculate the sloping length of the roof.
Give your answer correct to 2 decimal places.

6 Find the area of this isosceles triangle.
Give your answer correct to 1 decimal place.

7 The diagram shows a farm gate made from seven pieces of metal.

The gate is 2.6 m wide and 1.2 m high.

Calculate the total length of metal used to make the gate.
Give your answer correct to 2 decimal places.

8 The diagram shows the outline of a house.

All the measurements are in metres.
All the walls are vertical.
E, F, G, H and N are in the same horizontal plane.
(a) Using the axes on the diagram, write down the coordinates of these points.
   (i) B   **(ii)** H   **(iii)** G

The coordinates of Q are (11, 5, 9).
N is vertically below Q.
(b) Write down the coordinates of N.

11 → MENTAL METHODS

THIS CHAPTER IS ABOUT

- Developing strategies for mental calculation
- Recalling square numbers, cube numbers and square roots
- Rounding to a given number of significant figures
- Estimating answers to problems involving decimals
- Using π without a calculator
- Deriving unknown facts from those you know

YOU SHOULD ALREADY KNOW

- Number bonds and multiplication tables up to 10
- The meaning of *square numbers* and *square roots*
- How to calculate the circumference and area of circles

Mental strategies

You can develop your mental skills by practising them and by being open to new and better ideas.

Discovery 11.1

How many ways can you find to work out mentally the answers to each of the following calculations?

Make a note of the methods you use.

Which methods were most efficient?

(a) $39 + 47$	**(b)** $126 \div 3$	**(c)** $290 \div 5$	**(d)** $164 - 37$
(e) 23×16	**(f)** 21×19	**(g)** 13×13	**(h)** $10 - 1.7$
(i) $14.6 + 2.9$	**(j)** 3.6×30	**(k)** $-6 + (-4)$	**(l)** $-10 - (-7)$
(m) $0.7 + 9.3$	**(n)** 4×3.7	**(o)** $12 \div 0.4$	**(p)** 15% of £176

Compare your results and methods with the rest of the class.

Did anyone have ideas which you hadn't thought of and which you think work well?

Which calculations could you easily do completely in your head?

In which calculations did you want to make a note on paper of intermediate answers?

For adding and subtracting, there are a number of strategies you can use.

- Use number bonds that you know
- Count forwards or backwards from one number
- Use compensation: add or subtract too much, then compensate
  For example, to add 9, first add 10 and then subtract 1
- Use your knowledge of place value to help with adding or subtracting decimals
- Use partitioning
  For example, to subtract 63, first subtract 60 and then subtract 3
- Jot a number line down on paper

For multiplying and dividing, there are other strategies.

- Use factors
  For example, to multiply by 20, first multiply by 2 and then multiply the result by 10
- Use partitioning
  For example, to multiply by 13, first multiply the number by 10, then multiply the number by 3 and finally add the results
- Use your knowledge of place value to help with multiplying and dividing decimals
- Recognise special cases where doubling and halving can be used
- Use the relationship between multiplication and division
- Recall percentage and fraction relationships
  For example, 25% = $\frac{1}{4}$

> **TIP** Check your answers by working them out again, using a different strategy.

Square and cube numbers

You learned about square and cube numbers in Chapter 1.

Area of square = 3 × 3
= 3^2 = 9 cm²

Volume of cube = 4 × 4 × 4
= 4^3 = 64 cm³

Numbers such as 3^2 are called **square numbers**.
Numbers such as 4^3 are called **cube numbers**.

You learned in Chapter 1 that because 4^2 = 4 × 4 = 16, the **square root** of 16 is 4. This is written as $\sqrt{16}$ = 4.

You should learn the squares of the numbers 1 to 15 and the cubes of the numbers 1 to 5 and 10 by heart.

Knowing the square numbers up to 15^2 will help you when you need to work out a square root.
For example, if you know that $7^2 = 49$, you also know that $\sqrt{49} = 7$.

These facts can also be used in other calculations.

EXAMPLE 11.1

Work out 50^2 mentally.

Solution

$50^2 = (5 \times 10)^2$ $50 = 5 \times 10$.
$ = 5^2 \times 10^2$ Square each term inside the brackets.
$ = 25 \times 100 = 2500$ You know that $5^2 = 25$ and $10^2 = 100$.

This is one possible strategy. You may think of another.

EXERCISE 11.1

Work these out mentally. As far as possible, write down only the final answer.

1 (a) $9 + 17$ (b) $0.6 + 0.9$ (c) $13 + 45$ (d) $143 + 57$ (e) $72 + 8.4$
   (f) $13.6 + 6.5$ (g) $614 + 47$ (h) $6.2 + 3.9$ (i) $246 + 37$ (j) $92 + 183$

2 (a) $24 - 8$ (b) $1.5 - 0.6$ (c) $132 - 45$ (d) $76 - 18$ (e) $78 - 8.4$
   (f) $102 - 37$ (g) $165 - 96$ (h) $403 - 126$ (i) $98 - 12.3$ (j) $1200 - 204$

3 (a) 9×8 (b) 13×4 (c) 0.6×4 (d) 32×5 (e) 0.8×1000
   (f) 21×16 (g) 37×5 (h) 130×4 (i) 125×8 (j) 31×25

4 (a) $28 \div 7$ (b) $160 \div 2$ (c) $65 \div 5$ (d) $128 \div 8$ (e) $156 \div 12$
   (f) $96 \div 24$ (g) $8 \div 100$ (h) $3 \div 0.5$ (i) $4 \div 0.2$ (j) $1.8 \div 0.6$

5 (a) $5 + (-1)$ (b) $-6 + 2$ (c) $-2 + (-5)$ (d) $-10 + 16$ (e) $12 + (-14)$
   (f) $6 - (-4)$ (g) $-7 - (-1)$ (h) $-10 - (-6)$ (i) $12 - (-12)$ (j) $-8 - (-8)$

6 (a) 4×-2 (b) -6×2 (c) -3×-4 (d) 7×-5 (e) -4×-10
   (f) $6 \div -2$ (g) $-20 \div 5$ (h) $-12 \div -4$ (i) $18 \div -9$ (j) $-32 \div -2$

7 Write down the square of each of these numbers.
   (a) 6   (b) 5   (c) 11   (d) 10   (e) 13
   (f) 20   (g) 300   (h) 0.4   (i) 0.7   (j) 0.3

Mental strategies   171

8 Write down the square root of each of these numbers.
   (a) 16   (b) 9   (c) 49   (d) 169   (e) 225

9 Write down the cube of each of these numbers.
   (a) 1   (b) 5   (c) 2   (d) 40   (e) 0.3

10 Find 2% of £460.

11 A square has area 64 cm^2. How long is its side?

12 Jim spends £34.72. How much change does he get from £50?

13 A bottle contains 750 ml of water. Jo pours 330 ml into a glass. How much water is left in the bottle?

14 A rectangle has sides 4.5 cm and 4.0 cm. Work out
   (a) the perimeter of the rectangle.   (b) the area of the rectangle.

15 Find two numbers the sum of which is 13 and the product 40.

Rounding to 1 significant figure

We often use rounded numbers instead of exact ones.

Check up 11.1

In the following statements, which of these numbers are likely to be exact and which have been rounded?
(a) Yesterday, I spent £14.62.
(b) My height is 180 cm.
(c) Her new dress cost £40.
(d) The attendance at the Arsenal match was 32 000.
(e) The cost of building the new school is £27 million.
(f) The value of π is 3.142.
(g) The Olympic games were in Athens in 2004.
(h) There were 87 people at the meeting.

Discovery 11.2

Look at a newspaper.

Find five articles or advertisements where exact numbers have been used.

Find five articles or advertisements where rounded numbers have been used.

11 Mental methods

When estimating the answers to calculations, rounding to 1 significant figure is usually sufficient.

This means giving just one non-zero figure, with zeros as placeholders to make the number the correct size.

For example, 87 is 90 to 1 significant figure. It is between 80 and 90 but is nearer 90.

```
80   81   82   83   84   85   86   87   88   89   90
          ↑         ↑         ↑
         82.4      85        87
```

82.4 is 80 to 1 significant figure. It is between 80 and 90 but is nearer 80.
85 is 90 to 1 significant figure. It is halfway between 80 and 90. To avoid confusion, 5 is always rounded up.

The first significant figure is the first non-zero digit.

For example, the first significant figure in 6072 is 6.

So to round to 1 significant figure:

- Find the first non-zero digit. Look at the digit after it.
  If it is less than 5, leave the first non-zero digit as it is.
  If it is 5 or more, add 1 to the first non-zero digit.
- Then look at the place value of the first non-zero digit and add zeros as placeholders, if necessary, to make the number the correct size.

EXAMPLE 11.2

Round each of these numbers to 1 significant figure.
(a) £29.95
(b) 48 235
(c) 0.072

Solution

(a) £29.95 = £30 to 1 s.f.   The second non-zero digit is 9 so round 2 up to 3.
                              Looking at place value, the 2 is 20, so the 3 should be 30.

(b) 48 235 = 50 000 to 1 s.f. The second non-zero digit is 8 so round 4 up to 5.
                              Looking at place value, the 4 is 40 000, so the 5 should be 50 000.

(c) 0.072 = 0.07 to 1 s.f.   The second non-zero digit is 2 so 7 stays as it is.
                              Looking at place value, the 7 is 0.07, which stays as it is.

To estimate answers to problems, round each number to 1 significant figure.

Use mental or pencil and paper strategies to help you do the calculation.

EXAMPLE 11.3

Estimate the cost of four CDs at £7.95 each.

Solution

Cost = £8 × 4   £7.95 rounded to 1 significant figure is £8.
     = £32

> **TIP**
> In practical situations, it is often useful to know whether your estimate is too big or too small. Here, £32 is larger than the exact answer, because £7.95 has been rounded up.

EXAMPLE 11.4

Estimate the answer to this calculation.

$$\frac{4.62 \times 0.61}{52}$$

Solution

$$\frac{4.62 \times 0.61}{52} \approx \frac{5 \times 0.6}{50}$$ Round each number in the calculation to 1 significant figure.

$$= \frac{{}^{1}\cancel{5} \times 0.6}{\cancel{50}\,_{10}}$$ Cancel by dividing both 5 and 50 by 5.

$$= \frac{0.6}{10}$$

$$= 0.06$$

This is one possible strategy. You may think of another.

Rounding to a given number of significant figures

Rounding to a given number of significant figures involves using a similar method to rounding to 1 significant figure: just look at the size of the first digit which is not required.

For instance, to round to 3 significant figures, start counting from the first non-zero digit and look at the size of the fourth figure.

EXAMPLE 11.5

(a) Round 52 617 to 2 significant figures.
(b) Round 0.072 618 to 3 significant figures.
(c) Round 17 082 to 3 significant figures.

TIP Always state the accuracy of your answers, when you have rounded them.

Solution

(a) 52 |617 = 53 000 to 2 s.f.
To round to 2 significant figures, look at the third figure. It is 6, so the second figure changes from 2 to 3. Remember to add zeros for placeholders.

(b) 0.072 6|18 = 0.0726 to 3 s.f.
The first significant figure is 7. To round to 3 significant figures, look at the fourth significant figure. It is 1, so the third figure is unchanged.

(c) 17 0|82 = 17 100 to 3 s.f.
The 0 in the middle here is a significant figure. To round to 3 significant figures, look at the fourth figure. It is 8, so the third figure changes from 0 to 1. Remember to add zeros for placeholders.

EXERCISE 11.2

1 Round each of these numbers to 1 significant figure.
(a) 8.2　　(b) 6.9　　(c) 17　　(d) 25.1
(e) 493　　(f) 7.0　　(g) 967　　(h) 0.43
(i) 0.68　　(j) 3812　　(k) 4199　　(l) 3.09

2 Round each of these numbers to 1 significant figure.
(a) 14.9　　(b) 167　　(c) 21.2　　(d) 794
(e) 6027　　(f) 0.013　　(g) 0.58　　(h) 0.037
(i) 1.0042　　(j) 20 053　　(k) 0.069　　(l) 1942

3 Round each of these numbers to 2 significant figures.
(a) 17.6　　(b) 184.2　　(c) 5672　　(d) 97 520
(e) 50.43　　(f) 0.172　　(g) 0.0387　　(h) 0.006 12
(i) 0.0307　　(j) 0.994

4 Round each of these numbers to 3 significant figures.
(a) 8.261　　(b) 69.77　　(c) 16 285　　(d) 207.51
(e) 12 524　　(f) 7.103　　(g) 50.87　　(h) 0.4162
(i) 0.038 62　　(j) 3.141 59

For questions **5** to **12**, round the numbers in your calculations to 1 significant figure. Show your working.

5 At the school fête, Tony sold 245 ice-creams at 85p each. Estimate his takings.

6 Kate had £30. How many CDs, at £7.99 each, could she buy?

7 A rectangle measures 5.8 cm by 9.4 cm. Estimate its area.

8 A circle has diameter 6.7 cm. Estimate its circumference. $\pi = 3.142\ldots$.

9 A new car is priced at £14 995 excluding VAT. VAT at 17.5% must be paid on it. Estimate the amount of VAT to be paid.

10 A cube has side 3.7 cm. Estimate its volume.

11 Pedro drove 415 miles in 7 hours 51 minutes. Estimate his average speed.

12 Estimate the answers to these calculations.

(a) 46×82
(b) $\sqrt{84}$
(c) $\dfrac{1083}{8.2}$
(d) 7.05^2

(e) $43.7 \times 18.9 \times 29.3$
(f) $\dfrac{2.46}{18.5}$
(g) $\dfrac{29}{41.6}$
(h) 917×38

(i) $\dfrac{283 \times 97}{724}$
(j) $\dfrac{614 \times 0.83}{3.7 \times 2.18}$
(k) $\dfrac{6.72}{0.051 \times 39.7}$
(l) $\sqrt{39 \times 80}$

Challenge 11.1

Write a number which will round to 500 to 1 significant figure.
Write a number which will round to 500 to 2 significant figures.
Write a number which will round to 500 to 3 significant figures.
Compare your results with your classmates. What do you notice?

Using π without a calculator

When finding the area and circumference of a circle, you need to use π. Since $\pi = 3.141\,592\ldots$, you often round it to 1 significant figure when working without a calculator.

This is what you did in question **8** of Exercise 11.2.

An alternative is to give an exact answer by leaving π in the answer.

EXAMPLE 11.6

Find the area of a circle of radius 5 cm, leaving π in your answer.

Solution

Area = πr^2 You learned the formula for the area of a circle in Chapter 6.
       = $\pi \times 5^2$
       = $\pi \times 25 = 25\pi$ cm^2

EXAMPLE 11.7

A circular pond of radius 3 m is surrounded by a path 2 m wide.
Find the area of the path.
Give your answer as a multiple of π.

Solution

Area of path = area of large circle − area of small circle
               = $\pi \times 5^2 - \pi \times 3^2$
               = $25\pi - 9\pi$ You already know that you can **collect like terms**.
               = 16π m^2 You can treat π in the same way.

EXERCISE 11.3

Give your answers to these questions as simply as possible.
Leave π in your answers where appropriate.

1. (a) $2 \times 4 \times \pi$ (b) $\pi \times 8^2$ (c) $\pi \times 6^2$
     (d) $2 \times 13 \times \pi$ (e) $\pi \times 9^2$ (f) $2 \times \pi \times 3.5$

2. (a) $4\pi + 10\pi$ (b) $\pi \times 8^2 + \pi \times 4^2$ (c) $\pi \times 6^2 - \pi \times 2^2$
     (d) $2 \times 25\pi$ (e) $\dfrac{24\pi}{6\pi}$ (f) $2 \times \pi \times 5 + 2 \times \pi \times 3$

3. The circumferences of two circles are in the ratio $10\pi : 4\pi$. Simplify this ratio.

4. Find the area of a circle with radius 15 cm.

5. A circular hole of radius 2 cm is drilled in a square of side 8 cm.
   Find the area that is left.

Deriving unknown facts from those you know

Earlier in this chapter, you saw that knowing a square number means that you also know the corresponding square root. For example, if you know that $11^2 = 121$, you also know that $\sqrt{121} = 11$.

In a similar way, knowing addition facts means that you also know the corresponding subtraction facts. For example, if you know that $91 + 9 = 100$, you also know that $100 - 9 = 91$ and $100 - 91 = 9$.

Knowing multiplication facts means that you also know the corresponding division facts. For example, if you know that $42 \times 87 = 3654$, you also know that $3654 \div 42 = 87$ and $3654 \div 87 = 42$.

Your knowledge of place value, and of multiplying and dividing by powers of 10, means that you can answer other problems as well.

EXAMPLE 11.8

Given that $73 \times 45 = 3285$, work out these.

(a) 730×45

(b) $\dfrac{32.85}{450}$

Solution

(a) $730 \times 45 = 10 \times 73 \times 45$ You can break 730 down to 10×73.
$= 10 \times 3285 = 32\,850$ You know that $73 \times 45 = 3285$.

(b) $\dfrac{32.85}{450} = \dfrac{3285}{45\,000}$ Multiply the numerator and denominator by 100 so that the numerator is 3285.

$= \dfrac{3285}{1000 \times 45}$ You can break 45 000 down to 1000×45.

$= \dfrac{3285}{45} \div 1000$ You know that $73 \times 45 = 3285$, so you also know that $3285 \div 45 = 73$.

$= 73 \div 1000 = 0.073$

> **TIP** Check your answer by estimating. $\dfrac{32.85}{450}$ is a bit less than $\dfrac{45}{450}$ so the answer will be a bit less than 0.1.

Challenge 11.2

$352 \times 185 = 65\,120$

Write five other multiplication statements, with their answers, using this result.
Write five division statements, with their answers, using this result.

EXERCISE 11.4

1 Work out these.
- (a) 0.7×7000
- (b) 0.06×0.6
- (c) 0.8×0.05
- (d) $(0.04)^2$
- (e) $(0.2)^2$
- (f) 600×50
- (g) 70×8000
- (h) 5.6×200
- (i) 40.1×3000
- (j) 4.52×2000
- (k) 0.15×0.8
- (l) 0.05×1.2

2 Work out these.
- (a) $500 \div 20$
- (b) $10 \div 200$
- (c) $2.6 \div 20$
- (d) $35 \div 0.5$
- (e) $2.4 \div 400$
- (f) $2.7 \div 0.03$
- (g) $0.06 \div 0.002$
- (h) $7 \div 0.2$
- (i) $600 \div 0.04$
- (j) $80 \div 0.02$
- (j) $0.52 \div 40$
- (j) $70 \div 0.07$

3 Given that $1.6 \times 13.5 = 21.6$, work out these.
- (a) 16×135
- (b) $21.6 \div 16$
- (c) $2160 \div 135$
- (d) 0.16×0.0135
- (e) $216 \div 0.135$
- (f) 160×1.35

4 Given that $988 \div 26 = 38$, work out these.
- (a) 380×26
- (b) $98.8 \div 26$
- (c) $9880 \div 38$
- (d) $98.8 \div 2.6$
- (e) $9.88 \div 260$
- (f) $98.8 \div 3.8$

5 Given that $153 \times 267 = 40\,851$, work out these.
- (a) 15.3×26.7
- (b) $15\,300 \times 2.67$
- (c) $40\,851 \div 26.7$
- (d) 0.153×26.7
- (e) $408.51 \div 15.3$
- (f) $408\,510 \div 26.7$

WHAT YOU HAVE LEARNED

- How to use different mental strategies for adding and subtracting, and multiplying and dividing
- To round to a given number of significant figures, look at the size of the first digit which is not required
- When using π, round it to 1 significant figure, or give an exact answer by leaving π in the answer, simplifying the other numbers
- Knowing a square number means you also know the corresponding square root
- Knowing addition facts means you also know the corresponding subtraction facts
- Knowing multiplication facts means that you know the corresponding division facts

MIXED EXERCISE 11

1 Work these out mentally. As far as possible, write down only your final answer.
- (a) $16 + 76$
- (b) $0.7 + 0.9$
- (c) $135 + 6.9$
- (d) $12.3 + 8.8$
- (e) $196 + 245$
- (f) $13.6 - 6.4$
- (g) $205 - 47$
- (h) $12 - 3.9$
- (i) $601 - 218$
- (j) $15.2 - 8.3$

2 Work these out mentally. As far as possible, write down only your final answer.
(a) 17×9 (b) 0.6×0.9 (c) 0.71×1000 (d) 23×15 (e) 41×25
(f) $85 \div 5$ (g) $0.7 \div 2$ (h) $82 \div 100$ (i) $1.8 \div 0.2$ (j) $6 \div 0.5$

3 Work these out mentally. As far as possible, write down only your final answer.
(a) $2 + (-6)$ (b) $-3 + 9$ (c) $15 - (-2)$ (d) $-8 + (-1)$ (e) $-3 - (-4)$
(f) 7×-4 (g) -6×-5 (h) $18 \div -2$ (i) $-50 \div -10$ (j) $-12 \div 4$

4 Write down the square of each of these numbers.
(a) 7 (b) 0.9 (c) 12 (d) 100 (e) 14

5 Jackie spends £84.59. How much change does she get from £100?

6 Round each of these numbers to 1 significant figure.
(a) 9.2 (b) 3.9 (c) 26 (d) 34.9 (e) 582
(f) 6.0 (g) 985 (h) 0.32 (i) 0.57 (j) 45 218

7 A rectangle measures 3.9 cm by 8.1 cm. Estimate its area.

8 Pam drove for 2 hours 5 minutes and travelled 106 miles. Estimate her average speed.

9 Estimate the answer to each of these calculations.
(a) 46×82 (b) $\sqrt{107}$ (c) $\dfrac{983}{5.2}$ (d) 6.09^2 (e) $72.7 \times 19.6 \times 3.3$
(f) $\dfrac{2.46}{18.5}$ (g) $\dfrac{59}{1.96}$ (h) 307×51 (i) $\dfrac{586 \times 97}{187}$ (j) $\dfrac{318 \times 0.72}{5.1 \times 2.09}$

10 Round each of these numbers to 2 significant figures.
(a) 9.16 (b) 4.72 (c) 0.0137 (d) 164 600 (e) 507

11 Round each of these numbers to 3 significant figures.
(a) 1482 (b) 10.16 (c) 0.021 85 (d) 20.952 (e) 0.005 619

12 Simplify each of these calculations, leaving π in your answers.
(a) $2 \times 5 \times \pi$ (b) $\pi \times 7^2$ (c) $14\pi + 8\pi$
(d) $\pi \times 5^2 - \pi \times 4^2$ (e) $\pi \times 9^2 + \pi \times 2^2$ (f) $\pi \times 8^2 - \pi \times 1^2$

13 Work out these.
(a) 500×30 (b) 0.2×400 (c) 2.4×20 (d) 0.3^2 (e) 5.13×300
(f) $600 \div 30$ (g) $3.2 \div 20$ (h) $2.1 \div 0.03$ (i) $90 \div 0.02$ (j) $600 \div 0.05$

14 Given that $1.9 \times 23.4 = 44.46$, work out these.
(a) 19×234 (b) $44.46 \div 19$ (c) $4446 \div 234$
(d) 0.19×0.0234 (e) $444.6 \div 0.234$ (f) 190×0.0234

15 Given that $126 \times 307 = 38\,682$, work out these.
(a) 12.6×3.07 (b) $12\,600 \times 3.07$ (c) $38\,682 \div 30.7$
(d) 0.126×30.7 (e) $386.82 \div 12.6$ (f) $38.682 \div 30.7$

12 FORMULAE 1

THIS CHAPTER IS ABOUT

- Using simple formulae
- Writing down and creating formulae
- Rearranging formulae
- Solving equations using trial and improvement

YOU SHOULD ALREADY KNOW

- How to substitute numbers into simple formulae
- How to simplify and solve linear equations
- How to simplify a formula by, for example, collecting together 'like' terms

Using formulae

You already know how to **substitute** numbers into formulae. You have also used formulae in other chapters: for example, in Chapter 6 you found the area of circles using the formula $A = \pi r^2$.

Check up 12.1

The area of a circle is given by the formula $A = \pi r^2$.
Find A when $r = 10$ cm. Use $\pi = 3.14$.

You also know how to write a formula in letters for a given situation.
You solve these formulae in the same way, by substitution.

EXAMPLE 12.1

To work out the cost of hiring a car for a certain number of days, multiply the number of days by the daily rate and add the fixed charge.
(a) Write a formula using letters to work out the cost of hiring a car.
(b) If the fixed charge is £20 and the daily rate is £55, find the cost of hiring a car for five days.

Solution

(a) $c = nd + f$ This uses c to represent the cost, n to represent the number of days, d to represent the daily rate and f to represent the fixed rate.

(b) $c = 5 \times 55 + 20$ Substitute the numbers into the formula.
$c = 275 + 20$
$c = 295$
Cost = £295

EXERCISE 12.1

1. To find the time needed, in minutes, to cook a piece of beef, multiply the weight of the beef in kilograms by 40 and add 10.
   How many minutes are needed to cook a piece of beef weighing
   (a) 2 kilograms?
   (b) 5 kilograms?

2. The further you go up a mountain, the colder it gets.
   There is a simple formula which tells you roughly how much the temperature will drop.

   Temperature drop (°C) = height climbed in metres ÷ 200.

   If you climb 800 m, by about how much will the temperature drop?

3. The total coach fare, £P, for a group going to the airport is given by the formula

   $P = 8A + 5C$

   where A is the number of adults and C is the number of children.
   Calculate the cost for two adults and three children.

4. The average speed (s) of a journey is the distance (d) divided by the time (t).
   (a) Write the formula for this.
   (b) A car journey of 150 km took 2 hours 30 minutes.
   What was the average speed of the journey?

5. The distance, d, in metres, that a stone falls in t seconds when dropped is given by the formula
   $$d = \frac{9.8t^2}{2}.$$
   Find d when $t = 10$ seconds.

6. This formula tells you the number of heaters needed to heat an office.

   $$\text{Number of heaters} = \frac{\text{length of office} \times \text{width of office}}{10}$$

   An office measures 15 m by 12 m.
   How many heaters are needed?

7 The number of sandwiches, S, needed for a party is calculated by a bread shop using the formula $S = 3P + 10$, where P is the number of people expected.
   (a) How many sandwiches are needed when 15 people are expected?
   (b) How many people are expected when 70 sandwiches are provided?

8 The diagram shows a rectangle.
   (a) What is the perimeter of the rectangle in terms of x?
   (b) What is the area of the rectangle in terms of x?

$3x$ cm

x cm

9 The time, T minutes, needed to cook a leg of lamb is given by the formula
   $T = 50W + 30$
   where W is the weight of the leg in kilograms.
   (a) How long, in hours and minutes, does it take to cook a leg of lamb weighing 2 kilograms?
   (b) What is the weight of a leg of lamb that takes 105 minutes to cook?

10 The formula linking volume, area and length for a prism is $L = \dfrac{V}{A}$.
   If $V = 200$ and $A = 40$, find L.

11 Anne walks for 5 hours at an average speed of 3 mph.
   Use the formula $d = st$ to work out the distance she walked.
   d stands for distance in miles.
   s stands for average speed in mph.
   t stands for time in hours.

12 Connor is making an ornamental fence. He joins posts with chains as shown in the diagram.
   (a) Connor fixes 5 posts into the ground. How many chains will he need?
   (b) Copy and complete this table.

Number of posts, P	1	2	3	4	5	6
Number of chains, C	0	3	6			

   (c) Write down the formula which gives the number of chains for any number of posts.
       Let C = total number of chains, and P = the number of posts.
   (d) How many chains are needed for a fence with 30 posts?

13 The area of a parallelogram is equal to the base multiplied by the vertical height.
   What is the area of a parallelogram with these dimensions?
   (a) Base = 6 cm and vertical height = 4 cm
   (b) Base = 4.5 cm and vertical height = 5 cm

Using formulae

14 The volume of a cuboid is the length multiplied by the width multiplied by the height.
What is the volume of a cuboid with these dimensions?
  (a) Length = 5 cm, width = 4 cm and height = 6 cm
  (b) Length = 4.5 cm, width = 8 cm and height = 6 cm

15 The cost of a long taxi journey is a fixed charge of £20 plus £1 per mile travelled.
  (a) What is the cost of a journey of 25 miles?
  (b) The cost of a journey was £63. How far was the journey?

Challenge 12.1

Write down the 'formula' you get by following each of these sets of instructions.

(a)
- Choose any number
- Multiply it by two
- Add five
- Multiply by five
- Subtract twenty-five

(b)
- Choose any number
- Double it
- Add nine
- Add the original number
- Divide by three
- Subtract three

What answer do you get for each set if your starting number is ten?

Challenge 12.2

The Golden Ratio for rectangles is achieved when their lengths are (approximately) equal to 1.6 times their widths.

A golden rectangle has an area of 230 cm².
Find its dimensions. Give your answers correct to the nearest millimetre.

Rearranging formulae

Sometimes you need to find the value of a letter which is not on the left-hand side of the formula. To find the value of the letter, you first need to **rearrange** the formula.

For example, the formula $d = st$ links distance (d), speed (s) and time (t). If you know the distance covered during a journey and the time it took, and want to find the average speed, you need to get the s by itself.

The method used to rearrange a formula is similar to the method you use to solve equations. You learned how to do this in Chapter 7.

In this case, to get the s on its own, you need to divide by t. As with equations, you must do each operation to the whole of both sides of the formula.

$d = st$

$\dfrac{d}{t} = \dfrac{st}{t}$ Divide each side by t.

$\dfrac{d}{t} = s$

$s = \dfrac{d}{t}$ A formula is usually written with the single term (in this case, s) on the left-hand side.

s is now the **subject** of the formula.
The formula gives s in terms of d and t.

EXAMPLE 12.2

$y = mx + c$
Make x the subject.

Solution

$y = mx + c$
$y - c = mx + c - c$ Subtract c from each side.
$y - c = mx$

$\dfrac{y - c}{m} = \dfrac{mx}{m}$ Divide each side by m.

$\dfrac{y - c}{m} = x$

$x = \dfrac{y - c}{m}$ Turn the formula around so that x is on the left-hand side.

EXAMPLE 12.3

The formula for the volume, v, of a square-based pyramid of side a is $v = \tfrac{1}{3}a^2h$.
Rearrange the formula to make h the subject.

Solution

$v = \tfrac{1}{3}a^2h$ Get rid of the fraction first.
$3v = a^2h$ Multiply each side by 3.
$\dfrac{3v}{a^2} = h$ Divide each side by a^2.
$h = \dfrac{3v}{a^2}$ Turn the formula around so that h is on the left-hand side.

EXAMPLE 12.4

Rearrange the formula $A = \pi r^2$ to make r the subject.

Solution

$A = \pi r^2$

$\dfrac{A}{\pi} = r^2$ Divide each side by π.

$r^2 = \dfrac{A}{\pi}$ Turn the formula around so that r^2 is on the left-hand side.

$r = \sqrt{\dfrac{A}{\pi}}$ Take the square root of each side.

EXERCISE 12.2

1. Rearrange each of these formulae to make the letter in brackets the subject.
   (a) $a = b - c$ (b)
   (b) $4a = wx + y$ (x)
   (c) $v = u + at$ (t)
   (d) $c = p - 3t$ (t)
   (e) $A = p(q + r)$ (q)
   (f) $p = 2g - 2f$ (g)
   (g) $F = \dfrac{m + 4n}{t}$ (n)

2. Make u the subject of the formula $s = \dfrac{3uv}{bn}$.

3. Rearrange the formula $a = \dfrac{bh}{2}$ to give h in terms of a and b.

4. The formula for calculating simple interest is $I = \dfrac{PRT}{100}$.
   Make R the subject of this formula.

5. The volume of a cone is given by the formula $V = \dfrac{\pi r^2 h}{3}$, where V is the volume in cm³, r is the radius of the base in cm and h is the height in cm.
   (a) Rearrange the formula to make h the subject.
   (b) Calculate the height of a cone with radius 5 cm and volume 435 cm³.
       Use $\pi = 3.14$ and give your answer correct to 1 decimal place.

6. To change from degrees Celsius (°C) to degrees Fahrenheit (°F), you can use the formula:
   $F = \tfrac{9}{5}(C + 40) - 40$.
   (a) The temperature is 60°C. What is this in °F?
   (b) Rearrange the formula to find C in terms of F.

7 Rearrange the formula $V = \dfrac{\pi r^2 h}{3}$ to make r the subject.

8 **(a)** Make a the subject of the formula $v^2 = u^2 + 2as$.
  (b) Make u the subject of the formula $v^2 = u^2 + 2as$.

Solving equations by trial and improvement

Sometimes you will need to solve an equation by **trial and improvement**. This means that you substitute different values into the equation until you find a solution.

It is important that you work systematically and do not just choose the numbers you try at random.

First you need to find two numbers between which the solution lies. Next you try the number halfway between these two numbers. You continue this process until you find the answer to the required degree of accuracy.

EXAMPLE 12.5

Find a solution of the equation $x^3 - x = 40$.
Give your answer correct to 1 decimal place.

Solution

$x^3 - x = 40$
Try $x = 3$ $3^3 - 3 = 24$ Too small. Try a larger number.
Try $x = 4$ $4^3 - 4 = 60$ Too large. The solution must lie between 3 and 4.
Try $x = 3.5$ $3.5^3 - 3.5 = 39.375$ Too small. Try a larger number.
Try $x = 3.6$ $3.6^3 - 3.6 = 43.056$ Too large. The solution must lie between 3.5 and 3.6.
Try $x = 3.55$ $3.55^3 - 3.55 = 41.118\ldots$ Too large. The solution must lie between 3.5 and 3.55.

So the answer is $x = 3.5$, correct to 1 decimal place.

EXAMPLE 12.6

(a) Show that $x^3 - 3x = 6$ has a solution between $x = 2$ and $x = 3$.
(b) Find the solution correct to 1 decimal place.

Solution

(a) $x^3 - 3x = 6$

Try $x = 2$ $2^3 - 3 \times 2 = 2$ Too small.
Try $x = 3$ $3^3 - 3 \times 3 = 18$ Too large.

6 is between 2 and 18. Therefore there is a solution of $x^3 - 3x = 6$ between $x = 2$ and $x = 3$.

(b) Try $x = 2.5$ $2.5^3 - 3 \times 2.5 = 8.125$ Too large. Try a smaller number.
Try $x = 2.3$ $2.3^3 - 3 \times 2.3 = 5.267$ Too small. Try a larger number.
Try $x = 2.4$ $2.4^3 - 3 \times 2.4 = 6.624$ Too large. Try a smaller number.
Try $x = 2.35$ $2.35^3 - 3 \times 2.35 = 5.927 \ldots$ Very close, but still too small.

x must be greater than 2.35. Therefore the answer, correct to 1 decimal place, is $x = 2.4$.

EXERCISE 12.3

1 Find a solution, between $x = 1$ and $x = 2$, to the equation $x^3 = 5$.
   Give your answer correct to 1 decimal place.

2 (a) Show that a solution to the equation $x^3 - 5x = 8$ lies between $x = 2$ and $x = 3$.
   (b) Find the solution correct to 1 decimal place.

3 (a) Show that a solution to the equation $x^3 - x = 90$ lies between $x = 4$ and $x = 5$.
   (b) Find the solution correct to 1 decimal place.

4 Find a solution to the equation $x^3 + x = 15$.
   Give your answer correct to 1 decimal place.

5 Find a solution to the equation $x^3 + x^2 = 100$.
   Give your answer correct to 2 decimal places.

6 Which whole number, when cubed, gives the value closest to 10 000?

7 Use trial and improvement to find which number, when squared, gives 1000.
   Give your answer correct to 1 decimal place.

8 A number, added to the square of this number, gives 10.
   (a) Write this as a formula.
   (b) Find the number correct to 1 decimal place.

9 The product of two whole numbers, the difference of which is 4, is 621.
   (a) Write this as formula in terms of x.
   (b) Use trial and improvement to find the two numbers.

10 Use trial and improvement to find which number, when squared, gives 61.
   Give your answer correct to 1 decimal place.

Formulae 1

> **WHAT YOU HAVE LEARNED**
>
> - To rearrange a formula, do each operation to the whole of both sides of the formula until you get the required term on its own, on the left-hand side of the formula
> - To find the solution to an equation by trial and improvement you first need to find two numbers between which the solution lies. You then try the number halfway between these two numbers and continue the process until you find the answer to the required degree of accuracy

MIXED EXERCISE 12

1 To convert temperatures on the Celsius (°C) scale to the Fahrenheit (°F) scale you can use the formula $F = 1.8C + 32$.

Calculate the Fahrenheit temperature when the temperature is
(a) 40°C.
(b) 0°C.
(c) −5°C.

2 The cost of a child's ticket on a bus is half that of an adult plus 25p.
Find the cost of a child's ticket when the adult fare is £1.40.

3 The area of a rhombus is found by multiplying the lengths of the diagonals together and then dividing by 2.
Find the area of a rhombus with diagonals of length
(a) 4 cm and 6 cm.
(b) 5.4 cm and 8 cm.

4 The Trenton bus company estimates the time for its local bus journeys, in minutes, by using the formula $T = 1.2m + 2s$, where m is the number of miles in a journey and s is the number of stops.
Find T when
(a) $m = 5$ and $s = 14$.
(b) $m = 6.5$ and $s = 20$.

5 Rearrange each of these formulae to make the letter in brackets the subject.
(a) $p = q + 2r$ (q)
(b) $x = s + 5r$ (r)
(c) $m = \dfrac{pqr}{s}$ (r)
(d) $A = t(x - 2y)$ (y)

6 The cooking time, T minutes, for w kg of meat is given by the formula

$$T = 45w + 40.$$

(a) Make w the subject of the formula.
(b) What is the value of w when the cooking time is 2 hours 28 minutes?

7 The area of a triangle is given by the formula $A = b \times h \div 2$, where b is the base and h is the height.
  (a) Find the length of the base when $A = 12\,\text{cm}^2$ and $h = 6\,\text{cm}$.
  (b) Find the height when $A = 22\,\text{cm}^2$ and $b = 5.5\,\text{cm}$.

8 The cost in £ of an advert in a local paper is given by the formula $C = 12 + \dfrac{w}{5}$ where w is the number of words in the advert.

How many words can you have if you are willing to pay
  (a) £18?   **(b)** £24?

9 (a) Show that a solution to the equation $x^3 + 4x = 12$ lies between $x = 1$ and $x = 2$.
  (b) Find the solution correct to 1 decimal place.

10 (a) Show that a solution to the equation $x^3 - x^2 = 28$ lies between $x = 3$ and $x = 4$.
  (b) Find the solution correct to 1 decimal place.

11 A number, added to the cube of this number, gives 100.
  (a) Write this as a formula.
  (b) Find the number correct to 1 decimal place.

13 → TRANSFORMATIONS

THIS CHAPTER IS ABOUT
- Drawing, recognising and describing reflections, rotations, enlargements with positive fractional scale factors and translations

YOU SHOULD ALREADY KNOW
- The terms *object* and *image* as they apply to transformations
- How to draw the reflection of a simple shape
- How to rotate a simple shape
- How to recognise and draw an enlargement of a shape using a centre and a positive, integer scale factor
- Equations of straight lines such as $x = 2$, $y = 3$, $y = x$ and $y = -x$

Reflections

In a reflection, the object and image are **congruent**. Congruent means exactly the same shape and size.

Drawing reflections

Check up 13.1

Copy these diagrams. Reflect each of the shapes in the mirror line.

(a)

(b)

TIP: When you have drawn a reflection in a sloping line, check it by turning the page so that the line is vertical. You can also use a mirror or tracing paper.

Recognising and describing reflections

You also need to be able to recognise and describe reflections.

You can tell whether a shape has been reflected using tracing paper: if you trace the **object**, you will have to turn the tracing paper over to fit the tracing on to the **image**.

You also need to find the **mirror line**. You do this by measuring the distance between points on the object and image.

EXAMPLE 13.1

Describe the single transformation that maps shape ABC on to shape A'B'C'.

Solution

You can probably tell just by looking that the transformation is a reflection, but you could check using tracing paper.

To find the mirror line, put a ruler between two corresponding points (B and B') and mark the midpoint of the line between them. The midpoint is (3, 3).

Do the same for two other corresponding points (C and C'). The midpoint is (4, 4).

Join the points to find the mirror line. The mirror line passes through (1, 1), (2, 2), (3, 3), (4, 4) … .
It is the line $y = x$.

The transformation is a reflection in the line $y = x$.

> **TIP**: You must both state that the transformation is a reflection and give the mirror line.

> **TIP**: Check the line is correct by turning the page so that the mirror line is vertical.

mirror line can be any straight line.

ansformations

Check up 13.2

Draw a pair of axes and label them −4 to 4 for x and y.
Draw these lines on the graph and label them.

(a) $x = 2$ (b) $y = -3$ (c) $y = x$ (d) $y = -x$

EXERCISE 13.1

1 Draw a pair of axes and label them −4 to 4 for x and y.
   (a) Draw a triangle with vertices at (1, 0), (1, −2) and (2, −2). Label it A.
   (b) Reflect triangle A in the line $y = 1$. Label it B.
   (c) Reflect triangle B in the line $y = x$. Label it C.

2 Draw a pair of axes and label them −4 to 4 for x and y.
   (a) Draw a triangle with vertices at (1, 1), (2, 3) and (3, 3). Label it A.
   (b) Reflect triangle A in the line $y = 2$. Label it B.
   (c) Reflect triangle A in the line $y = -x$. Label it C.

3 For each part
   • copy the diagram carefully, making it larger if you wish.
   • reflect the shape in the mirror line.

   (a)   (b)   (c)

4 Describe fully the single transformation that maps
   (a) flag A on to flag B.
   (b) flag A on to flag C.
   (c) flag B on to flag D.

Reflections

5 Describe fully the single transformation that maps
   (a) triangle A on to triangle B.
   (b) triangle A on to triangle C.
   (c) triangle C on to triangle D.

Rotations

In a rotation, the object and image are congruent.

Drawing rotations

Check up 13.3

Rotate each of these shapes as described.

(a) Rotation of 90° anticlockwise about the origin.

(b) Rotation of 270° anticlockwise about its centre, A.

The centre of rotation can be any point. It does not have to be either the origin or the centre of the shape.

13 Transformations

EXAMPLE 13.2

Rotate the shape through 90° about the point C(1, 2).

Solution

Angles of rotation are anticlockwise unless you are told otherwise.

You can rotate the shape using tracing paper or you can count squares.

EXAMPLE 13.3

Rotate triangle ABC through 90° clockwise about C.

Solution

Because the triangle is not drawn on squared paper, you have to use a different method.

Measure an angle of 90° clockwise at C from the line AC, and draw a line.

Trace the shape ABC.
Put a pencil or pin at C to hold the tracing to the diagram at that point.
Rotate the tracing paper until AC coincides with the line drawn.
Use a pin or the point of your compasses to prick through the other corners, A and B.
Join up the new points to make the image.

When the centre of rotation is not on the shape the method is slightly different.

EXAMPLE 13.4

Rotate triangle ABC through 90° clockwise about point P.

Solution

Join P to a point C on the object. Measure an angle of 90° clockwise from PC and draw a line.

Trace the triangle ABC and the line PC.
Put a pencil or pin at P to hold the tracing to the diagram at that point.
Rotate the tracing paper until PC coincides with the line drawn.
Use a pin or the point of your compasses to prick through the corners A, B and C.
Join up the new points to make the image.

> **TIP** Corresponding points will be the same distance from the centre of rotation.

Recognising and describing rotations

Challenge 13.1

Which of the triangles B, C, D, E, F and G are reflections of triangle A and which are rotations of triangle A?

Hint: For reflections the tracing paper needs to be turned over, for rotations it does not.

To describe a rotation, you need to know the **angle of rotation** and the **centre of rotation**.

Sometimes you can tell the angle of rotation just by looking at the diagram.

If you can't, you need to identify a pair of sides that correspond in the object and image and measure the angle between them. You may need to extend the lines.

You can usually find the centre of rotation by counting squares or using tracing paper.

EXAMPLE 13.5

Describe fully the single transformation that maps flag A on to flag B.

Solution

It is clear that the transformation is a rotation and that the angle is 90° clockwise.
Clockwise rotations are described as negative.
This is a rotation of −90°.

Use tracing paper and a pencil or compass point to find the centre of rotation.
Trace flag A and use the pencil or compass point to hold the tracing to the diagram at a point.
Rotate the tracing paper and see if the tracing fits over flag B.
Keep trying different points until you find the centre of rotation.
Here, the centre of rotation is (6, 4).

The transformation is a rotation of 90° about (6, 4).

> **TIP**
> You must state that the transformation is a rotation and give the angle of rotation and the centre of rotation.

Rotations 197

EXERCISE 13.2

1. Copy the diagram.
   (a) Rotate shape A through 90° clockwise about the origin. Label it B.
   (b) Rotate shape A through 180° about the point (1, 2). Label it C.

2. Copy the diagram.
   (a) Rotate flag A through 90° anticlockwise about the origin. Label it B.
   (b) Rotate flag A through 90° clockwise about the point (1, 2). Label it C.
   (c) Rotate flag A through 180° about the point (2, 0). Label it D.

3. Draw a pair of axes and label them −4 to 8 for x and y.
   (a) Draw a triangle with vertices (0, 1), (0, 4) and (2, 3). Label it A.
   (b) Rotate triangle A through 180° about the origin. Label it B.
   (c) Rotate triangle A through 90° anticlockwise about the point (0, 1). Label it C.
   (d) Rotate triangle A through 90° clockwise about the point (2, −1). Label it D.

4. Copy the diagram.

   Rotate the triangle through 90° clockwise about point C.

5. Copy the diagram.

   Rotate the triangle through 90° clockwise about the point O.

6 Copy the diagram.

   Rotate the triangle through 120° clockwise about the point C.

7 Describe fully the single transformation that maps
   (a) triangle A on to triangle B.
   (b) triangle A on to triangle C.
   (c) triangle A on to triangle D.

8 Describe fully the single transformation that maps
   (a) flag A on to flag B.
   (b) flag A on to flag C.
   (c) flag A on to flag D.

9 Describe fully the single transformation that maps triangle A on to triangle B.

Rotations 199

10 Describe fully the single transformation that maps
  (a) triangle A on to triangle B.
  (b) triangle A on to triangle C.
  (c) triangle A on to triangle D.
  (d) triangle A on to triangle E.
  (e) triangle B on to triangle E.

  Hint: Some of these transformations are reflections.

Translations

A **translation** moves all points of an object the same distance in the same direction. The object and image are congruent.

Discovery 13.1

Triangle B is a translation of triangle A.
(a) How can you tell it is a translation?
(b) How far across has it moved?
(c) How far down has it moved?

TIP Take care with the counting. Choose a point on both the object and image and count the squares from one to the other.

How far a shape moves in a translation is written as a **column vector**.

The *top* number tells you how far the shape moves *across*, or in the x direction.
The *bottom* number tells you how far the shape moves *up or down*, or in the y direction.

A *positive* top number is a move to the *right*. A *negative* top number is a move to the *left*.
A *positive* bottom number is a move *up*. A *negative* bottom number is a move *down*.

A translation of 3 to the right and 2 down is written as $\begin{pmatrix} 3 \\ -2 \end{pmatrix}$.

EXAMPLE 13.6

Translate the triangle by $\begin{pmatrix} -3 \\ 4 \end{pmatrix}$.

Solution

$\begin{pmatrix} -3 \\ 4 \end{pmatrix}$ means move 3 units left, and 4 units up.

Point A moves from (1, −1) to (−2, 3).
Point B moves from (2, −1) to (−1, 3).
Point C moves from (2, −1.5) to (−1, 2.5).

EXAMPLE 13.7

Describe fully the single transformation that maps shape A on to shape B.

Solution

It is clearly a translation as the shape stays the same way up.

To find the movement choose one point on the object and image and count the squares moved.
For example, P moves from (1, 5) to (3, 2). This is a movement of 2 to the right and 3 down.

The transformation is a translation of $\begin{pmatrix} 2 \\ -3 \end{pmatrix}$.

> **TIP**
> You must both state that the transformation is a translation and give the column vector.

> **TIP**
> Try not to confuse the words *transformation* and *translation*.
>
> *Transformation* is the general name for all changes made to shapes.
>
> *Translation* is the particular transformation where all points of an object move the same distance in the same direction.

EXERCISE 13.3

1. Draw a pair of axes and label them −2 to 6 for x and y.
   (a) Draw a triangle with vertices at (1, 2), (1, 4), and (2, 4). Label it A.
   (b) Translate triangle A by vector $\begin{pmatrix} 2 \\ 1 \end{pmatrix}$. Label it B.
   (c) Translate triangle A by vector $\begin{pmatrix} 4 \\ -2 \end{pmatrix}$. Label it C.
   (d) Translate triangle A by vector $\begin{pmatrix} -2 \\ -3 \end{pmatrix}$. Label it D.

2. Draw a pair of axes and label them −2 to 6 for x and y.
   (a) Draw the trapezium with vertices at (2, 1), (4, 1), (3, 2) and (2, 2). Label it A.
   (b) Translate trapezium A by vector $\begin{pmatrix} 2 \\ 3 \end{pmatrix}$. Label it B.
   (c) Translate trapezium A by vector $\begin{pmatrix} -4 \\ 0 \end{pmatrix}$. Label it C.
   (d) Translate trapezium A by vector $\begin{pmatrix} -3 \\ 2 \end{pmatrix}$. Label it D.

3. Describe the single transformation that maps
   (a) triangle A on to triangle B.
   (b) triangle A on to triangle C.
   (c) triangle A on to triangle D.
   (d) triangle B on to triangle D.

202 13 Transformations

4 Describe the single transformation that maps
  (a) flag A on to flag B.
  (b) flag A on to flag C.
  (c) flag A on to flag D.
  (d) flag A on to flag E.
  (e) flag A on to flag F.
  (f) flag E on to flag G.
  (g) flag B on to flag E.
  (h) flag C on to flag D.

  Hint: Not all the transformations are translations.

Challenge 13.2

Draw a pair of axes and label them −6 to 6 for x and y.

(a) Draw a shape in the positive region near the origin. Label it A.

(b) Translate shape A by vector $\begin{pmatrix} 2 \\ 1 \end{pmatrix}$. Label it B.

(c) Translate shape B by vector $\begin{pmatrix} 3 \\ -2 \end{pmatrix}$. Label it C.

(d) Translate shape C by vector $\begin{pmatrix} -6 \\ -1 \end{pmatrix}$. Label it D.

(e) Translate shape D by vector $\begin{pmatrix} 1 \\ 2 \end{pmatrix}$. Label it E.

(f) What do you notice about shapes A and E? Can you suggest why this happens? Try to find other combinations of translations for which this happens.

Challenge 13.3

Sometimes you can apply different transformations to an object and get the same image.

(a) Describe all the different single transformations that will map A onto B.

(b) Try to find other pairs of shapes where the object, A, can be mapped on to the image, B, by more than one single transformation.

Enlargements

There is another kind of transformation: **enlargement**. In an enlargement, the object and image are not congruent, but they are **similar**. The lengths change but the angles in the object and the image are the same.

Check up 13.4

Draw a pair of axes and label them 0 to 6 for x and y.
(a) Draw a triangle with vertices at (1, 2), (3, 2) and (3, 3). Label it A.
(b) Enlarge the triangle by scale factor 2, with the origin as the centre of enlargement. Label it B.

Discovery 13.2

(a) (i) Think about what happens to the lengths of the sides of an object when it is enlarged by scale factor 2.
What do you think will happen to the lengths of the sides of an object if it is enlarged by scale factor $\frac{1}{2}$?
(ii) Think about the position of the image when an object is enlarged by scale factor 2. What happens to the distance between the centre of enlargement and the object? What do you think will be the position of the image if an object is enlarged by scale factor $\frac{1}{2}$?

(b) Draw a pair of axes and label them 0 to 6 for x and y.
(i) Draw a triangle with vertices at (2, 4), (6, 4) and (6, 6). Label it A.
(ii) Enlarge the triangle by scale factor $\frac{1}{2}$, with the origin as the centre of enlargement. Label it B.

(c) Compare your diagram with the diagram you drew in Check up 13.4. What do you notice?

An enlargement with scale factor $\frac{1}{2}$ is the **inverse** of an enlargement with scale factor 2.

> **TIP**
> Although the image is smaller than the object, an enlargement with scale factor $\frac{1}{2}$ is still called an enlargement.

You can also draw enlargements with other fractional scale factors.

EXAMPLE 13.8

Draw a pair of axes and label them 0 to 8 for both x and y.
(a) Draw a triangle with vertices at P(5, 1), Q(5, 7) and R(8, 7).
(b) Enlarge the triangle PQR by scale factor $\frac{1}{3}$, centre C(2, 1).

Solution

The sides of the enlargement are $\frac{1}{3}$ the lengths of the original.

The distance from the centre of enlargement, C, to P is 3 across.
So the distance from C to P' is $3 \times \frac{1}{3} = 1$ across.

The distance from C to Q is 3 across and 6 up.
So the distance from C to Q' is $3 \times \frac{1}{3} = 1$ across and $6 \times \frac{1}{3} = 2$ up.

The distance from C to R is 6 across and 6 up.
So the distance from C to R' is $6 \times \frac{1}{3} = 2$ across and $6 \times \frac{1}{3} = 2$ up.

EXAMPLE 13.9

Describe fully the single transformation that maps triangle PQR on to triangle P'Q'R'.

Solution

It is obvious that the shape has been enlarged. The length of each side of triangle P'Q'R' is half the length of the corresponding side of triangle PQR, so the scale factor is $\frac{1}{2}$.

To find the centre of enlargement, join the corresponding corners of the two triangles and extend the lines until they cross. The point where they cross is the centre of enlargement, C. Here, C is at (1, 2).

> **TIP**
> To check the centre of enlargement, find the distance from the centre of enlargement to a corresponding pair of points. For example, the distance from C to P is 2 across and 4 up, so the distance from C to P' should be 1 across and 2 up.

Enlargements 205

The transformation is an enlargement with scale factor $\frac{1}{2}$, centre (1, 2).

> **TIP**
> You must state that the transformation is an enlargement and give the scale factor and centre of enlargement.

EXERCISE 13.4

1 Draw a pair of axes and label them 0 to 6 for both x and y.
  (a) Draw a triangle with vertices at (4, 2), (6, 2) and (6, 6). Label it A.
  (b) Enlarge triangle A by scale factor $\frac{1}{2}$, with the origin as the centre of enlargement. Label it B.
  (c) Describe fully the single transformation that maps triangle B on to triangle A.

2 Draw a pair of axes and label them 0 to 8 for both x and y.
  (a) Draw a triangle with vertices at (4, 5), (4, 8) and (7, 8). Label it A.
  (b) Enlarge triangle A by scale factor $\frac{1}{3}$, with centre of enlargement (1, 2). Label it B.
  (c) Describe fully the single transformation that maps triangle B on to triangle A.

3 Draw a pair of axes and label them 0 to 8 for both x and y.
  (a) Draw a triangle with vertices at (0, 2), (1, 2) and (2, 1). Label it A.
  (b) Enlarge triangle A by scale factor 4, with the origin as the centre of enlargement. Label it B.
  (c) Describe fully the single transformation that maps triangle B on to triangle A.

4 Draw a pair of axes and label them 0 to 8 for both x and y.
  (a) Draw a triangle with vertices at (4, 3), (4, 5) and (6, 2). Label it A.
  (b) Enlarge triangle A by scale factor $1\frac{1}{2}$, with centre of enlargement (2, 1). Label it B.
  (c) Describe fully the single transformation that maps triangle B on to triangle A.

5 Describe fully the single transformation that maps
  (a) triangle A on to triangle B.
  (b) triangle B on to triangle A.
  (c) triangle A on to triangle C.
  (d) triangle C on to triangle A.

Hint: In questions **6**, **7** and **8**, not all the transformations are enlargements.

6 Describe fully the single transformation that maps
   (a) triangle A on to triangle B.
   (b) triangle A on to triangle C.
   (c) triangle C on to triangle D.
   (d) triangle A on to triangle E.
   (e) triangle A on to triangle F.
   (f) triangle G on to triangle A.

7 Describe fully the single transformation that maps
   (a) flag A on to flag B.
   (b) flag A on to flag C.
   (c) flag A on to flag D.
   (d) flag A on to flag E.
   (e) flag F on to flag E.
   (f) flag E on to flag G.

8 Describe fully the single transformation that maps
   (a) triangle A on to triangle B.
   (b) triangle A on to triangle C.
   (c) triangle B on to triangle D.
   (d) triangle C on to triangle E.
   (e) triangle F on to triangle G.
   (f) triangle H on to triangle G.
   (g) triangle G on to triangle H.

Challenge 13.4

A triangle ABC has sides AB = 9 cm, AC = 7 cm and BC = 6 cm.

A line XY is drawn parallel to BC through a point X on AB and a point Y on AC.

AX = 5 cm.

(a) Draw a sketch of the triangle.

(b) (i) Describe fully the transformation that maps ABC on to AXY.
   (ii) Work out the length of XY, correct to 2 decimal places.

WHAT YOU HAVE LEARNED

- In reflections, rotations and translations, the object and image are congruent
- To describe a reflection, you must state that the transformation is a reflection and give the mirror line
- How to find the mirror line
- Negative rotations are clockwise
- To describe a rotation, you must state that the transformation is a rotation and give the centre of rotation and the angle of rotation
- How to find the centre of rotation and the angle of rotation
- In a translation, the object and image are the same way around
- To describe a translation, you must state that the transformation is a translation and give the column vector.
- What the column vector $\begin{pmatrix} a \\ b \end{pmatrix}$ represents
- In an enlargement, the object and the image are similar. If the scale factor is fractional, the image will be smaller than the object
- To describe an enlargement, you must state that the transformation is an enlargement and give the scale factor and the centre of enlargement
- How to find the scale factor and the centre of enlargement

MIXED EXERCISE 13

1. Draw a pair of axes and label them −4 to 4 for x and y.
   (a) Draw a triangle with vertices at $(2, -1)$, $(4, -1)$ and $(4, -2)$. Label it A.
   (b) Reflect triangle A in the line $y = 0$. Label it B.
   (c) Reflect triangle A in the line $y = -x$. Label it C.

2. Copy these diagrams, making them larger if you wish.
   Reflect each shape in the mirror line.
   (a)   (b)

3. Copy the diagram.
   (a) Rotate shape A through 90° anticlockwise about the origin. Label it B.
   (b) Rotate shape A through 180° about the point $(2, -1)$. Label it C.

4. Copy the diagram.
   (a) Translate shape A by vector $\begin{pmatrix} 1 \\ -6 \end{pmatrix}$. Label it B.
   (b) Translate shape A by vector $\begin{pmatrix} -3 \\ 0 \end{pmatrix}$. Label it C.
   (c) Translate shape A by vector $\begin{pmatrix} -5 \\ -4 \end{pmatrix}$. Label it D.

5 Draw a pair of axes and label them 0 to 9 for both x and y.
   (a) Draw a triangle with vertices at (6, 3), (6, 6) and (9, 3). Label it A.
   (b) Enlarge the triangle by scale factor $\frac{1}{3}$, with centre of enlargement (0, 0). Label it B.

6 Draw a pair of axes and label them 0 to 8 for both x and y.
   (a) Draw a triangle with vertices at (6, 4), (6, 6) and (8, 6). Label it A.
   (b) Enlarge the triangle by scale factor $\frac{1}{2}$, with centre of enlargement (2, 0). Label it B.

7 Describe fully the single transformation that maps
   (a) flag A on to flag B.
   (b) flag A on to flag C.
   (c) flag A on to flag D.
   (d) flag B on to flag E.
   (e) flag F on to flag C.
   (f) flag C on to flag G.
   (g) flag B on to flag C.

8 Describe fully the single transformation that maps
   (a) triangle A on to triangle B.
   (b) triangle A on to triangle C.
   (c) triangle B on to triangle D.
   (d) triangle C on to triangle E.
   (e) triangle F on to triangle C.
   (f) triangle A on to triangle G.
   (g) triangle H on to triangle G.

14 PROBABILITY 1

> **THIS CHAPTER IS ABOUT**
> - Using the fact that the probability of an event not happening and the probability of the event happening add up to 1
> - Calculating expected frequency
> - Calculating relative frequency

> **YOU SHOULD ALREADY KNOW**
> - That probabilities are expressed as fractions or decimals
> - All probabilities lie on a scale between 0 and 1
> - How to find a probability from a set of equally likely outcomes
> - How to add decimals and fractions
> - How to subtract decimals and fractions from 1
> - How to multiply decimals

Probability of an outcome not happening

Discovery 14.1

There are three pens and five pencils in a box.
One of these is chosen at random.

(a) What is the probability that it is a pen, P(pen)?
(b) What is the probability that it is a pencil, P(pencil)?
(c) What is the probability that it is not a pen, P(not a pen)?
(d) What can you say about your answers to parts **(b)** and **(c)**?
(e) What is P(pen) + P(not a pen)?

> **TIP** P( ) is often used when writing probabilities because it saves time and space.

The probability of an event not happening = 1 − the probability of the event happening.

If p is the probability of an event happening, then this can be written as

$$P(\text{not happening}) = 1 - p.$$

EXAMPLE 14.1

(a) The probability that it will rain tomorrow is $\frac{1}{5}$.
What is the probability that it will not rain tomorrow?
(b) The probability that Phil scores a goal in the next match is 0.6.
What is the probability that Phil does not score a goal?

Solution

(a) P(not rain) = 1 − P(rain)
$= 1 - \frac{1}{5}$
$= \frac{4}{5}$

(b) P(not score) = 1 − P(score)
= 1 − 0.6
= 0.4

EXERCISE 14.1

1. The probability that Max will get to school late tomorrow is 0.1.
What is the probability that Max will not be late tomorrow?

2. The probability that Charlie has cheese sandwiches for his lunch is $\frac{1}{6}$.
What is the probability that Charlie does not have cheese sandwiches?

3. The probability that Ashley will pass her driving test is 0.85.
What is the probability that Ashley will fail her driving test?

4. The probability that Adam's Mum will cook dinner tonight is $\frac{7}{10}$.
What is the probability that she will not cook dinner?

5. The probability that City will win their next game is 0.43.
What is the probability that City will not win their next game?

6. The probability that Alec will watch TV one night is $\frac{32}{49}$.
What is the probability that he will not watch TV?

Probability involving a given number of different outcomes

Often there are more than two possible outcomes.
If you know the probability of all but one of the outcomes, you can work out the probability of the remaining outcome.

EXAMPLE 14.2

A bag contains only red, white and blue counters.
The probability of picking a red counter is $\frac{1}{12}$.
The probability of picking a white counter is $\frac{7}{12}$.
What is the probability of picking a blue counter?

Solution

You know that P(not happening) = 1 − P(happening).
So P(not happening) + P(happening) = 1

$$P(\text{not blue}) + P(\text{blue}) = 1$$
$$P(\text{red}) + P(\text{white}) + P(\text{blue}) = 1$$
$$P(\text{blue}) = 1 - [P(\text{red}) + P(\text{white})]$$
$$= 1 - (\tfrac{1}{12} + \tfrac{7}{12})$$
$$= 1 - \tfrac{8}{12}$$
$$= \tfrac{4}{12}$$
$$= \tfrac{1}{3}$$

There are only red, white and blue counters in the bag, so if a counter is not blue it must be red or white.

When there are a given number of possible outcomes, the sum of the probabilities is equal to 1.

For example, if there are four possible outcomes, A, B, C and D, then

$$P(A) + P(B) + P(C) + P(D) = 1$$

So, for example

$$P(B) = 1 - [P(A) + P(C) + P(D)]$$
or
$$P(B) = 1 - P(A) - P(C) - P(D)$$

EXERCISE 14.2

1. A shop has black, grey and blue dresses on a rail. Jen picks one at random.
   The probability of picking a grey dress is 0.2 and the probability of picking a black dress is 0.1. What is the probability of picking a blue dress?

2. Heather always comes to school by car, bus or bike.
   On any day, the probability that Heather will come by car is $\frac{3}{20}$ and the probability that she will come by bus is $\frac{11}{20}$.
   What is the probability that Heather will come to school by bike?

Probability involving a given number of different outcomes

3   The probability that the school hockey team will win their next match is 0.4.
    The probability that they will lose is 0.25.
    What is the probability that they will draw the match?

4   Pat has either boiled eggs, cereal or toast for breakfast.
    The probability that she will have toast is $\frac{2}{11}$ and the probability that she will have cereal is $\frac{5}{11}$.
    What is the probability that she will have boiled eggs?

5   The table shows the probability of getting some of the scores when a biased six-sided dice is thrown.

Score	1	2	3	4	5	6
Probability	0.27	0.16	0.14		0.22	0.1

    What is the probability of getting 4?

6   When it is Jack's birthday, Aunty Chris gives him money or a voucher, or forgets altogether.
    The probability that Aunty Chris will give Jack money for his birthday is $\frac{3}{4}$ and the probability that she will give him a voucher is $\frac{1}{5}$.
    What is the probability that she forgets?

Challenge 14.1

The weather forecast says the probability that it will be sunny tomorrow is 0.4.

Terry says this means that the probability that it will rain is 0.6.

Is Terry correct? Why?

Challenge 14.2

A cash bag contains only 5p, 10p and 50p coins.
The total amount of money in the bag is £5.

A coin is chosen from the bag at random.

$P(5p) = \frac{1}{2}$
$P(10p) = \frac{3}{8}$

(a) Work out P(50p).
(b) How many of each kind of coin is there in the bag?

Expected frequency

You can also use probability to predict how often an outcome will occur, or the **expected frequency** of the outcome.

EXAMPLE 14.3

Each time Ronnie plays a game of snooker, the probability that he will win is $\frac{7}{10}$.

In a season, Ronnie plays 30 games. How many of the games can he be expected to win?

Solution

The probability P(win) = $\frac{7}{10}$ tells us that Ronnie will win, on average, seven times in every ten games he plays. That is, he will win $\frac{7}{10}$ of the time.

In a season, he can be expected to win $\frac{7}{10}$ of 30 games.

$$\frac{7}{10} \times 30 = \frac{210}{10}$$
$$= 21$$

This is an example of an important result.

Expected frequency = Probability × Number of trials

EXAMPLE 14.4

The probability of a child catching measles is 0.2.

Out of the 400 children in a primary school, how many of them might you expect to catch measles?

Solution

Expected frequency = Probability × Number of trials
            = 0.2 × 400
            = 80 children

The number of 'trials' means the the number of times the probability is tested. Here each of the 400 children has a 0.2 chance of catching measles. The number of trials is the same as the number of children: 400.

EXERCISE 14.3

1. The probability that Beverley is late to work is 0.1.
   How many times would you expect her to be late in 40 working days?

2. The probability that it will be sunny on any day in April is $\frac{2}{5}$.
   On how many of April's 30 days would you expect it to be sunny?

3. The probability that United will win their next match is 0.85.
   How many of their next 20 games might you expect them to win?

4. When John is playing darts, the probability that he will hit the bull's eye is $\frac{3}{20}$.
   John takes part in a sponsored event and throws 400 darts.
   Each dart hitting the bull's eye earns £5 for charity.
   How much might he expect to earn for charity?

5. An ordinary six-sided dice is thrown 300 times.
   How many times might you expect to score
   (a) 5?
   (b) an even number?

6. A box contains two yellow balls, three blue balls and five green balls.
   A ball is chosen at random and its colour noted.
   The ball is then replaced. This is done 250 times.
   How many of each colour might you expect to get?

Challenge 14.3

(a) If you roll a dice 30 times, how many times would you expect to get a 6?

(b) Now roll a dice 30 times and see how many times you get a 6.
    Did a 6 come up as many times as you predicted?
    Do the same for another 30 throws of the dice.
    Check and discuss your results with your classmates.

Relative frequency

You already know how to **estimate** probabilities using **experimental evidence**.

$$\text{The experimental probability of an event} = \frac{\text{The number of times an event happens}}{\text{The total number of trials}}.$$

The probability you estimate is known as **relative frequency**.

Discovery 14.2

Copy this table and complete it by following the instructions below.

Number of trials	20	40	60	80	100
Number of heads					
Relative frequency = $\dfrac{\text{Number of heads}}{\text{Number of trials}}$					

- Toss a coin 20 times and record, using tally marks, the number of times it lands on heads.
- Now toss the coin another 20 times and enter the number of heads for all 40 tosses.
- Continue in groups of 20 and record the number of heads for 60, 80 and 100 tosses.
- Calculate the relative frequency of heads for 20, 40, 60, 80 and 100 tosses.
  Give your answers to 2 decimal places.

(a) What do you notice about the values of the relative frequencies?
(b) The probability of getting a head with one toss of a coin is $\frac{1}{2}$ or 0.5. Why is this?
(c) How does your final relative frequency value compare with this value of 0.5?

Relative frequency becomes more accurate the more trials you do.

When using experimental evidence to estimate probability it is advisable to perform at least 100 trials.

EXERCISE 14.4

1 Ping rolls a dice 500 times and records the number of times each score appears.

Score	1	2	3	4	5	6
Frequency	69	44	85	112	54	136

(a) Work out the relative frequency of each of the scores.
   Give your answers to 2 decimal places.
(b) What is the probability of obtaining each score on an ordinary six-sided dice?
(c) Do you think that Ping's dice is biased? Give a reason for your answer.

2 Rashid notices that 7 out of the 20 cars in the school car park are red.
He says there is a probability of $\frac{7}{20}$ that the next car to come into the car park will be red.
Explain what is wrong with this.

3 In a local election, 800 people were asked which party they would vote for.
The results are shown in the table.

Party	Labour	Conservative	Lib. Dem.	Other
Frequency	240	376	139	45

(a) Work out the relative frequency for each party.
Give your answers to 2 decimal places.
(b) Estimate the probability that the next person to be asked will vote Labour.

4 Emma and Rebecca have a coin that they think is biased.
They decide to do an experiment to check.
(a) Rebecca tosses the coin 20 times and gets a head 10 times.
She says that the coin is not biased.
Why do you think she has come to this conclusion?
(b) Emma tosses the coin 300 times and gets a head 102 times.
She says that the coin is biased.
Why do you think she has come to this conclusion?
(c) Who do you think is correct?
Give a reason for your answer.

5 Joe made a spinner numbered 1, 2, 3 and 4.
He tested the spinner to see if it was fair.
He spun it 600 times. The results are shown in the table.

Score	1	2	3	4
Frequency	160	136	158	146

(a) Work out the relative frequency of each of the scores.
Give your answers to 2 decimal places.
(b) Do you think that the spinner is fair?
Give a reason for your answer.
(c) If Joe were to test the spinner again and spin it 900 times, how many times would you expect each of the scores to appear?

6 Samantha carried out a survey into how students travel to school.
She asked 200 students. Here are her results.

Travel by ...	Bus	Car	Bike	Walk
Number of students	49	48	23	80

(a) Explain why it is reasonable for Samantha to use these results to estimate the probabilities of students travelling by the various methods.
(b) Estimate the probability that a randomly selected student will use each of the various methods of getting to school.

Challenge 14.4

Work in pairs.

Put 10 counters, some red and the rest white, in a bag.

Challenge your partner to work out how many counters there are of each colour.

Hint: You need to devise an experiment with 100 trials.
At the start of each trial, all 10 counters must be in the bag.

WHAT YOU HAVE LEARNED

- If three events, A, B and C, cover all possible outcomes then, for example, $P(A) = 1 - P(B) - P(C)$
- Expected frequency = Probability × Total number of trials
- Relative frequency = $\dfrac{\text{Number of times an outcome occurs}}{\text{Total number of outcomes}}$
- Relative frequency is a good estimate of probability if there are sufficient trials

MIXED EXERCISE 14

1. The probability that Peter can score 20 with one dart is $\frac{2}{9}$.
   What is the probability of him not scoring 20 with one dart?

2. The probability that Carmen will go to the cinema during any week is 0.65.
   What is the probability that she will not go to the cinema during one week?

3. Some of the probabilities of the length of time that any car will stay in a car park are shown below.

Time	Up to 30 minutes	30 minutes to 1 hour	1 hour to 2 hours	Over 2 hours
Probability	0.15	0.32	0.4	

   What is the probability that a car will stay in the car park for over 2 hours?

4. There are 20 counters in a bag. They are all red, white or blue in colour.
   A counter is chosen from the bag at random.
   The probability that it is red is $\frac{1}{4}$. The probability that it is white is $\frac{2}{5}$.
   (a) What is the probability that it is blue?
   (b) How many counters of each colour are there?

5 The probability that Robert goes swimming on any day is 0.4.
There are 30 days in the month of June.
On how many days in June might you expect Robert to go swimming?

6 Holly thinks that a coin may be biased.
To test this, she tosses the coin 20 times. Heads turns up 10 times.
Holly says 'The coin is fair.'
(a) Why does Holly say this?
(b) Is she correct? Give a reason for your answer.

7 In an experiment with a biased dice, the following results were obtained after 400 throws.

Score	1	2	3	4	5	6
Frequency	39	72	57	111	25	96

(a) If the dice was fair, what would you expect the frequency of each score to be?
(b) Use the results to estimate the probability of throwing this dice and getting
  (i) a 1.
  (ii) an even number.
  (iii) a number greater than 4.

15 ➔ GRAPHS 1

THIS CHAPTER IS ABOUT

- Drawing straight-line graphs from equations given in explicit or implicit form
- Distance–time graphs
- Drawing and interpreting graphs of real-life situations
- Drawing graphs of quadratic functions
- Solving equations using quadratic graphs

YOU SHOULD ALREADY KNOW

- How to plot and read points in all four quadrants
- How to substitute numbers into equations
- How to draw graphs with equations of the form $y = 2$, $x = 3$, etc.
- How to rearrange equations
- How to add, subtract and multiply negative numbers
- How to plot and interpret simple straight-line graphs involving conversions, distance–time and other real-life situations
- How to use the relationship between distance, speed and time

Drawing straight-line graphs

The most common straight-line graphs have equations of the form $y = 3x + 2$, $y = 2x - 3$, etc.

This can be written in a general form as

$$y = mx + c.$$

To draw a straight-line graph, work out three pairs of coordinates by substituting values of x into the formula to find y.

You can draw a straight line with only two points, but you should always work out a third point as a check.

EXAMPLE 15.1

Draw the graph of $y = -2x + 1$ for values of x from -4 to 2.

Solution

Find the values of y when $x = -4, 0$ and 2.

$y = -2x + 1$

When $x = -4$
$y = -2 \times -4 + 1$
$y = 9$

When $x = 0$
$y = -2 \times 0 + 1$
$y = 1$

When $x = 2$
$y = -2 \times 2 + 1$
$y = -3$

The y values needed are -3 to 9.
Draw the axes and plot the points $(-4, 9)$, $(0, 1)$ and $(2, -3)$.
Join them with a straight line. Label it $y = -2x + 1$.

TIP Always use a ruler to draw a straight-line graph.

TIP If axes have been drawn for you, check the scale before plotting points or reading values.

EXERCISE 15.1

1. Draw the graph of $y = 4x$ for values of x from -3 to 3.

2. Draw the graph of $y = x + 3$ for values of x from -3 to 3.

3. Draw the graph of $y = 3x - 4$ for values of x from -2 to 4.

4. Draw the graph of $y = 4x - 2$ for values of x from -2 to 3.

5. Draw the graph of $y = -3x - 4$ for values of x from -4 to 2.

Harder straight-line graphs

Sometimes you will be asked to draw graphs with equations of a different form.

For equations such as $2y = 3x + 1$, work out three points as before, remembering to divide by 2 to find the y value.

EXAMPLE 15.2

Draw the graph of $2y = 3x + 1$ for values of x from -3 to 3.

Solution

Find the values of y when $x = -3, 0$ and 3.

$2y = 3x + 1$

When $x = -3$
$2y = 3 \times -3 + 1$
$2y = -8$
$y = -4$

When $x = 0$
$2y = 3 \times 0 + 1$
$2y = 1$
$y = \frac{1}{2}$

When $x = 3$
$2y = 3 \times 3 + 1$
$2y = 10$
$y = 5$

The values of y needed are -4 to 5.

Draw the axes and plot the points $(-3, -4)$, $(0, \frac{1}{2})$ and $(3, 5)$. Join them with a straight line. Label it $2y = 3x + 1$.

For equations such as $4x + 3y = 12$, work out y when $x = 0$, and x when $y = 0$. These are easy to work out: you can find a third point as a check after you have drawn the line.

EXAMPLE 15.3

Draw the graph of $4x + 3y = 12$.

Solution

Find the value of y when $x = 0$ and the value of x when $y = 0$.

$4x + 3y = 12$

When $x = 0$
$\quad 3y = 12 \quad\quad 4 \times 0 = 0$ so the x term 'disappears'.
$\quad y = 4$

When $y = 0$
$\quad 4x = 12 \quad\quad 3 \times 0 = 0$ so the y term 'disappears'.
$\quad x = 3$

The values of x needed are 0 to 3. The values of y needed are 0 to 4.

Draw axes and plot the points (0, 4) and (3, 0).
Join them with a straight line. Label it $4x + 3y = 12$.

TIP: Take care when plotting the points. Do not put (0, 4) at (4, 0) by mistake.

Choose a point on the line you have drawn and check it by substituting the x and y values into the equation.

For example, the line passes through $(1\frac{1}{2}, 2)$.

$4x + 3y = 12$
$4 \times 1\frac{1}{2} + 3 \times 2 = 6 + 6 = 12$ ✓

EXERCISE 15.2

1. Draw the graph of $2y = 3x - 2$ for $x = -2$ to 4.
2. Draw the graph of $2x + 5y = 15$.
3. Draw the graph of $7x + 2y = 14$.
4. Draw the graph of $2y = 5x + 3$ for $x = -3$ to 3.
5. Draw the graph of $2x + y = 7$.

Challenge 15.1

The entry fee at Radium hot springs is $6.50 each. It costs $2 to hire towels.
A coach party of 40 people went in the hot springs and n of them hired towels.
 (a) Write down an equation for the total amount they spent, S, in terms of n.
 (b) Draw a graph of S against n, for values of n up to 40.
 (c) Use your graph to find how many towels were hired if the total spent was $310.

Distance–time graphs

Check up 15.1

James walked to the bus stop and waited for the bus.
When the bus arrived he got on the bus and it took him to school without stopping.
Which of these distance–time graphs best shows James' journey to school?
Explain your answer.

(a)

(b)

(c)

(d)

Discovery 15.1

James walked to the bus stop at 4 km/h.
This took him 15 minutes.
He waited 5 minutes at the bus stop.
The bus journey was 12 km and took 20 minutes.
The bus went at a constant speed.

(a) Copy these axes and draw an accurate graph of James' journey.
(b) What was the speed of the bus in km/h?
(c) After 30 minutes, how far was James away from home?

When a graph illustrates real quantities, how steeply it goes up or down is called the **rate of change**.

When the graph shows distance (vertical) against time (horizontal), the rate of change is equal to the **speed**.

> **TIP** Speed is also known as **velocity**.

Interpreting graphs

When you are asked to answer questions about a given graph, you should:
- look carefully at the labels on the axes to see what the graph represents.
- check what the units are on each of the axes.
- look to see whether the lines are straight or curved.

If the graph is straight, the rate of change is constant.
The steeper the line, the higher the rate of change.

A horizontal line represents a part of the graph where there is no change in the quantity on the vertical axis.

If the graph is a convex curve (viewed from below), the rate of change is increasing.

If the graph is a concave curve (viewed from below), the rate of change is decreasing.

EXAMPLE 15.4

The graph shows the cost of printing tickets.
(a) Find the total cost of printing 250 tickets.
(b) The cost consists of a fixed charge and an additional charge for each ticket printed.
   (i) What is the fixed charge?
   (ii) Find the additional charge for each ticket printed.
   (iii) Find the total cost of printing 800 tickets.

Solution

(a) £22 Draw a line from 250 on the Number of tickets printed axis, to meet the straight line. Then draw a horizontal line and read off the value where it meets the Cost axis.

(b) (i) £7 Read from the graph the cost of zero tickets (where the graph cuts the Cost axis).
   (ii) 250 tickets cost £22.
        Fixed charge is £7.
        So the additional charge for 250 tickets is 22 − 7 = £15.
        The additional charge per ticket is $\frac{15}{250}$ = £0.06 or 6p
   (iii) Cost in £ = 7 + number of tickets × 0.06   Work in either pounds or pence.
         Cost of 800 tickets = 7 + 800 × 0.06   If you work in pounds, you won't have to
                             = 7 + 48   convert your final answer back from pence.
                             = £55

EXERCISE 15.3

1 Jane and Halima live in the same block of flats and go to the same school.
The graphs represent their journeys home from school.
(a) Describe Halima's journey home.
(b) After how many minutes did Halima overtake Jane?
(c) Calculate Jane's speed in
   (i) kilometres per minute.
   (ii) kilometres per hour.
(d) Calculate Halima's fastest speed in
   (i) kilometres per minute.
   (ii) kilometres per hour.

Interpreting graphs

2 Anne, Britney and Catherine run a 10 km race.
Their progress is shown by the graph.

Imagine you are a commentator and give a description of the race.

3 A taxi driver charges according to the following rates.

A fixed charge of £a
+
x pence per kilometre for the first 20 km
+
40 pence for each kilometre over 20 km

The graph shows the charges for the first 20 km.

(a) What is the fixed charge, £a?
(b) Calculate x, the charge per kilometre for the first 20 km.
(c) Copy the graph and add a line segment to show the charges for distances from 20 km to 50 km.
(d) What is the total charge for a journey of 35 km?
(e) What is the average cost per kilometre for a journey of 35 km?

4 Water is poured into each of these glasses at a constant rate until they are full.

(a) (b) (c) (d)

These graphs show depth of water (d) against time (t).
Choose the most suitable graph for each glass

A   B   C   D
E   F   G   H

5 An office supplies firm advertises the following price structure for boxes of computer paper.

Number of boxes	1 to 4	5 to 9	10 or more
Price per box	£6.65	£5.50	£4.65

(a) How much do 9 boxes cost?
(b) How much do 10 boxes cost?
(c) Draw a graph to show the total cost of orders for 1 to 12 boxes.
Use a scale of 1 cm to 1 box on the horizontal axis and 2 cm to £1 on the vertical axis.

Interpreting graphs 229

6   The table shows the cost of sending first class mail.
    The graph shows the information in the first two rows in the table.

Maximum weight	First class cost
60 g	30p
100 g	46p
150 g	64p
200 g	79p
250 g	94p
300 g	£1.07

(a) What is the cost of sending a letter that weighs
   (i) 60 g?
   (ii) 60.1 g?
(b) (i) What is the meaning of the dot at the right of the lower line?
    (ii) What is the meaning of the circle at the left of the second line?
(c) Copy the graph and add lines to show the cost of sending
    first class mail weighing up to 300 g.
(d) Osman posted one letter weighing 95 g and another weighing 153 g.
    What was the total cost?

7   A water company makes the following charges for customers with a water meter.

Basic charge	£20.00
Charge per cubic metre for the first 100 cubic metres used	£1.10
Charge per cubic metre for water used over 100 cubic metres	£0.80

(a) Draw a graph to show the charge for up to 150 cubic metres.
    Use a scale of 1 cm to 10 cubic metres on the horizontal axis and 1 cm to £10 on the
    vertical axis.
(b) Customers can choose instead to pay a fixed amount of £120.
    For what amounts of water is it cheaper to have a water meter?

Challenge 15.2

The graph shows the speed (v m/s) of a train at time t seconds.

(a) What is happening between the times $t = 100$ and $t = 350$?
(b) (i) What is the rate of change between $t = 0$ and $t = 100$?
   (ii) What quantity does the rate of change represent?
   (iii) What are the units of the rate of change?
(c) (i) What is the rate of change between $t = 350$ and $t = 400$?
   (ii) What quantity does the rate of change represent?

Quadratic graphs

A **quadratic function** is a function where the highest power of x is 2.

So the function will have an x^2 term.
It may also have an x term and a numerical term.
It will *not* have a term with any other power of x.

The function $y = x^2 + 2x - 3$ is a typical quadratic function.

Check up 15.2

State whether or not each of these functions is quadratic.

(a) $y = x^2$
(b) $y = x^2 + 5x - 4$
(c) $y = \dfrac{5}{x}$
(d) $y = x^2 - 3x$
(e) $y = x^2 - 3$
(f) $y = x^3 + 5x^2 - 2$
(g) $y = x(x - 2)$

As with all graphs of functions of the form 'y = ', to plot the graph you must first choose some values of x and complete a table of values.

The simplest quadratic function is $y = x^2$.

TIP Remember that the square of a negative number is positive.

x	−3	−2	−1	0	1	2	3
$y = x^2$	9	4	1	0	1	4	9

The points can then be plotted and joined up with a smooth curve.

TIP The y scale does not have to be the same as the x scale.

TIP Turn your paper round and draw the curve from the inside. The sweep of your hand will give a smoother curve.

Draw the curve without taking your pencil away from the paper.

Look ahead to the next point as you draw the curve.

You can read off from your graph the value of y for any value of x or the value of x for any value of y.

For some quadratic graphs you may need extra rows in your table to get the final y values.

EXAMPLE 15.5

(a) Complete the table of values for $y = x^2 - 2x$.
(b) Plot the graph of $y = x^2 - 2x$.
(c) Use your graph to
  (i) find the value of y when $x = 2.6$.
  (ii) solve $x^2 - 2x = 5$.

Solution

(a)

x	-2	-1	0	1	2	3	4
x^2	4	1	0	1	4	9	16
$-2x$	4	2	0	-2	-4	-6	-8
$y = x^2 - 2x$	8	3	0	-1	0	3	8

> **TIP** The second and third rows are included in the table only to make the calculation of the y values easier: for this graph, add the numbers in the second and third rows to find the y values.
>
> The values you plot are the x values (first row) and y values (last row).

(b) $y = x^2 - 2x$

(c) (i) $y = 1.5$ Read up from $x = 2.6$.
  (ii) $x = -1.45$ or $x = 3.45$ $x^2 - 2x = 5$ means that $y = 5$.
Reading across from 5, you will see that there are two possible answers.

EXAMPLE 15.6

(a) Complete the table of values for $y = x^2 + 3x - 2$.
(b) Plot the graph of $y = x^2 + 3x - 2$.
(c) Use your graph to
   (i) find the value of y when $x = -4.3$.
   (ii) solve $x^2 + 3x - 2 = 0$.

Solution

(a)

x	−5	−4	−3	−2	−1	0	1	2
x^2	25	16	9	4	1	0	1	4
$3x$	−15	−12	−9	−6	−3	0	3	6
-2	−2	−2	−2	−2	−2	−2	−2	−2
$y = x^2 + 3x - 2$	8	2	−2	−4	−4	−2	2	8

(b)

> **TIP**
>
> The lowest y values in the table are both −4, but the actual curve goes below −4. In such situations, it is often useful to work out the coordinates of the lowest (or highest) point of the curve.
>
> Because the curve is symmetrical, the lowest point of $y = x^2 + 3x - 2$ must lie halfway between $x = -2$ and $x = -1$, that is, at $x = -1.5$.
>
> When $x = -1.5$, $y = (-1.5)^2 + 3 \times -1.5 - 2 = 2.25 - 4.5 - 2 = -4.25$.

(c) (i) $y = 3.5$ Read up from $x = -4.3$.
   (ii) $x = -3.6$ or $x = 0.6$ $x^2 + 3x - 2 = 0$ means that $y = 0$.
   Reading off the graph when $y = 0$, you will see that there are two possible answers.

All quadratic graphs are the same basic shape. This shape is called a **parabola**.

The three you have seen so far were ∪-shaped. In these graphs, the x^2 term was positive.

If the x^2 term is negative, the parabola is the other way up (∩).

> **TIP**
> If your graph is not shaped like a parabola, go back and check your table.

EXAMPLE 15.7

(a) Complete the table of values for $y = 5 - x^2$.
(b) Plot the graph of $y = 5 - x^2$.
(c) Use your graph to solve
   (i) $5 - x^2 = 0$.   (ii) $5 - x^2 = 3$.

Solution

(a)

x	−3	−2	−1	0	1	2	3
5	5	5	5	5	5	5	5
$-x^2$	−9	−4	−1	0	−1	−4	−9
$y = 5 - x^2$	−4	1	4	5	4	1	−4

(b)

(c) (i) $x = -2.25$ or $x = 2.25$ Read off at $y = 0$.
   (ii) $x = -1.4$ or $x = 1.4$ Read off at $y = 3$.

Quadratic graphs 235

EXERCISE 15.4

1 (a) Copy and complete the table of values for $y = x^2 - 2$.

x	−3	−2	−1	0	1	2	3
x^2	9					4	
−2	−2					−2	
$y = x^2 - 2$	7					2	

(b) Plot the graph of $y = x^2 - 2$.
Use a scale of 2 cm to 1 unit on the x-axis and 1 cm to 1 unit on the y-axis.

(c) Use your graph to
  (i) find the value of y when $x = 2.3$. **(ii)** solve $x^2 - 2 = 4$.

2 (a) Copy and complete the table of values for $y = x^2 - 4x$.

x	−1	0	1	2	3	4	5
x^2					9		
$-4x$					−12		
$y = x^2 - 4x$					−3		

(b) Plot the graph of $y = x^2 - 4x$.
Use a scale of 2 cm to 1 unit on the x-axis and 1 cm to 1 unit on the y-axis.

(c) Use your graph to
  (i) find the value of y when $x = 4.2$. **(ii)** solve $x^2 - 4x = -2$.

3 (a) Copy and complete the table of values for $y = x^2 + x - 3$.

x	−4	−3	−2	−1	0	1	2	3
x^2			4					
x			−2					
−3			−3					
$y = x^2 + x - 3$			−1					

(b) Plot the graph of $y = x^2 + x - 3$.
Use a scale of 2 cm to 1 unit on the x-axis and 1 cm to 1 unit on the y-axis.

(c) Use your graph to
  (i) find the value of y when $x = 0.7$. **(ii)** solve $x^2 + x - 3 = 0$.

4 (a) Make a table of values for $y = x^2 - 3x + 4$. Choose values of x from -2 to 5.
   (b) Plot the graph of $y = x^2 - 3x + 4$.
       Use a scale of 2 cm to 1 unit on the x-axis and 1 cm to 1 unit on the y-axis.
   (c) Use your graph to
       (i) find the minimum value of y.   (ii) solve $x^2 - 3x + 4 = 10$.

5 (a) Copy and complete the table of values for $y = 3x - x^2$.

x	-2	-1	0	1	2	3	4	5
$3x$				3			12	
$-x^2$				-1			-16	
$y = 3x - x^2$				2			-4	

   (b) Plot the graph of $y = 3x - x^2$.
       Use a scale of 2 cm to 1 unit on the x-axis and 1 cm to 1 unit on the y-axis.
   (c) Use your graph to
       (i) find the maximum value of y.   (ii) solve $3x - x^2 = -2$.

6 (a) Make a table of values for $y = x^2 - x - 5$. Choose values of x from -3 to 4.
   (b) Plot the graph of $y = x^2 - x - 5$.
       Use a scale of 2 cm to 1 unit on the x-axis and 1 cm to 1 unit on the y-axis.
   (c) Use your graph to solve
       (i) $x^2 - x - 5 = 0$.   (ii) $x^2 - x - 5 = 3$.

7 (a) Make a table of values for $y = 2x^2 - 5$. Choose values of x from -3 to 3.
   (b) Plot the graph of $y = 2x^2 - 5$.
       Use a scale of 2 cm to 1 unit on the x-axis and 1 cm to 1 unit on the y-axis.
   (c) Use your graph to solve
       (i) $2x^2 - 5 = 0$.   (ii) $2x^2 - 5 = 10$.

8 The total surface area (A cm^2) of this cube is given by $A = 6x^2$.
   (a) Make a table of values for $A = 6x^2$. Choose values of x from 0 to 5.
   (b) Plot the graph of $A = 6x^2$.
       Use a scale of 2 cm to 1 unit on the x-axis and 1 cm to 10 units on the A-axis.
   (c) Use your graph to find the side of a cube with surface area
       (i) 20 cm^2.   (ii) 80 cm^2.

Quadratic graphs

Challenge 15.3

The diagram shows a sheep pen. Three sides are made of fencing. A wall is used for the fourth side.

Wall

x m   *x* m

The sides of the pen are *x* metres in length.
A total of 50 metres of fencing are used.
(a) Explain why the area of the pen is given by $A = x(50 - 2x)$
(b) Make a table of values for A using 0, 5, 10, 15, 20, 25 as the values of x.
(c) Plot a graph with x on the horizontal axis and A on the vertical axis.
(d) Use your graph to find
  (i) the area of the pen when $x = 8$.
  (ii) the values of x when the area is 150 m².
  (iii) the maximum area of the pen.

WHAT YOU HAVE LEARNED

- You need only two points to draw a straight-line graph, but should always check with a third point
- When you are asked to answer questions about a given graph, look carefully at the labels and units on the axes and see whether the line is straight or curved
- A straight line represents a constant rate of change, and the steeper the line, the greater the rate of change
- A horizontal line means that there is no change in the quantity on the *y*-axis
- A convex curve (viewed from below) represents an increasing rate of change
- A concave curve (viewed from below) represents a decreasing rate of change
- The rate of change on a distance–time graph is the speed
- On a cost graph, the value where the graph cuts the cost axis is the fixed charge
- A quadratic function has x^2 as the highest power of x. It may also have an x term and a numerical term. It will not have a term with any other power of x
- The shape of all quadratic graphs is a parabola. If the x^2 term is positive the curve is U-shaped. If the x^2 term is negative the curve is ∩-shaped

MIXED EXERCISE 20

1 Draw the graph of $y = 2x - 1$ for values of x from -1 to 4.

2 Draw the graph of $2x + y - 8 = 0$ for values of x from 0 to 4.

3 The graph shows an energy supplier's quarterly charges for up to 500 kWh of electricity.
   (a) What is the cost if 350 kWh are used?
   The cost is made up of a fixed charge plus an amount per kWh of electricity used.
   (b) (i) What is the fixed charge?
   (ii) Calculate the cost per kWh in pence.

4 The same energy supplier makes a fixed charge for gas of £15 per quarter.
   In addition to this there is a charge of 2p per kWh.
   (a) Draw a graph to show the quarterly bill for up to 1500 kWh of gas used.
   Use a scale of 1 cm to 100 kWh on the horizontal axis and 2 cm to £10 on the vertical axis.
   (b) Look at this graph and the graph in question **3**.
   Which is cheaper: 400 kWh of electricity or 400 kWh of gas?
   By how much?

5 This table shows the cost of sending letters by second class post.
   (a) Look back at the graph for first class post in Exercise 15.3, question **6**.
   Draw a similar graph for second class post.
   Use a scale of 2 cm to 50 g on the horizontal axis and 1 cm to 10p on the vertical axis.
   (b) Wasim posted second class letters weighing 45 g, 60 g, 170 g, 200 g and 240 g.
   What was the total cost?

Maximum weight	Second class cost
60 g	21p
100 g	35p
150 g	47p
200 g	58p
250 g	71p
300 g	83p

6 Water is poured into these vases at a constant rate.
Sketch the graphs of depth of water (vertical) against time (horizontal).
(a)   (b)

7 The graph shows Kerry's Saturday morning shopping trip.

(a) What happened between 10 and 20 minutes after Kerry left home?
(b) How long did she spend at the shops?
(c) She caught a bus home. What was the speed of the bus?
(d) How far from Kerry's home is
   (i) the bus stop?   (ii) the shopping centre?

8 Which of these functions are quadratic?
For each of the functions that is quadratic, state whether the graph is ∪-shaped or ∩-shaped.
(a) $y = x^2 + 3x$
(b) $y = x^3 + 5x^2 + 3$
(c) $y = 5 + 3x - x^2$
(d) $y = (x + 1)(x - 3)$
(e) $y = \dfrac{4}{x^2}$
(f) $y = x^2(x + 1)$
(g) $y = x(5 - 2x)$

9 (a) Copy and complete the table of values for $y = x^2 + 3x$.

x	−5	−4	−3	−2	−1	0	1	2
x^2	25			4				4
$3x$	−15			−6				6
$y = x^2 + 3x$	10			−2				10

(b) Plot the graph of $y = x^2 + 3x$.
Use a scale of 2 cm to 1 unit on the x-axis and 1 cm to 1 unit on the y-axis.

(c) Use your graph to
  (i) find the minimum value of y.
  (ii) solve $x^2 + 3x = 3$.

10 (a) Copy and complete the table of values for $y = (x + 3)(x − 2)$.

x	−4	−3	−2	−1	0	1	2	3
$(x + 3)$			1		3			6
$(x − 2)$			−4		−2			1
$y = (x + 3)(x − 2)$			−4		−6			6

(b) Plot the graph of $y = (x + 3)(x − 2)$.
Use a scale of 2 cm to 1 unit on the x-axis and 1 cm to 1 unit on the y-axis.

(c) Use your graph to
  (i) find the minimum value of y.
  (ii) solve $(x + 3)(x − 2) = −2$.

11 (a) Make a table of values for $y = x^2 − 2x − 1$. Choose values of x from −2 to 4.
(b) Plot the graph of $y = x^2 − 2x − 1$.
Use a scale of 2 cm to 1 unit on the x-axis and 1 cm to 1 unit on the y-axis.
(c) Use your graph to solve
  (i) $x^2 − 2x − 1 = 0$.
  (ii) $x^2 − 2x − 1 = 4$.

12 (a) Make a table of values for $y = 5x − x^2$. Choose values of x from −1 to 6.
(b) Plot the graph of $y = 5x − x^2$.
Use a scale of 2 cm to 1 unit on the x-axis and 1 cm to 1 unit on the y-axis.
(c) Use your graph to
  (i) solve $5x − x^2 = 3$.
  (ii) find the maximum value of y.

16 ➔ MEASURES

> **THIS CHAPTER IS ABOUT**
> - Converting between measures, especially measures of area and volume
> - Accuracy of measurement
> - Giving answers to a sensible degree of accuracy
> - Using compound measures such as speed and density

> **YOU SHOULD ALREADY KNOW**
> - The common metric units for length, area, volume and capacity

Converting between measures

You already know the basic **linear** relationships between metric measures. Linear means 'of length'.

You can use these relationships to work out the relationships between metric units of area and volume.

For example:

1 cm = 10 mm   1 m = 100 cm

1 cm^2 = 1 cm × 1 cm   1 m^2 = 1 m × 1 m
1 cm^2 = 10 mm × 10 mm   1 m^2 = 100 cm × 100 cm
1 cm^2 = 100 mm^2 1 m^2 = 10 000 cm^2

1 cm^3 = 1 cm × 1 cm × 1 cm   1 m^3 = 1 m × 1 m × 1 m
1 cm^3 = 10 mm × 10 mm × 10 mm   1 m^3 = 100 cm × 100 cm × 100 cm
1 cm^3 = 1000 mm^3 1 m^3 = 1 000 000 cm^3

EXAMPLE 16.1

Change these units.
(a) 5 m^3 to cm^3
(b) 5600 cm^2 to m^2

242 16 Measures

Solution

(a) $5 \text{ m}^3 = 5 \times 1\,000\,000 \text{ cm}^3$
  $= 5\,000\,000 \text{ cm}^3$

Convert 1 m³ to cm³ and multiply by 5.

(b) $5600 \text{ cm}^2 = 5600 \div 10\,000 \text{ m}^2$
  $= 0.56 \text{ m}^2$

To convert m² to cm² you multiply, so to convert cm² to m² you divide. Make sure you have done the right thing by checking your answer makes sense. If you had multiplied by 10 000 you would have got 56 000 000 m², which is obviously a much larger area than 5600 cm².

EXERCISE 16.1

1 Change these units.
  (a) 25 m to cm
  (b) 42 cm to mm
  (c) 2.36 m to cm
  (d) 5.1 m to mm

2 Change these units.
  (a) 3 m² to cm²
  (b) 2.3 cm² to mm²
  (c) 9.52 m² to cm²
  (d) 0.014 cm² to mm²

3 Change these units.
  (a) 90 000 mm² to cm²
  (b) 8140 mm² to cm²
  (c) 7 200 000 cm² to m²
  (d) 94 000 cm² to m²

4 Change these units.
  (a) 3.2 m³ to cm³
  (b) 42 cm³ to m³
  (c) 5000 cm³ to m³
  (d) 6.42 m³ to cm³

5 Change these units.
  (a) 2.61 litres to cm³
  (b) 9500 ml to litres
  (c) 2.4 litres to ml
  (d) 910 ml to litres

6 What is wrong with this statement?

  The trench I have just dug is 5 m long, 2 m wide and 50 cm deep.
  To fill it in, I would need 500 m³ of concrete.

7 A pane of glass measures 32 cm by 65 cm and is 0.3 cm thick.
  What is the volume of the glass?

Challenge 16.1

Cleopatra is reputed to have had a bath filled with asses' milk.
Today her bath might be filled with cola!

Assuming a can of drink holds 33 centilitres, approximately how many cans would she need to have a bath in cola?

Converting between measures 243

Accuracy in measurement

All measurements are **approximations**. Measurements are given to the nearest practical unit.

Measuring a value to the nearest unit means deciding that it is nearer to one mark on a scale than another; in other words, that the value is within half a unit of that mark.

Look at this diagram.

```
├──┼──┼──┼──┼──┼──┼──┼──┼──┼──┼──┼──┤
4         4.5        5        5.5        6
```

Any value within the shaded area is 5 to the nearest unit.

The boundaries for this interval are 4.5 and 5.5. This would be written as $4.5 \leq x < 5.5$.

> **TIP**
>
> Remember that $4.5 \leq x < 5.5$ means all values, x, which are greater than or equal to 4.5 but less than 5.5.
>
> $x < 5.5$ because if $x = 5.5$ it would round up to 6.
> Even though x cannot equal 5.5, it can be as close to it as you like. So 5.5 is the upper bound. Do not use 5.499 or 5.4999, etc.

4.5 is the lower bound and 5.5 the upper bound.

Any value less than 4.5 is closer to 4 (4 to the nearest unit).
Any value greater than or equal to 5.5 is closer to 6 (6 to the nearest unit).

EXAMPLE 16.2

(a) Tom won the 100 m race with a time of 12.2 seconds, to the nearest tenth of a second.
What are the upper and lower bounds for this time?

(b) Copy and complete this statement.

> A mass given as 46 kg, to the nearest kilogram, lies between .... kg and .... kg.

Solution

(a) Lower bound = 12.15 seconds, upper bound = 12.25 seconds

(b) A mass given as 46 kg, to the nearest kilogram, lies between 45.5 kg and 46.5 kg.

EXERCISE 16.2

1 Copy and complete each of these statements.
  (a) A height given as 57 m, to the nearest metre, is between .... m and .... m.
  (b) A volume given as 568 ml, to the nearest millilitre, is between .... ml and .... ml.
  (c) A winning time given as 23.93 seconds, to the nearest hundredth of a second, is between .... seconds and .... seconds.

2 Copy and complete each of these statements.
  (a) A mass given as 634 g, to the nearest gram, is between .... g and .... g.
  (b) A volume given as 234 ml, to the nearest millilitre, is between .... ml and .... ml.
  (c) A height given as 8.3 m, to 1 decimal place, is between .... m and .... m.

3

> **Gloss Paint**
> Coverage from 7 to 8 square metres depending on surface
> 750 ml

  (a) What is the least and greatest surface area that 3 litres of the paint will cover?
  (b) How many cans of paint are needed to ensure coverage of an area of 100 m²?

4 Jessica measures the thickness of a metal sheet with a gauge.
The reading is 4.97 mm, accurate to the nearest $\frac{1}{100}$th of a millimetre.
  (a) What is the minimum thickness the sheet could be?
  (b) What is the maximum thickness the sheet could be?

5 Gina is fitting a new kitchen.
She has an oven which is 595 mm wide, to the nearest millimetre.
Will it definitely fit in a gap which is 60 cm wide, to the nearest centimetre?

6 Two metal blocks are placed together as shown.
The left-hand block is 6.3 cm long and the right-hand block is 8.7 cm.
Both blocks are 2 cm wide and 2 cm deep.
All measurements are correct to the nearest millimetre.
  (a) What is the least and greatest combined length of the two blocks?
  (b) What is the least and greatest depth of the blocks?
  (c) What is the least and greatest width of the blocks?

7 A company manufactures components for the car industry.
One component consists of a metal block with a hole drilled
into it. A plastic rod is fixed into the hole.

The hole is drilled to a depth of 20 mm, to the nearest millimetre.
The length of the rod is 35 mm, to the nearest millimetre.
What are the maximum and minimum values of d (the height of the rod above the block)?

8 The diagram shows a rectangle, ABCD.
AB = 15 cm and BC = 9 cm.
All measurements are correct to the nearest centimetre.
Work out the least and greatest values for the perimeter
of rectangle.

Working to a sensible degree of accuracy

Measurements and calculations should not be too accurate for their purpose.

It is obviously silly to claim that:
    a car journey took 4 hours, 56 minutes and 13 seconds.
or the distance between 2 houses is 93 kilometres, 484 metres and
    78 centimetres.

Answers such as these would be more sensible rounded to 5 hours and 93 km respectively.

When calculating a measurement, you need to give your answer to a **sensible degree of accuracy**.
As a general rule your final answer should not be given to a greater degree of accuracy than any of the values used in the calculation.

EXAMPLE 16.3

A table is 1.8 m long and 1.3 m wide. Both measurements are correct to
1 decimal place.

Work out the area of the table.
Give your answer to a sensible degree of accuracy.

Solution

Area = length × width
     = 1.8 × 1.3
     = 2.34   The answer has 2 decimal places.
     = 2.3 m² (to 1 d.p.) However, the answer cannot be more accurate
                                 than the original measurements. So you need to
                                 round the answer to 1 decimal place.

EXERCISE 16.3

1 Rewrite each of these statements using sensible values for the measurements.
   (a) It takes 3 minutes and 24.8 seconds to boil an egg.
   (b) It will take me 2 weeks, 5 days, 3 hours and 13 minutes to paint your house.
   (c) Helen's favourite book weighs 2.853 kg.
   (d) The height of the classroom door is 2 metres, 12 centimetres and 54 millimetres.

2 Give your answer to each of these questions to a sensible degree of accuracy.
   (a) Find the length of the side of a square field whose area is 33 m^2.
   (b) Three friends win £48.32. How much will each receive?
   (c) It takes 1.2 hours to fly between two cities at 554 km/h.
   How far apart are they?
   (d) A strip of card is 2.36 cm long and 0.041 cm wide.
   Calculate the area of the card.

Challenge 16.2

The health provision in different countries can be compared using various measures.

One measure uses the number of doctors per million people.
Another measure is the number of under-one-year-olds who died per 1000 live births.

Use this table, showing figures from 1990, to compare the health provision in these countries.

Country	Population (millions)	Total number of doctors	Live births in a year	Infant deaths in a year
Brazil	169.8	14 500	3 550 000	131 300
China	1237	1 040 000	19 500 000	885 000
Somalia	6.8	350	318 000	40 000
UK	59	95 300	708 000	6400

Compound measures

Some measures are calculated using the same type of measurements.
Area, for example, is calculated using length and width, which are both measures of length.

Compound measures are calculated using two different types of measure.
Speed is calculated using distance and time.

$$\text{Speed} = \frac{\text{Distance}}{\text{Time}}$$

Compound measures are written with **compound units**.
The units for speed are written in the form distance per time. For example, if the distance is in kilometres and the time is in hours, speed is written as kilometres per hour, or km/h.

Another compound measure is **density**. Density is linked to **mass** and **volume**.

$$\text{Density} = \frac{\text{Mass}}{\text{Volume}}$$

EXAMPLE 16.4

(a) Calculate the average speed of a car travelling 80 km in 2 hours.
(b) Gold has a density of 19.3 g/cm³.
   Calculate the mass of a gold bar with a volume of 30 cm³.

Solution

(a) $\text{Speed} = \frac{\text{Distance}}{\text{Time}}$

$= \frac{80}{2} = 40$ km/h

(b) $\text{Density} = \frac{\text{Mass}}{\text{Volume}}$ First rearrange the formula to make Mass the subject.

Mass = Density × Volume
= 19.3 × 30 = 579 g

EXERCISE 16.4

1. A train covers a distance of 1250 metres in a time of 20 seconds.
   Calculate its average speed.

2. Caroline's car travels 129 miles in 3 hours. Calculate her average speed.

3. Paula jogs at a steady 6 miles per hour.
   How far does she run in one and a quarter hours?

4 How long will it take a boat sailing at 12 km/h to travel 60 km?

5 The density of aluminium is 2.7 g/cm³. What is the volume of a block of aluminium with a mass of 750 g? Give your answer to the nearest whole number.

6 Find the average speed of a car which travelled 150 miles in two and a half hours.

7 Calculate the density of a rock of mass 780 g and volume 84 cm³.
Give your answer to a suitable degree of accuracy.

8 A car travels 20 km in 12 minutes. What is the average speed in km/h?

9 Calculate the density of a stone of mass 350 g and volume 45 cm³.

10 (a) Calculate the density of a 3 cm³ block of copper of mass 26.7 g.
 (b) What would be the mass of a 17 cm³ block of copper?

11 Gold has a density of 19.3 g/cm³. Calculate the mass of a gold bar of volume 1000 cm³.
Give your answer in kilograms.

12 Air at normal room temperature and pressure has a density of 1.3 kg/m³.
 (a) What mass of air is there in a room which is a cuboid measuring 3 m by 5 m by 3 m?
 (b) What volume of air would have a mass of
  (i) 1 kg? (ii) 1 tonne?

13 (a) Find the speed of a car which travels 75 km in 1 hour 15 minutes.
 (b) A car travels 15 km in 14 minutes. Find its speed in km/h.
  Give your answer correct to 1 decimal place.

14 Calculate the density of a stone of mass 730 g and volume 69 cm³.
Give your answer correct to 1 decimal place.

15 A town has a population of 74 000 and covers an area of 64 square kilometres.
Calculate the population density (number of people per square kilometre) of the town.
Give your answer correct to 1 decimal place.

WHAT YOU HAVE LEARNED

- **How to convert between metric measures of length, area and volume**
- **That all measurements are approximations**
- **When calculating a measurement, you need to give your answer to a sensible degree of accuracy. As a general rule your final answer should not be given to a greater degree of accuracy than any of the values used in the calculation**
- **Compound measures are calculated from two other measurements. Examples include speed, which is calculated using distance and time and expressed in units such as m/s, and density, which is calculated using mass and volume and expressed in units such as g/cm³**

MIXED EXERCISE 16

1 Change these units.
 (a) 12 m² to cm²
 (b) 3.71 cm² to mm²
 (c) 0.42 m² to cm²
 (d) 0.05 cm² to mm²

2 Change these units.
 (a) 3 m² to mm²
 (b) 412 500 cm² to m²
 (c) 9400 mm² to cm²
 (d) 0.06 m² to cm²

3 Change these units.
 (a) 2.13 litres to cm³
 (b) 5100 ml to litres
 (c) 421 litres to ml
 (d) 91.7 ml to litre

4 Give the lower and upper bounds of each of these measurements.
 (a) 27 cm to the nearest centimetre
 (b) 5.6 cm to the nearest millimetre
 (c) 1.23 m to the nearest centimetre

5 A policeman timed a car travelling along a 100 m section of road.
 The time taken was 6 seconds.
 The length of the road was measured accurate to the nearest 10 cm, and the time was measured accurate to the nearest second.
 What is the greatest speed the car could have been travelling at?

6 (a) A machine produces pieces of wood.
 The length of each piece measures 34 mm, correct to the nearest millimetre.
 Between what limits does the actual length lie?
 (b) Three of the pieces of wood are put together to make a triangle.
 What is the greatest possible perimeter of the triangle?

7 In a 10 km road race, one runner started at 11:48 and finished at 13:03.
 (a) How long did it take this runner to complete the race?
 (b) What was his average speed?

8 (a) Eleanor drives to Birmingham on a motorway.
 She travels 150 miles in 2 hours 30 minutes. What is her average speed?
 (b) Eleanor drives to Cambridge at an average speed of 57 mph.
 The journey takes 3 hours 20 minutes. How many miles is the journey?

9 The length of a field is 92.43 m and the width is 58.36 m.
 Calculate the area of the field.
 Give your answer to a sensible degree of accuracy.

17 → PLANNING AND COLLECTING

THIS CHAPTER IS ABOUT

- Posing statistical questions and planning how to answer them
- Primary and secondary data
- Choosing a sample and eliminating bias
- The advantages and problems of random samples
- Designing a questionnaire
- Collecting data
- Writing a statistical report

YOU SHOULD ALREADY KNOW

- How to make and use tally charts
- How to calculate the mean, median, mode and range
- How to draw diagrams to represent data, such as bar charts, pie charts and frequency diagrams

Statistical questions

Discovery 17.1

Are boys taller than girls?

Discuss how you could begin to answer this question.
- What information would you need to collect?
- How would you collect it?
- How would you analyse the results?
- How would you present the information in your report?

To answer a question using statistical methods, the first thing you need to do is make a written plan.

You need to decide which statistical calculations and diagrams are relevant to the problem. You should think about this before you start collecting data, so that you can collect it in a useful form.

It is a good idea to rewrite the question as a **hypothesis**. This is a statement such as 'boys are taller than girls'. Your report should present evidence either for or against your hypothesis.

> **TIP**
> If you are choosing your own problem, make sure there is more than one aspect to it that you can explore. This will help you to get higher marks.

Different types of data

When you investigate a statistical problem such as 'boys are taller than girls', there are two types of data which you can use.

- **Primary data** are data which you collect yourself. For example, you could measure the heights of a group of girls and boys.
- **Secondary data** are data which someone else has already collected. For example, you could use the internet database CensusAtSchool, which has a large number of students' heights already collected. Other sources of secondary data include books and newspapers.

Data samples

Most statistical investigations do not have a definite, obvious answer. For example, some girls are taller than some boys, and some boys are taller than some girls. What you are trying to find out is whether girls or boys are taller most often. You cannot measure the heights of all boys and all girls, but you can measure the heights of a group of boys and girls and answer the question for that group. In statistics, a group like this is called a **sample**.

The size of your sample is important. If your sample is too small, the results may not be very reliable. In general, the sample size needs to be at least 30. If your sample is too large, the data may take a long time to collect and analyse. You need to decide what is a reasonable sample size for the hypothesis you are investigating.

You also need to eliminate **bias**. A biased sample is unreliable because it means that certain results are more likely. For example, if all the boys in your sample were members of a basketball team, your data might appear to show that boys are taller than girls but the results would be unreliable because basketball players are often of above average height.

It is often a good idea to use a **random** sample, where every person or piece of data has an equal chance of being selected. You may want, however, to make sure that your sample has certain characteristics. For example, random sampling within the whole school could mean that all the boys selected happen to be in Year 7 and all the girls in Year 11: this would be a biased sample, as older children tend to be taller. So you may instead want to use random sampling to select five girls and five boys from within each year group.

Random numbers can be generated by your calculator or a spreadsheet. To select a random sample of five girls from Year 7, for example, you could allocate a random number to each Year 7 girl and then select the five girls with the smallest random numbers.

When you write your report, include reasons for your choice of sample.

EXAMPLE 17.1

Candace is doing a survey about school meals. She asks every tenth person going into lunch.

Why may this not be a good method of sampling?

Solution

She will not get the opinions of those who dislike school meals and have stopped having them.

Discovery 17.2

A borough council wants to survey public opinion about its library facilities.
How should it choose a sample of people to ask?
Discuss the advantages and disadvantages of each method you suggest.

When you collect large amounts of data, you may need to group it in order to analyse it or to present it clearly. It is usually best to use equal class widths for this. Tally charts are a good way of obtaining a frequency table, or you can use a spreadsheet or other statistics program to help you. Before you collect your data, make sure you design a suitable data collection sheet or spreadsheet. Two-way tables are often useful for both recording and presenting your data.

Designing a questionnaire

A **questionnaire** is often a good way of collecting data.

You need to think carefully about what information you need and how you will analyse the answers to each question. This will help you get the data in the form you need.

For instance, if you are investigating the hypothesis 'boys are taller than girls', you need to know a person's sex as well as their height. If you know their age as well you can find out whether your hypothesis is true for all ages of boys and girls. The data can be organised in a two-way table. However, asking people their height would probably not be the best way of finding this information – you would be more likely to get reliable results if you asked whether you could measure their height.

Here are some points to bear in mind when you design a questionnaire.
- Make the questions short, clear and relevant to your task.
- Only ask one thing at a time.
- Make sure your questions are not 'leading' questions. Leading questions show bias. They 'lead' the person answering them towards a particular answer: for example, 'do you agree that the cruel sport of fox-hunting should be illegal?'
- If you give a choice of answers, make sure there are neither too few nor too many.

EXAMPLE 17.2

Suggest a sensible way of asking an adult their age.

Solution

Please tick your age-group:

☐ 18–25 years   ☐ 26–30 years   ☐ 31–40 years
☐ 41–50 years   ☐ 51–60 years   ☐ Over 60 years

This means that the person does not have to tell you their exact age, which many adults don't like doing.

When you have written your questionnaire, test it out on a few people. This is called doing a **pilot survey**. Try also to analyse the data from this pilot, so that you can check whether it is possible. You may then wish to reword one or two questions, regroup your data, or change your method of sampling, before you do the proper survey.

If you encounter practical problems in collecting your data, describe them in your report.

Discovery 17.3

- Think of a survey topic about school lunches. Make sure that it is relevant to your own school or college. For instance, you may wish to test the hypothesis 'fish and chips is the favourite meal'.
- Write some suitable questions for a survey to test your hypothesis.
- Try them out in a pilot survey. Discuss the results and how you could improve your questions.

Writing up your report

Your report should begin with a clear statement of your aims and end with a conclusion. Your conclusion will depend on the results of the statistical calculations you have done with your data and on any differences or similarities illustrated by your statistical diagrams. Throughout the report, you should give your reasons for what you have done and describe any difficulties you encountered, and how you dealt with them.

Use this checklist to make sure that the whole project is clear.
- Use statistical terms whenever possible.
- Make sure you include a written plan.
- Explain how you selected your sample and why you chose to select it that way.

- Show how you found your data.
- Say why you have chosen to draw a particular diagram or table, and what it shows.
- Relate your findings back to the original problem. Have you proved or disproved your hypothesis?
- Aim to extend the original problem, using ideas of your own.

EXERCISE 17.1

1. State whether the following are primary data or secondary data.
   (a) Measuring people's foot length
   (b) Using school records of students' ages
   (c) A librarian using a library catalogue to enter new books on the system
   (d) A borrower using a library catalogue

2. A borough council wants to survey public opinion about the local swimming pool. Give one disadvantage of each of the following sampling situations.
   (a) Selecting people to ring at random from the local phone directory.
   (b) Asking people who are shopping on Saturday morning.

3. Paul plans to ask 50 people at random how long they spent doing homework yesterday evening.
   Here is the first draft of his data collection sheet.

Time spent	Tally	Frequency
Up to 1 hour		
1–2 hours		
2–3 hours		

   Give two ways in which Paul could improve his collection sheet.

4. For each of these survey questions
   - state what is wrong with it.
   - write a better version.
   (a) What is your favourite sport: cricket, tennis or athletics?
   (b) Do you do lots of exercise each week?
   (c) Don't you think this government should encourage more people to recycle waste?

5. Janine is doing a survey about how often people have a meal out in a restaurant.
   Here are two questions she has written.
   Q1. How often do you eat out?
   ☐ A lot   ☐ Sometimes   ☐ Never
   Q2. What food did you eat the last time you ate out?
   (a) Give a reason why each of these questions is unsuitable.
   (b) Write a better version of Q1.

6 Design a questionnaire to investigate use of the school library or resource centre.
   You need to know
   - which year group the student is in.
   - how often they use the library.
   - how many books they usually borrow on each visit.

   Design two-way tables to show how you could organise the data.

> **WHAT YOU HAVE LEARNED**
>
> - **Primary data are data which you collect yourself**
> - **Secondary data are data which someone else has already collected, and are found in books or on the internet, for example**
> - **You need to plan how to find evidence for or against your hypothesis, giving evidence of your planning**
> - **Avoid bias when sampling**
> - **In a random sample, every member of the population being considered has an equal chance of being selected**
> - **Make sure the size of the sample is sensible**
> - **In a questionnaire, questions should be short, clear and relevant to your task**
> - **You can do a pilot survey to test out a questionnaire or data collection sheet**
> - **In your report, you should give reasons for what you have done and relate your conclusions back to the original problem, saying whether your hypothesis has been shown to be correct or not**

MIXED EXERCISE 17

1 Jan uses train times from the internet.
   Are these data primary or secondary? Give a reason for your answer.

2 Ali wants to test the hypothesis 'older students at secondary school are better at estimating angles than younger ones'.
   (a) What could he ask people to do in order to test this hypothesis?
   (b) How should he choose a suitable sample of people?
   (c) Design a collection sheet for Ali to record his data.

3 Write three suitable questions for a questionnaire asking a sample of people about their favourite music or musicians.
   If you use questions without given categories for responses, show also how you would group the responses to the questions when analysing the data.

18 SEQUENCES

> **THIS CHAPTER IS ABOUT**
> - Using rules to find terms of sequences
> - Seeing patterns in sequences
> - Explaining how you have found another term in a sequence
> - Recognising common integer sequences such as square or triangular numbers
> - Finding the nth term of a linear sequence

> **YOU SHOULD ALREADY KNOW**
> - How to find terms of simple sequences using term-to-term rules and position-to-term rules

Using rules to find terms of sequences

You already know how to find the next **term** in a **sequence**.

For example, for this sequence: 3, 8, 13, 18, 23, 28, … ,

you find the next term by adding 5.

This is known as the **term-to-term** rule.

You also know how to find a term given its **position** in the sequence using a **position-to-term** rule.

For example, for the sequence: 3, 8, 13, 18, 23, 28, … ,
taking the position number (n), multiplying it by 5 and then subtracting 2 gives the term.

The term-to-term rule and position-to-term rule for any sequence can be expressed as formulae using the following notation.

T_1 represents the first term of a sequence,
T_2 represents the second term of a sequence,
T_3 represents the third term of a sequence,
and so on.

T_n represents the nth term of a sequence.

EXAMPLE 18.1

Marie makes some matchstick patterns. Here are her first three patterns.

To get the next pattern from the previous one, Marie adds three more matchsticks to complete another square.

She makes this table.

Pattern	1	2	3
Number of matchsticks	4	7	10

(a) Find the term-to-term rule.
(b) Find the position-to-term rule.

Solution

(a) First find the rule in words.

The first term is 4.   You must always state the value of the first
To find the next term, add 3.   term when giving a term-to-term rule.

Then write the rule using the notation.

$T_1 = 4$
$T_{n+1} = T_n + 3$ Add 3 to each term to find the next one.
  For example, $T_4 = T_3 + 3$
   $= 10 + 3 = 13$

(b) First find the rule in words.

Taking the position number (n), multiplying it by 3 and then adding 1 gives the term.

Then write the rule using the notation.

nth term $= 3n + 1$
or $T_n = 3n + 1$ For example, $T_4 = 3 \times 4 + 1$
   $= 12 + 1 = 13$

EXAMPLE 18.2

For a sequence, $T_1 = 10$ and $T_{n+1} = T_n - 4$.
Find the first four terms of the sequence.

Solution

$T_1 = 10$ $T_2 = T_1 - 4$ $T_3 = T_2 - 4$ $T_4 = T_3 - 4$
     $= 10 - 4$ $= 6 - 4$ $= 2 - 4$
     $= 6$ $= 2$ $= -2$

The first four terms are 10, 6, 2 and -2.

A position-to-term rule is very useful if you need to find a term a long way into the sequence, such as the 100th term. It means that you can find it straight away without having to find the previous 99 terms as you would using a term-to-term rule.

EXAMPLE 18.3

The nth term of a sequence is $5n + 1$.
(a) Find the first four terms of the sequence.
(b) Find the 100th term of the sequence.

Solution

(a) $T_1 = 5 \times 1 + 1$ $T_2 = 5 \times 2 + 1$ $T_3 = 5 \times 3 + 1$ $T_4 = 5 \times 4 + 1$
    $= 6$ $= 11$ $= 16$ $= 21$
The first four terms are 6, 11, 16 and 21.

(b) $T_{100} = 5 \times 100 + 1$
    $= 501$

EXERCISE 18.1

1. Look at this sequence of circles. The first four patterns in the sequence have been drawn.
   (a) Describe the position-to-term rule for this sequence.
   (b) How many circles are there in the 100th pattern?

2. Look at this sequence of matchstick patterns.
   (a) Copy and complete the table.

Pattern number	1	2	3	4	5
Number of matchsticks					

   (b) What patterns can you see in the numbers?
   (c) Find the number of matchsticks in the 50th pattern.

3. Here is a sequence of star patterns.
   (a) Draw the next pattern in the sequence.
   (b) Without drawing the pattern, find the number of stars in the 8th pattern. Explain how you found your answer.

Using rules to find terms of sequences

4 The numbers in a sequence are given by this rule:

Multiply the position number by 3, then subtract 5.

(a) Show that the first term of the sequence is −2.
(b) Find the next four terms in the sequence.

5 Find the first four terms of the sequences with these nth terms.
(a) $6n - 2$ (b) $4n + 1$ (c) $6 - 2n$

6 Find the first five terms of the sequences with these nth terms.
(a) n^2 (b) $n^2 + 2$ (c) n^3

7 The first term of a sequence is 2.
The general rule for the sequence is multiply a term by 2 to get to the next term.
Write down the first five terms of the sequence.

8 For a sequence, $T_1 = 5$ and $T_{n+1} = T_n - 3$.
Write down the first four terms of the sequence.

9 Draw suitable patterns to represent this sequence.

1, 5, 9, 13, …

10 Draw suitable patterns to represent this sequence.

1, 4, 9, 16, …

Challenge 18.1

Work in pairs.

Find as many different sequences as you can where $T_1 = 1$ and $T_2 = 3$

For each one, write down the first four terms on a separate piece of paper.
On the back of the paper, write the rule you have used.

Swap a sequence with your partner.
Try to find each other's rule.

Finding the nth term of a linear sequence

Look at this linear sequence.

4   9   14   19   24   …
 +5   +5   +5   +5

To get from one term to the next, you add 5 each time.

18 Sequences

Another way of saying this is that there is a **common difference** between the terms, 5.

A sequence like this, which has a common difference, is called a **linear sequence**.

If you plot the terms of a linear sequence on a graph, you get a straight line.

Term (n)	1	2	3	4	5
Value (y)	4	9	14	19	24

As 5 is added each time,

$$T_2 = T_1 + 5$$
$$= 4 + 5$$
$$T_3 = 4 + 5 \times 2$$
$$T_4 = 4 + 5 \times 3, \text{ etc.}$$

So $\quad T_n = 4 + 5(n - 1)$
$\quad\quad\quad = 5n - 1$

The nth term of this sequence is $5n - 1$.

Now look at some of the other linear sequences we have met so far in this chapter:

Sequence	Common difference	First term − Common difference	nth term
4, 7, 10, 13, …	3	$4 - 3 = 1$	$3n + 1$
6, 11, 16, 21, …	5	$6 - 5 = 1$	$5n + 1$
10, 6, 4, −2, …	−4	$10 - (-4) = 14$	$-4n + 14$
2, 4, 6, 8, …	2	$2 - 2 = 0$	$2n$
4, 10, 16, 22, …	6	$4 - 6 = -2$	$6n - 2$

Looking at the patterns in the table, you can see some evidence for this formula.

$$n\text{th term of a linear sequence} =$$
$$\text{Common difference} \times n + (\text{First term} - \text{Common difference})$$

This can be written as

$$n\text{th term} = An + b$$

where A represents the common difference and b is the first term minus A.

You can also find b by comparing An with any term in the sequence.

Finding the nth term of a linear sequence 261

EXAMPLE 18.4

Find the nth term of this sequence: 4, 7, 10, 13, ...

Solution

4   7   10   13   ...
 +3 +3   +3

The common difference (A) is 3, so the formula contains $3n$.

When $n = 1$, $3n = 3$. The first term is actually 4, which is 1 more. So the nth term is $3n + 1$.

You can check your answer using a different term.

When $n = 2$, $3n = 6$. The second term is actually 7, which is 1 more. This confirms that the nth term is $3n + 1$.

You can use sequences and position-to-term rules to solve problems.

EXAMPLE 18.5

Lucy has ten CDs. She decides to buy three more CDs each month.

(a) Copy and complete the table to show the number of CDs Lucy has after each of the first four months.

Number of months	1	2	3	4
Number of CDs				

(b) Find the formula for the number of CDs she will have after n months.

(c) After how many months will Lucy have 58 CDs?

Solution

(a)

Number of months	1	2	3	4
Number of CDs	13	16	19	22

(b) nth term $= An + b$
$A = 3$ A is the common difference.
$b = 10$ b is the first term minus the common difference.
nth term $= 3n + 10$

(c) $3n + 10 = 58$ Solve the equation to find n when the nth term is 58.
    $3n = 48$
    $n = 16$
Lucy will have 58 CDs after 16 months.

Some special sequences

You have already met some special sequences in the examples and Exercise 18.1.

Discovery 18.1

Look at each of these sequences.

Even numbers   2, 4, 6, 8, ...
Odd numbers   1, 3, 5, 7, ...
Multiples of 4   4, 8, 12, 16, ...
Powers of 2   2, 4, 8, 16, ...
Square numbers   1, 4, 9, 16, ...
Triangular numbers 1, 3, 6, 10, ...

Look for different patterns in each of the sequences.

(a) Describe the term-to-term rule.
(b) Describe the position-to-term rule.

For triangular numbers, you may find it helpful to look at these diagrams.

Finding the nth term of a linear sequence

EXERCISE 18.2

1 Find the nth term for each of these sequences.
(a) 5, 7, 9, 11, 13, ...
(b) 2, 5, 8, 11, 14, ...
(c) 7, 8, 9, 10, 11, ...

2 Find the nth term for each of these sequences.
(a) 17, 14, 11, 8, 5, ...
(b) 5, 0, −5, −10, −15, ...
(c) 0, −1, −2, −3, −4, ...

3 Which of these sequences are linear?
Find the next two terms of each of the sequences that are linear.
(a) 5, 8, 11, 14, ...
(b) 2, 4, 7, 11, ...
(c) 6, 12, 18, 24, ...
(d) 2, 6, 18, 54, ...

4 (a) Write the first five terms of the sequence with nth term $12 - 6n$.
(b) Write the nth term of this sequence: 8, 2, −4, −10, −16, ...

5 A theatre agency charges £15 per ticket, plus an overall booking charge of £2.
(a) Copy and complete the table.

Number of tickets	1	2	3	4
Cost in £				

(b) Write an expression for the cost, in pounds, of n tickets.
(c) Jenna pays £107 for her tickets. How many does she buy?

6 Write down the first ten triangular numbers.

7 The nth triangular number is $\dfrac{n(n+1)}{2}$. Find the 20th triangular number.

8 The nth term of a sequence is 10^n.
(a) Write down the first five terms of this sequence.
(b) Describe this sequence.

9 (a) Write down the first five square numbers.
(b) (i) Compare the following sequence with the sequence of square numbers.
    4, 7, 12, 19, 28, ...
(ii) Write down the nth term of this sequence.
(iii) Find the 100th term of this sequence.

10 (a) Compare the following sequence with the sequence of square numbers.
    3, 12, 27, 48, 75, ...
(b) Write down the nth term of this sequence.
(c) Find the 20th term of this sequence.

Challenge 18.2

Work in pairs.

You are going to use a spreadsheet to explore sequences. Don't let your partner see you input your formula. Make sure that they can't see the formula on the computer screen: click on View in the toolbar and make sure the Formula Bar is not checked.

1 Open a new spreadsheet.
2 Enter the number 1 in cell A1.
   Click on cell A1, and hold down the mouse key and drag down the column. Then click on Edit in the toolbar and select Fill, then Series to call up the Series dialogue box. Make sure that the Columns and Linear boxes are checked and that the Step value is 1. Click OK.
3 Enter a formula in cell B1. For example, **=A1*3+5** or **=A1^2**. Press the enter key.
   Click on cell B1, click on Edit in the toolbar and select Copy.
   Click on cell B2, and hold down the mouse key and drag down the column. Then click on Edit in the toolbar and select Paste.
4 Ask your partner to try to work out the formula and generate the same sequence in column C.

If you have time, you could explore some non-linear sequences as well. For example, enter the formula **=A1^2+A1**.

WHAT YOU HAVE LEARNED

- Sequences may be described by a list of numbers, diagrams in a pattern, a term-to-term rule (for example, $T_{n+1} = T_n + 3$ when $T_1 = 4$) or a position-to-term rule (for example, nth term = $3n + 1$ or $T_n = 3n + 1$)
- The nth term of a linear sequence = $An + b$, where A is the common difference and b is the first term minus A
- Here are some important sequences.

Name	Sequence	nth term	Term-to-term rule
Even numbers	2, 4, 6, 8, …	$2n$	Add 2
Odd numbers	1, 3, 5, 7, …	$2n - 1$	Add 2
Multiples e.g. multiples of 6	6, 12, 18, 24, …	$6n$	Add 6
Powers of 2	2, 4, 8, 16, …	2^n	Multiply by 2
Square numbers	1, 4, 9, 16, …	n^2	Add 3 then 5 then 7, etc. (the odd numbers)
Triangular numbers	1, 3, 6, 10, …	$\dfrac{n(n + 1)}{2}$	Add 2 then 3 then 4, etc. (consecutive integers)

Finding the nth term of a linear sequence

MIXED EXERCISE 18

1 Look at this sequence of circles. The first four patterns in the sequence have been drawn.

  (a) How many circles are there in the 100th pattern?
  (b) Describe a rule for this sequence.

2 Here is a sequence of star patterns.
  (a) Draw the next pattern in the sequence.
  (b) Without drawing the pattern, find the number of stars in the 8th pattern. Explain how you found your answer.

3 The numbers in a sequence are given by this rule:

  Multiply the position number by 6, then subtract 2.

  (a) Show that the first term of the sequence is 4.
  (b) Find the next four terms in the sequence.

4 Find the first four terms of the sequences with these nth terms.
  (a) $5n + 2$
  (b) $n^2 + 1$
  (c) $90 - 2n$

5 The first term of a sequence is 4.
  The general rule for the sequence is multiply a term by 2 to get to the next term.
  Write down the first five terms of the sequence.

6 Find the nth term for each of these sequences.
  (a) 5, 8, 11, 14, 17, …
  (b) 1, 7, 13, 19, 25, …
  (c) 2, −3, −8, −13, −18, …

7 Which of these sequences are linear?
  Find the next two terms of each of the sequences that are linear.
  (a) 4, 9, 14, 19, …
  (b) 3, 6, 10, 15, …
  (c) 5, 10, 20, 40, …
  (d) 12, 6, 0, −6, …

8 The nth term of a sequence is 3^n.
  (a) Write down the first five terms of this sequence.
  (b) Describe this sequence.

9 Draw suitable diagrams to show the first five triangular numbers.
  Write the triangular numbers under your diagrams.

10 (a) Write down the first five terms of the sequence with nth term n^2.
  (b) Hence find the nth term of the following sequence.
        5, 8, 13, 20, 29, …

19 CONSTRUCTIONS AND LOCI

THIS CHAPTER IS ABOUT

- Constructing the perpendicular bisector of a line
- Constructing the perpendicular from a point on a line
- Constructing the perpendicular from a point to a line
- Constructing the bisector of an angle
- Knowing that a locus is a line, a curve or a region of points
- Knowing the four basic loci results
- Locating a locus of points that follow a given rule or rules

YOU SHOULD ALREADY KNOW

- How to use a protractor and compasses
- How to make scale drawings
- How to construct a triangle given three facts about its sides and angles

Constructions

You already know how to **construct** angles and triangles.

You can use these skills in other constructions.

Four important constructions

You need to know four important constructions.

Construction 1: The perpendicular bisector of a line

Use the following method to construct the **perpendicular bisector** of line AB.

> **TIP**
> *Perpendicular* means 'at right angles to'.
> A *bisector* is something that divides into 'two equal parts'.

1 Open your compasses to a radius more than half the length of the line AB.
Put the point of your compasses on A.
Draw one arc above the line, and one arc below.

2 Keep your compasses open to the same radius.
Put the compass point on B.
Draw two more arcs, cutting the first arcs at P and Q.

3 Join the points P and Q.
This line divides AB into two equal parts and is at right angles to AB.

Discovery 19.1

(a) (i) Draw a triangle. Make it big enough to fill about half of your page.
  (ii) Construct the perpendicular bisector of each of the three sides.
  (iii) If you have drawn them accurately enough, the bisectors should meet at one point. Put your compass point on this point, and the pencil on one of the corners of the triangle.
Draw a circle.

(b) You have drawn the **circumcircle** of the triangle.
What do you notice about this circle?

Construction 2: The perpendicular from a point on a line

Use the following method to construct the perpendicular from point P on the given line.

1 Open your compasses to any radius.
Put the compass point on P.
Draw an arc on each side of P, cutting the line at Q and R.

2 Open your compasses to a larger radius.
Put the compass point on Q.
Draw an arc above the line.
Now put the compass point on R and draw another arc, with the same radius, cutting the first arc at X.

3 Join the points P and X.
This line is at right angles to the original line.

268 19 Constructions and loci

Discovery 19.2

(a) Draw a line 10 cm long. Label it AB.
(b) At A, draw a circle of radius 5 cm.
Label the point where the circle crosses the line P.
(c) Construct the perpendicular from P.

This perpendicular is the **tangent** to the circle at P.

Construction 3: The perpendicular from a point to a line

Use the following method to construct the perpendicular from point P to the given line.

1. Open your compasses to any radius.
   Put the compass point on P.
   Draw two arcs, cutting the line at Q and R.

2. Keep your compasses open to the same radius.
   Put the compass point on Q.
   Draw an arc below the line.
   Now put the compass point on R and draw another arc, cutting the first arc at X.

3. Line up your ruler with points P and X.
   Draw the line PM.
   This line is at right angles to the original line.

Discovery 19.3

(a) (i) Draw a line across your page. Put a cross on one side of the line and label it P.
   (ii) Construct the perpendicular from P to the line. Make sure you keep your compasses open to the same radius all the time.
   This time, join P to X, don't stop at the original line.

(b) (i) Measure PM and XM.
   (ii) What do you notice?
   What can you say about P and X?

Construction 4: The bisector of an angle

Use the following method to construct the bisector of the given angle.

1. Open your compasses to any radius.
   Put the compass point on A.
   Draw two arcs, cutting the 'arms' of the angle at P and Q.

2. Open your compasses to any radius.
   Put the compass point on P.
   Draw an arc inside the angle.
   Now put the compass point on Q and draw another arc, with the same radius, cutting the first arc at X.

3. Join the points A and X.
   This line divides the given angle into two equal parts.

Discovery 19.4

(a) (i) Draw a triangle. Make it big enough to fill about half of your page.
   (ii) Construct the bisector of each of the three angles.
   (iii) If you have drawn them accurately enough, the bisectors should meet at one point. Label this point A.
   Construct the perpendicular from A to one of the sides of the triangle.
   Label the point where the perpendicular meets the side of the triangle B.
   (iv) Put your compass point on A, and the pencil on point B.
   Draw a circle.

(b) You have drawn the **incircle** of the triangle.
   (i) What do you notice about this circle?
   (ii) What can you say about the side of the triangle to which you have drawn the perpendicular from A?
   Hint: Look at your diagram from Discovery 19.2.
   (iii) What can you say about each of the other two sides of the triangle?

Constructing a locus

A **locus** is a line, curve or region of points that satisfy a certain rule.
The plural of locus is **loci**.

Four important loci

You need to know four important loci.

Locus 1: The locus of points that are the same distance from a given point

The locus of points that are 2 cm from point A is a circle, with centre A and radius 2 cm.

> **TIP** The locus of points that are less than 2 cm from A is the region inside the circle.
>
> The locus of points that are more than 2 cm from A is the region outside the circle.

> **TIP** When trying to identify a particular locus, find several points that satisfy the required rule and see what sort of line, curve or region they form.

Locus 2: The locus of points that are the same distance from two given points

The locus of points that are the same distance from the points A and B is the perpendicular bisector of the line joining A and B.

> **TIP** You learned how to construct a perpendicular bisector earlier in this chapter.

Locus 3: The locus of points that are the same distance from two, given, intersecting lines

The locus of points that are the same distance from AB and AC is the bisector of the angle BAC.

> **TIP** You learned how to construct the bisector of an angle earlier in this chapter.

Proof 19.1

(a) Prove that locus 2 works.
(b) Prove that locus 3 works.

Locus 4: The locus of points that are the same distance from a given line

The locus of points that are 3 cm from the line AB is a pair of lines, parallel to AB and 3 cm away from it on either side; at each end of the line there is a semicircle with centre A or B and radius 3 cm.

You can use constructions and loci to solve problems.

EXAMPLE 19.1

Two towns, P and Q, are 5 km apart.
Toby lives exactly the same distance from P as from Q.
(a) Construct the locus of where Toby could live. Use a scale of 1 cm to 1 km.

Toby's school is closer to P than to Q.
(b) Shade the region where Toby's school could be.

Solution

The locus of where Toby lives is the perpendicular bisector of the line joining P and Q.

Any point to the left of the line drawn in part **(a)** is closer to point P than to point Q. Any point to the right of the line is closer to point Q than to point P.

EXAMPLE 19.2

A security light is attached to a wall.
The light illuminates an area up to 20 m.

Construct the region illuminated by the light. Use a scale of 1 cm to 5 m.

Solution

Remember that the light cannot illuminate the area behind the wall.

19 Constructions and loci

EXAMPLE 19.3

The diagram shows a port, P, and some rocks.

To leave the port safely, a boat must keep the same distance from each set of rocks.

Copy the diagram and construct the path of a boat from the port.

Solution

EXERCISE 19.1

1. Draw the locus of points that are less than 5 cm from a fixed point A.

2. Two rocks are 100 m apart.
   A boat passes between the rocks so that it is always the same distance from each of them.
   Construct the locus of the path of the boat.
   Use a scale of 1 cm to 20 m.

3. In a farmer's field, a tree is 60 m from a long hedge.
   The farmer decides to build a fence between the tree and the hedge.
   The fence must be as short as possible.
   Make a scale drawing of the tree and the hedge.
   Construct the locus of where the fence must be built.
   Use a scale of 1 cm to 10 m.

4. Draw an angle of 60°.
   Construct the bisector of the angle.

5 Draw a square, ABCD, with side 5 cm.
Draw the locus of points inside the square that are less than 3 cm from corner C.

6 A rectangular shed measures 4 m by 2 m.
A path, 1 m wide and perpendicular to the shed, is to be built from the door of the shed.
Construct the locus showing the edges of the path.
Use a scale of 1 cm to 1 m.

7 Construct a compass like the one opposite.
 • Draw a circle with radius 4 cm.
 • Draw a horizontal diameter of the circle.
 • Construct the perpendicular bisector of the diameter.
 • Bisect each of the four angles.

8 Draw a line 7 cm long.
Construct the region of points that are less than 3 cm from the line.

9 Construct a triangle ABC with AB = 8 cm, AC = 7 cm and BC = 6 cm.
Shade the locus of points inside the triangle that are closer to AB than to AC.

10 The owner of a theme park decides to build a moat 20 m wide around a castle.
The castle is a rectangle measuring 80 m long by 60 m wide.
Draw accurately an outline of the castle and the moat.

Challenge 19.1

Sketch the locus for each of the following.
 (a) The tip of the hour hand of a clock.
 (b) A ball thrown vertically up.
 (c) A ball thrown at an angle.
 (d) The middle of a bicycle wheel as it is ridden along a level road.
 (e) A nail stuck in the tyre of a bicycle as it is ridden along a level road.
 (f) A door handle as the door opens.
 (g) The lower edge of an 'up-and-over' garage door as it is opened.

Intersecting loci

Often a locus is defined by more than one rule.

EXAMPLE 19.4

Two points, P and Q, are 5 cm apart.
Find the locus of points that are less than 3 cm from P and equidistant from P and Q.

> **TIP:** *Equidistant* means 'equal distance'.

Solution

The locus of points that are less than 3 cm from P is within a circle with centre P and radius 3 cm.

The locus of points that are equidistant from P and Q is the perpendicular bisector of the line joining P and Q.

The points that satisfy both rules lie within the circle *and* on the line.

EXAMPLE 19.5

A rectangular garden is 25 m long and 15 m wide.
A tree is to be planted in the garden so that it is more than 2.5 m from the boundary and less than 10 m from the south-west corner.
Using a scale of 1 cm to 5 m, make a scale drawing of the garden and find the region where the tree can be planted.

Solution

Draw a rectangle measuring 5 cm by 3 cm to represent the garden.

The locus of points more than 2.5 m from the boundary is a smaller rectangle inside the first. Each side of the smaller rectangle is 0.5 cm inside the sides of the larger rectangle.

The locus of points less than 10 m from the south-west corner is an arc with the corner as its centre and radius 2 cm.

The points that satisfy both rules lie within the smaller rectangle *and* the arc.

EXERCISE 19.2

1. Draw a point and label it A.
   Draw the region of points that are more than 3 cm from A but less than 6 cm from A.

2. Two towns, P and Q, are 7 km apart.
   Amina wants to buy a house that is within 5 km of P and also within 4 km of Q.
   Make a scale drawing to indicate the region where Amina could buy a house.
   Use a scale of 1 cm to 1 km.

3. Draw a square ABCD with side 5 cm.
   Find the region of points that are more than 3 cm from AB and AD.

4. Steve is using an old map to locate treasure.
   He is searching a rectangular plot of land, EFGH, which measures 8 m by 5 m.
   The map says that the treasure is hidden 6 m from E on a line equidistant from F and H.
   Using a scale of 1 cm to 1 m, make a scale drawing to locate the treasure.
   Mark the position where the treasure is hidden with the letter T.

5. Construct triangle ABC with AB = 11 cm, AC = 7 cm and BC = 9 cm.
   Construct the locus of points, inside the triangle, that are closer to AB than to AC and equidistant from A and B.

6. The diagram shows the corner of a farm building, which stands in a field.
   A donkey is tethered at a point D with a rope 5 m long.
   Shade the region of the field that the donkey can graze.

7. A sailor is shipwrecked at night. She is 140 m from the straight coastline.
   She swims straight for the shore.

   (a) Make a scale drawing of the path she swims.

   The coastguard is standing on the beach exactly where the sailor will come ashore.
   He has a searchlight that can illuminate up to a distance of 50 m.

   (b) Mark on your diagram the part of the sailor's swim that will be lit up.

8. The positions of three radio stations, A, B and C, form a triangle such that AB = 7 km, BC = 9.5 km and angle ABC = 90°.
   The signal from each radio station can be received up to 5 km away.
   Make a scale drawing to locate the region where none of the three radio stations can be received.

9 A rectangular garden measures 20 m by 14 m.
The house wall is along one of the shorter sides of the garden.
Pete is going to plant a tree. It must be more than 10 m from the house and more than 8 m from any corner of the garden.
Find the region of the garden where the tree can be planted.

10 Two towns, H and K, are 20 miles apart.
A new leisure centre is to be built within 15 miles of H, but nearer to K than to H.
Using a scale of 1 cm to 5 miles, draw a diagram to show where the leisure centre could be built.

Challenge 19.2

(a) Describe the 3-D locus produced when each of the following 2-D shapes is rotated 360° about the edge XY.

(i) (ii) (iii)

(b) In 3-D, P and Q are points 16 cm apart.
  (i) Describe the 3-D locus of a point that is always 10 cm from P.
  (ii) Describe the locus of a point that is always 10 cm from P and 10 cm from Q.

WHAT YOU HAVE LEARNED

- How to construct the perpendicular bisector of a line
- How to construct the perpendicular from a point on a line
- How to construct the perpendicular from a point to a line
- How to construct the bisector of an angle
- That the locus of points that are the same distance from a given point is a circle
- That the locus of points that are the same distance from two points is the perpendicular bisector of the line joining the two points
- That the locus of points which are the same distance from two intersecting lines is the bisector of the angle formed by the two lines
- That some loci must satisfy more than one rule

MIXED EXERCISE 19

1 Draw an angle of 100°.
Construct the bisector of the angle.

2 Draw a line 8 cm long.
Construct the locus of the points that are the same distance from each end of the line.

3 Draw a line 7 cm long.
Draw the locus of points which are 3 cm away from this line.

4 Draw the triangle ABC with AB = 9 cm, BC = 8 cm and CA = 6 cm.
Construct the perpendicular line from C to AB.
Measure the length of this line and hence work out the area of the triangle.

5 Draw the rectangle PQRS with PQ = 8 cm and QR = 5 cm.
Shade the region of points which are nearer to QP than to QR.

6 Two radio stations are 40 km apart. Each station can transmit signals up to 30 km.
Construct a scale drawing to show the region which can receive signals from both radio stations.

7 A garden is a rectangle ABCD with AB = 5 m and BC = 3 m.
A tree is planted so that it is within 5 m of A and within 3 m of C.
Indicate the region where the tree could be planted.

8 Draw triangle EFG with EF = 8 cm, EG = 6 cm and angle E = 70°.
Construct the point which is equidistant from F and G and is also 5 cm from G.

9 A lawn is a square with side 5 m.
A water sprinkler covers a circle of radius 3 m.
If the gardener puts the sprinkler at each corner, will the whole lawn get watered?

10 The gardener in question **9** loans his water sprinkler to a neighbour.
The neighbour has a large garden with a rectangular lawn measuring 10 m by 8 m.
She moves the sprinkler slowly around the edge of the lawn. Draw a scale diagram to show the region of the lawn which will be watered.

20 SOLVING PROBLEMS

THIS CHAPTER IS ABOUT

- Understanding the order in which your calculator does calculations
- Using your calculator efficiently to do more difficult calculations
- Estimating and checking your answers
- Selecting suitable strategies and techniques in problem-solving
- Applying your knowledge to solving problems using ratio, proportion and percentages and to compound measures such as speed and density
- Conversion between measures such as time
- Interpreting social statistics such as the retail price index

YOU SHOULD ALREADY KNOW

- How to work with ratios
- How to use proportion
- How to find and use percentages
- How to use speed and density
- How to round numbers, for example to 1 significant figure

Order of operations

Your calculator always follows the correct order of operations. This means that it does brackets first, then powers (such as squares), then multiplication and division and lastly addition and subtraction.

If you want to change the normal order of doing things you need to give your calculator different instructions.

Sometimes the simplest way of doing this is to press the $=$ button in the middle of a calculation. This is shown in the following example.

EXAMPLE 20.1

Work out $\dfrac{5.9 + 3.4}{3.1}$.

Solution

You need to work out the addition first.

Press [5][.][9][+][3][.][4][=].

You should see 9.3.

Now press [÷][3][.][1][=].

The answer is 3.

Using brackets

Sometimes you need other ways of changing the order of operations.

For example, in the calculation $\dfrac{5.52 + 3.45}{2.3 + 1.6}$, you need to add 5.52 + 3.45, then add 2.3 + 1.6 before doing the division.

One way to do this is to write down the answers to the two addition sums and then do the division

$$\dfrac{5.52 + 3.45}{2.3 + 1.6} = \dfrac{8.97}{3.9} = 2.3$$

A more efficient way to do it is to use brackets.

You do the calculation as (5.52 + 3.45) ÷ (2.3 + 1.6).

This is the sequence of keys to press.

[(][5][.][5][2][+][3][.][4][5][)][÷][(][2][.][3][+][1][.][6][)][=]

Check up 20.1

Enter the sequence above in your calculator and check that you get 2.3.

EXAMPLE 20.2

Use your calculator to work out these calculations without writing down the answers to middle stages.

(a) $\sqrt{5.2 + 2.7}$ (b) $\dfrac{5.2}{3.7 \times 2.8}$

Solution

(a) You need to work out 5.2 + 2.7 before finding the square root.
You use brackets so that the addition is done first.
$\sqrt{(5.2 + 2.7)} = 2.811$ correct to 3 decimal places.

(b) You need to work out 3.7 × 2.8 before doing the division.
You use brackets so that the multiplication is done first.
$5.2 \div (3.7 \times 2.8) = 0.502$ correct to 3 decimal places.

EXERCISE 20.1

Work these out on your calculator without writing down the answers to middle stages.
If the answers are not exact, give them correct to 2 decimal places.

1 $\dfrac{5.2 + 10.3}{3.1}$

2 $\dfrac{127 - 31}{25}$

3 $\dfrac{9.3 + 12.3}{8.2 - 3.4}$

4 $\sqrt{15.7 - 3.8}$

5 $6.2 + \dfrac{7.2}{2.4}$

6 $(6.2 + 1.7)^2$

7 $\dfrac{5.3}{2.6 \times 1.7}$

8 $\dfrac{2.6^2}{1.7 + 0.82}$

9 $2.8 \times (5.2 - 3.6)$

10 $\dfrac{6.2 \times 3.8}{22.7 - 13.8}$

11 $\dfrac{5.3}{\sqrt{6.2 + 2.7}}$

12 $\dfrac{5 + \sqrt{25 + 12}}{6}$

Estimating and checking

Discovery 20.1

Without working them out, write down whether or not each of these calculations is correct.

Give your reason in each case.

(a) 1975 × 43 = 84 920
(b) 697 × 0.72 = 5018.4
(c) 3864 ÷ 84 = 4.6
(d) 19 × 37 = 705
(e) 306 ÷ 0.6 = 51
(f) 6127 × 893 = 54 714.11

Compare your reasons with the rest of the class.
Did you all use the same reasons each time?
Did anyone have ideas which you hadn't thought of and which you think work well?

There are a number of facts that you can use to check a calculation.

- odd × odd = odd, even × odd = even, even × even = even
- A number multiplied by 5 will end in 0 or 5
- The last digit in a multiplication comes from multiplying the last digits of the numbers
- Multiplying by a number between 0 and 1 makes the original number smaller
- Dividing by a number greater than 1 makes the original number smaller
- Calculating an estimate by rounding the numbers to 1 significant figure shows whether the answer is the correct size

When checking a calculation, there are three main strategies that you can use.

- Common sense
- Estimates
- Inverse operations

Using **common sense** is often a good first check: is your answer about the size you expected?

You may already use **estimates** when you are shopping, to make sure you have enough money and to check you are given the correct change.

> **TIP**
>
> Get into the habit of checking your answers to calculations when solving problems, to see if your answer is sensible.

EXAMPLE 20.3

Estimate the cost of five CDs at £5.99 and two DVDs at £14.99.

Solution

CDs: 5 × 6 = 30   Split the calculation into two parts and round
DVDs: 2 × 15 = 30   the numbers to 1 significant figure.

Total = 30 + 30
      = £60

EXAMPLE 20.4

Estimate the answer to $\dfrac{\sqrt{394} \times 3.7}{49.2}$.

Solution

$$\frac{\sqrt{394} \times 3.7}{49.2} \approx \frac{\sqrt{400} \times 4}{50}$$

$$= \frac{20 \times 4}{50}$$

$$= \frac{80}{50}$$

$$= \frac{8}{5}$$

$$= 1.6$$

TIP: $\approx$ means 'is approximately equal to'.

Inverse operations can be particularly useful when you are working with a calculator and want to check that you pressed the correct keys first time.

For example, to check the calculation $920 \div 64 = 14.375$, you can do $14.375 \times 64 = 920$.

Accuracy of answers

Sometimes, you are asked to give your answers to a **given degree of accuracy**. For example, you may be asked to round your answer to 3 decimal places.

Sometimes you are asked to give the answer to a **sensible degree of accuracy**. You learned in Chapter 16 that your final answer should not be given to a greater degree of accuracy than any of the values used in the calculation.

EXAMPLE 20.5

Calculate the hypotenuse of a right-angled triangle, given that the other two sides are 4.2 cm and 5.8 cm.

Solution

Using Pythagoras' theorem,

$c^2 = 4.2^2 + 5.8^2$

$c^2 = 51.28$

$c = \sqrt{51.28}$

$c = 7.161\,005 \ldots$

$c = 7.2$ cm (to 1 decimal place)

Estimating and checking 283

Challenge 20.1

In Example 20.5, the answer was given to 1 decimal place, which is to the nearest millimetre.

Think of a situation where it would be most appropriate to give the answer correct to
(a) 2 decimal places.
(b) the nearest 100.

EXERCISE 20.2

Do not use your calculator for questions **1** to **4**.

1 These calculations are all wrong. This can be spotted quickly without working them out. For each one, give a reason why it is wrong.
   (a) $6.3 \times -5.1 = 32.13$
   (b) $8.7 \times 0.34 = 29.58$
   (c) $3.7 \times 60 = 22.2$
   (d) $\sqrt{62.41} = 8.9$

2 These calculations are all wrong. This can be spotted quickly without working them out. For each one, give a reason why it is wrong.
   (a) $5.4 \div 0.9 = 60$
   (b) $-7.2 \div -0.8 = -9$
   (c) $5.7^2 = 44.89$
   (d) $13.8 + 9.3 = 22.4$

3 Estimate the answer to each of these calculations. Show your working.
   (a) 972×18
   (b) 0.39^2
   (c) $-19.6 \div 5.2$

4 Estimate the answers to each of these calculations. Show your working.
   (a) The cost of 7 CDs at £8.99.
   (b) The cost of 29 theatre tickets at £14.50.
   (c) The cost of 3 meals at £5.99 and 3 drinks at £1.95.

You may use your calculator for questions **5** to **9**.

5 Use inverse operations to check these calculations. Write down the operations you use.
   (a) $762.5 \times 81.4 = 62\,067.5$
   (b) $38.3^2 = 1466.89$
   (c) $66.88 \div 3.8 = 17.6$
   (d) $69.1 \times 4.3 - 18.2 = 278.93$

6 Work these out. Round your answers to 2 decimal places.
   (a) $(48.2 - 19.5) \times 16.32$
   (b) $\dfrac{14.6 + 17.3}{13.8 \times 0.34}$

7 Work these out. Round your answers to 3 decimal places.
   (a) $\dfrac{47.3}{6.9 - 3.16}$
   (b) $\dfrac{17.6^3 \times 94.1}{572}$

8 Work these out. Round your answers to 1 decimal place.
   (a) 6.3×9.7
   (b) 57×0.085

9 (a) Use rounding to 1 significant figure to estimate the answer to each of these calculations. Show your working.
   (b) Use your calculator to find the correct answer to each of these calculations. Where appropriate, round your answer to a sensible degree of accuracy.
   (i) 39.2^3
   (ii) 18.4×0.19
   (iii) $\sqrt{7.1^2 - 3.9^2}$
   (iv) $\dfrac{11.6 + 30.2}{0.081}$

Challenge 20.2

In question **9** of Exercise 20.2, the estimates and actual answers agree to 1 significant figure, except for part **(ii)**.

Make up some more estimation and calculation questions of your own.

Try to find other examples where the estimates and accurate answers do not agree to 1 significant figure.

Compound measures

In Chapter 16 you learned about two **compound measures**, **speed** and **density**. Another compound measure you are likely to meet is **population density**. This measures the number of people living in a certain area.

EXAMPLE 20.6

The 2001 census showed that 129 701 people were living in the borough of Guildford.
The area of the borough is 271 km².
Calculate the population density of Guildford in 2001.

Solution

Population density $= \dfrac{\text{population}}{\text{area}}$

$= \dfrac{129\,701}{271}$

$= 478.601\ ...$

$= 479$ people/km² (to nearest whole number)

TIP: When your final answer is a rounded number, make sure you state the accuracy you have used.

> **Challenge 20.3**
>
> From the internet, or elsewhere, find the population and area of your town or village.
>
> Calculate the population density for your area.
>
> Compare the population densities of two different places locally – perhaps a town and a village, or either of these with a city.

Time

When solving a problem using measures, make sure you check which units you are using. You may need to convert between units.

EXAMPLE 20.7

A train is travelling at 18 metres per second.
Calculate its speed in kilometres per hour.

Solution

18 metres per second = 18 × 60 metres per minute   1 minute = 60 seconds
                    = 18 × 60 × 60 metres per hour   1 hour = 60 minutes
                    = 64 800 metres per hour
                    = 64.8 km/h   1 km = 1000 m

EXAMPLE 20.8

Penny's journey to her holiday destination has three stages.
The stages take 3 hours 43 minutes, 1 hour 29 minutes and 4 hours 17 minutes.
How long does her journey take altogether?

Solution

Add the hours and the minutes separately.
3 + 1 + 4 = 8 hours
43 + 29 + 17 = 89 minutes

89 minutes = 1 hour 29 minutes   There are 60 minutes in 1 hour.

8 hours + 1 hour 29 minutes = 9 hours 29 minutes

> **TIP**
>
> Take care when using your calculator for time problems.
> For example, 3 hours 43 minutes is not 3.43 hours, since there are 60 minutes in an hour, not 100.
> It is safer to add the minutes separately, as in Example 20.8.

EXAMPLE 20.9

Pali travels 48 miles at an average speed of 30 miles per hour. How long does his journey take? Give your answer in hours and minutes.

Solution

Time = $\dfrac{\text{distance}}{\text{speed}}$

= $\dfrac{48}{30}$ = 1.6 hours

0.6 hours = 0.6 × 60 minutes
= 36 minutes

So Pali's journey takes 1 hour 36 minutes.

Discovery 20.2

Some calculators have a $\boxed{\,`\,"\,}$ button. You can use this for working with time on your calculator.

When you do a calculation and the answer is a time in hours but your calculator shows a decimal, you change it to hours and minutes by pressing $\boxed{\,`\,"\,}$ and then the $\boxed{=}$ button.

To change a time in hours and minutes back to a decimal time, use the $\boxed{\text{SHIFT}}$ key.

The $\boxed{\text{SHIFT}}$ key is usually the top left button on your calculator, but it might be called something else.

To enter a time of 8 hours 32 minutes on your calculator, press this sequence of keys.

$\boxed{8}$ $\boxed{\,`\,"\,}$ $\boxed{3}$ $\boxed{2}$ $\boxed{\,`\,"\,}$ $\boxed{=}$

The display should look like this. $\boxed{8° 32° 0}$

You may wish to experiment with this button and learn how to use it to enter and convert times.

Solving problems

When solving a problem, break it down into steps.

Read the question carefully and then ask yourself these questions.
- What am I asked to find?
- What information have I been given?
- What methods can I apply?

If you can't see how to find what you need straight away, ask yourself what you can find with the information you are given. Then, knowing that information, ask yourself what you can find next that is relevant.

Many of the complex problems that you meet in everyday life concern money. For example, people have to pay **income tax**. This is calculated as a percentage of what you earn.

Everyone is entitled to a personal allowance (income that is not taxed). For the tax year 2004–2005 this was £4745.

Income in excess of the personal allowance is known as taxable income and is taxed at different rates. For the tax year 2004–2005 the rates were as follows.

Tax bands	Taxable income (£)
Starting rate 10%	0–2020
Basic rate 22%	2021–31 400
Higher rate 40%	over 31 400

EXAMPLE 20.10

In the tax year 2004–2005, Stacey earned £28 500. Calculate how much tax she had to pay.

Solution

Taxable income = £28 500 − £4745 = £23 755

First subtract the personal allowance from Stacey's total income to find her taxable income.

Tax payable at starting rate = 10% of £2020
= 0.1 × £2020
= £202

Calculate the tax Stacey must pay on the first £2020 of her taxable income.

Income to be taxed at basic rate = £23 755 − £2020
= £21 735

Stacey's taxable income is less than £31 400. So the rest of her taxable income will all be taxed at the basic rate, 22%. To calculate the amount to be taxed at this rate, subtract the £2020 taxed at the starting rate from Stacey's total taxable income.

Tax payable at basic rate = 22% of £21 735
= 0.22 × £21 735
= £4781.70

Calculate the tax Stacey must pay on the remaining £21 735 of her taxable income.

Total tax payable = £202 + £4781.70
= £4983.70

Finally, add the two lots of tax together to find the total Stacey must pay.

20 Solving problems

Index numbers

The **Retail Price Index** (RPI) is used by the government to help keep track of how much certain basic items cost. It helps to show how much your money is worth year on year.

The system started in the 1940s and the base price was reset to 100 in January 1987. You can think of this base RPI number as being 100% of the price at the time.

In October 2004 the RPI for all items was 188.6. This showed that there had been an 88.6% increase in the price of these items since January 1987.

However, the RPI for all items excluding housing costs was 171.3, showing that there had been a smaller increase of 71.3% if housing costs were not included.

The RPI is often referred to in the media, when monthly figures are published: people need price increases to be kept small, otherwise they will in effect be poorer unless their income increases.

As well as the RPI, there are other index numbers in use, such as the **Average Earnings Index**. This has a base set to 100 in the year 2000, so the current index values show comparisons with earnings in the year 2000.

You can find more information about these and other index numbers on the government's statistics website, www.statistics.gov.uk.

> **TIP**
> This may seem complicated, but index numbers are really just percentages. You learned about percentage increase and decrease in Chapter 4.

EXAMPLE 20.11

In October 2003, the RPI for all items excluding mortgage payments was 182.6.
In October 2004, this same RPI was 188.6.
Calculate the percentage increase during that 12 month period.

Solution

Increase in RPI during year = 188.6 − 182.6
　　　　　　　　　　　　　= 6　　　　First work out the increase in the RPI.

Percentage increase = $\dfrac{\text{Increase}}{\text{Original price}} \times 100$　　Then calculate the percentage increase in relation to the 2003 figure.

　　　　　　　　　= $\dfrac{6}{182.6} \times 100 = 3.29\%$ (to 2 decimal places)

Solving problems

EXERCISE 20.3

1. Write each of these times in hours and minutes.
   (a) 2.85 hours
   (b) 0.15 hours

2. Write each of these times as a decimal.
   (a) 1 hour 27 minutes
   (b) 54 minutes

3. Jason took part in a three-stage race. His times for the three stages were 43 minutes, 58 minutes and 1 hour 34 minutes.
   What was his total time for the race? Give your answer in hours and minutes.

4. A courier travelled from Barnsley to Rotherham and then from Rotherham to Sheffield, before driving straight back from Sheffield to Barnsley.

   The journey from Barnsley to Rotherham took 37 minutes.
   The journey from Rotherham to Sheffield took 29 minutes.
   The journey from Sheffield to Barnsley took 42 minutes.

   How long did the courier spend travelling in total?
   Give your answer in hours and minutes.

5. Pierre bought 680 g of cheese at £7.25 a kilogram. He also bought some peppers at 69p each. The total cost was £8.38. How many peppers did he buy?

6. Two families share the cost of a meal in the ratio 3 : 2. They spend £38.40 on food and £13.80 on drinks. How much do the families each pay for the meal?

7. A recipe for four people uses 200 ml of milk.
   Janna makes this recipe for six people. She uses milk from a full 1 litre carton.
   How much milk is left after she has made the recipe?

8. At the beginning of a journey, the mileometer in Steve's car read 18 174.
   At the end of the journey it read 18 309.
   His journey took 2 hours 30 minutes.
   Calculate his average speed.

9. Mr Brown's electricity bill showed that he had used 2316 units of electricity at 7.3p per unit.
   He also pays a standing charge of £12.95. VAT on the total bill was at the rate of 5%.
   Calculate the total bill including VAT.

10. The population density of Broughton was 832 people/km^2 in 2005.
    The area of Broughton is 73 km^2. How many people lived in Broughton in 2005?

11. In January 2003 the Retail Price Index (RPI) excluding housing was 166.8.
    During the next 12 months it increased by 1.5%.
    What was this RPI in January 2004?

12 In June 1999, the average earnings index (AEI) was 99.7. In June 2004 it was 117.9.
Calculate the percentage increase in earnings over this five-year period.

13 A wooden toy brick is a cuboid measuring 2 cm by 3 cm by 5 cm.
Its mass is 66 g. Calculate the density of the wood.

14 A cylindrical water jug has a base radius of 5.6 cm.
Calculate the depth of the water when the jug contains 1.5 litres.

Challenge 20.4

Work in pairs.

Use data from a newspaper or your own experience to write a money problem.

Write the problem on one side of a sheet of paper then, on the other side, solve your problem.

Swap problems with your partner and solve each other's problems.

Check your answers against the solutions provided and discuss instances where you have used different methods.

If you have time, repeat this activity with another problem: perhaps one involving speed, or where you need to change the units.

WHAT YOU HAVE LEARNED

- How to change the order of operations by using the = button and brackets
- Three good strategies for checking answers are common sense, estimates and using inverse operations
- Compound measures include speed, density and population density
- When solving a problem, break it down into steps. Consider what you have been asked to find, what information you have been given and what methods you can apply. If you can't immediately see how to find what you need, consider what you can find with the given information and then look at the problem again
- To check you have used the correct units

MIXED EXERCISE 20

1 Work out these calculations without writing down the answers to any middle stages.

(a) $\dfrac{7.83 - 3.24}{1.53}$

(b) $\dfrac{22.61}{1.7 \times 3.8}$

2 Work out $\sqrt{5.6^2 - 4 \times 1.3 \times 5}$.
Give your answer correct to 2 decimal places.

3 These calculations are all wrong.
This can be spotted quickly without working them out.
For each one, give a reason why it is wrong.
(a) $7.8^2 = 40.64$
(b) $2.4 \times 0.65 = 15.6$
(c) $58\,800 \div 49 = 120$
(d) $-6.3 \times 8.7 = 2.4$

4 Estimate the answers to these calculations. Show your working.
(a) 894×34
(b) 0.58^2
(c) $-48.2 \div 6.1$

5 Work out these using your calculator. Round your answers to 2 decimal places.
(a) $(721.5 - 132.6) \times 2.157$
(b) $\dfrac{19.8 + 31.2}{47.8 \times 0.37}$

6 (a) Use rounding to 1 significant figure to estimate the answer to each of these calculations. Show your working.
(b) Use your calculator to find the correct answer to each of these calculations. Where appropriate, round your answer to a sensible degree of accuracy.

(i) 21.4^3
(ii) 26.7×0.29
(iii) $\sqrt{8.1^2 - 4.2^2}$
(iv) $\dfrac{31.9 + 48.2}{0.039}$

You may use a calculator for questions **7** to **11**.

7 Ken bought 400 g of meat at £6.95 a kilogram. He also bought some melons at £1.40 each. He paid £6.98. How many melons did he buy?

8 Write each of these times in hours and minutes.
(a) 3.7 hours
(b) 2.75 hours
(c) 0.8 hours
(d) 0.85 hours

9 Stefan's journey to work took him 42 minutes. He travelled 24 miles.
Calculate his average speed in miles per hour.

10 The density of a block of wood is 3.2 g/cm³. Its mass is 156 g.
Calculate the volume of the block of wood.

11 Mrs Singh's electricity bill showed that she had used 1054 units of electricity at 7.5p per unit. She also had to pay a standing charge of £13.25. VAT on the total bill was at the rate of 5%. Calculate the total bill including VAT.

12 A glass contains 300 ml of water. It is a cylinder with depth of water 11 cm.
Find the radius of the cylinder.

21 GRAPHS 2

THIS CHAPTER IS ABOUT

- Finding the gradient of a straight-line graph
- Finding the equation of a line in the form $y = mx + c$, given the gradient and intercept
- Solving simultaneous equations graphically
- Solving simple simultaneous equations algebraically

YOU SHOULD ALREADY KNOW

- How to plot and read points in all four quadrants
- How to draw straight-line graphs from equations given in explicit or implicit form
- How to substitute numbers into equations
- How to rearrange equations
- How to add, subtract and multiply negative numbers

Finding the gradient of a straight-line graph

The **gradient** of a graph is the mathematical way of measuring its steepness or rate of change.

$$\text{Gradient} = \frac{\text{increase in } y}{\text{increase in } x}$$

To find the gradient of a straight-line graph, mark two points, then draw a horizontal line and a vertical line to form a right-angled triangle.

For this line, gradient = $\frac{4}{3}$
= 1.33 (correct to 2 decimal places)

> **TIP**
> Choose two points which are as far apart as possible. Make sure the increase in x is a whole number. This will make the arithmetic easier.

For this line, *y decreases* by 8 between the two points chosen. So the *increase* is −8.

gradient = $\dfrac{-8}{2}$
        = −4

> **TIP**
> A line sloping up from left to right has a positive gradient. A line sloping down from left to right has a negative gradient.

> **TIP**
> When calculating gradients from a graph, count the number of units on the axes not the number of squares on the grid.

You can find the gradient of a line without drawing a diagram.

EXAMPLE 21.1

Find the gradient of the line joining each of these pairs of points.
(a) (3, 5) and (8, 7)
(b) (2, 7) and (6, 1)

Solution

(a) (3, 5) and (8, 7)
Increase in $y = 7 − 5$
            $= 2$
Increase in $x = 8 − 3$
            $= 5$
Gradient $= \tfrac{2}{5}$
         $= 0.4$

(b) (2, 7) and (6, 1)
Increase in $y = 1 − 7$ Take care with the signs.
            $= −6$
Increase in $x = 6 − 2$
            $= 4$
Gradient $= \dfrac{-6}{4}$
         $= −1.5$

You may prefer, however, to draw the diagram first.

EXAMPLE 21.2

Find the gradient of this distance–time graph.

Solution

Gradient $= \frac{30}{20}$
$= 1.5$

For a distance–time graph, $\frac{\text{increase in } y}{\text{increase in } x} = \frac{\text{distance travelled}}{\text{time passed}}$.

You know that velocity (speed) $= \frac{\text{distance}}{\text{time}}$.

So the gradient of a distance–time graph gives the velocity.

In this example the units are metres and seconds.
So the velocity $= 1.5$ m/s.

EXERCISE 21.1

1 Find the gradient of each of these lines.

(a) (b) (c)

2 Find the gradient of the line joining each of these pairs of points.
   (a) (3, 2) and (4, 8)   (b) (5, 3) and (7, 7)   (c) (0, 4) and (2, −6)
   (d) (3, −1) and (−1, −5)   (e) (1, 1) and (6, 1)

3 Find the gradient of each side of the triangle ABC.

Finding the gradient of a straight-line graph

4 Find the gradient of each of these lines.

(a) [graph: line from (0,0) to (4,8)]

(b) [graph: line from (0,5) to (8,17)]

(c) [graph: line from (0,15) to (30,0)]

5 Draw the graph of each of these straight lines and find its gradient.
  (a) $y = 2x + 3$
  (b) $y = 5x - 2$
  (c) $y = -2x + 1$
  (d) $y = -x$
  (e) $3x + 2y = 12$

6 Find the velocity for each of these distance–time graphs.

(a) [graph: Distance (km) vs Time (hours), line from (0,0) to (3,15)]

(b) [graph: Distance (m) vs Time (seconds), line from (0,50) to (4,0)]

Finding the equation of a straight-line graph

Look again at the answers to question **5** in Exercise 21.1. Can you see a connection between the equation of a line and its gradient?

Discovery 21.1

(a) Draw a pair of axes and label them −10 to 10 for both x and y.
Draw each of these lines on the same axes.

$y = 2x$ $y = 2x + 1$ $y = 2x + 2$ $y = 2x + 4$ $y = 2x - 2$ $y = 2x - 4$

  (i) What do you notice about the gradient of the lines?
  (ii) What do you notice about where the lines cut the y-axis?
  The point where a straight line cuts the y-axis is called the **y-intercept**.
  (iii) Check your ideas with these lines.

$y = x$ $y = x + 1$ $y = x + 2$ $y = x - 3$ $y = x - 4$ $y = x - 1$

(b) Write down the gradient and y-intercept of each of these lines without drawing a diagram.
  (i) $y = 4x + 2$
  (ii) $y = 5x - 3$
  (iii) $y = 2x$
  (iv) $y = -3x + 2$
  (v) $y = x + 4$
  (vi) $y = -4x + 6$

---

21 Graphs 2

Parallel lines have the same gradient.

An equation of the form $y = mx + c$ has gradient m and y-intercept c.

You can use this fact to find the equation of a line from its graph.

EXAMPLE 21.3

Find the equation of this line.

Solution

Gradient, $m = \frac{6}{2} = 3$

y-intercept, $c = -1$ The line crosses the y-axis at $(0, -1)$.

So the equation is $y = 3x - 1$.

You can also find the gradient and y-intercept of a line from its equation. Sometimes you will have to rearrange the equation first.

EXAMPLE 21.4

The equation of a straight line is $5x + 2y = 10$.
(a) Find the gradient of the line.
(b) Find the y-intercept of the line.

Solution

First you need to rewrite the equation in the form $y = mx + c$.

$5x + 2y = 10$
$\quad 2y = -5x + 10$ Subtract $5x$ from each side so that the y term is on its own.
$\quad\ y = -2.5x + 5$ Divide each side by 2.

(a) Gradient, $m = -2.5$

(b) y-intercept, $c = 5$

Finding the equation of a straight-line graph

EXERCISE 21.2

1 Write down the equations of straight lines with these gradients and y-intercepts.
   (a) Gradient 3, y-intercept 2
   (b) Gradient −1, y-intercept 4
   (c) Gradient 5, y-intercept 0

2 Find the equation of each of these lines.
   (a) [graph through (0,2) and (2,10)]
   (b) [graph through (0,4) and (6,6)]
   (c) [graph through (0,7) and (4,3)]

3 Find the gradient and y-intercept of each of these lines.
   (a) $y = 3x - 2$
   (b) $y = 2x + 4$
   (c) $y = -x + 3$
   (d) $y = -3x + 2$
   (e) $y = 2.5x - 6$

4 Find the gradient and y-intercept of each of these lines.
   (a) $y + 2x = 5$
   (b) $4x + 2y = 9$
   (c) $6x + 5y = 12$
   (d) $3x - 2y = 6$
   (e) $3x + 4y = 12$

5 Find the equation of each of these lines.
   (a) [graph with y from 0 to 20, x from 0 to 4]
   (b) [graph with y from 0 to 8, x from 0 to 4]
   (c) [graph with y from −5 to 20, x from 0 to 40]

Solving simultaneous equations graphically

Discovery 21.2

(a) (i) Draw the graph of $y = 2x - 4$ for values of x from 0 to 6.
   (ii) On the same axes draw the graph of $2x + 3y = 12$.
(b) Write down the coordinates of the point where the two lines cross.
(c) What can you say about the values of x and y that you have found?

The coordinates of the point where two lines cross satisfy the equations of both lines. You can check this by substituting the values into the equations.

For example, when $x = 3$ and $y = 2$
$y = 2x - 4$ $2x + 3y = 12$
$2 = 2 \times 3 - 4$ $2 \times 3 + 3 \times 2 = 12$
$2 = 2$ ✓ $12 = 12$ ✓

Only the point with these coordinates lie on both the line $y = 2x - 4$ and the line $2x + 3y = 12$. Only the values $x = 3$ and $y = 2$ satisfy both equations at the same time.
The values $x = 3$ and $y = 2$ are the solution of the **simultaneous equations** $y = 2x - 4$ and $2x + 3y = 12$. *Simultaneous* means at the same time.

EXAMPLE 21.5

Solve graphically the simultaneous equations $y = 2x$ and $y = 3x - 4$.
Use values of x from 0 to 5.

Solution

Work out and plot three points on each of the lines.
Three points on $y = 2x$ are $(0, 0)$ $(2, 4)$ and $(5, 10)$.
Three points on $y = 3x - 4$ are $(0, -4)$, $(2, 2)$, and $(5, 11)$.

Find the point where the lines cross and write down its coordinates.
The lines cross at $(4, 8)$.

So the solution to the simultaneous equations $y = 2x$ and $y = 3x - 4$ is $x = 4$, $y = 8$.

EXERCISE 21.3

Solve graphically each of these pairs of simultaneous equations.

1 $y = x + 1$ and $y = 4x - 5$. Use values of x from 0 to 5.

2 $y = 2x$ and $y = 8 - 2x$. Use values of x from -2 to 4.

3 $y = 3x + 5$ and $y = x + 3$. Use values of x from -3 to 2.

4 $y = 2x - 7$ and $y = 5 - x$. Use values of x from -1 to 5.

5 $2y = 2x + 1$ and $x + 2y = 7$. Use values of x from 0 to 7.

Challenge 21.1

Delaney's Cabs charge £20 plus £2 per mile to hire a mini-bus.
Tracey's Cars charge £50 plus £1.50 per mile to hire a mini-bus.

(a) Write down an equation for the cost, C, of a mini-bus for n miles from
  (i) Delaney's Cabs. **(ii)** Tracey's Cars.

(b) On one graph draw the two lines for the equations connecting C and n, for values of n up to 100.

(c) Use your graph to find the number of miles for which the two firms charge the same amount.

Solving simultaneous equations algebraically

You can also solve simultaneous equations using algebra.

By adding or subtracting the two equations, you can eliminate either the x term or the y term from one of them. You can then go on to find x and y. This is known as solving simultaneous equations by the **method of elimination**.

EXAMPLE 21.6

Use algebra to solve the simultaneous equations $x + y = 4$ and $2x - y = 5$.

Solution

$x + y = 4$ (1)   Set out the two equations one under the other and label them.
$2x - y = 5$ (2)

Look to see whether either of the unknowns (x or y) has the same **coefficient** in both equations. The coefficient of x is the number in front of the x. The coefficient of y is the number in front of the y.

In this case there is y in (1) and $-y$ in (2).
Because the signs are different, the two y terms will be eliminated (cancel each other out) if the two equations are added.

$x + y = 4$ (1)
$2x - y = 5$ (2)
$3x = 9$ (1) + (2)
$x = 3$ Divide by 3 to find the value of x.

Now that you know the value of x, you can find the value of y by substituting $x = 3$ into one of the equations. In this case, it is easiest to use equation (1).

$x + y = 4$
$3 + y = 4$
$y = 1$

So the solution to the simultaneous equations $x + y = 4$ and $2x - y = 5$ is $x = 3$, $y = 1$.

To check your answer, substitute the solution into the second equation.
In this case, substitute $x = 3$ and $y = 1$ into equation (2).
$2x - y = 2 \times 3 - 1 = 5$ ✓

EXAMPLE 21.7

Use algebra to solve the simultaneous equations $2x + 5y = 9$ and $2x - y = 3$.

Solution

$2x + 5y = 9$ (1)   Set out and label the equations.
$2x - y = 3$ (2)

This time $2x$ occurs in both equations. Because the signs are the same, the two x terms will be eliminated if the two equations are subtracted.

$2x + 5y = 9$ (1)
$2x - y = 3$ (2)
$6y = 6$ (1) − (2) Take care with the signs: $5y - (-y) = 5y + y$.
$y = 1$ Divide by 6 to find the value of y.

Substitute $y = 1$ into equation (1).
$2x + 5y = 9$
$2x + 5 = 9$
$2x = 4$
$x = 2$

So the solution to the simultaneous equations $2x + 5y = 9$, $2x - y = 3$ is $x = 2$, $y = 1$.

> **TIP** Make sure you read the question. If it says 'use algebra', you must use algebra!

Check your answer in equation (2).
$2x - y = 2 \times 2 - 1 = 3$ ✓

EXERCISE 21.4

Use algebra to solve each of these pairs of simultaneous equations.

1. $x + y = 5$
   $2x - y = 7$

2. $3x + y = 9$
   $2x + y = 7$

3. $2x + 3y = 11$
   $2x + y = 5$

4. $2x + y = 7$
   $4x - y = 5$

5. $x + 3y = 8$
   $x - y = 4$

6. $3x + y = 7$
   $3x + 2y = 8$

7. $2x - 3y = 0$
   $4x + 3y = 18$

8. $2x + 3y = 17$
   $2x - 3y = -1$

9. $x + y = 4$
   $4x - y = 11$

10. $2x - y = 7$
    $3x + y = 8$

Solving simultaneous equations algebraically 301

Challenge 21.2

(a) Two numbers, x and y, have a sum of 57, and twice the first number minus the second is equal to 24.
  (i) Write down two equations in x and y.
  (ii) Solve them to find x and y.

(b) At Corner Café, John bought two teas and one coffee and paid £3.30.
Erica bought two teas and three coffees and paid £5.90.
  (i) Let x be the cost of a tea and y the cost of a coffee. Write down two equations involving x and y.
  (ii) Solve the equations and find the cost of a tea.

Solving harder simultaneous equations algebraically

Sometimes neither of the unknowns (x or y) has the same coefficient in both equations. In such cases you first need to multiply one of the equations.

EXAMPLE 21.8

Use algebra to solve the simultaneous equations $x + 3y = 10$ and $3x + 2y = 16$.

Solution

$x + 3y = 10$ (1)
$3x + 2y = 16$ (2)

In this example the coefficients of x and y are different in the two equations.

Multiply equation (1) by 3 to make the coefficient of x the same as in equation (2).

$x + 3y = 10$ (1)
$3 \times x + 3 \times 3y = 3 \times 10$ (1) × 3   Remember to multiply *each* term in the equation by 3.
$3x + 9y = 30$ (3)   Label the new equation.

You can now subtract equation (2) from equation (3) to eliminate the x term.

$3x + 9y = 30$ (3)
$3x + 2y = 16$ (2)
$\overline{7y = 14}$ (3) − (2)
$y = 2$ Divide by 7 to find the value of y.

TIP When subtracting you can do either (3) − (2) or (2) − (3). It is better to do the one that leaves the remaining term positive.

Substitute $y = 2$ into equation (1).
$$x + 3y = 10$$
$$x + 3 \times 2 = 10$$
$$x + 6 = 10$$
$$x = 4$$

So the solution to the simultaneous equations $x + 3y = 10$, $3x + 2y = 16$ is $x = 4$, $y = 2$.

Check your answer in equation (2).
$$3x + 2y = 3 \times 4 + 2 \times 2$$
$$= 12 + 4$$
$$= 16 \checkmark$$

You must always write down clearly what you are doing, but you do not need to write as much detail as in Example 21.8. The next example shows what is required.

EXAMPLE 21.9

Use algebra to solve the simultaneous equations $4x - y = 10$ and $3x + 2y = 13$.

Solution

$$4x - y = 10 \quad (1)$$
$$3x + 2y = 13 \quad (2)$$

$$8x - 2y = 20 \quad (1) \times 2 = (3)$$
$$\underline{3x + 2y = 13} \quad (2)$$
$$11x \phantom{{}+2y} = 33 \quad (3) + (2)$$
$$x \phantom{{}+2y} = 3$$

Substitute $x = 3$ in (1)
$$12 - y = 10$$
$$-y = -2$$
$$y = 2$$

Solution is $x = 3$, $y = 2$

Check in (2)
$$3x + 2y = 9 + 4$$
$$= 13 \checkmark$$

EXERCISE 21.5

Use algebra to solve each of these pairs of simultaneous equations.

1 $x + 3y = 5$
  $2x - y = 3$

2 $3x + y = 9$
  $x + 2y = 8$

3 $x + 3y = 9$
  $2x - y = 4$

4 $2x + y = 7$
  $x - 2y = -4$

5 $2x + 3y = 13$
  $x - y = 4$

6 $3x + y = 7$
  $2x + 3y = 7$

7 $2x - 3y = 2$
  $3x + y = 14$

8 $2x + 3y = 5$
  $x + 2y = 4$

9 $x + y = 4$
  $4x - 2y = 7$

10 $4x - 2y = 10$
  $3x + y = 5$

Challenge 21.3

Solve each of these pairs of simultaneous equations.

(a) $3x + 4y = 10$
  $5x - 3y = 7$

(b) $2x + 3y = 3$
  $3x + 4y = 5$

(c) $3x + 5y = 15$
  $5x - 3y = 8$

WHAT YOU HAVE LEARNED

- Gradient of a straight line = $\dfrac{\text{increase in } y}{\text{increase in } x}$
- Lines with positive gradient slope up from left to right (╱)
- Lines with negative gradient slope down from left to right (╲)
- Lines with the same gradient are parallel
- The equation of a line can be written in the form $y = mx + c$, where m is the gradient of the line and c is the y-intercept
- To solve simultaneous equations graphically, draw the lines and find the point where they cross
- To solve simultaneous equations algebraically, make the coefficient of one of the letters the same in both equations, if necessary. If the signs are the same subtract the equations. If they are different, add the equations

MIXED EXERCISE 21

1. Find the gradient of the line joining each of these pairs of points.
   (a) (1, 3) and (3, 6)
   (b) (2, 1) and (6, −3)

2. Find the gradient of each of these lines.
   (a)
   (b)

3. Find the gradient and y-intercept of each of these lines.
   (a) $y = 3x - 2$
   (b) $2y = 5x - 4$
   (c) $3x + 2y = 8$
   (d) $2x - y = 7$

4. Find the equation of each of these lines.
   (a)
   (b)

5. Solve each of these pairs of simultaneous equations graphically.
   (a) $y = 3x - 1$ and $y = 4x - 3$. Use values of x from −1 to 4.
   (b) $2x + 3y = 12$ and $y = 3x - 7$. Use values of x from 0 to 6.

6. Solve each of these pairs of simultaneous equations algebraically.
   (a) $x + y = 6$
       $2x + y = 10$
   (b) $2x + 5y = 13$
       $2x + 3y = 11$
   (c) $3x + y = 14$
       $x - y = 2$
   (d) $x + 4y = 11$
       $x + y = 2$
   (e) $x + y = 5$
       $2x + 3y = 12$
   (f) $x + y = 1$
       $3x - 2y = 8$
   (g) $x + 3y = 5$
       $7x + 2y = -3$
   (h) $4x - 3y = 9$
       $2x + y = 7$

22 → FURTHER PERCENTAGES

THIS CHAPTER IS ABOUT

- Repeated percentage and proportional change
- Reverse percentage problems

YOU SHOULD ALREADY KNOW

- How to use fraction, decimal and percentage notation
- How to increase and decrease a quantity by a given percentage
- How to find a fraction of a quantity
- How to multiply and divide by fractions and mixed numbers

Repeated percentage change

In Chapter 4 you learned how to increase and decrease a quantity by a given percentage.

> **Check up 22.1**
>
> What must you multiply an amount by to
> (a) increase it by 5%?
> (b) increase it by 2.5%?
> (c) decrease it by 5%?
> (d) decrease it by 2.5%?
> (e) increase it by x%?
> (f) decrease it by x%?

In Chapter 4 you also met repeated percentage change.

A common use of repeated percentage increase is compound interest. This differs from simple interest. When compound interest is paid it is added to the account. The interest is worked out each year on the total in the account, rather than just the original amount.

A common use of repeated percentage decrease is depreciation.

Check up 22.2

(a) Charlotte put £2400 into a savings account.
Each year the savings earn interest of 4.5% of the amount in the account at the beginning of the year.
How much will be in her account after 3 years?
Give your answer to the nearest penny.

(b) Each year a car loses 11% of its value at the start of the year.
The car was worth £15 000 when it was new.
What was its value after 2 years?

Challenge 22.1

(a) Investigate how many years it will take for an amount to double at different rates of compound interest.

(b) Investigate how many years it will take for the value of an object to halve at various rates of depreciation.

Repeated fractional change

In the same way as you increase a quantity by a given percentage, you increase a quantity by a given fraction by multiplying it by 1 + the fraction. You learned how to multiply by mixed numbers in Chapter 4.
To decrease a quantity by a given fraction you divide by 1 − the fraction.

EXAMPLE 22.1

(a) Increase £45 by $\frac{1}{5}$.
(b) Decrease £63 by $\frac{1}{3}$.

Solution

(a) The multiplier is $1 + \frac{1}{5} = \frac{6}{5}$.
Do not convert $\frac{6}{5}$ to a mixed number.
£45 increased by $\frac{1}{5} = 45 \times \frac{6}{5} = £54$.

(b) The multiplier is $1 - \frac{1}{3} = \frac{2}{3}$.
£63 decreased by $\frac{1}{3} = 63 \times \frac{2}{3} = £42$.

Check up 22.3

(a) What do you multiply a quantity by to increase it by
   (i) $\frac{1}{6}$?   (ii) $\frac{1}{10}$?   (iii) $\frac{3}{5}$?   (iv) $\frac{3}{7}$?   (v) $\frac{5}{11}$?

(b) What do you multiply a quantity by to decrease it by
   (i) $\frac{1}{6}$?   (ii) $\frac{1}{10}$?   (iii) $\frac{3}{5}$?   (iv) $\frac{3}{7}$?   (v) $\frac{5}{11}$?

You use powers to work out repeated fractional change in the same way that you do to work out repeated percentage change.

EXAMPLE 22.2

Andrew said that he would increase his donation to a charity by $\frac{1}{25}$ each year.
His first donation was £120.
How much was his donation after 5 years?

Solution

The multiplier is $1 + \frac{1}{25} = \frac{26}{25}$.

After 5 years his donation is $120 \times \left(\frac{26}{25}\right)^5 = £146.00$ (to the nearest penny).

These are the keys to press on your calculator.

[1] [2] [0] [×] [(] [2] [6] [÷] [2] [5] [)] [^] [5] [=]

EXAMPLE 22.3

The distance that Patricia can walk in a day is reducing by $\frac{1}{15}$ each year.
This year she can walk 12 miles in a day.
How far will she be able to walk in 5 years' time?
Give your answer to 2 decimal places.

Solution

The multiplier is $1 - \frac{1}{15} = \frac{14}{15}$.

In five years the distance is $12 \times \left(\frac{14}{15}\right)^5 = 8.50$ miles to 2 decimal places.

EXERCISE 22.1

1 Calculate how much these items are worth if they increase by the given fraction each year for the given number of years.

Give your answers to the nearest penny.

	Original value	Fractional increase	Number of years
(a)	£280	$\frac{1}{5}$	5
(b)	£3500	$\frac{4}{15}$	7
(c)	£1400	$\frac{2}{9}$	4

2 Calculate how much these items are worth if they decrease by the given fraction each year for the given number of years.

Give your answers to the nearest penny.

	Original value	Fractional decrease	Number of years
(a)	£280	$\frac{1}{5}$	5
(b)	£3500	$\frac{4}{15}$	7
(c)	£1400	$\frac{2}{9}$	4

3 An investment company claims it will add $\frac{1}{5}$ to your savings each year.

Jasmine invests £3000.

How much should her savings be worth after 10 years?

Give your answer to the nearest pound.

4 In a sale a clothes shop reduced the price of goods by $\frac{1}{3}$ each day until they were sold.

A coat was originally priced at £60.

What was its price after 3 days, to the nearest penny.

5 It is claimed that the number of rabbits in Freeshire is increasing by $\frac{1}{12}$ each year.

It is estimated there are currently 1700 rabbits.

How many rabbits will there be after 4 years if the statement is true?

Give your answer correct to three significant figures.

Challenge 22.2

(a) Ellie bought a painting for £5000.
During the first year its value increased by $\frac{1}{10}$ and during the second year it increased by $\frac{1}{8}$ of its new value.
What was its value after the two years?

(b) Francis invested in a bond.
The value increased by $\frac{1}{20}$ in the first year, but then dropped by $\frac{1}{15}$ of the new value in the second year.
What was the overall fractional increase or decrease of the original value over the two years?

Reverse percentage and fraction problems

If a quantity is increased by a percentage, $x\%$, the new amount is $1 + x\%$ of the original amount. The multiplier is $\left(1 + \dfrac{x}{100}\right)$.

To find the original amount when you are given the new amount, you divide by the multiplier, $\left(1 + \dfrac{x}{100}\right)$.

If a quantity is decreased by a percentage, $x\%$, the new amount is $1 - x\%$ of the original amount. The multiplier is $\left(1 - \dfrac{x}{100}\right)$.

To find the original amount when you are given the new amount, you divide by the multiplier, $\left(1 - \dfrac{x}{100}\right)$.

EXAMPLE 22.4

Ben received a 20% increase in his salary.
After the increase his salary was £31 260.
What was his salary before the increase?

Solution

New salary = old salary × 1.2   The multiplier is 1.2.

Old salary = new salary ÷ 1.2   To reverse the process, divide by the
= 31 260 ÷ 1.2   multiplier.
= £26 050

22 Further percentages

EXAMPLE 22.5

In a sale everything was reduced by 7.5%.

(a) David bought a jacket in the sale.
It was originally priced at £85.
What was the sale price?

(b) Irene paid £38.70 for a skirt in the sale.
What was the original price of the skirt?

Give your answers to a sensible degree of accuracy.

Solution

Since 1p is the smallest coin, a sensible degree of accuracy is to the nearest penny.

(a) Sale price = original price × 0.925   The multiplier is
Sale price = 85 × 0.925   1 − 0.075 = 0.925.
         = £78.63 (to the nearest penny)

(b) Original price = sale price ÷ 0.925
                   = £38.70 ÷ 0.925
                   = £41.84 (to the nearest penny)

> **TIP**
> When you are asked to give an answer to a sensible degree of accuracy, look at how accurate the figures are given in the question.

Just as with percentages, if a quantity is increased by a fraction, the new amount is (1 + fraction) × the original amount.
To find the original amount when you are given the new amount, you divide by the multiplier, (1 + fraction).

If a quantity is decreased by a fraction, the new amount is
(1 − fraction) × the original amount.
To find the original amount when you are given the new amount, you divide by the multiplier, (1 − fraction).

You learned how to divide by a fraction in Chapter 4.

Check up 22.4

Work out these.

(a) $45 \div \frac{5}{6}$ **(b)** $26 \div \frac{4}{3}$ **(c)** $31.5 \div \frac{9}{7}$ **(d)** $46.2 \div \frac{7}{4}$ **(e)** $297 \div \frac{2}{3}$

Reverse percentage and fraction problems

EXAMPLE 22.6

On a jar of coffee it says 'Now contains $\frac{1}{5}$ more'.
The new size contains 564 g.
How much did a jar contain before the increase?

Solution

New amount = old amount $\times \frac{6}{5}$

Old amount = new amount $\div \frac{6}{5}$
$= 564 \div \frac{6}{5}$
$= 564 \times \frac{5}{6}$ To divide by $\frac{6}{5}$ you multiply by $\frac{5}{6}$.
$= 470$ g

EXERCISE 22.2

Give your answers to a sensible degree of accuracy.

1 Copy and complete this table.

	Original value	Percentage increase	New value
(a)	£80	15%	
(b)		12%	£52.64
(c)	£185	4%	
(d)		7.5%	£385.50

2 Copy and complete this table.

	Original value	Percentage decrease	New value
(a)	£800	13%	
(b)		8%	£113.16
(c)	£227	2.5%	
(d)		4.5%	£374.50

3 Alan invested in a bond that increased by 7.5% each year. After one year his investment was worth £875. How much did he invest?

4 A coat originally cost £79. In a sale it was reduced by 5%. What was the sale price?

5 Mrs Dale made a profit of £13 250 this year. This was 6% more than her profit last year.
What was her profit last year?

6 In a sale all items were reduced by 2.5%. A computer cost £740 in the sale.
What was the pre-sale price of the computer?

7 Henry was given a pay rise of 7%. His salary after the rise was £36 850.
What was his salary before the rise?

8 In a local election last year, Labour received 1375 votes. The number of votes they received this year was 12% greater.
How many votes did Labour receive this year?

9 A holiday cost £584 including VAT at 17.5%.
What was the cost before VAT?

10 At Jane's café all the prices were increased by 5% (to the nearest penny).
   (a) A cup of tea cost 75p before the increase. What is the new price?
   (b) The new price of a cup of coffee is £1.30. What was the old price?

11 During a special offer, a train company reduces all its fares by a third.
   (a) A journey usually costs £84. What is the cost of the journey during the special offer?
   (b) During the special offer a journey costs £36.50. What is the usual cost of the journey?

12 A computer servicing company increased all charges by $\frac{1}{8}$. After the increase Sam paid £94.50 to have his computer serviced.
How much would it have cost before the increase?

Challenge 22.3

(a) A jumper was reduced by 12.5% in a sale.
The reduction was £7.50.
What was the sale price?

(b) Sarah invested in a bond which increased by 4.5% each year for 5 years.
At the end of that time her bond was worth £10 530.24.
How much did she invest?

(c) There are 36 more girls than boys in a school.
54% of the students at the school are girls.
How many girls are there at the school?

continues ...

Challenge 22.3 continued

(d) Joe invests £1000 in a savings account that pays 4.5% compound interest annually.
He invests a further £1000 at the end of each year for 4 years.
He then leaves his money in the account for a further 3 years without adding to it.
How much has he in the account at the end of this time?

(e) Maria has £12 000 in a savings account that pays 4.75% compound interest annually.
Each year she takes £1000 out of the account immediately after the interest has been added.
  (i) After how many years does she first have less than £5000 in her account?
  (ii) How much is there then in the account?

(f) The value of a car decreased by $\frac{1}{5}$ each year for 5 years. At the end of that time the car was worth £6144. How much was it worth when new?

(g) A canal boat increased in value by $\frac{1}{15}$ each year for 2 years.
The overall increase was £3100. What was the original value of the boat?

WHAT YOU HAVE LEARNED

- When a quantity is increased by x% for n years, the multiplier is $\left(1 + \dfrac{x}{100}\right)^n$
- When a quantity is decreased by x% for n years, the multiplier is $\left(1 - \dfrac{x}{100}\right)^n$
- The multiplier for fractional increase is (1 + fraction)
- The multiplier for fractional decrease is (1 − fraction)
- To find the original amount when given the new amount and the increase, you divide by the multiplier

MIXED EXERCISE 22

Give your answers to a sensible degree of accuracy.

1. A population of bacteria is growing at a rate of 5% a day. There are 1450 bacteria on Tuesday. How many are there 3 days later?

2. A newspaper reported that the number of people taking their main holiday in Britain had reduced by 10% a year over the last 5 years. Five years ago, 560 people from a small town took their main holiday in Britain. If the report is true, how many of them would you expect to take their main holiday in Britain now?

3 Copy and complete this table.

	Original value	Increase or decrease	New value
(a)	£700	Increase of 3.5%	
(b)		Increase of 4.5%	£28.54
(c)	£365	Decrease of 5%	
(d)		Decrease of 7%	£840
(e)		Increase of $\frac{2}{9}$	£92.40

4 Damien sold his bicycle for £286, at a loss of 45% on what he paid for it. How much did he pay?

5 A magazine sold 10 240 copies this month. This was an increase of $\frac{1}{9}$ on the number sold last month. How many were sold last month?

6 At the Star theatre, the seating plan was changed and the number of seats in the stalls was increased by a third. There are now 312 seats in the stalls. How many were there before the increase?

7 Calculate how much £5000 invested with compound interest would be worth in each of the following cases.
   (a) 4.5% for 3 years   (b) 3.1% for 5 years   (c) 3.8% for 8 years

8 A bond pays 4% compound interest annually for the first 2 years and 6% each year for the next three years. Jenny invested £2000 in the bond. What was the bond worth
   (a) after 2 years?   (b) after 5 years?

9 In a sale, all the prices were reduced by 10%.
   (a) A coat cost £125 before the sale. What was its sale price?
   (b) The sale price of a suit was £156.42. What the pre-sale price?

10 A car manufacturer claims that for its latest model, the number of miles per gallon has increased by $\frac{1}{5}$. The new model travels 48 miles per gallon. How many miles per gallon did the old model travel?

23 → SAMPLING

> **THIS CHAPTER IS ABOUT**
> - Deciding on an appropriate sample size
> - Simple random sampling
> - Systematic random sampling
> - Stratified random sampling
> - Bias

> **YOU SHOULD ALREADY KNOW**
> - That data are collected to answer a question
> - How to write a questionnaire and carry out a survey
> - That data collected in a survey are analysed to answer the question posed

Sampling

A survey is often carried out to investigate a characteristic of a **population**. In statistics the word 'population' is used for a collection, set or group of objects being studied. It does not necessarily mean people.

Surveys are undertaken for many reasons. Here are some examples.
- Political parties wanting to know how people intend to vote in an election.
- Manufacturers wanting to know if a new flavour of crisps will appeal to the public.
- Doctors wanting to know how effective a new drug is.

When the whole population is large, it is not possible, or practical, to collect data from every member of that population. Not only would it take a long time to complete the survey, it would also be very expensive. It is therefore necessary to select a smaller group, called a **sample**, from the population. Any conclusions drawn from this sample will be applied to the whole population. For these conclusions to be meaningful, the sample must be representative of the population. Any variations in the population should be reflected in the sample. Any sample drawn from the population must be of sufficient size. The larger the sample, the more representative the sample will be of the population. A small sample will not give confidence that the results can be applied to the whole population.

There are various methods of choosing a representative sample. In this chapter three methods are presented: simple random sampling, systematic random sampling and stratified random sampling.

Notice that in the name of each of these methods the word 'random' appears. You can see, therefore, how important the random selection of the sample is to it being representative of the population.

Simple random sampling

In simple random sampling every member of the population has an equal chance of being selected. There are two main methods of selecting the sample: using random number tables and using the random number generating function of a computer or calculator. How these methods work is demonstrated in Examples 23.1 and 23.2.

EXAMPLE 23.1

The staff at a school want to find out how students would react to a change in the timing of the school day.
There are 500 students in the school.
A sample of ten students is to be selected and their views sought.

Method 1

- Each student in the school is given a three-digit number from 001 to 500.

(Notice that the members of the population are given a three-digit number because the number in the population is a three-digit number. If there were only 47 people then a two-digit number would be assigned to each person and the numbering would be from 01 to 47.)

- Consult a table of random numbers.
- Starting from a random position in the table, read numbers in groups of three digits.
- List all values in the range 001 to 500 and ignore any outside this range.
- Ignore any values that are repeated.
- Stop when you have ten different values.

This is part of a table of random numbers.

3063	7752	4300	0803	8080	6022	4280	6735	5278
0635	2656	2407	8314	4676	2411	3704	3481	8594
4519	3873	4674	2190	7024	8702	1671	6357	2223
7218	7119	9237	5344	9887	3865	0254	2516	0136
8113	7222	9927	7557	...				

Solution

Starting from the top left-hand corner, you get these numbers.

| 306 | 377 | 524 | 300 | 080 | 380 |
| 806 | 022 | 428 | 067 | 355 | 278 |

So, ignoring those numbers over 500, the students to be surveyed are those with these numbers.

| 306 | 377 | 300 | 080 | 380 |
| 022 | 428 | 067 | 355 | 278 |

Check up 23.1

Choose a different starting point in the random number table and make another selection of ten numbers in the range 001 to 500.

Do you think the sample is large enough?

EXAMPLE 23.2

The staff at a school want to find out how students would react to a change in the timing of the school day.
There are 500 students in the school.
A sample of ten students is to be selected and their views sought.

Method 2

- Again, each student in the school is given a three-digit number from 001 to 500.
- Use the random number button on a calculator to generate a number between 0.0…01 and 0.9…99. (The number will have as many digits as your calculator can show.) Alternatively, you could use a computer to generate random numbers.
- Multiply this value by 500, the number of items in the population.
- Add 1 and then take the whole number part of the answer. (This is called the integer part of the answer.)
- List all values.
- Ignore any values that are repeated.
- Stop when you have ten different values.

Solution

To obtain a random number press [SHIFT] [Ran#].

For example, a calculator gives a random number of 0.579 139 694.

The calculation is $0.579\,139\,694 \times 500 + 1 = 290.569\,847$.

The value chosen is 290.

Notice how there is no rounding involved. The value is truncated at the decimal point.

> **Check up 23.2**
>
> Follow the instructions above to select the other nine students to be surveyed.

Systematic random sampling

When you use systematic random sampling, you select the individuals at given intervals from a list of the population. For example, if you wanted to select 10% of the population you would number each member of the population and then, from a suitable starting point, choose every tenth item or individual.

The drawback of this method is that it will only provide a representative sample if the population is arranged in a random way.

EXAMPLE 23.3

A garage has 40 cars of a particular model. The manufacturer thinks that there is a fault in the brakes of this model and asks the garage to check the brakes of a 10% sample (four cars).

Method

- Each car in the garage is given a two-digit number from 01 to 40.
- Consult a table of random numbers. Starting from a random position in the table, read the numbers in groups of two digits.
- Find the first two-digit number between 01 and 10. (This is because a 10% sample is '1 in every 10'.)
- Alternatively use a calculator to generate a random number, multiply it by 10 and add 1. Take the integer part of the number.

(Note that for a 20% sample you would choose a start value between 1 and 5, for a 5% sample the start value should be between 01 and 20 and for a 1% sample the start value should be between 001 and 100.)

- From the start value, keep adding on 10 until the sample of 4 is achieved.

Solution

Starting from the top left-hand corner of the random number table on page 317, you get these numbers.

30   63   77   52   43   00   08

So, the starting value is 8.

The sample will be the cars with these numbers.

08   18   28   38

These cars will have their brakes tested.

Sampling 319

Check up 23.3

Use the instructions in Example 23.3 to find the car numbers for these systematic random samples.
(a) Start at the beginning of row 2 of the random number table on page 317. Choose a 20% sample.
(b) Start at the beginning of row 3 of the random number table on page 317. Choose a 5% sample.
(c) Start at the beginning of row 1 of the random number table on page 317. Choose a 50% sample.

Stratified random sampling

Some populations divide naturally into sub-groups. For example people can be divided by age, cars can be divided by engine size, apples can be divided by variety. These sub-groups are called **strata** and reflect the make-up of the population being investigated. Provided that the strata are distinct and that every member of the population belongs to one stratum only, then the population can be sampled using the method of stratified random sampling.

EXAMPLE 23.4

There are 240 people living in a small village.
Their views are sought by the council about the building of a new community centre.
A stratified random sample of 30 people is to be selected and interviewed.
The villagers are divided into three age groups.

Age (years)	Under 25	25 to 50	Over 50
Number of people	70	115	55

Method

- Find the proportion of the population in each of the strata.
- Work out what proportion of the sample needs to be selected from each stratum.
- Select a sub-sample of the appropriate size from each stratum using a simple random sampling method.

Solution

Under 25: $\frac{70}{240} \times 30 = 8.75$ Choose 9 people.
25 to 50: $\frac{115}{240} \times 30 = 14.375$ Choose 14 people.
Over 50: $\frac{55}{240} \times 30 = 6.875$ Choose 7 people.

- In the under 25 age group, number the people between 01 and 70. Choose a random start in a random number table and list the first 9 two-digit numbers in the required range. Alternatively, generate random numbers using a calculator. Interview the people with these numbers.
- Repeat this random sampling for the other strata.

Check up 23.4

Using the table of random numbers on page 317 or a calculator, find the code numbers of the people to be interviewed from each stratum in Example 23.4.

EXERCISE 23.1

1. Identify which type of sampling has been used in each of the following cases.
   (a) In order to determine whether the sports facilities in a leisure centre are satisfactory, all the members are numbered and questionnaires are sent to 100 who are selected using random numbers.
   (b) A car manufacturer employs 2000 people in the assembly plant, 400 in the parts department and 500 in the offices. A sample is taken containing 20 assembly plant workers, 4 people from the parts department and 5 from the offices.

2. The table shows the number of students in Years 9 to 13 of a school.

Year 9	Year 10	Year 11	Year 12	Year 13
162	161	157	63	58

   Students are to be interviewed about exam stress.
   A stratified sample of 60 students is to be taken.
   How many students from each of the year groups should be interviewed?

3. A biologist wants to estimate the average number of worms per square metre in a field. The field is divided into 100 metre squares and each square has a two-digit identification number between 00 and 99.
   For example, square 56 (row 5, column 6) has 9 worms.

	0	1	2	3	4	5	6	7	8	9
0	5	6	4	7	4	7	6	4	8	3
1	2	6	4	8	4	6	5	6	6	3
2	7	8	4	3	2	7	8	9	3	3
3	6	4	5	5	8	3	2	1	4	6
4	8	6	3	6	4	5	6	3	7	8
5	4	3	4	6	5	8	9	2	4	3
6	7	6	4	1	2	3	5	5	4	3
7	3	7	6	4	2	3	6	3	4	2
8	6	5	5	6	3	4	3	3	6	7
9	5	4	7	6	9	4	3	5	6	4

You are asked to select a sample of ten squares and find the mean number of worms in those squares. You are asked to use two methods.

Method 1: Starting at the beginning of the first row of the random number table on page 317, choose a simple random sample of ten squares.
Find the mean number of worms in these squares.

Method 2: Starting at the beginning of the second row of the random number table on page 317, choose the first value between 00 and 09.

Use this as the starting number of a systematic random sample of size 10.
Find the mean number of worms in these squares.

(a) Select the samples as described above and find the mean of each sample.
(b) How do the two samples compare?
(c) Find the mean of the population by finding the mean of all 100 squares.
(d) How do the means of the samples compare with the mean of the population of worms?

4 A company owns five factories. It wishes to select a stratified sample of 100 of its workers to interview about a new pension scheme.

Factory	1	2	3	4	5
Number of workers	409	207	1985	1011	398

How many workers should be selected from each factory?

Challenge 23.1

Measure the height of every student in the class.
Find the mean height for the class.
Choose a random sample of students in the class and find the mean height of this sample.
How does the sample mean compare to the population mean?
Discuss how other students' sample means compare to the population mean.

Bias

If each member of the population does not have an equal chance of being selected for a sample then the sample is said to be biased. A biased sample will not be representative of the population.

Bias can come from a variety of sources.
- When a sample is not chosen randomly.
- When people do not reply to a questionnaire. Bias is introduced into the results as it may mean that only those who have time for filling in the form or those who wish to influence the result of the investigation have replied.

- When a replacement item is included. If you were interviewing every tenth householder in a street and one was not at home, it would be wrong to interview another householder instead. The characteristics of the person at home may be different from the one who was out.
- How, where and when data are collected. Using the internet excludes those without a computer; questioning people at a particular location excludes those who do not frequent that location; the time of day may mean people are excluded who are not in the vicinity at that time.
- When the questions posed are not clear or are leading questions (see page 253).

When you take part in a statistical exercise you must show what measures you have taken to avoid bias in the sample you have chosen.

EXERCISE 23.2

1. In each of the following, decide whether or not the method of sampling is appropriate. If it is not satisfactory, say why not.
   (a) A newspaper editor wishes to gauge the public's reaction to a matter discussed in Parliament.
   She asks readers of her newspaper to write in and express their views.
   (b) To find out drivers' opinions of a car park, the drivers of 50 cars in the car park are asked to complete a questionnaire.
   (c) A councillor wishes to know the opinion of householders on a certain local issue.
   His plan is to visit every tenth house in each street. If there is no reply he has decided to call at the house next door.
   (d) A supermarket thinks that as many men as women shop at their store. To investigate this they set up a survey one Saturday morning between 9 a.m. and 10 a.m. where they count the number of men and women going in to the store.

2. A sample of 1000 people is to be interviewed about what books they read. Comment on the following methods for obtaining the sample.
   (a) Choose 1000 names from the telephone directory.
   (b) Ask 1000 people at random at a local railway station one evening.
   (c) Ask 100 librarians each to supply the names of 10 people.

Challenge 23.2

Look back at Exercise 23.2.

For each question, suggest a more suitable method for selecting a representative sample.

> **WHAT YOU HAVE LEARNED**
>
> - The importance of sample size
> - How to select samples by simple random sampling, systematic random sampling and stratified random sampling
> - How to avoid bias when selecting a sample

MIXED EXERCISE 23

1. A government officer is investigating whether there is a link between the income of families and the number of children they have.
   The table shows the information in her database of families.

Number of children	0	1	2	3	4 and over
Number of families	123	179	457	88	45

   She plans to interview a sample of 60 families.
   How many should she select from each group to make the sample representative?

2. The manager of a newly-opened gym wants to find out how successful it is. He decides to interview a sample of 50 of the members of the gym.
   Describe how he might choose the 50 members using each of these methods.
   (a) Simple random sampling
   (b) Systematic random sampling
   (c) Stratified random sampling

3. There are 180 students in Year 10 of a school.
   The P.E. department decides to interview a sample of 30 of these students to find out about the amount of exercise they take in a week.
   They intend to conduct the survey during a P.E. lesson when 80 of the students are playing football, 63 are playing hockey and 37 are playing badminton.
   How many of each group do they need to interview to make the sample representative?

4. A politician wants to find out how people feel about regional assemblies.
   She considers these four survey methods.
   (a) Put questionnaires in the Town Halls of 20 randomly selected towns across the country.
   (b) Randomly select 20 areas in the country and telephone every 50th person in their telephone directories.
   (c) Put an advert in 20 randomly selected local newspapers asking people to respond.
   (d) Send e-mails to every Member of Parliament asking their views.

   Criticise each of these methods of sampling.

24 → TRIGONOMETRY 1

THIS CHAPTER IS ABOUT
- Calculating the distance between two points
- Finding length of sides and size of angles in right-angled triangles

YOU SHOULD ALREADY KNOW
- How to measure angles and make scale drawings
- How to solve simple equations
- How to use Pythagoras' theorem

The distance between two points

You can use Pythagoras' theorem to find the distance between two points on a graph.

EXAMPLE 24.1

Find the length AB.

Solution

First make a right-angled triangle by drawing across from A and down from B.

By counting squares, you can see that the lengths of the short sides are 5 and 3.

You can then use Pythagoras' theorem to work out the length of AB.

$AB^2 = 5^2 + 3^2$
$AB^2 = 25 + 9 = 34$
$AB = \sqrt{34} = 5.83$ units (correct to 2 d.p.)

EXAMPLE 24.2

A is the point $(-5, 4)$ and B is the point $(3, 2)$. Find the length AB.

Solution

Plot the points and complete the right-angled triangle.

Then use Pythagoras' theorem to work out the length of AB.

$AB^2 = 8^2 + 2^2$
$AB^2 = 64 + 4 = 68$
$AB = \sqrt{68} = 8.25$ units (correct to 2 d.p.)

It is also possible to answer Example 24.2 without drawing a diagram.

From $A(-5, 4)$ to $B(3, 2)$ the x value has been increased from -5 to 3. That is, it has been increased by 8.

From $A(-5, 4)$ to $B(3, 2)$ the y value has been decreased from 4 to 2. That is, it has been decreased by 2.

So the short sides of the triangles are 8 units and 2 units.

As before, you can now use Pythagoras' theorem to work out the length of AB. You may prefer, however, to draw the diagram first.

EXERCISE 24.1

1 Find the length of each of the lines in the diagram.

Where the answer is not exact, give your answer correct to 2 decimal places.

2 Find the length of the line joining each of these pairs of points.
You can draw a diagram to help you.
Where the answer is not exact, give your answer correct to 2 decimal places.
   (a) A(1, 4) and B(6, 8)
   (b) C(1, 7) and D(6, 2)
   (c) E(4, 1) and F(6, −3)
   (d) G(−3, −4) and H(0, 2)
   (e) I(−5, −1) and J(1, 1)
   (f) K(−5, 0) and L(0, 12)

Labelling sides

You already know that the longest side is called the **hypotenuse**.

The side opposite the angle you are using (θ) is called the **opposite**.

The remaining side is called the **adjacent**.

TIP

Label in the order hypotenuse, opposite, adjacent.

To identify the opposite side, go straight out from the middle of the angle. The side you hit is the opposite.

You can shorten the labels to 'H', 'O' and 'A'.

Check up 24.1

Label each of the three sides in these triangles.

(a)   (b)   (c)

(d)   (e)   (f)

Labelling sides **327**

Discovery 24.1

- Make four drawings of this triangle.
  Draw the angles accurately but make each triangle a different size.
- Label the sides H, O, and A appropriately.
- Measure each of the sides of all your triangles.
- Use your calculator to work out $\dfrac{\text{Opposite}}{\text{Hypotenuse}}$ for each triangle.

What do you notice?

Repeat the task with four right-angled triangles each containing an angle of 70°.

You should have found that your answers for each set of triangles were very close to each other. This is because all your first four triangles were similar to each other and all your second four triangles were similar to each other.

The ratio you worked out, $\dfrac{\text{Opposite}}{\text{Hypotenuse}}$, is called the **sine** of the angle.

This is often shortened to 'sin'.

$$\sin \theta = \dfrac{\text{Opposite}}{\text{Hypotenuse}}$$

> **TIP**: Notice that the ratio of the lengths is written as a fraction, $\dfrac{\text{Opposite}}{\text{Hypotenuse}}$, rather than Opposite : Hypotenuse.

Find the [sin] button on your calculator.

Find sin 40° on your calculator by pressing these keys.

[sin] [4] [0] [=]

Now find sin 70°.

Check that your answers in Discovery 24.1 are close to these answers.

> **TIP**: Make sure that your calculator is set to degrees. This is the default setting but, if you see 'rad' or 'R' or 'grad' or 'G' in the window, change the setting using the [DRG] button.

Discovery 24.2

Use again the first four triangles you drew in Discovery 24.1.

Use your calculator to work out the ratio $\dfrac{\text{Adjacent}}{\text{Hypotenuse}}$ for each triangle.

What do you notice?

Repeat this for the second group of four triangles you drew in Discovery 24.1.

The ratio you worked out, $\dfrac{\text{Adjacent}}{\text{Hypotenuse}}$, is called the **cosine** of the angle.

This is often shortened to 'cos'.

$$\cos \theta = \dfrac{\text{Adjacent}}{\text{Hypotenuse}}$$

Find the [cos] button on your calculator.

Find cos 40° on your calculator by pressing these keys.

[cos] [4] [0] [=]

Now find cos 70°.

Check that your answers in Discovery 24.2 are close to these answers.

Discovery 24.3

Use again the first four triangles you drew in Discovery 24.1.

Use your calculator to work out the ratio $\dfrac{\text{Opposite}}{\text{Adjacent}}$ for each triangle.

What do you notice?

Repeat this for the second group of four triangles you drew in Discovery 24.1.

The ratio you worked out, $\dfrac{\text{Opposite}}{\text{Adjacent}}$, is called the **tangent** of the angle.

This is often shortened to 'tan'.

$$\tan \theta = \dfrac{\text{Opposite}}{\text{Adjacent}}$$

Find the tan button on your calculator.

Find tan 40° on your calculator by pressing these keys.

tan 4 0 =

Now find tan 70°.

Check that your answers in Discovery 24.3 are close to these answers.

> **TIP**
>
> You need to learn the three ratios
>
> $\sin \theta = \dfrac{O}{H}$, $\cos \theta = \dfrac{A}{H}$ and $\tan \theta = \dfrac{O}{A}$.
>
> There are various ways of remembering these but one of the most popular is to learn the 'word' '**SOHCAHTOA**'.
>
> This stands for
>
> | S O H | C A H | T O A |
> |---|---|---|
> | i p y | o d y | a p d |
> | n p p | s j p | n p j |
> | e o o | i a o | g o a |
> | s t | n c t | e s c |
> | i e | e e e | n i e |
> | t n | n n | t t n |
> | e u | t u | e t |
> | s | s | |
> | e | e | |

Using the ratios 1

When you need to solve a problem using one of the ratios, you should follow these steps.

- Draw a clearly labelled diagram.
- Label the sides H, O and A.
- Decide which ratio you need to use.
- Solve the equation.

In one type of problem you will encounter you are required to find the numerator (top) of the fraction. This is demonstrated in the following examples.

EXAMPLE 24.3

Find the length marked x.

8 cm

50°

x

330   24 Trigonometry 1

Solution

Draw a diagram and label the sides H, O and A.

Since you know the hypotenuse (H) and want to find the opposite (O), you use the sine ratio.

$$\sin 50° = \frac{O}{H} = \frac{x}{8}$$

$8 \times \sin 50° = x$ Multiply both sides by 8.

Press these keys on your calculator to find x.   [8] [×] [sin] [5] [0] [=]

$x = 6.128\,35... = 6.13$ cm correct to 3 significant figures.

EXAMPLE 24.4

In triangle ABC, BC = 12 cm, angle $B = 90°$ and angle $C = 35°$.
Find the length AB.

Solution

Draw the triangle and label the sides.

Since you know the adjacent (A) and want to find the opposite (O), you use the tangent ratio.

$$\tan 35° = \frac{O}{A} = \frac{x}{12}$$

$12 \times \tan 35° = x$ Multiply both sides by 12.

Press these keys on your calculator to find x.   [1] [2] [×] [tan] [3] [5] [=]

$x = 8.402\,49... = 8.40$ cm correct to 3 significant figures.

EXERCISE 24.2

1 In these diagrams find the lengths marked a, b, c, d, e, f, g and h.

Using the ratios 1   331

2 The ladder in the picture is 6 metres long.
The angle between the ladder and the ground is 70°.
How far from the wall is the foot of the ladder?

3 **(a)** Find the height, h, of the triangle.
   (b) Use the height you found in part **(a)** to find the area of the triangle.

Challenge 24.1

The length of the crane's arm is 20 metres.

The crane can operate with the arm anywhere between 15° and 80° to the vertical.

Calculate the minimum and maximum values of x, the distance from the crane at which a load can be lowered.

24 Trigonometry 1

Using the ratios 2

Check up 24.2

(a) Find x in each of these equations.

(i) $4 = \dfrac{8}{x}$ (ii) $4 = \dfrac{12}{x}$ (iii) $2 = \dfrac{20}{x}$

(iv) $3 = \dfrac{15}{x}$ (v) $2 = \dfrac{18}{x}$ (vi) $6 = \dfrac{24}{x}$

(b) Copy and complete this general statement.

If $a = \dfrac{b}{x}$ then $x = \ldots\ldots\ldots$.

In the second type of problem you will encounter you are required to find the denominator (bottom) of the fraction. This is demonstrated in the following examples.

EXAMPLE 24.5

Find the length marked x.

Solution

Draw the triangle and label the sides.

Since you know the A and want to find the H, you use the cosine ratio.

$$\cos 40° = \dfrac{A}{H} = \dfrac{12}{x}$$

$$x = \dfrac{12}{\cos 40°} \quad \text{Using the rule you found in Check up 24.2}$$

Press these keys on your calculator to find x.

[1] [2] [÷] [cos] [4] [0] [=]

$x = 15.664\,88\ldots = 15.7$ cm correct to 3 significant figures.

EXAMPLE 24.6

Find the length marked x.

Solution

Draw the triangle and label the sides.

Since you know O and want to find A, you use the tangent ratio.

$$\tan 27° = \frac{O}{A} = \frac{5.3}{x}$$

$$x = \frac{5.3}{\tan 27°}$$ Using the rule you found in Check up 24.2.

$x = 10.401\ 83\ldots$ Using your calculator.

$x = 10.4$ cm correct to 3 significant figures.

TIP Always look to see whether the length you are trying to find should be longer or shorter than the one you are given. If your answer is obviously wrong you have probably multiplied instead of dividing.

EXERCISE 24.3

1 In these diagrams find the lengths marked a, b, c, d, e, f, g and h.

334 24 Trigonometry 1

2 The bearing of A from B is 040°.
   A is 8 kilometres east of B.
   Calculate how far A is north of B.

3 The diagram shows a lean-to shed.
   (a) Find the length d.
   (b) The length of the shed is 2.5 m.
       Find the area of the roof.

Challenge 24.2

Mr Jones wants to buy a ladder.
His house is 5.3 metres high and he needs to reach the top.
The ladders are in two sections, each section being the same length.
When extended there must be an overlap of 1.5 metres between the two sections.

The safe operating angle between the ladder and the ground is 76°.

Calculate the length of each of the sections of ladder he needs to buy.

Using the ratios 3

In the third type of problem you will encounter, you are given the value of two sides and are required to find the angle. This is demonstrated in the following examples.

EXAMPLE 24.7

Find the angle θ.

Solution

Draw the triangle and label the sides.

This time, look at the two sides you know.

Since they are O and H, you use the sine ratio.

$$\sin \theta = \frac{O}{H} = \frac{5}{8}$$

Work out $5 \div 8 = 0.625$ on your calculator and leave this number in your display.

You have worked out the sine of the angle and now need to work back to the angle.

To do this, you use the $\sin^{-1}$ function (the inverse of sin).

You will find $\sin^{-1}$ above the [sin] button on your calculator.

To use this function you press the button labelled SHIFT, INV or 2nd F, followed by the [sin] button.

With 0.625 still in your display, press [SHIFT] [sin] [=], or the equivalent on your calculator.

You should see 38.682 18... .

So $\theta = 38.7°$ correct to 3 significant figures or $39°$ correct to the nearest degree.

Check that you do get this answer using your calculator.

You can also do the calculation in one stage by pressing these buttons, or the equivalent on your calculator. Note that you *must* use the brackets.

[SHIFT] [sin] [(] [5] [÷] [8] [)] [=]

EXAMPLE 24.8

Find the angle θ.

Solution

Draw the triangle and label the sides.

The two sides you know are O and A so you use the tangent ratio.

$$\tan \theta = \frac{O}{A} = \frac{15}{7} \quad \text{so} \quad \theta = \tan^{-1} \frac{15}{7}$$

This is the sequence of keys to press on your calculator.

[SHIFT] [tan] [(] [1] [5] [÷] [7] [)] [=]

This gives the answer $\theta = 64.983... = 65.0°$ correct to 3 significant figures.

EXAMPLE 24.9

Find the angle θ.

Solution

Since this is an isosceles triangle, not a right-angled triangle, you need to draw in the line of symmetry. This splits the triangle into two equal right-angled triangles.

The sides you know are A and H so you use the cosine ratio.

$$\cos \theta = \frac{A}{H} = \frac{6}{8} \quad \text{so} \quad \theta = \cos^{-1} \frac{6}{8}$$

This is the sequence of keys to press on your calculator.

[SHIFT] [cos] [(] [6] [÷] [8] [)] [=]

This gives the answer $\theta = 41.4°$ correct to 3 significant figures.

> **TIP**
> Example 24.9 shows how to deal with isosceles triangles. You use the line of symmetry to split the triangle into two equal right-angled triangles. This works only with isosceles triangles because they have a line of symmetry.

EXERCISE 24.4

1 In these diagrams find the angles marked *a*, *b*, *c*, *d*, *e*, *f*, *g* and *h*.

2 The diagram represents a ladder leaning against a wall. Find the angle the ladder makes with the horizontal.

3 In the picture the kite is 15 metres above the girl.
The string is 25 metres long.

Find the angle the string makes with the horizontal.

4 The diagram represents a pair of step ladders standing on a horizontal floor.

Find the angle, θ, between the two parts of the step ladder.

― Challenge 24.3 ―

A television mast is 54 metres high and stands on horizontal ground.
Six guy wires keep the mast upright.
Three of these are attached to the top and a point on the ground.
These three make an angle of 16.5° with the vertical.

(a) Calculate the total length of these three wires.

(b) The other three wires are attached $\frac{2}{3}$ of the way up the mast.

They are attached to the same points on the ground as the previous three.
Calculate the angle these make with the vertical.

WHAT YOU HAVE LEARNED

- How to find the distance between two points using Pythagoras' theorem
- The sides of a right-angled triangle are labelled hypotenuse, opposite and adjacent, usually abbreviated to H, O and A
- $\sin \theta = \dfrac{O}{H}$, $\cos \theta = \dfrac{A}{H}$, $\tan \theta = \dfrac{O}{A}$
- The steps used to solve a trigonometry problem are as follows
  1. Draw a clearly labelled diagram
  2. Label the sides H, O and A
  3. Decide which ratio you need to use
  4. Solve the equation

MIXED EXERCISE 24

1 Find the length of the line joining each of these pairs of points.
You can draw a diagram to help you.
Where the answer is not exact, give your answer correct to 2 decimal places.
    (a) A(2, 2) and B(4, 7)   **(b)** C(2, 9) and D(7, 2)   **(c)** E(5, 3) and F(7, −1)

2 In these diagrams find the lengths marked a, b, c, d, e and f.

3 In these diagrams find the angles marked a and b.

4 **(a)** Find the length a in this diagram.

    (b) Find the angle b in this diagram.

5 The picture shows a ladder leaning against a wall.
   (a) For safety the angle the ladder makes with the horizontal should be between 75° and 77°.
       Is this ladder safe? Show your working.
   (b) Find the length of the ladder.
   (c) A man is standing on the ladder.
       His feet are 3.5 metres from the bottom of the ladder.
       How far above the ground are his feet?

6 A ship sails on a bearing of 070° for 120 kilometres.
   (a) Draw a diagram to show this.
   (b) Calculate how far the ship is
       (i) east of its starting point.
       (ii) north of its starting point.

7 Find the acute angle between the diagonals of a rectangle with sides 7 cm and 10 cm.

8 Calculate the length of the equal sides in this isosceles triangle.

9 (a) Find angle θ in this trapezium.
   (b) Find the area of the trapezium.

10 A survey is being made of tall building.

The surveyor measures the angle of elevation of the top of the building as 15°.

The surveyor is 125 metres from the foot of the building.

The sighting device is 1.8 metres above the ground.

Calculate the height of the building.

11 The diagrams show a bascule bridge in the closed and open positions.

Calculate the distance, x, the two parts of the bridge are apart in the open position.

25 REPRESENTING AND INTERPRETING DATA

THIS CHAPTER IS ABOUT

- Constructing and interpreting cumulative frequency diagrams and box plots
- Using the median and interquartile range
- Constructing and interpreting histograms
- Calculating moving averages
- Interpreting a wide range of statistical diagrams and graphs
- Comparing distributions

YOU SHOULD ALREADY KNOW

- How to find the mean, median, mode and range of a set of discrete data
- How to construct bar graphs and frequency polygons
- How to find the modal class for grouped continuous or discrete data
- How to calculate an estimate of the mean of grouped continuous or discrete data

Cumulative frequency diagrams

Check up 25.1

The heights of 60 plants were measured.
Look at these data and calculate an estimate of the mean height of the plants.

Height (h cm)	$0 < h \leq 10$	$10 < h \leq 20$	$20 < h \leq 30$	$30 < h \leq 40$	$40 < h \leq 50$
Frequency	15	31	8	2	4

Why may the mean not be a good average to use here?

When you have a set of grouped continuous data, you can analyse it by calculating an estimate of the mean. However, sometimes the median is a more appropriate measure of average to use. For this and other purposes, you can use a **cumulative frequency** graph.

The data in Check up 25.1 can be combined to give this table.

Height (h cm)	$h \leq 0$	$h \leq 10$	$h \leq 20$	$h \leq 30$	$h \leq 40$	$h \leq 50$
Cumulative frequency	0	15	46	54	56	60

This tells you that, for instance, there are 54 plants which are 30 cm or less in height, obtained from 15 + 31 + 8 or 46 + 8.

> **TIP** When you look at a cumulative frequency table, make sure that you understand what information is given by the cumulative frequencies in the context of the data.

You use the table to draw a cumulative frequency graph, plotting (0, 0), (10, 15), (20, 46), (30, 54), (40, 56) and (50, 60).

Make sure that you use the top end of the class to plot a cumulative frequency graph and not the midpoints as you would for a frequency polygon.

This point shows that 56 of the plants have a height of 40 cm or less.

With 60 plants, the median is the average of the heights of the 30th and 31st plants. From the graph, find the value of the height at a cumulative frequency of 30.5. With a large set of data, the approximation $\frac{60}{2} = 30$ may be used. Cumulative frequency graphs are only suitable for large sets of data, so you should be able to use this approximation.

The graph shows that the median is about 15 cm.

Some statisticians prefer to join the points of the graph with straight lines rather than curves, showing that the graph is used for estimates. For GCSE, either method is accepted.

The cumulative frequency graph may also be used to find other information. For instance, reading the frequency corresponding to 25 on the horizontal axis, you can see that 52 plants are less than or equal to 25 cm in height.

344 25 Representing and interpreting data

The graph may also be used to find the **interquartile range**. This measures the spread of the middle 50% of the plants.

You need to read values for the lower quartile and the upper quartile, $\frac{1}{4}$ and $\frac{3}{4}$ of the way through the data respectively. Here, $\frac{1}{4}$ of 61 = 15.25, and $\frac{3}{4}$ of 61 = 45.75, so these are at the 15th and the 45th or 46th plants, approximately.

Lower quartile (LQ) = 10 cm

Upper quartile (UQ) = 19.5 cm

Interquartile range (IQR) = UQ − LQ
$$= 19.5 - 10 \text{ cm}$$
$$= 9.5 \text{ cm}$$

You can see here that the interquartile range is small, compared to the whole range. This tells you that the middle 50% of the data are closely bunched together. The steep curve between the quartiles also shows this.

Since the data are grouped and you do not have the original data, you cannot tell what the smallest and largest values of the data are, so you can only estimate the range. It could be as large as 50 − 0 = 50 cm and its lower bound is 40 − 10 = 30 cm.

The following notation is sometimes useful.
The lower quartile is Q_1 ($\frac{1}{4}$ of the way through the data).
The median is Q_2 ($\frac{2}{4}$ or $\frac{1}{2}$ way through the data).
The upper quartile is Q_3 ($\frac{3}{4}$ through the data).
The interquartile range is $Q_3 - Q_1$.

Cumulative frequency diagrams 345

Note: Mathematicians and software packages vary as to the cumulative frequencies they use for the quartiles. In this chapter $\frac{n+1}{2}$ is used for the median and $\frac{n+1}{4}$ and $\frac{3(n+1)}{4}$ are used for the lower and upper quartiles as the most accurate values to be used with $\frac{n}{2}, \frac{n}{4}$ and $\frac{3n}{4}$ being used as approximations when n is large. When interpreting a cumulative frequency graph for a large data set, there is unlikely to be much difference between the values for these definitions, and the acceptable values in GCSE questions will make allowance for these differences. For small data sets, the quartiles have only limited value and you are advised to use them with caution in these circumstances.

Cumulative frequency graphs can only be used with continuous data. The following example illustrates the use of the interquartile range for a small set of discrete data.

EXAMPLE 25.1

This stem-and-leaf diagram shows the number of passengers on a bus on 15 of its journeys.

```
1 | 8 9
2 | 0 3 5 5 6 6 7 9
3 | 1 2 3 3
4 | 5
```

Key:
3|2 represents 32 passengers

Find the range, the median and the interquartile range of these data.

Solution

Range = greatest value − least value
= 45 − 18 = 27 passengers

The median, Q_2 has a cumulative frequency of $\frac{15+1}{2}$ so Q_2 is the 8th value = 26 passengers.

Q_1 has a cumulative frequency of $\frac{15+1}{4}$ so Q_1 is the 4th value = 23 passengers.

Q_3 has a cumulative frequency of $\frac{3(15+1)}{4}$ so Q_3 is the 12th value = 32 passengers.

Interquartile range = $Q_3 - Q_1$
= 32 − 23 = 9 passengers

Example 25.1 shows also how one outlying value (45 passengers) affects the range but not the interquartile range.

> **Check up 25.2**
>
> Collect data from at least 50 students. (Or use data that has already been collected.) For instance, you could find the heights of students or the weight of their school bags. Group the data suitably into equal classes and find the frequencies.
> Make a cumulative frequency table and draw the cumulative frequency graph.
> Leave blank at least 5 cm underneath your graph. You will need this later in the chapter.
>
> From your graph, find the median and the quartiles, the range and the interquartile range.

Box plots

These are a way of showing the median, the quartiles, the range and the interquartile range.

A box shows the size of the interquartile range, with a line to show the position of the median.
'Whiskers' outside the box show the upper and lower values, so that the whole diagram shows the range.

If you are drawing a cumulative frequency diagram, it can be helpful to draw a box plot directly underneath it, using the same scale. The median and quartiles on the graph are then in line with their positions on the box plot. The next diagram shows this for the data on plants used earlier in the chapter.

Note that, as the data were grouped, you cannot be sure of the exact end points for the whiskers.

Cumulative frequency diagrams 347

Check up 25.3

Use the cumulative frequency graph you drew in Check up 25.2.
In the space you left below your graph, draw a box to show the median, the quartiles and the interquartile range.
Look back at the raw data you used and find the greatest and least values.
Use these to draw the whiskers on your diagram to complete the box plot.

EXAMPLE 25.2

Draw a box plot to represent the distribution with these summary statistics.

Smallest value   5.6 cm
Q_1 8.2 cm
Q_2 10.3 cm
Q_3 12.1 cm
Largest value   14.8 cm

Solution

Draw a scale from 0 to 15 cm.
Draw lines at each of the values given.
You can draw the line for the median as a dotted or dashed line.
Make a box between the lower and upper quartiles.

EXAMPLE 25.3

These box plots summarise the reaction times for a sample of one hundred students, for left and right hands.
Compare the distributions.

348   25 Representing and interpreting data

Solution

The median for the right hand is smaller. This shows that, on average, students were quicker at reacting using their right hand. However, the shortest reaction time was from a student using their left hand.

The interquartile range for the right hand is smaller. This shows that there was less variation between the students when reacting using their right hand.

> **TIP** When commenting on a distribution, your comments must relate to the context and not just mention the statistics.

You could also comment that both distributions are **positively skewed**. This means there is relatively little variation in the reaction times for the lower half of the distribution, but the box (and the whisker) is stretched out in the top half, showing that some students took much longer than the median. This idea is not required for GCSE but can be useful when describing a distribution.

Negatively skewed
$Q_2 - Q_1 > Q_3 - Q_2$
Often a longer tail in the negative direction

Symmetrical distribution
$Q_2 - Q_1 = Q_3 - Q_2$

Positively skewed
$Q_2 - Q_1 < Q_3 - Q_2$
Often a longer tail in the positive direction

The range is of less use than the interquartile range when comparing distributions, since the range may be affected by one or two extreme values.

Outliers are extreme values which occur in a distribution, such as the 45 minutes in Example 25.1. There may be good reason for them to occur (in that example, caused by a traffic jam resulting from an accident). However, sometimes outliers may be errors in recording results and you may wish to discount them.

A rule for outliers is that they are values whose distance from the nearest quartile is more than $1.5 \times$ interquartile range. If you discount outliers when doing a statistics project, make sure you mention them and give your reasons for ignoring them.

Here are the box plots for Example 25.3 showing the outliers. The whiskers have been drawn of length $1.5 \times$ interquartile range, and the outliers shown as separate plotted points.

Challenge 25.1

Look at your data from Check up 25.2 and the box plots you drew in Check up 25.3.
How long are the whiskers of your box plots compared to the interquartile range?
Are there any outliers in the data?
Discuss the reasons which have led to the outliers.

EXERCISE 25.1

1   This cumulative frequency graph shows the heights of 200 girls and 200 boys.

Find the median, the quartiles and the interquartile range for the girls and for the boys.

350   25 Representing and interpreting data

2. The table on the left shows information about the masses of 200 potatoes.
   (a) Copy and complete the cumulative frequency table on the right.

Mass (m grams)	Frequency
$0 < m \leq 50$	16
$50 < m \leq 100$	22
$100 < m \leq 150$	43
$150 < m \leq 200$	62
$200 < m \leq 250$	40
$250 < m \leq 300$	13
$300 < m \leq 350$	4

Mass (m grams)	Cumulative frequency
$m \leq 50$	16
$m \leq 100$	38
$m \leq 150$	
$m \leq 200$	
$m \leq 250$	
$m \leq 300$	
$m \leq 350$	

   (b) Draw the cumulative frequency graph.
   (c) Use your graph to find the median and interquartile range of these masses.

3. The table on the left shows the ages of people in a netball club.
   (a) Copy and complete the cumulative frequency table on the right.

Age (years)	Frequency
11–15	7
16–18	10
19–24	15
25–34	20
35–49	12
50–64	7

Age (y years)	Cumulative frequency
$y < 11$	0
$y < 16$	7
$y < 19$	17
$y <$	
$y <$	

   Note: the upper boundary of the 11–15 age group is the 16th birthday.

   (b) Draw the cumulative frequency graph.
   (c) How many people in this club are aged under 30?
   (d) How many people in this club are aged 40 or over?
   (e) Find the median and the quartiles.

Cumulative frequency diagrams   351

4 The cumulative frequency graph shows the head circumferences of a sample of 50 girls and 50 boys.

Make two comparisons between these distributions.

5 The stem-and-leaf diagram represents the marks gained by 23 students in a test.

```
4 | 1 8
5 | 0 2 3 6
6 | 2 4 5 6 7 7
7 | 0 1 1 3 5 6 8 9
8 | 2 5
9 | 3
```
Key: 5|4 represents 54 marks.

Copy and complete this table for the distribution.

Minimum (Q_0)	LQ (Q_1)	Median (Q_2)	UQ (Q_3)	Maximum (Q_4)

6 This table shows the earnings for a group of students one week.

Earnings (£w)	$0 < w \leq 20$	$20 < w \leq 40$	$40 < w \leq 60$	$60 < w \leq 80$	$80 < w \leq 100$
Frequency	5	15	26	30	6

Draw a cumulative frequency graph and a box plot to represent this distribution.

7 Here is a summary for a distribution of marks gained by a year-group in an examination.

Minimum (Q_0)	LQ (Q_1)	Median (Q_2)	UQ (Q_3)	Maximum (Q_4)
23	52	65	73	98

Draw a box plot for this distribution.

8 The cumulative frequency graph represents the heights of trees in a park.

(a) How many trees are there in the park?
(b) Draw a box plot for this distribution.

9 These box plots represent the time, in minutes, spent making mobile phone calls by samples of 50 boys and 50 girls one week.

Make two comparisons between the times spent making mobile phone calls by the boys and the girls, stating which statistics you use.

10 A company tested a sample of 500 light bulbs of each of two types it produces.
The table summarises the results, showing the time, in hours, that each light bulb lasted.

Time (t hours)	Frequency for type A	Frequency for type B
$0 < t \leq 250$	12	2
$250 < t \leq 500$	88	58
$500 < t \leq 750$	146	185
$750 < t \leq 1000$	184	223
$1000 < t \leq 1250$	63	29
$1250 < t \leq 1500$	7	3

(a) On the same axes, draw cumulative frequency graphs to represent these distributions. Below your graphs, draw box plots for the distributions.
(b) Which of the two types of light bulb is more reliable?

Histograms

Discovery 25.1

This frequency table summarises the data for the earnings one week of a group of students (from question **6** in Exercise 25.1).

Earnings (£w)	$0 < w \leq 20$	$20 < w \leq 40$	$40 < w \leq 60$	$60 < w \leq 80$	$80 < w \leq 100$
Frequency	5	15	26	30	6

Work in pairs, with one drawing a bar chart to represent these data and the other drawing a frequency polygon.
Compare your graphs and discuss the advantages and disadvantages of each type of graph.

The data may be grouped differently and presented like this.

Earnings (£w)	$0 < w \leq 10$	$10 < w \leq 30$	$30 < w \leq 50$	$50 < w \leq 70$	$70 < w \leq 100$
Frequency	2	8	24	32	16

How could you present this information on a graph?
Try out your ideas and discuss the results.

You may have realised in the task above that our eyes take area into account when judging relative size. So, when the width of the groups is unequal, you need to consider the impact of the area of the bars in a bar chart.

A histogram is a bar chart which uses the *area* of each bar to represent frequency. In doing this it represents fairly the frequencies of groups of unequal widths.

The table shows the ages of people in the netball club from question **3** of Exercise 25.1.

Age in years	11–15	16–18	19–24	25–34	35–49	50–64
Frequency	7	10	15	20	12	7

The histogram below shows the distribution of the ages of the members. Remember that the upper boundary of the 11–15 age group is the 16th birthday. So the boundaries of the bars in the histogram are at 11, 16, 19, 25, 35, 50 and 65.

Width = 15 years
Frequency = 12
Height = $\frac{12}{15} = 0.8$

The calculation of the frequency density for one group has been added to the histogram to show you how it was done. Sometimes, instead of frequency densities being shown, a key is given, showing what each unit of area represents. On this histogram, one rectangle of the grid represents two people.

Usually the calculations for the frequency densities are done in a table, as in the next example.

EXAMPLE 25.4

Draw a histogram to represent this distribution for the money raised for charity by runners in a sponsored race.

Amount raised (£x)	Frequency
$0 < x \leq 50$	6
$50 < x \leq 100$	22
$100 < x \leq 200$	31
$200 < x \leq 500$	42
$500 < x \leq 1000$	15

Solution

You add two columns to the table, one to work out the width of each group and the other to work out the frequency density.

You calculate the frequency density using

$$\text{Frequency density} = \frac{\text{Frequency}}{\text{Width of group}}.$$

Amount raised (£x)	Frequency	Group width	Frequency density (people per £)
$0 < x \leq 50$	6	50	$6 \div 50 = 0.12$
$50 < x \leq 100$	22	50	$22 \div 50 = 0.44$
$100 < x \leq 200$	31	100	$31 \div 100 = 0.31$
$200 < x \leq 500$	42	300	$42 \div 300 = 0.14$
$500 < x \leq 1000$	15	500	$15 \div 500 = 0.03$

356 25 Representing and interpreting data

> **TIP**
>
> An alternative method is to calculate the group widths as multiples of £50 (or £10).
>
> Using £50 would give group widths (×£50) of 1, 1, 2, 6 and 10.
>
> The frequency densities (people per £50) would be 6, 22, 15.5, 7 and 1.5.
>
> This avoids the need for a decimal scale.
>
> You may wish to draw the histogram using this scale and compare it with the one drawn in the solution above.

EXAMPLE 25.5

The histogram shows the distribution of money raised in another sponsored race.

The key has not been shown, but you are given that 15 people raised £50 or less.

(a) Calculate the frequencies for each group.
(b) Calculate also an estimate of the total amount raised.
(c) Make two comparisons with the distribution for the sponsored race in Example 25.4.

Solution

(a) The bar for the first group has a width of $\frac{1}{2}$ a rectangle on the grid and a height of 6 rectangles.
Its area is $\frac{1}{2} \times 6 = 3$ grid rectangles.
So 1 grid rectangle represents 5 people.

The 50–100 group has an area of 5 rectangles, which represents 25 people.
The 100–200 group has an area of 6 rectangles, which represents 30 people.
The 200–500 group has an area of 9 rectangles, which represents 45 people.
The 500–800 group has an area of $1.2 \times 3 = 3.6$ rectangles, which represents 18 people.

Alternatively, frequency density could be used.
The frequency density for the first group = $15 \div 50 = 0.3$, so now label the scale on the frequency density axis accordingly.
For the second group, the frequency density is 0.5, so the frequency = $0.5 \times 50 = 25$.
For the third group, the frequency density is 0.3, so the frequency = $0.3 \times 100 = 30$, etc.

(b)

Amount raised (£x)	Frequency	Midpoint	Midpoint × Frequency
$0 < x \leq 50$	15	25	375
$50 < x \leq 100$	25	75	1 875
$100 < x \leq 200$	30	150	4 500
$200 < x \leq 500$	45	350	15 750
$500 < x \leq 800$	18	650	11 700
Total	**133**		**34 200**

So a total of approximately £34 200 was raised.

(c) More people took part in the second race: 133 in the second race compared with 116 in the first.
Both groups had a positively skewed distribution, with the majority of people raising less than £200, but with a few people raising much larger amounts.

Challenge 25.2

Discuss other comparisons between these two distributions.

EXERCISE 25.2

1 The table shows the earnings for a group of students one week.

Earnings (£w)	0 < w ≤ 20	20 < w ≤ 40	40 < w ≤ 70	70 < w ≤ 100	100 < w ≤ 150
Frequency	5	15	26	30	6

Draw a histogram to represent this distribution.
Label your vertical scale or key clearly.

2 This distribution shows the ages of people watching a local football team one week.

Age (years)	Under 10	10–19	20–29	30–49	50–89
Frequency	24	46	81	252	288

(a) Explain why the boundary of the 10–19 group is 20 years.
(b) Calculate the frequency densities and draw a histogram to represent this distribution.

3 This histogram represents a distribution of waiting times in an outpatients department one day.

(a) Make a frequency table for this distribution.
(b) Calculate an estimate of the mean waiting time.

4 The histograms represent the time spent on mobile phone calls for a sample of girls and boys one week.

Histogram to show the time spent on mobile phone calls by girls

Histogram to show the time spent on mobile phone calls by boys

(a) Find how many girls and how many boys spent between 20 and 40 minutes on the phone.
(b) Compare the distributions.

5 The members of a gym were weighed. The histogram represents their masses.

(a) How many members of the gym were weighed?
(b) Calculate an estimate of their mean mass.

Time series

The table shows the takings in a café over a four-week period.

	M	Tu	W	Th	F	Sa
Week 1	£270	£302	£268	£342	£406	£432
Week 2	£286	£298	£237	£352	£425	£486
Week 3	£254	£283	£251	£364	£397	£459
Week 4	£273	£304	£258	£372	£410	£501

The graph below represents these data. The points are joined with dotted lines, since there is no meaning to 'in-between' values.

The graph shows the variation in the takings during the week and that they have a cyclic pattern. For instance, the takings are highest on Saturdays and lowest on Wednesdays.

To help 'iron out' the variation and to enable any long-term trends to be spotted more easily, **moving averages** are used. Since in this example the variation is over a 6-day cycle, a 6-point moving average is used.

The next graph shows the moving averages superimposed on the time-series graph.

The moving averages show that, over the four-week period, takings have been fairly stable, with a slight increase near the end.

To calculate moving averages, first find the mean of the takings for the first 6 days, Monday to Saturday.

$$\frac{270 + 302 + 268 + 342 + 406 + 432}{6} = 366.7 \text{ to 1 d.p.}$$

For the next moving average, you drop the first day and add on the next day to find the mean of the takings on Tuesday to Monday.

$$\frac{302 + 268 + 342 + 406 + 432 + 286}{6} = 339.3 \text{ to 1 d.p.}$$

Similarly, the next one is for Wednesday to Tuesday.

$$\frac{268 + 342 + 406 + 432 + 286 + 298}{6} = 338.7 \text{ to 1 d.p.}$$

And so on for the rest of the moving averages plotted on the graph.

You plot a moving average in the middle of the period to which it relates. So the first moving average is plotted in the middle of Monday and Saturday, halfway between Wednesday and Thursday.

A spreadsheet is useful for these repetitive calculations! If you are doing them by hand, the process is quicker if you notice that, from the first to the second moving average, the change is $(286 - 270) \div 6$. From the second to the third, it is $(298 - 302) \div 6$. So, having worked out the first one, the rest may be obtained using the day which has changed.

Using this method:

Monday–Saturday = $\dfrac{270 + 302 + 268 + 342 + 406 + 432}{6} = 336.666\ldots = 336.7$ to 1 d.p.

Tuesday–Monday = $366.666\ldots + \dfrac{286 - 270}{6} = 339.333\ldots = 339.3$ to 1 d.p.

Wednesday–Tuesday = $339.333\ldots + \dfrac{298 - 302}{6} = 338.666\ldots = 338.7$ to 1 d.p.

Thursday–Wednesday = $338.666\ldots + \dfrac{237 - 268}{6} = 333.499\ldots = 333.5$ to 1 d.p.

and so on.

Check your calculations by doing the last one, for Week 4 Monday − Saturday, by the long method as well as the short method.

> **TIP**
>
> Keep all the figures on your calculator and use the answer function for the next calculation, so you do not use rounded answers in further working. Take care, too, to use brackets when doing the divisions.

Discovery 25.2

Discuss situations when it might be suitable to use these.
- **(a)** 7-point moving average
- **(b)** 4-point moving average
- **(c)** 12-point moving average
- **(d)** 5-point moving average

EXAMPLE 25.6

This graph shows the number of units of electricity used each quarter by the Peters' family over 5 years, together with the 4-point moving averages.

TIP: The quarters 1 to 4 are winter, spring, summer and autumn.

(a) Describe the seasonal variation.
(b) Describe the long-term trend.

Solution

(a) Each year, the greatest use of electricity by the Peters' family is in the first quarter (winter) with the least use being in the third quarter (summer).

(b) The general trend is for slightly reduced use of electricity.

Interpreting other graphs and diagrams

Statistical information is often illustrated using graphs in newspapers, reports and other publications. Sometimes the graphs may be misleading, as in this example.

Large increase in profits

With no vertical scale given, the increase looks impressive. However, compare this with the two graphs below, which both represent the same information.

Large increase in profits

Large increase in profits

Discovery 25.3

Look at some newspapers and find some graphs and diagrams representing statistical information.

Discuss how clearly they show the information.

Discuss how fairly they show the information.

Read the accompanying newspaper articles.

Do they interpret the statistics accurately?

Are there comparisons made between distributions? If so, are they valid?

Share your results.

EXERCISE 25.3

1. The table shows the number of people visiting a leisure centre each day for a 4-week period.

	Su	M	Tu	W	Th	F	Sa
Week 1	1037	542	731	1084	832	905	1617
Week 2	1405	741	750	905	794	927	1392
Week 3	1605	763	801	928	937	1017	1854
Week 4	2047	694	728	861	904	935	1532

   (a) Plot a time-series graph of these figures.
   (b) Calculate the 7-day moving averages and add these to the graph.
   (c) Describe the trend.

2. The table shows the number of people visiting a doctors' surgery each day for a 4-week period.

	M	Tu	W	Th	F
Week 1	105	71	63	84	92
Week 2	126	86	71	94	115
Week 3	142	91	84	88	104
Week 4	115	82	73	84	91

   (a) Plot a time-series graph of these figures.
   (b) Calculate the 5-day moving averages and add these to the graph.
   (c) Describe the trend over this period.

3. These figures show the number of units of gas used by the Peters' family over a period of 3 years.

	1st quarter	2nd quarter	3rd quarter	4th quarter
Year 1	201	157	54	135
Year 2	192	161	63	173
Year 3	207	141	71	158

   (a) Describe the seasonal variation.
   (b) Calculate the 4-point moving averages.
   (c) Describe the trend.

4 The graph shows a shop's quarterly sales of rainwear.

Sales of rainwear

(a) Use readings from this graph to show how the fifth moving average has been calculated.
(b) Comment on the seasonal variation and trends shown on the graph.

5 The graph shows the variation in currency conversion rates during part of 2004 and 2005.

Exchange rate: British pounds to 1 US dollars

(a) On approximately what date did the US dollar buy fewest British pounds?
(b) Approximately, what was the most British pounds that 1 dollar would buy during February 2005?
(c) On 14 April 2005, the exchange rate was 0.531 745 British pounds to 1 US dollar. How many US dollars did 1 British pound buy then?
Give your answer correct to the nearest cent.

> **WHAT YOU HAVE LEARNED**
>
> - Frequencies can be combined to give cumulative frequencies, showing how many there are in that group or below
> - Cumulative frequency graphs can be drawn by plotting the cumulative frequency at the top end of each group
> - The values of the median, the upper quartile and the lower quartiles can be obtained from a cumulative frequency graph
> - Interquartile range = Upper quartile − Lower quartile
> - A box plot can be drawn to summarise a distribution
> - A histogram is a bar chart which uses the area of each bar to represent frequency
> - The vertical axis of a histogram is frequency density
> - Frequency density = $\dfrac{\text{Frequency}}{\text{Width of group}}$
> - A time-series graph represents discrete values over a period of time
> - Moving averages are used to help 'iron out' the variation and to enable any long-term trends to be spotted more easily
> - A moving average is plotted in the middle of the period to which it relates

MIXED EXERCISE 25

1 The table on the left shows information about the heights of 200 children in a primary school.

(a) Copy and complete the cumulative frequency table on the right.

Height (h cm)	Frequency
$120 < h \leqslant 130$	5
$130 < h \leqslant 140$	27
$140 < h \leqslant 150$	39
$150 < h \leqslant 160$	62
$160 < h \leqslant 170$	45
$170 < h \leqslant 180$	18
$180 < h \leqslant 190$	4

Height (h cm)	Cumulative frequency
$h \leqslant 120$	0
$h \leqslant 130$	5
$h \leqslant 140$	
$h \leqslant 150$	
$h \leqslant 160$	
$h \leqslant 170$	
$h \leqslant 180$	
$h \leqslant 190$	

(b) Draw the cumulative frequency graph.

(c) Use your graph to find the median and the interquartile range of these heights.

2 The heights of some tomato seedlings were measured.
Here is a summary of the results.

Smallest value	6.1 cm
Q_1	9.3 cm
Q_2	12.3 cm
Q_3	14.8 cm
Largest value	17.2 cm

Draw a box plot to represent the distribution.

3 The cumulative frequency graph shows how far a group of people, each using a pedometer, walked one day.

(a) How many people walked less than 4 kilometres?
(b) How many people walked more than 12 km?
(c) What was the median distance?

4 This stem-and-leaf diagram represents the total number of letters delivered to houses in a road by the postman each day for one month.

```
14 | 1 5 8
15 | 0 1 4 6 9
16 | 2 4 5 6 7 7
17 | 0 1 2 3 4 6 6 8 9
18 | 1 5 6 7
19 | 3 8
20 | 0 5
```

Key:
15 | 4 represents 154 letters.

Copy and complete this table for the distribution.

Minimum (Q_0)	LQ (Q_1)	Median (Q_2)	UQ (Q_3)	Maximum (Q_4)

5 The distribution shows the ages of people watching a rugby match one week.

Age (years)	Under 10	10–19	20–29	30–49	50–89
Frequency	240	1460	2080	4950	6120

Calculate the frequency densities and draw a histogram to represent this distribution.

6 The histogram shows the distance run one week by some people in training for a charity race.

Calculate the frequencies for each group and hence calculate an estimate of the mean distance run.

7 The histogram shows the distance run one week by another group of people.

Compare this distribution with that in question **6**.
Make at least two comparisons.

8 The table shows the number of people borrowing books from a library each day for 3 weeks.

	M	Tu	W	Th	F	Sa
Week 1	92	143	89	92	105	161
Week 2	83	122	76	94	116	132
Week 3	88	119	94	99	132	146

(a) Calculate the last 6-day moving average for this three week period (i.e. for Monday to Saturday of Week 3).
(b) The next moving average, for Tuesday of Week 3 to Monday of Week 4, is 111. How many people borrowed books on Monday of Week 4?

9 The table shows the number of people visiting a dentists' surgery each day for a 4-week period.

	M	Tu	W	Th	F
Week 1	35	42	63	24	51
Week 2	33	24	60	26	48
Week 3	38	44	66	29	46
Week 4	35	47	65	27	49

(a) Plot a time-series graph of these figures.
(b) One of the dentists works part-time. On which day does he not work?
(c) On one day in this period, a dentist was ill and her patients' appointments were postponed. When was this?
(d) Calculate the 5-day moving averages and add these to the graph.

10 The graphs show the percentiles for body mass index (BMI) for children. For instance they show that 75% of girls aged 12 years have a body mass index of 21 or less.

Boys: Body mass index

Girls: Body mass index

Graphics courtesy of Kidshealth.org/The Nemours Foundation. All rights reserved. © 2005

(a) What is the 75th percentile BMI for boys aged 14 years?
(b) Peter is 9 years old. He has a BMI of 18.
   Between which two percentile lines on the graph is his BMI?
(c) Sumita is 11 years old. Her BMI is on the lower quartile.
   What is her BMI?

26 → INDICES AND STANDARD FORM

> **THIS CHAPTER IS ABOUT**
> - Using the rules of indices
> - Dealing with negative and fractional indices
> - Dealing with very large and very small numbers

> **YOU SHOULD ALREADY KNOW**
> - How to use index notation
> - $a^m \times a^n = a^{m+n}$
> - $a^m \div a^n = a^{m-n}$

Raising a power to another power

In Chapter 1 you learned that $a^m \times a^n = a^{m+n}$. From this rule for multiplication you can work out the following.

$$(a^4)^3 = a^4 \times a^4 \times a^4$$
$$= a^{4+4+4}$$
$$= a^{3 \times 4}$$
$$= a^{12}$$

This result can be written in the general form

$$(a^m)^n = a^{m \times n}.$$

Other powers

Discovery 26.1

(a) Copy and complete this table for $y = 2^x$.

x	5	4	3	2	1
$y = 2^x$			8		2

(b) What is the rule for getting from one term to the next along the bottom row?
(c) Use this rule to find the last four entries in this table.

x	5	4	3	2	1	0	−1	−2	−3
$y = 2^x$			8		2				

Two to the power zero is 1.

$$2^0 = 1$$

This fits with the rules for multiplication and division. For example

$2^0 \times 2^3 = 2^{0+3} = 2^3$ which means that $2^0 = 1$.
$2^4 \div 2^4 = 2^{4-4} = 2^0$ which again means $2^0 = 1$ because $2^4 \div 2^4 = 1$.

Discovery 26.2

Use the multiplication and division rules to show that $3^0 = 1$ and $4^0 = 1$.

This is the general rule.

$$a^0 = 1, \text{ whatever the value of } a.$$

Here is the completed table from Discovery 26.1.

x	5	4	3	2	1	0	-1	-2	-3
$y = 2^x$	32	16	8	4	2	1	$\frac{1}{2}$	$\frac{1}{4}$	$\frac{1}{8}$

From the table you can see that

$$2^{-1} = \frac{1}{2}, \; 2^{-2} = \frac{1}{4} = \frac{1}{2^2} \text{ and } 2^{-3} = \frac{1}{8} = \frac{1}{2^3}.$$

These fit with the division rule. For example

$$2^2 \div 2^5 = 2^{2-5} = 2^{-3} \text{ and } \frac{2^2}{2^5} = \frac{4}{32} = \frac{1}{8} = \frac{1}{2^3}.$$

Discovery 26.3

Use the division rule to show that $3^{-2} = \frac{1}{3^2}$.

This is the general rule for negative powers.

$$a^{-n} = \frac{1}{a^n}$$

26 Indices and standard form

Discovery 26.4

Here again is a table for $y = 2^x$.

x	0	1	2	3	4
$y = 2^x$	1	2	4	8	16

(a) Plot a graph of $y = 2^x$.

(b) Use your graph to suggest values for $2^{\frac{1}{2}}$, $2^{\frac{1}{3}}$ and $2^{\frac{3}{2}}$.
Use the rule $(a^m)^n = a^{m \times n}$ to find the value of $\left(2^{\frac{1}{2}}\right)^2$.
What does this suggest that $2^{\frac{1}{2}}$ means?
Does this agree with the answer you read off the graph?

(c) Similarly use the rule $(a^m)^n = a^{m \times n}$ to find the value of $\left(2^{\frac{1}{3}}\right)^3$.
What does this suggest that $2^{\frac{1}{3}}$ means?
Does this agree with the value you read off the graph.

(d) Again use the rule $(a^m)^n = a^{m \times n}$ to find the value of $\left(2^{\frac{3}{2}}\right)^2$.
What does this suggest that $2^{\frac{3}{2}}$ means?
Does this agree with the value you read off the graph.

Discovery 26.5

Use the rule $(a^m)^n = a^{m \times n}$ to find the meaning of $3^{\frac{1}{2}}$ and $4^{\frac{1}{3}}$.

This is the general rule for fractional powers with one as the numerator.

$$a^{\frac{1}{n}} = \sqrt[n]{a}$$

This is the general rule for any fractional power.

$$a^{\frac{m}{n}} = \sqrt[n]{a^m}$$

Now $8^{\frac{2}{3}} = \sqrt[3]{8^2} = \sqrt[3]{64} = 4$.

But also $\left(\sqrt[3]{8}\right)^2 = 2^2 = 4$.

This suggests that you can do the root and the power in either order $\sqrt[3]{8^2}$ or $\left(\sqrt[3]{8}\right)^2$.

So the general rule above becomes as follows.

$$a^{\frac{m}{n}} = \sqrt[n]{a^m} = \left(\sqrt[n]{a}\right)^m$$

EXAMPLE 26.1

Write the following in index form.
(a) The cube root of x
(b) The reciprocal of x^2
(c) $\sqrt[5]{x^2}$

Solution

(a) $x^{\frac{1}{3}}$ (b) x^{-2} (c) $x^{\frac{2}{5}}$

EXAMPLE 26.2

Work out these:
(a) $49^{\frac{1}{2}}$ (b) 5^{-2} (c) $125^{\frac{1}{3}}$
(d) $4^{\frac{5}{2}}$ (e) $\left(\frac{1}{3}\right)^{-2}$

Solution

(a) $49^{\frac{1}{2}} = \sqrt{49} = 7$ (b) $5^{-2} = \frac{1}{5^2} = \frac{1}{25}$

(c) $125^{\frac{1}{3}} = \sqrt[3]{125} = 5$ (d) $4^{\frac{5}{2}} = (\sqrt{4})^5 = 2^5 = 32$

(e) $\left(\frac{1}{3}\right)^{-2} = \frac{1}{\left(\frac{1}{3}\right)^2} = \frac{1}{\left(\frac{1}{9}\right)} = 9$

TIP

If you have to work out the square root of the cube of a number it is usually easier to find the square root first.

If you want a fraction to a negative power, you can use the reciprocal of the fraction to the positive power.

$\left(\frac{a}{b}\right)^{-n} = \left(\frac{b}{a}\right)^n$

Check up 26.1

Match each number in index form to an ordinary number.
You may not need all of the numbers but you may need some more than once.

2^3 $\left(\frac{1}{2}\right)^{-2}$ $1000^{\frac{2}{3}}$ $64^{\frac{1}{2}}$ 10^2 $64^{\frac{1}{3}}$ $(0.5)^{-1}$ $8^{\frac{2}{3}}$ $4^{\frac{1}{2}}$ $64^{\frac{2}{3}}$ $64^{\frac{1}{6}}$ 7^0 $36^{\frac{1}{2}}$ $64^{\frac{5}{6}}$

0   1   2   4   6   8   9   10   16   20   32   64   100   200

376 26 Indices and standard form

EXERCISE 26.1

1 Write these in index form.
   (a) The square root of x
   (b) $\dfrac{1}{x^4}$
   (c) $\sqrt{x^5}$

2 Work out these. Give your answers as whole numbers or fractions.
   (a) 4^{-1}
   (b) $4^{\frac{1}{2}}$
   (c) 4^0
   (d) 4^{-2}
   (e) $4^{\frac{3}{2}}$
   (f) $100^{\frac{3}{2}}$
   (g) $64^{\frac{2}{3}}$
   (h) $81^{-\frac{1}{2}}$
   (i) 12^0
   (j) $32^{\frac{4}{5}}$
   (k) $8^{\frac{1}{3}}$
   (l) 8^{-1}
   (m) $8^{\frac{4}{3}}$
   (n) $\left(\frac{1}{8}\right)^{-1}$
   (o) $8^{-\frac{1}{3}}$

3 Work out these. Give your answers as whole numbers or fractions.
   (a) $3^2 \times 4^{\frac{1}{2}}$
   (b) $3^4 \times 9^{\frac{1}{2}}$
   (c) $125^{\frac{1}{3}} \times 5^{-2}$
   (d) $16^{\frac{1}{2}} \times 6^2 \times 2^{-3}$
   (e) $2^3 + 4^0 + 49^{\frac{1}{2}}$
   (f) $\left(\frac{1}{2}\right)^{-3} \times 27^{\frac{2}{3}}$
   (g) $6^2 \div 25^{\frac{1}{2}}$
   (h) $5^2 + 8^{\frac{1}{3}} - 7^0$

Challenge 26.1

Expand and simplify these.
   (a) $p^{\frac{3}{2}}(3p^{\frac{1}{2}} + 2p^{-2})$
   (b) $(3a^{\frac{1}{2}} - 2)(5a^{\frac{1}{2}} + 1)$

Using a calculator

The power button on a calculator is usually labelled $\boxed{\wedge}$ or $\boxed{x^y}$ or $\boxed{y^x}$.
You can use your calculator to work out any number to any power.

EXAMPLE 26.3

Work out $3.1^{2.4}$.

Solution

This is the sequence of keys to press.

$\boxed{3}\,\boxed{.}\,\boxed{1}\,\boxed{\wedge}\,\boxed{2}\,\boxed{.}\,\boxed{4}\,\boxed{=}$

You should get 15.110… .

Even if the power button on your calculator is labelled $\boxed{x^y}$ or $\boxed{y^x}$ rather than $\boxed{\wedge}$ you may see the symbol ^ in your display.

Check up 26.2

Practise using the power button on your calculator using simple examples such as 2^4 and 2^{-3}.

You can combine the use of the power button with the fraction button $\boxed{a^{b/c}}$ for powers such as $\frac{3}{4}$.

Above the power button you may see $\sqrt[x]{}$ or $\sqrt[x]{y}$ or $y^{1/x}$. These are usually in yellow. They allow you to find any root of a number. The yellow functions are operated using the $\boxed{\text{SHIFT}}$ or $\boxed{\text{INV}}$ or $\boxed{\text{2nd F}}$ button (usually yellow) before the main button.

EXAMPLE 26.4

Find the cube root of 27.

Solution

The cube root of 27 in index form is $27^{\frac{1}{3}}$.

This is the sequence of keys to press.

$\boxed{3}$ $\boxed{\text{SHIFT}}$ $\boxed{\wedge}$ $\boxed{2}$ $\boxed{7}$ $\boxed{=}$

You should get 3.

Check up 26.3

Practise with calculations you can do in your head such as $\sqrt[4]{16}$ and $125^{\frac{1}{3}}$.

You can practise further by checking the calculations you did in Exercise 26.1.

EXAMPLE 26.5

Work out the following. Give your answers exactly or to 5 significant figures:
- (a) 4.7^4
- (b) 2.3^5
- (c) 2.1^{-2}
- (d) $17.8^{\frac{1}{4}}$
- (e) $729^{\frac{5}{6}}$

Solution

(a) $4.7^4 = 487.968\,1 = 487.97$
(b) $2.3^5 = 64.363\,43 = 64.363$
(c) $2.1^{-2} = 0.226\,757\ldots = 0.226\,76$
(d) $17.8^{\frac{1}{4}} = 2.054\,021\ldots = 2.0540$
(e) $729^{\frac{5}{6}} = 243$

> **TIP**
>
> When you find a root using a calculator, it is very helpful to check by working backwards.
>
> For example, in part **(d)** above, work out $2.054\,021^4 = 17.799\,98\ldots$ to confirm your answer.

EXERCISE 26.2

1 Work out these. Give your answers exactly or to 5 significant figures.

(a) 4.2^3
(b) 0.52^4
(c) 2.01^6
(d) 3.24^{-3}
(e) $16\,807^{\frac{1}{5}}$
(f) $5.32^{\frac{1}{4}}$
(g) $\sqrt[3]{23}$
(h) $243^{\frac{3}{5}}$

2 Work out these. Give your answers exactly or to 5 significant figures.

(a) 200×1.03^4
(b) $1.3^5 \times 3.2^4$
(c) $2.5^5 \div 1.3^{-4}$
(d) $(5.6 \times 2.3^3)^{\frac{1}{4}}$
(e) $2.3^5 + 1.2^6$
(f) $2.3^{\frac{1}{3}} - 1.9^{\frac{1}{5}}$
(g) $5.2^4 + 0.3^{-3}$
(h) $15^3 - 225^{\frac{3}{2}}$

Challenge 26.2

The number of bacteria in a petri dish doubles every 2 hours.
There are 400 bacteria in the dish at midday.

(a) How many will there be at 4 p.m.?
(b) How many will there be at midnight?
Write your answer in the form 400×2^t.
Use the $\boxed{\wedge}$ button on your calculator to work out the answer.

Using the rules of indices with numbers and letters

The rules you have learned can be used with numbers or letters.

Here are the rules again.

- $a^m \times a^n = a^{m+n}$
- $a^m \div a^n = a^{m-n}$
- $(a^m)^n = a^{m \times n}$

> **TIP**
> A common mistake is trying to simplify an addition or subtraction.
> There is no rule for simplifying $a^x + a^y$ or $a^x - a^y$.
> Also, there is no rule for simplifying $a^x \times b^y$ or $a^x \div b^y$ because the **base** is different. This is another way of saying that they are unlike terms.

EXAMPLE 26.6

Where possible, write these as single powers of 2.

(a) $2\sqrt{2}$ (b) $(\sqrt[3]{2})^2$ (c) $2^3 \div 2^{\frac{1}{2}}$ (d) $2^3 + 2^4$
(e) $8^{\frac{3}{4}}$ (f) $2^3 \times 4^{\frac{3}{2}}$ (g) $2^n \times 4^3$

Solution

(a) $2\sqrt{2} = 2^1 \times 2^{\frac{1}{2}} = 2^{\frac{3}{2}}$

(b) $(\sqrt[3]{2})^2 = (2^{\frac{1}{3}})^2 = 2^{\frac{2}{3}}$

(c) $2^3 \div 2^{\frac{1}{2}} = 2^{3-\frac{1}{2}} = 2^{2\frac{1}{2}} = 2^{\frac{5}{2}}$

(d) $2^3 + 2^4$ (these cannot be added)

(e) $8^{\frac{3}{4}} = (2^3)^{\frac{3}{4}} = 2^{3 \times \frac{3}{4}} = 2^{\frac{9}{4}}$

(f) $2^3 \times 4^{\frac{3}{2}} = 2^3 \times (2^2)^{\frac{3}{2}} = 2^3 \times 2^3 = 2^6$

(g) $2^n \times 4^3 = 2^n \times (2^2)^3 = 2^n \times 2^6 = 2^{n+6}$

EXERCISE 26.3

1 Write these as powers of 3 as simply as possible.

(a) 81   (b) $\frac{1}{3}$ (c) $3 \times \sqrt{3}$ (d) $3^4 \times 9^{-1}$
(e) 9^n (f) 27^{3n} (g) $9^n \times 27^{3n}$

2 Where possible, write these as powers of 5 as simply as possible.

(a) 0.2   (b) 125   (c) 25^2 (d) $125 \times 5^{-2} \times 25^2$
(e) $5^4 - 5^3$ (f) $25^{3n} \times 125^{\frac{n}{3}}$

3 Write these in the form $2^a \times 3^b$.

(a) 18   (b) 72   (c) $18^{\frac{1}{3}}$ (d) $\frac{4}{9}$ (e) $13\frac{1}{2}$

4 Write each of these numbers as a product of prime numbers. Use indices where possible.

For example, $\frac{8}{\sqrt{3}} = 8 \times \frac{1}{\sqrt{3}} = 2^3 \times 3^{-\frac{1}{2}}$

(a) 75   (b) 288   (c) 500   (d) 3240

Challenge 26.3

Simplify these.

(a) $x^2 \times x^{\frac{1}{2}}$
(b) $x^{\frac{1}{2}} \div x^2$
(c) $x^3 \times x^{-2}$
(d) $x^4 \div x^{-2}$
(e) $\sqrt{\dfrac{8a^3}{2a^2}}$
(f) $\sqrt[3]{x^6}$

Challenge 26.4

The numbers of a certain species of animal are reducing by 15% every 10 years.
In 1960 there were 30 000.
How many will there be
(a) in 2010?
(b) in 2050?
(c) n years after 1960?

Standard form

Standard form is a very important use of indices. It is a way of making very large numbers and very small numbers easy to deal with.

In standard form, numbers are written as a number between 1 and 10 multiplied by a power of 10.

Large numbers

EXAMPLE 26.7

Write these numbers in standard form.
(a) 500 000
(b) 6 300 000
(c) 45 600

Solution

(a) $500\,000 = 5 \times 100\,000 = 5 \times 10^5$
(b) $6\,300\,000 = 6.3 \times 1\,000\,000 = 6.3 \times 10^6$
(c) $45\,600 = 4.56 \times 10\,000 = 4.56 \times 10^4$

TIP

You can write down the answer without any intermediate steps.

Move the decimal point until the number is between 1 and 10.

Count the number of places the point has moved: that is the power of 10.

Small numbers

EXAMPLE 26.8

Write these numbers in standard form.
(a) 0.000 003 (b) 0.000 056 (c) 0.000 726

Solution

(a) $0.000\,003 = \dfrac{3}{1\,000\,000} = 3 \times \dfrac{1}{1\,000\,000} = 3 \times \dfrac{1}{10^6} = 3 \times 10^{-6}$

(b) $0.000\,056 = \dfrac{5.6}{100\,000} = 5.6 \times \dfrac{1}{100\,000} = 5.6 \times \dfrac{1}{10^5} = 5.6 \times 10^{-5}$

(c) $0.000\,726 = \dfrac{7.26}{10\,000} = 7.26 \times \dfrac{1}{10\,000} = 7.26 \times \dfrac{1}{10^4} = 7.26 \times 10^{-4}$

TIP

You can write down the answer without any intermediate steps.

Move the decimal point until the number is between 1 and 10.

Count the number of places the point has moved: put a minus sign in front and that is the power of 10.

Discovery 26.6

Find the approximate distance, in kilometres, of each of the planets from the sun.

Write the distances in standard form.

(You will find the distances in books such as atlases or encyclopaedias or on the internet.)

EXERCISE 26.4

1 Write these numbers in standard form.
(a) 7000 (b) 84 000 (c) 563 (d) 6 500 000
(e) 723 000 (f) 27 (g) 8 million (h) 39.2 million

2 Write these numbers in standard form.
(a) 0.003 (b) 0.056 (c) 0.000 38
(d) 0.000 006 3 (e) 0.000 082 (f) 0.000 000 38

3 These numbers are in standard form. Write them as ordinary numbers.
(a) 5×10^4 (b) 3.7×10^5 (c) 7×10^{-4} (d) 6.9×10^6
(e) 6.1×10^{-3} (f) 4.73×10^4 (g) 2.79×10^7 (h) 4.83×10^{-5}
(i) 1.03×10^{-2} (j) 9.89×10^8 (k) 2.61×10^{-6} (l) 3.7×10^2

Calculating with numbers in standard form

When you need to multiply or divide numbers in standard form you can use your knowledge of the laws of indices.

EXAMPLE 26.9

Work out these. Give your answers in standard form.
(a) $(7 \times 10^3) \times (4 \times 10^4)$
(b) $(7 \times 10^7) \div (2 \times 10^{-3})$
(c) $(3 \times 10^8) \div (5 \times 10^3)$

Solution

(a) $(7 \times 10^3) \times (4 \times 10^4) = 7 \times 4 \times 10^3 \times 10^4 = 28 \times 10^{3+4} = 28 \times 10^7 = 2.8 \times 10^8$

(b) $(7 \times 10^7) \div (2 \times 10^{-3}) = \dfrac{7 \times 10^7}{2 \times 10^{-3}} = 3.5 \times 10^{7-(-3)} = 3.5 \times 10^{10}$

(c) $(3 \times 10^8) \div (5 \times 10^3) = \dfrac{3 \times 10^8}{5 \times 10^3} = 0.6 \times 10^{8-3} = 0.6 \times 10^5 = 6 \times 10^4$

When you need to add or subtract numbers in standard form it is much safer to change to ordinary numbers first.

EXAMPLE 26.10

Work out these. Give your answers in standard form.
(a) $(7 \times 10^3) + (1.4 \times 10^4)$ (b) $(7.2 \times 10^5) + (2.5 \times 10^4)$
(c) $(5.3 \times 10^{-3}) - (4.9 \times 10^{-4})$

Solution

(a)
```
  7 0 0 0
+1 4 0 0 0
─────────
 2 1 0 0 0 = 2.1 × 10⁴
```

(b)
```
  7 2 0 0 0 0
+   2 5 0 0 0
─────────────
  7 4 5 0 0 0 = 7.45 × 10⁵
```

(c)
```
   0.0 0 5 3 0
-  0.0 0 0 4 9
──────────────
   0.0 0 4 8 1 = 4.81 × 10⁻³
```

Standard form on your calculator

You can do all the calculations above on your calculator using the $\boxed{\text{EXP}}$ button.

EXAMPLE 26.11

Find $(7 \times 10^7) \div (2 \times 10^{-3})$ using your calculator.

Solution

This is part **(b)** of Example 26.9. These are the keys to press on your calculator.

$\boxed{7}$ $\boxed{\text{EXP}}$ $\boxed{7}$ $\boxed{\div}$ $\boxed{2}$ $\boxed{\text{EXP}}$ $\boxed{(-)}$ $\boxed{3}$ $\boxed{=}$

You should see 3.5×10^{10}.

TIP: When using the $\boxed{\text{EXP}}$ button, do not enter 10 as well.

On some calculators the $\boxed{(-)}$ button is marked $\boxed{+/-}$.

Sometimes your calculator will give you an ordinary number which you will have to write in standard form, if asked to give your answer in standard form. Otherwise your calculator will give you the answer in standard form.

Modern calculators usually give the correct version of standard form, for example 2.8×10^8.

Older calculators often give a calculator version such as 2.8^{08}. You must write this in proper standard form, 2.8×10^8, for your answer.

Some graphical calculators display standard form as, for example, 2.8 E 08.

Again you must write this in proper standard form for your answer.

Check up 26.4

Practise by checking the rest of Example 26.9 and Example 26.10 on your calculator.

EXERCISE 26.5

1 Work out these. Give your answers in standard form.
   (a) $(4 \times 10^3) \times (2 \times 10^4)$
   (b) $(6 \times 10^7) \times (2 \times 10^3)$
   (c) $(7 \times 10^3) \times (8 \times 10^2)$
   (d) $(4.8 \times 10^3) \div (1.2 \times 10^{-2})$
   (e) $(4 \times 10^3) \times (1.3 \times 10^4)$
   (f) $(4 \times 10^9) \div (8 \times 10^4)$
   (g) $(4 \times 10^3) + (6 \times 10^4)$
   (h) $(6.2 \times 10^5) - (3.7 \times 10^4)$

2 Work out these. Give your answers in standard form.
   (a) $(6.2 \times 10^5) \times (3.8 \times 10^7)$
   (b) $(6.3 \times 10^7) \div (4.2 \times 10^2)$
   (c) $(6.67 \times 10^8) \div (4.6 \times 10^{-3})$
   (d) $(3.7 \times 10^{-4}) \times (2.9 \times 10^{-3})$
   (e) $(1.69 \times 10^8) \div (5.2 \times 10^3)$
   (f) $(7.63 \times 10^5) + (3.89 \times 10^4)$
   (g) $(3.72 \times 10^6) - (2.8 \times 10^4)$
   (h) $(5.63 \times 10^{-3}) - (4.28 \times 10^{-4})$

Challenge 26.5

Light takes approximately 3.3×10^{-9} seconds to travel 1 metre.
The distance from the Earth to the Sun is 150 000 000 km.

(a) Write 150 000 000 km in metres using standard form.
(b) How long does it take for light to reach Earth from the Sun?

Challenge 26.6

Paper is 0.08 mm thick

(a) Write this thickness in metres using standard form.
(b) A library has 4.6×10^4 metres of shelf space.
Assuming 80% of this is filled with paper, the rest being the covers of the books, estimate how many sheets of paper there are on the shelves.
Give your answer in standard form.

Challenge 26.7

The table shows information about the Earth.

Distance from the Sun	149 503 000 km
Circumference of solar orbit	9.4×10^8 km
Speed of the Earth in solar orbit	0.106×10^6 km/h
Speed of the solar system	20.1 km/s

continues …

Challenge 26.7 continued

(a) The speed of the Earth is given in index form but not standard form.
Write the speed of the Earth in standard form.
(b) How far does the Earth travel at this speed in one day?
Give your answer in standard form correct to three significant figures.
(c) How far does the solar system travel in one day?
Give your answer in standard form correct to three significant figures.
(d) An object travels from the Earth to the Sun and back.
How far does it travel?
Give your answer in standard form correct to three significant figures.

WHAT YOU HAVE LEARNED

- **The rules of indices**
  - $a^m \times a^n = a^{m+n}$
  - $a^m \div a^n = a^{m-n}$
  - $(a^m)^n = a^{m \times n}$
  - $a^0 = 1$, whatever the value of a
  - $a^{-n} = \dfrac{1}{a^n}$
  - $a^{\frac{1}{n}} = \sqrt[n]{a}$
  - $a^{\frac{m}{n}} = \sqrt[n]{a^m} = (\sqrt[n]{a})^m$

- **Standard form is used to deal with very large and very small numbers**
  - Numbers are written as $a \times 10^n$ where a is between 1 and 10
  - Large numbers such as 93 million (93 000 000) are written as 9.3×10^7
  - Small numbers such as 0.000 007 82 are written as 7.82×10^{-6}
  - You can enter numbers in standard form in your calculator using the [EXP] button

MIXED EXERCISE 26

1 Work out these. Give your answers as whole numbers or fractions.
  (a) $9^{\frac{1}{2}}$ (b) $27^{\frac{2}{3}}$ (c) 3^{-2} (d) $16^{-\frac{1}{2}}$ (e) $100^{\frac{5}{2}}$

2 Work out these. Give your answers as whole numbers or fractions.
  (a) $5^{-1} \times 4^{\frac{1}{2}}$
  (b) $81^{\frac{1}{2}} \times 3^0 \times 144^{-\frac{1}{2}}$
  (c) $16^{\frac{3}{4}} + 5^0 + 1000^{\frac{2}{3}}$
  (d) $8^{-\frac{1}{3}} \times 49^{\frac{1}{2}} \times 3^{-1}$

3 Work out these. Give your answers to 4 significant figures.
   (a) 2.6^3
   (b) $4.3^{\frac{1}{2}}$
   (c) 3.8^{-2}
   (d) $\sqrt[5]{867}$
   (e) $50^{\frac{2}{3}}$

4 Work out these. Give your answers to 4 significant figures.
   (a) $5.8^4 \div 2.6^3$
   (b) $2.8^{\frac{1}{2}} \times 7.6^{-2}$
   (c) $(3.8 \times 1.7^4)^{\frac{1}{3}}$
   (d) $5^{\frac{1}{2}} + 3^{-2} - 6^{0.7}$

5 Write these numbers as powers of prime numbers.
   (a) 49
   (b) $\frac{1}{25}$
   (c) $8^{-\frac{2}{3}}$
   (d) $\sqrt[3]{121}$
   (e) $\frac{1}{\sqrt{3}}$

6 Write each of these numbers as a product of powers of prime numbers. Use indices where possible.

   For example, $\frac{8}{\sqrt{3}} = 8 \times \frac{1}{\sqrt{3}} = 2^3 \times 3^{-\frac{1}{2}}$

   (a) 12^3
   (b) $4^2 \times 18$
   (c) $\frac{8}{81}$
   (d) $\frac{125}{36}$
   (e) $\sqrt[3]{15}$

7 Write these numbers in standard form.
   (a) 16 500
   (b) 0.000 869
   (c) 53 million
   (d) 0.000 000 083

8 Write these as ordinary numbers.
   (a) 5.3×10^5
   (b) 6.32×10^{-3}
   (c) 7.26×10^8
   (d) 1.28×10^{-6}

9 Work these out. Write your answers in standard form.
   (a) $(2 \times 10^3) \times (4 \times 10^5)$
   (b) $(6 \times 10^8) \times (4 \times 10^{-3})$
   (c) $(9 \times 10^7) \div (4 \times 10^3)$
   (d) $(5 \times 10^6) \div (2 \times 10^{-3})$
   (e) $(4 \times 10^7) \div (5 \times 10^2)$
   (f) $(7 \times 10^{-3}) \times (3 \times 10^{-5})$
   (g) $(4 \times 10^4) + (6 \times 10^3)$
   (h) $(7 \times 10^{-4}) + (6 \times 10^{-5})$
   (i) $(6 \times 10^7) - (4 \times 10^5)$
   (j) $(8 \times 10^{-4}) - (3 \times 10^{-5})$

10 Work these out. Give your answers in standard form to 3 significant figures.
   (a) $(5.32 \times 10^5) \times (1.28 \times 10^3)$
   (b) $(6.23 \times 10^{-5}) \times (4.62 \times 10^{-6})$
   (c) $(2.8 \times 10^5) \div (3.2 \times 10^{-3})$
   (d) $(6.1 \times 10^4) \div (7.3 \times 10^8)$
   (e) $(6.53 \times 10^5) + (7.26 \times 10^4)$
   (f) $(2.87 \times 10^{-4}) - (8.26 \times 10^{-5})$

27 → SIMILARITY AND ENLARGEMENT

THIS CHAPTER IS ABOUT
- Recognising and working with similar triangles
- Enlarging triangles and other plane shapes using negative scale factors
- Area and volume of similar figures

YOU SHOULD ALREADY KNOW
- The angle facts for parallel lines: alternate angles, a and b, are equal and corresponding angles, a and c, are equal

- The angles in a triangle add up to 180°
- The angles on a straight line add up to 180°
- The exterior angle of a triangle equals the sum of the opposite, interior angles

Similarity of triangles and other plane shapes

Two triangles are **similar** if the angles in one triangle are equal to the angles in the other.

For other polygons, the test for similarity is that the angles in the two shapes are equal *and* the corresponding sides are in proportion.

In this diagram, triangle ABC is similar to triangle PQR because angles A, B and C equal angles P, Q and R.

For similar triangles the ratios of the corresponding sides are equal. As you did in Chapter 24, you can write the ratios as fractions.

$$\frac{a}{p} = \frac{b}{q} = \frac{c}{r} = k$$

The ratio k is the scale factor.

The heights are also in the same ratio.

$$\frac{h}{H} = k$$

EXAMPLE 27.1

The diagram shows two triangles, triangle ABC and triangle XYZ.

(a) Explain why the two triangles are similar.
(b) Calculate the values of y and z.

Solution

(a) Angle BAC = 52°   Angles in a triangle add up to 180°.
Angle ZXY = 30°   Angles in a triangle add up to 180°.

Therefore the corresponding angles in each triangle are equal.
Therefore the triangles are similar.

(b) AB and ZY are corresponding sides, joining the angles of 98° and 52°.

$$\frac{ZY}{AB} = \frac{4}{5} \text{ so } \frac{YX}{BC} \text{ also } = \frac{4}{5}$$

$$YX = \frac{4}{5} \times BC$$
$$= \frac{4}{5} \times 8$$
$$= 0.8 \times 8$$
$$= 6.4$$

$z = 6.4$ cm

Similarly,

$$\frac{ZX}{AC} = \frac{4}{5}$$

$$ZX = \frac{4}{5} \times AC$$
$$= \frac{4}{5} \times 10$$
$$= 0.8 \times 10$$
$$= 8$$

$y = 8$ cm

Similarity of triangles and other plane shapes

EXERCISE 27.1

1 Which of the triangles in this diagram are similar?

2 These two triangles are similar.

Calculate the lengths of XY and YZ.

3 In triangle ABC, XY is parallel to AC, AB = 12 cm, YC = 3 cm, YB = 5 cm and XY = 3 cm.
Calculate the lengths of AC, AX and XB.

4 At noon a radio mast of height 12 m has a shadow length of 16 m. Calculate the height of a tower with a shadow length of 56 m.

390 27 Similarity and enlargement

5 Calculate the lengths *x* and *y* in this diagram.

6 Calculate the lengths *x* and *y* in this diagram.

7 A stand for a small statue is made from part of a cone (called a frustum).
The circular top of the stand has a diameter of 12 cm; the base has a diameter of 18 cm.
The slant height of the stand is 9 cm.
Calculate the slant height of the complete cone.

8 **(a)** Explain how you know that the two triangles in the diagram are similar.
(b) Calculate the lengths of AC and CB.

Challenge 27.1

This definition was given at the beginning of this chapter.

Two triangles are **similar** if the angles in one triangle are equal to the angles in the other.

For other polygons, the test for similarity is that the angles in the two shapes are equal *and* the corresponding sides are in proportion.

Can you explain why the definition needs extending for polygons?

Challenge 27.2

The diagram shows a inclined block of wood with a groove, ABCD, cut in it.

As part of an experiment a ball is rolled down the groove from A to D when the block is placed on a table.

(a) Use similar triangles to calculate the length of the groove.
    Give your answer to the nearest centimetre.
(b) Calculate the angle the path from C to D makes with the table.
    Give your answer to the nearest degree.

Enlargement

To carry out an enlargement you need two pieces of information

- the scale factor
- the centre of enlargement.

In Chapter 13 you learned about enlargements with fractional scale factors. The next example reminds you about this.

EXAMPLE 27.2

Plot the coordinates A(4, 4), B(16, 4), C(16, 8) and D(4, 8) and join them to form a rectangle.

Enlarge rectangle ABCD by a scale factor of $\frac{1}{2}$ using the origin as the centre of enlargement.

Solution

You draw the rectangle ABCD and join each of the vertices to the centre of enlargement.

Then you mark the position of the image of each of the vertices.

OA′ = $\frac{1}{2}$ × OA measured along OA.
OB′ = $\frac{1}{2}$ × OB measured along OB.
OC′ = $\frac{1}{2}$ × OC measured along OC.
OD′ = $\frac{1}{2}$ × OD measured along OD.

392   27 Similarity and enlargement

Alternatively, since the centre of enlargement is the origin, you can work out the coordinates of the image without drawing lines from the vertices. You simply multiply each of the coordinates of the image by the scale factor.

A(4, 4) maps to A'(2, 2).
B(16, 4) maps to B'(8, 2).
C(16, 8) maps to C'(8, 4).
D(4, 8) maps to D'(2, 4).

If the scale factor of an enlargement is negative, the image is on the opposite side of the centre of enlargement from the object, and the image is inverted. This is shown in the next example.

EXAMPLE 27.3

Plot the coordinates A(2, 2), B(4, 2) and C(2, 4) and join them to form a triangle.

Enlarge triangle ABC by a scale factor of −3 using the point O(1, 1) as the centre of enlargement.

You plot the triangle.

Then you draw a line from each of the vertices through the centre of enlargement O and extend it on the other side.

You measure the distance from the vertex A and multiply it by 3.

You then mark the point A' at a distance of 3 × OA along OA extended on the other side of the centre of enlargement.

TIP

You can find the position of the image points by counting squares from the centre of enlargement as you have done previously so long as you remember the image will be on the opposite side from the object. For example, from the centre of enlargement to point B is 3 units in the positive x direction and 1 unit in the positive y direction. Multiplying by the scale factor, point B' is 9 units in the negative x direction and 3 unit in the negative y direction.

If you are given both the original shape and the enlarged shape you can find the centre of enlargement as you have previously. You join corresponding points on the two shapes with straight lines. The centre of enlargement is where the lines cross.

EXERCISE 27.2

1 Draw a set of axes with the x-axis from −16 to 6 and the y-axis from −6 to 4.

Plot the points A(2, 2), B(5, 0), C(5, −1) and D(2, −1) and join them to form a quadrilateral.

Enlarge the quadrilateral by a scale factor of −3 using the origin as the centre of enlargement.

2 Copy the diagram and find
   (a) the centre of enlargement.
   (b) the scale factor.

3 Draw a set of axes with the x-axis from −16 to 6 and the y-axis from −8 to 4.

Plot the points A(2, 8), B(6, 8), C(6, 4) and D(2, 4) and join them to form a square.

Enlarge the square by a scale factor of −2 using the point O(5, 6) as the centre of enlargement.

4 Copy the diagram and find
   (a) the centre of enlargement.
   (b) the scale factor.

5 The diagram shows a quadrilateral, ABCD, and its image A′B′C′D′.

Copy the diagram and find
   (a) the centre of enlargement.
   (b) the scale factor.

394 27 Similarity and enlargement

Challenge 27.3

(a) Draw a scalene triangle.
Choose a centre and enlarge the triangle by a scale factor of –1.
Can the same result be achieved with other transformations?

(b) Can you find another transformation that gives the same result if the triangle has symmetry?

The area and volume of similar figures

Figure is a mathematical term for a shape.

Discovery 27.1

Here are two similar figures. The sides of the larger are three times the length of those of the smaller. (The linear scale factor is 3.)

Tessellate the small triangle into the larger. How many will fit?

What is the area scale factor?

What is the connection between the area scale factor and the linear scale factor?

Discovery 27.2

Use some centimetre cubes to make a larger cube with each side three times as long. (The linear scale factor is 3.)

Are the small cube and the large cube similar figures?

What is the volume scale factor?

What is the connection between the volume scale factor and the linear scale factor?

The results of Discoveries 27.1 and 27.2 can be generalised.

> For similar shapes, the area scale factor is the square of the linear scale factor.
>
> For similar solids, the volume scale factor is the cube of the linear scale factor.

TIP: The word 'similar' in ordinary usage can mean 'like' or 'roughly the same'. This chapter is about mathematical similarity, as defined at the beginning of the chapter, but, for simplicity 'mathematical' is omitted in this section.

EXAMPLE 27.4

Two cuboids are similar, with a linear scale factor of 2.5.
(a) The volume of the smaller cuboid is 10 cm³.
 Find the volume of the larger cuboid.
(b) The total surface area of the larger cuboid is 212.5 cm².
 Find the surface area of the smaller cuboid.

Solution

(a) The linear scale factor is 2.5.
 The volume scale factor is 2.5^3.
 The volume of the larger cuboid = $10 \times 2.5^3 = 156.25$ cm³

(b) The linear scale factor is 2.5.
 The area scale factor is 2.5^2.
 The surface area of the smaller cuboid = $212.5 \div 2.5^2 = 34$ cm²

EXERCISE 27.3

1 Triangles PQR and XYZ are similar.
 (a) What is the linear scale factor of the enlargement?
 (b) Find the height of triangle XYZ.
 (c) Calculate the area of triangle PQR.
 (d) Calculate the area of triangle XYZ.
 (e) What do you notice about the ratio of the areas?

2 State the area scale factor and the volume scale factor for each of these linear scale factors.
   (a) 2 **(b)** 5 **(c)** 10 **(d)** 0.5

3 Find the linear scale factor and the volume scale factor for each of these area scale factors.
   (a) 36 **(b)** 64 **(c)** 50 **(d)** 0.1

4 A carton of cream holds 125 ml.
   A similar carton is 1.5 times as tall.
   How much cream does it hold?

5 A model car is built to a scale of 1 : 24.
   It is 15 cm long.
   (a) How long is the real car?
   (b) 10 ml of paint are required to paint the model.
   How many litres of paint will be needed for the real car?

6 An artist makes a model for a large sculpture. It is 24 cm high.
   The finished sculpture will be 3.6 m high.
   (a) Find the linear scale factor.
   (b) Find the area scale factor.
   (c) The model has a volume of 1340 cm^3.
   What is the volume of the sculpture?

7 A wine glass is 12 cm high.
   How tall is a similar glass which holds twice as much?

8 A model aircraft is made to a scale of 1 : 48.
   The area of the wing of the real aircraft is 52 m^2.
   What is the area of the wing of the model?

9 Barrels to hold liquid come in various sizes with different names.
   - An ordinary barrel (b) holds 36 gallons.
   - A firkin (f) holds 9 gallons.
   - A hogshead (h) holds 54 gallons.

   All the barrels are similar.
   Find the ratio of their heights.

10 A square is enlarged by increasing the length of its sides by 10%.
   The area of the square was originally 64 cm^2.
   What is the area of the enlarged square?

Challenge 27.4

(a) A simple model for the heat lost by birds is that it is proportional to their surface area.

Also, the energy a bird can produce, to replace the heat loss, is proportional to its volume.

Investigate whether similar birds (meaning birds of the same species) are larger or smaller in colder climates.

(b) Investigate the relationship for similar aircraft between wing area (which gives the lift) and volume (which is closely associated with its mass).

WHAT YOU HAVE LEARNED

- Triangles are similar if the corresponding angles in each are equal
- A negative enlargement moves the image to the opposite side of the centre of enlargement from the original and inverts it
- The area scale factor for similar figures is the square of the linear scale factor
- The volume scale factor for similar figures is the cube of the linear scale factor

MIXED EXERCISE 27

1 Calculate the lengths a, b, c, d and e in these diagrams.

2. Triangle ADE has an area of 24 cm².
   (a) Calculate the area of triangle ABC.
   (b) Calculate the length of BC.

3. Draw a set of axes with the x-axis from 0 to 16 and the y-axis from 0 to 8.
   Plot the points A(4, 5), B(9, 5), C(9, 2) and D(4, 2) and join them to form a rectangle.
   Enlarge the rectangle by a scale factor of -1.5 using the point O(8, 4) as the centre of enlargement.
   Write down the coordinates of the enlarged rectangle.

4. Copy the diagram and find
   (a) the centre of enlargement.
   (b) the scale factor.

5. P and Q are two regular octagons. Q is an enlargement of P with a scale factor of 3.
   The area of octagon Q is 90 cm². What is the area of octagon P?

6. An architect has made a model of a new hotel complex using a scale of 1 : 100.
   (a) The area of the garden on the model is 650 cm².
       Find the area of the real garden.
   (b) The real swimming pool will hold 500 000 litres of water.
       How much water is needed in the model?

7. Two bottles of lemonade are similar.
   One holds 2 litres and the other holds 1.5 litres.
   (a) Find the ratio of their heights.
   (b) The label on the larger bottle has an area of 75 cm².
       What is the area of the label on the smaller bottle?

28 → ALGEBRAIC MANIPULATION 2

THIS CHAPTER IS ABOUT
- Cancelling algebraic expressions
- Factorising quadratic expressions
- Manipulating expressions involving indices

YOU SHOULD ALREADY KNOW
- How to carry out operations on numerical fractions
- How to factorise linear expressions
- How to use index notation

Simplifying algebraic fractions

You already know how to **simplify**, or cancel, **numerical fractions**: you divide the **numerator** and **denominator** by a **common factor**.

Algebraic fractions follow the same rules as numerical fractions. However, it is important to realise that in a fraction such as $\frac{x+2}{2x+3}$, both the numerator and the denominator are expressions in their own right.

It is not possible to cancel individual terms in the numerator with individual terms in the denominator. In the fraction $\frac{x+2}{2x+3}$, there is an x in both the numerator and the denominator, but it is not a factor of either expression and so cannot be cancelled. Only complete factors can be cancelled.

In order to cancel an algebraic fraction, you must first **factorise** the numerator and denominator. For the fraction $\frac{x+2}{2x+3}$, this is not possible: it is already in its **simplest form**.

EXAMPLE 28.1

Simplify $\frac{x^2 + 5x}{x^2 - 2x}$.

Solution

$$\frac{x^2 + 5x}{x^2 - 2x} = \frac{x(x+5)}{x(x-2)}$$ First factorise the expressions.

$$= \frac{\cancel{x}(x+5)}{\cancel{x}(x-2)}$$ Cancel the common factor x.

$$= \frac{x+5}{x-2}$$ The expression is now in its simplest form.

EXAMPLE 28.2

Simplify $\dfrac{2x+6}{x^2+3x}$.

Solution

$$\frac{2x+6}{x^2+3x} = \frac{2(x+3)}{x(x+3)}$$ First factorise the expressions.

$$= \frac{2}{x}$$ Cancel the common factor $(x+3)$.

EXERCISE 28.1

Simplify each of these algebraic fractions. If this is not possible, say so.

1 $\dfrac{3x-9}{6x-3}$ **2** $\dfrac{2x+6}{5x-10}$ **3** $\dfrac{8+2x}{6-4x}$ **4** $\dfrac{12-4x}{6-9x}$

5 $\dfrac{3x^2-x}{2x^2+x}$ **6** $\dfrac{2x^2-4x}{6x^2-8x}$ **7** $\dfrac{9x-6x^2}{2x^2+8x}$ **8** $\dfrac{5x^2+15x}{10x-5}$

Challenge 28.1

Work in pairs.

Write your own algebraic fraction (either one that will factorise or one that will not).

Challenge your partner to say if it factorises or not, and to carry out the factorisation if it does.

If they are correct they score one point, if they are wrong they score nothing.

The first to score five points wins.

Factorising quadratic expressions

In Chapter 2 you learned how to **expand** expressions such as $(x + 1)(x + 7)$, to give the **quadratic** expression $x^2 + 8x + 7$. You also need to be able to factorise quadratic expressions, which is the reverse of that process.

EXAMPLE 28.3

Factorise $x^2 + 7x + 12$.

Solution

$x^2 + 7x + 12 = x^2 + 4x + 3x + 12$ The 'trick' is to look for **factor pairs** of **12** (the **constant term**): 1×12, 2×6, 3×4. Choose the pair that can be added or subtracted to give **7** (the **coefficient of x**).
From 1 and 12 it is possible to make 11 or 13.
From 2 and 6 it is possible to make 4 or 8.
From 3 and 4 it is possible to make 1 or **7** so the required factors are 3 and 4.

$ = x(x + 4) + 3(x + 4)$
$ = (x + 3)(x + 4)$

> **TIP**
> The *coefficient* is the number part of a term in an expression.

Check that you have factorised the expression correctly by expanding the brackets.

$(x + 3)(x + 4) = x^2 + 4x + 3x + 12$
$ = x^2 + 7x + 12$ ✓

You do not need to write out all the steps of your solution as in Example 28.3. However, you should always expand the brackets to check your solution.

EXAMPLE 28.4

Factorise $x^2 + 3x - 10$.

Solution

$x^2 + 3x - 10 = (x + 5)(x - 2)$ The factor pairs of 10 are 1×10 and 2×5. To make 3 you need to use 5 and -2.

Check by expanding the brackets.

$(x + 5)(x - 2) = x^2 - 2x + 5x - 10$
$ = x^2 + 3x - 10$ ✓

EXAMPLE 28.5

Factorise $x^2 - 6x + 8$.

Solution

$x^2 - 6x + 8 = (x - 2)(x - 4)$ The factor pairs of 8 are 1×8 and 2×4.
To make -6 you need to use -2 and -4.

Check by expanding the brackets.

$(x - 2)(x - 4) = x^2 - 4x - 2x + 8$
$= x^2 - 6x + 8$

EXERCISE 28.2

Factorise each of these expressions.

1. (a) $x^2 + 3x + 2$ (b) $x^2 + 6x + 5$ (c) $x^2 + 8x + 12$ (d) $x^2 + 8x + 15$
   (e) $x^2 + 10x + 9$ (f) $x^2 + 6x + 9$ (g) $x^2 + 9x + 20$ (h) $x^2 + 14x + 24$

2. (a) $x^2 + 5x - 6$ (b) $x^2 + 9x - 10$ (c) $x^2 + 2x - 8$ (d) $x^2 + 4x - 12$
   (e) $x^2 + 2x - 15$ (f) $x^2 + 8x - 20$ (g) $x^2 + 5x - 24$ (h) $x^2 + 2x - 24$

3. (a) $x^2 - 7x + 10$ (b) $x^2 - 9x + 8$ (c) $x^2 - 3x + 2$ (d) $x^2 - 9x + 14$
   (e) $x^2 - 10x + 16$ (f) $x^2 - 14x + 24$ (g) $x^2 - 11x + 30$ (h) $x^2 - 5x + 6$

Challenge 28.2

Work in pairs.

Write your own quadratic expression (either one that will factorise or one that will not).

Challenge your partner to say if it factorises or not, and to carry out the factorisation if it does. If they are correct they score one point, if they are wrong they score nothing.

The first to score five points wins.

Difference of two squares

Expressions such as $x^2 - 16$ look as though they cannot be factorised. However, this is a special case quadratic expression known as the **difference of two squares** (the expression represents the difference between two squares, in this case x^2 and 16).

To factorise such an expression, find the square root of each term. Because the numerical term in the expanded expression is negative, the numerical term is positive in one of the brackets and negative in the other.

$$x^2 - a = (x + \sqrt{a})(x - \sqrt{a})$$

For example, $x^2 - 16 = (x + 4)(x - 4)$.

This can be checked by expanding the brackets.

$(x + 4)(x - 4) = x^2 - 4x + 4x - 16 \qquad -4x + 4x = 0$
$\qquad\qquad\qquad = x^2 - 16$

EXAMPLE 28.6

Factorise $x^2 - 9$.

Solution

$x^2 - 9 = (x + 3)(x - 3)$ Find the square root of each term in the expression.

Check by expanding the brackets.
$(x + 3)(x - 3) = x^2 - 3x + 3x - 9 \qquad -3x + 3x = 0$
$\qquad\qquad\qquad = x^2 - 9$ ✓

EXAMPLE 28.7

Factorise $8x^2 - 8$.

Solution

$8x^2 - 8 = 8(x^2 - 1)$ The terms are not squares but there is a common factor.
$\qquad\quad = 8(x + 1)(x - 1)$ Factorise the expression in brackets.

Check by expanding the brackets.
$8(x + 1)(x - 1) = 8(x^2 - x + x - 1) \qquad -x + x = 0$
$\qquad\qquad\qquad = 8(x^2 - 1)$
$\qquad\qquad\qquad = 8x^2 - 8$ ✓

EXERCISE 28.3

Factorise each of these expressions.

1. (a) $x^2 - 9$ (b) $x^2 - 16$ (c) $x^2 - 49$
   (d) $x^2 - 81$ (e) $x^2 - 100$ (f) $x^2 - 144$

2. (a) $3x^2 - 12$ (b) $5x^2 - 45$ (c) $3x^2 - 108$
   (d) $7x^2 - 343$ (e) $10x^2 - 4000$ (f) $8x^2 - 200$

Challenge 28.3

Factorise each of these expressions.

(a) $\dfrac{2x + 14}{x^2 - 49}$ (b) $\dfrac{10x + 15}{4x^2 - 9}$ (c) $\dfrac{3x^2 - 108}{2x^2 + 12x}$

(d) $\dfrac{5x^3 + 5x^2 - 30x}{3x^3 - 12x}$ (e) $\dfrac{10x^3 - 5x^2 - 30x}{12x^3 - 27x}$

Simplifying algebraic fractions involving indices

You should already be familiar with the laws of indices:

$$a^m \times a^n = a^{m+n} \text{ (add the indices)}$$
and
$$a^m \div a^n = a^{m-n} \text{ (subtract the indices)}$$

These laws can be applied when simplifying algebraic fractions.

Remember that only complete factors can be cancelled, parts of factors cannot.

EXAMPLE 28.8

Simplify $\dfrac{5x^3y^2}{2z^4} \times \dfrac{8z^2}{15xy^3}$.

Solution

$\dfrac{5x^3y^2}{2z^4} \times \dfrac{8z^2}{15xy^3} = \dfrac{x^2}{z^2} \times \dfrac{4}{3y}$ Look for common factors: 5 in 5 and 15
    2 in 2 and 8
    x in x^3 and x
    y^2 in y^2 and y^3
    z^2 in z^4 and z^2

$= \dfrac{4x^2}{3yz^2}$ Simplify.

EXAMPLE 28.9

Simplify $\dfrac{4a^5b^3}{15c^2} \div \dfrac{8a^2b^5}{9c^4}$.

Solution

$\dfrac{4a^5b^3}{15c^2} \div \dfrac{8a^2b^5}{9c^4} = \dfrac{4a^5b^3}{15c^2} \times \dfrac{9c^4}{8a^2b^5}$ As with division of numerical fractions it is easier to change the operation to multiplication and to invert the fraction after the division sign.

$= \dfrac{a^3}{5} \times \dfrac{3c^2}{2b^2}$ Look for common factors: 4 in 4 and 8
    3 in 15 and 9
    a^2 in a^5 and a^2
    b^3 in b^3 and b^5
    c^2 in c^2 and c^4

$= \dfrac{3a^3c^2}{10b^2}$ Simplify.

EXERCISE 28.4

Simplify each of these expressions.

1 $\dfrac{6a^4b}{5c^2} \times \dfrac{10c^3}{9a^2b^3}$

2 $\dfrac{12x^5y^4}{7z^5} \times \dfrac{14z^3}{15x^3y^2}$

3 $\dfrac{6a^4b^5}{9c^3} \div \dfrac{10a^2b^3}{3c^6}$

4 $\dfrac{8a^7b^5}{15c^4} \div \dfrac{4ab^2}{9c}$

5 $\dfrac{6t^5v^2}{5w^2} \div \dfrac{8t^2v^5}{15w^4}$

6 $\dfrac{12e^6f^2}{5g^3} \times \dfrac{10g^4}{8e^4f^3}$

7 $\dfrac{5a^3b^2}{2c^4} \times \dfrac{8c^2d^4}{15ae^3} \times \dfrac{3e^2}{2b^3d^2}$

8 $\dfrac{8t^3v^2}{3x^5z^4} \times \dfrac{5x^2}{12v^4y^3} \div \dfrac{10t^4}{9y^2z^5}$

9 $\left(\dfrac{4a^5b^6}{5c^2d^4} \div \dfrac{12a^2b^5}{25c^4}\right) \times \dfrac{8d^2}{15ab^3}$

28 Algebraic manipulation 2

Challenge 28.4

Work in pairs.

Write your own algebraic fraction problem (using either multiplication or division only).

Challenge your partner to simplify the problem to a single algebraic fraction.

Factorising quadratic expressions where the coefficient of $x^2 \neq 1$

Earlier in this chapter you learned how to factorise expressions such as $x^2 + 7x + 12$, to give $(x + 3)(x + 4)$. In all the examples, the coefficient of x^2 was 1.

It is also possible to factorise quadratic expressions where the coefficient of x^2 is not 1 in a similar way.

EXAMPLE 28.10

Factorise $3x^2 + 14x + 8$.

Solution

$3x^2 + 14x + 8 = (3x + 2)(x + 4)$ The factor pairs of 8 are 1×4 and 2×4.
When forming the x term, one of the two factors will also be multiplied by 3 (the coefficient of x^2).
To make 14 you need to use 2 and 4 with the 3, $(2 + 3 \times 4)$.
The 4 is multiplied by the 3 so the $3x$ must not be in the same bracket as the 4.

Check by expanding the brackets.

$(3x + 2)(x + 4) = 3x^2 + 12x + 2x + 8$
$\qquad\qquad\qquad\; = 3x^2 + 14x + 8$ ✓

EXAMPLE 28.11

Factorise $2x^2 + 3x - 20$.

Solution

$2x^2 + 3x - 20 = (2x - 5)(x + 4)$ The factor pairs of 20 are 1×20, 2×10 and 4×5.
To make 3 you need to use 4 and -5 with the 2, $(2 \times 4 - 5)$.
The 4 is multiplied by the 2 so the $2x$ must not be in the same bracket as the 4.

Check by expanding the brackets.

$(2x - 5)(x + 4) = 2x^2 + 8x - 5x - 20$
$\qquad\qquad\qquad\; = 2x^2 + 3x - 20$

EXERCISE 28.5

Factorise each of these expressions.

1 (a) $3x^2 + 17x + 20$ (b) $2x^2 + 7x + 6$ (c) $3x^2 + 13x + 4$
   (d) $5x^2 + 18x + 9$ (e) $4x^2 + 6x + 2$ (f) $3x^2 + 11x + 10$
   (g) $2x^2 + 5x + 2$ (h) $4x^2 + 17x + 15$ (i) $5x^2 + 8x + 3$

2 (a) $2x^2 - x - 15$ (b) $3x^2 + x - 14$ (c) $5x^2 - 17x - 12$
   (d) $3x^2 - 5x - 12$ (e) $4x^2 - 3x - 10$ (f) $2x^2 - 7x - 15$
   (g) $4x^2 - 7x - 2$ (h) $3x^2 - 16x - 12$ (i) $4x^2 + 21x - 18$

3 (a) $3x^2 - 14x + 8$ (b) $5x^2 - 19x + 12$ (c) $3x^2 - 26x + 35$
   (d) $2x^2 - 21x + 40$ (e) $2x^2 - 11x + 12$ (f) $4x^2 - 11x + 6$
   (g) $2x^2 - 21x + 40$ (h) $3x^2 - 5x + 2$ (i) $3x^2 - 7x + 4$

Challenge 28.5

Factorise each of these expressions.
(a) $8x^2 + 10x + 3$
(b) $15x^2 + 2x - 8$
(c) $8x^2 - 2x - 15$
(d) $6x^2 - 29x + 35$

Simplifying fractions involving quadratic expressions

Earlier in this chapter you learned that, to cancel an algebraic fraction, you must first factorise the numerator and denominator. Sometimes the fraction will involve quadratic expressions.

EXAMPLE 28.12

Simplify $\dfrac{2x + 14}{x^2 + 6x - 7}$.

Solution

$\dfrac{2x + 14}{x^2 + 6x - 7} = \dfrac{2(x + 7)}{(x - 1)(x + 7)}$ First factorise the expressions.

$\qquad\qquad\quad = \dfrac{2}{x - 1}$ Cancel the common factor, $(x + 7)$.

28 Algebraic manipulation 2

EXAMPLE 28.13

Simplify $\dfrac{x^2 - 25}{x^2 + 3x - 10}$.

Solution

$\dfrac{x^2 - 25}{x^2 + 3x - 10} = \dfrac{(x + 5)(x - 5)}{(x + 5)(x - 2)}$ First factorise the expressions.

$\qquad\qquad\quad = \dfrac{x - 5}{x - 2}$ Cancel the common factor, $(x + 5)$.

EXAMPLE 28.14

Simplify $\dfrac{2x^2 + 4x - 16}{x^2 - 7x + 10}$.

Solution

$\dfrac{2x^2 + 4x - 16}{x^2 - 7x + 10} = \dfrac{2(x^2 + 2x - 8)}{x^2 - 7x + 10}$ Take the common factor, 2, out of the numerator.

$\qquad\qquad\qquad = \dfrac{2(x + 4)(x - 2)}{(x - 5)(x - 2)}$ Factorise the expressions.

$\qquad\qquad\qquad = \dfrac{2(x + 4)}{x - 5}$ Cancel the common factor, $(x - 2)$.

EXAMPLE 28.15

Simplify $\dfrac{2(x^2 + 4)^2}{3x^2 + 12}$.

Solution

$\dfrac{2(x^2 + 4)^2}{3x^2 + 12} = \dfrac{2(x^2 + 4)(x^2 + 4)}{3(x^2 + 4)}$ Rewrite the numerator and take the common factor, 3, out of the denominator.

$\qquad\qquad\quad = \dfrac{2(x^2 + 4)}{3}$ Cancel the common factor, $(x^2 + 4)$.

Simplifying fractions involving quadratic expressions

EXERCISE 28.6

Simplify each of these algebraic fractions.

1. $\dfrac{3x + 15}{x^2 + 3x - 10}$
2. $\dfrac{6x - 18}{x^2 - x - 6}$
3. $\dfrac{x^2 - 5x + 6}{x^2 - 4x + 3}$
4. $\dfrac{x^2 - 3x - 4}{x^2 - 4x - 5}$
5. $\dfrac{x^2 - 2x - 3}{x^2 - 9}$
6. $\dfrac{3x^2 - 12}{x^2 + 2x - 8}$
7. $\dfrac{3x^2 + 5x + 2}{2x^2 - x - 3}$
8. $\dfrac{2x^2 + x - 6}{x^2 + x - 2}$
9. $\dfrac{6x^2 - 3x}{(2x - 1)^2}$
10. $\dfrac{5(x + 3)^2}{x^2 - 9}$
11. $\dfrac{(x - 3)(x + 2)^2}{x^2 - x - 6}$
12. $\dfrac{2x^2 + x - 6}{(2x - 3)^2}$

WHAT YOU HAVE LEARNED

- When simplifying algebraic fractions only complete factors may be cancelled
- How to factorise quadratic expressions
- How to factorise the difference of two squares

MIXED EXERCISE 28

1. Simplify each of these algebraic fractions.
   (a) $\dfrac{5x + 10}{15 - 5x}$
   (b) $\dfrac{8x + 12}{10 + 6x}$
   (c) $\dfrac{6x^2 - 4x}{10x^2 + 15x}$
   (d) $\dfrac{8x - 12x^2}{12x^2 + 8x}$
   (e) $\dfrac{9x + 15x^2}{5x^2 - 10x}$
   (f) $\dfrac{4x + 8}{3x^2 + 6x}$
   (g) $\dfrac{6x - 9}{4x^2 - 9}$
   (h) $\dfrac{5x^2 + 15x}{4x + 12}$

2. Factorise each of these expressions.
   (a) $x^2 + 5x + 4$
   (b) $x^2 + 7x + 12$
   (c) $x^2 + 9x + 14$
   (d) $x^2 + 8x + 7$
   (e) $x^2 + 7x + 10$
   (f) $x^2 + 6x + 5$
   (g) $x^2 + 17x + 30$
   (h) $x^2 + 20x + 36$

3. Factorise each of these expressions.
   (a) $x^2 - 81$
   (b) $x^2 - 64$
   (c) $x^2 - 169$
   (d) $x^2 - 225$
   (e) $3x^2 - 48$
   (f) $5x^2 - 45$
   (g) $7x^2 - 343$
   (h) $10x^2 - 1000$

28 Algebraic manipulation 2

4 Simplify each of these algebraic fractions.

(a) $\dfrac{5a^3b^2}{2c^4} \times \dfrac{8c^2}{15ab^3}$

(b) $\dfrac{6x^3}{5y^3z^4} \times \dfrac{25y^2z^2}{18x}$

(c) $\dfrac{4q^5r^3}{15s^2} \div \dfrac{8q^2r^5}{9s^4}$

(d) $\dfrac{6t^4v^5}{15w^3} \div \dfrac{4t^5v^3}{21w^2}$

(e) $\dfrac{3x^4y^2}{5z^3} \times \dfrac{4x}{9y^5z^2} \times \dfrac{5yz^7}{8x^3}$

(f) $\dfrac{2e^2n}{3t^4} \times \dfrac{3t^5}{e^4n^6} \div \dfrac{8t^2}{4en^4}$

5 Factorise each of these expressions.

(a) $5x^2 + 27x + 10$
(b) $3x^2 + 16x + 21$
(c) $3x^2 - 22x + 24$
(d) $4x^2 - 13x + 3$
(e) $2x^2 + 3x - 14$
(f) $6x^2 + x - 7$
(g) $3x^2 - 4x - 32$
(h) $5x^2 - 12x - 9$
(i) $7x^2 - 2x - 5$

6 Simplify each of these algebraic fractions.

(a) $\dfrac{2x + 8}{x^2 + x - 12}$

(b) $\dfrac{6x - 18}{3x^2 + 6x}$

(c) $\dfrac{x^2 + 3x - 4}{x^2 + 6x + 8}$

(d) $\dfrac{x^2 - 2x - 3}{x^2 - 1}$

(e) $\dfrac{10x^2 + 15x}{2x^2 - x - 6}$

(f) $\dfrac{6x^2 + 5x - 4}{2x^2 + 5x - 3}$

(g) $\dfrac{4(x-5)^2}{2x^2 - 50}$

(h) $\dfrac{2x(x+3)^2}{x^2 + x - 6}$

29 USING A CALCULATOR

THIS CHAPTER IS ABOUT

- Using your calculator to perform more complex calculations efficiently
- Exploring examples of exponential growth and decay
- The upper and lower bound of measurements and the effect of these on a calculation

YOU SHOULD ALREADY KNOW

- How to use the basic functions on your calculator
- How to round answers to a given number of decimal places or significant figures
- How to write a number in standard index form

The efficient use of a calculator

You can use your calculator to perform complex calculations quickly and efficiently.

> **TIP**
> Investigate how your calculator works and the functions that it has. Different makes and models work in different ways. You should practise using your calculator regularly so that you can use it efficiently and effectively.

EXAMPLE 29.1

Use your calculator to work out these. Give your answers to 3 significant figures.

(a) $\dfrac{14.73 + 2.96}{15.25 - 7.14}$

(b) $\sqrt{17.8^2 + 4.3^2}$

Solution

There are many ways to do these calculations. Here is a direct method for each.

(a) `( 1 4 . 7 3 + 2 . 9 6 )`
`÷ ( 1 5 . 2 5 − 7 . 1 4 ) =` 2.181 257 ...
= 2.18 (to 3 s.f.)

(b) `√ ( 1 7 . 8 x² + 4 . 3 x² ) =` 18.312 018 ...
= 18.3 (to 3 s.f.)

> **TIP**
> Notice the use of brackets. These make sure that calculations are performed in the correct order.

Here are some other useful function buttons that you need to be aware of.

$\boxed{x^{-1}}$ $\boxed{1/x}$ — This is the **reciprocal** button.
This button is not essential. You could do $1 \div x$ instead.

$\boxed{\wedge}$ $\boxed{x^y}$ $\boxed{y^x}$ — This is the **power** button.

$\boxed{\sqrt[x]{}}$ $\boxed{y^{1/x}}$ — This is the **root** button.
Again, this button is not essential. You could use the 'power' button, with a power of $\frac{1}{x}$, instead.

$\boxed{\sin}$ $\boxed{\cos}$ $\boxed{\tan}$
$\boxed{\sin^{-1}}$ $\boxed{\cos^{-1}}$ $\boxed{\tan^{-1}}$ — These are the **trigonometry** buttons.

$\boxed{\text{EXP}}$ $\boxed{\text{EE}}$ — This is the **standard form** button.
Once again, this button is not essential. You could use $\boxed{\times}$ $\boxed{1}$ $\boxed{0}$ $\boxed{\wedge}$ instead.

EXAMPLE 29.2

Use your calculator to work out these. Give your answers to 3 significant figures.

(a) $\dfrac{1}{1.847}$ (b) 4.2^3 (c) $\sqrt[4]{15}$
(d) $\cos 73°$ (e) $\cos^{-1} 0.897$ (f) $(3.7 \times 10^{-5}) \div (8.3 \times 10^6)$

Solution

(a) $\boxed{1}\boxed{.}\boxed{8}\boxed{4}\boxed{7}\boxed{x^{-1}}\boxed{=}$ 0.541 (to 3 s.f.)

(b) $\boxed{4}\boxed{.}\boxed{2}\boxed{\wedge}\boxed{3}\boxed{=}$ 74.1 (to 3 s.f.)

(c) $\boxed{1}\boxed{5}\boxed{\sqrt[x]{}}\boxed{4}\boxed{=}$ 1.97 (to 3 s.f.)

(d) $\boxed{\cos}\boxed{7}\boxed{3}\boxed{=}$ 0.292 (to 3 s.f.)

(e) $\boxed{\text{SHIFT}}\boxed{\cos}\boxed{0}\boxed{.}\boxed{8}\boxed{9}\boxed{7}\boxed{=}$ 26.2° (to 3 s.f.)

(f) $\boxed{3}\boxed{.}\boxed{7}\boxed{\text{EXP}}\boxed{(-)}\boxed{5}\boxed{\div}\boxed{8}\boxed{.}\boxed{3}\boxed{\text{EXP}}\boxed{6}\boxed{=}$ 4.46×10^{-12} (to 3 s.f.)

The efficient use of a calculator

EXERCISE 29.1

Use your calculator to work out these. Give all your answers to 3 significant figures.

1. (a) $\dfrac{1}{7.2} + \dfrac{1}{14.6}$ (b) $\dfrac{1}{0.961} \div \dfrac{1}{0.412}$ (c) $4.2\left(\dfrac{1}{5.5} - \dfrac{1}{7.6}\right)$

2. (a) 1.562^5 (b) 6.8^{-4} (c) $0.32^3 + 0.51^2$

3. (a) $\sqrt[4]{31.8}$ (b) $\sqrt[3]{0.9316}$ (c) $\sqrt[5]{8.6 \times 9.71}$

4. (a) $\sin 46.2°$ (b) $\tan 51.6°$ (c) $\sin 12° - \cos 31°$

5. (a) $\cos^{-1} 0.832$ (b) $\sin^{-1} 0.910$ (c) $\tan^{-1}\left(\dfrac{43.9}{16.3}\right)$

6. (a) $(5.7 \times 10^4) \times (8.2 \times 10^3)$ (b) $\dfrac{4.6 \times 10^5}{7 \times 10^{-3}}$ (c) $(1.8 \times 10^{12}) \times (2 \times 10^{-20})$

7. (a) $\dfrac{8.71 \times 3.65}{0.84}$ (b) $\dfrac{0.074 \times 9.61}{23.1}$ (c) $\dfrac{41.78}{0.0537 \times 264}$

8. (a) $\dfrac{114}{27.6 \times 58.9}$ (b) $\dfrac{0.432 - 0.317}{0.76}$ (c) $\dfrac{6.51 - 0.1114}{7.24 + 1.655}$

9. (a) $3\cos 14.2° - 5\sin 16.3°$ (b) $\dfrac{3.5 \times 4.4 \times \sin 18.7°}{2}$ (c) $\cos^{-1} \dfrac{2.7^2 + 3.6^2 - 1.9^2}{2 \times 2.7 \times 3.6}$

10. (a) $(4.7 \times 10^5)^2$ (b) $\sqrt{6.4 \times 10^{-3}}$ (c) $\dfrac{(9.6 \times 10^4) \times (3.75 \times 10^7)}{8.87 \times 10^{-6}}$

Challenge 29.1

Sometimes, when the display on a calculator is turned upside down, the inverted figures 'spell' a word.

Find the words that these calculations reveal.

(a) $(84 + 17) \times 5$ (b) $566 \times 711 - 23\,617$ (c) $\dfrac{9999 + 319}{8.47 + 2.53}$

(d) $\dfrac{27 \times 2000 - 2}{0.63 \div 0.09}$ (e) $0.008 - \dfrac{0.3^2}{10^5}$

See if you can find more calculations that result in 'calculator words'. Check them with your partner.

Challenge 29.2

Using trial and improvement, or otherwise, solve each of these equations.

Give your answers correct to 2 decimal places.

(a) $1.5^x = 6$　　　　(b) $\log x = 1.5$　　　　(c) $\sin 2x° = 0.9$
　　　　　　　　　　　　　　　　　　　　　　　　Find two values for x.

Exponential growth and decay

When a number is repeatedly multiplied by a fixed value **greater than one** we have **exponential growth**.

When a number is repeatedly multiplied by a fixed value **less than one** we have **exponential decay**.

The formula is the same for exponential growth and decay:

$$y = A \times b^x$$

where A is the initial value and b is the rate of growth or decay (**multiplier**).

In Chapter 22 you learned about **compound interest** and **depreciation**. These are examples of exponential growth and decay.

EXAMPLE 29.3

£2000 is invested in a bank and receives 6% per year compound interest.
(a) Write down a formula for the amount of money in the bank, y, after x years.
(b) How much money will there be after 5 years?
(c) After how many years will the amount of money in the bank be more than doubled?

TIP: Remember that to increase by 6%, the multiplier is 1.06.

Solution

(a) $y = A \times b^x$　　　The initial value, A, is 2000 and the rate of
　　$y = 2000 \times 1.06^x$　　growth, b is 1.06.

(b) $y = 2000 \times 1.06^5$
$= £2676.45$ (to the nearest penny)

(c) 12 years Using trial and improvement, you will find that after 12 years the investment will be worth £4024.39.
Note that you do not need to do the whole calculation for each value of x: the investment will be more than double the initial value when $b^x > 2$, i.e. when $1.06^x > 2$, and you will find that $1.06^{12} = 2.012 \ldots$.

EXAMPLE 29.4

The population of a rare species of animal is falling by 2% per year.
In 2005 there were 30 000 of these animals.
(a) Write down a formula for the number of animals, p, after t years.
(b) How many of these animals will there be after 10 years?
(c) How long will it be before the population is halved?

Solution

(a) $p = 30\,000 \times 0.98^t$

(b) $p = 30\,000 \times 0.98^{10}$
$= 24\,512$

(c) 35 years Using trial and improvement, we find that when $t = 35$, $b^t < 0.5$. The population will be 14 792.

EXERCISE 29.2

1 £5000 is invested at 3% compound interest.
   (a) Write down a formula for the amount, a, the investment is worth after t years.
   (b) Calculate the value of the investment after
       (i) 4 years.   (ii) 20 years.

2 Elaine buys a car for £9000. It depreciates in value by 12% each year.
   (a) Write down a formula for the value of the car, v, after t years.
   (b) Calculate the value of the car after
       (i) 3 years.   (ii) 8 years.
   (c) Elaine wants to sell the car when its value has reduced to £5000.
       Use trial and improvement to work out how many years she will keep the car.

3 The number of a strain of bacteria decays exponentially following the formula

$$N = 1\,000\,000 \times 2^{-t}$$

where N is the number of bacteria present and t is the time in hours.
- **(a)** How many bacteria were present originally?
- **(b)** How many bacteria were present after
   - **(i)** 5 hours?
   - **(ii)** 12 hours?
- **(c)** After how many hours will the bacteria no longer exist: that is, after how many hours will be the number of bacteria be less than 1?

4 A bank pays Phil compound interest on the money he invests.
Phil works out the formula that the bank will use.

$$A = 2000 \times 1.08^n$$

- **(a)** How much did Phil invest?
- **(b)** What was the rate of interest?
- **(c)** What does the letter n stand for in the formula?
- **(d)** How much will the investment be worth after
   - **(i)** 5 years?
   - **(ii)** 15 years?

5 The population of a country is increasing at a rate of 5% per year.
In 2005 the population was 60 million.
- **(a)** Write down a formula for the population size, P, after t years.
- **(b)** What will the population be in
   - **(i)** 2010?
   - **(ii)** 2100?
- **(c)** How long will it take for the population to double from its 2005 size?

6 A radioactive element has a mass of 50 g.
Its mass reduces by 10% each year.
- **(a)** Write down a formula for the mass, m, of the element after t years.
- **(b)** Calculate the mass after
   - **(i)** 3 years.
   - **(ii)** 10 years.
- **(c)** Use trial and improvement to find how long it takes for the mass to halve. This is known as the half-life of the element.

Challenge 29.3

The curve $y = Ab^x$ passes through the points (0, 5) and (3, 20.48).

Find the values of A and b.

Bounds of measurements

In Chapter 16 you learned that when a value is measured to the nearest unit, the value is within half a unit of that mark.

Another way of expressing this is to say that any measurement expressed to a given unit is in **possible error** of half that unit.

EXAMPLE 29.5

A piece of wood measures 26 cm, correct to the nearest centimetre. What are the upper and lower bounds of the length of the piece of wood?

Solution

Upper bound = 26.5 cm
Lower bound = 25.5 cm

The bounds are half a centimetre above and below the given length. The actual length could be anywhere between 25.5 and 26.5.

> **TIP**
> The lower bound is included in the range of possible lengths, but the upper bound is excluded. This is because, when rounding, a 5 is rounded up. For example, if you round 26.5 you get 27.
>
> Bounds can be written as an inequality. For example, $25.5 \leq \text{length} < 26.5$.

Measurements are not always given correct to the nearest unit: often they are measured correct to the nearest *part* of a unit; for example, to the nearest 0.1 cm. Such measurements are in possible error of half of the part unit: in the case of a length measured to the nearest 0.1 cm, the possible error is ±0.05 cm.

EXAMPLE 29.6

A supermarket sells chickens. Each chicken weighs 4.2 kg, correct to the nearest 0.1 kg.
(a) What are the upper and lower bounds of the weight of one chicken?
    These chickens can be bought in boxes of 10.
(b) What are the upper and lower bounds of a box of these chickens?

Solution

(a) Upper bound = 4.25 kg
    Lower bound = 4.15 kg

(b) Upper bound = 4.25 × 10   Multiply the bounds of one item by the number
                = 42.5 kg   of items.
    Lower bound = 4.15 × 10
                = 41.5 kg

29 Using a calculator

EXERCISE 29.3

1. Find the upper and lower bounds for each of these measurements.
   (a) The height of a tree is 4.7 m, to the nearest 0.1 m.
   (b) A dog weighs 37 kg to the nearest kilogram.
   (c) A door measures 1.95 m to the nearest centimetre.
   (d) The winning time for the 200 m race was 28.45 seconds to the nearest hundredth of a second.
   (e) The volume of cola in a can is 330 ml to the nearest millilitre.

2. A ladder is measured as 3 m to the nearest centimetre.
   Write the possible length of the ladder as an inequality.

3. A square birthday card of side 12.5 cm, to the nearest 0.1 cm, is to be put into a square envelope of side 13 cm, to the nearest centimetre.
   Is it certain that the card will fit into the envelope? Show how you decide.

4. Find the upper and lower bounds for each of these measurements.
   (a) The total weight of 10 coins, each coin weighing 6 g to the nearest gram.
   (b) The total length of 20 pipes, each measuring 10 m to the nearest metre.
   (c) The total time to make 100 cakes when each cake takes 13.6 seconds to make, to the nearest tenth of a second.

Further calculations involving bounds of measurements

You need to be able to work out the bounds of the answer to a calculation involving more than one measurement. You do this by performing the calculation using the bounds of the measurements involved.

When adding:
- to find the upper bound, add the upper bounds.
- to find the lower bound, add the lower bounds.

When subtracting:
- to find the upper bound, subtract the lower bound from the upper bound.
- to find the lower bound, subtract the upper bound from the lower bound.

EXAMPLE 29.7

Chen and Samantha are carrying out a survey of the length of worms in a plot of land.
Chen measures a worm as 12 cm to the nearest cm and Samantha measures another worm as 10 cm to the nearest cm.
Calculate the upper and lower bound of
(a) the total length of the two worms.
(b) the difference in length of the two worms.

Solution

(a) Upper bound = 12.5 + 10.5   The longest possible total length occurs
                    = 23 cm   with the longest possible individual lengths.
    Lower bound = 11.5 + 9.5   The shortest possible total length occurs
                    = 21 cm   with the shortest possible individual lengths.

(b) Upper bound = 12.5 − 9.5   The greatest possible difference occurs with
                    = 3 cm   the longest possible longer length and the
                                                shortest possible shorter length.
    Lower bound = 11.5 − 10.5   The least possible difference occurs with
                    = 1 cm   the shortest possible longer length and the
                                                longest possible shorter length.

When multiplying:
- to find the upper bound, multiply the upper bounds.
- to find the lower bound, multiply the lower bounds.

When dividing:
- to find the upper bound, divide the upper bound by the lower bound.
- to find the lower bound, divide the lower bound by the upper bound.

EXAMPLE 29.8

$p = 3$ and $q = 7$, both correct to the nearest whole number.

Calculate the upper and lower bounds of (a) pq. (b) $\dfrac{q}{p}$.

Solution

(a) Upper bound = 3.5 × 7.5   The largest possible value of pq occurs
                    = 26.25   with the largest possible individual values.
    Lower bound = 2.5 × 6.5   The smallest possible value of pq occurs
                    = 16.25   with the smallest possible individual values.

(b) Upper bound = $\dfrac{7.5}{2.5}$ The largest possible value of $\dfrac{q}{p}$ occurs when
                    = 3   the largest possible value of q is divided by
                                               the smallest possible value of p.
    Lower bound = $\dfrac{6.5}{2.5}$ The smallest possible value of $\dfrac{q}{p}$ occurs when
                    = 1.86 (to 2 d.p.)   the smallest possible value of q is divided by
                                               the largest possible value of p.

EXERCISE 29.4

1 A triangle has sides of length 7 cm, 8 cm and 10 cm.
All measurements are correct to the nearest centimetre.
Work out the upper and lower bounds of the perimeter of the triangle.

2 Work out the largest and smallest possible areas of a rectangle measuring 27 cm by 19 cm, where both lengths are correct to the nearest centimetre.

3 Stuffing weighing 0.5 kg is added to a chicken weighing 2.4 kg.
   Both weights are correct to the nearest 0.1 kg.
   What is the maximum and minimum possible weight of the stuffed chicken?

4 Phil and Ruby each drew a line 15 cm long, to the nearest centimetre.
   What is the greatest and least possible difference between the lengths drawn?

5 Given that $p = 5.1$ and $q = 8.6$, correct to 1 decimal place, work out the largest and smallest possible values of
   (a) $p + q$.   **(b)** $q - p$.

6 Jasbinder runs 100 m in 12.8 seconds.
   The distance is correct to the nearest metre and the time is correct to the nearest 0.1 seconds.
   Work out the upper and lower bound of Jasbinder's speed.

7 A bar of gold is a cuboid measuring 8.6 cm by 4.1 cm by 2.4 cm.
   All the measurements are correct to the nearest millimetre.
   (a) Work out the largest and smallest possible volume of the bar of gold.
   (b) The density of gold is 19.3 g/cm³, correct to the nearest 0.1 g/cm³.
   Work out the greatest and least possible mass of the gold bar.

8 The population of a town is 108 000, correct to the nearest 1000.
   The town covers an area of 120 square miles, to the nearest square mile.
   Work out the greatest and least possible population density of the town.

9 Use the formula $P = \dfrac{V^2}{R}$ to work out the upper and lower bounds of P when $V = 6$ and $R = 1$ and both values are correct to the nearest whole number.

10 Work out the upper and lower bounds of the calculation
    $$\dfrac{8.1 - 3.6}{11.4}.$$
    Each value in the calculation is correct to 1 decimal place.

WHAT YOU HAVE LEARNED

- How to use some of the function keys on your calculator
- How to calculate exponential growth and decay
- How to find the bounds of measurements
- How to calculate the bounds in calculations involving more than one measurement

Further calculations involving bounds of measurements

MIXED EXERCISE 29

Give your answers to questions **1** to **4** correct to 3 significant figures.

1 (a) $\dfrac{1}{9.7} + \dfrac{1}{0.035}$ (b) $9.5^3 + 3.9^5$ (c) $\sqrt[4]{108.6}$

2 (a) $3 \cos 21°$ (b) $\tan^{-1} 1.46$ (c) $\dfrac{8.5 \times \sin 57.1°}{\sin 39.2°}$

3 (a) $\dfrac{555}{10.4 + 204}$ (b) $\dfrac{23.7 \times 0.0042}{12.4 - 1.95}$ (c) $\dfrac{88.71 - 35.53}{26.42 + 9.76}$

4 (a) $(4.2 \times 10^5) \times (3.9 \times 10^6)$ (b) $\sqrt{4.29 \times 10^{-8}}$

    (c) $\dfrac{(8.66 \times 10^4) + (2.98 \times 10^5)}{1.57 \times 10^{-3}}$

5 Jack invests a sum of money at a fixed percentage yearly interest rate.
He is told that the formula the firm will use is $A = 3000 \times 1.05^t$.
 (a) How much did Jack invest?
 (b) What was the rate of interest?
 (c) What does the letter *t* stand for in the formula?
 (d) How much will the investment be worth after
    (i) 4 years?   (ii) 12 years?

6 A car costs £12 000 when new. Its value depreciates by 13% per year.
 (a) Write down a formula for the value, *v*, of the car after *t* years.
 (b) Calculate the value after
    (i) 3 years.   (ii) 8 years.
 (c) Use trial and improvement to find how long it takes for the value to halve.

7 Find the upper and lower bounds for each of these measurements.
 (a) A book weighs 1.7 kg to the nearest 0.1 kg.
 (b) The total weight of 10 sacks of corn, each sack weighing 25 kg to the nearest kg.

8 A rectangular room measures 4.3 m and 6.2 m. Both measurements are correct to the nearest 0.1 m. Work out the upper and lower bounds of the perimeter of the room.

9 A lorry driver travels 157 km in 2.5 hours. The distance is correct to the nearest kilometre and the time is correct to the nearest 0.1 hour. Work out the upper and lower bound of the average speed of the lorry.

30 EQUATIONS AND INEQUALITIES 2

THIS CHAPTER IS ABOUT
- Solving more difficult linear equations
- How to represent an inequality on a graph
- Solving linear inequalities with one or two unknowns

YOU SHOULD ALREADY KNOW
- How to write a formula using letters
- How to manipulate algebraic expressions
- How to expand brackets
- How to solve simple equations and inequalities
- How to manipulate fractions
- How to draw graphs of straight lines

Equations

You learned how to solve simple equations in Chapter 7.

Check up 30.1

Solve each of these equations.
(a) $5x + 2 = 12$
(b) $3x - 9 = x + 4$
(c) $2(4x - 3) = 14$
(d) $x - 2 = 3x + 6$

The equations that follow will bring together all the ideas you met in Chapter 7 and extend them.

Equations with brackets on both sides

In Chapter 7 you learned how to solve equations involving brackets, and equations with x on both sides. You can use the strategies needed to solve both of these types of equation to solve more complex equations.

EXAMPLE 30.1

Solve the equation $3(4x - 5) = 2(3x - 2) - 4x - 3$.

Equations 423

Solution

$$3(4x - 5) = 2(3x - 2) - 4x - 3$$
$$12x - 15 = 6x - 4 - 4x - 3$$ First expand the brackets.
$$12x - 6x + 4x = 15 - 4 - 3$$ Collect all the x terms on the left-hand side of the equation, and the numerical terms on the right.
$$10x = 8$$
$$x = \tfrac{8}{10}$$ Divide each side of the equation by the coefficient of x, 10.
$$x = \tfrac{4}{5}$$ Give the answer in its simplest form.

> **TIP**
> A common error is to go from $10x = 8$ to $x = \dfrac{10}{8}$ rather than $\dfrac{8}{10}$.
> Make sure you divide by the coefficient of x.

Equation involving fractions

You learned in Chapter 7 how to solve equations involving fractions and a single x term.

When an equation involves a fraction and more than one x term you need to get rid of the fraction first, by multiplying each side of the fraction by the denominator of the fraction.

EXAMPLE 30.2

Solve the equation $\dfrac{x}{3} = 2x - 3$.

Solution

$$\tfrac{x}{3} = 2x - 3$$
$$x = 3(2x - 3)$$ First multiply each side of the equation by the denominator, 3.
$$x = 6x - 9$$ Expand the brackets.
$$6x - 9 = x$$ Swap the sides of the equation so that the x term with the larger positive coefficient is on the left. You could do this at a later stage.
$$5x = 9$$ Collect all the x terms on the left-hand side of the equation, and the numerical terms on the right.
$$x = \tfrac{9}{5}$$ Divide each side of the equation by the coefficient of x, 5.
$$x = 1\tfrac{4}{5}$$ Give the answer as a mixed number.

424 30 Equations and inequalities 2

When an equation involves more than one fraction, you need to multiply each side of the equation by the lowest common multiple (LCM) of all the denominators.

EXAMPLE 30.3

Solve the equation $\dfrac{x}{4} = \dfrac{3x}{2} - \dfrac{5}{3}$.

Solution

$$\dfrac{x}{4} = \dfrac{3x}{2} - \dfrac{5}{3}$$

$12 \times \dfrac{x}{4} = 12 \times \left(\dfrac{3x}{2} - \dfrac{5}{3}\right)$ Multiply each side of the equation by the LCM of 4, 2 and 3, which is 12.

$3x = 18x - 20$

$18x - 20 = 3x$ Swap the sides of the equation so that the x term with the larger positive coefficient is on the left.

$15x = 20$ Collect all the x terms on the left-hand side of the equation, and the numerical terms on the right.

$x = \dfrac{20}{15}$ Divide each side of the equation by the coefficient of x, 15.

$x = \dfrac{4}{3}$ Cancel the fraction by dividing by the common factor, 5.

$x = 1\dfrac{1}{3}$ Give the answer as a mixed number.

> **TIP**
>
> A common error when multiplying through by a number is to multiply just the first term.
>
> Use brackets to make sure.

EXAMPLE 30.4

Solve the equation $\dfrac{2x-3}{6} + \dfrac{x+2}{3} = \dfrac{5}{2}$.

Solution

$$\frac{2x-3}{6} + \frac{x+2}{3} = \frac{5}{2}$$

$6 \times \left(\frac{2x-3}{6} + \frac{x+2}{3}\right) = 6 \times \frac{5}{2}$ Multiply each side of the equation by the LCM of 6, 3 and 2, which is 6.

$2x - 3 + 2(x + 2) = 15$

$2x - 3 + 2x + 4 = 15$ Expand the brackets.

$4x + 1 = 15$ Simplify by collecting like terms.

$4x = 14$ Subtract 1 from each side of the equation.

$x = \frac{14}{4}$ Divide each side of the equation by the coefficient of x, 4.

$x = \frac{7}{2}$ Cancel the fraction by dividing by the common factor, 2.

$x = 3\frac{1}{2}$ Give the answer as a mixed number.

EXERCISE 30.1

Solve each of these equations.

1 $5(x - 4) = 4x$

2 $4(2x - 2) = 3(x + 4)$

3 $2(4x - 5) = 2x + 6$

4 $\frac{x}{2} = 3x - 10$

5 $\frac{x}{3} = x - 2$

6 $\frac{3x}{2} = 7 - 2x$

7 $\frac{4x}{3} = 4x - 2$

8 $\frac{2x}{3} = x - \frac{4}{3}$

9 $\frac{x}{2} = \frac{3x}{4} - 6$

10 $\frac{x}{3} = \frac{3x}{4} - \frac{1}{6}$

11 $\frac{3x}{2} = \frac{3x-2}{5} + 4$

12 $\frac{2x-1}{6} = \frac{x-3}{2} + \frac{2}{3}$

13 $\frac{x-2}{3} + \frac{2x-1}{2} = \frac{17}{6}$

14 $\frac{2x-3}{3} - \frac{2x+1}{6} + \frac{3}{2} = 0$

15 $\frac{3x-2}{2} = \frac{x-3}{3} + \frac{7}{6}$

Challenge 30.1

(a) Mr Watson left his assets to be shared amongst three people.
He left one third to John, one half to Sylvia and the rest, £75 000, to Maxine.
Use algebra to find how much he left altogether.

(b) At a sports club there are seven more men than women.
A quarter of the number of women is the same as one fifth of the number of men.
Use algebra to find how many women there are at the sports club.

Equations where the unknown is the denominator

In some equations the unknown will be the denominator. The first step towards solving equations of this sort is to multiply through by the denominator.

EXAMPLE 30.5

Solve the equation $\dfrac{200}{x} = 8$.

Solution

$\dfrac{200}{x} = 8$

$200 = 8x$ First multiply each side of the equation by the denominator, x.

$8x = 200$ Swap the sides of the equation so that the x term is on the left.

$x = 25$ Divide each side of the equation by the coefficient of x, 25.

If the equation involves more than one fraction, you need to multiply through by the LCM of all the denominators.

EXAMPLE 30.6

Solve the equation $\dfrac{3}{2x} = \dfrac{6}{5}$.

Solution

$\dfrac{3}{2x} = \dfrac{6}{5}$

$10x \times \dfrac{3}{2x} = 10x \times \dfrac{6}{5}$ Multiply each side of the equation by the LCM of $2x$ and 5, which is $10x$.

$15 = 12x$ Swap the sides of the equation so that the x term is on the left.

$12x = 15$

$x = \dfrac{15}{12}$ Divide each side of the equation by the coefficient of x, 12.

$x = \dfrac{5}{4}$ Cancel the fraction by dividing by the common factor, 3.

$x = 1\tfrac{1}{4}$ Give the answer as a mixed number.

> **TIP**
>
> These equations are not difficult if all the steps are carried out.
> Avoid the common error of going from, for example, $\frac{2}{x} = 8$ to $x = 4$ rather than $x = \frac{1}{4}$.

Equations involving decimals

When an equation involves decimals, the solution may not be exact.

EXAMPLE 30.7

Solve the equation $3.6x = 8.7$.
Give your answer correct to 3 significant figures.

Solution

$3.6x = 8.7$
$\quad x = 8.7 \div 3.6$ Divide each side of the equation by 3.6.
$\quad x = 2.416\,666\,...$
$\quad x = 2.42$ (to 3 s.f.)   Round your answer to the given degree of accuracy.

EXERCISE 30.2

Solve each of these equations.
Where the answer is not exact, give your answer correct to 3 significant figures.

1. $\frac{20}{x} = 5$
2. $\frac{4}{x} = 12$
3. $\frac{75}{2x} = 3$
4. $\frac{16}{3x} = \frac{1}{6}$
5. $\frac{2}{3x} = \frac{4}{3}$
6. $3.5x = 9.6$
7. $5.2x = 25$
8. $\frac{x}{3.4} = 2.7$
9. $2.3(x - 1.2) = 4.6$
10. $\frac{3.4}{x} = 12$

Challenge 30.2

A piece of string is 84 cm long. It is cut into x pieces of equal length.

Another piece of string is 60 cm long and cut into eight pieces, each of which is $\frac{1}{2}$ cm longer than the pieces from the 84 cm string.

Use algebra to find the value of x.

Inequalities

In Chapter 7 you also learned how to solve simple inequalities.

> **Check up 30.2**
>
> Solve each of these inequalities.
>
> (a) $4x < 5$ (b) $2x - 4 > 5$ (c) $3(2x - 5) < 6$

In general, inequalities follow the same rules as equations. For example, you deal with fractions in inequalities in the same way as you do fractions in equations.

EXAMPLE 30.8

Solve the inequality $\frac{x}{3} \leq 2x - 3$.

Solution

$\frac{x}{3} \leq 2x - 3$

$x \leq 3(2x - 3)$ Multiply each side of the inequality by the denominator, 3.

$x \leq 6x - 9$ Expand the brackets.

$9 \leq 5x$ Collect the x terms on the side with the higher x term and the numerical terms on the other side.

$1.8 \leq x$ Divide each side of the inequality by the coefficient of x, 5.

$x \geq 1.8$ Rewrite the inequality so that x is on the left.
Remember to turn the inequality sign round as well.

There is, however, one way in which the rules for inequalities are different from the rules for equations: when you multiply or divide by a negative number, you need to turn the inequality sign around.

EXAMPLE 30.9

Solve the inequality $2 - 3x > 8$.

Solution

$2 - 3x > 8$

$-3x > 6$ Subtract 2 from each side of the inequality.

$x < -2$ Divide each side of the inequality by the coefficient of x, -3.
Because you are dividing by a negative number, you need to turn the inequality sign around.

Discovery 30.1

(a) To see why the method used in Example 30.9 works, solve the inequality $2 - 3x > 8$ by adding $3x$ to each side.

(b) Now try both methods to solve these inequalities.
  (i) $4 - x < 7$
  (ii) $4 > 3 - 7x$

TIP

If you are not sure which way round the inequality sign should be, check by testing a number that satisfies the solution in the original inequality.

For instance, in Example 30.9, the solution is $x < -2$.
Choose a number that satisfies this solution, for example $n = -10$.
Substitute the number into the original inequality, $2 - 3x > 8$.

When $x = -10$, $2 - 3 \times (-10) > 8$
$$32 > 8 \checkmark$$

EXERCISE 30.3

Solve each of these inequalities.

1 $3(2x - 6) > 12 - 4x$

2 $12(x - 4) \leq 3(2x - 6)$

3 $\dfrac{x}{2} < 3x - 10$

4 $\dfrac{2x}{3} < 3x - 14$

5 $\dfrac{3x}{2} > \dfrac{x}{4} + 2$

6 $\dfrac{x}{2} \geq \dfrac{3x}{4} - 2$

7 $\dfrac{1}{2}(2 - x) < 9$

8 $7 - \dfrac{x}{3} \geq 3$

9 $4 - x \leq 7 - 2x$

10 $3.4x - 5 \leq 2.1x$

Challenge 30.3

Natasha wants to organise a disco for as many of her friends as possible.

It costs £75 to hire the disco equipment and the buffet cost £3.50 for each person. She has only £150 to spend.

Use algebra to find the largest number of people that can go to the disco.

Solving inequalities with two unknowns

Discovery 30.2

For each of these inequalities, write down three or four possible pairs of values for x and y.

(a) $x + y < 5$ (b) $3x + y > 10$ (c) $2x + 3y \leq 12$

There are infinitely many possible answers to Discovery 30.2!

Discovery 30.3

For each of these pairs of inequalities, write down two possible pairs of values for x and y.

The values must satisfy both the inequalities at the same time.

(a) $2x + 3y \leq 6$ and $x > y$
(b) $4x - 2y > 5$ and $x + y < 6$
(c) $5x + 4y < 20$ and $2x + y > 4$

As the many possible answers cannot be listed, it is much better to draw them on a graph and show the possible values by shading.

Discovery 30.4

(a) Draw a pair of axes and label them −4 to 4 for both x and y.
Draw and label the line $x = 2$, and label the regions $x \leq 2$ and $x \geq 2$ clearly.

(b) Draw a pair of axes and label them −4 to 4 for both x and y.
Draw and label the line $y = x + 2$, and label the regions $y \leq x + 2$ and $y \geq x + 2$ clearly.

(c) Draw a pair of axes and label them 0 to 6 for both x and y.
Draw and label the line $3x + 2y = 12$, and label the regions $3x + 2y \leq 12$ and $3x + 2y \geq 12$ clearly.

You can represent an inequality on a graph by drawing the graph of the line and labelling the region that satisfies the inequality.

Often the region that *does not* satisfy the inequality is shaded; the region that *does* satisfy the inequality is left unshaded.

Several inequalities can be represented on the same axes and the region where the values of x and y satisfy all of them found.

EXAMPLE 30.10

Draw a pair of axes and label them 0 to 8 for both x and y.
Show, by shading, the region where $x \geq 0$, $y \geq 0$ and $x + 2y \leq 8$.

Solution

First draw the line $x + 2y = 8$.

Then shade out the regions $x \leq 0$, $y \leq 0$, and $x + 2y \geq 8$. These are the regions which are *not required* for the solution; that is, where the values of x and y do *not* satisfy the inequalities.

The required region, where the values of x and y satisfy all three inequalities, is labelled R.

> **TIP** When you have drawn a line, test which side is the required region: choose a simple point on one side of the line and see whether or not it satisfies the inequality.

When an inequality involves the signs $<$ or $>$, the points on the line are *not* included in the solution. For example, if $x < 2$, the points $(2, -2)$, $(2, -1)$, $(2, 0)$, $(2, 1)$, $(2, 2)$ and so on do not satisfy the inequality. Inequalities involving the signs $<$ or $>$ are represented on a graph using a broken line.

EXAMPLE 30.11

Draw a pair of axes and label them from 0 to 5 for both x and y.
Show, by shading, the region where $x \geq 0$, $y \geq 0$, $5x + 4y < 20$ and $2x + y > 4$.

Solution

Draw the two lines $5x + 4y = 20$ and $2x + y = 4$.

Because they represent the inequalities $5x + 4y < 20$ and $2x + y > 4$ the lines should be broken, not solid.

Label them clearly.

Shade out the regions $x \leq 0$, $y \leq 0$, $5x + 4y > 20$ and $2x + y < 4$.

The required region is labelled R.

EXERCISE 30.4

1. Draw a pair of axes and label them 0 to 6 for both x and y.
   Show, by shading, the region where $x \geq 0$, $y \geq 0$ and $x + 2y \leq 6$.

2. Draw a pair of axes and label them -3 to 4 for both x and y.
   Show, by shading, the region where $x \geq 0$, $y \leq 3$ and $y \geq 2x - 3$.

3. Draw a pair of axes and label them -4 to 4 for both x and y.
   Show, by shading, the region where $x > -2$, $y < 3$ and $y > 2x$.

4. Draw a pair of axes and label them 0 to 6 for both x and y.
   Show, by shading, the region where $x < 4$, $y < 3$ and $3x + 4y > 12$.

5. Draw a pair of axes and label them -1 to 5 for both x and y.
   Show, by shading, the region where $y \geq 0$, $y \leq x + 1$ and $3x + 5y < 15$.

Challenge 30.4

At James' and Nicola's wedding, 56 people need to be taken to the reception.

Harry's Hire Cars has nine four-seater cars costing £25 each and five eight-seater cars costing £35 each.

James and Nicola hire x four-seater and y eight-seater taxis.

(a) One inequality is $x \leq 9$.
    Write down two other inequalities that must be satisfied.

(b) Draw these three inequalities on a graph and shade out the regions not required.

(c) Find the combination of cars that will cost the least.
    State how many of each type of car James and Nicola should hire, and the total cost.

WHAT YOU HAVE LEARNED

- To solve equations involving fractions, first multiply every term in the equation by the lowest common multiple of the denominators, expand any brackets and then rearrange as usual
- Linear inequalities are solved using the same rules as equations, except that when you multiply or divide by a negative number the inequality sign must be changed around
- To illustrate a number of inequalities on a graph, draw the lines and shade out the regions not required. Inequalities involving the signs < or > are represented using a broken line

MIXED EXERCISE 30

For questions 1 to 15, solve the equation.
Where the answer is not exact, give your answer correct to 3 significant figures.

1 $4(2x - 5) = 3(4 - x) + 1$

2 $2(x - 3) = x - 1$

3 $\dfrac{3x}{2} = 2 + x$

4 $\dfrac{x}{2} = 3x + 5$

5 $\dfrac{x}{2} = \dfrac{3x}{4} - \dfrac{1}{2}$

6 $\dfrac{3x}{2} = \dfrac{3x - 2}{5} + 1$

7 $\dfrac{2x - 1}{6} = \dfrac{2(x - 3)}{3} + 1$

8 $\dfrac{4}{x} = 24$

9 $\dfrac{75}{2x} = 5$

10 $7.3x = 18.2$

11 $3.6x - 2.4 = 7.6$

12 $\dfrac{7x}{2} < 3x + 2$

13 $2(x - 4) \leq 3(2x - 3)$

14 $2.5x - 7.3 > 4.2$

15 Draw a pair of axes and label them 0 to 6 for x and -2 to 10 for y.
Show, by shading, the region where $x > 0$, $y > 3x - 2$ and $4x + 3y < 24$.

31 THREE-DIMENSIONAL GEOMETRY

THIS CHAPTER IS ABOUT

- Using right-angled triangles to find lengths and angles in 3D
- Finding angles between lines and planes

YOU SHOULD ALREADY KNOW

- Pythagoras' theorem:

$$c^2 = a^2 + b^2$$

- The trigonometrical ratios:

$$\sin \theta = \frac{\text{opposite}}{\text{hypotenuse}} \qquad \cos \theta = \frac{\text{adjacent}}{\text{hypotenuse}}$$

$$\tan \theta = \frac{\text{opposite}}{\text{adjacent}}$$

Finding lengths and angles in three dimensions

You can find lengths and angles of **3-D** objects by identifying **right-angled triangles** within the object and using **Pythagoras' theorem** or **trigonometry**.

EXAMPLE 31.1

A vertical flagpole, VO, which is 12 m high, is attached to the ground by three ropes of equal length.

The ropes reach the ground at A, B and C, 2 m from the foot of the flagpole.

The ground is horizontal.

Calculate
(a) the length of a rope, VA.
(b) the angle which it makes with the ground, VAO.

Solution

First draw a diagram.

TIP: In a 3-D diagram, right angles often don't look their true size.

Work out where the right angles are and draw a 2-D diagram of a relevant triangle.

(a) $r^2 = 12^2 + 2^2$
$r^2 = 148$
$r = \sqrt{148}$
$r = 12.2$ m (to 1 d.p.)

Use Pythagoras' theorem to find the length of the rope.

(b) $\tan \text{VAO} = \dfrac{12}{2}$
$= 6$

Use trigonometry to find angle VAO.

Angle VAO $= \tan^{-1} 6$
$= 80.5°$ (to 1 d.p.)

Use the [SHIFT] [tan] keys on your calculator to obtain the inverse function. It may be labelled arctan, invtan or $\tan^{-1}$.

EXAMPLE 31.2

Calculate the length of the diagonal of this cuboid.

Solution

First identify a relevant right-angled triangle.

$d^2 = b^2 + 3^2$ (1)

Use Pythagoras' theorem to link the sides of the triangle. You cannot solve this equation yet because you don't know the value of b, so label the equation (1).

b is the length of the diagonal of the base of the cuboid.

31 Three-dimensional geometry

$b^2 = 5^2 + 2^2$ (2) Use Pythagoras' theorem to form a second equation linking
$b^2 = 29$ the sides of this triangle, and use it to find b^2.
$d^2 = b^2 + 3^2$ (1)   Substitute for b^2 in equation (1).
$d^2 = 29 + 9$
$d^2 = 38$
$d = \sqrt{38}$
$d = 6.2$ cm (to 1 d.p.)

TIP Don't forget to include the units in your answer.

Proof 31.1

Use a similar method to that used in Example 31.2 to show that the length of diagonal of a cuboid measuring a cm by b cm by c cm is $\sqrt{a^2 + b^2 + c^2}$.

You can use the formula:

Diagonal of a cuboid measuring a cm by b cm by c cm = $\sqrt{a^2 + b^2 + c^2}$

when working with coordinates in three dimensions.

EXAMPLE 31.3

Calculate the distance between the points $(-1, 0, 3)$ and $(2, 4, 7)$.

Solution

To get from the first point to the second you need to move 3 in the positive x direction, 4 in the positive y direction and 4 in positive z direction.

Finding lengths and angles in three dimensions

Think of the two points as being at the vertices of a 3 by 4 by 4 cuboid.

So the distance between the points (−1, 0, 3) and (2, 4, 7) is

$\sqrt{3^2 + 4^2 + 4^2} = \sqrt{9 + 16 + 16}$
$= \sqrt{41}$
$= 6.4$ units (to 1 d.p)

EXERCISE 31.1

1. Calculate the length of the diagonal of a cuboid measuring 5 cm by 8 cm by 3 cm.

2. Calculate the length of the diagonal of a cube with sides 5.6 cm.

3. A box is a cuboid with base 6 cm by 15 cm.
   A pencil 17 cm long just fits in the box.
   Calculate the height of the box.

4. A square-based pyramid has sloping edges of length 9.5 cm.
   Its base has diagonals of length 8.4 cm.
   Calculate the vertical height of the pyramid.

5. A pyramid has a rectangular base of sides 8.2 cm and 7.6 cm. Its height is 6.5 cm.
   All its sloping edges are the same length. Calculate the length of a sloping edge.

6. ABCDEF is a triangular wedge.
   The faces ABFE, BCDF and ACDE are rectangles.
   (a) Calculate the length CE.
   (b) Calculate each of these angles.
      (i) CAB
      (ii) CEB

438 31 Three-dimensional geometry

7 Calculate the distance between each of these pairs of points.
   (a) (4, 1, 5) and (2, 4, −5)
   (b) (−2, 3, 6) and (2, 4, −4)
   (c) (0, 2, −3) and (1, 5, 12)

8 The distance of the point (2, 5, k) from the origin is $\sqrt{65}$.
   Find the value of k.

9 The pyramid OABCD has a horizontal rectangular base ABCD as shown.
   O is vertically above A.
   Calculate
   (a) the length of OC.
   (b) angle OCA.

10 A vertical mast, MT, has its foot, M, on horizontal ground.
   It is supported by a wire, AT, which makes an angle of 65°
   with the horizontal and is of length 12 m, and two more
   wires, BT and CT, where A, B and C are on the ground.
   BM = 4.2 m.
   Calculate
   (a) the height of the mast.
   (b) the angle which BT makes with the ground.
   (c) the length of wire BT.

The angle between a line and a plane

So far in this chapter, the angles found have been identified by letters.
You also need to be able to find the **angle between a line and a plane**
without the angle being identified for you.

To find the angle between a line and a plane:
- Draw a perpendicular to the plane from a point on the line.
- Join the two lines to make a right-angled triangle.

The angle required is the angle between the line and the plane in this triangle.

These diagrams show in each case the angle between the line, L, and the shaded plane.

The first line you draw is shown in red, the second in blue.

To find the size of the angle, use trigonometry.

EXAMPLE 31.4

Calculate the angle between the diagonal and the base of this cuboid.

Solution

This is the same cuboid as in Example 31.2. You need to use the same triangle.

$\sin \theta = \dfrac{3}{d}$ Use trigonometry to find θ.

$\sin \theta = \dfrac{3}{\sqrt{38}}$ You found $d = \sqrt{38}$ in Example 31.2.

$\theta = \sin^{-1} \dfrac{3}{\sqrt{38}}$

$\theta = 29.1°$ (to 1 d.p.)

TIP

When using the results of calculations in further working, use unrounded answers if possible, to avoid rounding errors.

For example, your final answer to Example 31.4 will be more accurate if you use $d = \sqrt{38}$ than if you use $d = 6.2$ cm.

EXERCISE 31.2

1. A square-based pyramid has sloping edges of length 9.5 cm.
   Its base has diagonals of length 8.4 cm.
   Calculate the angle between a sloping edge and the base.
   Hint: See Exercise 31.1, question **4**.

2. A box is a cuboid with base 6 cm by 15 cm.
   A pencil 17 cm long just fits in the box.
   Calculate the angle which the pencil makes with the base.
   Hint: See Exercise 31.1, question **3**.

3. A cube has side 10 cm.
   Calculate the angle between a diagonal of the cube and a face of the cube.
   Explain why your answer is true for all cubes.

4. A cuboid has a base of sides 5.6 cm by 8.2 cm. Its height is 4.3 cm.
   Calculate the angle between a diagonal of the cuboid and
   (a) the base.
   (b) a 5.6 cm by 4.3 cm face.

5. A pyramid is 8 cm high and has a square base of side 6 cm.
   Its sloping edges are all of equal length.
   Calculate the angle between a sloping edge and the base.

6. A square-based pyramid has height 8.3 cm.
   Its sloping faces each make an angle of 55° with the base.
   (a) Find the length of the sides of the square.
   (b) Find the length of the sloping edges of the pyramid.

7. ABCDEF is a triangular wedge.
   The base ABFE is a horizontal rectangle.
   C is vertically above B.
   (a) Calculate the length AD.
   (b) Calculate the angle which AD makes with
       (i) the base ABEF.   (ii) the face ABC.

8. Sketch the right-angled triangle and label the angle required in each case to find the angle between the following lines and planes in this cuboid.
   (a) HB and ABCD
   (b) ED and ABFE
   (c) FD and BCGF
   (d) FD and ABFE

Challenge 31.1

Work in pairs.

Look at some 3-D shapes in the classroom, particularly some which have sloping faces or edges.

Take it in turns to describe to your partner the angle between a line and a plane, in words, and challenge them to identify it on the shape.

WHAT YOU HAVE LEARNED

- How to find lengths and angles in 3-D shapes by finding right-angled triangles and using Pythagoras' theorem or trigonometry as appropriate
- That the length of diagonal of a cuboid measuring a cm by b cm by c cm is $\sqrt{a^2 + b^2 + c^2}$

- How to find the angle between a line and a plane, using a perpendicular to the plane from a point on the line

MIXED EXERCISE 31

1. Calculate the length of the diagonal of a cuboid measuring 5.8 cm by 6.7 cm by 3.8 cm.

2. The length of a diagonal of a cuboid is 12.4 cm.
   The base of the cuboid is a square of side 5.3 cm.
   Calculate the height of the cuboid.

3. Calculate the distance between each of these pairs of points.
   (a) (0, 1, 4) and (2, 6, 5)
   (b) (3, 2, −4) and (−1, 6, 7)

4. A cylinder has base radius 3.7 cm.
   A pencil 15.6 cm long just fits in the cylinder.
   (a) Calculate the angle between the pencil and the base of the cylinder.
   (b) Calculate the height of the cylinder.

31 Three-dimensional geometry

5   Amy stands 30 m west of a church tower.
    She measures the angle of elevation of the top of the tower from ground level as 52°.
    (a) Calculate the height of the tower.
    Amy then walks 25 m due south to point B.
    (b) Calculate how far she is, at B, from the tower.
    (c) Calculate the angle of elevation of the top of the tower from B.

6   In this cuboid, AB = 12 cm, BC = 5 cm and CG = 7 cm.
    Calculate
    (a) angle ABE.
    (b) length EG.
    (c) length EC.
    (d) angle GEC.

7   This 'lean-to' conservatory is a prism with a trapezium as its cross-section.
    (a) Calculate the length of the sloping edge of the roof.
    (b) Calculate the angle between the roof and the wall against which the conservatory is built.

8   A pyramid has height 7.5 cm and a square base of side 6.3 cm.
    (a) Calculate the length of a sloping edge of the pyramid.
    (b) Calculate the angle that a sloping edge makes with the vertical.

9   A pyramid has a rectangular base of sides 3.6 cm and 5.2 cm.
    The faces with base 5.2 cm make an angle of 62° with the base.
    Calculate
    (a) the height of the pyramid.
    (b) the angle made with the base by a sloping edge of the pyramid.

10 The diagram shows the roof of a house
    The base, ABCD, is a rectangle measuring 12.4 m by 7.6 m.
    The sloping edges are all of equal length.
    The ridge of the roof, EF, is 8.2 m. EF is 3.4 m above the base ABCD.
    (a) Calculate the length of a sloping edge of the roof.
    (b) Calculate the angle between a sloping edge and the base.
    (c) Calculate the angle between face EDA and the base.
    (d) Calculate the angle between face ABFE and the base.

32 FORMULAE 2

> **THIS CHAPTER IS ABOUT**
> - Rearranging formulae where the new subject occurs more than once
> - Rearranging formulae where the new subject is raised to a power

> **YOU SHOULD ALREADY KNOW**
> - How to factorise simple expressions
> - How to expand brackets and manipulate simple algebraic expressions
> - How to rearrange simple formulae

Formulae where the new subject occurs more than once

In all the formulae you have rearranged so far, the new subject has occurred only once. For example, you already know how to make t the subject of $v = u + at$.

You also need to be able to rearrange formulae where the new subject occurs more than once. In such cases, all terms containing the new subject must be collected together.

EXAMPLE 32.1

Rearrange the formula $mxy = y + 4x$ to make x the subject.

Solution

$mxy = y + 4x$
$mxy - 4x = y$ Subtract $4x$ from each side so that all the x terms are together.
$x(my - 4) = y$ Factorise the left-hand side, taking out the common factor, x.
$x = \dfrac{y}{my - 4}$ Divide each side by $(my - 4)$.

Sometimes, it is not immediately obvious that the new subject occurs more than once.

EXAMPLE 32.2

Rearrange the formula $m = \dfrac{1}{x} + \dfrac{4}{y}$ to make x the subject.

Solution

$$m = \frac{1}{x} + \frac{4}{y}$$
$$mxy = y + 4x \qquad \text{Multiply each side by } xy \text{ to get rid of the fractions.}$$
$$mxy - 4x = y \qquad \text{The formula is now in the form it was in Example 32.1.}$$
$$x(my - 4) = y$$
$$x = \frac{y}{my - 4}$$

Formulae like the one in Example 32.2 can also be rearranged using a different approach.

EXAMPLE 32.3

Rearrange the formula $m = \dfrac{1}{x} + \dfrac{4}{y}$ to make x the subject.

Solution

$$m = \frac{1}{x} + \frac{4}{y}$$

$$m - \frac{4}{y} = \frac{1}{x} \qquad \text{Subtract } \frac{4}{y} \text{ from each side.}$$

$$\frac{1}{x} = m - \frac{4}{y} \qquad \text{Swap the sides so that the } x \text{ term is on the left.}$$

$$\frac{1}{x} = \frac{my - 4}{y} \qquad \text{Arrange the right-hand side over a common denominator.}$$

$$x = \frac{y}{my - 4} \qquad \text{Invert each side.}$$
$$\text{Remember that you can only do this if each side is a single fraction.}$$

Formulae where the new subject occurs more than once

EXERCISE 32.1

Rearrange each of these formulae to make the letter in brackets the subject.

1. $pq - rs = rt$ (r)
2. $A = P + \dfrac{PRT}{100}$ (P)
3. $3(x - 5) = y(4 - 3x)$ (x)
4. $pq + r = rq - p$ (p)
5. $pq + r = rq - p$ (r)
6. $y = x + \dfrac{px}{q}$ (x)
7. $s = ut + \dfrac{at}{2}$ (t)
8. $\dfrac{a}{2x + 1} = \dfrac{b}{3x - 1}$ (x)
9. $s = \dfrac{uv}{u + v}$ (u)
10. $\dfrac{1}{f} = \dfrac{1}{u} + \dfrac{1}{v}$ (v)

Formulae where the new subject is raised to a power

You also need to be able to rearrange formulae where the new subject is raised to a power.

In these cases you will need, at the appropriate stage, to use the inverse operation. For example, for $\sqrt{x}$, you need to square; for x^2, you need to take the square root.

EXAMPLE 32.4

Rearrange the formula $v = y + \sqrt{\dfrac{p}{x}}$ to make x the subject.

Solution

$v = y + \sqrt{\dfrac{p}{x}}$ When a formula involves a power or root, rearrange the formula to get that term by itself.

$v - y = \sqrt{\dfrac{p}{x}}$ In this case, subtract y from each side so that $\sqrt{\dfrac{p}{x}}$ is by itself.

$(v - y)^2 = \dfrac{p}{x}$ Square each side. In this case you do not need to expand $(v - y)^2$.

$x(v - y)^2 = p$ Multiply each side by x.

$x = \dfrac{p}{(v - y)^2}$ Divide each side by $x(v - y)^2$.

32 Formulae 2

EXERCISE 32.2

1 Rearrange each of these formulae to make the letter in brackets the subject.

(a) $y = 3x^2 - 4$ (x)

(b) $t = 2\pi \sqrt{\dfrac{l}{g}}$ (l)

(c) $A = \pi r \sqrt{h^2 + r^2}$ (h)

(d) $v^2 - u^2 = 2as$ (u)

(e) $V = \frac{1}{3}\pi r^2 h$ (r)

(f) $s = 15 - \frac{1}{2}at^2$ (t)

2 The formula for the volume of a cylinder is $V = \pi r^2 h$, where r is the radius of the cylinder and h is its height.
  (a) Find the volume of a cylinder of radius 12 cm and height 20 cm
      Give your answer to 2 significant figures.
  (b) Rearrange the formula to make r the subject.
  (c) What is the radius of a cylinder of volume 500 cm² and height 5 cm?
      Give your answer to 3 significant figures.

3 The formula for finding the length, d, of the diagonal of a cuboid whose dimensions are x, y and z is $d = \sqrt{x^2 + y^2 + z^2}$.
  (a) Find d when $x = 2$, $y = 3$ and $z = 4$.
  (b) How long is the diagonal of a cuboid block of concrete with dimensions 2 m, 3 m and 75 cm?
  (c) Rearrange the formula to make x the subject.
  (d) Find x when $d = 0.86$ m, $y = 0.25$ m, and $z = 0.41$ m.

Challenge 32.1

(a) The formula for the surface area of a closed cyliner is $A = 2\pi r(r + h)$, where r is the radius of the cylinder and h is its height.
What happens if you try to make r the subject?

(b) $S = \frac{1}{2}n(n + 1)$ gives the sum, S, of the first n positive integers.
Find n when $S = 325$.

WHAT YOU HAVE LEARNED

- When rearranging a formula where the new subject occurs more than once, collect together all terms containing the new subject
- When a formula involves a power or root, rearrange the formula to get that term by itself
- When the new subject is raised to a power, use the inverse operation. For example, for $\sqrt{x}$, square; for x^2, take the square root

MIXED EXERCISE 32

1 Rearrange each of these formulae to make the letter in brackets the subject.

(a) $r = \dfrac{a}{a+b}$ $\quad (a)$

(b) $t = 2\pi\sqrt{\dfrac{l}{g}}$ $\quad (g)$

(c) $\dfrac{1}{f} = \dfrac{1}{u} + \dfrac{1}{v}$ $\quad (u)$

(d) $x + a = \dfrac{x+b}{c}$ $\quad (x)$

(e) $a - b = \dfrac{a+2}{b}$ $\quad (a)$

(f) $\dfrac{y+x}{y-x} = 3$ $\quad (y)$

(g) $ab + bc + a = 0$ $\quad (a)$

(h) $2x = \sqrt{x^2 + y}$ $\quad (x)$

(i) $\sqrt{\dfrac{x+1}{x}} = y$ $\quad (x)$

(j) $p = 2\left[\dfrac{n-(r+1)}{n-1}\right]$ $\quad (n)$

(k) $y = \dfrac{x - np}{\sqrt{npq}}$ $\quad (q)$

(l) $F = \dfrac{x^2}{1-x^2}$ $\quad (x)$

(m) $s = \sqrt{\dfrac{x^2 + y^2}{n}}$ $\quad (y)$

(n) $m = \dfrac{ax + by}{a + b}$ $\quad (b)$

2 The formula for the volume of a sphere is $V = \tfrac{4}{3}\pi r^3$.
  (a) Find V if $r = 5$.
  (b) Make r the subject of the formula.
  (c) Find the radius of a sphere of volume 3500 m^3.

33 ➔ PROPORTION AND VARIATION

THIS CHAPTER IS ABOUT
- Solving problems using simple proportion
- Solving problems using more complex proportion (variation)

YOU SHOULD ALREADY KNOW
- How to use ratio
- How to use fractions as multipliers
- How to manipulate simple algebraic expressions

Direct proportion

You met **proportion** in Chapter 8, where you learned how to solve problems using ratios.

In this sort of problem, both quantities increase at the same rate: for example, if you need 200 g of oats to make a small batch of 10 flapjacks, you need 400 g of oats to make a large batch of 20 flapjacks.

Amount of oats needed for the large batch = amount of oats needed for the small batch × 2
Number of flapjacks in the large batch = number of flapjacks in the small batch × 2
Both quantities are multiplied by the same number, called the **multiplier**.

To find the multiplier, you divide either pair of quantities. For example, $\frac{400}{200} = 2$ or $\frac{20}{10} = 2$.

So a quicker way to solve this type of problem is to find the multiplier and use it to find the unknown quantity. This second method is quicker than the first method because it combines two steps in one.

EXAMPLE 33.1

A car uses 20 litres of petrol when making a journey of 160 miles. How many litres of petrol would be used making a similar journey of 360 miles?

Solution

Method 1

This is the method you learned in Chapter 8.

$160 : 360 = 4 : 9$	First write down the ratio linking the distance travelled in the two journeys and divide by 40 so that it is in its lowest terms.
$20 \div 4 = 5$	Divide the amount of petrol needed for the first journey by the first part of the ratio, 4.
$5 \times 9 = 45$	Multiply the second part of the ratio by 5.

45 litres of petrol would be used making a journey of 360 miles.

Method 2

$\dfrac{360}{160} = \dfrac{9}{4}$	Write the distance travelled in the two journeys as a fraction. You want to find the petrol needed for a 360 mile journey, so make 360 the numerator and 160 the denominator. Cancel the fraction so that it is in its simplest form.
$20 \times \dfrac{9}{4} = 45$	Multiply the amount of petrol needed for the first journey by the multiplier.

45 litres of petrol would be used making a journey of 360 miles.

Notice that in Method 1 you divided by 4 then multiplied by 9.

In Method 2 you multiplied by $\dfrac{9}{4}$, combining the two steps into one.

Questions of this type are examples of **direct proportion**. As one quantity increases (miles travelled, x) so must the other (petrol used, y). Simply, the more miles you travel, the more petrol you use.

This relationship can be written as $y \propto x$, which is expressed in words as 'y is proportional to x' or 'y varies as x'.

This graph shows direct proportion.

The gradient of the line could be any positive value (dependent on the multiplier) but the line will always pass through the origin.

The multiplier is sometimes called the **constant of proportionality** and given the letter k.

EXAMPLE 33.2

An excavator can dig a trench that is 560 metres long in 21 days.
How long would it take the excavator to dig a trench that is 240 metres long?

Solution

$\dfrac{240}{560} = \dfrac{3}{7}$ First find the multiplier and cancel so that it is in its simplest form.

You want to find the time required to dig a 240 m trench, so make 240 the numerator of the fraction and 560 the denominator.

$21 \times \dfrac{3}{7} = 9$ days Multiply the known time by the multiplier to find the unknown time.

EXERCISE 33.1

For each of these questions
(a) write down the multiplier.
(b) calculate the required quantity.

1. An express train travels 165 metres in 3 seconds.
   How far would it travel in 8 seconds?

2. An aeroplane travels 216 miles in 27 minutes.
   How far did it travel in 12 minutes?

3. £50 is worth $90.
   How much is £175 worth?

4. A ladder that is 7 metres long has 28 rungs.
   How many rungs would there be in a ladder that is 5 metres long?

5. A piece of string 27 metres long has a mass of 351 grams.
   What is the mass of 15 metres of the string?

6. A rabbit can dig a tunnel that is 4 metres long in a total of 26 hours.
   How long would it take in total to dig a tunnel 7 metres long?

7. A landscape gardener can paint 15 fence panels in 6 hours.
   How many hours would it take him to paint 40 fence panels?

8. The cost of 12 printer cartridges is £90.00.
   What is the cost of five of these cartridges?

9 A carpet with an area of 18 m² costs £441.
What is the cost of 14 m² of the same carpet?

10 A piece of balsa wood with a volume of 2.5 m³ has a mass of 495 kilograms.
What is the mass of a piece of balsa wood with a volume of 0.9 m³?

Inverse proportion

It is not always the case with proportion that, as one quantity increases, so does the other.

Sometimes, as one quantity increases, the other decreases.

In such cases, you need to divide by the multiplier, rather than multiply.

EXAMPLE 33.3

If three excavators can dig a hole in 8 hours, how long would it take four excavators to dig the hole?

Solution

Clearly, as more excavators are to be used, the digging will take less time.

The multiplier is $\frac{4}{3}$.

$8 \div \frac{4}{3} = 6$ Divide the known time by the multiplier to find the unknown time.

Questions of this type are examples of **inverse proportion**. As one quantity increases (number of diggers, x) the other quantity decreases (hours taken, y). Simply, the more excavators you have the less time you need to dig the hole.

This relationship can be written as $y \propto \frac{1}{x}$, which is expressed in words as 'y is inversely proportional to x' or 'y varies inversely as x'.

This graph shows inverse proportion.

EXERCISE 33.2

For each of these questions
(a) write down the multiplier.
(b) calculate the required quantity.

1 A journey takes 18 minutes at a constant speed of 32 kilometres per hour.
   How long would the journey take at a constant speed of 48 kilometres per hour?

2 It takes a team of 8 men six weeks to paint a bridge.
   How long would the painting take if there were 12 men?

3 A pool is normally filled using four inlet valves in a period of 18 hours.
   One of the inlet valves is out of action.
   How long will it take to fill the pool using just three inlet valves?

4 A journey can be completed in 44 minutes at an average speed of 50 miles per hour.
   How long would the same journey take at an average speed of 40 miles per hour?

5 A supply of hay is enough to feed 12 horses for 15 days.
   How long would the same supply feed 20 horses?

6 It takes three harvesters 6 hours to harvest a crop of wheat.
   How long would it take to harvest the wheat if only two harvesters were available?

7 On the outward leg of a journey a cyclist travels at an average speed of 12 kilometres per hour for a period of 4 hours.
   The return journey took 3 hours.
   What was the average speed for the return journey?

8 It takes a team of 18 men 21 weeks to dig a canal.
   How long would it take to dig the canal if there were 14 men?

9 A tank can be emptied using six pumps in a period of 18 hours.
   How long will it take to empty the tank using eight pumps?

10 A gang of 9 bricklayers can build a wall in 20 days.
   How long would a gang of 15 bricklayers take to build the wall?

Challenge 33.1

The time taken to complete a race is inversely proportional to the speed.

What happens to the time taken if the speed is

(a) doubled?   (b) halved?   (c) increased by 20%?

Finding formulae

In Example 33.2, y is proportional to x ($y \propto x$).

The variables are metres and days, and can be written in a table.

x (metres)	560	240
y (days)	21	9

The first pair of x and y values are 560 and 21. The ratio $\frac{y}{x}$ is $\frac{21}{560}$, or $\frac{3}{80}$ in its simplest form.

The second pair of x and y values are 240 and 9. The ratio $\frac{y}{x}$ is $\frac{9}{240}$, or $\frac{3}{80}$ in its simplest form.

The same constant ratio (k) would apply to all pairs of x and y values.

So the formula for this relationship is $y = \frac{3}{80}x$.

The formula for any relationship of direct proportion is $y = kx$.

In Example 33.3, y is inversely proportional to x $\left(y \propto \frac{1}{x}\right)$.

The variables are excavators (x) and hours (y), and can be written in a table.

x (excavators)	3	4
y (hours)	8	6

The first pair of x and y values are 3 and 8. The value xy is 24.
The second pair of x and y values are 4 and 6. The value xy is 24.

The same constant (k) would apply to all pairs of x and y values.

So the formula for this relationship is $xy = 24$ or $y = \frac{24}{x}$.

The formula for any relationship of inverse proportion is $xy = k$ or $y = \frac{k}{x}$.

EXAMPLE 33.4

For each of these relationships
(i) state the type of proportion.
(ii) find the formula.
(iii) find the missing y value in the table.

(a)
x	6	10	22
y	15	25	

(b)
x	20	15	12
y	6	8	

Solution

(a) (i) Direct proportion — As x increases, so does y.

$\dfrac{15}{6} = \dfrac{5}{2}, \dfrac{25}{10} = \dfrac{5}{2}$

(ii) $y = \dfrac{5}{2}x$

(iii) $y = \dfrac{5}{2} \times 22$
$= 55$

(b) (i) Inverse proportion — As x decreases, y increases.

$20 \times 6 = 120, 15 \times 8 = 120$

(ii) $y = \dfrac{120}{x}$

(iii) $y = \dfrac{120}{12}$
$= 10$

EXERCISE 33.3

For each of these relationships
(a) state the type of proportion.
(b) find the formula.
(c) where appropriate, find the missing y value in the table.

1
x	40	200	
y	3	15	

2
x	4	7	10
y	28	49	

3
x	12	20	
y	16	25	

4
x	20	90	150
y	8	36	

5
x	18	15	
y	66	55	

6
x	40	24	15
y	6	10	

7

x	30	18.75
y	5	8

8

x	60	80	200
y	24	18	

9

x	10	24
y	36	15

10

x	72	96	160
y	25	18.75	

Challenge 33.2

The variables A and B are such that $B = 50$ when $A = 20$.

(a) (i) Write down a formula where A is directly proportional to B.
 (ii) Write down a formula where A is inversely proportional to B.

(b) Calculate B when $A = 25$ for each of the two formulae you have found.

Other types of proportion

You have seen that, if $y \propto x$, then as x increases so does y.

For the following relationship, as the value of x increases so does the value of y.

x	4	12
y	8	72

However, there is no constant linking each pair of x and y values.

For the first pair of values the multiplier is 2.
For the second pair of values the multiplier is 6.
This is therefore not an example of $y \propto x$.

This relationship is an example of $y \propto x^2$.

This graph shows $y \propto x^2$

The gradient of the curve will be positive and the curve will always pass through the origin.

EXAMPLE 33.5

$y \propto x^2$

Find the formula for

x	4	12
y	8	72

Solution

The formula for this relationship is $y = kx^2$, where k is a constant (the constant of proportionality).

$y = kx^2$ To find the value of k, substitute the x value of 4 and
$8 = k \times 4^2$ the y value of 8 into the equation.
$8 = k \times 16$ You could use $x = 12$ and $y = 72$ instead.
$k = 0.5$

The formula is $y = \frac{1}{2}x^2$.

Check the formula by substituting the second pair of values into the equation.

$y = \frac{1}{2}x^2$
$72 = \frac{1}{2} \times 12^2$
$72 = 72$ ✓

You have seen that, if $y \propto \frac{1}{x}$, then as x increases, y decreases.

For the following relationship, as the value of x increases, the value of y decreases.

x	5	10
y	8	2

However, for the first pair of values $xy = 40$.
For the second pair of values $xy = 20$

This is therefore not an example of $y \propto \frac{1}{x}$.

This relationship is an example of $y \propto \frac{1}{x^2}$.

This graph shows $y \propto \frac{1}{x^2}$.

The gradient of the curve is negative.

Other types of proportion 457

EXAMPLE 33.6

$y \propto \dfrac{1}{x^2}$

Find the formula for

x	5	10
y	8	2

Solution

The formula for this relationship is $x^2y = k$, where k is a constant.

$x^2y = k$
$5^2 \times 8 = k$
$25 \times 8 = k$
$k = 200$

To find the value of k, substitute the x value of 5 and the y value of 8 into the equation. You could use $x = 10$ and $y = 2$ instead.

The formula is $x^2y = 200$ or $y = \dfrac{200}{x^2}$.

Check the formula by substituting the second pair of values into the equation.

$x^2y = 200$
$10^2 \times 2 = 200$
$200 = 200$ ✓

EXERCISE 33.4

For each of these relationships
(a) state the type of proportion.
(b) find the formula.
(c) where appropriate, find the missing y value in the table.

Hint: This exercise includes all four types of proportion that you have met in this chapter.

1

x	4	6
y	16	36

2

x	2	5	8
y	8	50	

3

x	6	9
y	12	27

4

x	5	25	35
y	10	250	

5

x	3	6
y	10.8	43.2

6

x	3	6	15
y	25	6.25	

7

x	5	10
y	50	12.5

8

x	2	5	10
y	5	0.8	

9

x	10	20
y	8	2

10

x	8	10	16
y	4	2.56	

Challenge 33.3

There are yet more types of proportion other than $y \propto x$, $y \propto \dfrac{1}{x}$, $y \propto x^2$ and $y \propto \dfrac{1}{x^2}$.

For each of the relationships in parts **(a)** to **(d)**
(i) state the type of proportion.
(ii) find the formula.

(a)

x	2	5
y	24	375

(b)

x	4	25
y	5	12.5

(c)

x	2	4
y	256	32

(d)

x	4	25
y	5	2

(e) A truck is tested in a wind tunnel.
  The wind resistance is proportional to the square of the speed of the truck.
  What happens to the wind resistance if the speed of the truck is
  (i) halved?
  (ii) increased by 50%?

(f) A marble is rolled down a slope.
  After travelling d metres down the slope the speed of the marble is v metres per second, where v is proportional to the square root of d.
  Given that $v = 3.5$ when $d = 3$, calculate v when $d = 5$.

Other types of proportion

Challenge 33.4

The tables below show examples of the following variations.

$$y \propto x^2,\ y \propto \frac{1}{x^2},\ y \propto \sqrt{x}\ \text{and}\ y \propto x^3$$

For each of these relationships
(i) state the type of proportion.
(ii) find the formula.

(a)
x	16	25
y	12	15

(b)
x	2	4
y	12	48

(c)
x	2	3
y	40	135

(d)
x	3	6
y	4	1

(e)
x	3	6
y	9	72

(f)
x	4	16
y	8	16

(g)
x	3	10
y	5	0.45

(h)
x	10	8
y	150	96

Challenge 33.5

(a) It takes a team of eight men six days to dig a trench 60 metres long.
How long would it take 10 men to dig a similar trench 50 metres long?
(b) A 2250 m³ pool is normally filled using four inlet valves in a period of 18 hours.
How long will it take to fill a 1500 m³ pool using three similar inlet valves?
(c) A total of 3200 washers can be made in 42 minutes using five punch machines.
How long would it take three similar machines to make 4800 washers?
(d) A total of 90 bales of hay is enough to feed 12 horses for 15 days.
How many bales of hay would be needed to feed 10 horses for 8 days?

WHAT YOU HAVE LEARNED

- Direct proportion is a linear relationship where, as one quantity increases, so does the other
  y is directly proportional to x, $y \propto x$, the equation is $y = kx$ where k is a constant
- Inverse proportion is a non-linear relationship where, as one quantity increases, the other decreases.
  y is inversely proportional to x, $y \propto \dfrac{1}{x}$, the equation is $y = \dfrac{k}{x}$ where k is a constant
- Other forms of variation include $y \propto x^2$ and $y \propto \dfrac{1}{x^2}$

MIXED EXERCISE 33

1 **(a)** A bicycle wheel rotates 115 times in a journey of 300 metres.
How many revolutions will the wheel make during a journey of 420 metres?

(b) An express train travels 260 metres in 5 seconds.
How far would it travel at the same speed in 19 seconds?

(c) A car travelling at a constant speed covers 38 miles in 57 minutes.
How far did it travel in 24 minutes?

(d) A piece of card with an area of 640 square centimetres has a mass of 16 grams.
What is the mass of 1000 square centimetres of the card?

(e) Painting a wall with an area of 18 m^2 uses 6.3 litres of paint.
How much paint is needed to paint a wall with an area of 28 m^2?

2 **(a)** It takes a team of five men 8 hours to lay a path.
How long would it take to lay the path if there were four men?

(b) A tank can be emptied using five pumps in a period of 21 hours.
How long will it take to empty the tank using six pumps?

(c) A stack of hay can feed 33 horses for 12 days.
For how long would the same stack of hay feed 44 horses?

(d) A supply of oil is enough to run six generators for 12 days.
How long would the same supply run eight generators?

(e) A gang of 15 bricklayers can build a wall in 8 days.
How long would a gang of 12 bricklayers take to build the wall?

3 For each of these relationships
  (i) state the type of proportion.
  (ii) find the formula.
  (iii) where appropriate, find the missing y value in the table.

(a)
x	2	10
y	8	40

(b)
x	4	20	32
y	15	75	

(c)
x	6	15
y	4	10

(d)
x	30	125	275
y	6	25	

(e)
x	3	6
y	4	2

(f)
x	4	6	10
y	6	4	

(g)
x	8	2
y	5	20

(h)
x	18	24	32
y	4	3	

(i)
x	10	8
y	12	15

(j)
x	7	28	63
y	4	16	

(k)
x	9	36
y	8	32

(l)
x	8	36	48
y	9	2	

(m)
x	40	180
y	12	54

(n)
x	30	16	12
y	8	15	

34 LINEAR EQUATIONS

THIS CHAPTER IS ABOUT
- The equation of a straight line in the form $y = mx + c$
- Gradients of straight lines that are perpendicular to each other

YOU SHOULD ALREADY KNOW
- How to draw straight line graphs from equations
- How to find the gradient of straight-line graphs
- How to find the equation of a line in the form $y = mx + c$, given the gradient and y-intercept
- That parallel lines have the same gradient
- How to substitute in equations and manipulate them

Finding the equation of a straight line in the form $y = mx + c$

Check up 34.1

Find the gradient of the line joining each of these pairs of points.
- (a) (0, 2) and (2, 8)
- (b) (2, 3) and (3, 7)
- (c) (0, 2) and (2, −2)
- (d) (−3, −1) and (−1, −5)
- (e) (−1, 1) and (−5, −1)

Check up 34.2

Find the gradient and y-intercept of each of these lines.
- (a) $y = 2x - 5$
- (b) $2y = 4x - 9$
- (c) $6x + 2y = 5$
- (d) $3x - 4y = 6$
- (e) $2x + 4y = 5$

You learned how to find the equation of a straight line in Chapter 21.

EXAMPLE 34.1

Find the equation of this straight line.

Solution

Gradient, $m = \dfrac{\text{increase in } y}{\text{increase in } x}$ First find the gradient of the line.

$= \dfrac{-6}{4} = -\dfrac{3}{2}$

y-intercept, $c = 6$ The line crosses the y-axis at $(0, 6)$.

$y = mx + c$ Substitute m and c into the equation for a straight line.

$y = -\tfrac{3}{2}x + 6$ Multiply each side of the equation by 2 to get rid of the fraction.

$2y = -3x + 12$ Add $3x$ to both sides of the equation to get rid of the negative term.

$3x + 2y = 12$

EXAMPLE 34.2

Find the equation of the line with gradient $-\tfrac{2}{3}$, passing through the point $(4, 0)$.

Solution

The equation of a straight line is $y = mx + c$.

The equation is $y = -\tfrac{2}{3}x + c$.   You are given the gradient, m.

$y = -\tfrac{2}{3}x + c$ To find the y-intercept, c, substitute the coordinates of the given point ($x = 4$ and $y = 0$) into the equation.

$0 = -\tfrac{2}{3} \times 4 + c$

$0 = -\tfrac{8}{3} + c$

$c = \tfrac{8}{3}$

So $y = -\tfrac{2}{3}x + \tfrac{8}{3}$ Multiply each side of the equation by 3 to get rid of the fraction.

$3y = -2x + 8$ Add $2x$ to both sides to get rid of the negative term.

$2x + 3y = 8$

EXAMPLE 34.3

Find the equation of the line that passes through (4, 6) and (6, 2).

Solution

Gradient, $m = \dfrac{\text{increase in } y}{\text{increase in } x}$ First find the gradient of the line.

$= \dfrac{2-6}{6-4}$

$= \dfrac{-4}{2}$

$= -2$

The equation is $y = -2x + c$

$y = -2x + c$
$6 = -2 \times 4 + c$
$6 = -8 + c$
$6 + 8 = c$
$c = 14$

To find the y-intercept, c, substitute the coordinates of either of the given points (here, $x = 4$ and $y = 6$) into the equation.

So $y = -2x + 14$ Add $2x$ to each side of the equation to get rid of the negative term.
$2x + y = 14$

You could also have found the equation of the line in Example 34.3 by drawing the line through the two points and extending it to where it cuts the y-axis, then finding the gradient and y-intercept from the graph.

> **TIP**
> You should be able to find the equation of a line without drawing it, but it is useful to do a sketch as a check.

EXERCISE 34.1

Find the equation of each of these straight lines.

1

2

Finding the equation of a straight line in the form $y = mx + c$ 465

3

[graph: line from (0,8) to (3,0)]

4

[graph: line from (0,4) to (8,0)]

5 A line with gradient $\frac{2}{3}$, passing through the point (2, 3).

6 A line with gradient $-\frac{3}{4}$, passing through the point (3, 0).

7 A line passing through (1, 4) and (4, 7).

8 A line passing through (2, 3) and (5, 9).

9 A line passing through (−1, 5) and (3, −7).

10 A line passing through (3, 1), (6, −1).

Challenge 34.1

(a) Look at these graphs.

[Distance–Time graph and Velocity–Time graph]

What does the gradient of each of these graphs represent?
Hint: *Velocity* is another word for *speed*.

(b) A particle is accelerating at 40 m/s² (metres per second squared).
Its initial velocity was 25 m/s.
Find the equation connecting the velocity, v, and the time, t.

(c) A ball is thrown into the air.
Its velocity after two seconds is 15 m/s.
The deceleration due to gravity is 10 m/s². (To decelerate means to slow down.)
Find the equation connecting the velocity, v, and the time, t.

Exploring gradients

Discovery 34.1

(a) Draw each of the following pairs of lines on a separate pair of axes.
Use values of x and y from -6 to 6.

   (i) $y = x$ and $y = -x$
   (ii) $y = 2x$ and $y = -\frac{1}{2}x$
   (ii) $y = 5x$ and $y = -\frac{1}{5}x$
   (iv) $y = 4x$ and $y = -0.25x$
   (v) $y = 2x$ and $x + 2y = 6$

(b) What do you notice about each pair you have drawn?
Can you spot a connection between them?
Find more pairs that give you the same result.

You learned in Chapter 21 that **parallel lines** have the same gradient.

There is also a connection between the gradients of **perpendicular lines**:

If a line has gradient m, then the perpendicular line has gradient $-\dfrac{1}{m}$.

The product of the two gradients is -1.

Proof 34.1

Use the properties of triangles to prove that if a line has gradient m, then the perpendicular line has gradient $-\dfrac{1}{m}$.

Solution

Two lines, AB and CD, cross at right angles at P.

Let the gradient of AB be $m = \dfrac{BC}{AC}$ and the gradient of CD be $n = -\dfrac{AD}{AC}$.

In triangles ABC and ADC:
Angle ACB = angle DAC   Both are 90°.
Angle BAC = angle ADC   Both are 90° − angle PAD.
So triangles ABC and ADC are similar   They are equiangular.

continues ...

Proof 34.1 continued

Therefore $\dfrac{BC}{AC} = \dfrac{AC}{AD}$ Ratio of corresponding sides.

So $m = -\dfrac{1}{n}$ or $mn = -1$ $-\dfrac{1}{n} = -\dfrac{1}{-\frac{AD}{AC}} = \dfrac{AC}{AD}$.

Check up 34.3

On a pair of axes, draw two lines that are perpendicular.
Check that their gradients satisfy the rule above.

Repeat this for a number of different pairs of lines.

TIP When drawing perpendicular lines, make sure the scale is the same on both axes.

If you know the equation of a line, you can find the equation of any line that is either parallel or perpendicular to it.

EXAMPLE 34.4

Find the equation of the line that is parallel to the line $2y = 3x + 4$ and passes through the point $(3, 2)$.

Solution

The gradient of the line $2y = 3x + 4$ is 1.5.
So the equation of the parallel line is $y = 1.5x + c$.
(The parallel line has the same gradient.)

$y = 1.5x + c$	To find the y-intercept, c, substitute the
$2 = 1.5 \times 3 + c$	coordinates of the given point ($x = 3$ and $y = 2$)
$2 = 4.5 + c$	into the equation.
$c = 2 - 4.5$	
$c = -2.5$	

So $\quad y = 1.5x - 2.5$ Multiply each side of the equation by 2 to get rid
$\quad\quad 2y = 3x - 5$ of the decimals.

EXAMPLE 34.5

Find the equation of the line that crosses the line $y = 2x - 5$ at right angles at the point (3, 1).

Solution

The gradient of the line $y = 2x - 5$ is 2.

The gradient of the perpendicular line is $-\frac{1}{2}$. (Since the gradient of the perpendicular line is $-\frac{1}{m}$.)

So the equation of the perpendicular line is $y = -\frac{1}{2}x + c$.

$y = -\frac{1}{2}x + c$ To find the y-intercept, c, substitute the
$1 = -\frac{1}{2} \times 3 + c$ coordinates of the given point ($x = 3$, $y = 1$) into
$2 = -3 + 2c$ the equation.
$2c = 5$
$c = 2.5$

So $y = -\frac{1}{2}x + 2.5$ Multiply each side of the equation by 2 to get rid
    $x + 2y = 5$ of the decimals.

TIP

A line parallel to $y = mx + c$ will be of the form $y = mx + d$, where c and d are constants.

A line perpendicular to $y = mx + c$ will be of the form $y = -\frac{1}{m}x + e$, where c and e are constants.

EXAMPLE 34.6

Draw a pair of axes and label them 0 to 4 for x and -1 to 7 for y.
Draw the line $y = 2x - 1$. Draw
(a) a line parallel to $y = 2x - 1$.
(b) a line perpendicular to $y = 2x - 1$.
Find the equations of the two lines.

Solution

There are many solutions to this question.

The lines drawn on this diagram are

(a) $y = 2x + 1$ Parallel to $y = 2x - 1$: same gradient, y-intercept is 1.

(b) $y = -\frac{1}{2}x + 4$ Perpendicular to $y = 2x - 1$: gradient is $-\frac{1}{2}$, y-intercept is 4.
      $x + 2y = 8$

EXERCISE 34.2

1 Find the gradient of a line perpendicular to the line joining each of these pairs of points.
   (a) $(1, 2)$ and $(5, -6)$ (b) $(2, 4)$ and $(3, 8)$ (c) $(-2, 1)$ and $(2, -4)$

2 Find the equation of the line that passes through $(1, 5)$ and is parallel to $y = 3x - 3$.

3 Find the equation of the line that passes through $(0, 3)$ and is parallel to $3x + 2y = 7$.

4 Draw the line $y = 2x$.
   On the same graph, draw a line parallel to it and a line perpendicular to it.
   Find the equation of each of these two lines.

5 (a) Draw the line $x + 3y = 6$. State its gradient.
   (b) Draw a line perpendicular to this. State its gradient.

6 Find the equation of the line that passes through $(1, 5)$ and is perpendicular to $y = 3x - 1$.

7 Find the equation of the line that passes through $(0, 3)$ and is perpendicular to $2y + 3x = 7$.

8 Which of these lines are
   (a) parallel?   (b) perpendicular?
   $y = 4x + 3$ $2y - 3x = 5$ $6y + 4x = 1$ $4x - y = 5$

9 Two lines cross at right angles at the point $(5, 3)$. One passes through $(6, 0)$.
   What is the equation of the other line?

10 In the diagram AB and BC are two sides of a square, ABCD.

Work out

(a) the equation of the line AD.
(b) the equation of the line DC.
(c) the coordinates of D.

Challenge 34.2

(a) What happens when you try to solve these simultaneous equations?

$$2x - y = 2$$
$$2x - y = -1$$

(b) Explain the result in terms of the graphs of the lines.

WHAT YOU HAVE LEARNED

- How to find the equation of any straight line in the form $y = mx + c$
- That if perpendicular lines have gradients m and n, then $m = -\dfrac{1}{n}$

Exploring gradients 471

MIXED EXERCISE 34

1 Draw each of these lines on a separate pair of axes. Use values of x and y as stated.
  (a) $2x + 3y = 9$ x: 0 to 5 y: 0 to 5
  (b) $5x + 2y + 10 = 0$ x: −2 to 0 y: −5 to 0

2 Find the equation of each of these lines.
  (a)
  (b)
  (c)

3 Find the equation of each of these lines.
  (a) A line with gradient 3, passing through (0, 2).
  (b) A line with gradient −2, passing through (1, 4).
  (c) A line with gradient $\frac{1}{2}$, passing through (2, 6).

4 Find the gradient of each of these lines.
  (a) $y = 4x - 1$ (b) $5y = 2x + 3$ (c) $2x + 3y = 18$ (d) $6x + y = 4$

5 Find the equation of the line that joins each of these pairs of points.
  (a) (4, 0) and (6, 5)   (b) (1, 2) and (6, 4)   (c) (2, 3) and (5, −6)

472 34 Linear equations

6 Find the equation of each of the three sides of the triangle ABC.

7 Find the equation of these lines.
   (a) A line parallel to $y = 7x + 4$, passing through $(5, 1)$.
   (b) A line parallel to $2y = 5x + 4$, passing through $(4, 0)$.
   (c) A line parallel to $5x + 4y = 3$, passing through $(2, -1)$.

8 Find the equation of each of these lines.
   (a) A line perpendicular to $y = 2x + 4$, passing through $(2, 1)$.
   (b) A line perpendicular to $3y = 2x + 7$, passing through $(0, 1)$.
   (c) A line perpendicular to $2x + 5y = 4$, passing through $(1, -3)$.

9 Draw axes and label them 0 to 8 for both x and y.
   (a) (i) Draw the line passing through $(0, 8)$ and $(6, 0)$.
       (ii) What is the equation of this line?
   (b) (i) Draw the parallel line that passes through $(0, 6)$.
       (ii) Where does this line cross the x-axis?
   (c) (i) Draw the line perpendicular to both these lines that passes through the origin.
       (ii) What is the equation of this line?

10 Three corners of a parallelogram are $A(1, 6)$, $B(3, 4)$ and $C(5, 8)$.
   (a) Find the equation of AD.
   (b) Without drawing the graph, find the coordinates of D.

35 CONGRUENCE AND PROOF

THIS CHAPTER IS ABOUT

- Solving problems in geometry and giving reasons/proof for your solutions
- Recognising and working with congruent triangles

YOU SHOULD ALREADY KNOW

- The angle facts for parallel lines: alternate angles, *a* and *b*, are equal and corresponding angles, *a* and *c* are equal

- The angles in a triangle add up to 180°
- The sum of the angles on a straight line is 180°
- The exterior angle of a triangle is equal to the sum of the opposite, interior angles

Angle properties of triangles

In Chapter 3 you learned how to use the properties of parallel lines to prove that the angles in a triangle add up to 180°.

Check up 35.1

Use the diagram to write a proof that the angles in a triangle add up to 180°. Remember to give a reason for each step.

In Chapter 3 you saw one proof that the exterior angle of a triangle is equal to the sum of the opposite, interior angles. There is an alternative proof of this fact using the properties of parallel lines.

Proof 35.1

Using the properties of parallel lines, prove that the exterior angle of a triangle is equal to the sum of the opposite, interior angles.

Solution

A line parallel to AB from C is constructed, as shown in the diagram.

$a = y$ Corresponding angles.
$b = x$ Alternate angles.

So
$a + b = x + y$ Since angles in a triangle add up to 180° and angles on a straight line add up to 180°.

This proves that the exterior angle of a triangle is equal to the sum of the opposite, interior angles.

Congruent triangles

In Chapter 27 you learned that two triangles are **similar** if all their angles are the same. If the angles of two triangles are the same, all their sides are in the same ratio. They are the same shape but not necessarily the same size.

Two triangles are **congruent** if they are the same shape and the same size. This means that they will fit exactly on to each other when one of them is rotated, reflected or translated.

Discovery 35.1

For each of the following triangles.
  (i) Construct the triangle.
      You will need to use compasses for some of them.
  (ii) Compare each of your triangles with your neighbours'.
      Are they all congruent?

(a) $a = 4$ cm, $b = 5$ cm, $c = 6$ cm
(b) $A = 50°$, $b = 5$ cm, $c = 6$ cm
(c) $A = 50°$, $B = 60°$, $c = 6$ cm
(d) $A = 90°$, $a = 10$ cm, $b = 6$ cm
(e) $A = 20°$, $a = 6$ cm, $b = 10$ cm

Angle properties of triangles

Two triangles are congruent if any of these conditions are satisfied.

- The three sides of one triangle are equal to the corresponding three sides of the other triangle
  (side, side, side or SSS).
- Two sides and the included angle of one triangle are equal to two sides and the included angle of the other triangle
  (side, angle, side or SAS).
- Two angles and the side between them of one triangle are equal to two angles and the side between them in the other triangle
  (angle, side, angle or ASA).
- Each triangle is right-angled and the hypotenuse and one other side of one triangle is equal to the hypotenuse and one side of the other triangle
  (right angle, hypotenuse, side or RHS).

EXAMPLE 35.1

State whether or not each of these pairs of triangles are congruent. If the triangles are congruent, give a reason for your answer.

(a)

(b)

(c)

(d)

(e)

(f)

476 35 Congruence and proof

Solution

(a) Congruent: SSS
(b) Congruent: SAS
(c) Not congruent
(d) Congruent: ASA
(e) Not congruent
(f) Congruent: the missing third angles are also equal, ASA

Proof 35.2

Triangle XYZ is isosceles with XY = XZ.

The bisector of angle Y meets XZ at M; the bisector of angle Z meets XY at N.

Prove that YM = ZN.

Solution

Angle XYZ = angle XZY	Base angles of an isosceles triangle are equal.
so angle MYZ = angle NZY.	Since YM bisects angle XYZ and ZN bisects angle XZY.

In triangles YMZ and ZNY, YZ is common.

So triangles YMZ and ZNY are congruent.   ASA

So YM = ZN.

EXERCISE 35.1

1 ABC is an isosceles triangle with AC = BC.
X and Y are points on AC and BC so that CX = CY.

Prove that triangle CXB is congruent to triangle CYA.

2 In this diagram, DX = XC, DV = ZC and AB is parallel to DC.

Prove that triangle DBZ is congruent to triangle CAV.

3 These two triangles are congruent.

(a) Write down the length of sides *a* and *b*.
(b) Write down the size of angles *x* and *y*.

4 PQRS is a rhombus. PQ = QR = RS = SP.
PQ is parallel to RS, QR is parallel to PS.
(a) Prove that
  (i) triangles PQX and RSX are congruent.
  (ii) triangles PSX and QRX are congruent.
(b) Prove that X is the midpoint of SQ and of PR, and hence that the diagonals of a rhombus intersect at right angles.

5 Which two of these triangles are congruent?

6 ABCD is a square. P, Q, R and S are the midpoints of the sides.

Prove that the quadrilateral PQRS is a square.

478 **35 Congruence and proof**

7 In the diagram, AB = AC, angle XAE = 140° and CE = CF.

Find angle ADE, giving reasons for your answer.

8 In this diagram, CD is the bisector of angle ACB and AE is parallel to DC.

Prove that AC = CE.

9 In this diagram, AB = AC, CD is parallel to BA, CD = CB and angle BAC = 40°.

Calculate the size of angle DBC, giving reasons for your answer.

10 In this diagram, angle CBX = 122°, angle DEC = 33° and AX is parallel to DY.

Calculate the size of angles BAD and BCY, giving reasons for your answers.

11 In triangle ABC, BD bisects angle ABC, angle ACB = 80° and BD = BC.

Prove that angle BAC = 60°.

Angle properties of triangles

12 ABC is a right-angled triangle. Angle ACB = 55° and angle PQC = 90°.

Prove that angle a = 145°.

Challenge 35.1

Draw a triangle with one side 6 cm and angles 35°, 66° and 79°.

Compare your triangle with your neighbours'. Are they all congruent?
If the answer is 'No', how many different triangles are there?

Are all the triangles similar?

Challenge 35.2

Plane figures other than triangles, for example, rectangles and octagons, can be congruent.

Two rectangles have the same area and the same perimeter.
Does this mean that they must be congruent?
Explain your answer.

WHAT YOU HAVE LEARNED

- Two triangles are congruent is one of these four statements is true:
  - the corresponding three sides of each triangle are equal (SSS)
  - two sides and the included angle in each triangle are equal (SAS)
  - two angles and the side between them in each triangle are equal (ASA)
  - each triangle is right-angled and the hypotenuse and one other side in each triangle is equal (RHS)

MIXED EXERCISE 35

1. In this diagram PQ is parallel to SR, SP = SR, angle SPR = 66° and angle PQS = 22°.

   Find the size of angles x, y, z, giving reasons for your answers.

2. Calculate the size of angles x, y and z, giving reasons for your answers.

3. ABCD is a quadrilateral. Angle CBA = 70°, angle BAD = 80° and angle ADC = 130°. CA bisects angle DCB.

   Prove that triangle CAB is isosceles.

4. Find the size of angles a and b, giving reasons for your answers.

5. Find the size of x, giving reasons for your answer.

6. Use congruent triangles to prove that the diagonals of a kite cross at right angles.

7. Two straight lines, AB and CD, bisect each other at right angles at E. Prove that the straight lines AC, CB, BD and DA are equal in length.

36 → QUADRATIC EQUATIONS

THIS CHAPTER IS ABOUT
- Solving quadratic equations by factorising, completing the square and using the formula

YOU SHOULD ALREADY KNOW
- How to factorise expressions such as:
  $x^2 + 3x$ $4x^2 - 9$
  $x^2 - 5x + 6$ $2x^2 - 7x - 15$
- How to multiply out brackets such as:
  $(x + 3)^2$ $(x - 4)^2$

Solving quadratic equations

You learned in Chapter 15 that a **quadratic** function is a function where the highest power of x is 2, and in Chapter 28 you learned how to **factorise** a quadratic expression.

You also need to be able to solve quadratic equations.

Discovery 36.1

Find two numbers which multiply together to give zero.

If two numbers, A and B, are such that A × B = 0, either A = 0 or B = 0.

We can use this fact to solve equations where the left-hand side is factorised and the right-hand side is zero.

EXAMPLE 36.1

Solve each of these quadratic equations.
(a) $x(x - 3) = 0$
(b) $(x + 2)(x - 3) = 0$
(c) $(2x - 5)(x + 1) = 0$

Solution

(a) $x(x - 3) = 0$
    Either $x = 0$ or $x - 3 = 0$ The two factors are x and $x - 3$.
                       If $x - 3 = 0$
                       $x = 3$
    There are two possible solutions to the equation: $x = 0$ or $x = 3$.
    Both these answers are valid solutions to the equation.

(b) $(x + 2)(x - 3) = 0$
    Either $x + 2 = 0$ or $x - 3 = 0$
    If $x + 2 = 0$ If $x - 3 = 0$
    $x = -2$ $x = 3$

    Solutions: $x = -2$ or $x = 3$

(c) $(2x - 5)(x + 1) = 0$
    Either $2x - 5 = 0$ or $x + 1 = 0$
    If $2x - 5 = 0$ If $x + 1 = 0$
    $2x = 5$ $x = -1$
    $x = 2\frac{1}{2}$

    Solutions: $x = 2\frac{1}{2}$ or $x = -1$

> **TIP** A quadratic equation always has two solutions, although they may be the same.

> **TIP** The sign of the answer is opposite to the sign in the bracket.

EXERCISE 36.1

Solve each of these quadratic equations.

1 $x(x + 2) = 0$

2 $(x - 5)(x - 1) = 0$

3 $(x - 4)(x + 3) = 0$

4 $(x + 2)(x + 7) = 0$

5 $2x(x - 3) = 0$

6 $(x + 4)(x - 4) = 0$

7 $(x + 10)(x - 6) = 0$

8 $(x - 7)(2x - 3) = 0$

9 $(x + 4)(2x - 1) = 0$

10 $(2x - 5)(3x + 1) = 0$

11 $(3x + 7)(2x - 9) = 0$

12 $5x(4x + 1) = 0$

Solving quadratic equations by factorising

If the left-hand side of the quadratic equation is not already factorised, factorise it first.

EXAMPLE 36.2

Solve each of these quadratic equations
(a) $x^2 + 5x = 0$
(b) $x^2 - 25 = 0$
(c) $x^2 - 5x + 6 = 0$
(d) $2x^2 - 7x - 15 = 0$
(e) $x^2 - 6x + 9 = 0$

Solution

(a) $x^2 + 5x = 0$
$x(x + 5) = 0$ Take out the common factor, x.
$x = 0$ or $x + 5 = 0$
                  $x = -5$

Solutions: $x = 0$ or $x = -5$

(b) $x^2 - 25 = 0$
$(x - 5)(x + 5) = 0$ This is the difference of two squares.
$x - 5 = 0$ or $x + 5 = 0$
$x = 5$ $x = -5$

Solutions: $x = 5$ or $x = -5$

> **TIP** These solutions can be written as $x = \pm 5$.

(c) $x^2 - 5x + 6 = 0$
$(x - 2)(x - 3) = 0$ Factorise using two brackets.
$x - 2 = 0$ or $x - 3 = 0$
$x = 2$ $x = 3$

Solutions: $x = 2$ or $x = 3$

(d) $2x^2 - 7x - 15 = 0$
$(2x + 3)(x - 5) = 0$ Factorise using two brackets.
$2x + 3 = 0$ or $x - 5 = 0$
$2x = -3$ $x = 5$
$x = -1\frac{1}{2}$

Solutions: $x = -1\frac{1}{2}$ or $x = 5$

(e) $x^2 - 6x + 9 = 0$
$(x - 3)(x - 3) = 0$ Factorise using two brackets
$x - 3 = 0$ or $x - 3 = 0$
$x = 3$ $x = 3$

Solution: $x = 3$ The two solutions are the same when the quadratic expression factorises into a 'perfect square', in this case $(x - 3)^2$. This is sometimes called a 'repeated solution'.

TIP

The difference of two squares can be solved by another method.

For example, $x^2 - 25 = 0$
$x^2 = 25$ Add 25 to each side.
$x = \pm 5$ Take the square root of each side.

If you use this method, make sure you don't forget about the negative solution.

EXERCISE 36.2

Solve each of these quadratic equations.

1   $x^2 + 3x + 2 = 0$ 2 $x^2 - 6x + 8 = 0$ 3 $x^2 + 3x - 4 = 0$

4   $x^2 - 4x - 5 = 0$ 5 $x^2 + x - 12 = 0$ 6 $x^2 + 7x = 0$

7   $x^2 - 8x + 15 = 0$ 8 $x^2 - 4x - 21 = 0$ 9 $2x^2 - 8x = 0$

10   $x^2 - 36 = 0$ 11 $x^2 + 10x + 16 = 0$ 12 $x^2 - 5x - 24 = 0$

13   $x^2 + 5x - 6 = 0$ 14 $x^2 - 11x + 18 = 0$ 15 $4x^2 - 25 = 0$

16   $x^2 + 8x - 20 = 0$ 17 $3x^2 - x = 0$ 18 $x^2 - 7x - 30 = 0$

19   $3x^2 + 15x = 0$ 20 $x^2 - 9x + 20 = 0$ 21 $3x^2 + 4x + 1 = 0$

22   $2x^2 - 7x + 3 = 0$ 23 $2x^2 + 3x - 5 = 0$ 24 $3x^2 + 7x + 2 = 0$

25   $2x^2 - x - 6 = 0$ 26 $3x^2 - 11x + 6 = 0$ 27 $5x^2 - 24x - 5 = 0$

28   $6x^2 + x - 2 = 0$ 29 $x^2 - 10x + 25 = 0$ 30 $15x^2 - 4x - 3 = 0$

31   $2x^2 - 200 = 0$ 32 $81 - 4x^2 = 0$ 33 $6x^2 - 5x - 6 = 0$

Equations that need rearranging first

If the equation is not in the form where the right-hand side is zero, rearrange it before factorising.

EXAMPLE 36.3

Solve each of these quadratic equations
(a) $x^2 + 4x = 5$ (b) $x^2 = 5x - 6$ (c) $3x - x^2 - 2 = 0$

Solution

(a)
$x^2 + 4x = 5$
$x^2 + 4x - 5 = 0$ Subtract 5 from each side.
$(x + 5)(x - 1) = 0$ Factorise using two brackets.

$x + 5 = 0$ or $x - 1 = 0$
$x = -5$ $x = 1$

Solutions: $x = -5$ or $x = 1$

(b)
$x^2 = 5x - 6$
$x^2 - 5x = -6$ Subtract $5x$ from each side.
$x^2 - 5x + 6 = 0$ Add 6 to each side.
$(x - 2)(x - 3) = 0$

$x - 2 = 0$ or $x - 3 = 0$
$x = 2$ $x = 3$

Solutions: $x = 2$ or $x = 3$

(c)
$3x - x^2 - 2 = 0$ Although the right-hand side of this equation is zero, the order of the terms and the fact that the x^2 term is negative is a problem.
$3x - 2 = x^2$ Add x^2 to each side.
$-2 = x^2 - 3x$ Subtract $3x$ from each side.
$0 = x^2 - 3x + 2$ Add 2 to each side.
$x^2 - 3x + 2 = 0$ Swap the sides so that the zero is on the right.
$(x - 2)(x - 1) = 0$ Factorise using two brackets.

$x - 2 = 0$ or $x - 1 = 0$
$x = 2$ $x = 1$

Solutions: $x = 2$ or $x = 1$

> **TIP**
> Instead of rearranging the equation in Example 36.3 part **(c)**, you could have multiplied each side by -1, giving $-3x + x^2 + 2 = 0$.

EXERCISE 36.3

Solve each of these quadratic equations.

1. $x^2 - x = 12$
2. $x^2 = 3x + 10$
3. $x^2 = 5x + 14$
4. $x^2 = 7x - 6$
5. $x^2 = 6x$
6. $x^2 = 5 - 4x$
7. $x^2 = 8 + 2x$
8. $2x^2 = 2 - 3x$
9. $15 + 2x - x^2 = 0$
10. $4 - 3x - x^2 = 0$

Challenge 36.1

I think of a number. I add 6 to it. I multiply the result by the original number and add 3. The answer is 58.

Write down an equation and solve it to find the original number.

Challenge 36.2

The diagram shows a rectangular pen made of fencing on three sides and a wall on the fourth side.

(a) If 50 m of fencing is used, find the length of the pen in terms of x.

(b) If the area of the pen is 272 m², write down an equation in x and show that it simplifies to
$x^2 - 25x + 136 = 0$.

(c) Solve your equation to find the length and width of the pen.

Challenge 36.3

The area of the triangle is 6.5 cm².

(a) Write down an equation in x and simplify it.
(b) Hence solve the equation to find the lengths of AB and BC.

Triangle with AB = $x + 3$, BC = $2x - 5$, right angle at B.

Completing the square

Discovery 36.2

(a) Expand and simplify each of these expressions.
   (i) $(x + m)^2$
   (ii) $(x - m)^2$

(b) Copy and fill in the gaps in each of these equations. Use your answers to part (a).
   (i) $(x + 1) = x^2 + \text{.......} + 1$
   (ii) $(x + 3)^2 = x^2 + \text{.......} + 9$
   (iii) $(x - 2)^2 = x^2 - \text{.......} + 4$
   (iv) $(x - 5)^2 = x^2 - \text{.......} + 25$
   (v) $(x + 4)^2 = x^2 + \text{.......} + \text{.......}$
   (vi) $(x - 10)^2 = x^2 - \text{.......} + \text{.......}$
   (vii) $(x + \frac{1}{2})^2 = x^2 + \text{.......} + \text{.......}$

(c) Look at your answers to part (b).
   (i) If $(x + m)^2 = x^2 + nx + m^2$, what is the relationship between m and n?
   (ii) If $(x - m)^2 = x^2 - nx + m^2$, what is the relationship between m and n?

(d) Copy and fill in the gaps in each of these equations. Use your answers to part (c).
   (i) $x^2 + 4x + 4 = (x + \text{.......})^2$
   (ii) $x^2 - 6x + 9 = (x - \text{.......})^2$
   (iii) $x^2 + 10x + 25 = (x + \text{.......})^2$
   (iv) $x^2 - 12x + 36 = (x - \text{.......})^2$
   (v) $x^2 - 8x + 16 = (x - \text{.......})^2$
   (vi) $x^2 + 14x + 49 = (x + \text{.......})^2$

(e) Copy and fill in the gaps in each of these equations. Use your answers to part (d).
   (i) $x^2 + 4x = (x + \text{.......})^2 - \text{.......}$
   (ii) $x^2 - 6x = (x - \text{.......})^2 - \text{.......}$
   (iii) $x^2 + 10x = (x + \text{.......})^2 - \text{.......}$
   (iv) $x^2 - 12x = (x - \text{.......})^2 - \text{.......}$
   (v) $x^2 - 8x = (x - \text{.......})^2 - \text{.......}$
   (vi) $x^2 + 14x = (x + \text{.......})^2 - \text{.......}$

You can solve a quadratic equation that does not factorise by **completing the square**.

This involves writing the left-hand side of the equation in the form $(x \pm m)^2 \pm n$, as you did in part (e) of Discovery 36.2.

EXAMPLE 36.4

(a) Write each of these quadratic expressions in the form $(x \pm m)^2 \pm n$.
   (i) $x^2 + 6x$
   (ii) $x^2 - 2x$
   (iii) $x^2 + 3x$

(b) Write each of these quadratic expressions in the form $(x \pm m)^2 \pm n$. Use your answers to part (a).
   (i) $x^2 + 6x + 10$
   (ii) $x^2 - 2x - 3$
   (iii) $x^2 + 3x - 2$

Solution

(a) (i) $m = 6 \div 2$ m is always half the coefficient of x.
   $= 3$
   $n = 3^2$ n is always equal to m^2.
   $= 9$
   So $x^2 + 6x = (x + 3)^2 - 9$ The sign in the bracket is always the same as the one in front of the x term.

(ii) $m = 2 \div 2$
   $= 1$
   $n = 1^2$
   $= 1$
   So $x^2 - 2x = (x - 1)^2 - 1$

(iii) $m = 3 \div 2$
   $= 1.5$
   $n = 1.5^2$
   $= 2.25$
   So $x^2 + 3x = (x + 1.5)^2 - 2.25$

(b) (i) Since $x^2 + 6x = (x + 3)^2 - 9$
   then $x^2 + 6x + 10 = (x + 3)^2 - 9 + 10$ As 10 has been added to the left-hand side, you need to add 10 to the right-hand side, to maintain equality.
       $x^2 + 6x + 10 = (x + 3)^2 + 1$

(ii) Since $x^2 - 2x = (x - 1)^2 - 1$
   then $x^2 - 2x - 3 = (x - 1)^2 - 1 - 3$ This time you need to subtract 3 from the right-hand side.
       $= (x - 1)^2 - 4$

(iii) Since $x^2 + 3x = (x + 1.5)^2 - 2.25$
   then $x^2 + 3x - 4 = (x + 1.5)^2 - 2.25 - 4$ Subtract 4 from the right-hand side.
       $= (x + 1.5)^2 - 6.25$

> **TIP**
>
> You may be asked to write a quadratic expression in the form $(x + m)^2 + n$. Remember that m and n could be positive or negative.
>
> Alternatively, you may simply be asked to 'complete the square'. This means 'write the quadratic expression in the form $(x + m)^2 + n$'.

EXERCISE 36.4

1 (a) Write each of these quadratic expressions in the form $(x + m)^2 + n$.
   (i) $x^2 + 8x$ (ii) $x^2 - 10x$ (iii) $x^2 + 12x$ (iv) $x^2 + x$
  (b) Write each of these quadratic expressions in the form $(x + m)^2 + n$.
   Use your answers to part **(a)**.
   (i) $x^2 + 8x - 3$ (ii) $x^2 - 10x + 31$ (iii) $x^2 + 12x - 5$ (iv) $x^2 + x + 2$

2 For each of these quadratic expressions, complete the square.
  (a) $x^2 + 2x - 3$
  (b) $x^2 + 4x - 1$
  (c) $x^2 - 6x + 12$
  (d) $x^2 + 10x - 6$
  (e) $x^2 - 20x - 50$
  (f) $x^2 + 12x - 1$
  (g) $x^2 + 8x + 19$
  (h) $x^2 - 3x - 3$
  (i) $x^2 + 5x + 10$

Challenge 36.4

(a) Complete the square to express $4x^2 + 12x - 7$ in the form $(kx + m)^2 - n$, where k, m and n are positive integers.

(b) Use your answer to part **(a)** to solve $4x^2 + 12x - 7 = 0$.

Challenge 36.5

(a) Complete the following to write $3x^2 + 6x - 10$ in the form $k(x + m)^2 - n$, where k, m and n are positive integers.

$$\begin{aligned} 3x^2 + 6x - 10 &= 3(x^2 + \text{.......}) - 10 \\ &= 3[(x + \text{.......})^2 - \text{.......}] - 10 \\ &= 3(x + \text{.......})^2 - \text{.......} - 10 \\ &= 3(x + \text{.......})^2 - \text{.......} \end{aligned}$$

(b) Use a similar method to write $2x^2 + 8x - 5$ in the form $k(x + m)^2 - n$, where k, m and n are positive integers.

Challenge 36.6

(a) What is the smallest possible value of $(x - 3)^2$?
What would be the value of x in that case?

(b) What is the smallest possible value of $(x - 3)^2 + 5$?

(c) What is the smallest possible value of $(x - 3)^2 - 2$?

(d) What is the smallest possible value of $(x + 2)^2 + 4$?
What would be the value of x in that case?

(e) What is the smallest possible value of $(x - 1)^2 - 6$?
What would be the value of x in that case?

(f) What is the smallest possible value of $(x + m)^2 + n$?
What would be the value of x in that case?

Solving quadratic equations by completing the square

Some quadratic equations do not factorise. However, if it is in the form of a completed square, it can easily be solved. Remember to do the same operation to the whole of both sides.

EXAMPLE 36.5

Solve each of these quadratic equations.
(a) $(x-3)^2 - 8 = 0$
(b) $(x+2)^2 - 11 = 0$

Solution

(a) $(x-3)^2 - 8 = 0$
$(x-3)^2 = 8$ Add 8 to each side.
$x - 3 = \pm\sqrt{8}$ Take the square root of each side
$x = \pm\sqrt{8} + 3$ Add 3 to each side.
$x = +5.83$ or $x = 0.17$ (to 2 d.p.)

> **TIP**
> Since the number 8 is not a perfect square, the final answer to part (a) is not exact and has to be rounded. The exact answer is seen in the previous line of the solution, where it is given in **surd form**: $x = \pm\sqrt{8} + 3$. You will learn more about surds in Chapter 38.

(b) $(x+2)^2 - 11 = 0$
$(x+2)^2 = 11$ Add 11 to each side.
$x + 2 = \pm\sqrt{11}$ Take the square root of each side.
$x = \pm\sqrt{11} - 2$ Subtract 2 from each side.
$x = 1.32$ or $x = -5.32$ (to 2 d.p.)

If the equation is not in the form of a completed square, you need to complete the square first.

EXAMPLE 36.6

Solve each of these quadratic equations.
(a) $x^2 - 8x + 10 = 0$
(b) $x^2 + 10x - 9 = 0$

Solution

(a)
$$x^2 - 8x + 10 = 0$$
$$(x - 4)^2 - 16 + 10 = 0 \qquad \text{First complete the square.}$$
$$(x - 4)^2 - 6 = 0$$
$$(x - 4)^2 = 6 \qquad \text{Add 6 to each side.}$$
$$x - 4 = \pm\sqrt{6} \qquad \text{Take the square root of each side.}$$
$$x = \pm\sqrt{6} + 4 \qquad \text{Add 4 to each side.}$$
$$x = 6.45 \text{ or } x = 1.55 \text{ (to 2 d.p.)}$$

(b)
$$x^2 + 10x - 9 = 0$$
$$(x + 5)^2 - 25 - 9 = 0 \qquad \text{First complete the square.}$$
$$(x + 5)^2 - 34 = 0$$
$$(x + 5)^2 = 34 \qquad \text{Add 34 to each side.}$$
$$x + 5 = \pm\sqrt{34} \qquad \text{Take the square root of each side.}$$
$$x = \pm\sqrt{34} - 5 \qquad \text{Subtract 5 from each side.}$$
$$x = 0.83 \text{ or } x = -10.83 \text{ (to 2 d.p.)}$$

TIP If you are asked to solve a quadratic equation giving your solutions to a number of decimal places or significant figures, it almost certainly will not factorise.

EXERCISE 36.5

In this exercise, give all your answers correct to 2 decimal places.

1 Solve each of these quadratic equations.
(a) $(x - 3)^2 - 10 = 0$
(b) $(x + 1)^2 - 2 = 0$
(c) $(x + 6)^2 - 28 = 0$
(d) $(x + 4)^2 - 17 = 0$

2 For each of the quadratic equations, first complete the square and then solve the equation.
(a) $x^2 - 4x - 10 = 0$
(b) $x^2 + 8x + 11 = 0$
(c) $x^2 - 2x - 7 = 0$
(d) $x^2 - 10x + 19 = 0$
(e) $x^2 - 12x + 21 = 0$
(f) $x^2 + 4x - 6 = 0$
(g) $x^2 + 8x + 13 = 0$
(h) $x^2 + 20x + 50 = 0$
(i) $x^2 - 3x - 11 = 0$

Solving quadratic equations by using the formula

The method of completing the square can be used to solve the general quadratic equation

$$ax^2 + bx + c = 0.$$

This leads to the general solution of this quadratic equation, known as the **quadratic formula**.

$$x = \frac{-b \pm \sqrt{b^2 - 4ac}}{2a}$$

> **TIP**
> Remember that $\pm$ means 'plus or minus'. You obtain the two solutions of the equation by using the formula with $+$ and $-$ separately.

You do not need to know the proof of this formula, but it can be done by completing the square.

The formula can be used to solve quadratic equations which do not factorise.

EXAMPLE 36.7

Solve each of these quadratic equations. Give your answers correct to two decimal places.
(a) $x^2 + 6x + 2 = 0$ (b) $2x^2 - 9x + 5 = 0$ (c) $3x^2 - 2x - 7 = 0$

Solution

(a) $x^2 + 6x + 2 = 0$
$a = 1, b = 6$ and $c = 2$

$$x = \frac{-b \pm \sqrt{b^2 - 4ac}}{2a}$$

> **TIP**
> If you write out the formula each time you do the first few questions, you will learn it much more easily.

$$x = \frac{-6 \pm \sqrt{6^2 - 4 \times 1 \times 2}}{2 \times 1}$$ Substitute $a = 1, b = 6$ and $c = 2$ into the equation.

$$x = \frac{-6 \pm \sqrt{36 - 8}}{2} = \frac{-6 \pm \sqrt{28}}{2}$$

$$x = \frac{-6 + \sqrt{28}}{2} \quad \text{or} \quad x = \frac{-6 - \sqrt{28}}{2} \quad \text{Find both solutions.}$$

$x = -0.35$ or $x = -5.65$ (to 2 d.p.)

(b) $2x^2 - 9x + 5 = 0$
$a = 2$, $b = -9$ and $c = 5$

$$x = \frac{-b \pm \sqrt{b^2 - 4ac}}{2a}$$

$$x = \frac{9 \pm \sqrt{(-9)^2 - 4 \times 2 \times 5}}{2 \times 2}$$ Substitute $a = 2$, $b = -9$ and $c = 5$ into the equation.

$$x = \frac{9 \pm \sqrt{81 - 40}}{4}$$

$$x = \frac{9 \pm \sqrt{41}}{4}$$

$$x = \frac{9 + \sqrt{41}}{4} \quad \text{or} \quad x = \frac{9 - \sqrt{41}}{4}$$ Find both solutions.

$x = 3.85$ or $x = 0.65$ (to 2 d.p.)

> **TIP**
> When doing a calculation such as $\frac{9 - \sqrt{41}}{4}$ on your calculator, always press the $\boxed{=}$ button after working out the top and before dividing by 4, otherwise you will get the wrong answer.

(c) $3x^2 - 2x - 7 = 0$
$a = 3$, $b = -2$ and $c = -7$

$$x = \frac{-b \pm \sqrt{b^2 - 4ac}}{2a}$$

$$x = \frac{2 \pm \sqrt{(-2)^2 - 4 \times 3 \times (-7)}}{2 \times 3}$$ Substitute $a = 3$, $b = -2$ and $c = -7$ into the equation.

$$x = \frac{2 \pm \sqrt{4 + 84}}{6}$$

$$x = \frac{2 \pm \sqrt{88}}{6}$$

$$x = \frac{2 + \sqrt{88}}{6} \quad \text{or} \quad x = \frac{2 - \sqrt{88}}{6}$$ Find both solutions.

$x = 1.90$ or $x = -1.23$ (to 2 d.p.)

> **TIP**
> If the square root works out exactly then the equation would have factorised.

Quadratic equations with no real solutions

If you square a number, the result will always be positive, because $+ \times + = +$ and $- \times - = +$. This means that the square root of a negative number is not a **real** number.

Therefore, if you are using the formula to solve a quadratic equation and the number inside the square root ($b^2 - 4ac$) works out to be negative, then there are no real solutions to the equation.

The graph of such a quadratic equation could look like this.

Notice that the curve does not cross the x-axis, so there is no point where $y = 0$.

> **TIP**
> In Exercise 36.6 there are a few equations with no real solutions. However, if you are asked to solve an equation it will usually have solutions. If the number inside the square root works out to be negative, you may have made a mistake: go back and check your working.

EXERCISE 36.6

Solve each of these quadratic equations using the formula.
Give your answers correct to two decimal places.
If there are no real solutions, say so.

1 $x^2 + 8x + 5 = 0$
2 $x^2 - 5x + 3 = 0$
3 $x^2 + 7x - 5 = 0$
4 $x^2 - x - 3 = 0$
5 $2x^2 + 10x + 5 = 0$
6 $x^2 + 3x + 6 = 0$
7 $2x^2 + 4x - 7 = 0$
8 $3x^2 + 8x + 1 = 0$
9 $3x^2 - 6x - 4 = 0$
10 $2x^2 - 9x + 8 = 0$
11 $6x^2 + 3x - 1 = 0$
12 $5x^2 + 8x - 5 = 0$
13 $4x^2 - 12x + 7 = 0$
14 $3x^2 - 5x + 4 = 0$
15 $2x^2 + x - 20 = 0$
16 $7x^2 + 3x - 1 = 0$
17 $x^2 - 2x - 100 = 0$
18 $5x^2 + 11x + 3 = 0$
19 $4x^2 + 7x + 6 = 0$
20 $3x^2 - 6x - 8 = 0$
21 $x^2 + 10x + 11 = 0$

Challenge 36.7

Jane's Mum is twice as old as Jane.

Jane works out that in 5 year's time the product of their ages will be approximately 1000.

(a) Write down an equation in x.

(b) Solve your equation to find Jane's present age.

WHAT YOU HAVE LEARNED

- To solve a quadratic equation by factorising, collect all the terms on one side, factorise the quadratic expression and obtain the solutions by equating each factor to zero
- You can solve a quadratic equation which does not factorise by completing the square: write the equation in the form $(x \pm m)^2 = n$, where m is equal to half the coefficient of x and n is equal to m^2; then square root each side
- You can also solve a quadratic equation which does not factorise by using the formula
$x = \dfrac{-b \pm \sqrt{b^2 - 4ac}}{2a}$, where a, b and c are the coefficients in the equation
$ax^2 + bx + c = 0$
- If $b^2 - 4ac < 0$, then there are no real solutions

MIXED EXERCISE 36

1 Solve each of these quadratic equations.
 (a) $x(x - 6) = 0$
 (b) $(x + 3)(x - 7) = 0$
 (c) $(2x + 5)(x - 4) = 0$
 (d) $(3x + 4)(5x + 1) = 0$

2 Solve each of these quadratic equations by factorising.
 (a) $x^2 + 9x = 0$
 (b) $x^2 - 49 = 0$
 (c) $x^2 + 5x + 4 = 0$
 (d) $x^2 + 7x - 8 = 0$
 (e) $x^2 - 9x + 14 = 0$

3 Solve each of these quadratic equations by factorising.
 (a) $3x^2 - 12x = 0$
 (b) $4x^2 - 25 = 0$
 (c) $2x^2 - 5x - 3 = 0$
 (d) $3x^2 - 7x + 2 = 0$
 (e) $3x^2 - 5x - 12 = 0$

4 Solve each of these quadratic equations by rearranging and factorising.
 (a) $x^2 = 7x$
 (b) $x^2 + 3x = 4$
 (c) $x^2 + 7 = 8x$
 (d) $x^2 = 9x - 20$
 (e) $6x^2 = 1 - x$

5 Write each of these expressions in the form $(x + m)^2 + n$.
  (a) $x^2 - 2x + 7$
  (b) $x^2 + 8x - 10$
  (c) $x^2 - 4x - 9$
  (d) $x^2 - 5x + 1$

6 Solve each of these equations by completing the square.
Give your answers correct to 2 decimal places.
  (a) $x^2 - 6x + 4 = 0$
  (b) $x^2 + 10x + 5 = 0$
  (c) $x^2 - 4x - 3 = 0$
  (d) $x^2 + 3x - 1 = 0$

7 Solve each of these equations using the quadratic formula.
Give your answers correct to 2 decimal places.
  (a) $x^2 - 4x + 2 = 0$
  (b) $x^2 + 9x + 5 = 0$
  (c) $x^2 - 7x - 4 = 0$
  (d) $3x^2 + 6x - 5 = 0$

8 Which of these equations have no solutions? Show your calculations.
  (a) $x^2 - 4x - 7 = 0$
  (b) $x^2 + 3x + 4 = 0$
  (c) $x^2 - 5x + 8 = 0$
  (d) $4x^2 + 3x - 1 = 0$

9 The area of this rectangle is 33 cm².

Write down an equation in x and solve it to find the dimensions of the rectangle.

$x + 1$ cm

$x - 7$ cm

10 I think of a number. I double it and take away 3.
I then multiply by the number I first thought of.
The answer is 77.
Assume the number I started with was x.
Write down an equation in x and solve it to find the number I started with.

Mixed exercise 36

37 SIMULTANEOUS EQUATIONS

> **THIS CHAPTER IS ABOUT**
> - Solving simultaneous equations when the equations are both linear
> - Solving simultaneous equations where one is linear and the other quadratic

> **YOU SHOULD ALREADY KNOW**
> - How to solve quadratic equations by factorisation

Solving simultaneous equations using the method of elimination

You learned how to solve **simultaneous equations** using the method of elimination in Chapter 21.

EXAMPLE 37.1

Solve each of these pairs of simultaneous equations
(a) $3x - 2y = 14$
$x + 2y = 10$
(b) $2x + 3y = 21$
$2x + y = 11$

Solution

(a) $3x - 2y = 14$ (1)
$x + 2y = 10$ (2)
$4x = 24$ (1) + (2)
$x = 6$

Remember to label the equations (1) and (2).
y has the same **coefficient**, 2, in both equations. Because the signs are different, the two y terms will be eliminated (cancel each other out) if the two equations are added.

Substitute $x = 6$ in (2)
$6 + 2y = 10$
$2y = 4$
$y = 2$

You could substitute $x = 6$ in equation (1) instead, but in this example it is easier to use equation (2).

Solution is $x = 6$, $y = 2$

Check in (1)
$3x - 2y = 18 - 4$
$= 14$ ✓

> **TIP** Always check your solution using the other equation.

(b) $2x + 3y = 21$ (1)
    $2x + y = 11$ (2)
    $2y = 10$ (1) − (2)
    $y = 5$

This time x has the same coefficient, 2, in both equations. Because the signs are the same, the two x terms will be eliminated if the two equations are subtracted.

Substitute $y = 5$ in (1)
$2x + 15 = 21$
$2x = 6$
$x = 3$

Solution is $x = 3$, $y = 5$

Check in (2)
$2x + y = 6 + 5$
$ = 11$ ✓

> **TIP**
> The coefficients of either x or y must be the same value, positive or negative.
> If the signs are different, add the equations. If the signs are the same, subtract the equations.

You also learned how to solve simultaneous equations where neither of the unknowns (x or y) has the same coefficient in both equations. In such cases you first need to multiply one of the equations.

EXAMPLE 37.2

Solve each of these pairs of simultaneous equations.
(a) $5x + 3y = 4$
    $2x − y = −5$

(b) $4x + 5y = 30$
    $2x − 3y = 4$

Solution

(a) $5x + 3y = 4$ (1)
    $2x − y = −5$ (2)

$6x − 3y = −15$ (2) × 3 = (3)

In this example the coefficients of x and y are different in the two equations.

Multiply equation (2) by 3 to make the coefficient of y the same as in equation (1).
Remember to multiply *each* term in the equation by 3.
The signs are different, so add.

$5x + 3y = 4$ (1)
$6x − 3y = −15$ (3)
$11x = −11$ (1) + (3)
$x = −1$

Substitute $x = −1$ in (1)
$−5 + 3y = 4$
$3y = 9$
$y = 3$

Solution is $x = −1$, $y = 3$

Check in (2)
$2x − y = −2 − 3$
$ = −5$ ✓

Solving simultaneous equations using the method of elimination

(b) $4x + 5y = 30$ (1)
$2x - 3y = 4$ (2)
$4x - 6y = 8$ (2) × 2 = (3)   Multiply equation (2) by 2 to make the coefficient of x the same as in equation (1).

$4x + 5y = 30$ (1)   The signs are the same, so subtract.
$4x - 6y = 8$ (3)   Take care with the signs. $5y - (-6y) = 11y$.
$11y = 22$ (1) − (3)
$y = 2$

Substitute $y = 2$ in (1)
$4x + 10 = 30$
$4x = 20$
$x = 5$

Solution is $x = 5$, $y = 2$

Check in (2)
$2x - 3y = 10 - 6$
$= 4$ ✓

In both pairs of equations in Example 37.2, you can make the coefficient of one of the values (x or y) the same by multiplying one of the equations. Sometimes this is not possible, and you have to multiply each of the equations by a different number.

EXAMPLE 37.3

Solve the simultaneous equations $2x + 5y = -4$ and $3x + 4y = 1$.

Solution

$2x + 5y = -4$ (1)
$3x + 4y = 1$ (2)

In this example, you cannot make the coefficient of either the x terms or the y terms the same by multiplying just one equation. This is because 2 is not a factor of 3 (the x terms) and 4 is not a factor of 5 (the y terms).

Instead, look at the coefficients of the x terms. You know that $2 \times 3 = 6$. So if you multiplying equation (1) by 3 and multiply equation (2) by 2, the x terms in both equations will be the same, $6x$.

Alternatively, you could make the y terms the same by multiplying equation (1) by 4 and equations (2) by 5, but these numbers are larger: for this pair of equations, the arithmetic will be easier if you make the x terms the same.

$6x + 15y = -12$ (1) × 3 = (3)   The signs are the same, so subtract.
$6x + 8y = 2$ (2) × 2 = (4)
$7y = -14$ (3) − (4)
$y = -2$

Substitute $y = -2$ in (1)
$2x - 10 = -4$
$2x = 6$
$x = 3$

Check in (2)
$3x + 4y = 9 - 8$
$= 1$ ✓

EXERCISE 37.1

Solve each of these pairs of simultaneous equations.

1 $5x + y = 7$
$3x + y = 5$

2 $4x - 3y = 7$
$2x + 3y = 17$

3 $4x + 2y = 16$
$x + 2y = 10$

4 $2x + 3y = 3$
$2x - y = 7$

5 $3x + 2y = 7$
$3x - y = -8$

6 $2x + 3y = 14$
$4x - 3y = 1$

7 $-3x + 2y = 0$
$3x - 4y = 6$

8 $x + 5y = 9$
$2x + 3y = 11$

9 $5x - 2y = 19$
$3x + y = 18$

10 $4x + y = 8$
$7x + 3y = 9$

11 $2x - 3y = 8$
$x + 2y = -10$

12 $2x + 6y = 34$
$4x - 2y = 5$

13 $2x + 3y = 10$
$5x - 6y = 16$

14 $2x + 3y = 0$
$8x + 9y = -1$

15 $7x + 8y = 19$
$3x - 2y = -19$

16 $3x + 4y = 15$
$x - 6y = -6$

17 $3x - 4y = 14$
$5x - 8y = 30$

18 $3x + 5y = 21$
$4x + 3y = 17$

19 $3x - 2y = 17$
$2x + 7y = 3$

20 $5x - 2y = 26$
$3x - 5y = 27$

21 $2x + 4y = 5$
$5x + 7y = 8$

Challenge 37.1

Mr and Mrs Brown went to the cinema with their three children. Their total entrance fee was £20.

Mr and Mrs Khan also went to the cinema with their grown-up son and his wife and two grandchildren. Their total entrance fee was £28.

Let £x be the entrance fee for an adult and £y be the entrance fee for a child.

(a) Write down two equations in x and y.

(b) Solve your equations simultaneously to find the entrance fee for adults and children.

Challenge 37.2

Mrs Jones is buying cans of coke and lemonade for her daughter's birthday party.

She buys x cans of coke and y cans of lemonade. Altogether she buys 32 cans.

Coke costs 50p per can and lemonade 40p per can. Altogether she spends £14.80.

Write down a pair of simultaneous equations and solve them to find how many of each can Mrs. Jones buys.

Hint: Take care with the units and simplify one of the equations before solving it.

Solving simultaneous equations by substitution

Simultaneous equations can also be solved algebraically by **substitution**.

This involves making x or y the subject of one equation, and substituting this into the other equation.

For some forms of equation this is the easier method, or the only method possible.

EXAMPLE 37.4

Solve the simultaneous equations $2x + 3y = 21$ and $2x + y = 11$.

Solution

$2x + 3y = 21$ (1)
$2x + y = 11$ (2)
$y = 11 - 2x$ (2)   First make y the subject of equation (2) by subtracting $2x$ from each side.

Substitute for y in equation (1).

$$2x + 3y = 21 \quad (1)$$
$$2x + 3(11 - 2x) = 21$$

$2x + 33 - 6x = 21$	Expand the brackets.
$33 - 4x = 21$	Collect the x terms together.
$33 = 21 + 4x$	Add 4x to each side.
$12 = 4x$	Subtract 21 from each side.
$3 = x$	Divide each side by 4.

Substitute $x = 3$ in the rearranged version of equation (2).
$y = 11 - 2x$
$y = 11 - 6$
$y = 5$

Solution is $x = 3$, $y = 5$

If you look back at Example 37.1 part **(b)** you will see that this is the same solution as we got using the method of elimination.

Substitution is usually a longer, more difficult method than elimination, especially as rearranging one of the equations often creates fractions.

If, however, x or y is the subject of one or both of the given equations, it is the easier method.

EXAMPLE 37.5

Solve each of these pairs of the simultaneous equations.
(a) $2x + 5y = 4$
$x = 3y - 9$

(b) $y = 3x - 17$
$y = 8 - 2x$

Solution

(a) $2x + 5y = 4 \quad (1)$
$x = 3y - 9 \quad (2)$

Substitute for x from equation (2) in equation (1)
$2(3y - 9) + 5y = 4$

$6y - 18 + 5y = 4$	Expand the brackets.
$11y - 18 = 4$	Collect the y terms together.
$11y = 22$	Add 18 to each side.
$y = 2$	Divide each side by 2.

Substitute $y = 2$ in equation (1)
$x = 6 - 9$
$x = -3$

Solution is $x = -3$, $y = 2$

Solving simultaneous equations by substitution

(b) $y = 3x - 17$ (1)
$y = 8 - 2x$ (2)

Substitute for y from equation (1) in equation (2)
$3x - 17 = 8 - 2x$
$5x - 17 = 8$ Add $2x$ to each side.
$5x = 25$ Add 17 to each side.
$x = 5$ Divide each side by 5.

Substitute $x = 5$ in equation (1)
$y = 15 - 17$
$y = -2$

Solution is $x = 5$, $y = -2$

Solving one linear and one quadratic equation

So far in this chapter the simultaneous equations have both been **linear** equations. That is, if their graphs are plotted, they are both straight lines. As you saw in Chapter 21, the solution of the equations represents the point where the two lines cross.

Challenge 37.3

Look at the circle in the diagram.

The centre is the origin and the radius is 5.

The coordinates of the point P are (x, y).

Explain why $x^2 + y^2 = 25$ is true for any point P on the circle.

The equation of a circle with centre the origin and radius r is

$$x^2 + y^2 = r^2.$$

To find where the graph of a circle and a straight line intersect, solve the simultaneous equations. You can do this either graphically or algebraically.

EXAMPLE 37.6

Find, graphically, the coordinates of the points where the circle $x^2 + y^2 = 25$ and the line $y = x + 1$ intersect.

Solution

First draw the graph of $x^2 + y^2 = 25$.
Then, on the same axes, draw the graph of $y = x + 1$.
Read off the coordinates of the points where the two graphs meet.

The circle and the line intersect at the points $(-4, -3)$ and $(3, 4)$.

When you solve the simultaneous equations algebraically, as one equation is quadratic, you must use the **substitution** method.

EXAMPLE 37.7

The diagram shows the circle $x^2 + y^2 = 5^2$ and the line $y = x + 1$.

Find the points where the two graphs intersect.

Solution

$$x^2 + y^2 = 5^2 \quad (1)$$
$$y = x + 1 \quad (2)$$

Substitute for y from equation (2) in equation (1)

$$x^2 + (x + 1)^2 = 5^2$$
$$x^2 + x^2 + 2x + 1 = 25 \quad \text{Expand the brackets.}$$
$$2x^2 + 2x + 1 = 25 \quad \text{Collect the } x^2 \text{ terms together}$$
$$2x^2 + 2x - 24 = 0 \quad \text{This is a quadratic equation, so subtract 25 from each side so that the right-hand side is equal to zero.}$$
$$x^2 + x - 12 = 0 \quad \text{Divide each side of the equation by 2.}$$
$$(x + 4)(x - 3) = 0 \quad \text{Factorise using two brackets.}$$

$x + 4 = 0$ or $x - 3 = 0$
$x = -4$ $\quad\quad\quad x = 3$

Solutions: $x = -4$ or $x = 3$

Substitute $x = -4$ or $x = 3$ in equation (2)
$y = -4 + 1$ or $y = 3 + 1$
$y = -3$ $\quad\quad\quad y = 4$

So the circle $x^2 + y^2 = 5^2$ and the line $y = x + 1$ intersect at $(-4, -3)$ and $(3, 4)$.

EXERCISE 37.2

1. Solve each of these pairs of simultaneous equations by substitution.
   - (a) $y = 2x - 3$
     $y = 3x - 5$
   - (b) $y = 2x - 7$
     $y = 8 - 3x$
   - (c) $y = x + 7$
     $2x + y = 1$
   - (d) $y = 3x - 9$
     $5x + 2y = 4$
   - (e) $7x - y = 10$
     $y = x + 2$
   - (f) $y = 2x - 10$
     $7x - 2y = 29$

2. Find the coordinates of the points where each of these circles and straight lines intersect both graphically and algebraically using the substitution method.
   - (a) $x^2 + y^2 = 25$
     $y = x + 7$
   - (b) $x^2 + y^2 = 100$
     $y = x - 2$
   - (c) $x^2 + y^2 = 169$
     $y = x + 7$

3. Solve each of these pairs of equations by substitution.
   - (a) $x + y = 3$
     $y = x^2 + x$
   - (b) $y = 3x + 1$
     $y = 5x^2$
   - (c) $y = x$
     $y = x^2$

4. Find the coordinates of the points where the line $y = 3 - x$ intersects the curve $y = 2x^2$.

5. Find the coordinates of the points where the straight line $x + 2y - 4 = 0$ meets the curve $y = x^2 - 4$.

Challenge 37.4

The sum of two numbers is 16. The product of the two numbers is 48.

Let the two numbers be x and y.

(a) Write down two equations in x and y.

(b) Solve your equations simultaneously to find the two numbers.

Challenge 37.5

The area of this rectangle is 28 cm².

The perimeter is 22 cm.

(a) Write down two equations in a and b.

(b) Solve your equations simultaneously to find the length and width of the rectangle.

WHAT YOU HAVE LEARNED

- To solve simultaneous equations by elimination, make the coefficients of either x or y take the same value, positive or negative, in both equations by multiplying one equation (or occasionally both) by a number, then add or subtract the equations. If the signs are different, add the equations. If the signs are the same, subtract the equations. Then substitute the value of x or y you have found into either of the equations to find the value of the other value
- To solve simultaneous equations by substitution, first make x or y the subject of one of the equations, then substitute from this equation into the other equation. Solve the new equation to find y or x, then substitute this value into the transformed equation to find the other value
- If one of the equations is quadratic and one is linear, always start by making x or y the subject of the linear equation

MIXED EXERCISE 37

1 Solve each of these pairs of simultaneous equations by elimination.
  (a) $3x - y = 10$
      $2x + y = 5$
  (b) $2x + 3y = -3$
      $4x - y = 8$
  (c) $3x - 2y = -11$
      $x + 5y = 2$
  (d) $4x - 3y = 7$
      $3x + 2y = 18$

2 Solve each of these pairs of simultaneous equations by substitution.
  (a) $y = 3x + 5$
      $x = y - 3$
  (b) $y = 4x + 1$
      $y = x - 11$

3 (a) Find the radius of the circle with equation $x^2 + y^2 = 17$.
  (b) By drawing graphs, find the coordinates of the points where the line $y = x - 3$ intersects the circle $x^2 + y^2 = 17$.
  (c) By solving simultaneous equations, find the coordinates of the points where the line $y = x - 3$ intersects the circle $x^2 + y^2 = 17$.

4 Find the coordinates of the points where the line $y = 2x + 6$ intersects the curve $y = x^2 + 3$.

5 Jamie and Sasha went to the stationery shop.

Jamie bought three pens and two exercise books. The total cost was £1.55.
Sasha bought four pens and one exercise book. The total cost was £1.40.

Let x pence be the cost of a pen and y pence be the cost of an exercise book.
  (a) Write down two equations in x and y to represent Jamie and Sasha's purchases.
      Hint: Take care with the units.
  (b) Solve the equations to find the cost of a pen and the cost of an exercise book.

38 → DECIMALS AND SURDS

THIS CHAPTER IS ABOUT

- **Distinguishing between terminating and recurring decimals**
- **Representing recurring decimals as fractions**
- **Using surds in exact calculations**
- **Rationalising a denominator which has a surd in it**

YOU SHOULD ALREADY KNOW

- How to write terminating decimals as fractions in their simplest form
- How to find the prime factors of a number
- How to work with indices
- How to expand quadratic expressions
- How to solve a quadratic equation which does not factorise

Terminating and recurring decimals

Check up 38.1

Without using a calculator, find the decimal equivalent of each of these fractions.

(a) $\frac{2}{5}$ (b) $\frac{2}{3}$ (c) $\frac{3}{8}$ (d) $\frac{7}{40}$ (e) $\frac{2}{9}$ (f) $\frac{7}{16}$

Some of the decimals recur.

Did you know before you began which decimals would terminate and which recur?

You learned in Chapter 4 that if the denominator of a fraction has only factors which are factors of 10, it will give a terminating decimal. If the denominator of a fraction has factors which are not factors of 10, it will give a recurring decimal.

This is because, when a terminating decimal is written as a fraction, the denominator must be a power of 10.

The prime factors of 10 are 2 and 5. So the prime factors of a power of 10 are powers of 2 and 5.

If the fraction is cancelled down, the numerator and denominator can only be divided by powers of 2 and/or 5.

Thus the prime factors of the denominator must be powers of 2 and/or 5.

For example, $0.265 = \frac{265}{1000}$ The prime factors of 1000 are 2^3 and 5^3.
$= \frac{53}{200}$ The highest common factor (HCF) of 265 and 1000 is 5.

The prime factors of 200 are 2^3 and 5^2.

So, to see whether a fraction can be written as a terminating decimal, write it in its simplest terms and look at the factors of its denominator. If 2 and 5 are the only prime factors, the decimal will terminate. If 2 and 5 are not the only prime factors, the decimal will recur.

EXAMPLE 38.1

State whether each of these fractions will give a terminating decimal or a recurring decimal.

(a) $\frac{4}{25}$ (b) $\frac{3}{15}$ (c) $\frac{7}{40}$ (d) $\frac{8}{11}$ (e) $\frac{29}{30}$

Solution

(a) $\frac{4}{25}$ terminates. $25 = 5^2$

(b) $\frac{3}{15}$ terminates. $\frac{3}{15} = \frac{1}{5}$

(c) $\frac{7}{40}$ terminates. $40 = 2^3 \times 5$

(d) $\frac{8}{11}$ recurs.   11 is prime

(e) $\frac{29}{30}$ recurs. $30 = 2 \times 3 \times 5$

Dots are used to show that a decimal recurs.

If only one digit occurs, a dot is placed over that digit the first time it occurs after the decimal place. For example, 0.166 666 ... is written as $0.1\dot{6}$ and 3.333 333 ... is written as $3.\dot{3}$.

If a group of digits recurs, a dot is placed over the first and last digits in the group. For example, 0.012 612 6 12 ... is written as $0.0\dot{1}2\dot{6}$.

A group of recurring digits is also known as a **period**.

EXAMPLE 38.2

Write $\frac{3}{11}$ as a recurring decimal.

Solution

$$\begin{array}{r} 0.2\,7\,2\,7\,2 \\ 11\overline{)3.0^80^30^80^30^8} \end{array}$$

So $\frac{3}{11} = 0.\dot{2}\dot{7}$

Challenge 38.1

(a) Write each of these fractions as a decimal.

$$\frac{1}{7}, \frac{2}{7}, \frac{3}{7}, \frac{4}{7}, \frac{5}{7}, \frac{6}{7}$$

These decimals recur. What patterns do you notice?

(b) Write each of these fractions as a decimal.

$$\frac{1}{13}, \frac{2}{13}, \frac{3}{13}, \frac{4}{13}, \frac{5}{13}$$

Can you predict the results for $\frac{6}{13}$ to $\frac{12}{13}$?

Work them out to check your predictions.

(c) Write the fractions $\frac{1}{17}$ to $\frac{4}{17}$ as decimals and predict the results for $\frac{5}{17}$ to $\frac{16}{17}$.

Decimals which recur can all be written as fractions.

EXAMPLE 38.3

Write $0.\dot{4}0\dot{2}$ as a fraction in its simplest form.

Solution

Let $a = 0.\dot{4}0\dot{2}$ (1)	
$1000a = 402.\dot{4}0\dot{2}$ (2)	Multiply a by 1000 to move the recurring pattern on by a whole period.
$1000a = 402.\dot{4}0\dot{2}$ $a = 0.\dot{4}0\dot{2}$	Subtract a from $1000a$. This will eliminate the digits after the decimal point. Even though they go on forever, they are the same.
$999a = 402$ (2) − (1)	You now have a simple equation which can easily be solved.
$a = \frac{402}{999}$	Divide each side by 999.
$a = \frac{134}{333}$	Remember to give your answer in its simplest form.

TIP Check your answer by dividing 134 by 333 on your calculator.

The same method can be used for all recurring decimals.

If only part of the decimal recurs, make sure you multiply by a power of 10 such that the recurring pattern is moved on by exactly one whole period.

EXAMPLE 38.4

Write $0.4\dot{2}$ as a fraction in its simplest form.

Solution

Let $a = 0.4\dot{2}$ (1)
$10a = 4.2\dot{2}$ (2)   Multiply a by 10 to move the recurring pattern on by a whole period. You do not need to move the pattern on so that it appears before the decimal point, although often it will, as in Example 38.3.

$10a = 4.2\dot{2}$ (2)   Subtract a from $10a$ to eliminate the recurring digits.
$\underline{a = 0.4\dot{2}}$ (1)
$9a = 3.8$ (2) − (1)   Solve the resulting equation.
$a = \frac{3.8}{9}$

$a = \frac{38}{90}$ Multiply the numerator and denominator of the fraction by 10 to get rid of the decimal.

$a = \frac{19}{45}$ Remember to give your answer in its simplest form.

EXERCISE 38.1

1 Which of these fractions are equivalent to recurring decimals?
    (a) $\frac{4}{15}$ (b) $\frac{3}{20}$ (c) $\frac{4}{35}$ (d) $\frac{9}{125}$ (e) $\frac{11}{16}$

2 Find the decimal equivalent of each of the fractions in question **1**.

3 When these fractions are written as decimals, which of them terminate?
    (a) $\frac{2}{5}$ (b) $\frac{17}{20}$ (c) $\frac{38}{125}$ (d) $\frac{7}{18}$ (e) $\frac{3}{8}$

4 Find the decimal equivalent of each of the fractions in question **3**.

5 Find the fractional equivalent of each of these terminating decimals. Write each fraction in its simplest form.
    (a) 0.12   (b) 0.205   (c) 0.375   (d) 0.3125

6 Find the fractional equivalent of each of these recurring decimals. Write each fraction in its simplest form.
    (a) $0.\dot{4}$ (b) $0.\dot{7}$ (c) $0.1\dot{2}$ (d) $0.4\dot{7}$

7 Find the fractional equivalent of each of these recurring decimals. Write each fraction in its simplest form.
    (a) $0.\dot{3}\dot{5}$ (b) $0.\dot{5}\dot{4}$ (c) $0.\dot{1}\dot{2}$ (d) $0.\dot{1}\dot{7}$

8 Find the fractional equivalent of each of these recurring decimals.
  Write each fraction in its simplest form.
  (a) $0.1\dot{0}\dot{8}$ (b) $0.1\dot{2}\dot{3}$ (c) $0.0\dot{7}$ (d) $0.0\dot{9}\dot{3}$

Challenge 38.2

Work in pairs.

Practise your division skills by writing some fractions as recurring decimals.
Hint: Remember that any fraction whose denominator has prime factors other than 2 or 5 will recur.

Give your recurring decimals to your partner and challenge them to turn them back into fractions.

Challenge 38.3

(a) Given that $\frac{5}{33} = 0.\dot{1}\dot{5}$, write $\frac{5}{330}$ as a recurring decimal.

(b) Given that $\frac{70}{333} = 0.\dot{2}1\dot{0}$, write $\frac{7}{333}$ as a recurring decimal.

Surds

A **rational** number is a number that can be written as an ordinary fraction, $\frac{m}{n}$, where m and n are integers.

An **irrational** number cannot be written in this form. Decimals which neither terminate nor recur are irrational numbers. For example, π and $\sqrt{6}$ are irrational numbers.

Surds are irrational numbers expressed in root form.
For example, $\sqrt{c}$ or $a + b\sqrt{c}$, where c is an integer which is not a perfect square and a and b are rational.

You met surds in Chapter 36, when solving quadratic equations which do not factorise.

When working with surds, you deal with the rational and irrational parts of the expression separately.

38 Decimals and surds

EXAMPLE 38.5

Write each of these in the form $\sqrt{a}$.
(a) $\sqrt{3} \times \sqrt{5}$ (b) $(\sqrt{2})^3$

Solution

(a) $\sqrt{3} \times \sqrt{5} = \sqrt{15}$ Use the result $\sqrt{a} \times \sqrt{b} = \sqrt{ab}$.
(b) $(\sqrt{2})^3 = \sqrt{8}$

Some surds may be simplified by taking out perfect square factors.

EXAMPLE 38.6

Simplify these.
(a) $\sqrt{18}$ (b) $\sqrt{48}$

Solution

(a) $\sqrt{18} = \sqrt{9 \times 2}$ 18 is the product of 9, which is a perfect square, and 2.
$= \sqrt{9} \times \sqrt{2}$
$= 3\sqrt{2}$

(b) $\sqrt{48} = \sqrt{16 \times 3}$ 48 is the product of 16, which is a perfect square, and 3.
$= \sqrt{16} \times \sqrt{3}$
$= 4\sqrt{3}$

TIP

If you did not spot that 16 is a factor of 48, you could have simplified $\sqrt{48}$ in stages.
$\sqrt{48} = \sqrt{4 \times 12}$
$= \sqrt{4 \times 4 \times 3}$
$= 4\sqrt{3}$

EXAMPLE 38.7

Simplify $\sqrt{50} + \sqrt{8}$.

Solution

$\sqrt{50} + \sqrt{8} = \sqrt{25 \times 2} + \sqrt{4 \times 2}$
$= 5\sqrt{2} + 2\sqrt{2}$
$= 7\sqrt{2}$

Sometimes you will need to use your skills at expanding quadratic expressions.

EXAMPLE 38.8

$p = 3 + 5\sqrt{2}$ and $q = 4 - 7\sqrt{2}$.

Find, in the form $a + b\sqrt{2}$, the value of
(a) $p + q$. **(b)** pq. **(c)** p^2.

Solution

(a) $p + q = 3 + 5\sqrt{2} + 4 - 7\sqrt{2}$
$= 7 - 2\sqrt{2}$

$3 + 4 = 7$ and $5\sqrt{2} - 7\sqrt{2} = -2\sqrt{2}$.

(b) $pq = (3 + 5\sqrt{2})(4 - 7\sqrt{2})$
$= 12 + 20\sqrt{2} - 21\sqrt{2} - 35 \times 2$
$= -58 - \sqrt{2}$

Expand the brackets in the usual way.
When you multiply $5\sqrt{2}$ and $-7\sqrt{2}$, use the result $\sqrt{a} \times \sqrt{a} = a$.

(c) $p^2 = (3 + 5\sqrt{2})(3 + 5\sqrt{2})$
$= 9 + 15\sqrt{2} + 15\sqrt{2} + 25 \times 2$
$= 59 + 30\sqrt{2}$

Expand the brackets in the usual way.
Again, use the result $\sqrt{a} \times \sqrt{a} = a$.

When there is a square root in the denominator of a fraction, you may be asked to simplify by **rationalising the denominator**.

This involves multiplying the numerator and denominator by a factor such that the denominator of the fraction becomes a rational number. Remember that when you multiply both numerator and denominator by the same number, the value of the fraction is unchanged.

If the denominator is of the form $a\sqrt{b}$, simply multiply the numerator and denominator by $\sqrt{b}$, and simplify.

EXAMPLE 38.9

Simplify each of these by rationalising the denominator.

(a) $\dfrac{2}{\sqrt{6}}$ **(b)** $\dfrac{8\sqrt{3}}{\sqrt{2}}$

Solution

(a) $\dfrac{2}{\sqrt{6}} = \dfrac{2}{\sqrt{6}} \times \dfrac{\sqrt{6}}{\sqrt{6}}$

Multiply the numerator and denominator by $\sqrt{6}$.

$= \dfrac{2\sqrt{6}}{6}$

Use the result $\sqrt{a} \times \sqrt{a} = a$.

$= \dfrac{\sqrt{6}}{3}$

(b) $\dfrac{8\sqrt{3}}{\sqrt{2}} = \dfrac{8\sqrt{3}}{\sqrt{2}} \times \dfrac{\sqrt{2}}{\sqrt{2}}$ Multiply the numerator and denominator by $\sqrt{2}$.

$= \dfrac{8\sqrt{6}}{2}$

$= 4\sqrt{6}$

EXERCISE 38.2

1 Simplify these.
   (a) $\sqrt{3} + 5\sqrt{3}$
   (b) $12\sqrt{5} - 3\sqrt{5}$
   (c) $6\sqrt{5} - \sqrt{5}$
   (d) $\sqrt{2} \times 6\sqrt{2}$
   (e) $5\sqrt{3} \times \sqrt{7}$
   (f) $3\sqrt{2} \times \sqrt{8}$

2 Write each of these expressions in the form $a\sqrt{b}$, where b is an integer which is as small as possible.
   (a) $\sqrt{50}$
   (b) $2\sqrt{125}$
   (c) $6\sqrt{32}$
   (d) $5\sqrt{54}$
   (e) $\sqrt{90}$
   (f) $\sqrt{2000}$

3 Simplify these.
   (a) $\sqrt{12} + 5\sqrt{3}$
   (b) $8\sqrt{5} - \sqrt{45}$
   (c) $\sqrt{8} + 3\sqrt{2}$
   (d) $\sqrt{60} \times 2\sqrt{3}$
   (e) $\sqrt{32} \times \sqrt{18}$
   (f) $5\sqrt{30} \times \sqrt{60}$

4 Expand and simplify these.
   (a) $\sqrt{3}(2 + \sqrt{3})$
   (b) $2\sqrt{5}(\sqrt{2} + \sqrt{5})$
   (c) $4\sqrt{7}(3 + \sqrt{14})$
   (d) $5\sqrt{2}(\sqrt{8} + \sqrt{6})$

5 Expand and simplify these.
   (a) $(1 + 2\sqrt{3})(2 + 5\sqrt{3})$
   (b) $(3 - \sqrt{2})(5 + \sqrt{2})$
   (c) $(6 - 2\sqrt{5})(3 + \sqrt{5})$
   (d) $(\sqrt{6} + 2)(\sqrt{6} + 3)$
   (e) $(\sqrt{11} + 1)(\sqrt{11} - 1)$
   (f) $(10 - \sqrt{7})(3 - 2\sqrt{7})$

6 Find the value of each of these expressions, when $m = 2 + 5\sqrt{3}$ and $n = 3 - 7\sqrt{3}$.
   (a) $4m$
   (b) $m + n$
   (c) $3m - 2n$
   (d) mn

7 Find the value of each of these expressions, when $p = 3 + 5\sqrt{2}$ and $q = 3 - 5\sqrt{2}$.
   (a) $3q$
   (b) $\sqrt{2}p$
   (c) $p + q$
   (d) pq
   (e) p^2
   (f) q^2

8 Show that $(10 - 3\sqrt{7})(10 + 3\sqrt{7})$ is rational, finding its value.

9 Rationalise the denominator and simplify each of the following.

(a) $\dfrac{10}{\sqrt{2}}$ (b) $\dfrac{2}{\sqrt{10}}$ (c) $\dfrac{4}{3\sqrt{10}}$

(d) $\dfrac{14}{5\sqrt{8}}$ (e) $\dfrac{2\sqrt{3}}{3\sqrt{2}}$ (f) $\dfrac{12\sqrt{6}}{7\sqrt{15}}$

10 Rationalise the denominator and simplify each of the following.

(a) $\dfrac{6 + 3\sqrt{2}}{\sqrt{2}}$ (b) $\dfrac{15 + \sqrt{5}}{2\sqrt{5}}$

(c) $\dfrac{12 + 3\sqrt{2}}{2\sqrt{3}}$ (d) $\dfrac{5 + 2\sqrt{3}}{\sqrt{6}}$

Challenge 38.4

You can rationalise a denominator in the form $a \pm b\sqrt{c}$ by multiplying the numerator and denominator of the fraction by $a \mp b\sqrt{c}$.

For example, to rationalise the denominator of $\dfrac{3\sqrt{5}}{2 + \sqrt{5}}$, multiply by $\dfrac{2 - \sqrt{5}}{2 - \sqrt{5}}$.

To rationalise the denominator of $\dfrac{\sqrt{3}}{6 - 5\sqrt{3}}$, multiply by $\dfrac{6 + 5\sqrt{3}}{6 + 5\sqrt{3}}$.

Why does this method work?

WHAT YOU HAVE LEARNED

- A fraction can be written as a terminating decimal if, in its simplest form, 2 and 5 are the only prime factors of its denominator
- A recurring decimal can be written as a fraction by multiplying by the correct power of 10 to move the recurring pattern on by a whole 'period', then subtracting the original decimal and dividing your resulting equation to obtain the fraction
- Surds are irrational numbers which can be expressed in root form
- Surds may be added and subtracted by adding their rational and irrational parts separately
- Some surds may be simplified by taking a perfect square factor out from the square root
- When multiplying or dividing or simplifying surds you often need to use these results:

  $\sqrt{a} \times \sqrt{a} = a$ and $\sqrt{a} \times \sqrt{b} = \sqrt{ab}$

- When a surd is a fraction with a denominator of the form $a\sqrt{b}$, you can rationalise the denominator by multiplying both numerator and denominator by $\sqrt{b}$

MIXED EXERCISE 38

1 Which of these fractions are equivalent to recurring decimals?
   (a) $\frac{5}{6}$ (b) $\frac{5}{8}$ (c) $\frac{5}{18}$ (d) $\frac{11}{25}$ (e) $\frac{11}{15}$

2 Find the decimal equivalents of each of the fractions in question **1**.

3 Find the fractional equivalents of each of these terminating decimals.
   Write each fraction in its simplest form.
   (a) 0.72   (b) 0.325   (c) 0.625   (d) 0.192

4 Find the fractional equivalents of each of these recurring decimals.
   Write each fraction in its simplest form.
   (a) $0.\dot{4}$ (b) $0.5\dot{4}$ (c) $0.\dot{5}\dot{4}$ (d) $0.\dot{5}0\dot{4}$

5 Write each of these in the form $a\sqrt{b}$, where b is an integer which is as small as possible.
   (a) $\sqrt{32}$ (b) $2\sqrt{75}$ (c) $5\sqrt{18}$
   (d) $\sqrt{108}$ (e) $\sqrt{60}$ (f) $\sqrt{675}$

6 Simplify these.
   (a) $\sqrt{18} + 4\sqrt{2}$ (b) $6\sqrt{5} - \sqrt{20}$ (c) $\sqrt{48} + 3\sqrt{3}$
   (d) $\sqrt{90} \times 2\sqrt{10}$ (e) $\sqrt{8} \times \sqrt{24}$ (f) $4\sqrt{15} \times \sqrt{3}$

7 Expand and simplify these.
   (a) $\sqrt{2}(5 + \sqrt{2})$ (b) $3\sqrt{5}(\sqrt{3} + 2\sqrt{5})$ (c) $2\sqrt{11}(1 + \sqrt{22})$ (d) $3\sqrt{3}(\sqrt{6} + \sqrt{12})$

8 Expand and simplify these.
   (a) $(1 + 5\sqrt{3})(2 + \sqrt{3})$ (b) $(4 - \sqrt{2})(1 + \sqrt{2})$ (c) $(4 - 3\sqrt{5})(1 + \sqrt{5})$
   (d) $(\sqrt{7} + 5)(\sqrt{7} + 2)$ (e) $(\sqrt{5} + 1)(\sqrt{5} - 1)$ (f) $(8 - \sqrt{3})(5 - 2\sqrt{3})$

9 Find the value of each of these expressions, when $p = 7 + 2\sqrt{3}$ and $q = 7 - 2\sqrt{3}$.
   (a) $6q$ (b) $5\sqrt{3}p$ (c) $p - q$
   (d) pq (e) p^2 (f) q^2

10 Rationalise the denominator and simplify each of the following.
   (a) $\dfrac{8}{\sqrt{2}}$ (b) $\dfrac{6}{\sqrt{15}}$ (c) $\dfrac{5}{4\sqrt{10}}$
   (d) $\dfrac{2 + \sqrt{5}}{\sqrt{5}}$ (e) $\dfrac{12 + \sqrt{3}}{\sqrt{3}}$ (f) $\dfrac{42 + \sqrt{21}}{3\sqrt{7}}$

39 → GRAPHS 3

> **THIS CHAPTER IS ABOUT**
> - Velocity–time graphs
> - Solving simultaneous equations graphically
> - Drawing the graphs of simple functions

> **YOU SHOULD ALREADY KNOW**
> - How to use your calculator efficiently
> - How to draw graphs of straight lines
> - How to interpret simple real-life graphs, including rate of change

Velocity–time graphs

In Chapter 15 you looked at some real-life graphs, including distance–time graphs. You also saw how the rate of change was represented on the graph. In the case of distance–time graphs the rate of change is the speed or, more correctly, **velocity**. Velocity has a direction whereas speed does not. The reverse direction has a negative gradient, as you saw in Chapter 21.

EXAMPLE 39.1

This is a distance–time graph for a small particle moving in a straight line.

Describe the motion of the particle.

Solution

From O to A the particle moves 9 metres in 4 seconds at a constant velocity.

(Constant velocity means the velocity is the same at all times.)

From A to B the particle is stationary.

From B to C the particle moves back towards the start so it has a negative velocity. The velocity is not constant. The distance decreases slowly at first and then more rapidly.

In Example 39.1, the rate of change of distance is the velocity but the velocity from B to C is not constant.

> **Discovery 39.1**
>
> **(a)** Work out the average velocity of the particle in Example 39.1 between the times
>   **(i)** 0 and 2 seconds. **(ii)** 2 and 4 seconds.
>   What do you notice?
>
> **(b)** Now work out the average velocity of the particle between the times
>   **(i)** 8 and 9 seconds. **(ii)** 9 and 10 seconds.
>   **(iii)** 10 and 11 seconds. **(iv)** 11 and 12 seconds.
>   What do you notice now?

When velocity is not constant, there is an acceleration (sometimes called deceleration when it is negative). The rate of change of velocity is called **acceleration**.

EXAMPLE 39.2

This graph is a velocity–time graph for the movement of the particle. Describe the movement.

When $t = 4$ the velocity instantly becomes zero. This could not actually happen, of course, but it is usual to show rapid changes in velocity in this way for simplicity.

Solution

From $t = 0$ to $t = 4$, the velocity is constant at 2.2 m/s. There is no acceleration.
From $t = 4$ to $t = 8$, the velocity is zero.
From $t = 8$ to $t = 12$, the velocity decreases (increases backwards) with constant acceleration.
The acceleration is the gradient of the line $= \dfrac{-4}{4} = -1$ m/s^2.

> **TIP**
> The units of velocity are metres per second, written m/s or ms^{-1}. The units of acceleration are metres per second per second, written m/s^2 or ms^{-2}.

EXERCISE 39.1

1 (a) Draw a velocity–time graph with the Time axis (t) from 0 to 10 seconds and the Velocity axis (v) from 0 to 20 m/s.
Show the velocity increasing from 0 m/s at $t = 0$ to 18 m/s when $t = 10$.
(b) Calculate the acceleration.

2 (a) Draw a velocity–time graph with the Time axis (t) from 0 to 10 seconds and the Velocity axis (v) from -10 to 10 m/s.
Show a constant velocity of 6 m/s from $t = 0$ to $t = 3$ and a constant acceleration of -1.5 m/s² from $t = 3$ to $t = 10$.
(b) What is the velocity when $t = 10$?

3 Describe what is happening in this velocity–time graph.
Take appropriate readings and show your calculations.

4 Here is a distance–time graph.
Draw the equivalent velocity–time graph.

Challenge 39.1

Look back to Example 39.1 and Discovery 39.1.
You worked out some average velocities over one-second intervals.
The velocity kept changing.
Can you find the velocity at the instant when $t = 10$? Between what bounds will it lie?
The velocity is the gradient of the graph.
How can you find or estimate the gradient at the point where $t = 10$?

Solving simultaneous equations graphically

In Chapter 21 you saw that you could solve a pair of linear equations graphically by finding where the lines intersected (crossed). In Chapter 15 you drew some quadratic graphs. You can solve a pair of simultaneous equations where one is linear and one is quadratic by drawing the graphs and finding where the line crosses the curve. You will see that, in most cases, the line crosses the curve twice.

EXAMPLE 39.3

Solve the simultaneous equations $y = x^2 + 3x - 7$ and $y = x - 3$ graphically. Take values of x from -5 to 2.

Solution

First make tables of values for the two equations.

x	-5	-4	-3	-2	-1	0	1	2
x^2	25	16	9	4	1	0	1	4
$+3x$	-15	-12	-9	-6	-3	0	3	6
-7	-7	-7	-7	-7	-7	-7	-7	-7
$y = x^2 + 3x - 7$	3	-3	-7	-9	-9	-7	-3	3

x	-5	0	2
$y = x - 3$	-8	-3	-1

You can see from the graph that the line and the curve cross at $(-3.2, -6.2)$ and $(1.2, -1.8)$.

The solutions are, approximately, $x = -3.2$, $y = -6.2$ and $x = 1.2$, $y = -1.8$.

EXERCISE 39.2

1. (a) Draw the graph of $y = x^2 - 5x + 5$ for values of x from -2 to 5.
   (b) On the same axes, draw the line $y = 9 - 2x$.
   (c) Write down the coordinates of the points where the line and the curve intersect.

2. (a) Draw the graph of $y = x^2 - 3x - 1$ for values of x from -4 to 3.
   (b) On the same axes, draw the line $y + 4x = 5$.
   (c) Write down the coordinates of the points where the line and the curve intersect.

3. (a) Draw the graph of $y = x^2 + 3$ for values of x from -2 to 5.
   (b) On the same axes, draw the line $y = 3x + 7$.
   (c) Write down the coordinates of the points where the line and the curve intersect.

4. (a) Draw the graph of $y = x^2 - 2x + 3$ for values of x from 0 to 6.
   (b) On the same axes, draw the line $y = 4x + 1$.
   (c) Write down the coordinates of the points where the line and the curve intersect.

Using graphs to solve quadratic equations

Sometimes you may have drawn a quadratic graph and then need to solve an equation that is different from the graph you have drawn. Rather than drawing another graph, it may be possible to rearrange the equation to obtain the one you have drawn.

EXAMPLE 39.4

(a) Draw the graph of $y = 2x^2 - x - 3$ for values of x between -3 and 4.
(b) Use this graph to solve these equations.
   (i) $2x^2 - x - 3 = 6$ (ii) $2x^2 - x = x + 5$

Solution

(a)

(b) (i) To solve $2x^2 - x - 3 = 6$ you draw the line $y = 6$ on the same axes.
At the points of intersection of the line and the curve $y = 6$ and $2x^2 - x - 3$ and therefore $2x^2 - x - 3 = 6$.
The curve and line cross at approximately $x = -1.9$ and $x = 2.4$.

(ii) To solve $2x^2 - x = x + 5$ you must rearrange the equation so that you have $2x^2 - x - 3$ on the left-hand side.
You do this by subtracting 3 from both sides.

$$2x^2 - x = x + 5$$
$$2x^2 - x - 3 = x + 5 - 3$$
$$2x^2 - x - 3 = x + 2$$

Now draw the line $y = x + 2$.
The points where the line and the curve intersect are the solution to $2x^2 - x = x + 5$.

The curve and line cross at approximately $x = -1.2$ and $x = 2.2$.

EXERCISE 39.3

1 (a) Draw the graph of $y = x^2 - 2x - 3$ for values of x from -2 to 4.
   (b) Use your graph to solve these equations.
   (i) $x^2 - 2x - 3 = 0$ **(ii)** $x^2 - 2x - 3 = -2$
   (iii) $x^2 - 2x - 3 = x$ **(iv)** $x^2 - 2x - 5 = 0$

2 (a) Draw the graph of $y = x^2 - 2x + 2$ for values of x from -2 to 4.
   (b) Use your graph to solve these equations.
   (i) $x^2 - 2x + 2 = 8$ **(ii)** $x^2 - 2x + 2 = 5 - x$
   (iii) $x^2 - 2x - 5 = 0$

3 (a) Draw the graph of $y = 2x^2 + 3x - 9$ for values of x from -3 to 2.
   (b) Use your graph to solve these equations.
   (i) $2x^2 + 3x - 9 = -1$ **(ii)** $2x^2 + 3x - 4 = 0$

4 (a) Draw the graph of $y = x^2 - 5x + 3$ for values of x from -2 to 8.
   (b) Use your graph to solve these equations.
   (i) $x^2 - 5x + 3 = 0$ **(ii)** $x^2 - 5x + 3 = 5$
   (iii) $x^2 - 7x + 3 = 0$

For the remaining questions, do not draw the graphs.

5 The graph of $y = x^2 - 8x + 2$ has been drawn.
What other line needs to be drawn to solve the equation $x^2 - 8x + 6 = 0$?

6 The graph of $y = x^3 - 2x^2$ has been drawn.
What other curve needs to be drawn to solve the equation $x^3 - x^2 - 4x + 3 = 0$?

Challenge 39.2

(a) Draw the graph of $y = x^3 - x$.

(b) What are the roots of $x^3 - x = 0$?

(c) On the same axes, draw these lines.
   (i) $y = \frac{1}{2}$ (ii) $y = 5$ (iii) $y = 2x$

(d) Write down the equations whose roots (or solutions) are given by the various intersections.

(e) How many roots does each equation have?

(f) What can you say about the number of roots of the equations $x^3 - x = kx$ and $x^3 - x = k$?

Drawing and recognising other curves

There are different types of functions and each type has its own characteristic shape. So far you have met linear functions, which give straight-line graphs, and quadratic functions, which, as you saw in Chapter 15, give a parabola when drawn. You will meet the graphs of trigonometrical functions in Chapter 40.

In this section you will meet the graphs of cubic, exponential and reciprocal functions. Cubic functions are functions which have x cubed as the highest power of x.

EXAMPLE 39.5

Draw the graph of $y = x^3$.

Solution

First draw up a table of values.

x	−3	−2	−1	0	1	2	3
y	−27	−8	−1	0	1	8	27

Then plot the points and join them with a smooth curve.

The next two examples are of exponential functions. You met these in Chapter 29.

EXAMPLE 39.6

The number of bacteria in a solution doubles each hour.
The number present at the start of timing is 300.
Draw a graph to show the number of bacteria in the solution over a 4-hour period.

Solution

First make a table of values for the number of bacteria in the solution.

Number of hours (h)	0	1	2	3	4
Number of bacteria (n)	300	600	1200	2400	4800

Then plot the points and join them with a smooth curve.

The graph in Example 39.6 is an exponential curve.

The equation is $n = 300 \times 2^h$.

The 300 in the equation is because this is the initial value.

The 2 results because the number of bacteria doubles each hour.

$n = 300 \times 2^h$ is a typical exponential equation.

Drawing and recognising other curves

> **EXAMPLE 39.7**
>
> (a) Draw the graph of $y = 3^x$ for values of x from -2 to 3.
> (b) Use your graph to estimate the value of y when $x = 2.4$.
> (c) Use your graph to estimate the solution to the equation $3^x = 20$.
>
> **Solution**
>
> First make a table of values.
>
> | x | -2 | -1 | 0 | 1 | 2 | 3 |
> |---|---|---|---|---|---|---|
> | y | 0.111 | 0.333 | 1 | 3 | 9 | 27 |
>
> (b) You read values from the graph in the usual way.
>   When $x = 2.4$, $y = 13.5$.
>
> (c) The solution to the equation $3^x = 20$ is the value of x when $y = 20$.
>   From the graph you can see this is $x = 2.7$.

Another function you have met before is the reciprocal function. The graph of a reciprocal function has two branches, as is shown in the next example.

EXAMPLE 39.8

Draw the graph of $y = \dfrac{2}{x}$ for values of x from -4 to 4.

Solution

The table of values is shown below.

x	-4	-3	-2	-1	0	1	2	3	4
y	-0.5	-0.7	-1	-2	–	2	1	0.7	0.5

Notice when x is zero the value of y cannot be found – the value is at infinity.

It is difficult to judge where to draw the line between the values -1 and $+1$ so it is helpful to calculate the values of y when x is -0.5 and $+0.5$.

When $x = -0.5$, $y = -4$.
When $x = 0.5$, $y = 4$.

EXERCISE 39.4

1. (a) Draw the graph of $y = x^3$ for values of x between -4 and 4.
   (b) Use your graph to solve the equation $x^3 - 4x = 0$.
   (c) Draw the graph of $y = x^3 - 4x$.

2. The population of a species of bird is dropping by 20% every 10 years.
   (a) Copy and complete this table of values.

Year (y)	1970	1980	1990	2000	2010
Number of birds (n)	50 000		32 000		

   (b) Draw a graph to show this relationship.
   (c) Write down the equation for this relationship.

Drawing and recognising other curves

3 (a) Draw a graph of $y = 2^{-x}$ for values of x from -4 to 2.
   (b) Use your graph to estimate
      (i) the value of y when $x = 0.5$.
      (ii) the solution to the equation $2^{-x} = 10$.

4 The number of a species of animal in a park is shown in the table.

Year (y)	2000	2001	2002	2003	2004	2005
Number of animals (n)	2	6	18	54		

   (a) Find the formula for n in terms of y.
   (b) Copy and complete the table.

5 (a) Plot the graph of $y = 2^x$ for values of x from -2 to 5.
   (b) Use your graph to estimate
      (i) the value of y when $x = 3.2$.
      (ii) the solution of the equation $2^x = 10$.

6 (a) Draw the graph of $y = \dfrac{3}{x}$.
   (b) Use your graph to estimate the value of y when $x = 1.8$.

Challenge 39.3

On the same axes, draw the graphs $y = 2^x$ and $x = 2^y$.

What do you notice?

Is this true for all inverse functions?

Challenge 39.4

(a) Radon is a naturally occurring gas which seeps out of some rocks in some parts of the country.

The gas is radioactive with a half-life of 4 seconds.

This means that if there are 500 atoms of radon in a sample of gas, 4 seconds later there will be half that number so there will be 250 atoms of radon in the sample.

The formula for n, the number of atoms left after time t seconds, is $n = 1000 \times 2^{-\frac{1}{4}t}$.
   (i) Copy and complete this table of values.

t	0	4	8	12	16	20
n						

continues ...

Challenge 39.4 continued

  (ii) Draw the graph of n against t.
  (iii) Use your graph to estimate the time, in seconds, when the number of atoms is 300.
(b) Another radioactive element now has a mass of 50 grams.
  Its decay rate reduces its mass, m grams, by 20% each year.
  (i) Write down a formula for the mass after t years.
  (ii) By drawing the graph of m against t, estimate the times when the mass was 70 g and when it will be 35 g.
    Give your answers correct to the nearest tenth of a year.

WHAT YOU HAVE LEARNED

- How to interpret velocity–time graphs
- To solve simultaneous equations graphically, plot the graphs and find the points of intersection
- When using graphs to solve equations, rearrange the equation to be solved so that the equation already plotted is on the left-hand side
- The shape of cubic, exponential and reciprocal graphs

MIXED EXERCISE 39

1 Describe what is happening in this velocity–time graph.

2 (a) Draw the graph of $y = x^2 - 5x + 3$ for values of x from -2 to 4.
  (b) On the same axes draw the line $7x + 2y = 11$.
  (c) Write down the coordinates of the points where the line and the curve intersect.

3 (a) Draw the graph of $y = x^2 - 2x$ for values of x from -1 to 4.
  (b) Use your graph to solve the equation $x^2 - 2x = x + 1$.

4 (a) Draw the graph of $y = x^2 - 7x$ for values of x from 0 to 7.
   (b) Use your graph to solve these equations.
      (i) $x^2 - 7x + 9 = 0$ (ii) $x^2 - 5x + 1 = 0$

5 (a) Draw the graph of $y = x^2 - 4x + 3$ for values of x from -2 to 8.
   (b) Use your graph to solve the equation $x^2 - 4x + 1 = 0$.

6 (a) Draw the graph of $y = x^3 - 1$ for values of x from -3 to 3.
   (b) Use your graph to solve these equations.
      (i) $x^3 - 2 = 0$ (ii) $x^3 - x - 1 = 0$

7 (a) Copy and complete the table of values for $y = 4^{-x}$.

x	-2.5	-2	-1.5	-1	-0.5	0	0.5	1
y		16		4			0.5	

   (b) Plot the graph of $y = 4^{-x}$ for values of x from -2.5 to 1.
   (c) Use your graph to estimate
      (i) the value of y when $x = -1.8$.
      (ii) the solution of the equation $4^{-x} = 25$.

40 → TRIGONOMETRY 2

THIS CHAPTER IS ABOUT
- Finding areas, angles and lengths in non-right-angled triangles
- Graphs of trigonometrical functions

YOU SHOULD ALREADY KNOW
- How to find the area of a right-angled triangle
- Basic trigonometry within right-angled triangles

The area of a triangle

For any right-angled triangle, you can find the area of the triangle using the formula

$$\text{Area} = \tfrac{1}{2} \times \text{base} \times \text{height} = \tfrac{1}{2} \times AB \times AC.$$

For a non-right-angled triangle, you can use the formula to find the area of the triangle if you know the perpendicular height of the triangle. This is because the triangle can be divided into two right-angled triangles.

$$\begin{aligned}\text{Area} &= (\tfrac{1}{2} \times AD \times CD) + (\tfrac{1}{2} \times DB \times CD) \\ &= (\tfrac{1}{2} \times CD) \times (AD + DB) \\ &= \tfrac{1}{2} \times CD \times AB \\ &= \tfrac{1}{2} \times \text{base} \times \text{height}\end{aligned}$$

You cannot find the area of a triangle using the formula when you do not know the perpendicular height. An alternative method is required.

There is a convention to label the sides and angles of a triangle. The angles are labelled with capital letters. The side opposite an angle is labelled with the same letter but in lower case.

The area of a triangle 531

Discovery 40.1

- Draw any non-right-angled triangle.
- Label it according to convention.
- Measure accurately each of the sides and each of the angles of your triangle.
- For your triangle calculate $ab \sin C$, $bc \sin A$ and $ac \sin B$.

(a) What do you notice?
(b) Compare your answers with those of other students.

> **TIP**: $ab \sin C$ means $a \times b \times \sin C$.

General formula for the area of a triangle

ACD is a right-angled triangle.

As you learned in Chapter 24, you can find the length of CD using simple trigonometry.

$$\sin A = \frac{O}{H} = \frac{CD}{b}$$

so $\quad CD = b \sin A$

Now you can work out a formula to find the area of any triangle.

$$\begin{aligned} \text{Area} &= \tfrac{1}{2} \times \text{base} \times \text{height} \\ &= \tfrac{1}{2} \times AB \times CD \\ &= \tfrac{1}{2} \times c \times b \sin A \\ &= \tfrac{1}{2} bc \sin A \end{aligned}$$

Using different sides as the base you get three alternative versions of the formula.

$$\text{Area} = \tfrac{1}{2} bc \sin A$$
$$\text{Area} = \tfrac{1}{2} ac \sin B$$
$$\text{Area} = \tfrac{1}{2} ab \sin C$$

EXAMPLE 40.1

Find the area of this triangle.

(Triangle with A at top, angle 134° at A, side AC = 3.8 cm, side AB = 8.7 cm)

Solution

Angle A is given so the version of the formula to use is

Area $= \frac{1}{2} \times b \times c \sin A$
$= \frac{1}{2} \times 3.8 \times 8.7 \times \sin 134°$
$= 11.9 \text{ cm}^2$

EXERCISE 40.1

1 Find the area of each of these triangles.

(a) Triangle ABC with angle C = 77°, CA = 6.3 cm, CB = 4.9 cm

(b) Triangle ABC with angle A = 55°, AB = 9.9 cm, AC = 8.2 cm

(c) Triangle ABC with angle B = 52°, BA = 7.3 cm, BC = 5.8 cm

(d) Triangle PQR with angle R = 69°, RP = 12.3 cm, RQ = 8.7 cm

(e) Triangle XYZ with angle Y = 98°, YX = 5.6 cm, YZ = 7.8 cm

(f) Triangle ABC with angle A = 62°, AC = 5 cm, AB = 11 cm

(g) Triangle PQR with angle P = 73°, PQ = 10.5 cm, PR = 11.9 cm

(h) Triangle XYZ with angle Z = 115°, ZY = 12.6 cm, ZX = 9.3 cm

2 **(a)** In triangle ABC, $a = 5$ cm, $b = 6$ cm and the area is 11 cm^2.
Find the size of angle C.
(b) In triangle PQR, $p = 6.4$ cm, $r = 7.8$ cm and the area is 23.4 cm^2.
Find the size of angle Q.
(c) In triangle XYZ, $y = 10.7$ cm, $z = 7.6$ cm and the area is 16.9 cm^2.
Find the size of angle X.

3 **(a)** In triangle ABC, $a = 27$ cm, angle B is 54° and the area is 345 cm^2.
Find the length of side c.
(b) In triangle PQR, $r = 9.3$ cm, angle P is 123° and the area is 74.1 cm^2.
Find the length of side q.

Challenge 40.1

(a) A triangle ABC has side AC of length 13.7 cm, side BC of length 8.7 cm and an area of 50 cm^2.
Calculate the size of angle ACB.

(b) A triangle ABC has side AB of length 8.9 cm, angle ABC of 78° and an area of 29.2 cm^2.
Calculate the length of side BC.

The sine rule

The general formula works for finding the area of any triangle where the lengths of two sides and the angle between them (the **included** angle) are known.

If the angle given is a non-included angle or if two angles are given and the length of just one side, it is necessary to find the missing information first.

There are two rules which you can use to find missing information in non-right-angled triangles. They are called the **sine rule** and the **cosine rule** because of the trigonometrical function they each rely upon.

The sine rule is based upon the relationship between an angle and the side opposite it in the triangle.

The sine rule takes two forms. For finding sides you use this form.

$$\frac{a}{\sin A} = \frac{b}{\sin B} = \frac{c}{\sin C}$$

For finding angles you use this form.

$$\frac{\sin A}{a} = \frac{\sin B}{b} = \frac{\sin C}{c}$$

You use any two of the fractions at the same time.

It is useful to learn and remember the sine rule but it is not essential that you do so. The first version will be provided in an examination and the second version is just the first version inverted.

The sine rule works for any triangle in which you know
- the lengths of two sides and the non-included angle.
- the length of one side and the sizes of any two angles (because this means you in fact know the size of all the angles).

Proof 40.1

It is easy to prove the sine rule, although you will not be required to do so in an examination.

In triangle ADC,   AD = $b \sin C$.
In triangle ADB,   AD = $c \sin B$.

Therefore $b \sin C = c \sin B$

or $\dfrac{b}{\sin B} = \dfrac{c}{\sin C}$

Using another perpendicular will involve a and A.

EXAMPLE 40.2

Find the size of the missing angles and sides in these diagrams.

(a) Triangle with A = 47°, C = 36°, AB = 5.2 cm, side b, side a opposite A, BC = a.

(b) Triangle with AC = 8.6 cm, C = 42°, AB = 6.1 cm, side a opposite A.

The sine rule 535

Solution

(a) Side *a*

The fractions to use are $\dfrac{a}{\sin A} = \dfrac{c}{\sin C}$.

$$\dfrac{a}{\sin 47} = \dfrac{5.2}{\sin 36}$$

$$a = \dfrac{5.2 \times \sin 47}{\sin 36}$$

$$a = 6.47 \text{ cm}$$

Angle *B*

Angle $B = 97°$, because the angles of a triangle add up to 180°.

Side *b*

$$\dfrac{b}{\sin B} = \dfrac{c}{\sin C}$$

$$\dfrac{b}{\sin 97} = \dfrac{5.2}{\sin 36}$$

$$b = \dfrac{5.2 \times \sin 97}{\sin 36}$$

$$b = 8.78 \text{ cm}$$

(b) Angle *B*

Use the alternative form of the sine rule since you want to find an angle.

$$\dfrac{\sin B}{b} = \dfrac{\sin C}{c}$$

$$\dfrac{\sin B}{8.6} = \dfrac{\sin 42}{6.1}$$

$$\sin B = \dfrac{8.6 \times \sin 42}{6.1}$$

$$B = 70.6°$$

Angle *A*

Angle $A = 67.4°$, because the angles of a triangle add up to 180°.

Side *a*

$$\dfrac{a}{\sin A} = \dfrac{c}{\sin C}$$

$$\dfrac{a}{\sin 67.4} = \dfrac{6.1}{\sin 42}$$

$$a = \dfrac{6.1 \times \sin 67.4}{\sin 42}$$

$$a = 8.42 \text{ cm}$$

> **TIP** In your calculations use the sides and angles that you are given, rather than ones you have calculated, where possible.

EXERCISE 40.2

1 Find the size of each of the angles and sides marked.

(a) Triangle ABC with AC = 8.4 cm, angle A = 49°, angle B = 64°, side a marked (BC).

(b) Triangle ABC with angle A = 53°, AB = 7.1 cm, BC = 7.3 cm.

(c) Triangle ABC with AC = 5.4 cm, angle A = 62°, BC = 7.6 cm.

(d) Triangle PQR with PR = 14.9 cm, angle Q = 65°, angle R = 79°, side r marked (PQ).

(e) Triangle PQR with PR = 8.6 cm, angle P = 54°, angle Q = 93°, side p marked (QR).

(f) Triangle XYZ with XZ = 8 cm, angle Z = 72°, XY = 14 cm.

2 Find the size of each of the sides and angles not given in these diagrams.

(a) Triangle PQR with PQ = 7.5 cm, angle Q = 73°, PR = 8.7 cm.

(b) Triangle XYZ with XZ = 9.6 cm, angle Z = 123°, XY = 23.4 cm.

(c) Triangle ABC with angle C = 83°, BC = 6 cm, angle A = 59°.

(d) Triangle ABC with AC = 8.2 cm, angle B = 61°, angle A = 38°.

(e) Triangle ABC with angle C = 72°, CB = 6.8 cm, AB = 8.6 cm.

(f) Triangle PQR with PR = 13 cm, angle P = 48°, angle R = 75°.

Challenge 40.2

The diagram represents a river.

The bearing of a tree on one bank is measured from two points, R and S, that are 50 metres apart on the opposite bank.

Calculate the width of the river.

Challenge 40.3

A farmer makes a triangular pen bounded by a fence 59 metres long, a hedge 68 metres long and a wall.

The angle between the wall and the hedge is 49°.

(a) Calculate the length of the wall, correct to the nearest metre.
(b) Find the area of the pen.

The cosine rule

The cosine rule is based upon the relationship between two sides of a triangle and the angle included between them.

For finding sides, the cosine rule is usually written as follows.

$$a^2 = b^2 + c^2 - 2bc \cos A$$
$$b^2 = a^2 + c^2 - 2ac \cos B$$
$$c^2 = a^2 + b^2 - 2ab \cos C$$

For finding angles, the cosine rule is usually written as follows.

$$\cos A = \frac{b^2 + c^2 - a^2}{2bc}$$
$$\cos B = \frac{a^2 + c^2 - b^2}{2ac}$$
$$\cos C = \frac{a^2 + b^2 - c^2}{2ab}$$

Again, it is useful to learn the cosine rule but it is not essential that you do so. One version of each of the forms of the cosine rule will be provided in an examination. You will, however, need to remember how to manipulate them.

The cosine rule works for any triangle in which you know
- the lengths of all three sides.
- the lengths of two sides and the size of the included angle.

Proof 40.2

Again, you do not need to be able to prove the cosine rule in an examination. It is, however, quite easy to prove using Pythagoras.

In triangle ADC, $b^2 = AD^2 + DC^2$
                     $DC = a - BD$
Therefore $DC^2 = a^2 - 2aBD + BD^2$

In triangle ADB: $AD^2 = c^2 - BD^2$
and $BD = c \cos B$
Therefore $DC^2 = a^2 - 2ac \cos B + BD^2$
so $b^2 = c^2 - BD^2 + a^2 - 2ac \cos B + BD^2$
so $b^2 = c^2 + a^2 - 2ac \cos B$

EXAMPLE 40.3

Find the size of each of the missing angles and sides in these diagrams.

(a) Triangle with A = 58°, AC = 7 cm, AB = 5.4 cm, side a opposite A.

(b) Triangle with AC = 8 cm, CB = 11 cm, AB = 9 cm.

Solution

(a) **Side a**
$a^2 = b^2 + c^2 - 2bc \cos A$
$a^2 = 7^2 + 5.4^2 - 2 \times 7 \times 5.4 \times \cos 58°$
$a^2 = 49 + 29.16 - 40.06$
$a^2 = 38.1$
$a = 6.2$ cm

Angle B

$$\cos B = \frac{a^2 + c^2 - b^2}{2ac}$$

$$\cos B = \frac{38.1 + 5.4^2 - 7^2}{2 \times 6.2 \times 5.4}$$

$$\cos B = \frac{18.26}{66.96}$$

$$B = 74.2°$$

Angle C
Angle C = 47.8°, because the angles of a triangle add up to 180°.

(b) **Angle A**

$$\cos A = \frac{b^2 + c^2 - a^2}{2bc}$$

$$\cos A = \frac{8^2 + 9^2 - 11^2}{2 \times 8 \times 9}$$

$$\cos A = \frac{24}{144}$$

$$A = 80.4°$$

Angle B

$$\cos B = \frac{a^2 + c^2 - b^2}{2ac}$$

$$\cos B = \frac{11^2 + 9^2 - 8^2}{2 \times 11 \times 9}$$

$$\cos B = \frac{138}{198}$$

$$B = 45.8°$$

Angle C
Angle C = 53.8°, because the angles of a triangle add up to 180°.

EXERCISE 40.3

1 Find the size of each of the sides and angles marked in these diagrams.

(a) Triangle with AC = 8 cm, AB = 9 cm, angle A = 49°, side a (= BC) to find.

(b) Triangle with AC = 7 cm, BC = 4 cm, AB = 9 cm, angle A marked.

(c) Triangle with AC = b, CB = 9.8 cm, AB = 13.2 cm, angle C = 27°.

(d) Triangle with AC = 8.7 cm, AB = 7.4 cm, BC = 6.2 cm.

2 Find the size of each of the sides and angles not given in these diagrams.

(a) Triangle ABC: AC = 6 cm, CB = 5 cm, angle C = 83°

(b) Triangle ABC: AC = 8 cm, CB = 6 cm, AB = 9 cm

(c) Triangle ABC: CB = 6.5 cm, AB = 7.2 cm, angle B = 46°

(d) Triangle ABC: AC = 6.7 cm, AB = 6.3 cm, CB = 5.5 cm

(e) Triangle PQR: PQ = 5.6 cm, QR = 7.8 cm, angle Q = 98°

(f) Triangle PQR: PR = 5 cm, RQ = 9 cm, PQ = 11 cm

(g) Triangle PQR: PR = 11.4 cm, PQ = 10.5 cm, QR = 11.9 cm

(h) Triangle XYZ: XZ = 12.6 cm, ZY = 9.3 cm, angle Z = 115°

(i) Triangle XYZ: XZ = 8.2 cm, XY = 6.3 cm, YZ = 6.3 cm

(j) Triangle XYZ: ZY = 5.4 cm, ZX = 13.6 cm, angle Z = 119°

The cosine rule 541

3 (a) In triangle ABC, $a = 23$ cm, $b = 19.4$ cm and angle C is $54°$.
Find the length of AB.
(b) In triangle PQR, $p = 12$ cm, $q = 13.4$ cm and $r = 15.6$ cm.
Find the size of angle Q.

4 ABCDEFGH is a cuboid.
ACH is a triangle contained within the cuboid.
Calculate the size of these angles.
(a) Angle ACH
(b) Angle AHC
(c) Angle CAH

Challenge 40.4

A runner takes part in a race. The course is in the shape of a triangle.
Three posts, X, Y and Z, mark the corners of the triangle.
Angle XYZ is $54°$, XY is 100 metres and YZ is 120 metres.
What is the length of the race?

Challenge 40.5

A harbour (H) is 1500 metres due south of a lighthouse (L).
A speedboat is travelling towards H.
When the speedboat is first seen from the lighthouse it is on a bearing of $060°$ and at a distance of 2800 m from L.
Calculate the distance of the speedboat from the harbour at the time when the speedboat is first seen from the lighthouse.

Graphs of trigonometrical functions

When using the sine and cosine rules in the previous sections you will, from time to time, have been dealing with angles greater than 90° and your calculator will have given you the sin or cos value of these angles. This is possible because the values of sin and cos follow a repeating pattern. Consider the following situation.

$$\sin \theta = \frac{h}{r}$$

Rotating the radius anticlockwise until the height of P is again h gives rise to the diagram on the left.

$$\sin (180 - \theta) = \frac{h}{r}$$

Rotating the radius anticlockwise until the height of P is again h gives rise to the diagram on the left.

$$\sin (180 + \theta) = \frac{-h}{r}$$

A further rotation to $(360 - \theta)$ would produce $\sin (360 - \theta) = \frac{-h}{r}$

This pattern can be repeated for any height h (different values of θ). Plotting the value of h against the value of θ, for all angles θ, produces the graph shown below. It is called the **sine curve**.

The height (or depth) of the wave from zero is known as the **amplitude**. The distance over which the wave repeats itself is known as the **period**.

It is a useful skill to be able to sketch the sine curve and, for this reason, you should try to remember the basic features of the curve.

The cosine curve takes a similar form, as can be seen in the diagram below.

40 Trigonometry 2

Challenge 40.6

The curve of cos θ is simply the curve of sin x translated by 90°.

Why do you think that this is the case?

A similar diagram can be drawn for tan θ but this does not produce a continuous curve, as can be seen in the diagram below.

The diagram for the tan θ function does have a repeating pattern, like that for sin θ and cos θ. Its period is 180°, as shown by the dashed vertical lines known as **asymptotes**.

EXAMPLE 40.4

Draw accurately the graph of $y = \sin \theta$ for values of θ from $-180°$ to $180°$.
From your graph read off all the values of θ in this range for which $\sin \theta = 0.4$.

Solution

Draw the curve and the line $y = 0.4$.

Read off the values of θ where the curve and the line intersect.
The approximate possible solutions from the graph are 24° and 156°.

Note that, if you were to find $\sin^{-1} 0.4$ using a scientific calculator you would only obtain the one solution of 23.6°.

Drawing the curve and the line on a graphic calculator would enable you to see both solutions. Check that you know how to use the ZOOM, TRACE and INTERSECT functions on your graphic calculator.

EXERCISE 40.4

1. (a) Sketch the graph of $y = \sin \theta$ for values of θ from 0° to 540°.
   (b) For what values of θ in this range does $\sin \theta = 0.5$?

2. (a) Sketch the graph of $y = \cos \theta$ for values of θ from $-180°$ to 360°.
   (b) For what values of θ in this range does $\cos \theta = -0.5$?

3. (a) Draw accurately the graph of $y = \sin \theta$ for values of θ from $-180°$ to 180°.
   (b) From your graph read off all the values of θ for which $\sin \theta = 0.7$.

4. (a) Draw accurately the graph of $y = \cos \theta$ for values of θ from 0° to 540°.
   (b) From your graph read off all the values of θ for which $\cos \theta = -0.4$.

5. One solution to $\sin \theta = 0.8$ is approximately 53°.
   Using only the symmetry of the sine curve, find the other angles between 0° and 720° that also satisfy the equation $\sin \theta = 0.8$.

6. (a) Draw a sketch graph of $y = \tan \theta$ for values of θ from 0° to 360°.
   (b) Find, from your graph, the angles for which $\tan \theta = 1.2$.

Other trigonometrical functions

The graph below shows the curves $y = \sin \theta$ and $y = 4 \sin \theta$, i.e. $4 \times (\sin \theta)$.

You can see that the amplitude of the green curve, $y = 4\sin\theta$, is four times the amplitude of the curve $y = \sin\theta$. This is because you are plotting 4 times $\sin\theta$ and this has the effect of stretching the curve in the y direction by a scale factor of 4.

Fractional scale factors such as $y = \frac{1}{2}\sin\theta$ have the effect of compressing the curve as the amplitude is halved and all the y values are consequently reduced.

In both cases the period of the graph remains unchanged.

The graph below shows the curves $y = \cos\theta$ and $y = \cos 4\theta$ i.e. $\cos(4 \times \theta)$. Note the difference between this graph and the graph above.

You will see that the period of the green curve, $y = \cos 4\theta$, is one quarter the period of the curve $y = \cos\theta$. This is because you are plotting $\cos(4 \times \theta)$ and this has the effect of compressing the curve in the θ direction by a scale factor of 4.

Fractional scale factors, such as $y = \cos\frac{1}{2}\theta$ have the effect of stretching the curve in the θ direction. This is because the angle is effectively halved and all the θ values are consequently reduced.

In both cases the amplitude of the graph remains unchanged.

For all graphs of the type $y = A\sin B\theta$ and $y = A\cos B\theta$, the amplitude of the curve is A and the period of the curve is $\dfrac{360}{B}$.

Other trigonometrical functions 547

EXAMPLE 40.5

Draw the graph of $y = 2 \sin 3\theta$ between $0°$ and $360°$.
Find the solutions of $2 \sin 3\theta = 1.5$ between $150°$ and $270°$
(a) from your graph.
(b) from your calculator, giving your answers to 1 decimal place.

Solution

(a) Approximately $165°$ and $255°$
(b) $166.2°$ and $253.8°$

EXERCISE 40.5

1. Find the amplitude and the period of each of these curves.
   (a) $y = 3 \sin \theta$
   (b) $y = \cos 5\theta$
   (c) $y = 3 \sin 4\theta$
   (d) $y = 4 \sin \frac{1}{2}\theta$
   (e) $y = 5 \cos 3\theta$
   (f) $y = 2 \cos 0.8\theta$

2. Draw the graph of $y = 3 \cos \theta$ for values of θ from $0°$ to $180°$.

3. Draw the graph of $y = \sin 2\theta$ for values of θ from $0°$ to $180°$.

4. Sketch the graph of $y = \cos 2\theta$ for values of θ from $0°$ to $360°$.

5. Sketch the graph of $y = 2.5 \sin \theta$ for values of θ from $0°$ to $360°$.

6. Find the solutions of $\cos 3\theta = -0.5$ between $0°$ and $180°$.

Challenge 40.7

Using a scale of 1 cm to represent 30°, draw the curve of $y = \sin 2x$ for values of x from 0° to 360°.

The flow of tides on any given day can be modelled by the curve $y = \sin 2x$.

The first high tide of a day occurs at 3 a.m.

What is the time of

(a) the next high tide?

(b) the low tides that day?

Challenge 40.8

(a) On one set of axes, draw sketch graphs of $y = 1.2 \sin \theta$ and $y = \cos 0.8\theta$ for values of θ from 0° to 360°.

(b) Find, from your graph, the solutions to the equation $1.2 \sin \theta = \cos 0.8\theta$.

WHAT YOU HAVE LEARNED

- **The convention for labelling angles and sides in a triangle**

- **Area of any triangle** $= \frac{1}{2} bc \sin A$
- **The sine rule is used for calculating sides or angles in non-right-angled triangles when you know either**
  - **the lengths of two sides and the non-included angle**
  - **the length of one side and the sizes of any two angles**
- **The sine rule can be written** $\dfrac{a}{\sin A} = \dfrac{b}{\sin B} = \dfrac{c}{\sin C}$ or $\dfrac{\sin A}{a} = \dfrac{\sin B}{b} = \dfrac{\sin C}{c}$
- **The cosine rule is used for calculating sides or angles in non-right-angled triangles when you know either**
  - **the lengths of all three sides**
  - **the length of two sides and the size of the included angle**
- **The cosine rule can be written** $\cos A = \dfrac{b^2 + c^2 - a^2}{2bc}$

- **The amplitude of a trigonometrical graph is the maximum height (or depth) of the curve**
- **The period of a trigonometrical graph is the distance over which the curve repeats**

- **For all graphs of the type $y = A \sin B\theta$ and $y = A \cos B\theta$, the amplitude is A and the period, in degrees, is $\dfrac{360}{B}$**

MIXED EXERCISE 40

1 Work out the area of each of these triangles.

(a) Triangle ABC with AC = 6.4 cm, AB = 7.3 cm, angle A = 47°

(b) Triangle ABC with CB = 8 cm, AB = 9 cm, angle B = 59°

(c) Triangle XYZ with XZ = 9.8 cm, YZ = 12.3 cm, angle Z = 51°

(d) Triangle ABC with BA = 6.8 cm, BC = 7.3 cm, angle B = 139°

2 (a) In triangle ABC, $a = 9$ cm, $b = 11$ cm and the area is 20 cm^2.
Find the size of angle C.
(b) In triangle PQR, $p = 10.4$ cm, $r = 12.4$ cm and the area is 33.2 cm^2.
Find the size of angle Q.
(c) In triangle XYZ, $y = 15.3$ cm, $z = 9.4$ cm and the area is 68.8 cm^2.
Find the size of angle X.

3 (a) In triangle ABC, $a = 15$ cm, angle B is 49° and the area is 45 cm^2.
Find the length AB.
(b) In triangle XYZ, $x = 18.4$ cm, angle Y is 96° and the area is 148.2 cm^2.
Find the length XY.

4 Find the size of each of the marked angles and sides in these diagrams.

(a) Triangle ABC with angle A = 59°, angle B = 98°, side BC = 7 cm, side AC = b.

(b) Triangle PQR with angle P = 75°, PQ = 6.4 cm, PR = 12.8 cm, angle R marked.

(c) Triangle XYZ with angle X = 105°, XY = 7 cm, YZ = 8.5 cm, angle Z marked.

(d) Triangle ABC with angle C = 112°, angle B = 48°, CB = 19.8 cm, AC = b.

5 Find the size of each of the sides and angles not given in these diagrams.

(a) Triangle PQR with PQ = 12 cm, PR = 14.5 cm, angle Q = 73°.

(b) Triangle XYZ with angle Z = 108°, ZX = 24.1 cm, XY = 28.6 cm.

(c)

(d)

6 In the triangle XYZ, angle XYZ is 43°, angle ZXY is 65° and side YZ is 8.3 cm. Calculate the length of the longest side of the triangle.

7 Find the size of each of the marked angles and sides in these diagrams.

(a)

(b)

(c)

(d)

8 Find the size of each of the sides and angles not given in these diagrams.

(a)

(b)

552 40 Trigonometry 2

(c)
R
67°
4.5 cm   5.6 cm
P
Q

(d)
X 13.3 cm Z
12.4 cm   11.5 cm
Y

9 A scalene triangle has sides of 53 metres, 74 metres and 85 metres.
   Calculate the sizes of the angles of the triangle.

10 ABCDEFGH is a cuboid. M is the midpoint of CD. AHM is a triangle contained within the cuboid.
   Calculate the size of these angles.
   (a) Angle AHM
   (b) Angle HMA

11 (a) (i) Sketch the graph of $y = \sin\theta$ for values of θ from 0° to 360°.
   (ii) For what values of θ in this range does $\sin\theta = 0.7$?
   (b) (i) Draw accurately the graph of $y = \cos\theta$ for values of θ from −180° to 180°.
   (ii) For what values of θ in this range does $\cos\theta = -0.3$?
   (c) One solution to $\cos\theta = -0.6$ is approximately 127°.
   Using only the symmetry of the cosine curve, find the other angles between 0° and 720° that also satisfy the equation $\cos\theta = -0.6$.
   (d) (i) Sketch the graph of $y = \tan\theta$ for values of θ from −180° to 180°.
   (ii) Find, from your graph, the angles for which $\tan\theta = 2$.
   (e) Find the amplitude and period of each of these curves.
      (i) $y = 3\sin\theta$ **(ii)** $y = \cos 5\theta$ **(iii)** $y = 3\sin 4\theta$
      (iv) $y = 4\sin\frac{1}{2}\theta$ **(v)** $y = 5\cos\frac{2}{3}\theta$ **(vi)** $y = 2\cos 0.8\theta$
      (vii) $y = 5\cos 3\theta$ **(viii)** $y = 2\cos 0.6\theta$
   (f) Sketch these graphs.
      (i) $y = 3\sin\theta$ for values of θ from 0° to 180°.
      (ii) $y = \cos 4\theta$ for values of θ from 0° to 180°.
      (iii) $y = 3\cos 2\theta$ for values of θ from 0° to 360°.
      (iv) $y = 0.5\sin 3\theta$ for values of θ from 0° to 360°.
   (g) Find the solutions of $\sin 5\theta = 0.4$ between −180° and 180°.

41 FUNCTIONS

THIS CHAPTER IS ABOUT
- Function notation
- Transforming graphs

YOU SHOULD ALREADY KNOW
- How to draw graphs of linear, quadratic and cubic functions
- How to draw graphs of trigonometrical functions
- The shape of basic graphs such as $y = x^2$, $y = x^3$ and $y = \sin \theta$
- How to transform shapes by reflection, translation and one-way stretch
- How to expand brackets

Function notation

$y = f(x)$ means that y is a **function** of x. You read $f(x)$ as 'f of x'. For any value of x, a function only has one value.

If $y = x^2 + 2$ then $f(x) = x^2 + 2$.
The value of the function when $x = 3$ is written $f(3)$.
So $f(3) = 3^2 + 2 = 9 + 2 = 11$.

EXAMPLE 41.1

$f(x) = 3x^2 + 2$. Find the value of each of these.
(a) $f(4)$ (b) $f(-1)$

Solution

(a) $f(4) = 3 \times 4^2 + 2$
$= 3 \times 16 + 2$
$= 48 + 2 = 50$

(b) $f(-1) = 3 \times (-1)^2 + 2$
$= 3 \times 1 + 2$
$= 3 + 2 = 5$

EXAMPLE 41.2

$g(x) = 5x + 6$
(a) Solve $g(x) = 8$
(b) Write an expression for each of these.
   (i) $g(3x)$ (ii) $3g(x)$

Solution

(a) $5x + 6 = 8$
$5x = 2$
$x = \frac{2}{5}$

(b) (i) To find $g(3x)$, you replace x with $3x$.
$g(3x) = 5 \times (3x) + 6$
$= 15x + 6$
  (ii) To find $3g(x)$, you multiply $g(x)$ by 3.
$3g(x) = 3 \times (5x + 6)$
$= 15x + 18$

EXAMPLE 41.3

$h(x) = x^2 - 6$. Write an expression for each of these.
(a) $2h(x)$ (b) $h(2x)$ (c) $h(x) + 3$ (d) $h(x + 3)$

Solution

(a) $2h(x) = 2 \times (x^2 - 6)$
$= 2x^2 - 12$

(b) $h(2x) = (2x)^2 - 6$
$= 4x^2 - 6$

(c) $h(x) + 3 = x^2 - 6 + 3$
$= x^2 - 3$

(d) $h(x + 3) = (x + 3)^2 - 6$
$= x^2 + 6x + 9 - 6$
$= x^2 + 6x + 3$

EXERCISE 41.1

1 $f(x) = x^2 - 5$. Find the value of each of these.
   (a) $f(3)$ (b) $f(-2)$

2 $g(x) = 3x^2 - 2x + 1$. Find the value of each of these.
   (a) $g(3)$ (b) $g(-2)$ (c) $g(0)$

3 h(x) = $2x - 5$
  (a) Solve h(x) = 7
  (b) Write an expression for each of these.
      (i) h($x - 2$)   (ii) h($2x$)

4 f(x) = $7 - 3x$
  (a) Solve f(x) = 1.
  (b) Write an expression for each of these.
      (i) 3f(x)   (ii) f($x + 3$)

5 g(x) = $4x - 3$
  (a) Solve g(x) = 0.
  (b) Write an expression for each of these.
      (i) g($x + 5$)   (ii) g(x) + 5

6 h(x) = $x^2 - 2$
  (a) Solve h(x) = 7.
  (b) Write an expression for each of these.
      (i) h($x + 1$)   (ii) h(x) + 1

7 f(x) = $3x^2 - 2x$
  (a) Find the value of f(-4).
  (b) Write an expression for each of these.
      (i) f($x - 1$)   (ii) f($2x$)

8 g(x) = $x^2 - 3x$
  (a) Solve g(x) = 4.
  (b) Write an expression for each of these.
      (i) g($2x$)   (ii) g($x + 1$)

Challenge 41.1

Function of a function

fg(x) means first find g(x) = y and then find f(y).
You always start with the function nearest the brackets.
For example, f(x) = $2x - 5$ and g(x) = $x^2 - 1$.
To find fg(3) you find g(3) = 8, then f(8) = 11.
To find fg(x) you find f($x^2 - 1$) = $2(x^2 - 1) - 5 = 2x^2 - 7$.
To find gf(x) you find g($2x - 5$) = $(2x - 5)^2 - 1 = 4x^2 - 20x + 24$.
Now try these.
Given f(x) = $3x + 2$, g(x) = x^2 and h(x) = $x^2 - 2x$, work out these.
  (a) fg(2)   (b) gf(2)   (c) gh(3)   (d) gh(-2)   (e) fgh(-1)
  (f) fg(x)   (g) gf(x)   (h) fh(x)   (i) hg(x)   (j) fgh(x)

Translations

Discovery 41.1

If possible, use graph-drawing software to draw the graphs in this task and print them out. Otherwise, draw the graphs on graph paper.

If your grid gets too crowded, start a new one.

Section 1

(a) For the function $f(x) = x^2$
   - plot the graph of $y = f(x)$.
   - on the same axes, plot the graph of $y = f(x) + 2$.

(b) What transformation maps $y = f(x)$ on to $y = f(x) + 2$?

(c) On the same axes, plot some other graphs of the form $y = f(x) + a$, where a can take any value. Try values of a that are positive, negative and fractional.

(d) Describe the transformation that maps the graph of $y = f(x)$ on to $y = f(x) + a$.

Section 2

(a) For the function $f(x) = x^2$
   - plot the graph of $y = f(x)$ on a new grid.
   - on the same axes, plot the graph of $y = f(x + 1)$.

(b) What transformation maps $y = f(x)$ on to $y = f(x + 1)$?

(c) On the same axes, plot $y = f(x - 2)$ and $y = f(x + 2)$.

(d) Experiment further until you can describe the transformation that maps the graph of $y = f(x)$ on to $y = f(x + a)$, for any value of a.

Section 3

What happens if you change the function?

Work through sections 1 and 2 again, using $y = \sin \theta$ for $\theta = -360°$ to $\theta = 360°$.

Describe what you find.

Translations parallel to the y-axis

The diagram shows the graphs of $y = x^2$, $y = x^2 + 4$ and $y = x^2 - 5$.

The graph of $y = x^2$ passes through the origin.

The graph of $y = x^2 + 4$ is the same shape and passes through the point (0, 4).

The graph of $y = x^2 - 5$ is also the same shape but passes through the point $(0, -5)$.

You can see that $y = x^2 + 4$ is the graph of $y = x^2$ translated by $\begin{pmatrix} 0 \\ 4 \end{pmatrix}$ and that $y = x^2 - 5$ is the graph of $y = x^2$ translated by $\begin{pmatrix} 0 \\ -5 \end{pmatrix}$.

This applies to all families of graphs. You can generalise the result.

The graph of $y = f(x) + a$ is the graph of $y = f(x)$ translated by $\begin{pmatrix} 0 \\ a \end{pmatrix}$.

> **TIP**
> The graphs in this section are drawn accurately but you can sketch graphs unless you are told to do otherwise.

Translations parallel to the x-axis

The diagram shows the graphs of $y = x^2$, $y = (x + 3)^2$ and $y = (x - 2)^2$.

The graph of $y = x^2$ passes through the origin.

The graph of $y = (x + 3)^2$ is the same shape and passes through $(-3, 0)$.

The graph of $y = (x - 2)^2$ is also the same shape but passes through $(2, 0)$.

You can see that $y = (x + 3)^2$ is the graph of $y = x^2$ translated by $\begin{pmatrix} -3 \\ 0 \end{pmatrix}$ and that $y = (x - 2)^2$ is the graph of $y = x^2$ translated by $\begin{pmatrix} 2 \\ 0 \end{pmatrix}$.

This applies to all families of graphs. You can generalise the result.

The graph of $y = f(x + a)$ is the graph of $y = f(x)$ translated by $\begin{pmatrix} -a \\ 0 \end{pmatrix}$.

> **TIP**
> It is useful to learn these results but you should also be able to work them out when needed.

41 Functions

EXAMPLE 41.4

(a) Sketch these graphs on the same diagram.
  (i) $y = x^2$ **(ii)** $y = x^2 - 4$
(b) State the transformation that maps $y = x^2$ on to $y = x^2 - 4$.

Solution

(a)

[Graph showing $y = x^2$ and $y = x^2 - 4$ on the same axes]

(b) The transformation is a translation of $\begin{pmatrix} 0 \\ -4 \end{pmatrix}$.

EXAMPLE 41.5

This graph is a transformed sine curve. Find its equation.

[Graph of a transformed sine curve from $-90°$ to $360°$, with maximum at 2 and minimum at 0]

Solution

The graph of $y = \sin \theta$ passes through the origin.

The graph in the diagram has been translated by $\begin{pmatrix} 0 \\ 1 \end{pmatrix}$ so its equation is $y = \sin \theta + 1$.

EXAMPLE 41.6

Find the translation that maps $y = x^3$ on to $y = (x - 5)^3 + 6$.

Solution

The transformation that maps $y = x^3$ on to $y = (x - 5)^3$ is a translation by $\begin{pmatrix} 5 \\ 0 \end{pmatrix}$.

The transformation that maps $y = (x - 5)^3$ on to $y = (x - 5)^3 + 6$ is a translation by $\begin{pmatrix} 0 \\ 6 \end{pmatrix}$.

So the transformation that maps $y = x^3$ on to $y = (x - 5)^3 + 6$ is a translation by $\begin{pmatrix} 5 \\ 6 \end{pmatrix}$.

EXERCISE 41.2

1. (a) Sketch these graphs on the same diagram.
   (i) $y = x^2$ (ii) $y = (x - 5)^2$
   (b) State the transformation that maps $y = x^2$ on to $y = (x - 5)^2$.

2. (a) Sketch these graphs on the same diagram.
   (i) $y = -x^2$ (ii) $y = -x^2 - 4$
   (b) State the transformation that maps $y = -x^2$ on to $y = -x^2 - 4$.

3. (a) Sketch these graphs on the same diagram.
   (i) $y = x^2$ (ii) $y = (x + 2)^2$ (iii) $y = (x + 2)^2 - 3$
   (b) State the transformation that maps $y = x^2$ on to $y = (x + 2)^2 - 3$.

4. (a) Sketch the result of translating the graph of $y = \sin \theta$ by $\begin{pmatrix} 0 \\ -1 \end{pmatrix}$ for $\theta = 0°$ to $\theta = 360°$.
   (b) State the equation of the transformed graph.

5. State the equation of $y = x^2$ after it has been translated by
   (a) $\begin{pmatrix} 0 \\ -5 \end{pmatrix}$.   (b) $\begin{pmatrix} 2 \\ 0 \end{pmatrix}$.

6. The diagram shows the graph of $y = f(x)$.
   Copy the diagram and draw these graphs on the same axes.
   (a) $y = f(x) - 2$
   (b) $y = f(x - 2)$

7 The diagram shows the graph of $y = g(x)$.
Copy the diagram and sketch these graphs on the same axes.

(a) $y = g(x + 1)$
(b) $y = g(x) + 1$

8 State the equation of the graph $y = x^2$ after it has been translated by $\begin{pmatrix} 1 \\ 2 \end{pmatrix}$.

9 The diagram shows the graph of a transformed cosine curve. State its equation.

10 The graph of $y = x^2$ is translated by $\begin{pmatrix} -2 \\ 3 \end{pmatrix}$.

(a) State the equation of the transformed graph.
(b) Show that this equation may be written as $y = x^2 + 4x + 7$.

Challenge 41.2

(a) Sketch the graphs of $y = \sin \theta$ and $y = \cos \theta$ on the same axes.
(b) (i) By considering the transformation necessary, find a value for a so that $\cos \theta = \sin (\theta + a)$.
   (ii) Investigate whether there are other possible values of a.
(c) Investigate possible values of b so that $\sin \theta = \cos (\theta + b)$.

Translations 561

One-way stretches

> ### Discovery 41.2
>
> If possible, use graph-drawing software to draw the graphs in this task and print them out. Otherwise, draw the graphs on graph paper.
>
> If your grid gets too crowded, start a new one.
>
> #### Section 1
> (a) For the function $f(x) = x^2 - 2x$
> • plot the graph of $y = f(x)$.
> • on the same axes, plot the graphs of $y = 2f(x)$ and $y = 3f(x)$.
> (b) Experiment further until you can describe the transformation that maps the graph of $y = f(x)$ on to $y = kf(x)$, for any value of k.
>
> #### Section 2
> (a) For the function $f(x) = x^2 - 2x$
> • plot the graph of $y = f(x)$.
> • on the same axes, plot the graph of $y = f(2x)$ (i.e. $y = 4x^2 - 4x$).
> • also on the same axes, plot $y = f\left(\dfrac{x}{2}\right)$ and $y = f(-3x)$.
> (b) Experiment further until you can describe the transformation that maps the graph of $y = f(x)$ on to $y = f(kx)$, for any value of k.

The diagram shows the graphs of $y = \sin \theta$ and $y = 3 \sin \theta$.

To get from $y = \sin \theta$ to $y = 3 \sin \theta$, the graph has been stretched parallel to the y-axis by a scale factor of 3.

This is an example of the following general principle.

The graph of $y = kf(x)$ is a one-way stretch of the graph $y = f(x)$ parallel to the y-axis with a scale factor of k.

The diagram shows the graphs of $y = \cos\theta$ and $y = \cos 2\theta$.

The graph of $y = \cos\theta$ shows one period of the curve. By comparison, the graph of $y = \cos 2\theta$ shows two periods of the curve over the same range. This is a one-way stretch parallel to the x-axis with a scale factor of $\frac{1}{2}$.

This is an example of the following general principle.

> The graph of $y = f(kx)$ is a one-way stretch of the graph of $y = f(x)$ parallel to the x-axis with a scale factor of $\frac{1}{k}$.

A one-way stretch with a scale factor of $k = -1$ can be more simply described as a reflection.

If $y = f(x)$ is $y = x^2$ then $y = -f(x)$ is $y = -x^2$.

You can see that the graph of $y = -x^2$ is the reflection of $y = x^2$ in the x-axis.

This is an example of the following general principle.

> The graph of $y = -f(x)$ is a reflection of the graph of $y = f(x)$ in the x-axis.

If $y = f(x)$ is $y = 2x + 3$ then $y = f(-x)$ is $y = -2x + 3$.

You can see that $y = -2x + 3$ is a reflection of $y = 2x + 3$ in the y-axis.

This is an example of the following general principle.

> The graph of $y = f(-x)$ is a reflection of the graph of $y = f(x)$ in the y-axis.

TIP
It is useful to learn these results but you should also be able to work them out when needed.

One-way stretches 563

EXAMPLE 41.7

(a) Sketch on the same diagram the graphs of $y = \cos \theta$ and $y = -\cos \theta$, for $0° \leq \theta \leq 360°$.
(b) Describe the transformation that maps $y = \cos \theta$ on to $y = -\cos \theta$.

Solution

(a)

(b) The transformation that maps $y = \cos \theta$ on to $y = -\cos \theta$ is a reflection in the x-axis.

EXAMPLE 41.8

Describe the transformation that maps the graph of $y = h(x)$ on to each of these graphs.
(a) $y = h(x) - 2$ **(b)** $y = 3h(x)$ **(c)** $y = h(0.5x)$ **(d)** $y = 4h(2x)$

Solution

(a) A translation of $\begin{pmatrix} 0 \\ -2 \end{pmatrix}$.

(b) A one-way stretch parallel to the y-axis with a scale factor of 3.

(c) A one-way stretch parallel to the x-axis with a scale factor of 2.

(d) A one-way stretch parallel to the x-axis of scale factor 0.5 and a one-way stretch parallel to the y-axis with a scale factor of 4.

EXAMPLE 41.9

The equation of this graph is $y = k \sin m\theta$. Find k and m.

Solution

The graph is stretched parallel to the y-axis by a scale factor of 3, so $k = 3$.

The period of this sine curve is $60°$.

The graph of $y = \sin \theta$ has a period of $360°$. So the scale factor is $\frac{1}{6}$.

The graph is stretched parallel to the x-axis by a scale factor of $\frac{1}{6}$, so $m = 6$.

EXERCISE 41.3

1. (a) Sketch on the same axes the graphs of $y = \sin \theta$ and $y = -\sin \theta$ for $0 \leq \theta \leq 360°$.
   (b) Describe the transformation that maps $y = \sin \theta$ on to $y = -\sin \theta$.

2. (a) Sketch on the same axes the graphs of $y = \sin \theta$ and $y = \sin \frac{\theta}{2}$ for $0 \leq \theta \leq 360°$.
   (b) Describe the transformation that maps $y = \sin \theta$ on to $y = \sin \frac{\theta}{2}$.

3. Describe the transformation that maps
   (a) $y = \cos \theta + 1$ on to $y = -\cos \theta - 1$.
   (b) $y = x + 2$ on to $y = -x + 2$.
   (c) $y = x^2$ on to $y = 5x^2$.

4 The graph of $y = \cos \theta$ is transformed by a one-way stretch parallel to the x-axis with a scale factor of $\frac{1}{3}$.
State the equation of the resulting graph.

5 State the equation of the graph $y = x^2 + 5$ after these transformations.
   (a) A reflection in the y-axis
   (b) A reflection in the x-axis

6 State the equation of the graph of $y = x + 2$ after these transformations.
   (a) A one-way stretch parallel to the y-axis with a scale factor of 3
   (b) A one-way stretch parallel to the x-axis with a scale factor of $\frac{1}{2}$

7 Describe the transformation that maps the graph of $y = f(x)$ on to each of these graphs.
   (a) $y = f(x) + 1$
   (b) $y = 3f(x)$
   (c) $y = f(2x)$
   (d) $y = 5f(3x)$

8 $y = -x^2 + 2x$. Find the equation of the graph after these transformations.
   (a) A reflection in the x-axis
   (b) A reflection in the y-axis
   (c) A translation of 3 parallel to the x-axis

9 The graph of $y = x^2$ is stretched parallel to the x-axis by a scale factor of 2.
   (a) State the equation of the resulting graph.
   (b) What does the point (1, 1) map on to under this transformation?
   (c) What is the scale factor of a stretch parallel to the y-axis that maps $y = x^2$ on to the same graph?
   (d) What does the point (1, 1) map on to under this transformation?

10 The equation of this graph is $y = \sin k\theta$. Find k.

> **WHAT YOU HAVE LEARNED**
>
> - The graph of f(x) + a is the graph of f(x) translated by $\begin{pmatrix} 0 \\ a \end{pmatrix}$
> - The graph of y = f(x + a) is the graph of y = f(x) translated by $\begin{pmatrix} -a \\ 0 \end{pmatrix}$
> - The graph of y = kf(x) is a one-way stretch of the graph y = f(x) parallel to the y-axis with a scale factor of k
> - The graph of y = f(kx) is a one-way stretch of the graph of y = f(x) parallel to the x-axis with a scale factor of $\frac{1}{k}$
> - The graph of y = −f(x) is a reflection of the graph of y = f(x) in the x-axis
> - The graph of y = f(−x) is a reflection of the graph of y = f(x) in the y-axis

MIXED EXERCISE 41

1 f(x) = 2x − 1.
 (a) Solve f(x) = 0.
 (b) Find an expression for each of these.
  (i) f(x + 5)   (ii) f(x) + 5

2 g(x) = x^2 + 6.
 (a) Solve g(x) = 7.
 (b) Find an expression for each of these.
  (i) g(x + 1)   (ii) g(2x) + 1

3 h(x) = x^2 − 2x.
 (a) Find the value of h(−4).
 (b) Find an expression for each of these.
  (i) h(x − 2)   (ii) h(2x) + 3

4 (a) On the same set of axes, sketch the graphs of y = x^2 and y = x^2 − 4.
 (b) Describe the transformation that maps y = x^2 on to y = x^2 − 4.

5 The graph of y = 2x − 3 is translated by $\begin{pmatrix} 1 \\ 2 \end{pmatrix}$.
 Find the equation of the transformed graph.

6 Sketch the graph of y = sin θ after it has been translated by $\begin{pmatrix} 0 \\ -1 \end{pmatrix}$.

7 Describe the transformation that maps the graph of $y = g(x)$ on to each of these graphs.
   (a) $y = g(x + 1)$
   (b) $y = g(3x)$
   (c) $y = 4g(x)$
   (d) $y = g(-x)$

8 State the equation of the graph of $y = \cos \theta$ after each of these transformations.
   (a) A translation of $\begin{pmatrix} 0 \\ 3 \end{pmatrix}$
   (b) A one-way stretch parallel to the x-axis with a scale factor of 0.25

9 State the equation of the graph of $y = x^3 + 5$ after it has been
   (a) reflected in the x-axis.
   (b) reflected in the y-axis.

10 The graph of $y = x^2$ is translated by $\begin{pmatrix} 3 \\ 1 \end{pmatrix}$ and then stretched with a scale factor of 2 parallel to the y-axis.
   (a) Find the equation of the resulting curve and write it as simply as possible.
   (b) Find the coordinates of the minimum point of this curve.

42 LENGTH, AREA AND VOLUME

THIS CHAPTER IS ABOUT

- Using dimension analysis to distinguish between formulae for length, area and volume
- Finding arc length and the area of a sector of a circle
- Calculating the surface area and volume of cones, pyramids and spheres
- Calculating the surface area and volume of compound shapes

YOU SHOULD ALREADY KNOW

- For a circle of radius r, the circumference $= 2\pi r$
- For a circle of radius r, the area $= \pi r^2$
- The area of a trapezium $= \frac{1}{2}(a + b)h$
- The volume of a prism = area of cross-section × length
- The area of triangle ABC $= \frac{1}{2}ab \sin C$
- How to rearrange formulae
- How to find the length of the diagonal of a cuboid

Dimension analysis

Discovery 42.1

Write down all the formulae you can remember for length, area and volume, keeping each of these categories in a separate list.

Include the formulae given above.

Look at the formulae in each group, to see what they have in common.

Looking at the dimensions of the formulae:

number × length = length (1 dimension)
length + length = length (1 dimension)
length × length = area (2 dimensions)
length × length × length = volume (3 dimensions)
area × length = volume (3 dimensions)

TIP Looking at dimensions can help you to remember formulae. For example, you can find out whether the area of a circle is πr^2 or $2\pi r$ if you have forgotten which it is. Remember that π is a number and has no dimensions.

Check that these rules fit all the formulae you remembered in Discovery 42.1.

Looking at the number of dimensions can also help you to remember which units to use. For example

cm for length (1 dimension)
cm² for area (2 dimensions)
cm³ for volume (3 dimensions).

EXAMPLE 42.1

a, b, h and r are lengths.
Decide whether each of these formulae represents a length, an area, a volume or none of these.

(a) $r + 2h$ (b) $\frac{1}{2}(a + b)h$ (c) $r^2 + 2\pi r$ (d) $\frac{4}{3}\pi r^3$

Solution

(a) length + length = length
(b) (length + length) × length = length × length = area
(c) area + length = nonsense
(d) length³ = volume

EXERCISE 42.1

Throughout this exercise, letters in algebraic expressions represent lengths and numbers have no dimensions.

1. Which of the following expressions could be a length?
   (a) $3r$ (b) $a + 2b$ (c) rh

2. Which of the following expressions could be an area?
   (a) $bc - a^2$ (b) $\pi h(a^2 + b^2)$ (c) $\frac{1}{3}\pi r^2$

3. Which of the following expressions could be a volume?
   (a) $2\pi r^2$ (b) $3ab(c + d)$ (c) $\frac{1}{3}\pi r^2 h$

4. State whether each of these expressions represents a length, an area or a volume.
   (a) $a + p$ (b) $\pi r^2 h$ (c) $\pi r l$

5. State whether each of these expressions represents a length, an area, a volume or is nonsense.
   (a) $8c^3$ (b) $6c^2$ (c) $4c + \pi r^2$ (d) $12c$

Check up 42.1

Make up some formulae which would be dimensionally possible for length, area, volume and none of these.

Then swap formulae with a partner.

Work out which of your partner's formulae are for length, area, volume and none of these.

Arcs and sectors

An **arc** is part of the circumference of a circle.

The shape in the diagram is a **sector** of a circle. It is formed by an arc and two radii.

Challenge 42.1

How many of the sectors in the diagram above would fit into a circle of radius 5 cm?

Use your answer to work out the area of one of these sectors and the arc length of the sector.

How would you find the perimeter of the sector?

Any sector is a fraction $\frac{\theta}{360}$ of a circle, where θ is the sector angle, as shown in the diagram.

The area of the sector is this fraction of the area of the circle.

The length of the arc is this fraction of the circumference of the circle.

$$\text{Area of a sector} = \frac{\theta}{360} \times \pi r^2$$

$$\text{Length of the arc of the sector} = \frac{\theta}{360} \times 2\pi r$$

EXAMPLE 42.2

Calculate the area and the perimeter of this sector.

Solution

Sector area $= \dfrac{\theta}{360} \times \pi r^2$

$= \dfrac{75}{360} \times \pi \times 4.6^2$

$= 13.8 \text{ cm}^2$ to 1 decimal place

Perimeter $=$ arc length $+ 2 \times 4.6$

$= \dfrac{\theta}{360} \times 2\pi r + 2 \times 4.6$

$= \dfrac{75}{360} \times 2\pi \times 4.6 + 2 \times 4.6$

$= 15.2 \text{ cm}$ to 1 decimal place

EXAMPLE 42.3

A sector has area 92 cm². The sector angle is 210°. Find the radius of the circle.

Solution

Area of the sector $= \dfrac{\theta}{360} \times \pi r^2$

$92 = \dfrac{210}{360} \times \pi r^2$

$\dfrac{92 \times 360}{210 \times \pi} = r^2$

$r = \sqrt{\dfrac{92 \times 360}{210 \times \pi}}$

$= 7.1 \text{ cm}$ to 1 decimal place

TIP Solving an equation like this involves rearranging the equation. If you prefer, you can rearrange the formula before substituting.

EXERCISE 42.2

1 Find the arc length of each of these sectors. Give your answers to the nearest millimetre.

(a) 5.4 cm, 5.4 cm, 65°

(b) 6.3 cm, 6.3 cm, 117°

(c) 10.5 cm, 10.5 cm, 230°

2 Find the area of each of the sectors in question **1**.

3 Find the sector angle of each of these sectors. Give your answers to the nearest degree.

(a) 6.5 cm, 7.2 cm, 7.2 cm

(b) 15.4 cm, 8.6 cm, 8.6 cm

(c) 3.6 cm, 3.6 cm, Area = 10.3 cm²

(d) 7.1 cm, 7.1 cm, Area = 113 cm²

4 Find the radius of each of these sectors.

(a) 3.8 cm, 24°

(b) 14.1 cm, 118°

(c) 21.8 cm, 145°

Arcs and sectors 573

5 Find the radius of each of these sectors.

(a) Area = 56 cm², 265°

(b) Area = 37.5 cm², 132°

(c) Area = 10.6 cm², 15°

(d) 316°, Area = 118 cm²

6 A sector of a circle of radius 6.2 cm has an arc length of 20.2 cm.
Calculate the angle of the sector and hence find the area of the sector.

7 A cushion is in the shape of a sector with a sector angle of 150°. The radius is 45 cm.
Edging is sewn all round the cushion. What length of edging is required?

Pyramids, cones and spheres

Discovery 42.2

(a) Cut out a sector of a circle of radius 12 cm. Each choose different sector angles.
(b) Stick the straight edges together to form a cone.
(c) Calculate the arc length of your sector.
This has become the circumference of the base of your cone.
(d) Work out the radius of the base of your cone.
Check your answer by measuring your cone.
(e) The sector area has become the curved surface area of the cone. Calculate this too.

Challenge 42.2

Replace 12 cm in Discovery 42.2 with the slant height, ℓ, of the cone.
Using a sector angle of θ, find the radius, r, of the base of the cone in terms of ℓ and θ.
Then find the area of the sector in terms of r and ℓ.

42 Length, area and volume

Here are some formulae for pyramids and cones.

> Curved surface area of a cone = $\pi r \ell$

> Volume of a pyramid = $\frac{1}{3} \times$ area of base $\times$ height

A cone is a special sort of pyramid with a circular base.

> Volume of a cone = $\frac{1}{3} \pi r^2 h$

EXAMPLE 42.4

A pyramid has a rectangular base 8 cm by 5 cm and a height of 9 cm. Calculate its volume.

Solution

Volume = $\frac{1}{3} \times$ area of base $\times$ height

$= \frac{1}{3} \times (8 \times 5) \times 9$

$= 120 \text{ cm}^3$

EXAMPLE 42.5

A cone has a slant height of 6.8 cm and its curved surface area is 91 cm². Find the radius, r, of its base.

Solution

Curved surface area = $\pi r \ell$

$91 = \pi r \times 6.8$

$r = \dfrac{91}{\pi \times 6.8}$

$= 4.3$ cm to the nearest millimetre

The other shape you meet in this section is a **sphere**. Proving the formulae for a sphere is beyond the scope of this course, but here are the results you will need.

Volume of sphere $= \frac{4}{3}\pi r^3$

Surface area of sphere $= 4\pi r^2$

EXAMPLE 42.6

A bowl is in the shape of a hemisphere of diameter 25 cm. Calculate its volume, in litres.

Solution

Volume of hemisphere $= \frac{1}{2} \times$ Volume of sphere
$= \frac{2}{3}\pi r^3$
$= \frac{2}{3}\pi \times 12.5^3$
$= 4090.6\ldots$ cm^3 (1 litre = 1000 cm^3)
$= 4.09$ litres to 3 significant figures

EXERCISE 42.3

1 Find the curved surface area of each of these cones. Give your answers to 3 significant figures.

(a) 4 cm, 5 cm, 3 cm

(b) 7.5 cm, 8.5 cm, 4.0 cm

(c) 6 cm, 6.5 cm, 2.5 cm

2 Calculate the volume of each of the cones in question **1**.

3 Calculate the volume of each of these square- or rectangular-based pyramids.

(a) 6 cm, 4 cm, 4 cm

(b) 9 cm, 8 cm, 10 cm

(c) 5.5 cm, 12 cm, 4.8 cm

576 42 Length, area and volume

4 A solid cone has a base of radius 4.2 cm and a slant height of 7.8 cm.
Calculate its total surface area.

5 A pyramid has a square base with sides of 8 cm. Its volume is 256 cm^3. Find its height.

6 Find the radius of the base of each of these cones.
  (a) Volume 114 cm^3, height 8.2 cm
  (b) Volume 52.9 cm^3, height 5.4 cm
  (c) Volume 500 cm^3, height 12.5 cm

7 A sector of a circle is joined to form a cone (as in Discovery 42.2).
Find the radius of the base of the cone made with these sectors.
  (a) Radius 5.8 cm, angle 162°
  (b) Radius 9.7 cm, angle 210°
  (c) Radius 12.1 cm, angle 295°

8 Find the surface area of each of these spheres.
  (a) Radius 5.1 cm
  (b) Radius 8.2 cm
  (c) Diameter 20 cm

9 Find the volume of each of the spheres in question **8**.

10 Find the radius of each of these spheres.
  (a) Surface area 900 cm^2
  (b) Surface area 665 cm^2
  (c) Volume 1200 cm^3
  (d) Volume 8000 cm^3

Challenge 42.3

How many glass marbles of radius 8 mm can be made from 500 cm^3 of molten glass?

Challenge 42.4

A sphere of radius 12.8 cm has the same volume as a cone of base radius 8.0 cm.
Find the height of the cone.

Compound shapes and problems

In this section you apply what you have learned already to more complex shapes and to problems involving shapes.

Two important examples of compound shapes are a segment of a circle and a frustum of a cone.

A line drawn between any two points on the circumference of a circle is called a **chord**.

A chord divides a circle into two **segments**.

The larger segment (white) is called the **major** segment; the smaller segment (green) is called the **minor** segment.

Area of the shaded segment = Area of sector AOB − Area of triangle AOB

EXAMPLE 42.7

Calculate the area of the segment shown in the diagram.

Solution

Area of the sector $= \dfrac{\theta}{360} \times \pi r^2$

$= \dfrac{74}{360} \times \pi \times 6.2^2$

$= 24.823\ldots \text{ cm}^2$

Area of triangle $= \frac{1}{2} ab \sin C$

$= \frac{1}{2} \times 6.2^2 \times \sin 74°$

$= 18.475\ldots \text{ cm}^2$

Area of segment = Area of sector − Area of triangle

$= 24.823\ldots - 18.475\ldots$

$= 6.35 \text{ cm}^2$ to 3 significant figures

The **frustum** of a cone is the shape remaining when the top of a cone has been removed.

The circle on the top of the frustum is in a plane parallel to the base.

Volume of frustum = Volume of whole cone − Volume of missing cone

42 Length, area and volume

EXAMPLE 42.8

Find the volume of the frustum remaining when a cone of height 8 cm is removed from a cone of height 12 cm and base radius 6 cm.

Solution

First, use similar triangles to find the base radius, r cm, of the cone which has been removed.

$$\frac{r}{8} = \frac{6}{12}$$
$$r = 4$$

Then find the volume of the frustum.

Volume of frustum = Volume of whole cone − Volume of missing cone
$$= \tfrac{1}{3}\pi r^2 h_1 - \tfrac{1}{3}\pi r^2 h_2$$
$$= \tfrac{1}{3}\pi \times 6^2 \times 12 - \tfrac{1}{3}\pi \times 4^2 \times 8$$
$$= 318 \text{ cm}^3 \text{ to 3 significant figures}$$

Other shape problems may use simpler shapes but require several steps to solve the problem, as in the next example.

EXAMPLE 42.9

A cone has a base of radius 5.6 cm and a volume of 82 cm³.
(a) Calculate its height.
(b) Calculate also its slant height and hence find its curved surface area.

Solution

Volume of cone $= \tfrac{1}{3}\pi r^2 h$

$$82 = \tfrac{1}{3}\pi \times 5.6^2 \times h$$
$$\frac{3 \times 82}{\pi \times 5.6^2} = h$$
$$h = 2.496...$$
$$= 2.5 \text{ cm to 1 decimal place}$$

Use Pythagoras' theorem,
$$\ell^2 = r^2 + h^2 = 5.6^2 + 2.496...^2$$
$$= 37.59...$$
$$\ell = \sqrt{37.59...} = 6.13...$$
$$= 6.1 \text{ cm to 1 decimal place}$$

Curved surface area $= \pi r \ell = \pi \times 5.6 \times 6.13...$
$$= 108 \text{ cm}^2 \text{ to 3 significant figures}$$

TIP: When using a result in further working, make sure you use the unrounded value. Do not clear your calculator until you are sure that you do not need the result again.

Compound shapes and problems

Some problems may use algebra, as in the next challenge.

Challenge 42.5

The curved surface area of a particular cylinder of radius r cm and height h cm has the same surface area as a cube of side r cm.

Find h in terms of r.

EXERCISE 42.4

1. Calculate the area of each of the orange segments.
   (a) 50°, 6.7 cm
   (b) 8.2 cm, 104°
   (c) 116°, 9.1 cm

2. A grain silo is in the shape of a cylinder of height 25 m and radius 4 m topped by a hemisphere.
   Calculate the volume of the silo.

3. Calculate the area of each of the green major segments.
   (a) 120°, 8.1 cm
   (b) 5.4 cm, 136°
   (c) 12.4 cm, 175°

4. A piece of cheese is a prism of height 7 cm.
   Its cross-section is a sector of a circle with radius 15 cm and sector angle 72°.
   Calculate the volume of the piece of cheese.

42 Length, area and volume

5 Calculate the perpendicular height of each of these cones and hence find their volumes.

(a) 9.1 cm, 5.4 cm

(b) 5.8 cm, 3.6 cm

(c) 13.2 cm, 8.6 cm

6 A solid cone has a base of radius 6.9 cm and a height of 8.2 cm.
  (a) Calculate its volume.
  (b) Find its slant height and hence its total surface area.

7 The top of a flowerpot is a circle of radius 10 cm.
  Its base is a circle of radius 8 cm.
  The height of the flowerpot is 10 cm.
  (a) Show that the flowerpot is a frustum of an inverted cone of complete height 50 cm and base radius 10 cm.
  (b) Calculate how many litres of soil the flowerpot can contain.

8 A cone has a height of 20 cm and a base radius of 12 cm.
  The top 15 cm of the cone is removed to leave a frustum of height 5 cm.
  Find the volume of this frustum.

9 A pyramid has a square base of side 10.4 cm and its sloping edges are all 8.8 cm long.
  Calculate the perpendicular height and the volume of the pyramid.

10 A sector with angle 300° and radius 12.5 cm is joined to form a hollow cone.
   Showing your method clearly, calculate the volume of the cone.

WHAT YOU HAVE LEARNED

- Curved surface area of a cylinder = $2\pi rh$
- Dimensions of formulae:
  - number × length = length (1 dimension)
  - length + length = length (1 dimension)
  - length × length = area (2 dimensions)
  - length × length × length = volume (3 dimensions)
  - area × length = volume (3 dimensions)
- Area of a sector = $\dfrac{\theta}{360} \times \pi r^2$
- Arc length of a sector = $\dfrac{\theta}{360} \times 2\pi r$

- **Volume of a pyramid** = $\frac{1}{3} \times$ area of base $\times$ height
- **Volume of a cone** = $\frac{1}{3}\pi r^2 h$
- **Curved surface area of a cone** = $\pi r \ell$
- **Volume of a sphere** = $\frac{4}{3}\pi r^3$
- **Surface area of a sphere** = $4\pi r^2$
- **Area of a minor segment** = Area of sector − Area of triangle
- **Volume of a frustum** = Volume of whole cone − Volume of missing cone

MIXED EXERCISE 42

1 A prism has a height of 72 cm and a volume of 13 320 cm³.
Calculate the area of its cross-section.

2 A cube has a volume of 729 cm³.
Calculate the length of its diagonal and its total surface area.

3 A wastepaper bin is a cylinder with a diameter of 22 cm and a height of 36 cm.
Calculate the total surface area of the outside of the bin.

4 The letters in these formulae all represent lengths.
Which of the formulae represent a length?
 (a) $\sqrt{6a^2}$ (b) $\dfrac{4bc}{d}$ (c) $2a(c + d)$ (d) $\dfrac{2\pi a}{5}$

5 Classify these formulae into those representing length, area, volume or none of these.
The letters in the formulae all represent lengths.
 (a) $\sqrt{a^2 + b^2}$ (b) $a^2(2a + b)$ (c) $\pi(4a + 3bc)$ (d) $\pi a^2 + 3ac$

6 Calculate the arc length and the area of each of these sectors.
 (a) Radius 6.2 cm, sector angle 62°
 (b) Radius 7.8 cm, sector angle 256°

7 Find the sector angle of each of these sectors.
 (a) Radius 4.6 cm, arc length 9.2 cm
 (b) Radius 5.7 cm, area 85.6 cm²

8 A spinning top is a solid inverted cone of height 12.5 cm and base radius 6.7 cm.
Find its total surface area.

9 A sphere has a volume of 127 cm³.
Find its radius.

10 A wastepaper bin is the frustum of a cone.
It has a top radius of 20 cm, a bottom radius of 15 cm and a height of 40 cm.
Find the volume of rubbish that it can contain.

43 → PROBABILITY 2

THIS CHAPTER IS ABOUT

- The addition rule for mutually exclusive events, P(A or B) = P(A) + P(B)
- The multiplication rule for independent events, P(A and B) = P(A) × P(B)
- Probability tree diagrams
- Finding probabilities of dependent events

YOU SHOULD ALREADY KNOW

- That a probability can be expressed as a fraction or as a decimal
- How to find probability from a set of equally likely outcomes
- P(an outcome not happening) = 1 − P(the outcome happening)
- How to add, subtract and multiply decimals
- How to add, subtract and multiply fractions

The addition rule for mutually exclusive events

Events A and B are **mutually exclusive** if A and B cannot both occur at the same time.

For mutually exclusive events A and B,

$$P(A \text{ or } B) = P(A) + P(B).$$

TIP Remember: P(A) means the probability of A happening.

The addition rule is sometimes also called the 'or' rule.

EXAMPLE 43.1

The probability that the school hockey team will win their next match is 0.4.
The probability that the school hockey team will draw their next match is 0.3.
What is the probability that they will win or draw their next match?

Solution

The results are mutually exclusive since they can't both win and draw their next match.

P(win or draw) = P(win) + P(draw)
             = 0.4 + 0.3 = 0.7

Sometimes two events are not completely separate so they are not mutually exclusive. In these cases you cannot just add the probabilities of the two events.

> **EXAMPLE 43.2**
>
> One card is drawn at random from an ordinary pack of 52.
> What is the probability that it will be
> (a) a red card?
> (b) an ace?
> (c) a red card or an ace?
>
> **Solution**
> (a) P(red card) = $\frac{26}{52} = \frac{1}{2}$
>
> (b) P(an ace) = $\frac{4}{52} = \frac{1}{13}$
>
> (c) There are 26 red cards (including 2 aces) and 2 black aces. This makes 28 favourable outcomes.
> P(red card or ace) = $\frac{28}{52} = \frac{7}{13}$

It would be wrong to use the addition rule in Example 43.2 because the two events, red card and ace, are not mutually exclusive. They can occur together (when the card is the ace of hearts or the ace of diamonds). Because of this you have to work out the required probability by working out the number of favourable outcomes.

Notice that $\frac{26}{52} + \frac{4}{52} \neq \frac{28}{52}$

> **TIP**
> It is important to note that many questions involving mutually exclusive events can be answered without using the addition rule. Sometimes it just requires you to count up the number of favourable outcomes.

Check up 43.1

A fair dice is thrown.

Put the following events into pairs so that each of the events in a pair are mutually exclusive.

A: Getting a 6
B: Getting a prime number
C: Getting a factor of 4
D: Getting a 2
E: Getting an odd number
F: Getting a number greater than 4

The multiplication rule for independent events

Two events are **independent** when the outcome of the second event is not affected by the outcome of the first.

For two independent events A and B,

$$P(A \text{ and } B) = P(A) \times P(B).$$

The multiplication rule is sometimes also called the 'and' rule.

EXAMPLE 43.3

A dice is thrown twice.
What is the probability that a six occurs on both throws?

Solution

Since the outcome of the second throw is unaffected by the outcome of the first throw, these are independent events.

$P(\text{two sixes}) = P(\text{six and six}) = P(\text{six}) \times P(\text{six}) = \frac{1}{6} \times \frac{1}{6} = \frac{1}{36}$

EXAMPLE 43.4

It is known that the probability that a certain type of seed will germinate is 0.8.
What is the probability that four seeds sown will all germinate?

Solution

$P(\text{4 seeds germinate}) = P(\text{seed 1 and seed 2 and seed 3 and seed 4 germinate})$
$\qquad\qquad\qquad\qquad\; = 0.8 \times 0.8 \times 0.8 \times 0.8$
$\qquad\qquad\qquad\qquad\; = 0.4096$

EXAMPLE 43.5

There are six black counters and four white counters in a bag.
Elaine chooses a counter at random, notes its colour and replaces it.
She then chooses another counter.
What is the probability that she chooses one counter of each colour?

Solution

Since the counter is replaced, the second choice is independent of the first. The probabilities stay the same each time she chooses.

One counter of each colour could arise in two different ways:

　　　black then white
or　　white then black.

P(one counter of each colour) = P(black **and** white) **or** P(white **and** black)
$$= P(black) \times P(white) + P(white) \times P(black)$$
$$= \tfrac{6}{10} \times \tfrac{4}{10} + \tfrac{4}{10} \times \tfrac{6}{10}$$
$$= \tfrac{24}{100} + \tfrac{24}{100}$$
$$= \tfrac{48}{100} = \tfrac{12}{25}$$

Check up 43.2

This is the answer sheet to the multi-choice section of a pub quiz.

Bill's team are not very good and decide to randomly guess the answers.

What is the probability that they guess all five answers correctly?

ANSWER SHEET

1. (a)　(b)　(c)
2. (a)　(b)
3. (a)　(b)　(c)
4. (a)　(b)　(c)　(d)
5. (a)　(b)

EXERCISE 43.1

1 A bag contains ten red balls, five blue balls and eight green balls.
What is the probability of selecting
　(a) a red ball or a blue ball?　　　(b) a green ball or a red ball?

2 When Mrs Smith goes to town the probability that she goes by bus is 0.5, in a taxi is 0.35 and on foot is 0.15.
What is the probability that she goes to town
　(a) by bus or taxi?　　　(b) by bus or on foot?

3 In any batch of computers made by a company, the probabilities of the number of faults per computer are as follows.

Number of faults	0	1	2	3	4	5
Probability	0.44	0.39	0.14	0.02	0.008	0.002

What is the probability that any particular computer will have
　(a) 1 or 2 faults?　　(b) 2, 3 or 4 faults?　　(c) an odd number of faults?
　(d) fewer than 2 faults?　　(e) at least 1 fault?

4 Channel 10 weather report says

> The probability of rain on Saturday is $\frac{3}{5}$ and the probability of rain on Sunday is $\frac{1}{2}$. This means it is certain to rain on Saturday or Sunday.

Explain why the report is wrong. What mistake have they made?

5 A coin is tossed and a dice is thrown.
What is the probability of getting a head on the coin and an odd number on the dice?

6 A spinner is numbered 1 to 5.
The spinner is spun three times.
What is the probability that the spinner lands on 1 each time?

7 The probability that Holly wins the 100-metre race is 0.4.
The probability that Robert wins the 400-metre race is 0.3.
What is the probability that
  (a) Holly and Robert both win their race?
  (b) neither of them wins their race?

8 Each of the letters of the word INDEPENDENT is written on a card.
The cards are shuffled and one is selected.
This card is returned to the pack which is again shuffled.
A second card is selected.
What is the probability that the two cards are
  (a) both P?   **(b)** both N?   **(c)** both a vowel?

9 A box contains a large number of red counters and a large number of black counters.
25% of the counters are red.
A counter is chosen from the box, its colour is noted and it is replaced.
A second counter is then chosen.
What is the probability that
  (a) both counters are red?
  (b) both counters are black?
  (c) one counter of each colour is chosen?

10 The probability that a darts player hits the bull's eye is 0.6.
He has three throws at the dartboard.
What is the probability that
  (a) he hits the bull's eye each time?
  (b) he misses the bull's eye each time?
  (c) he hits the bull's eye on two of his three throws?

Probability tree diagrams

When you are dealing with two or more events occurring, you can show the possible outcomes and their probabilities on a tree diagram. 'Branches' are drawn to show the possibilities for each event. Some of the questions in Exercise 43.1 could have been answered using a probability tree diagram.

This method can be a useful way of setting out the different possible outcomes of a series of events and can be extended, if necessary, to take account of any subsequent events.

> **TIP** A tree diagram can look very messy if you are not careful with your presentation. Give yourself plenty of space and make sure that you don't draw the branches too close together.

EXAMPLE 43.6

The probability that I am woken by my alarm any morning is 0.7.
(a) Draw a probability tree diagram to show whether I am woken by my alarm on two days.
(b) Use the tree diagram to work out the probability that
  (i) I am woken by my alarm on both days.
  (ii) I am woken by my alarm on just one of the two days.

Solution

(a)

First day	Second day	Outcome	Probability
Woken (0.7)	Woken (0.7)	WW	$0.7 \times 0.7 = 0.49$
Woken (0.7)	Not woken (0.3)	WN	$0.7 \times 0.3 = 0.21$
Not woken (0.3)	Woken (0.7)	NW	$0.3 \times 0.7 = 0.21$
Not woken (0.3)	Not woken (0.3)	NN	$0.3 \times 0.3 = 0.09$

> **TIP** Notice how you can use letters to make the work less cluttered.

You *multiply* the probabilities when you follow each path *along* the branches of the tree.

You *add* the probabilities *down* when you are interested in more than one possible outcome.

> **TIP:** A good check to see if you have completed the tree correctly is to add the final probabilities together. The total should be 1.

(b) (i) P(woken both days) = $0.7 \times 0.7 = 0.49$
(ii) P(woken one of the days) = $0.7 \times 0.3 + 0.3 \times 0.7$
$= 0.21 + 0.21 = 0.42$

EXAMPLE 43.7

A bag contains five red balls and three green balls.
A ball is selected from the bag at random. Its colour is checked and it is returned to the bag.
A second ball is then selected.
What is the probability that
(a) both balls are green?
(b) both balls are the same colour?
(c) at least one of the balls is red?

Solution

First ball	Second ball	Outcome	Probability
red ($\frac{5}{8}$)	red ($\frac{5}{8}$)	RR	$\frac{5}{8} \times \frac{5}{8} = \frac{25}{64}$
	green ($\frac{3}{8}$)	RG	$\frac{5}{8} \times \frac{3}{8} = \frac{15}{64}$
green ($\frac{3}{8}$)	red ($\frac{5}{8}$)	GR	$\frac{3}{8} \times \frac{5}{8} = \frac{15}{64}$
	green ($\frac{3}{8}$)	GG	$\frac{3}{8} \times \frac{3}{8} = \frac{9}{64}$

(a) P(both green) = $\frac{9}{64}$

(b) P(both same colour) = P(both green) + P(both red)
$= \frac{9}{64} + \frac{25}{64}$
$= \frac{34}{64} = \frac{17}{32}$

> **TIP:** Do not cancel fractions until your final answer. You will find it easier to add them when they have the same denominator.

(c) P(at least one red) = P(one red) + P(two reds)
$= \frac{15}{64} + \frac{15}{64} + \frac{25}{64} = \frac{55}{64}$

Or
P(at least one red) = 1 − P(no red)
$= 1 - \frac{9}{64} = \frac{55}{64}$

EXERCISE 43.2

1 Terry is playing a board game where two dice are thrown each turn.
To start the game he must throw the two dice and get two sixes.

(a) Copy and complete the tree diagram.

```
First dice        Second dice      Outcome      Probability

                    Six              SS
        Six  <
                    Not a six        SN

                    Six              NS
        Not a six <
                    Not a six        NN
```

(b) Use the tree diagram to work out the probability that
  (i) Terry gets two sixes.
  (ii) Terry gets just one six.

2 The probability that the bus to school is late on any day is 0.2.
  (a) Draw a tree diagram to show the bus being late or not late on two days.
  (b) Work out the probability that the school bus is
  (i) not late on either of the days.
  (ii) late on one of the two days.

3 There are seven black discs and three white discs in a bag.
A disc is selected, its colour is noted and it is then replaced in the bag.
A second disc is then selected.
  (a) Draw a probability tree diagram to show the outcomes of the two selections.
  (b) Use the tree diagram to find the probability that
  (i) both discs are black.
  (ii) both discs are the same colour.
  (iii) at least one disc is white.

4 The probability that the school team win, draw or lose any match is 0.5, 0.3 and 0.2 respectively.

 (a) Copy and complete the tree diagram to show the outcomes of the next two matches.

```
    First match    Second match   Outcome    Probability
                        W
              W ───── D
                        L
                        W
              D ───── D
                        L
                        W
              L ───── D
                        L
```

 (b) Work out the probability that
   (i) the team win both of their matches.
   (ii) the team win one of the two matches.
   (iii) the results of the two matches are the same.

5 A coin is tossed three times.
 (a) Draw a tree diagram with three sets of branches to show all the possible outcomes.
 (b) Work out the probability that
   (i) the result is three heads.
   (ii) exactly two heads are obtained.
   (iii) at least two tails are obtained.

Challenge 43.1

There are x red balls and y blue balls in a bag.
A ball is chosen at random from the bag.
The ball is replaced and another is chosen.
What is the probability of choosing
(a) one ball of each colour?
(b) two balls of the same colour?
Give your answers in terms of x and y as a single fraction in its simplest form.

Dependent events

So far in this chapter, the outcome of the second event was not influenced by the result of the first event. There are, however, many situations where the outcome of the second event is dependent on what happened in the first event. These are called **dependent events**. Since the probability of the second event is influenced by the outcome of the first event it is called a **conditional probability**.

Tree diagrams can be used to represent dependent events, as is illustrated in the next examples.

EXAMPLE 43.8

There are 10 boys and 15 girls in a Maths class.
Two students are to be chosen at random to represent the class in a competition.
What is the probability that the team will consist of one boy and one girl?

Solution

The probabilities for the second event are out of 24 since one of the students has already been selected in the first choice and so only 24 remain to be chosen from.

First choice	Second choice	Outcome	Probability
Boy ($\frac{10}{25}$)	Boy ($\frac{9}{24}$)	BB	$\frac{10}{25} \times \frac{9}{24} = \frac{90}{600}$
	Girl ($\frac{15}{24}$)	BG	$\frac{10}{25} \times \frac{15}{24} = \frac{150}{600}$
Girl ($\frac{15}{25}$)	Boy ($\frac{10}{24}$)	GB	$\frac{15}{25} \times \frac{10}{24} = \frac{150}{600}$
	Girl ($\frac{14}{24}$)	GG	$\frac{15}{25} \times \frac{14}{24} = \frac{210}{600}$

P(one boy and one girl) $= \frac{150}{600} + \frac{150}{600} = \frac{300}{600} = \frac{1}{2}$

EXAMPLE 43.9

Whether I catch the bus to work or not depends on the weather.
The probability that it rains on any day is 0.3.
When it rains the probability that I catch the bus to work is 0.9.
When it doesn't rain the probability that I catch the bus is 0.2.
What is the probability that I catch the bus on any given day?

Solution

```
              Weather        Transport      Outcome     Probability

                         0.9    Bus          RB         0.3 × 0.9 = 0.27
                 Rain
         0.3
                         0.1    Not bus      RN         0.3 × 0.1 = 0.03

                         0.2    Bus          NB         0.7 × 0.2 = 0.14
         0.7
                Not rain
                         0.8    Not bus      NN         0.7 × 0.8 = 0.56
```

P(catch the bus) = 0.27 + 0.14 = 0.41

EXERCISE 43.3

1. There are seven yellow balls and four red balls in a box.
   A ball is selected at random and not replaced.
   A second ball is then selected.
   (a) Draw a probability tree diagram to show all the possible outcomes.
   (b) Find the probability that the two balls are
      (i) both yellow.
      (ii) one of each colour.

2. There are 500 electronic components in a box.
   It is known that 100 are defective.
   Two components are selected at random without replacement.
   What is the probability that
   (a) both are defective?
   (b) at least one is defective?

3. Judith and Suki play two games of tennis.
   The probability of Judith winning the first game is 0.7.
   If she wins the first game, the probability of her winning the second game is 0.7. If she loses the first game, however, the probability of her winning the second game is 0.5.
   (a) Draw a probability tree diagram to show the possible outcomes.
   (b) What is the probability of
      (i) Judith winning both games?
      (ii) Suki winning both games?
      (iii) Judith and Suki winning one game each?

4 The probability that the school basketball team will win their next match is 0.6.
If they win the next match, the probability that they will win the following match is 0.7, otherwise it is 0.4.
What is the probability that
   (a) they win their next two matches?
   (b) they win one of their next two matches?

5 At a school fair, thirty tickets numbered 1 to 30 are placed in a box.
People pay to choose a ticket from the box.
A ticket, drawn from the box wins a prize if its number is a multiple of 5.
Once drawn, a ticket is not replaced.
John chooses three tickets, one after the other, from the box.
What is the probability that
   (a) none of his tickets win?
   (b) at least one of his tickets wins?
   (c) two of his tickets win a prize?

Challenge 43.2

Frodo is searching a castle for the treasure room.
He has a bunch of five keys, only one of which will open the door to the treasure.
He does not know which key will open the door.
Frodo tries the keys in turn.
What is the probability that
(a) the first key he tries opens the door?
(b) the first key does not open the door but the second key does?
(c) the third key he tries opens the door?
(d) the fourth key he tries opens the door?
(e) the fifth key he tries opens the door?

Challenge 43.3

There are x red balls and y blue balls in a bag.
A ball is chosen at random from the bag.
Then another is chosen, without replacing the first.
What is the probability of choosing
(a) one ball of each colour?
(b) two balls of the same colour?
Give your answers in terms of x and y as a single fraction in its simplest form.

WHAT YOU HAVE LEARNED

- For mutually exclusive events A and B, P(A or B) = P(A) + P(B)
- For independent events A and B, P(A and B) = P(A) × P(B)
- How to use probability tree diagrams
- For dependent events, conditional probabilities are used

MIXED EXERCISE 43

1 In a school, every student has to take art, music or drama.
60% of the students study art and 25% of the students study music.
A student is chosen at random.
What is the probability that they study
   (a) art or music?
   (b) drama or music?

2 A tin of biscuits contains ten chocolate biscuits, eight cream biscuits and seven plain biscuits.
A biscuit is chosen at random from the tin.
What is the probability that it is
   (a) a chocolate or a plain biscuit?
   (b) a cream or a plain biscuit?

3 During any week, I take sandwiches for my school lunch, have a meal in the school canteen or go home for my lunch.
The probability that I take sandwiches for my school lunch is 0.4 and the probability that I have a meal in the school canteen is 0.1.
What is the probability that, for my lunch one day
   (a) I either take sandwiches or go to the school canteen?
   (b) I either take sandwiches or go home?

4 A spinner is numbered 1 to 5.
In two spins, what is the probability that I get
   (a) a 1 on the first spin and a 5 on the second spin?
   (b) a 3 or a 4 on each of the two spins?
   (c) an even number on the first spin and an odd number on the second spin?

5 One bag contains two red sweets, one orange sweet and four yellow sweets.
A second bag contains one green sweet, two black sweets and three purple sweets.
One sweet is taken at random from each bag.
What is the probability that
   (a) one is orange and one is green?
   (b) one is red and one is purple?
   (c) one is either red or yellow and one is either black or purple?

6 An ordinary dice is thrown three times.
What is the probability of obtaining three sixes?

7 There are two black discs and three white discs in a bag.
A disc is selected, its colour noted and it is then replaced in the bag.
A second disc is then selected.
   (a) Draw a probability tree diagram to show the outcomes of the two selections.
   (b) Use the tree diagram to find the probability that
      (i) both discs are black.
      (ii) both discs are the same colour.
      (iii) there is one disc of each colour.

8 70% of the plants grown from a large batch of seeds will have a red flower.
Two plants grown from this batch are selected at random and the colour of the flowers produced noted.
   (a) Copy and complete the tree diagram.

   First plant   **Second plant**   **Outcome**   **Probability**

   Red — Red → RR
   Red — Not red → RN
   Not red — Red → NR
   Not red — Not red → NN

   (b) Use the tree diagram to work out the probability that
      (i) neither plant has red flowers.
      (ii) one of the plants has red flowers.

9 A small box of chocolates contains four chocolates with hard centres and five chocolates with soft centres.
One chocolate is taken at random from the box and eaten.
Then a second one is taken.
What is the probability that
   (a) both centres are of the same type?   **(b)** there is one of each type of centre?

10 There are two fuses in a circuit.
The probability that the first fuse will blow is 0.2.
If the first fuse blows, the probability that the next fuse will blow is 0.7, otherwise it is 0.1.
What is the probability that
   (a) both fuses will blow?   **(b)** one of the two fuses will blow?

44 VECTORS

THIS CHAPTER IS ABOUT
- Column vectors
- Vectors representing quantities that have magnitude and direction
- Addition and subtraction of vectors
- Multiplying a vector by a scalar quantity
- Using vectors to solve geometry problems

YOU SHOULD ALREADY KNOW
- How to use column vectors to represent translations
- The geometry of triangles, squares, rectangles and parallelograms
- How to simplify and factorise algebraic expressions

The definition of a vector

A vector is any quantity that has **magnitude** and **direction**.

Vector quantities include translation (change of position), velocity, acceleration and force.

Since an arrow has magnitude (length) and direction, vectors are represented on a diagram by an arrow.

Vectors are labelled either by using the end points and an arrow or using a small letter.

$\overrightarrow{AB} = \mathbf{a}$

In text books and examination papers when vectors are represented using a single letter that letter is in bold type. When you write a vector in this form you should use a line under the letter: $\overrightarrow{AB} = \underline{a}$.

Column vectors

If a vector is drawn on a grid then it can be represented by a column vector $\begin{pmatrix} p \\ q \end{pmatrix}$, where p is the displacement in the x direction and q is the displacement in the y direction.

The definition of a vector 597

In the diagram

$$\vec{AB} = \begin{pmatrix} 3 \\ 2 \end{pmatrix}, \vec{CD} = \begin{pmatrix} -1 \\ 3 \end{pmatrix} \text{ and } \vec{EF} = \begin{pmatrix} -4 \\ 1 \end{pmatrix}.$$

Notice that the conventions are the same as for coordinates.

x (horizontal) direction first: to the right positive, to the left negative.
y (vertical) direction second: up positive, down negative.

With vectors, the numbers are written vertically rather than side by side as in coordinates. Note also that coordinates are relative to an origin whereas vectors are relative to the start point of the vector.

Check up 44.1

(a) Write down the column vectors representing each of these vectors.
$\vec{AB}, \vec{BA}, \vec{AC}, \vec{EB}, \vec{BC}, \vec{CA}, \vec{EC}, \vec{CD}, \vec{DE}$ and $\vec{ED}$

(b) $\vec{XY} = \begin{pmatrix} a \\ b \end{pmatrix}$.

Write down the column vector for $\vec{YX}$.

Multiplying a vector by a scalar

Discovery 44.1

(a) Draw the vectors $\begin{pmatrix} 2 \\ 3 \end{pmatrix}, \begin{pmatrix} 4 \\ 6 \end{pmatrix}, \begin{pmatrix} 6 \\ 9 \end{pmatrix}, \begin{pmatrix} -2 \\ -3 \end{pmatrix}$ and $\begin{pmatrix} -4 \\ -6 \end{pmatrix}$ on squared paper.

Do not forget the arrows.
What do you notice?

(b) On another piece of squared paper draw these vectors.

$\begin{pmatrix} -1 \\ 2 \end{pmatrix}, \begin{pmatrix} -2 \\ 4 \end{pmatrix}, \begin{pmatrix} -3 \\ 6 \end{pmatrix}, \begin{pmatrix} 1 \\ -2 \end{pmatrix}$ and $\begin{pmatrix} 2 \\ -4 \end{pmatrix}$

What do you notice?

A quantity that has magnitude but not direction is called a **scalar**.

Look again at the vectors you drew in Discovery 44.1.

The first three vectors in each case were parallel to each other, that is, in the same direction, and the last two were in the opposite direction.

This is because, for example, $\binom{4}{6} = 2\binom{2}{3}$ and $\binom{6}{9} = 3\binom{2}{3}$.

$\binom{4}{6}$ is twice as long as $\binom{2}{3}$ and $\binom{6}{9}$ is three times as long as $\binom{2}{3}$.

Multiplying a vector by a scalar produces a vector in the same direction but longer by a factor equal to the scalar.

The last two vectors in each set are in the opposite direction to the original vector.

This is because, for example, $\binom{1}{-2} = -\binom{-1}{2}$ and $\binom{2}{-4} = -2\binom{-1}{2}$.

In this diagram, the vector **b** is in the same direction as **a** and is three times as long.

So   **b** = 3**a**.

The vector **c** is in the opposite direction to **a** and is twice as long.

So   **c** = −2**a**.

Challenge 44.1

Use the vectors **a**, **b** and **c** from the diagram above to find the scalar, k, in each of these cases.
(Hint: you will need fractions.)
(a) **a** = k**c**   (b) **a** = k**b**   (c) **b** = k**c**   (d) **c** = k**b**

EXAMPLE 44.1

Find the column vector that maps
(a) (2, 1) on to (5, 6).
(b) (−1, 6) on to (5, 2).

Multiplying a vector by a scalar   599

Solution

(a) The *x*-coordinate has changed from 2 to 5 so the increase is 3.
The *y*-coordinate has changed from 1 to 6 so the increase is 5.

The vector is $\begin{pmatrix} 3 \\ 5 \end{pmatrix}$.

(b) The *x*-coordinate has changed from −1 to 5 so the increase is 6.
The *y*-coordinate has changed from 6 to 2 so the decrease is 4.

The vector is $\begin{pmatrix} 6 \\ -4 \end{pmatrix}$.

> **TIP** As you can see, it is not necessary to plot the points to do this question. However, you may prefer to do so.

EXAMPLE 44.2

Write each of these vectors in terms of **a**.
$\vec{AB}, \vec{CD}, \vec{EF}, \vec{GH}, \vec{IJ}$

Solution

$\vec{AB} = 2\mathbf{a}, \quad \vec{CD} = -\mathbf{a}, \quad \vec{EF} = -3\mathbf{a}, \quad \vec{GH} = \tfrac{3}{2}\mathbf{a}, \quad \vec{IJ} = -\tfrac{1}{2}\mathbf{a}$

If you know that $\vec{AB} = k\vec{CD}$, you can conclude that
- $\vec{AB}$ is parallel to $\vec{CD}$
- $\vec{AB}$ is *k* times the length of $\vec{CD}$.

If you know that $\vec{AB} = k\vec{AC}$ and there is a common point A, you can conclude that
- A, B and C are in a straight line
- $\vec{AB}$ is *k* times the length of $\vec{AC}$.

600 44 Vectors

EXERCISE 44.1

1 On squared paper, draw and label vectors to represent these column vectors.
Do not forget to put the arrows on.

$\mathbf{a} = \begin{pmatrix} 5 \\ 2 \end{pmatrix}$, $\mathbf{b} = \begin{pmatrix} 3 \\ -4 \end{pmatrix}$, $\mathbf{c} = \begin{pmatrix} -3 \\ 1 \end{pmatrix}$, $\mathbf{d} = \begin{pmatrix} 4 \\ 0 \end{pmatrix}$, $\mathbf{e} = \begin{pmatrix} 0 \\ -3 \end{pmatrix}$, $\mathbf{f} = \begin{pmatrix} -2 \\ -4 \end{pmatrix}$

2 Write down column vectors to represent these vectors.
(a) $\vec{AB}$ (b) $\vec{BA}$ (c) $\vec{EA}$ (d) $\vec{AC}$
(e) $\vec{BC}$ (f) $\vec{ED}$ (g) $\vec{AD}$ (h) $\vec{BE}$

3 Find the column vector that maps the point
(a) (2, 5) on to (6, 5). (b) (0, 2) on to (5, 5). (c) (6, 2) on to (2, 7).
(d) (−1, 4) on to (5, 1). (e) (5, 1) on to (3, −4). (f) (−6, 3) on to (−2, −1).

4 Write each of these vectors in terms of **a** or **b** as shown in the diagram.
(a) $\vec{AB}$ (b) $\vec{CD}$ (c) $\vec{EF}$ (d) $\vec{GH}$
(e) $\vec{IJ}$ (f) $\vec{KL}$ (g) $\vec{MN}$ (h) $\vec{PQ}$

5 OABC is a parallelogram.
D, E, F and G are the midpoints of the sides.
$\overrightarrow{OA} = \mathbf{a}$ and $\overrightarrow{OC} = \mathbf{c}$.

Write down each of these vectors in terms of **a** or **c**.

(a) $\overrightarrow{AO}$ (b) $\overrightarrow{CF}$ (c) $\overrightarrow{AB}$
(d) $\overrightarrow{DA}$ (e) $\overrightarrow{BE}$ (f) $\overrightarrow{BF}$

6 Copy and complete this table.

	Original point	Vector	New point
(a)	(2, 4)	$\binom{3}{2}$	
(b)	(3, 2)	$\binom{5}{-1}$	
(c)	(6, 3)	$\binom{-4}{-2}$	
(d)	(−1, 5)	$\binom{3}{-4}$	
(e)	(−4, −3)	$\binom{5}{-2}$	
(f)	(6, −2)	$\binom{2}{-4}$	

Addition and subtraction of vectors

Vectors are added and subtracted using the triangle rule.

Addition

In the diagram,
$$\overrightarrow{AB} + \overrightarrow{BC} = \overrightarrow{AC}$$
or $\mathbf{p} + \mathbf{q} = \mathbf{r}$.

In this diagram, ABCD is a parallelogram and so $\overrightarrow{AB} = \overrightarrow{DC}$ and $\overrightarrow{BC} = \overrightarrow{AD}$.

Notice that

$$\overrightarrow{AB} + \overrightarrow{BC} = \overrightarrow{AC} \text{ and } \overrightarrow{AD} + \overrightarrow{DC} = \overrightarrow{AC}.$$

This means that

$\mathbf{p} + \mathbf{q} = \mathbf{r}$ and $\mathbf{q} + \mathbf{p} = \mathbf{r}$.

In other words it does not matter in which order you do vector addition.

The rule can be extended to adding more than two vectors.

$\overrightarrow{AB} + \overrightarrow{BC} + \overrightarrow{CD} + \overrightarrow{DE} = \overrightarrow{AE}$

Notice that the last letter of each vector is the same as the first letter of the next.

Subtraction

To do subtraction you use the fact that $\mathbf{p} - \mathbf{q} = \mathbf{p} + (-\mathbf{q})$.

Addition and subtraction with column vectors

In the diagram, $\mathbf{a} = \begin{pmatrix} 3 \\ 1 \end{pmatrix}$ and $\mathbf{b} = \begin{pmatrix} 2 \\ -3 \end{pmatrix}$.

You can see that

$\mathbf{a} + \mathbf{b} = \begin{pmatrix} 3 \\ 1 \end{pmatrix} + \begin{pmatrix} 2 \\ -3 \end{pmatrix} = \begin{pmatrix} 5 \\ -2 \end{pmatrix}$

and $\mathbf{a} - \mathbf{b} = \mathbf{a} + (-\mathbf{b}) = \begin{pmatrix} 3 \\ 1 \end{pmatrix} - \begin{pmatrix} 2 \\ -3 \end{pmatrix} = \begin{pmatrix} 1 \\ 4 \end{pmatrix}$.

So, to add or subtract column vectors, you simply add or subtract the components.

$$\begin{pmatrix} a \\ b \end{pmatrix} + \begin{pmatrix} c \\ d \end{pmatrix} = \begin{pmatrix} a + c \\ b + d \end{pmatrix} \text{ and } \begin{pmatrix} a \\ b \end{pmatrix} - \begin{pmatrix} c \\ d \end{pmatrix} = \begin{pmatrix} a - c \\ b - d \end{pmatrix}$$

Addition and subtraction of vectors

Challenge 44.2

Find five different routes from A to E using one or more of the points B, C and D.

For each of your routes write down the vector additions and check that all the column vectors add up to the column vector for $\vec{AE}$.

EXAMPLE 44.3

OABC is a parallelogram.
D, E, F and G are the midpoints of the sides.
$\vec{OA} = \mathbf{a}$ and $\vec{OC} = \mathbf{c}$
Write down each of these vectors in terms of **a** or **c**.
(a) $\vec{OB}$ (b) $\vec{OE}$ (c) $\vec{AC}$
(d) $\vec{GA}$ (e) $\vec{BD}$ (f) $\vec{EF}$

Solution

(a) $\vec{OB} = \vec{OA} + \vec{AB} = \mathbf{a} + \mathbf{c}$ (b) $\vec{OE} = \vec{OA} + \vec{AE} = \mathbf{a} + \frac{1}{2}\mathbf{c}$

When you go in the opposite direction to the arrow, you use the negative vector.

(c) $\vec{AC} = \vec{AO} + \vec{OC} = -\mathbf{a} + \mathbf{c}$ (d) $\vec{GA} = \vec{GO} + \vec{OA} = -\frac{1}{2}\mathbf{c} + \mathbf{a}$

(e) $\vec{BD} = \vec{BA} + \vec{AD} = -\mathbf{c} - \frac{1}{2}\mathbf{a}$ (f) $\vec{EF} = \vec{EB} + \vec{BF} = \frac{1}{2}\mathbf{c} - \frac{1}{2}\mathbf{a}$

> **TIP**
> When you are working out a vector such as $\vec{GA}$ above, there may have been another route going through other points. For example, you could have used $\vec{GC} + \vec{CB} + \vec{BA}$ but $\vec{GO} + \vec{OA}$ is shorter and does not require simplifying.

To simplify vectors you use the normal rules of algebra. This is shown in the next example.

EXAMPLE 44.4

In the diagram, M is the midpoint of AB.
$\overrightarrow{OA} = \mathbf{a}$ and $\overrightarrow{OB} = \mathbf{b}$
Find each of these vectors as simply as possible, in terms of **a** and **b**.
(a) $\overrightarrow{AB}$ (b) $\overrightarrow{OM}$

Solution

(a) $\overrightarrow{AB} = \overrightarrow{AO} + \overrightarrow{OB}$
$= -\mathbf{a} + \mathbf{b}$

(b) $\overrightarrow{OM} = \overrightarrow{OA} + \overrightarrow{AM}$
$= \mathbf{a} + \frac{1}{2}(-\mathbf{a} + \mathbf{b})$
$= \mathbf{a} - \frac{1}{2}\mathbf{a} + \frac{1}{2}\mathbf{b}$
$= \frac{1}{2}\mathbf{a} + \frac{1}{2}\mathbf{b}$

EXERCISE 44.2

1 The diagram shows the vectors **a** and **b**.
   (a) Draw vectors **a** and **b** on squared paper.
   (b) Draw vectors to represent the following.
       (i) $\mathbf{a} + \mathbf{b}$ (ii) $\mathbf{a} - \mathbf{b}$ (iii) $\mathbf{a} + 2\mathbf{b}$
       (iv) $\mathbf{b} - 2\mathbf{a}$ (v) $\mathbf{b} + \frac{1}{2}\mathbf{a}$

2 $\mathbf{a} = \begin{pmatrix} 4 \\ 2 \end{pmatrix}, \mathbf{b} = \begin{pmatrix} 2 \\ -5 \end{pmatrix}$ and $\mathbf{c} = \begin{pmatrix} -3 \\ 0 \end{pmatrix}$.
   Work out these.
   (a) $\mathbf{a} + \mathbf{b}$
   (b) $\mathbf{a} - \mathbf{b}$
   (c) $3\mathbf{a} + 2\mathbf{b}$
   (d) $2\mathbf{b} - \mathbf{c}$
   (e) $\mathbf{b} + \frac{1}{2}\mathbf{a} - 2\mathbf{c}$
   (f) $3\mathbf{c} - 2\mathbf{b} + \mathbf{a}$

3 ABCD is a rectangle.
   E, F, G and H are the midpoints of the sides.
   $\overrightarrow{AB} = \mathbf{p}$ and $\overrightarrow{AD} = \mathbf{q}$.
   Find each of these vectors in terms of **p** and **q**.
   (a) $\overrightarrow{AC}$
   (b) $\overrightarrow{HB}$
   (c) $\overrightarrow{GA}$
   (d) $\overrightarrow{FE}$

Addition and subtraction of vectors

4 ABCDEF is a regular hexagon.
O is the centre of the hexagon.
$\vec{OA} = \mathbf{a}$ and $\vec{OB} = \mathbf{b}$
Find each of these vectors in terms of **a** and/or **b**.
(a) $\vec{FA}$ (b) $\vec{BD}$
(c) $\vec{AB}$ (d) $\vec{AC}$

5 In the diagram, P is one third of the way along AB.
$\vec{OA} = \mathbf{a}$ and $\vec{OB} = \mathbf{b}$
Find each of these vectors, as simply as possible, in terms of **a** and **b**.
(a) $\vec{AB}$ (b) $\vec{AP}$ (c) $\vec{OP}$

6 In the diagram, A and B are the midpoints of OC and OD respectively.
$\vec{OA} = \mathbf{a}$ and $\vec{OB} = \mathbf{b}$
(a) Find each of these vectors in terms of **a** and **b**.
  (i) $\vec{AB}$ (ii) $\vec{CD}$
(b) What can you conclude about the lines AB and CD?

7 Write each of these vectors in terms of **a** and **b**.
(a) $\vec{CD}$
(b) $\vec{EF}$
(c) $\vec{GH}$
(d) $\vec{IJ}$
(e) $\vec{KL}$

8 In the diagram, $\vec{OA} = \vec{AD} = \vec{CB} = \vec{BE} = \mathbf{a}$ and $\vec{OC} = \vec{AB} = \vec{DE} = \mathbf{c}$.
F is one third of the way along AC.
  (a) Find each of these vectors in terms of **a** and **c**.
      Simplify your answers where possible.
      (i) $\vec{OE}$ (ii) $\vec{AC}$ (iii) $\vec{OF}$
  (b) What two facts can you conclude about the points O, F and E?

Challenge 44.3

A ship sails 80 km on a bearing of 030°, from A to B.

It then sails for 100 km on a bearing of 110°, from B to C.

(a) Make a *sketch* showing the ship's journey.

Take 1 km to the East to represent 1 unit in the *x* direction and 1 km to the North to represent 1 unit in the *y* direction.

(b) Use trigonometry to find column vectors for $\vec{AB}$ and $\vec{BC}$.

(c) Find the column vector for $\vec{AC}$.

(d) Find the distance AC and the bearing of C from A.

(e) Calculate angle ABC.

(f) Use the cosine rule and sine rule to check your answers to part **(d)**.

Challenge 44.4

D, E and F are the midpoints of the sides of triangle ABC.
$\vec{OA} = \mathbf{a}$ and $\vec{OB} = \mathbf{b}$

(a) Find the vectors $\vec{OE}$, $\vec{AF}$ and $\vec{BD}$ in terms of **a** and **b**.
    Simplify your answers.

(b) (i) The point P divides OE in the ratio 2 : 1.
        Find $\vec{OP}$ in terms of **a** and **b**.
        Simplify your answer.

  (ii) The point Q divides AF in the ratio 2 : 1.
        Find $\vec{OQ}$ in terms of **a** and **b**.
        Simplify your answer.

  (iii) The point R divides BD in the ratio 2 : 1.
        Find $\vec{OR}$ in terms of **a** and **b**.
        Simplify your answer.

(c) What can you conclude about the points P, Q and R?

WHAT YOU HAVE LEARNED

- A vector has both magnitude and direction
- A vector can be represented by a column vector $\begin{pmatrix} p \\ q \end{pmatrix}$ where p is the displacement in the x direction and q is the displacement in the y direction
- Vectors are labelled using their end points with an arrow over or using small bold letters (underlined small letters when handwritten)

$\overrightarrow{AB} = \mathbf{a}$

- If two vectors are equal they are in the same direction and the same length
- If $\mathbf{b} = -\mathbf{a}$ then vector $\mathbf{b}$ is the same length as $\mathbf{a}$ but in the opposite direction
- If $\overrightarrow{AB} = k\overrightarrow{CD}$ then $\overrightarrow{AB}$ is parallel to $\overrightarrow{CD}$ and is k times the length of $\overrightarrow{CD}$
- If $\overrightarrow{AB} = k\overrightarrow{AC}$ then A, B and C are in a straight line and $\overrightarrow{AB}$ is k times the length of $\overrightarrow{AC}$
- To multiply a column vector by a scalar (or number), multiply both components by that number
- Vectors are added and subtracted using the triangle rule
  $\overrightarrow{AB} + \overrightarrow{BC} = \overrightarrow{AC}$
  or $\mathbf{p} + \mathbf{q} = \mathbf{r}$
- To subtract a vector, you add the negative vector
- To add or subtract column vectors, you add or subtract each component

MIXED EXERCISE 44

1 (a) On a coordinate grid with both axes labelled from 0 to 8, plot the points A(2, 1), B(6, 3), C(8, 8) and D(4, 6) and join them to form the quadrilateral ABCD.
(b) Find the vectors $\overrightarrow{AB}$, $\overrightarrow{BC}$, $\overrightarrow{DC}$ and $\overrightarrow{AD}$.
(c) What do you notice?
(d) What special name has the quadrilateral ABCD?

2 (a) Find the column vector that maps the point
   (i) (1, 4) on to (3, 7).   (ii) (5, 4) on to (2, 6).   (iii) (−1, 5) on to (−3, −1).
(b) Find the coordinates of the new point when the point (3, −2) is translated by these vectors.
   (i) $\begin{pmatrix} 2 \\ 5 \end{pmatrix}$ (ii) $\begin{pmatrix} 4 \\ -3 \end{pmatrix}$ (iii) $\begin{pmatrix} -5 \\ -2 \end{pmatrix}$

3. The diagram shows the vectors **a** and **b**.
   (a) Draw vectors **a** and **b** on squared paper.
   (b) Draw vectors to represent the following.
   (i) 3**a**   (ii) −2**b**   (iii) **a** + 3**b**
   (iv) 3**b** − **a**   (v) 2**b** + 1½**a**

4. Write each of these vectors in terms of **a** and/or **b**.
   (a) $\vec{AB}$
   (b) $\vec{CD}$
   (c) $\vec{EF}$
   (d) $\vec{GH}$
   (e) $\vec{IJ}$

5. $\mathbf{a} = \begin{pmatrix} 0 \\ 2 \end{pmatrix}$, $\mathbf{b} = \begin{pmatrix} -3 \\ 4 \end{pmatrix}$ and $\mathbf{c} = \begin{pmatrix} 2 \\ -6 \end{pmatrix}$.

   Work out these.
   (a) **a** + **b**
   (b) **a** − **c**
   (c) 3**b** + ½**c**
   (d) **b** − 3**c** + 2**a**
   (e) 3**c** + 2**b** + 5**a**

6. In the diagram, $\vec{OA}$ = **a** and $\vec{OB}$ = **b**.
   OC = 2 × CB
   Find each of these vectors in terms of **a** and **b**.
   (a) $\vec{BA}$
   (b) $\vec{CA}$

7. The lines AB and CD bisect each other.
   $\vec{AB}$ = **p** and $\vec{CD}$ = **q**.
   (a) Find each of these vectors in terms of **p** and **q**.
   (i) $\vec{AD}$ (ii) $\vec{CB}$
   (b) What can you conclude about the shape ADBC?

8 P divides AB in the ratio 3 : 2.
$\vec{OA} = \mathbf{a}$ and $\vec{OB} = \mathbf{b}$
Find each of these vectors in terms of **a** and **b**.
(a) $\vec{AB}$ (b) $\vec{AP}$ (c) $\vec{OP}$

9 ABCD is a rectangle and M is the midpoint of BC.
$\vec{DE} = 2\vec{DC}$, $\vec{AB} = \mathbf{p}$ and $\vec{AD} = \mathbf{q}$.
(a) Find each of these vectors in terms of **p** and **q**.
    (i) $\vec{AM}$ (ii) $\vec{AE}$
(b) What two facts can you conclude about the points A, M and E?

10 P, Q, R and S are the midpoints of the sides of the quadrilateral OABC.
$\vec{OA} = \mathbf{a}$, $\vec{OB} = \mathbf{b}$ and $\vec{OC} = \mathbf{c}$.
(a) Find each of these vectors in terms of **a** and/or **b**.
Simplify your answer where possible.
    (i) $\vec{PA}$ (ii) $\vec{AB}$
    (iii) $\vec{AQ}$ (iv) $\vec{PQ}$
(b) Find each of these vectors in terms of **b** and/or **c**.
Simplify your answer where possible.
    (i) $\vec{SC}$ (ii) $\vec{CB}$
    (iii) $\vec{CR}$ (iv) $\vec{SR}$
(c) What can you conclude about the quadrilateral PQRS?

45 ALGEBRAIC FRACTIONS

THIS CHAPTER IS ABOUT

- Factorising and cancelling algebraic expressions
- Manipulating algebraic fractions
- Solving equations involving algebraic fractions

YOU SHOULD ALREADY KNOW

- How to carry out operations on number fractions
- How to factorise linear expressions
- How to factorise quadratic expressions
- How to solve equations

Adding and subtracting algebraic fractions

When adding numerical fractions, such as $\frac{3}{8} + \frac{7}{13}$, the first step is to write the fractions with a common denominator. In the example above, the common denominator is 104 (8×13) and the numerator and denominator of each term needs to be multiplied by the appropriate factor to give this denominator.

$$\frac{3}{8} + \frac{7}{13} = \frac{3 \times 13}{104} + \frac{7 \times 8}{104}$$ Write the fractions with a common denominator.

$$= \frac{39 + 56}{104}$$ Add the numerators.

$$= \frac{95}{104}$$

The rules for dealing with algebraic fractions are exactly the same as those for dealing with numerical fractions, as is shown in the next examples. In Example 45.1 the denominators are both numbers; in Example 45.2 one of the denominators is an algebraic expression but, as is shown, the technique is still the same.

EXAMPLE 45.1

Simplify $\dfrac{x+3}{2} + \dfrac{x+2}{3}$.

Solution

$\dfrac{x+3}{2} + \dfrac{x+2}{3}$ Find the common denominator: 6.

$= \dfrac{3(x+3)}{6} + \dfrac{2(x+2)}{6}$ Multiply each numerator and denominator by the appropriate factor.

$= \dfrac{3x + 9 + 2x + 4}{6}$ Expand the brackets and combine the fractions (since the denominators are now the same).

$= \dfrac{5x + 13}{6}$ Simplify by collecting like terms.

EXAMPLE 45.2

Simplify $\dfrac{2}{x-3} + \dfrac{x+2}{5}$.

Solution

$\dfrac{2}{x-3} + \dfrac{x+2}{5}$ Find the common denominator by multiplying the two denominators together: $5(x-3)$.

$= \dfrac{2 \times 5}{5(x-3)} + \dfrac{(x+2)(x-3)}{5(x-3)}$ Multiply each numerator and denominator by the appropriate factor.

$= \dfrac{10 + x^2 - 3x + 2x - 6}{5(x-3)}$ Expand the brackets in the numerator and combine the fractions.

$= \dfrac{x^2 - x + 4}{5(x-3)}$ Simplify by collecting like terms.

The numerator will not factorise and therefore the expression cannot be simplified further.

EXERCISE 45.1

Simplify these.

1 $\dfrac{x+1}{2} + \dfrac{x-2}{3}$ **2** $\dfrac{x+3}{5} - \dfrac{x+1}{2}$ **3** $\dfrac{x-2}{4} + \dfrac{x-5}{3}$

4 $\dfrac{3x+2}{4} - \dfrac{2x-5}{2}$ 5 $\dfrac{x+2}{3} + \dfrac{2}{x-1}$ 6 $\dfrac{1}{x-2} - \dfrac{x+3}{4}$

7 $\dfrac{2x+3}{3} - \dfrac{2}{x-5}$ 8 $\dfrac{3x+2}{4x-1} + \dfrac{2}{7}$ 9 $\dfrac{5+3x}{2x-3} + \dfrac{1}{4}$

Adding and subtracting more complex algebraic fractions

In the previous section you learned how to add and subtract algebraic fractions when both denominators are numbers and when just one of the denominators is an algebraic expression.

In this section, both of the denominators are algebraic expressions. The key to dealing with these fractions is still to find the common denominator and, as before, the way to do this is to multiply the denominators.

EXAMPLE 45.3

Simplify $\dfrac{2}{x} + \dfrac{3}{x+2}$.

Solution

$\dfrac{2}{x} + \dfrac{3}{x+2}$ Find the common denominator: $x(x+2)$.

$= \dfrac{2(x+2)}{x(x+2)} + \dfrac{3(x)}{x(x+2)}$ Multiply each numerator and denominator by the appropriate factor.

$= \dfrac{2x + 4 + 3x}{x(x+2)}$ Expand the brackets and combine the fractions.

$= \dfrac{5x + 4}{x(x+2)}$ Simplify by collecting like terms.

EXAMPLE 45.4

Simplify $\dfrac{x-3}{x+2} + \dfrac{x-4}{x+1}$.

Solution

$\dfrac{x-3}{x+2} + \dfrac{x-4}{x+1}$ — Find the common denominator: $(x+2)(x+1)$.

$= \dfrac{(x-3)(x+1)}{(x+2)(x+1)} + \dfrac{(x-4)(x+2)}{(x+2)(x+1)}$ — Multiply each numerator and denominator by the appropriate factor.

$= \dfrac{x^2 + x - 3x - 3 + x^2 + 2x - 4x - 8}{(x+2)(x+1)}$ — Expand the brackets in the numerators and combine the fractions.

$= \dfrac{2x^2 - 4x - 11}{(x+2)(x+1)}$ — Simplify by collecting like terms.

In the next example an extra step is required because the numerator will factorise.

EXAMPLE 45.5

Simplify $\dfrac{8-9x}{2x-1} + \dfrac{6x+23}{x+4}$.

Solution

$\dfrac{8-9x}{2x-1} + \dfrac{6x+23}{x+4}$ — Find the common denominator: $(2x-1)(x+4)$.

$\dfrac{(8-9x)(x+4)}{(2x-1)(x+4)} + \dfrac{(6x+23)(2x-1)}{(2x-1)(x+4)}$ — Multiply each numerator and denominator by the appropriate factor.

$\dfrac{-9x^2 - 28x + 32 + 12x^2 + 40x - 23}{(2x-1)(x+4)}$ — Expand the brackets in the numerators and combine the fractions.

$\dfrac{3x^2 + 12x + 9}{(2x-1)(x+4)}$ — Simplify by collecting like terms.

$\dfrac{3(x+1)(x+3)}{(2x-1)(x+4)}$ — Factorise the numerator.

EXERCISE 45.2

Simplify these.

1. $\dfrac{2}{x+1} + \dfrac{1}{x+2}$
2. $\dfrac{2}{x+3} + \dfrac{x+1}{x}$
3. $\dfrac{x+2}{3x} + \dfrac{x}{x+3}$
4. $\dfrac{x+3}{x-4} + \dfrac{x-3}{x+4}$
5. $\dfrac{3}{x+2} - \dfrac{2}{x-1}$
6. $\dfrac{1}{x-2} - \dfrac{x+3}{x-4}$
7. $\dfrac{2x+3}{x-3} - \dfrac{x-2}{x-5}$
8. $\dfrac{x+2}{3x-4} + \dfrac{x-3}{x+2}$
9. $\dfrac{2}{2x+1} + \dfrac{3x+5}{x+2}$
10. $\dfrac{4x+17}{x+3} - \dfrac{2x-15}{x-3}$
11. $\dfrac{2x-5}{3x-2} - \dfrac{3x+2}{5x-4}$
12. $\dfrac{3x-4}{x+1} - \dfrac{x+2}{5x+3}$

Challenge 45.1

Simplify these.

(a) $\dfrac{3}{x+2} + \dfrac{x}{x+3} + \dfrac{3}{4}$

(b) $\dfrac{x+2}{3x} + \dfrac{x-3}{x+2} - \dfrac{4}{x-1}$

(c) $\dfrac{x+1}{x-6} - \dfrac{x-3}{3x+4} - \dfrac{x+5}{5x-2}$

Solving equations involving algebraic fractions

The rules for dealing with equations involving algebraic fractions are exactly the same as those for dealing with equations involving numerical fractions, as is shown in the next examples.

EXAMPLE 45.6

Solve $\dfrac{2x-3}{4} - \dfrac{x+1}{3} = 1$.

Solution

$\dfrac{2x-3}{4} - \dfrac{x+1}{3} = 1$ Find a common denominator: 12.

$3(2x-3) - 4(x+1) = 12 \times 1$ Multiply every term of the equation by the common denominator.

$6x - 9 - 4x - 4 = 12$ Expand the brackets.

$2x = 25$ Simplify by collecting like terms.

$x = 12.5$ Solve the equation.

EXAMPLE 45.7

Solve $\dfrac{x+4}{x-1} = \dfrac{x}{x-3}$.

Solution

$\dfrac{x+4}{x-1} = \dfrac{x}{x-3}$ Find the common denominator: $(x-1)(x-3)$.

$(x+4)(x-3) = x(x-1)$ Multiply each side of the equation by the common denominator.

$x^2 + 4x - 3x - 12 = x^2 - x$ Expand the brackets.

$2x = 12$ Simplify by collecting like terms.

$x = 6$ Solve the equation.

In the next example, the equation that results after you have eliminated the fractions is a quadratic equation (meaning that it has a term in x^2). You learned how to solve quadratic equations in Chapter 36.

EXAMPLE 45.8

Solve $\dfrac{2}{x} - \dfrac{3}{2x-1} = \dfrac{1}{3x+2}$.

Solution

$\dfrac{2}{x} - \dfrac{3}{2x-1} = \dfrac{1}{3x+2}$ Find the common denominator: $x(2x-1)(3x+1)$.

$2(2x-1)(3x+2) - 3(x)(3x+2) = x(2x-1)$ Multiply each term in the equation by the common denominator.

$12x^2 + 2x - 4 - 9x^2 - 6x = 2x^2 - x$ Expand the brackets.

$x^2 - 3x - 4 = 0$ Simplify by collecting like terms.

$(x-4)(x+1) = 0$ Factorise the resulting expression.

$x = 4$ or $x = -1$ Solve by finding *both* solutions.

EXAMPLE 45.9

Solve $\dfrac{2x+3}{x-1} = \dfrac{x+1}{2x+3}$.

Solution

$\dfrac{2x+3}{x-1} = \dfrac{x+1}{2x+3}$ Find the common denominator: $(x-1)(2x+3)$.

$(2x+3)^2 = (x-1)(x+1)$ Multiply each term in the equation by the common denominator.

$4x^2 + 12x + 9 = x^2 - 1$ Expand the brackets.

$3x^2 + 12x + 10 = 0$ Simplify by collecting like terms.

$x = \dfrac{-12 \pm \sqrt{12^2 - 4 \times 3 \times 10}}{2 \times 3}$ Solve the equation using the formula, since the expression will not factorise.

$x = -1.18$ or $x = -2.82$, correct to 3 significant figures.

EXERCISE 45.3

Solve these.

1 $\dfrac{x+3}{2} - \dfrac{x+4}{3} = 1$

2 $\dfrac{6}{x-4} = \dfrac{5}{x-3}$

3 $\dfrac{1}{2x+3} = \dfrac{1}{3x-2}$

4 $\dfrac{4}{x} + \dfrac{1}{x-3} = 1$

5 $\dfrac{x}{x+3} - \dfrac{x-2}{8} = \dfrac{1}{4}$

6 $\dfrac{2x}{x-3} - \dfrac{x}{x-2} = 3$

7 $\dfrac{2}{x} + \dfrac{1}{x+1} = 5$

8 $\dfrac{x}{x-2} - 2x = 3$

9 $\dfrac{2x}{x-5} + \dfrac{x-1}{3x} = 2$

Challenge 45.2

The cost of hiring a mini-bus for a trip one Wednesday was £120.

Each of the people travelling paid the same amount.

On Saturday, the cost of hiring the mini-bus remained the same but two fewer people travelled and each person had to pay £2 more than they had paid on Wednesday.

How many people made the journey on Wednesday?

> **WHAT YOU HAVE LEARNED**
>
> - To add or subtract algebraic fractions, first write the fractions with a common denominator and then simplify
> - To solve equations involving algebraic fractions, first multiply every term in the equations by the common denominator, then simplify, rearrange and solve

MIXED EXERCISE 45

1 Simplify these.

(a) $\dfrac{x-3}{3} + \dfrac{x+2}{2}$

(b) $\dfrac{x-3}{2} - \dfrac{x+5}{3}$

(c) $\dfrac{x+4}{5} - \dfrac{3}{2x}$

(d) $\dfrac{3}{4x-1} + \dfrac{1}{3x+2}$

2 Simplify these.

(a) $\dfrac{5}{x+4} - \dfrac{3}{x+2}$

(b) $\dfrac{x}{x+2} + \dfrac{x-1}{3}$

(c) $\dfrac{x-2}{x} + \dfrac{3x}{x+2}$

(d) $\dfrac{2x+3}{x-1} + \dfrac{4-x}{3x-5}$

3 Solve these.

(a) $\dfrac{x+2}{3} - \dfrac{x-3}{2} = 2$

(b) $\dfrac{3}{2(2x-1)} = \dfrac{4}{3x+2}$

(c) $\dfrac{2x-1}{3} + \dfrac{x-2}{6} = \dfrac{3x}{4}$

(d) $2 - \dfrac{2}{x-3} = \dfrac{8}{x}$

4 Solve these. Give your answers correct to 3 decimal places.

(a) $\dfrac{1}{3x-2} = \dfrac{2x+3}{x-1}$

(b) $\dfrac{3x-1}{x+2} = \dfrac{1-2x}{x+1}$

46 CIRCLE THEOREMS

THIS CHAPTER IS ABOUT
- The seven main properties of angles in a circle; their proof and applications

YOU SHOULD ALREADY KNOW
- The meaning of the terms *chord*, *tangent*, *arc*, *sector* and *segment*
- That the tangent to a circle is perpendicular to the radius at the point of contact
- The four cases for proving triangles are congruent
- Angle facts about triangles, angles on a straight line and angles round a point

The perpendicular from the centre to a chord bisects the chord

In Chapter 35 you learned how to prove that triangles are **congruent**. The proof that the perpendicular from the centre of a circle to a chord bisects the chord uses congruent triangles. Remember, **bisect** means to divide exactly in two.

Proof 46.1

Look at triangles OAM and OBM.

OM is common to both triangles.

OA = OB   (Both are radii of the circle.)

Angle OMA = Angle OMB = 90°   (Given)

So triangles OAM and OBM are congruent.   (RHS)

Therefore AM = BM.

So the chord is bisected.

You can use the properties of circles to solve geometry problems. The next example shows how the fact that the perpendicular from the centre of a circle to a chord bisects the chord can be used.

EXAMPLE 46.1

Find the length of the chord PQ.
Give a reason for each step of your work.

Solution

$MQ = \sqrt{13^2 - 5^2}$ (By Pythagoras' theorem)
$ = \sqrt{144}$
$ = 12$ cm

$PQ = 2MQ$ (The perpendicular from the centre bisects the chord.)
$ = 24$ cm

The angle subtended by an arc at the centre of a circle is twice the angle that it subtends at any point on the circumference

The proof that the angle subtended by an arc at the centre of a circle is twice the angle that it subtends at any point on the circumference uses the facts about triangles that you met in Chapter 3. **Subtended by** is a mathematical expression meaning 'opposite to'.

Proof 46.2

Let angle CAO = x and angle BAO = y.

Then angle CAB = $x + y$.

Triangles OAB and OAC are isosceles
(OA, OB and OC are radii of the circle.)

Angle ACO = x and Angle ABO = y
(Base angles of isosceles triangles)

Angle DOC = Angle OAC + Angle OCA = $2x$ (The exterior angle of a triangle
Angle DOB = Angle OAB + Angle OBA = $2y$ equals the sum of opposite interior angles.)

Angle COB = Angle DOC + Angle DOB
$ = 2x + 2y = 2(x + y)$
$ = 2 \times$ Angle CAB

So the angle at the centre is equal to twice the angle at the circumference.

620 46 Circle theorems

Example 46.2 shows a common application of the fact that the angle subtended by an arc at the centre of a circle is twice the angle that it subtends at any point on the circumference.

EXAMPLE 46.2

Find angle ACB.
Give a reason for each step of your work.

Solution

Triangle OAB is isosceles.   (OA and OB are radii.)
Angle BOA = 180 − (50 + 50) = 80° (The angle sum of a triangle is 180°.)
Angle BCA = 40°   (The angle at the centre is twice the angle at the circumference.)

The angle subtended at the circumference in a semicircle is a right angle

This proof is a special case of the proof that the angle subtended by an arc at the centre of a circle is twice the angle that it subtends at any point on the circumference.

Proof 46.3

Angle AOB = 2 × Angle APB   (The angle at the centre is twice the angle at the circumference.)

Angle AOB = 180°   (AB is a diameter.)
Angle APB = 90°   (Half of angle AOB)
So the angle in a semicircle is 90°.

This theorem is often used in conjunction with the angle sum of a triangle, as is shown in the next example.

EXAMPLE 46.3

Work out the size of angle x.
Give a reason for each step of your work.

Solution

Angle ACB = 90°   (The angle in a semicircle is a right angle.)
$x = 180 - (90 + 37)$ (The angle sum of a triangle is 180°.)
$x = 53°$

Angles in the same segment of a circle are equal

The proof that angles in the same segment of a circle are equal also uses the proof that the angle at the centre is twice the angle at the circumference. In Chapter 6 you learned that a **segment** is formed when a chord divides a circle into two pieces. In the diagram in Proof 46.4, the chord is between A and B.

Proof 46.4

Angle AOB = 2 × Angle APB   (The angle at the centre is twice the angle at the circumference.)

Angle AOB = 2 × Angle AQB   (The angle at the centre is twice the angle at the circumference.)

Angle APB = Angle AQB   (Since they both equal $\frac{1}{2}$ × Angle AOB.)

So angles in the same segment are equal.

To use this property, you have to identify angles subtended by the same arc since these are in the same segment. This is shown in the next example.

EXAMPLE 46.4

Find the sizes of angles a, b and c.
Give a reason for each step of your work.

Solution

a = Angle BDC = 40°   (Angles in the same segment are equal.)

$b = 180 - (40 + 85) = 55°$ (The angle sum of a triangle is 180°.)

$c = b = 55°$ (Angles in the same segment are equal.)

Challenge 46.1

Alan (A), Ben (B), Clive (C) and Dave (D) are fishing on the edge of a circular lake.

There is a small island (I) in the centre of the lake.

Alan, the island and Dave lie in a line running due South to due North.

Ben, the island and Clive lie in a straight line.

Clive is on a bearing of 038° from Alan.

(a) What is the bearing of Clive from Ben?
(b) Find the angles DBC and CDA.

Give a reason for each step of your work.

The opposite angles of a cyclic quadrilateral add up to 180°

A **cyclic quadrilateral** is one with each of its vertices on the circumference of a circle. The proof that the opposite angles of a cyclic quadrilateral add up to 180° relies, yet again on the proof that the angle at the centre is twice the angle at the circumference.

Proof 46.5

Angle ABC = $\frac{1}{2}x$ (The angle at the centre is twice the angle at the circumference.)

Angle ADC = $\frac{1}{2}y$ (The angle at the centre is twice the angle at the circumference.)

$x + y = 360°$ (The angles around a point add up to 360°.)

Angle ABC + Angle ADC = $\frac{1}{2}(x + y)$
Angle ABC + Angle ADC = $180°$

So opposite angles of a cyclic quadrilateral add up to 180°.

The next example shows a typical application of the proof that the opposite angles of a cyclic quadrilateral add up to 180°.

EXAMPLE 46.5

Find the sizes of angles c and d.
Give a reason for each step of your work.

Solution

$c = 180 - 96 = 84°$ (Opposite angles of a cyclic quadrilateral add up to 180°.)

Angle ABC = $180 - 101 = 79°$ (Angles on a straight line add up to 180°.)

$d = 180 - 79 = 101°$ (Opposite angles of a cyclic quadrilateral add up to 180°.)

When you are presented with a geometry problem you have to decide which of the theorems you need to use. The next exercise gives you practice choosing and using the theorems you have met so far.

EXERCISE 46.1

In each of the questions, find the size of the angle or length marked with a letter.
Set out your answers as in the examples, giving a reason for each step of your work.

1. Circle with chords AC and BD intersecting at X. Angle DAB (at A) = 20°, angle BCA (at C) = 40°. Angles marked: a at D, b at B, c at X.

2. Cyclic quadrilateral PQRS. Angle P = 76°, angle S = 95°. Angles marked: e at Q, d at R.

3. Triangle ABC inscribed in circle with centre O. Angle B = 55°. Angle f at O (AOC), angle g at A.

4. Circle with centre O. Points R, S, T on circle. Angle at O = 24°. Angle h at R.

5. Cyclic quadrilateral ABCD with diagonals meeting at E. Angle BEC = 84°, angle BAC (at A) = 50°, angle CDB... angle at D = 40°. Angles i at B, j at B, k at D.

6. Circle with centre O. Triangle EFG with FG passing through... Angle at O = 98°. Angles m at F, n at G.

7. Cyclic quadrilateral ABCD. Angle DAB = 3p, angle ABC = 2q, angle BCD = p, angle CDA = q.

8. Circle centre O. Chord XY with OP ⊥ XY, P on XY. OP = 12 cm, PY = 32 cm. Find r = OY.

9. Circle with centre O. Points A, B, C, D on circle. Angle B = 40°. Angles s, t, u marked.

10. Cyclic quadrilateral PQRS. Angle Q = 126°, angle P = 95°. Angles v at R, w at S.

11. Circle centre O. Points E, F, G on circle. Angle EOF (reflex or at O) = 84°, angle x at O.

12. Circle centre O. Points A, B, C on circle. Angle BAO area marked y, angle at C marked $2y$.

The opposite angles of a cyclic quadrilateral add up to 180°

The two tangents to a circle from an external point are equal in length

You learned in Chapter 6 that a tangent to a circle is a line that just touches the circle and that it is perpendicular to the radius at the point of contact. This fact is used to prove that the two tangents to a circle from an external point are equal in length.

626 46 Circle theorems

Proof 46.6

Look at triangles OAT and OBT.

OT is common to both triangles.

Angle OAT = Angle OBT = 90° (A tangent perpendicular to the radius.)

OA = OB (Both are radii of the circle.)

Therefore triangles OAT and OBT are congruent. (RHS)

AT = BT (Corresponding sides of congruent triangles)

So the tangents are of equal length.

It is easy to spot when you need to use this theorem as there will be two tangents (or more) drawn to the circle. The next example shows one application.

EXAMPLE 46.6

Work out the size of angle OBA.
Give a reason for each step of your work.

Solution

TA = TB (Equal length tangents)

Angle TBA = Angle TAB (Base angles of an isosceles triangle)

Angle TBA = $\frac{1}{2}(180 - 50) = 65°$ (The angle sum of a triangle is 180°.)

Angle OBT = 90° (A tangent is perpendicular to the radius.)

Angle OBA = 90 − 65 = 25°

The two tangents to a circle from an external point are equal in length

Challenge 46.2

A sphere of ice-cream is put into a hollow cone.

The diagram shows a section through the centre of the ice-cream and the cone.

The sides of the cone are tangents to the sphere.

(a) Find angle x.

(b) Calculate the slant height, y cm, of the cone.

Give a reason for each step of your work.

The angle between a tangent and a chord is equal to the angle subtended by the chord in the alternate segment

Look at the diagram in Proof 46.7 and identify first the angles and segments that are being referred to. The point of contact of the tangent is A. The chord is drawn from the point of contact, A, to another point on the circle, B. The angle between the tangent and the chord is labelled x. The chord divides the circle into two segments. One segment lies between the chord and the tangent, in this case the minor or smaller segment. The other segment is called the **alternate segment**.

Proof 46.7

Draw the diameter from A to meet the circle again at C.

Angle ABC = 90° (The angle in a semicircle is 90°.)

$y + r = 90°$ (The angle sum of a triangle is 180°.)

$y + x = 90°$ (A tangent is perpendicular to the radius.)

So $x = r$

$r = p$ (Angles in the same segment)

So $x = p$

So the angle between a tangent and a chord is equal to the angle in the alternate segment.

628 46 Circle theorems

EXAMPLE 46.7

Find angles x and y.
Give a reason for each step of your work.

Solution

$x = 180 - (55 + 65) = 60°$ (Angles in a triangle add up to 180°.)
$y = 60°$ (Angle in the alternate segment)

EXERCISE 46.2

In each of the questions, find the size of the angles marked with a letter.
Set out your answers as in the examples, giving a reason for each step of your work.

The angle between a tangent and a chord is equal to the angle subtended by the chord in the alternate segment

629

7

8

9

10

> **WHAT YOU HAVE LEARNED**
>
> **In a circle**
> - The perpendicular from the centre to a chord bisects the chord
> - The angle subtended by an arc at the centre is twice the angle subtended at the circumference
> - The angle in a semicircle is a right angle
> - Angles in the same segment are equal
> - The opposite angles of a cyclic quadrilateral add up to 180°
> - The two tangents from a point are equal
> - The angle between a tangent and a chord is equal to the angle in the alternate segment

MIXED EXERCISE 46

In each of the questions, find the size of the angle or length marked with a letter.
Set out your answers as in the examples, giving a reason for each step of your work.

INDEX

acceleration 519
accuracy 246, 283
  in measurements 244, 418–20
adding, mental methods 170
adjacent sides 45
  of triangles 327
algebraic fractions 400–1, 408–9, 611–12, 613–14, 615–17
allied angles 38
alternate angles 38
altitude of a triangle 32
amplitude of a wave 544
angles
  between a line and a plane 439–40
  in circles 620–4
  constructing bisectors 270
  finding by trigonometry 335–8
  of parallel lines 37–8
  of rotation 195, 197
  of three-dimensional objects 435–8
arc of a circle 93, 571–2
area
  of a circle 95–6
  of complex shapes 97
  of a parallelogram 34–5
  surface area of a cylinder 104–6
  of a triangle 31–2, 531–3
  units 242, 243
arrowheads 44
asymptotes 545
Average Earnings Index 289

bias in data samples 252, 253
bisector of an angle 270, 271
bounds, upper and lower 244, 418, 419–20
box plots 347–50
brackets
  in equations 115, 423–4
  expanding 19–20, 21–3, 25–6
  factorising 24–5
  using brackets on a calculator 280–1

calculators 412–13
  brackets 280–1

fractions 64–6
  order of operations 279–81
  powers 377–9
  reciprocals 15, 62
  standard form 384
cancelling 66, 122
centre of enlargement 205–6
centre of rotation 194, 195–6, 197
checking calculations 281–3, 379
chord of a circle 93, 578, 619–20, 628–9
circles 93, 95–6, 571–2
circle theorems 619–24, 626–9
circumcircle of a triangle 268
circumference of a circle 93, 93–5, 94–5
coefficients 402
co-interior angles 38
column vectors 200, 597–8
common denominator 53, 54
common difference, sequences 261
completing the square 488–9, 491–2
compound interest 75, 415–16
compound measures 247–8, 285
conditional probability 592–3
cones 574–5, 578, 579
congruence 191, 475–7
constant of proportionality 450
continuous data
  data display 79–80, 83
  estimation of mean 148–9
coordinates, three-dimensional 163, 437–8
correlation 87–9
corresponding angles 37
cosine 329, 330, 333, 337, 413
cosine curve 544, 547, 564
cosine rule 538–40
cube numbers 11, 170
cube roots 11, 12, 378
cubes (powers) 11
cubic functions 524
cuboids 99, 436–7, 440
cumulative frequency graphs 343–5
cyclic quadrilaterals 623–4
cylinders 104, 104–6

data collection 252–4
data types 252
decimals
  conversion from fractions 67–8
  in equations 428
  mental arithmetic 69
  multiplying and dividing decimals 70–1, 72–3
  terminating and recurring 68, 508–11
density 248
dependent events 592–3
diameter of a circle 93
difference of two squares 403–4, 485
dimension analysis 569–70
direct proportion 449–51
distance between two points 325–6
distance, speed and time 184–5
distance–time (travel) graphs 225–6, 518
division, mental strategies 170

elevations 107–9
elimination method, simultaneous equations 498–501
enlargements 204–6, 392–3
equations, solving 114–18, 187–8, 423–6, 427–8
equivalent fractions 53
estimation 282–3
  of probability 216–17
even numbers 263, 265
expected frequency 215
experimental probability 216–17
exponential functions 525–6
exponential growth and decay 415–16
expressions, simplifying 19–20, 21–3, 25–6
exterior angles 41, 48–9

factorising 24–5, 402–4
factors 1–2, 4–5
formulae
  for proportional relationships 454–5, 457–8

rearranging 184–6, 444–6
using letters 181–2
fractional powers 375–6
fractions
  adding and subtracting 54–7
  algebraic 400–1, 408–9, 611–12, 613–14, 615–17
  comparing fractions 53–4
  conversion from decimals 510–11
  conversion to decimals 67–8
  division by 60–1
  in equations 118, 424–6, 427–8
  multiplying fractions 59–60
  as scale factors 204–6
  using a calculator 64–6
frequency density 355–8
frequency diagrams 79–80
frequency polygons 83
frequency tables 136–9, 143–5, 148–9
frustum of cone 578, 579
function notation 554–5

Golden Ratio 184
gradients 464, 465, 467–70
graphs, interpreting 226–7
grouped data, statistical calculations 143–5

highest common factor (HCF) 4–5, 6
histograms 354–8
hypotenuse 156, 327
hypothesis 251

improper fractions 62, 66
incircle of a triangle 270
income tax 288
independent events 585–6
index notation 3, 28
  see also powers
index numbers 289
inequalities 119–20, 429–30, 431–2
inspection, finding by 4
interior angles 41, 42–3, 46–8
interquartile range 345–7
intersecting loci 275
inverse of enlargements 204
inverse operations 16, 283
inverse proportion 452
irrational numbers 512
isosceles trapezium 44
isosceles triangles, trigonometry 337–8

kites 44

leading questions 253
lengths, of three-dimensional objects 435–8

like terms 21
linear sequences, finding the nth term 260–3
line of best fit 88, 89
loci 270–3, 275
lowest common multiple (LCM) 5–6, 54
lowest terms 122

mean 136–9, 143–5, 148–9
measurement, accuracy 244, 418–20
median 80, 138, 143, 344
mental strategies 169–71
midpoint of a line 161
mirror line, how to find 192
mixed numbers
  adding and subtracting 56–7
  multiplying and dividing 62–3
modal class 80, 143
mode 138, 143
moving averages 362–4
multiple outcomes, probabilities 212–13
multiplication, mental strategies 170
multiplier
  exponential growth and decay 415
  percentage increase and decrease 74, 75, 76
  ratio and proportion 127, 128, 449
mutually exclusive events 583–4

negative numbers, multiplying and dividing 7–10
negative powers 374
negative scale factors 393

odd numbers 263, 265
opposite side, triangles 327
order of operations 279–81
outliers 349–50

parabolas 235
parallel lines 37–8, 467
parallelograms 34–5, 44
percentage increase and decrease 74–6
period
  of recurring decimal 509
  of a wave 544
perpendicular height, triangles 32
perpendicular lines 271, 467
  construction of 267–9
pi (π) 94, 176–7
pilot surveys 254
plans 107–9
polygons, angles in 46–50
population density 285
position-to-term rules, sequences 257–8

powers 11–12, 13, 374, 380
  in algebraic expressions 405–6
  fractional 375–6
  multiplication and division 13
  negative 374
  raising to another power 373
  rearranging formulae 446–7
  using a calculator 377–9, 413
primary data 252
prime factors 1–2
prime numbers 1
prism, volume of 101
probability of an event not happening 211–12
problem-solving 178, 287–9
proportions 456–8
  comparison of 132–3
  direct proportion 449–51
  finding formulae 454–5
  inverse 452
pyramids, volume 575
Pythagoras' theorem 155–6, 157–8, 325–6, 435–8
Pythagorean triples 160

quadratic equations 482–3, 484–5, 486
  completing the square 488–9, 491–2
  graphical solution 522–3
  with no real solutions 495
  quadratic formula 483–4
  simultaneous equations 504–5
quadratic expressions 402–4, 407–9
quadratic functions 231–5
quadrilaterals 42–3, 44–5
quartiles 345–7
questionnaires 253–4

radius of a circle 93
random data samples 252
range of data 138, 143
rate of change 226
rationalising the denominator 514–15
rational numbers 512
ratios 122–4, 126–8
  $1:n$ form 125
  dividing in a given ratio 130–1
  rearranging formulae 184–6
reciprocal functions 526–7
reciprocals 15, 16, 60–1, 61, 413
  in proportional relationships 457–8
rectangles 44, 97
recurring decimals 68, 508–11
reflections 191, 192, 564
regular polygons 48–50
relative frequency 216–17
Retail Price Index (RPI) 289

Index 633

rhombuses 44
roots 11–12, 375–6, 413
rotations 194–7
rounding numbers 172–5

samples of data 252–3
scalars 599
scale factors 388, 392–3
   area and volume 395–6
   fractional 204–6
   graphs of trigonometrical functions 546–8, 562–3, 565
   one-way stretches 562–5
scale of graphs 365
scatter diagrams 87–9
secondary data 252
sector of a circle 93, 571–2
segment of a circle 93, 578
sequences 257–9, 265
   finding the nth term 260–3
similar figures 204, 388–9, 475
   area and volume 395–6
simplifying expressions 21–3
simultaneous equations
   graphical solution 504, 521–2
   method of elimination 498–501
   substitution method 502–5
sine 328, 330–1, 336, 413
sine curve 543–4, 545–6, 547, 548, 565
sine rule 534–6
skewed distributions 349
speed 184–5, 226, 248
spheres 576–7
spreadsheets
   exploring sequences 265
   finding the mean of data 138–9, 144–5
squared terms in equations 114

square numbers 11, 170, 263, 265
square roots 11, 12, 170, 171, 375–6
squares (2-D shapes) 44
squares (powers) 11
   in proportional relationships 456–7
standard form 381–2, 383–4, 413
statistical questions
   planning 251–2
   writing a report 254–5
stem-and-leaf diagrams 84–6, 87, 346
straight line, equation of 221–2, 463–5
straight-line graphs 221–2, 223–4
subject of a formula 185
   changing 444–7
substitution method, simultaneous equations 502–5
subtraction, mental methods 170
surds 512–15
surface area of a cylinder 104–6

tangent (of a circle) 93, 269, 626–9
tangent (trigonometry) 329–30, 331, 334, 337, 413
   graph of 545
terminating decimals 68, 508–9
term-to-term rules, sequences 257–8
three-dimensional coordinates 163
three-dimensional objects, finding lengths and angles 435–8
time, problems involving 184–5, 286–7
time series graphs 361–2, 364
transformations
   enlargements 204–6, 392–3
   one-way stretches 562–5
   reflections 191–2, 564
   rotations 194–7

translations 200–2, 557–60
trapezium 44
tree diagrams 588–9
trial and improvement, solving equations
   by 187–8
triangle rule, vectors 602
triangles
   angles of 40–2, 474–5
   area of 31–2, 97, 531–3
   congruent 475–7
   labelling sides 327
   Pythagoras' theorem 155–6, 157–8
   similar 388–9
triangular numbers 263, 265
two-way tables 253

unit cost comparisons 132–3
units
   of area and volume 242–3
   in ratios 122, 123

values, comparison of 132–3
vectors 597–8
   addition and subtraction 602–5
   multiplication by scalars 598–600
velocity 226, 518–19
velocity–time graphs 519
vertex of a polygon 48
volume
   of complex shapes 99
   of a cylinder 103
   metric units 242, 243
   of a prism 101

y-intercept 464